CW00958675

CO 1 60 00717 7E

'Koonings and Kruijt have assembled a provocative and wide-ranging collection of first-rate case studies on the political roles armies have played and still play around the world. The choice of countries included is very original and the wide ambit of issues it covers makes it the most comprehensive book existing today on this ongoing debate. This timely volume is essential for understanding the importance of the military factor in current processes of democratization as it gives a cautionary sign about the ever-existing prospects of authoritarian regression.'
Patricio Silva, editor of *The Soldier and the State in South America*

'Political Armies lays bare the important truth about civil-military relations in the post-cold war world. In many countries, the military have remained the main guardians of the state. The façade of democracy that has been the guiding principle of political development since the end of military rule should remind us that, without civilian political leadership in times of transition, the military will remain the only presence of the state for the majority of citizens. Given the increase in violent conflict, crime and political unrest in many parts of the world, military forces still remain the "government" of choice in some recent public opinion polls. What does this mean for the future of democracy? Civilians will have to bear the responsibility to build local capacity to protect citizens from internal threats and allow civil society to thrive and have a voice.'
Johanna Mendelson Forman, Research Professor, American University, Washington, DC

'This timely volume raises hugely important issues for the aftermath of political armies which cannot be ignored. The particular forte of the contributors lies in their ability to penetrate the thinking of the military and to highlight their capacity for "strategic" responses to the dilemmas resulting from the dismantling of the Cold War and the surge of democracy … Quite probably the most important and sophisticated comparative volume on the subject of the military and politics to emerge in recent years.'
Professor Eboe Hutchful, Wayne State University

# Political Armies

## The Military
## and Nation Building
## in the Age of Democracy

Edited by
KEES KOONINGS AND DIRK KRUIJT

Zed Books
LONDON & NEW YORK

*Political Armies* was first published in 2002 by
Zed Books Ltd, 7 Cynthia Street, London N1 9JF, UK and
Room 400, 175 Fifth Avenue, New York, NY 10010, USA

Distributed in the USA exclusively by Palgrave, a division of
St Martin's Press, LLC, 175 Fifth Avenue, New York, NY 10010, USA.

Editorial copyright © Kees Koonings and Dirk Kruijt, 2002
Copyright © Individual contributors, 2002

Cover designed by Andrew Corbett
Set in 10/11 pt Bembo
by Long House, Cumbria, UK
Printed and bound in Malaysia

The rights of the authors of this work have been asserted by them
in accordance with the Copyright, Designs and Patents Act, 1988

All rights reserved

A catalogue record for this book
is available from the British Library

US CIP has been applied for


ISBN    Hb 1 85649 979 0
         Pb 1 85649 980 4

| Durham County Council Arts, Libraries & Museums | |
| --- | --- |
| CO 1 60 OO717 7E | |
| Askews | |
| 322.5 | |
| | |

# Contents

# List of Tables and Boxes

# Acknowledgements

This book is the result of intensive cooperation between 14 researchers who have focused on the political role of military institutions across the world. In mid-1999 we launched the idea of an international workshop dedicated to the phenomenon of political armies. We were gratified by the enthusiastic response of the invited authors and by their willingness to prepare their draft papers on the basis of a set of common issues to facilitate a comparative approach through a careful analysis of key country cases. In April 2000 we organized a very fruitful and pleasant two-day meeting at Utrecht University, during which we discussed the draft country papers and opening chapter of the book. The workshop was in large part made possible by generous financial support from the Netherlands Ministry of Foreign Affairs, particularly the Directorate for Human Rights and Peace Building. We specially thank Caroline Poldermans, head of its Division for Peace Building and Good Governance for offering advice and support. Additional funding was provided by Utrecht University, especially the Department of Anthropology and Development Studies, the Centre for Conflict Studies, and the CERES Research School for Development Studies. During the preparations for the workshop, Kootje Willemse and Mari Mar Azofra provided crucial and wholehearted organizational support. Daniela Digruber and Angelique Hornstra, graduate students in our department, offered invaluable logistic assistance during the proceedings.

After the workshop, the authors accepted our tight deadline for redrafting the chapters. They gracefully endured our constant harassment and complied with subsequent requests for missing details. We thank Helen Hintjens and Sandra Kramcha for their rapid and excellent translation of the Algeria chapter from the French original. The team from Zed Books, especially Robert Molteno, coached us smoothly and pleasantly through the process of the final editing and production of the book. Finally we owe a large debt of gratitude to Elisabet Rasch PhD, researcher at CERES, who worked with us in an intensive and very skilful way during the months of editing and completing the manuscript.

*Kees Koonings and Dirk Kruijt*

# About the Authors

*Lahouari Addi*, formerly Professor of Sociology at the University of Oran, is now Professor of Political Science at the Institute of Political Studies, University of Lyon-I. He works as *chercheur* at the CERIEP Centre for Political Science, Lyon.

*Felipe Agüero* is Associate Professor of Political Science at the School of International Studies and senior adjunct associate at the North–South Center, University of Miami. He taught political science at Ohio State University and has been a fellow of the Institute for Advanced Study, Princeton University; the Kellog Institute, University of Notre Dame; and at FLACSO, Chile. His areas of specialization include the comparative politics of authoritarianism and democratization; democratic transitions; and military politics.

*Celso Castro* is Researcher at the Research and Documentation Centre for Contemporary Brazilian History (CPDOC) of the Getúlio Vargas Foundation (FGV), Rio de Janeiro and Professor at the Catholic University (PUC-Rio) in the same city.

*J'Kayode Fayemi* is Director of the Centre for Democracy and Development in London. He studied civil–military relations at the universities of Lagos, Ife and London, where he received his PhD in War Studies. He is an adviser to various organizations on African affairs, including the British Parliamentary Human Rights Group, the International Crisis Group and the Norwegian Council for Africa.

*James Gow* is Reader in the Department of War Studies at King's College in London. Until 1993 he worked as a researcher at the Centre for Defence Studies and from 1994 to 1998 he acted as expert witness for the office of the Prosecutor at the International Criminal Tribunal for former Yugoslavia in The Hague. He is an expert on international order; the former Yugoslavia; and Central and East European Security.

*Aylin Güney* is Assistant Professor in the Department of Political Science at Bilkent University, Ankara. Her areas of specialization are Comparative Politics, European Politics and Civil–Military Relations.

*Emanuel de Kadt* was a professorial fellow and then academic director of the Institute of Development Studies at the University of Sussex. He has published on a variety of subjects on Latin American and African economy and society, and acted as senior adviser to the development community in the UK and the Netherlands. Currently he is Professor of Development Policy in the Faculty of Social Sciences, Utrecht University.

*Kees Koonings* is Associate Professor of Development Studies in the Faculty of Social Sciences at Utrecht University. An anthropologist and sociologist, he has written on development issues, Brazilian industrialization and militarism in Latin America.

*Dirk Kruijt* is Professor of Development Studies in the Faculty of Social Sciences at Utrecht University, and is currently vice-dean (research) of his faculty. A political sociologist and social anthropologist, his published work is mostly about poverty and informality, war and peace, and military governments.

*Robin Luckham* is a sociologist and political scientist. Currently he works as a research associate in political sociology in the Institute of Development Studies, University of Sussex. His specialisms are legal systems and the legal profession; Third World and African military institutions; disarmament and development; democratization in Africa and the Third World; and relationships between strategic issues and popular culture.

*Jennifer Schirmer*, an anthropologist, is Research Professor and Programme Leader of the Programme on Conflict Resolution and Peace Building at the International Peace Institute in Oslo, Norway. She is also a research fellow at the David Rockefeller Center for Latin American Studies, Harvard University. Her research has focused on military thinking, human rights and peace processes for the last decade, with a special emphasis on Latin America.

*Nico Schulte Nordholt* is Associate Professor in the Department of Development Studies at the University of Twente. He coordinates several research clusters in the Technology and Sustainable Development section, handling the institutional aspects of the transfer of technology, in particular in the field of natural resources (water and forestry); processes of democratization, in particular the role of NGOs in relation to civil society and responsive government; and corruption and legitimacy.

*Maria del Pilar Tello*, Doctor of Law and Political Sciences, was Professor of Political Sciences and International Relations in the Department of Law at the universities of San Marcos and San Martín de Porres. She is also a lawyer and journalist, and has worked on different journals. She is now political editor of *La República* newspaper in Lima.

# Abbreviations

| | |
|---|---|
| AP | Ausentes Pagados (Paid Absent) |
| AP | Acción Popular (Popular Action) |
| APRA | Alianza Popular Revolucionaria Americana (Popular Revolutionary American Aliance) |
| ARENA | Alianza Renovadora Nacional (National Renewal Alliance) |
| ASEAN | Association of South East Asian Nations |
| BIA | Burma Independence Army |
| BNA | Burma National Army |
| BSPP | Burma Socialist Programme Party |
| CAEM | Centro de Altos Estudios Militares (Centre of Advanced Military Studies) |
| CEH | Commissión de Esclaremiento Histórico (Commission for Historical Clarification) |
| CENIMAR | Centro de Informações da Marinha (Marine Intelligence Centre) |
| CFE | (Treaty of) Conventional Forces in Europe |
| CISA | Centro de Informações e Segurança da Aeronáutica (Air Force Intelligence and Security Centre) |
| CNI | Central Nacional de Informaciones (National Intelligence Centre) |
| COAP | Comité de Asesoramiento a la Presidencia (Committee of Presidential Assistance) |
| COMACA | (CO)mmanders, (MA)yors, (CA)ptains |
| COPWE | Commission for Organizing the Party of the Working People of Ethiopia |
| CPB | Communist Party of Burma |
| CPDOC | Centro de Pesquisa e Documentação da Historia Contemporânea do Brasil (Centre of Investigation and Documentation of the Contemporary History of Brazil) |
| CSN | Consejo de Seguridad Nacional (National Security Council) |
| DAB | Democratic Alliance of Burma |
| DDSI | Directorate of Defence Services Intelligence |
| DEA | (US) Drug Enforcement Agency |
| DHKP-C | Devrimici Halk Kurtulus Partisi Cephesi (Front of the Revolutionary People's Independence Party) |
| DIDE | Departamento de Información y Divulgación del Ejército (Department of Military Information and Disclosure) |

| | |
|---|---|
| DINA | Dirección de Inteligencia Nacional (National Intelligence Directorate) |
| DINCOTE | Dirección Nacional contra el Terrorismo (National Directorate against Terrrorism) |
| DOAN | Departemento de Operaciones Antinarcóticas (Department of Anti-Narcotic Operations) |
| DPA | Dewan Pertimbangan Agung (Supreme Advisory Board) |
| DPR | Dewan Perwakilan Rakyat (People's Representative Council) |
| DSI | Defence Services Institute |
| ECLAC | Economic Committee for Latin America and the Caribbean |
| EDORM | Ethiopian Democratic Officers Revolutionary Movement |
| EDU | Ethiopian Democratic Union |
| EFFORT | Endowment Fund for the Rehabilitation of Tigray |
| EGP | Ejército Guatemalteco de los Pobres (Guatemalan Army of the Poor) |
| ELF | Eritrean Liberation Front |
| EMDM | Dirección de Inteligencia de la Defensa Nacional (Intelligence Directorate of National Defence) |
| EMP | Estado Mayor Presidencial (Presidential Advisory Staff) |
| EPLF | Eritrean People's Liberation Front |
| EPRDF | Ethiopian People's Revolutionary Democratic Front |
| EPRP | Ethiopian People's Revolutionary Party |
| ERA | Eritrean Relief Association |
| ESAN | Escuela Superior de Administración de Negocios (Superior College of Business Administration) |
| ESTNA | Centro de Estudios de la Estabilidad Nacional (Study Centre of National Stability) |
| FEP | Fuerza Especial Policial (Special Police Forces) Guatemala |
| FFS | Socialist Forces Front |
| FINEP | Financiadora de Estudos e Projetos (Funding Agency for Studies and Projects) |
| FIS | Islamic Salvation Front |
| FLACSO | Facultad Latinoamericana de Ciencias Sociales (Latin American Faculty of Social Sciences) |
| FLN | National Liberation Front |
| FONAPAZ | Fondo Nacional de la Paz (National Peace Fund) |
| FONCODES | Fondo de Cooperación al Desarrollo (Fund for Development Cooperation) |
| FRG | Frente Republicano Guatemalteco (Guatemalan Republic Front) |
| FRY | Federal Republic of Yugoslavia |
| GEIN | Grupos Especiales de Inteligencia (Special Intelligence Forces) |
| GSI | Gabinete de Segurança Institucional (Department of Institutional Security) |
| IBDA-C | Islami Büyük Akincilar Cephesi (Great Islamic Raiders' Front) |
| ICMI | Ikatan Cendekiawan Muslim Indonesia (Association of Indonesian Muslim Intellectuals) |
| IU | Izquierda Unida (United Left Party) |
| JA | Jugoslovenska Armija (Yugoslav Army) |
| JNA | Jugoslovenska Narodna Armija (Regular Armed Forces of Yugoslavia) |
| KKN | Korupsi, Kolusi dan Nepotism (Corruption, Collusion and Nepotism) |
| KNU | Karen National Union |
| MA | Mahakam Agung (Supreme Court) |
| MDB | Movimento Democrático Brasileiro (Brazilian Democratic Movement) |
| MERCOSUR | Mercado Comun del Sur (Southern Common Market) |
| MINUGUA | Mission de las Naciones Unidas para Guatemala (United Nations Mission for Guatemala) |
| MIS | Military Intelligence Service |

| | |
|---|---|
| MPR | Majelis Permusyawaratan Rakyat (People's Consultative Assembly) |
| MRTA | Movimiento Revolucionario Tupac Amaru (Tupac Amaru Revolutionary Movement) |
| MUI | Majelis Ulama Indonesia (Board of Indonesian Ulamas) |
| NASAKOM | Nasionalis–Agama–Komunis (Nationalism–Religion–Communism) |
| NATO | North Atlantic Treaty Organization |
| NCO | Non-commissioned officer |
| NGO | Non-governmental organization |
| NIA | National Intelligence Agency |
| NLD | National League for Democracy |
| NSC | National Security Council |
| NSO | Nigerian Security Organization |
| NUP | National Unity Party |
| OAS | Organization of American States |
| OAU | Organization of African Unity |
| OLF | Oromo Liberation Front |
| OPDO | Oromo People's Democratic Organization |
| Opsus | Operasi Khusus (Special Force) |
| OSS | Office of Strategic Studies |
| OTS | Officer Training School |
| PAC | Patrulla de Autodefensa Civil (Civil Self-Defence Patrol) |
| PAEG | Programa de Ação Econômica do Governo (Government Programme of Economic Action) |
| PAN | Partai Amanat National (National Party) |
| PBB | Partai Bulan Bintang (Party of the Crescent Star) |
| PBF | Patriotic Burmese Forces |
| PCP | Partido Comunista del Perú (Communist Party of Peru) |
| PDI | Partai Demokrasi Indonesia (Indonesian Democracy Party) |
| PDI-P | Partai Demokrasi Indonesia – Perjuangan (Indonesian Democracy Party for Struggle) |
| PDRE | People's Democratic Republic of Ethiopia |
| PFDJ | People's Front for Democracy and Justice |
| PID | Partido Institucional Democrático (Institutional Democratic Party) |
| PK | Partai Keadilan (Justice Party) |
| PKB | Partai Kebangkitan Bangsa (People's Awakening Party) |
| PKK | Partita Karkaren Kurdistan (Kurdistan Workers' Party) |
| PMA | Policia Militar Ambulante  (Mobile Military Police Forces) |
| PMAC | Provisional Military Government |
| PMAO | Policia Militar Ambulante Ordinaria (Ordinary Mobile Military Police Forces) |
| PNC | Policia Nacional Civil (National Civil Police) |
| POLRI | Polisi Republik Indonesia (Police of the Republic of Indonesia) |
| POMOA | Provincial Office for Mass Organizational Affairs |
| PPC | Partido Popular Cristiana (Popular Christian Party) |
| PPP | Partai Persatuan Pembangunan (Unity and Development Party) |
| PRD | Partai Rakyat Demokratik (Democratic People's Party) |
| PRONAA | Programa Nacional de Alimentación (National Food Assistance Programme) |
| PRONEX | Programa de Apoio a Núcleos de Excelência (Programme to Support Research Centres of Excellence) |
| PUDI | Partai Uni Demokrasi Indonesia (Indonesian Democratic Union Party) |
| PVO | People's Volunteer Organzation |
| REMHI | Recuperación de la Memoria História (Recuperation of the Historical Memory) |

REST            Relief Society of Tigray
SARA          Suku, Agama, Ras, Antargolongan (Ethnic, Religious, Racial and Socio-Economic Differences)
SIE             Servicio de Inteligencia del Ejército (Army Intelligence Service)
SIN             Sistema de Inteligencia Nacional (National Intelligence System)
SINAMOS    Sistema Nacional de Movilización Social (National System for Social Mobilization)
SLORC        State Law and Order Council
SNI             Serviço Nacional de Informações (National Intelligence Service)
SPDC          State Peace and Development Council
SUNAT        Sistema Unitario Nacional Tributaria (National Unified Taxation System)
TGE            Transitional Government of Ethiopia
TNI             Tentara Nasional Indonesia (Indonesian Armed Forces)
TPLF           Tigray People's Liberation Front
URNG         Unidad Revolucionaria Nacional de Guatemala (National Revolutionary Unity of Guatemala)
USDA         Unity, Solidarity and Development Association
VJ              Vojska Jugoslavije (Army of Yugoslavia)
VRS            Vojska Republika Srpska (Army of the Serbian Republic)
WPE           Workers' Party of Ethiopia
WSLF          Western Somali Liberation Front

# Introduction

## KEES KOONINGS and DIRK KRUIJT

The military have played an important, if not a central role in the process of nation building and state formation over the past hundred years. In the majority of nation-states that have emerged and been consolidated during the nineteenth and twentieth centuries, military politics was the rule rather than the exception. We use the term 'political armies' for those military institutions that consider involvement in – or control over – domestic politics and the business of government to be a central part of their legitimate function. The non-political military should be seen as an exception, although a powerful one because it has turned into the dominant paradigm in North America, Western Europe, Japan, and to a certain degree also in the former Soviet Union, China, and most of the formerly communist countries of Eastern Europe.

The involvement of the military in domestic politics usually attracts sceptical or critical attention. Political armies are seen not only as a departure from the paradigm of the non-political military, but also as the antithesis of democratic governance. Criticism of political armies tends to disqualify them in terms of both military professionalism and the legitimization of rule in modern societies. Military dictatorships have become synonymous with widespread repression and violence directed by states against their own citizens, the systematic violation of human rights, unaccountable and often corrupt governments, and pariah status within the international community. These features seem to prevail under political armies. Close control of politics and the state by an institution built on hierarchy, the chain of command, monothetic ideology and deployment of the means of coercion is liable to fall short of the requirements of good governance. Political armies may quickly see political party competition as instability, public policy deliberations as inefficiency, and opposition to the established power hierarchy as dissent or even treason towards the state and the nation. The application of an uncontested military logic to politics in dealing with such perceived flaws and problems has in many cases produced the abject kind of dictatorship that excels in internal warfare, state terrorism, and murky politics.

Yet a case may be made for reaching a less severe verdict, probably applying to a much smaller number of countries, on the military role in nation building and state construction. Most political armies – and not only the more 'benign' specimens – claim that their actions are necessary to counter such dangers as economic disarray and increasing poverty, institutional breakdown or state collapse, or social disintegration and the proliferation of violent conflict. The more benign political armies refrain from state violence against political opponents and the violation of basic civil and social rights. They promote policies of development and social integration (making especial efforts towards poverty reduction) and accept civil participation in public life, eventually paving the way for democracy. Very few country cases of political armies would fit such criteria. Some of the examples that have a certain closeness to this ideal type may be Turkey (both during the foundational period led by Atatürk and during the past decade or so), Peru during the years of the Velasco government (1968–75), and perhaps Nigeria from 1966 until after the end of the civil war.

In practice, however, most political armies, including those of the countries mentioned, have found themselves facing the dilemmas that necessarily stem from seeking virtuous objectives by authoritarian means. In addition, political armies and the type of regime they ground are subject to change. Well-intended nationalist, developmentalist or social–reformist military regimes might degenerate into repressive, closed and corrupt autocracies. On the other hand, erstwhile hard-boiled dictatorships may initiate or accept degrees of liberalization and a return to civilian rule, to the point of setting the stage for a successful democratic transition.

Here, then, we have one of the reasons why a comparative study of political armies is relevant. Although political armies share a common core of characteristics and orientations (to be explored more fully in the first chapter), they also display significant differences. These differences can be found not only in the internal make-up of the military institutions but also in the variations in actual military political intervention or direct rule. Military rule does not depend only on the intrinsic nature of a political army but also on its relationship with civilian actors, the broader institutional context of military rule within the state, the public domain, civil society and various kinds of social contradictions and struggles. The chapters in this book aim to provide insight into the similarities and differences of political armies by looking at a selection of key countries from a longer-term historical perspective.

A second reason for studying the subject lies precisely in the current global wave of democratization. Rather than rendering scientific scrutiny of political armies obsolete, we feel that this further strengthens the need to pursue this theme. Political armies have been and still are one of the key variables shaping the origins and the course of democratic transitions. Democratic consolidation depends on, among other things, the manner in which political armies still interfere – or abstain from interfering – in civilian politics. Furthermore, in many cases, democracy has encountered tenacious obstacles, to the extent that even under the current global sway of pro-democracy forces and ideologies countries can relapse into military rule. Recent interventions in Pakistan or Côte d'Ivoire, and the ongoing political clout of the military in Peru, Guatemala, Ecuador, Algeria, Burma, and Indonesia, testify to that effect. This book devotes considerable attention to this key question of the position of political armies on the pressing issue of democratic governance.

Such a perspective will also allow us to re-examine current manifestations of political militarism in the post-Cold War era, precisely because recent global changes have dramatically altered the conventional parameters for political armies. Alongside the issue of democracy we have seen the rise of worldwide juridical concern with human rights violations and war crimes, often committed by military regimes. We have also seen the demise of economic nationalism as the preferred development strategy of political armies in the face of accelerating market-led globalization. Finally, a whole new array of problems for nation building and state formation have come to the fore on the basis of social and ethnic fragmentation, rising intra-state conflicts, and state collapse. Old and new political armies may appear to address such fundamental problems.

In view of the considerations outlined above, the book seeks to address four interrelated sets of questions. First, it explores the conditions, ingredients, and consequences of military projects for nation building (meaning economic development, state strengthening, and social and cultural integration) in the course of the twentieth century. How can similarities as well as differences across country cases be explained? What have been the specific forms and consequences of direct political intervention by the armed forces in different countries during the past decades?

Second, the book provides a specific focus on the recent (post-1990) economic, social, political, cultural and ideological changes that have affected the political role of the military and their nation-building agenda. How, especially, do political armies now cope with the problem of the threat of societal disintegration and conflict? How does this affect the agenda of political militarism in key areas such as the nature of the political regime, civil–military alliances, the notion of domestic threats and enemies, economic development, social integration, political ideologies and international relations?

Finally, with the second set of questions in mind, each of the country chapters asks how the past, present and future role of political armies can be assessed with respect to the problems of the consolidation of civil politics and democratic governance. In some cases this also brings in the related problem of conflict settlement, post-conflict conciliation, and reconstruction. Thus the book seeks to derive from the comparative analysis of political armies some insights for policy making in fields such as international stability, strengthening democratic governance, post-conflict reconstruction, institutional development, and the national and international dimensions of the rule of law.

The book is based upon a focused and comparative case study approach. Eleven country cases have been selected to offer a fairly illustrative sample of prominent political armies. The structure of the book is as follows. The first chapter sets out the basic assumptions and analytical considerations that have helped in guiding the conference papers and the subsequent redrafting of the country chapters. In this chapter we try to pinpoint some of the core characteristics of political armies such as their identification with nation building as a foundational mission, the effects of professionalization and military institutional strengthening on the political orientation of the military, the elaboration of specific military doctrines for political interventionism, the make-up of military rule, and the intricate relationships between political armies and the question of democracy. We have invited the authors of the country chapters to take up these issues in their respective case studies, but at the same time historical peculiarities of each country as well as specific preferences of the authors for a certain approach or aspect have allowed for differences in structure and tone in each of the country chapters.

The following four chapters deal with prominent country cases in Latin America. Peru and Guatemala share a long-term history of social cleavage based on ethnicity. Both countries have recently emerged from grim civil wars waged in part on the basis of the social schism between the urban *mestizo* sectors and the rural indigenous masses. Dirk Kruijt and Maria del Pilar Tello reconstruct, in Chapter 2, the dramatic cycle of rise, decline, and even decay of Peru's political army from the nationalist and reformist regime of General Velasco, through submersion in dirty counter-insurgent warfare, to the submission and ostracism of the military during the decade of civilian authoritarianism and intelligence service predominance under Fujimori and Montesinos. In Guatemala, as is shown by Jennifer Schirmer in Chapter 3, the military have managed to maintain their grip on the process of democratic transition, peace and reconstruction by elaborating a doctrinal framework and political practice of 'co-governance' that allowed the Guatemalan military to continue setting the political agenda despite their waging a brutal, genocidal civil war against the armed opposition and the Mayan population.

Chapters 4 and 5 deal with two countries that have been important examples of institutional transitions to democracy in Latin America. Both Brazil and Chile had long-lasting, foundational military regimes during the 1960s to the 1980s; in turn, these drew upon earlier systematic (Brazil) or periodic (Chile) manifestations of political militarism. Celso Castro, in Chapter 4, pays specific attention to the issue of intra-military factionalism in Brazil (a characteristic of the three main phases of the 21-year-long conservative dictatorship) and to the subsequent decline of the political role of the military. His analysis is based upon a careful reconstruction of 'military memory' and shows that the decline of the political role of the military – largely due to institutional and political factors – is reflected in the bitter recollections of the regime's protagonists. In Chile, by contrast, the political clout of the military has remained much stronger despite the apparent gradualism and smoothness of the transition. Felipe Agüero demonstrates in Chapter 5 that the authoritarian enclaves engendered by the Pinochet regime prior to its loss in the 1988 referendum preserved a tutelary role for the Chilean military during the 1990s. At the same time, this is forcing the civilian sectors and the military to come to a final settlement of civil–military relations compatible with consolidated democratic governance, something that was not achieved during the preceding period of democratic politics between 1932 and 1973.

The political role of the military in Indonesia has often been compared to that in Brazil. After a period of nationalist-populist orientation of the military, in the 1960s a conservative military coup was carried out against the threat of communism. Subsequently, a hybrid and centralizing military-civil regime was founded that was strongly oriented towards rapid capitalist development. This orientation was codified in a specific doctrine of security and development and was in part based upon a loyal civilian party alongside a dominant military 'quasi-party'. But, as Nico Schulte Nordholt shows in Chapter 6, differences between Indonesia and Brazil (or any other political army, for that matter) are perhaps even more important. Unlike Brazil, Indonesia has always been a very heterogeneous nation socially and culturally, so that the military were always facing the spectre of separatism and national disintegration. In addition, the Suharto dynasty (or 'sultanate') inserted a degree of personal prebendalism into the Indonesian regime unlike anything experienced in the institutional military regimes of Latin America. Both features have posed a particularly complex extrication problem for the

Indonesian military after Suharto's downfall, and it is not at all likely that they will be willing to give up their powerful position altogether.

Indonesia also brings to the fore another key problem: that of the force of politically organized religion that potentially can counteract the secular programmes of modern nation building championed by the military. While in Indonesia political Islam tried to develop ties to the regime, in Turkey and Algeria (chapters 7 and 8 respectively) the military chose to confront political Islam squarely during the 1990s because it was seen as posing a clear threat to the secular states that were the basis for the power and influence of political armies in both countries. Aylin Güney shows in Chapter 7 that the strongly tutelary role of the Turkish military has turned from a focus upon left-wing radicalism and civilian 'incompetence' in the 1960s, 1970s and 1980s to the party-political manifestation of Islamic fundamentalism in the 1990s. This, she argues, can be understood from the long-term key role the military reserved for themselves in building a modern and secular state on the remnants of the Ottoman Empire. Increasingly during the past decade military and important civilian sectors have seen this role as propitious for democratic consolidation. The challenge of democracy includes coming to terms not only with political Islam but with the thorny question of civil, social and cultural rights in general, as well as with the ending of military tutelage itself, one of the conditions imposed by the European Union for prospective Turkish membership.

In Algeria, the military barely maintain a thin veil of democratic commitment. Lahouari Addi shows in Chapter 8 that the key role of the Algerian military in the war of independence against France and the subsequent populist/socialist regime of Boumédiènne has turned it not only into a *de facto* political party but even into the self-proclaimed sole source of sovereignty and political legitimacy within Algerian politics and society. This explains to a large extent the repressive reaction of the Algerian military to the rise of political Islam in 1992 and the subsequent escalation of violence. This has left the Algerian military virtually on its own in countering Islamic radicalism because the army's usurpation of political legitimacy, together with the ruthless violence of the Islamic militias, has effectively stifled civilian politics and moderate civil society.

Political Islam is just one of the many problems that has been facing Nigeria in recent years. As is shown by J'Kayode Fayemi in Chapter 9, Nigeria's political scenario has been marked by regional, ethnic and religious contradictions since independence. From being the heirs to a typical British colonial army, the Nigerian military emerged as a full-fledged political army in 1966 to deal with such contradictions and with the ineffectiveness of civilian politics to contain them. Since then, the Nigerian military have been part of an often-vicious cycle of military takeover, moves towards restoration of civil rule, relapse into authoritarianism, and eventually the consolidation in the 1980s and 1990s, under the regimes of Babangida and Abacha, of military rule that was clearly personalist, prebendalist and corrupt. The longstanding economic and social problems of the country have not been adequately addressed. The recent demise of military rule in Nigeria therefore highlights a number of problems, among them the proliferation of a political psychology that sees recourse to violence as a normal instrument to solve social problems and to pursue political strategies.

The last three country cases (chapters 10–12) show fascinating common ingredients despite the considerable differences between the three countries.

Ethiopia (discussed in relation to Eritrea), Burma and Serbia (analysed in relation to the former Republic of Yugoslavia) all relate to pre-modern and pre-colonial polities – as well as to episodes of foreign or colonial occupation – in ways that still resonate in the current process of state formation and nation building or reconstruction. In addition, all three countries have been under the rule of Marxist-oriented military or military-backed regimes through the 1960s to the 1980s. Subsequent political militarism struggled with the redefinition of this ideological legacy. Finally, all three countries were the scene of permanent conflicts based on ethnicity or separatist nationalism questioning and threatening the military project of unitary nation building. A comparison of the three cases also brings out basic differences, not only with respect to regional contexts and historical legacies, but also in the way the military have tried to reshape the nation-building project in view of issues such as centralism versus decentralization (or even federalism or separatism), exclusionary ethnic nationalism versus the notion of a multicultural state, and the incorporation of the notion and the practice of democracy into the doctrinal framework of political militarism.

In Chapter 10, Robin Luckham discusses the complex trajectory of the political armies of Ethiopia and Eritrea. After the overthrow of the Ethiopian Empire the military took control of an originally popular Marxist-inspired uprising. The Derg military regime (*derg* means 'committee') formally invoked popular and socialist principles and support, but in practice degenerated rapidly into a terror regime that ended up entangled in separatist wars in Eritrea and Tigray and an increasingly strained project for enforced national unity. The institutional and moral collapse of this Marxist political army – hastened considerably by battlefield inadequacy, the exacerbation of repressive power, and the collapse of what popular support was left – paved the way for the appearance of two successor states and regimes in which renovated political armies played a key role. In Eritrea the originally popular-Marxist and separatist guerrilla movement EPLF (Eritrean People's Liberation Front) won independence on the battlefield against the Derg regime in 1991. It then faced the challenge of conjuring a new nation out of institutional nothingness and an ethnically diverse population. Furthermore, strong international pressure urged the new regime in the direction of adhering to the principles of democracy and 'good governance'. The EPLF also supported the armed opposition against the Derg within Ethiopia, particularly the Tigray People's Liberation Front (TPLF). The military and political collapse of the Derg regime brought a coalition led by the TPLF into power. The TPLF was transformed into a new centralizing Ethiopian defence force, the principal support of a new regime with the complicated agenda of building a multi-ethnic, federal nation-state on formally democratic principles, while Tigrean predominance continued within the military and the state apparatus. The recent war between the two 'new model army' regimes testifies to the fragility of state formation under such complex conditions in the Horn of Africa.

As Martin Smith shows in Chapter 11, the Burmese military have been much more successful, to date, in upholding institutional and political continuity as the self-proclaimed sole feasible national institution, all the way from anti-colonial struggle, through parliamentarianism and socialist military dictatorship, to the recent reformulation of the role of the army as the bedrock of authoritarian and centralist modernization and development. Three elements contributed to the virtual monopoly of the Burmese military over state power: the permanent armed resistance against the Burmese state put up by the Communist Party and the ethnic minorities; the ability of the military to engineer its doctrinal and institutional primacy within the nation-building process (first as tutors of civilian politics, and after 1962 as the sole ruling force); and the difficulties experienced by the civil opposition of the National Democratic League – led by founding father Aung San's daughter and Nobel Peace laureate Aung San Suu Kyi – in making effective headway against military rule. These difficulties did not derive only from the persistent repression exerted by the military regime, but also from the ongoing fragmentation of oppositional political groups and continuous armed conflict in the ethnic minority regions. At present, the Burmese military seem still in control of a Burmese-style 'transition agenda' based on the premise of ongoing military tutelage, a centralist perception of state consolidation, ethnic pacification, and 'guided democracy'.

In a certain way, the recent downfall of Milošević demonstrates perhaps the opposite principle, that of 'guided militarism'. The guides, in this case, appear to have been, first, the Serbian nationalist regime of Milošević, and then the protagonists and supporters of civil democracy who successfully opposed him late in 2000. A decade earlier Milošević took over the legacy of the Socialist Federal Republic of Yugoslavia. James Gow argues, in Chapter 12, that the regular armed forces of socialist Yugoslavia (the Jugoslovenska Narodna Armija, JNA) were given a formal role in Yugoslav politics on the premise that the Yugoslav military were uniquely dedicated to the preservation of this multi-national and socialist federal polity. The military failed, however, to put this watchdog role into effective practice after the onset of separatism and civil war in the early 1990s. In Serbia, the Milosević regime embarked upon a trajectory of nationalist expansion and cajoled the Yugoslav Army (successor to the JNA) into supporting this endeavour. This effectively destroyed any capacity the Yugoslav Army retained to uphold its role as keeper of the original federation. Instead, it faced the multiplication of regular and irregular armed forces, not only in the breakaway republics but also in Serbia itself, where the Milošević regime put into practice a kind of divide-and-rule strategy to subdue the by now fully 'Serbianized' military. Only after the Kosovo campaign did existing civil oppositional pressure against the Milošević regime erupt once more into mass demonstrations that resulted in a pact with the military leadership (possibly driven partly by rank-and-file dissent) to oust Milošević and support the new Koštunica government.

In Chapter 13, Emanuel de Kadt provides a conceptual overview of the findings of each of the country chapters. His stocktaking addresses a number of issues. After signalling the ongoing importance of military prerogatives in the era of reasserted civilian control, the chapter looks more closely at the variety of military regimes – characterized, following Hale, as moderator, guardian, or ruler regimes. The chapter relates evidence presented in the country chapters to such key features as the legitimization of political armies, the organization of military rule, the problem of societal support, and the consequences of military rule for the military as an institution. The chapter goes on to analyse the historical and doctrinal foundations of political armies, the transformations (but also the continuities) of the phenomenon in the post-Cold War period, and (particularly) the factors that complicate any full removal of the military from the political stage. These 'handovers' and 'leftovers' include the persistence of politically sensitive military doctrines, the role of violence in political contestation, the strong economic interests developed by the military, and extrication problems caused by the legacy of past repression and human rights violation under military rule.

In the Epilogue, we conclude the book with a brief round-up of key issues that follows closely upon the arguments presented in Chapter 13. In particular we look at some of the defining characteristics of political armies such as their foundational role, ideology, the organization of military rule, and the relation between political armies and democracy. We then try to discern current trends that emerge from the country studies on the basis of three possible scenarios (outlined in Chapter 1): the 'withering away', the 'institutional modification', and the 'perversion or corruption' of political armies in the age of democracy. Finally, we offer a brief review of relevant policy issues with respect to political armies that may concern both democratic governments or politicians and the members of the international community at large.

# 1

# Military Politics and the Mission of Nation Building

## KEES KOONINGS and DIRK KRUIJT[1]

## Political Armies Today

For those who were afraid that at the millennium's end political interventions by the military had become a thing of the past, the most recent *coup d'état* by the Pakistan armed forces may have come as a relief. The intervention of 12 October 1999 – the fourth in Pakistan's 52 years of independence, of which 25 have passed under direct military rule – rekindled a phenomenon that many had thought (or hoped) to be something of the past: the proclamation of a political army. Even a superficial survey of the coup and its immediate antecedents reveals a number of characteristics that have been shaping political armies, their interventions in national politics, and the establishment of institutional military rule in a large number of countries around the world for at least the past fifty years. In that sense, there was little new in the latest Pakistani military takeover.

The coup did not come as a surprise and was so predictable it might have been announced in the national press. Pakistan's economy was in disarray, with falling commodity prices and rising deficits and debts. Mass poverty and social fragmentation had evolved into widespread violence. Political strife was endemic, not only between the two major civilian parties but also in view of the rise of militant right-wing Islamic sectarianism. The toppled government had been unsuccessful in resolving the many problems of the country. The threat of ungovernability under the Sharif government, aggravated by corruption and the inability to address the economic crisis, put the military on edge. A high-voltage extra dimension was provided by the conflict with India and the regional nuclear arms race. This made the issue of national strength and development even more of a strategic military concern. But the trigger for the coup was the attempt by the ruling political class to blame the military for the recent Kashmir debacle and to intervene in the military command structure. This was seen by the leading generals as a threat to the unity and integrity of the armed forces and hence as the final disqualification of the regime. In his speech to the nation following the coup, General Musharraf presented the military's assessment of the situation (Box 1.1).[2]

**Box 1.1** General Pervez Musharraf's televised address to the nation on 13 October 1999

My dear countrymen ...

You are all aware of the kind of turmoil and uncertainty that our country has gone through in recent times. Not only have all the institutions been played around with, and systematically destroyed, the economy too is in a state of collapse. We are also aware of the self-serving policies being followed, which have rocked the very foundation of the Federation of Pakistan.... My singular concern has been the well-being of our country alone. This has been the sole reason that the army willingly offered its services for nation-building tasks, the results of which have already been judged by you. All my efforts and counsel to the government it seems were to no avail. Instead they now turned their attention on the army itself. Despite all my advice they tried to interfere with the armed forces, the last remaining viable institution in which all of you take so much pride and look up to, at all times, for the stability, unity and integrity of our beloved country.

... My dear countrymen, having briefly explained the background, I wish to inform you that the armed forces have moved in as a last resort, to prevent any further destabilization. I have done so with all sincerity, loyalty and selfless devotion to the country with the armed forces firmly behind me.... Dear brothers and sisters, your armed forces have never and shall never let you down, INSHALLAH. We shall preserve the integrity and sovereignty of our country to the last drop of our blood. I request you all, to remain calm and support your armed forces in the re-establishment of order to pave the way for a prosperous future for Pakistan.

May Allah guide us on the path of truth and honour.

Pakistan is one of a number of important countries in which political armies have dominated national politics during the twentieth century, playing an active and often decisive role in domestic politics and seeing this as a legitimate extension of their professional role as well as being of key importance for the fate of the nation. In the case of the Pakistan coup in 1999, but also in the example drawn from Brazil and presented in Box 1.2, a number of salient features of political armies come to the fore: strong identification of the armed forces with the fate of the nation and its core values, emphasis on the theme of order and especially the protection of the integrity of the state, national strength and the issue of development, and the incorporation of these issues into a military doctrine for political intervention that links the destiny of the nation and the interests of its people to the historic mission of the military. Often, transcendental national values derived from prevailing religious or ideological paradigms (Christianity, Islam, nationalism, socialism) are invoked to lend 'higher support' to intervention.

But one might argue that Pakistan is now an exception, given the extraordinary combination of economic disarray, social strife, political antagonism, failed governance, and the threat of regional geo-strategic rivalry and confrontation. Did former strongholds of political armies, like Indonesia, Nigeria, the Republic of

---

**Box 1.2   General Ibiapiana Lima, president of Brazil's Military Club: 'Are we reliving 1963?' (July 1999)**

It was the Marxist-syndicalist revolution on the march!... Brazil felt threatened; the middle class, in the streets in large numbers in various big cities, clamoured for an intervention by the 'vital forces' [*forças vivas*] of the Nation, to put an end to turmoil [*baderna*], to lack of discipline.... [H]ence, rapid, energetic and decisive MILITARY ACTION ... prevented the civil war, immobilized the activities of the extremist leaders inspired by a Marxist ideology following the instructions from Moscow, Peking, Havana, Prague and Tirana.... On 3 April 1964 the Revolution started.... MILITARY ACTION was directed against turmoil and terrorism ... against corruption and lack of ethics.... Many [enemies] of the Revolution fled or suffered the consequences of repression.... Worthy Brazilians were called upon and ... responded with efficiency and intelligence to the appeal of the Fatherland. The Country ... set out to conquer foreign markets ... made an effort in the war of construction and production of everything the Country needed: highways, railroads, ports, shipyards, modern communication equipment, machinery, steel, cellulose, paper, aircraft, coal, oil, wheat, cacao, soybeans, minerals, train wagons, locomotives, cars, trucks, tractors, ship engines, turbines, agricultural machinery, etc.... Thirty million Brazilians were saved from their predicament of misery!

[Turning to the present situation, the general continues:]

**The agents of disorder ... insist on revenge and hatred.** They caused agitation to return and they provoked renewed repression.... They took over the reigns of government when the Country was at its peak, steering it on a new course. So much irresponsibility led to Brazil once again begging for dollars; stagnating exports drag the Country into debt and recession; NGOs and multinationals made the decisions for the government; uncontrolled imports destroyed the national industry and agriculture; ... many businessmen of the 1960s, 1970s and 1980s went into bankruptcy, suffered extreme difficulties or sold their properties to foreigners and multinationals; ... the alcohol motor programme has been abandoned, the hatred of the citizenry against state-owned firms and even against farmers is nurtured.... We should not be pessimists and even less defeatists; **but are we not returning to circumstances similar to 1963?** Who is responsible? The military? Never! **The responsibility lies with the politicians and above all with the elites! There is no way of dodging it!**... Do they want to keep Brazil in disorder, impunity, irresponsibility, walking towards ungovernability?... Now it is time ... to awaken the NATIONAL WILL, to strengthen the citizenry, to love the Fatherland, to be a CITIZEN!

Korea, Turkey, and especially some of the most important countries in Latin America (Argentina, Brazil, Chile, Peru) not make a peaceful return to democratic institutions? The changes in Indonesia and Nigeria may be too recent for any bold assertion, but even in Latin America, where democratic transitions took place during the late 1970s and the 1980s, political interventionism by the armed forces is far from over, as the following examples demonstrate.[3]

In its most innocent form this is a nostalgic longing for past times in which the armed forces held the destiny of the nation in their hands. In Brazil, the Clube Militar gave in to reminiscing about the years of the military 'Revolution'. In the July 1999 issue of its *Revista do Clube Militar*, General Helio Ibiapiana Lima, the Clube's president, wrote an article that provides insights into the long-term endurance of military political views. By restating the military view on the origins and the results of military rule between 1964 and 1985 – views that are still widely held within the Brazilian armed forces – it is suggested that the present political, social and economic situation in Brazil is moving towards a comparable – though not identical – spectre of economic and political chaos posing a threat to national well-being. Box 1.2 quotes some assertions from the statement.

These bring to the fore a number of typical ingredients of the discourse of political armies. Furthermore, they illustrate that this discourse, and hence the political ambitions of the military, has far from disappeared even in countries that seem to have passed through successful and peaceful democratic transitions. In characteristic and unpolished military prose, the general shakes up the complete cocktail of mistrust and scorn that makes up his view of national problems: underdevelopment, dependency, cynical elites, chaotic politics, strikes, foreign agitation, precarious education, and weak government.[4]

Such problems continue to affect Latin America. In a number of countries, military interventionism still has a direct impact upon domestic politics. During the 1980s and early 1990s, military discontent with the civilian governments' performance erupted into barrack revolts or coup attempts in Argentina and Venezuela, while the military in Brazil and Chile staged occasional shows of force (alongside permanent backstage activism) to air their views on key issues such as constitutional reform, labour policy, or human rights. In Peru, the military backed the neo-populist self-coup of (elected) President Alberto Fujimori in 1992. In Guatemala, a similar coup intended by President Serrano and backed by the armed forces in 1993 failed and led to the appointment of a former human rights prosecutor as the new president. In Venezuela, former revolt leader Hugo Chavez was elected president in 1998 while in Bolivia former military strongman and dictator Hugo Banzer made a political comeback through the ballot box. After Guatemala's presidential elections in December 1999, Rios Montt, former dictator and colleague of Banzer, was invested with the presidency of the congress.

In Paraguay, would-be putschist Lino Oviedo was condemned to ten years' imprisonment after the failed attempt against President Wasmosy in 1996. However, Wasmosy's successor, Cubas, released the general. Interestingly, it was Lino Oviedo whose political intervention had finished the long-standing regime of the old dictator Alfredo Stroessner. Since then, he has been the key articulator of the political ambitions of the Paraguayan military. In March 1999, the country's vice-president Luis Maria Argana was assassinated; many suspected that Oviedo was involved in planning the assassination since Argana led the Colorado Party faction that sought President Cubas's impeachment. The Cubas government, meanwhile, made efforts to demonstrate its independence from military tutelage: in the fall of 1999, young supporters of Oviedo were arrested to suppress the outbreak of revolts, while the civilian authorities and the military high command denied rumours of new coup threats.

In November 1999, the chief of the joint staffs of the Ecuadorian armed forces, General Carlos Mendoza, expressed his concern over the current political problems of the government of President Jamil Mahuad and the popular protests this provoked, which presented a 'threat to the constitutive elements of the state, to the point that the prospects for its very survival hang in the balance'. In January 2000, a *pronunciamento* of the army's high command followed. The interesting point is that the participating officers supported the claims of the indigenous people's leadership, evoking memories of the leftist–nationalist revolutionary military governments of General Velasco in Peru and of Torrijos in Panama in the late 1960s and early 1970s.[5] After a couple of confused days, a formal military take-over in Ecuador was prevented by the resignation of the president, followed by his constitutional replacement by the former vice-president.

In fact, in Latin America political armies have been operating in many countries for at least the past hundred years. In other regions, the rise of political armies in a number of key countries followed the disintegration of old imperial states or the dissolution of the colonial empires of the Western industrial powers, roughly between 1918 and the 1960s. As a consequence, political armies have been a central factor in the development and nation-building process of a number of countries. Alongside the majority of Latin American nations that displayed varieties of the phenomenon during most of the twentieth century (with the exception of Costa Rica and until the 1970s Chile and Uruguay) we mention Turkey (an early example), Algeria, Burma, Egypt, Ethiopia, Ghana, Indonesia, Nigeria, Pakistan, South Korea, Sudan and Thailand. Additional examples of the phenomenon may be found in Iran, Iraq, Syria and a number of sub-Saharan African countries. In Europe, imperial Germany bore the seed of a political military during the First World War and the Weimar Republic, as we shall see below. In addition, the following countries showed traces of military political activism to a greater or lesser degree somewhere in the course of the past century: France, Greece, Poland, Portugal, Russia, Spain, Yugoslavia. This listing is by no means exhaustive and may not be completely accurate, either. It is clear, however, that political interventions by the military have been, to use Finer's still apt phrasing, 'distinctive, persistent and widespread'.[6]

In this chapter, we try to outline the main contours of political armies, their origins, their institutional and ideological constitution, and the nature of military rule established by them. We also address the issue of the current relevance of the phenomenon. Has political intervention by the military been superseded by the global wave of democratization, by global economic liberalism, and by the end of the Cold War? Pakistan's most recent coup testifies sufficiently to the contrary. Therefore, we first address the historical origins of political armies and their discussion in the scholarly debates since the 1950s. Then we examine the specific roots and institutional operationalization of political armies, the various dimensions of prolonged institutional military rule, and the relationship between militarism and democratization. Finally, we address the question of the possible demise of political armies by hypothesizing three scenarios for political armies in the post-Cold War context.

## Political Armies: a brief history

Contrary to what is sometimes suggested, the great armies of Europe's most authoritarian twentieth-century states, Hitler's Nazi Germany and Stalin's Soviet Union, did not become transformed into political armies. In both ironclad dictatorships, the party elite – under the inspiration and guidance of a personal, near-mythical leadership cult – took over the functions of the decisive institution in domestic politics and the ideological and political machinery behind the nation's development pattern.

Imperial Germany, however, showed a much clearer tendency towards the formation of a political army. Asprey's outstanding analysis of Germany's civil–military relations during Hindenburg's and Ludendorff's collective leadership shows the emergence of a military dictatorship, managed by the duo's Oberste Heeresleitung, slowly overtaking the civilian cabinet's prerogatives and decision making.[7] In 1917 the effective exercise of civilian control and civilian administration over the most encompassing aspects of warfare and related economy and politics was abolished. From 1917 until Germany's defeat in 1918, the Higher Army Command exercised through its regional commissioners most of the 'normal' economic and political functions as part of the 'total mobilization of the Nation'.[8] During the first ten years of its existence, the Weimar Republic had to cope with imperial Germany's military legacy and its politico–military dissolution. Torn apart by coup efforts from the left and right, and by attacks from the paramilitary Freikorpse, the leadership of the Weimar Republic had to rely once again on the political and military reputation of the now semi-senile Hindenburg, this time strongly influenced by political generals such as Ludendorff's successors Groener and Schleicher, protagonists of a more authoritarian Germany.[9] Ironically, the rise and consolidation of the Nazi Party in the early 1930s provided the scenario for a depoliticized and partly *gleichgeschalted* German Army and army command.

Imperial Japan before the Second World War repeats in some aspects the same military–civilian schism as that in First World War Germany under the Higher Army Command.[10] Formally, the emperor had plenary power. Again formally, under the Meji constitution, the emperor was commander-in-chief of the armed forces. However, according to tradition, once the cabinet and the military leaders had agreed on a policy, he could not withhold his approval. Out of the vague status and unclear political position of the emperor, the army and navy chiefs had consolidated an almost autocratic power for themselves. From the second half of the 1930s on, the influence of the military over the government and their dominance in the cabinet had been increasing, under a subservient prime minister. In fact, a handful of leaders of the armed forces already controlled national politics before the war with China, several years before Japan's participation in the Second World War.[11] Gradually, the army and the navy grasped even more political control over the nation's destiny, a situation that continued even during the last days of the war and was only ended by the emperor's radio message of surrender in August 1945.

The Red Army was born under strict party supervision and throughout its existence played a remarkably docile role as the instrument of the state rather than being a dominant institution within the state. During the Russian Civil War it was placed under the co-directorship of the political commissars because Trotsky, as

Minister of Defence, regarded that as the most effective survival strategy in an army commanded by former imperial officers. The same set-up continued, bolstered by the Stalinist purges of the army staff in the late 1930s[12] and the dual leadership of the generals of the armed forces and the party's political commissars that lasted until the successful battle of Stalingrad and Stalin's self-appointment as Minister of Defence[13] during the Great Patriotic War, until the days of the dissolution of the Soviet Union. In fact, the collaboration of its leadership during the aborted coup at the end of the Gorbachev period signified an acceleration of the dismantling of the Soviet Union.

In fact, the first modern political army after the German politicization of its armed forces during and after the First World War originated from the legacy of General, later Marshal, Kemal Atatürk: a remarkable soldier and statesman during the early decades of the twentieth century, the hero of the Gallipoli campaign in 1915, and after the First World War leader of the Turkish nationalist revolution. At the very beginning of the revolution, Atatürk drafted a document (Box 1.3) on the remnants of the Ottoman Empire in a language which recalls that used in boxes 1.1 and 1.2.[14]

---

**Box 1.3** Kemal Atatürk drafts the situation of the Ottoman Empire in September 1917

There are no bonds left between the present Turkish government and the people. Our 'people' are now nearly all women, disabled men and children. For all alike, the government is the power which insistently drives them to hunger and death. The administrative machine is devoid of authority. Public life is full of anarchy. Each new step taken by the government increases the general hatred against it. All officials accept bribes and are capable of all sorts of corruption and abuse. The machinery of justice has entirely broken down. The police forces do not function. Economic life is collapsing at a formidable speed. Neither the people nor the government employees have any confidence in the future. The urge to keep alive rids even the best and most honest people of every sort of sacred feeling. If the war lasts much longer the whole structure of the government and the dynasty, decrepit in all its parts, may suddenly fall in pieces.

---

In 1920 Atatürk was elected president of Turkey, the successor state of the Ottoman Empire. As the commander-in-chief of the Turkish forces which routed the Greeks during the Greek–Turkish War of 1921–2, he dedicated most of his politico-military career until his death in 1938 to the modernization of the Turkish state.[15] In this way, he is comparable with the Mexican general-presidents Calles and Cardenas, who in the late 1920s and 1930s built modern Mexico from the ruins of the Mexican Revolution (1910–17) and the civil wars thereafter by means of a unitary political party.[16] The difference between Mexico and Turkey is that Mexico's president Cardenas explicitly reduced the power and the privileges of the 'military sector' within the unified single-party state in such a way that his successor was able to dismantle the military sector as a political factor. Turkey, on the other hand, mostly relied upon civilian governments under 'military tutelage'.

From the 1930s and 1940s on, the National Security Council, formed by the military high command, has set the monthly political agenda for the national government. In fact, in Turkey modernization under military supervision has been a national mission firmly enshrined in the constitution.[17]

## Political Armies in the Scholarly Debate

After the Second World War the process of decolonization and the assertion of national independence around the globe inaugurated the heyday of political armies in a number of countries. From the 1950s onward, the phenomenon has been the object of a rapidly growing debate. Scholarly work on this theme over the past decades has been surprisingly cumulative. Successive approaches to the political role of the military in developing countries appear to draw fruitfully on earlier contributions, even if the latter were informed by a competing paradigm. As we shall see, many notions advanced by pioneering authors of the 1950s and 1960s still possess remarkable validity for the contemporary phenomenon of political armies. We may, in retrospect, discern three strands of argument that at the same time offer a rough chronology of work on political armies.

A first generation of authors set out to make a distinction between the apolitical professional armies of the advanced capitalist democracies represented in classical military sociology (and basically found in the North Atlantic area), and the blueprint 'modernizing' military of the 'new nations'.[18] These works have been, in one way or the other, informed by the modernization paradigm, since the rise of political armies was seen as related to the process of economic and social transition of these new nations, the 'incomplete' nature of their political system, and the self-ascribed modernizing role of their armed forces. Paraphrasing Finer, the overall process of modernization leads to the opportunity or the 'need' for military political intervention, while the organizational, technical and ideological make-up of the military provides them with means and motivation to become politically involved. The ultimate purpose of this type of analysis was to explain under what conditions the military failed to comply with the classical format of non-political armies, that is to say, armed forces that are subordinated to a civilian government and that are focused on defending the integrity of the nation against the threat of (mostly external) military enemies.[19] To explain this, both the social and political context of modernization and the origins and constitution of the armed forces in developing countries are taken into account.

Starting with the latter element, most authors working within the modernization tradition highlight the obvious fact that the military are armed: that is, they hold a formal monopoly on the legitimate means of violence.[20] Other organizational and institutional characteristics of the military give them a competitive advantage within the national unstable political structure: the armed forces' organizational unity, technical prowess and command hierarchy. To this should be added their ideological or doctrinal preoccupation with the 'national interest' which is further strengthened by the nation-wide patterns of recruitment and careers of (senior) officers. These elements lend the military in developing countries 'means and motive' for political intervention. But in addition there has to be 'opportunity' for the militarization of politics to come about. For this reason, we must look at the social and political insertion of the military, and at the issue of civil–military relations. Finer's formulation is still relevant today: military intervention in domestic politics becomes likely in times of crisis – emerging violent conflicts or protracted lack of legitimacy of rule – or in situations in which a power vacuum exists, leaving the military as the only viable institution to provide governance.[21]

Such situations are usually seen as symptoms of the overall initial 'backwardness' of developing countries or as results of rapid – and in many cases uneven – processes of modernization. The military are seen as being well placed to bridge the social and institutional divides that arise from the modernization process. At the same time, the military are presented as ideal modernizers themselves, given their organizational and doctrinal orientations. The more 'backward' the political system is and the lower the legitimacy of civil rule, the likelier the upsurge of military politics.[22] Huntington has described this syndrome using the concept of praetorianism: the underdevelopment of political institutions leads to a direct confrontation of mostly fragmented social interests. In this situation, the military may take on the task of modernization, which means seeking control of the state and domestic political life, especially if the military reflect (through recruitment) changing social structures and (through professionalization) increased identification with the idea of national strength and progress.[23]

This early scholarly work shared the notion of military involvement in domestic politics as in essence a temporary phenomenon. This notion was grounded on the dual assumption that, first, ongoing modernization would produce more mature political institutions and political culture so that the legitimacy and stability of civil rule would be permanently established; and, second, that the further professionalization of the military would bring them closer to the Huntingtonian ideal type of apolitical armies. Critics of the modernization approach of political armies emphasized the fact that military interventions reappeared even in relatively advanced societies, especially in Latin America. So another kind of explanation was needed. A new, second group of interpretations considered military interventions in politics as the outcome of specific social contradictions and problems of political domination and legitimacy experienced by developing countries. The source of these contradictions was to be found not in the modernization process but in the class composition of developing and dependent societies. Stated simply, this approach argued that, given the underdeveloped and dependent nature of Third World societies, there was no basis for stable and legitimate rule by the dominant class segments that were supposed to be the forerunners of modernity and democracy. Instead, these classes had their interests linked to exploitative and externally conditioned economic and social structures, which made their project for political domination in essence 'counter-revolutionary', to use the phrase of Fernandes.[24]

From this neo-Marxist paradigm arose a different view of political armies. The political intervention of the military in the context of underdevelopment and dependency served the interests of 'besieged' classes. Elites in developing countries took recourse to military intervention, and to prolonged periods of military rule, to safeguard their economic and social dominance or, in a milder formulation, to solve the problem of their failure to secure legitimacy as a ruling group.[25]

In the most radically Third-Worldist formulations, this analysis portrayed the Third World military as proto-fascists who protected the reactionary elites and therewith the hegemonic interests of the capitalist centres of the world economy. A more moderate perspective linked political militarism to nationalistic projects to overcome the constraints of dependency by setting up 'strong' or 'developmentalist' states that tried to alter the terms of insertion into the world economy. The military were seen as the only institution that could summon the necessary sense of common purpose in view of the fragmentation and weakness of the dominant classes.

This approach was pioneered in Latin America, first by Nun who advanced the notion of the 'middle-class military coup', and subsequently by O'Donnell with his concept of 'bureaucratic authoritarianism'.[26] According to Nun, the Latin American middle classes were not strong enough, economically, socially and politically, to fill the gap left by the breakdown of oligarchic hegemony during the early 1930s. Since the military, especially the officer corps, were increasingly recruited from the urban middle classes, the armed forces were inclined to intervene to assure the social and political position of 'their' class. O'Donnell's analytical framework has often been oversimplified as representing either a too-economic explanation of the rise of military-dominated authoritarian regimes or a form of latter-day Bonapartism in which the armed forces defend the position of the dominant class.[27] The merit of his analysis, however, is twofold. In the first place, he emphasized that more advanced modernization in Latin America could make military regimes more rather than less likely. In the second place, he underlined that the social and political strains of the effort to break out of classical dependency – mostly through a strategy of forced industrialization – brought the military into the political arena to deactivate antagonistic social forces and to reorganize the efforts of the state into 'deepening' the process of national industrialization. Therefore, a new kind of authoritarian developmentalism was founded upon civil–military alliances in which the so-called affinity between military and civilian technocrats helped to depoliticize the development strategy and thus responded to the felt need to deradicalize the political arena.[28]

A third, more recent approach is represented by the intra-institutional analysis of the military in relation to social context variables that drive the military towards systematic political interventions and towards specific civil–military alliances.[29] Problems of modernization, of structural dependency and of legitimate rule are, of course, highly relevant. However, it is necessary to understand when, how and why these kinds of concerns are taken up in such a way that political intervention and long-term military rule become a 'normal' option from a military perspective. In recent years, consideration of the military as an embedded political actor has also inspired the analysis of the democratic transition in Latin America and elsewhere.[30] This perspective suggests that the study of political armies should be guided by a series of intra-institutional characteristics of the armed forces.

It is interesting to note that several issues raised by the first generation of modernization authors have acquired a new lease on life. A first set of questions refers to the fundamental orientation of the military with respect to the fate of the nation, national destiny and national progress. A second theme is the transformation of such notions into quite specific doctrines that make political interference and military-controlled governance a normal part of the military profession. This leads to the military seeing the security of the state as their principal concern.[31] A third perspective is the identification of specific threats to this security and hence the identification of friends and enemies of the nation. Finally, the rise of specific military–civil alliances – or coup coalitions – that will serve as a point of reference for military interventions and as the basis of the subsequent organization and legitimization of military rule, is a key point of analysis. These elements are used to illustrate our overview of the formation of political armies and the nature of military rule in the following sections.

## The Formation of Political Armies

*The military and national destiny*
The starting point for the constitution of political armies is the profound identification of the military with the historical foundation and subsequent fate of the nation. This core point has been mentioned by seminal authors such as Finer and Janowitz and has been reiterated since: the military develop a strong identification with the nation they were 'called' to defend. The Huntingtonian ideal type of the non-political professional military has in fact been the exception, albeit a powerful one. Such a non-political professional military hierarchy regard themselves as 'civil servants in uniform', another functional category within the state bureaucracy with no specific public duty to develop historical, philosophical or moral notions about national destiny. Instead, their classic 'mission statement' calls for the technical execution of national territorial defence under the supervision of the legitimate civil authority. National destiny, if at all an active concept, is derived from the primacy of the national citizenry and its political institutions, widely seen as legitimate and beyond contestation. In contrast, political armies tend to take over some sort of steering monopoly of the national destiny. This mission is derived from the combination of two factors. First, there is the notion that the military institution is exceptionally well placed not only to defend but also to define the essence of the nation by birthright and competence. Second, the military 'know' that 'civilians', that is to say, civilian politicians, the institutional framework of civic governance, the actions of societal interest groups, and the overall political culture tend to be inadequate to address the needs of the nation. The first factor breaks down into two principles, the 'birthright principle' and the 'competence principle'.

The 'birthright principle', which we now elaborate at somewhat greater length, implies that the military are perceived to have been at the birth of the nation, or that without the sacrifices by the armed forces the nation would not have been formed or survived.[32] It matters less whether or not such a myth is historically correct. In fact, the foundational myth of armies may be derived from any of the following four historical situations.[33] The first situation refers to the armies of successor states to territorial empires that played a role in the military, institutional and ideological effort to construct this successor state. Turkey would be the best example, also Kuomintang China (with this myth aptly transferred to Taiwan after 1949), Pahlavi Iran, and possibly Meji Japan and Weimar Germany. The second situation occurs when armies were formed out of successful movements for independence from colonial domination or separation from existing nation-states or empires. Algeria, Burma, Indonesia, and more recently also Eritrea, are important examples. The third situation is represented by those armies that evolved from successful revolutionary movements within an existing state that, often through protracted civil war, succeeded in ousting the existing regime and taking control of the state, often to embark upon a course of profound societal transformation. The People's Army of the People's Republic of China would be the classical example, followed by the armed forces of Castro's Cuba, Sandinista Nicaragua, maybe Mengistu's Ethiopia or Ne Win's Burma, and – in quite different historical settings, although decolonization or liberation from foreign occupation were also involved – Ho's Vietnam and Tito's Yugoslavia. The fourth case involves armies that have been newly established as national institutions after the foundation of the independent state, so that the national armies did not play a role in the establishment of national sovereignty as such. These are Janowitz's post-liberation armies, such as those in South Korea and most of the former British and French colonies in Africa, sometimes formed in part out of ex-colonial armies, as in India, Pakistan and Egypt. The Latin American nations also belong to this type since there has been no real continuity between the forces that gained independence from Spain or Portugal in the early nineteenth century and the establishment of institutionalized national armies from about 1870 onward.

Whatever their 'true' origins, these so-called foundational myths lead to very strong forms of identification of the military with the nation, its core principles and basic values. In Latin American this has usually been expressed in terms of the military guarding over the 'permanent national objectives' rather than being involved in petty politics, factionalism or the pursuit of particularistic interests.[34] In actual practice, this role of the guardians of the nation means the self-perception of the military as protectors of the state on behalf of the people. This entails a shift from a territorial to a politico-institutional concept of security, focused upon the state as the nation's essential domain. In other regions, especially sub-Saharan Africa and in some South-east Asian countries, national unity and the design and feasibility of the post-colonial state were in themselves uncertain. Here, political armies emerged to take on nation building and state formation as more or less permanent military assignments: state construction rather than state protection. In many cases military institutions regard themselves as the essential core, the fundamental nucleus of the state. The military mission of security refers to the security of the state against any threat, internal or external. Permanent national objectives involve the military in modernization as its privileged field of action, for self-continuation and for state strengthening. These transformational projects, which have been added to the conventional security agenda, have historically been either of a conservative or a reformist nature, but always involved substantial state interventionism.[35]

Specific strategies of 'security and development' were given a clear doctrinal format. Along with these doctrines came notions of the actual versus desired social order, perceived threats to stability, and the ensuing identification of 'friends and foes' of the nation.[36] Additionally, political armies seek adherence to a broader, higher, moral order. Reference is often made to a set of basic values derived from the civilizational complex thought to be the foundation of national identity. In the recent history of political armies such values have been derived mostly from religion (Christianity, Islam), and political ideologies (socialism, populism, secularism, neo-liberalism), usually combined with idiosyncratic notions of national history and identity. Political armies develop such a moral order for guidance and legitimacy. To stress this functional dimension as something universal to political armies does not mean that we should ignore variations in content. These universal traits tend to be in tune with the overall project of national modernization but show significant differences in areas such as religion versus secularism, the role assigned to civil society and the private domain, national versus regional or ethnic identity, social conservatism versus reformism, economic internationalism versus self-reliance.

The 'competence principle' is based on the idea that the military are best placed to take care of national interests and hence the affairs of state because their organization and resources allow them to do so. Here the organizational characteristics repeated again and again in the literature come in: hierarchically structured, with unity of command; goal-oriented; efficient; and supported by the control of the means of coercion. In addition, owing to their functional role and modes of recruitment and training, the military see themselves as being perfectly in tune with national life and therefore able to overcome forms of sub-national particularism that may evolve into a threat to national interests. In contrast, the military may serve as a vehicle for national social and cultural integration and thereby for strengthening national loyalties and identity. Since the military may often be at the forefront of technical advancement, they develop a strong stake in technological and economic progress, to which very often concrete involvement in non-military administrative, logistic or developmentalist activities of the civic action type can be added. This leads to the conviction of the military that they are able to deal with such issues in a competent and especially non-political way.

The 'principle of civil inadequacy' states that civilians may be anything from inefficient, through divided, self-interested, and corrupt, down to disloyal and anti-national. Especially in times of crisis, but also as a more enduring component of the military outlook, civilian assumption of responsibility for national affairs is regarded with suspicion. The conduct of national affairs, thus, is too important to leave to civilians, especially in situations of crisis: collapse of governability or legitimacy of the existing regime, severe socio-economic problems and contradictions, internal conflicts or violent upheavals. We can observe a more generally ambiguous relation of the military with the notion of 'democracy'. Civilians are ultimately helpless. The nation is not a nation of citizens that seek active representation in its political institutions, but a nation of the people as an abstract category, held together – often precariously – by the state. The state can only rely on force and loyalty; so it has the armed forces as its sole and ultimate guarantor.

The mechanisms sketched above demarcate the basic orientation of political armies vis-à-vis the conduct of national life and the affairs of state. But an essential further ingredient of the constitution of political armies is that these generic notions are transformed into specific military doctrines that not only offer motivation and legitimacy to military intervention in politics, but also provide specific strategic guidance with respect to the form, content and timing of such interventions. Such doctrines have typically been developed by specialists within the armed forces who operate within specific institutional niches. This aspect is reviewed below.

*Military intellectuals, intelligence services and security doctrines*
Geopolitical schools were originally founded during the last decades of the nineteenth century in Germany, France and the United Kingdom.[37] Military theorists like von Clausewitz in the nineteenth century and Fuller[38] in the early twentieth century developed strategical innovations, with the German geopoliticians emphasizing more explicitly the concept of spatial supremacy – *Lebensraum* – for state and society. The leading theorists, geographers by profession, all received appointments to the (military) school of geopolitics in München. The German

tradition of military thinking became the most outspoken early example of military-cum-political aspirations. The Anglo-Saxon tradition emphasized more the strictly professional and technical advancements of the military profession. German, French, British and US war academies and related military training institutes became the example of and offered technical assistance to the professionalizing armed forces in late-nineteenth-century Latin America. In the 1880s, Chile was the first to call upon the service of training officers. Before long the arrival of European military missions in Latin America was common practice. Argentina, Bolivia, Chile and Uruguay had their armies trained by German officers. Brazil, Ecuador, Guatemala, and Peru engaged Frenchmen.

The US and the UK sent navy missions to Latin America from 1918 on. In Latin America, geopolitics gradually turned into an exclusively military affair from the 1940s onwards. The presence of the United States was felt more keenly after the Second World War, not only by way of military missions, but also through programmes of military and civilian development aid, complemented by training in the United States for a special cadre. After the Second World War, most newly independent countries in Africa and Asia received weaponry, training and technical assistance in the form of development aid and related purchases. American, British, French, Russian and even Chinese arms deliveries and technical assistance flooded Africa, Asia and the Middle East. Cuba, Israel and Taiwan discovered a niche in additional military assistance, and in the training of armed forces, national police and private security.

The Cold War reinforced the US hegemony in military and security-related assistance to Latin America, while the ties with European powers weakened under the enormous potential of military and other types of development aid from the US. This development aid was originally mostly military, and it was gradually combined with aid from the new intelligence community (especially the CIA). Under the umbrella thesis of 'continental security',[39] a complementary thesis of 'national security' merged with the Latin American tradition of geopoliticians. The writers of the thesis of national security were a new brand of Latin American officers, 'military intellectuals' of the staff schools and training institutes. Military intellectuals held staff functions in the general staff, at the military training schools and the higher military academies, and within the intelligence services. In Latin America, intelligence became preoccupied with internal rather than foreign enemies of the state. Another specialized US institution, the Drug Enforcement Agency (DEA) gradually took over from the CIA from the mid-1980s, when the 'war on drugs' acquired more political and financial support.

Three of the Latin American countries deeply affected by their military governments in the past decades, Brazil, Guatemala and Peru, created influential study centres, where military intellectuals lectured, wrote, thought and prospered.[40] After the end of military rule, the influence of the war colleges waned somewhat in Brazil and Peru, but now their role had been taken over by their heirs, the military intelligence agencies. In Brazil, the National Intelligence Service (Serviço Nacional de Informações, SNI) played a key role in policy formulation both during the last military government of João Figueiredo (1979–85) and during the civilian government of José Sarney (1985–90). The Peruvian intelligence chief Montesinos remained a powerful factor behind the Fujimori governments in the 1990s. In Guatemala, the Study Centre of National Stability (Centro de Estudios de La Estabilidad Nacional, Centro ESTNA) was founded in the late 1980s. Contrary to its counterparts in other Latin American countries, this centre aimed to develop a doctrine for post-authoritarian civil–military relations, rather than for underpinning authoritarian rule by the armed forces. Still, the supervisory role of the Guatemalan military over democratic consolidation has been exercised during the civilian governments of Cereso, Serrano, De Leon Carpio and Arzú.

The security thesis amplified the development and nation-building tasks of the military in the political arena and attributed to the national intelligence and security organizations the mission to prevent the 'internal enemy' from threatening the economic, social, and political order. As a consequence, we see the emergence of the 'military politicians' as a legitimate new role of the soldierly profession. Political armies define political intervention as the logical extension of military action.

The military do not usually see their political interventions as an explicit defence of specific class or ethnic interests, but as the autonomous representation of the 'national interests'. Yet, in their self-attributed tasks as national therapists the military are commonly engaged in alliances with other 'social sectors', to use here the special military jargon of analysis of the social structure. A military coup will normally be supported by a civilian–military 'coup coalition' that provides the legitimacy for direct intervention and institutional governance by the armed forces. Intervention in situations of political instability has become, if not prescribed, at least tolerated: military–civilian 'government pacts' have turned into normal practice.[41]

## The Consolidation of Prolonged Military Rule: similarities and variations

*The physiognomy of coups and the establishment of military governments*
The development of political doctrines as an integral part of the military *métier* is of course directly related to the armed forces' capacity to influence or control the national political arena. The stereotypical, although not the only, enforcement of military political clout is the coup. However, coups may occur under different formats, sometimes hidden by veils. Coups are prepared in secret, but are often preceded by some kind of announcement. Rumours of a possible coup sometimes circulate several weeks in advance in the national capital. It may happen that the military institutions 'go public' and make their worries about the nation's fate explicit even via press conferences. Or the chief-of-staff and the army commander may suddenly underline the 'granite unity between government and armed forces', for coup analysts often an early warning of the possibility of intervention by the armed forces. Reporters will sometimes be provided with the opportunity to interview the military brass: the general will almost certainly deny the very existence of preparations for a coup.

However, plans for a coup are often a regularly updated part of military contingency planning. Intelligence services prepare on a regular basis scenarios for various kinds of disasters. What to do in case of emergency? What to do in case of a strike in vital sectors (communications, transport)? What to do in case of sudden upheavals (students, slum dwellers, popular revolts)? Technically speaking, the implementation of a coup is a matter of relative routine. If the commanders of the army, marine and air forces can agree upon the necessity of a political intervention and can be sure of the loyalty of their regional commanders – nearly always members of the same cohort of cadets – the coup will be an 'institutional' one, initiated and supported by the armed forces as institutional actors. Smaller elite units will arrest the president, will oversee the house arrest of his most important advisers, politicians and trade union leaders, and will take control of the parliament buildings, the most important mass communication media and sometimes the supreme court of justice. Other units will be in charge of vital access and transport points and places where crowds gather. More operational plans are readily available, and modern coups may be directed by telephone or from a military plane.

A first indication of a possible coup may be the fact that prominent military intellectuals, linked to the national command structure, organize public or semi-public consultative sessions with civilian intellectuals and 'independent politicians, spokesmen of the national interests'. A more serious hint may be the request, stemming from the three military commanders, to dialogue with selected ministers in the core cabinet. The armed forces will then negotiate a package of requirements that are nearly impossible to disregard by the civilian government because a coup threat is implicit. In some countries, for example Honduras, there exists a kind of military parliament, formed by all commanding officers, which will advise – upon request or spontaneously – the president and the cabinet members on 'relevant matters'. In a more escalating avalanche of events, an 'emergency situation' will be proclaimed. In most countries this is the strict prerogative of the president. It implies, however, the delegation of civilian responsibilities to the military institutions. The armed forces partially substitute for the civilian police in urban areas; sometimes a curfew is announced. In the military regions, the regional commanders will be in charge of civilian governance tasks for the time being. In some countries such an emergency situation has become semi-permanent.

A new escalation occurs when military men replace civilian cabinet members with sensitive responsibilities: government or home affairs, transport and energy. The justification given may be that of 'support from the armed forces to the president by temporary assignments of the armed forces' most brilliant officers'. In fact it means the transfer of vital cabinet posts to the military. The next step may be the formal instalment of a civil–military cabinet, probably the favoured dream of many officers in Latin America. In such a case, all 'security sectors' such as home affairs, transport, communication and planning will be delegated to selected officers. In most Latin American countries long-term civil–military cabinets have been formed in the 1960s, 1970s and 1980s. The most extreme case has been the government structure of Uruguay in the 1970s, with a completely military cabinet headed by a civilian president (Bordaberry).

After a successful coup the country is usually governed by a military junta and a military president. The junta ('collective') is made up of the three military commanders, who at the same time are the (military) ministers of the army, the navy and the air force. The junta members will unanimously appoint or legitimate the president, usually an army general in active service or in retirement.[42] The military will distribute cabinet posts ('sectors') between the general officers of the army, the navy and the air force. Within these branches, the internal succession of retiring general-ministers will follow a strictly hierarchical procedure. The parliament will be disbanded or sent home for an undefined period of time. Law giving will occur by decree. Most Latin American countries have been governed, between the 1960s and the 1980s, by this kind of 'complete' military government. However, after the first years of pure military command, the ministerial functions which require explicit foreign negotiation (finance, foreign affairs) will be transferred to trusted 'civilian technicians'. The most far-reaching experiments in military technocracy were realized in Brazil, where the military inner circle decided to create several political parties as the substitute for parliamentary democracy, even with a co-opted, docile opposition.

### The politics of military rule

This final stage in the 'natural history' of interventions and coups leads to the establishment of long-term authoritarian regimes under military control. In many developing countries in the 1960s, 1970s and 1980s, these regimes have formed the apogee of the phenomenon of political armies. To understand the basic mechanisms as well as the varieties of (long-term) military rule one needs to take into account the fusion of the two constitutive factors of political armies elaborated above: the organizational and doctrinal formation of the military as a political actor – ultimately in the form of a 'quasi-party' – and the formation of 'coup coalitions' that call for and support the military intervention and the subsequent establishment of authoritarian rule. Both elements shape the form and content of such regimes in three crucial and obviously interlocking areas: legitimization, institutionalization, and strategy. Again we draw here on experience from Latin America, where two features were particularly salient: the tradition of legalism in society at large and also within the military; and the internalization of anti-communist warfare as a guiding principle during the Cold War.

Since political armies are so concerned with the protection of the state as the core national institution – and while this in itself is seen as lending automatic legitimacy to the political activism displayed by the military – the act of taking over the state by force and of the subsequent closure of politics requires specific forms of legitimization. It is one thing to be a permanent guardian of national values and institutions, but to take the state under direct political control and to design and implement routine policies goes further. The direct involvement in non-military affairs of state usually follows some sort of crisis situation and this will lend it a temporary air of legitimacy. But political armies have made considerable efforts at incorporating current political and administrative concerns into their 'core business'. Stepan has called this process 'role expansion' and it involves more than the mere shift from an external to an internal perception of threat and enemy.[43] It is role expansion precisely because non-military policy issues are drawn into the legitimate military field of action by a considerable widening of the notion of warfare as countering any threat to the 'permanent objectives' of the nation.

In Latin America, the overall doctrine of the military as national guardians was specified – by military intellectuals within the ambit of war schools and intelligence agencies as we noted above – in partly homespun national security doctrines, directed towards internal threats. This became the core of the 'new professionalism' that eventually set out to de-politicize politics by way of militarization. The latent threat to the state was increasingly broadened from 'real' rebels and subversives to any group or notion that could form a potential threat to the stability of the state. Military intervention usually finds self-confirmation in growing economic and social unrest and support for a coup. Social unrest is seen as sparked by 'subversive elements', giving additional space for internal enemies. At the same time, civilian allies of a military intervention rally behind the armed forces in times of crisis and upheaval, often to the point of actively seeking a military coup. A frequent pattern – and one that is a direct consequence of military role expansion – seems to be that a specific national crisis, making such threats acute, leads the military to intervention when they fear the crisis is going to contaminate or engulf the military institution itself. For political armies this is a clear sign of the degeneration and delegitimization of the incumbent regime. This in itself normally serves to disqualify the ousted civilian government: since they brought the country to the brink, they became irresponsible, treacherous or even illegal.

The new regime is often seen as an exceptional government, in itself acceptable in the short-run to the wider interest of the nation; but political armies tend to look for institutional mechanisms that can prolong their rule and give it a stable and permanent legitimate foundation. This normally implies two strategies. First, it means the militarization of the state at large and the adaptation of existing institutional and legal structures to that purpose. In practice this often means the formulation of new constitutional and legal arrangements and the creation of new – often parallel – state institutions so that military control of the state can be guaranteed. These arrangements are aimed basically at the neutralization of the existing political arena and the subordination of the state apparatus to the military hierarchy. In almost all regimes set up by political armies, the security notions engendered by military intellectuals and intelligence strategists were solidified into bodies specifically charged with the preservation of national security. In addition, these rearrangements often serve to deal with the issue of intra-military factionalism and intra-regime succession. The basis for such institutional and practical changes is usually provided by the 'revolutionary' nature of the military intervention. To confront the crisis, exceptional methods are called for and warranted.

Second, the military power holders face the task of constructing a political support base – an array of 'friends' – that may include civilian politicians, technocratic actors, elite segments, and mass movements. Janowitz has pointed at the inherent weakness of the military to organize a societal support base for long-term military rule.[44] However, this difficulty apparently only applied to a support base in the form of a mass movement or a stable political party. The Latin American context has shown that an 'apolitical' support base may well be both feasible and enduring. Crucial for this construction has been the rise to prominence of technocratic roles within bureaucratic authoritarianism, as noted by O'Donnell.[45] In the dictatorships of Brazil and the Southern Cone countries – but also under the reformist military regime in Peru – the alliances between the military, civilian technocrats, a handful of politicians, business sectors, and the urban middle classes gave medium-term stability to authoritarian rule as long as threat perceptions were maintained and economic progress secured.

This technocratic model appeared in its clearest form in Chile, where the model designed by the neo-liberal 'Chicago Boys' technocrats was directly welded to the political project of the junta (especially Pinochet); the widespread support from the business and middle classes was almost incidental. In Argentina, business had direct access to the military regime but political support, to the extent that it existed, was created mainly through the intensification of fear during the prolonged and vicious dirty war. In Peru, the military in the 1960s and 1970s dominated the state and the public sector, leaving certain agencies in charge of technocrats. The main effort at regime legitimization was channelled through the

National System of Social Mobilization (Sistema Nacional de Movilización Social, SINAMOS), a remarkable bureaucratic apparatus set up to organize mass social support for the regime and its reforms. In Brazil, the military regime went furthest in creating a broad support base. Not only were the usual 'bureaucratic rings' between military, technocrats and business interests put into place, but the regime also preserved as much as possible of the pre-coup political institutions, including a two-party system in which the government party played the role of sanctioning the decisions made within the military quasi-party. A possibly similar, even more tight-knit and pervasive support structure was set up in Indonesia, where military rule evolved into a complex set of relations between military institutional interests, business interests, the Suharto dynasty, and the Golkar party apparatus.

The strategy of regimes set up by political armies has typically involved two key domains. In the first place, the struggle against the internal enemies ('foes') on the basis of a pervasive but largely low-intensity counterinsurgency campaign (involving arbitrariness, coercion and violence against armed rebels, but more often against peaceful political, civil or religious opposition). In the second place, the pursuit of a development project that includes economic stability and growth, (limited but targeted) welfare, and in some cases social integration. The way these core strategies are handled often proves to be of crucial importance to the feasibility of long-term military rule. In addition, the legacy of both strategies powerfully affects the post-authoritarian democratic transitions, at least in Latin America. There, the new civilian governments have had to come to terms with economic and social imbalances left by the military model and to deal with the complicated issue of human rights violations by dictatorships that continue to be regarded as legitimate by still-powerful or at least influential military institutions. In Africa and Asia, this strategic component of military rule often went well beyond development in the strict sense to address the more fundamental problems of national unity and social cohesion, against centrifugal forces fuelled by ethnic strife, religious antagonism or regionalist dissent.

### The military and democratization

This brings us to a final aspect of the long-term rule of political armies, that is to say, the waning of such rule. We need not dwell on the vast body of literature that has been produced on issues of democratic transition and consolidation in Latin America, a region that has witnessed peaceful democratic transitions in a large number of countries.[46] We shall merely highlight some of the issues that link the military to the democratization process.

There is an overall ambiguity within the military perception of democracy as a desirable or feasible political system, as has been argued by Rial.[47] On the one hand, the military see democracy as running counter to notions of hierarchy, discipline and command that, when applied to politics, lead to the state taking precedence over the nation, and the nation taking precedence over the people and the citizenry. Democracy is a Pandora's box that may unleash all kinds of danger. On the other hand, democracy cannot be ignored since it constitutes a potent underpinning of the principle of national sovereignty. The rediscovery of civil society and the incorporation of democratic governance in new, desirable canons of modernity has been eroding the authoritarian-nationalist discourse. The Latin American military are not immune to such notions because they share a long-term identification with the values of 'Western civilization'. In other regions this may be less the case: the military may feel no commitment to liberal democracy, except under growing international pressure. In the post-Cold War period, international developments have in fact reinforced the linkage between democracy and sovereignty to the extent that democratic governance, the rule of law, and respect for human rights have become new conditionalities that may even prompt outside military intervention as in Bosnia, East Timor or Kosovo. As a result, democracy is now looming much larger over actual or potential forms of military political intervention than in the past.

A second set of observations relates to the mechanisms that erode military rule and bring back, if not full democracy, then at least the primacy of civilian government. In the Latin American transition scenarios – where in many cases a legacy of civic political institutions was available – these mechanisms can be summed up briefly as follows. First, prolonged military rule started to erode the institutional integrity of the armed forces. Political involvement increasingly came to be seen as running counter to the core values – such as unity, discipline, and untainted patriotism – embedded within the armed forces. The main undermining factors typically were: the exacerbation of intra-military factionalism; the involvement in widespread repression and human rights violations, that not only created so-called extrication problems but was also seen as a dirty business unworthy of real soldiers; and corruption that undermined the credibility of the regime and its dedication to the national interest.

Second, prolonged military rule heightens the possibility of 'casualties' within the military–civil alliance. Since military regimes are usually not more efficient in policy making and interest management than civilian governments, defection of civilian allies occurs sooner or later, especially if their estrangement is deepened by the continuing concentration of power in the hands of an increasingly unpopular and isolated military junta. In addition, the inability to build a stable political mass base for military rule, such as a movement or a party, erodes its social and political base. Third, the elimination of old threats and the resurgence of feasible and trustworthy civic alternatives among the opposition in civil society and political parties eases the way into power of the civilian opposition. If this opposition has a track record of peaceful institutional tactics, this will further widen the fissures in the military regime.

Last, international pressure in favour of democracy and human rights (notably stronger after the end of the Cold War) often serves to isolate authoritarian regimes and to strengthen domestic civilian opposition. Even hard-boiled military regimes grow weary of perpetual ostracism and pariah status in the development community of multilateral banks and bilateral donors. Initially, international pressure was generated by (some, not all) democratically governed nations in the North, or at least by their public opinion and civic associations. Later, countries of recent re-democratization developed some democratic scrutiny within their own ranks. This happened in the case of the Central American peace initiative of Esquipulas, within the MERCOSUR area – against Oviedo in Paraguay – or with the condemnation of authoritarian features in Peru and Ecuador.

However, the importance of international pressure should not be exaggerated. Not only is pressure exerted selectively, especially by the US and other rich countries, but its effectiveness also depends considerably on the importance a military-governed state accords to being an accepted player in the international order. In recent years countries such as Indonesia, Nigeria, South Korea and

Turkey have been in this position, with positive effects on the restoration of civic rule. In contrast, the Pakistan military were not sufficiently deterred from their recent intervention by the international financial and economic vulnerability of the country. In countries like Burma and Serbia, military – or at least strongly authoritarian – regimes persist because of their own marginal or antagonistic position *vis-à-vis* the dominant international order. In sub-Sahara Africa, the apparently chaotic movement in a number of countries from military or one-party rule to civil rule, or backwards, or into endemic intra-state violence, internecine warfare, and difficult regional peace enforcement efforts, seem to reflect an overall breakdown of institutions combined with a pattern of neglect by the international community. In Nigeria, but possibly also in Indonesia, the demise of open military rule may be unable to avert economic decline, internal conflicts and overall national disintegration, factors that continue to complicate democratic consolidation.

But even in countries where democratic consolidation has proceeded along fairly stable institutional channels, the legacy of political armies continues to influence national politics. For reasons of space we will not elaborate on the various post-transition problems faced by many Latin American countries that we touched on briefly at the beginning of this chapter. Turkey is another example of a country where the consolidation of democratic institutions and practices goes hand in hand with social conflicts and military 'tutors' who maintain an active political role. The legacy of political armies to the 'new' democracies includes this so-called tutelage problem, when the military continue to exert considerable influence over the political process and are able to dictate or draw bottom lines in key policy areas. Related to this problem is the issue of reformulating civil–military relations. The main difficulties here lie in the reluctance of the military to accept civil supremacy over military matters and to give up existing prerogatives, and conversely in the lack of experience or courage in civilian circles to take military matters seriously in hand. As a result, the demarcation of military institutional interests often remains strong; these include not accepting responsibility or allowing prosecution for human rights violations, the preservation of institutional prestige including recognition of the military's past role as national 'saviours', and the preservation of current prerogatives and resources. This leads to the difficult question of whether it is possible to redefine the role of the military in an apolitical direction. Kruijt has argued that below the surface of many processes of democratic consolidation in Latin America the armed forces are looking for new roles (preservation of public order and law enforcement, combating drugs, environmental patrolling, civic action) that may well preserve their tradition of inward-looking political and administrative involvement.[48]

## The Demise of Political Armies?

Despite the tensions built into the reconstruction of democracy in many countries that have had long experience with political armies, the recent climate of opinion seems confident about the prospects of democracy worldwide. Authoritarian military regimes that adhere to explicit anti-democratic doctrines, and base their rule on systematic repression, have become few in number. Instead, for the past ten or twenty years, the issue of democratic transition and consolidation has occupied the centre of scholarly attention. We witnessed consecutive rounds of democratic transitions: in Southern Europe in the 1970s, in Latin America in the

1980s, and in Eastern Europe and parts of South, Central and East Asia in the 1990s. This does not mean, however, that the process of democratic consolidation now goes unchallenged: poverty and social exclusion, governability problems, globalization, and conflicts of all kind (ethnic, religious, environmental, poverty-related) continue to put democratic governance under strain. Outright military dictatorships, however, are no longer counted, in most countries, among the most pressing threats to democratic rule.

Does this also mean the end of the military as a relevant actor in the domestic political arenas of the developing world, or as a force in the more general process of national development and nation building? Is it indeed true that the combined impact of the worldwide wave of democratization, economic globalization, supra-nationalism, and post-Cold War ideological liberalism has made the issue of 'military politics' something of the past, no longer worthy of scholarly or policy-oriented scrutiny?

We believe that this is not the case, for three reasons. In the first place, there is ample evidence that in a number of countries the military as a class or as an institution are still very influential in national politics, and still cling to the self-ascribed long-term task of shaping the fate of the nation. This stems from the long history of military political dominance, especially in those countries in which the military still exert considerable tutelage over civilian politics. It is important to understand this present-day military political involvement in relation to each country's specific social, political and cultural history, including the history and special features of its armed forces, but also in view of the recent global trends mentioned above.

Second, even in countries in which the military have now returned to the barracks as part of the reassertion of civilian politics, current societal problems still make the consolidation of democratic governance an uncertain endeavour. Is it not possible that, if real or perceived threats to the social or political integrity of the nation are sufficiently strong, a reversal may take place that would bring the military back into politics, even to the point of again assuming direct control of government? An examination of military involvement in politics in the (recent) past, as well as – in some cases – their apparent withdrawal from politics and explicit adherence to democratic norms, will shed light on the prospects for and threats to the consolidation of democracy in so-called 'transitional' polities.

We can add a third, long-term analytical consideration. It is worthwhile to continue studying political armies from a historical and comparative point of view precisely because the terms of reference for military politics have been changing dramatically during the past ten to fifteen years. That is why it is still highly relevant to investigate the ongoing military preoccupation with nation building, possible 'threats' to this project (as they may be perceived), and the resulting refurbishing of political armies in a globalizing world of the post-Cold War era.

The basic change of parameters for political armies has less to do with the rise of democracy as a valued form of political regime than with the fact that, because of the weakening of the notion of nationalist development and the virtual disappearance of anti-communism as a credible doctrine, a large part of the conventional legitimacy of military rule seems to have disappeared too. As we have seen, prior to this recent doctrinal shift, developmentalist 'modernization' and anti-communism had left their mark on military projects of nation building. In many cases (as will be shown for many of the countries discussed in later chapters), such projects espoused economic growth on the basis of market capitalism, political conservatism in defence of the status quo of social relations, and a general adherence to the strategic dominance of the advanced industrial powers. However, there have also been a number of cases in which the military project aimed at economic and social reform, with a non-aligned or even anti-imperialist doctrine.

The changes that have occurred during the past decade have provided a new context for this old phenomenon. Increasing economic globalization has called into question the relevance of national development objectives. New patterns of social instability, that may run counter to the military notion of national unity, strength, and order, now come from social exclusion, environmental degradation, regionalism, religious movements, ethnic conflicts, etcetera. This poses the question if and how such new threats may be met by political armies. Are these new issues indeed pushing political militarism to the side? Do the military address them in ways similar to the familiar patterns of pre-1990 militarism (which would imply a military posing as the ultimate guarantor of national well-being against explicitly defined internal threats and enemies)? Or do they provoke a qualitative change in military projects for nation building in general and political involvement in particular, and if so, how? It is important to consider how these changes affect the military 'mission' in countries with a strong legacy of the involvement of the armed forces in domestic politics.

## Scenarios for Political Armies in the Post-Cold War Era

The changing conditions in the post-Cold War period may give rise to at least three current trends and possible scenarios for the near future, with respect to the phenomenon of political armies. First, the *withering away scenario*. If the forces that work against the classical project of military politics are strong enough (like economic liberalization, globalization, disappearance of Cold-War battlegrounds and ideological polarization, democratization supported by an interstate system that – selectively – seeks to enforce democratic governance and the rule of law), this may lead to the gradual but effective demise of military involvement in politics to the benefit of civil and democratic control of political life and public administration. A crucial condition for this scenario to materialize would be that these forces do not 'backlash', that is to say, civil supremacy, democracy, and political pluralism are grounded on national political and institutional structures and processes that are regarded as 'effective'. Effectiveness here would mean being able to safeguard governability, to accommodate social differences and conflicts in a peaceful way, thus facilitating stability and order.

Second, the *institutionalized modification scenario*. This scenario means the preservation of the political role of the military, either openly (with old doctrines and legitimations or with new ones in terms of the military project and its immediate threats), or more hidden, backstage, through tutelary powers or notions of 'guided democracy'. In this scenario there are forces that may alter the profile of political armies but still keep their politicization clearly within corporate and institutional boundaries. This means the identification of new threats to national unity and stability in social, religious or ethnic radicalism or separatism, or in regional interstate rivalries. It also means the identification of new missions: humanitarian aid, environmental control, crime fighting, the war on drugs (pressed by external interests, mainly the US).

Finally, the *perversion and corruption scenario* of military politics is one in which the armed forces embark upon a destructive course while reluctant to yield real power despite strong pressures (internally or externally) to do so. A number of specific dynamics fit into this picture: degeneration into rogue regimes; having recourse to paramilitary forces to do the dirty work while the military are cloaked in formal respectability and compliance with democratization; or, alternatively, the marginalization of institutional militarism by a more shady proliferation of armed actors. In short, there are forces that may produce *new forms* of institutional or perverted military rule: governance failure, state collapse, intra-state violent conflicts, economic interests, rent seeking, association with paramilitary forces, uniformed gangsterism.

This last tendency seems to be on the rise. Its basic problem is that it removes the militarization of politics from public scrutiny and from a clearly demarcated institutional arena. As a result, formal democratic transitions or peace and reconstruction processes can be undermined. While formally adhering to democratic consolidation and civilian rule, the military may also secretly scheme to preserve their political leverage, partly through delegation to 'rogue' paramilitary groups, while officially denying all involvement in ongoing political violence. There are many indications that this may be the role of the military in countries like Algeria, Colombia, Indonesia, Peru and Serbia. Not least among the factors that contribute to this reluctance to yield is the desire to maintain deep-rooted military prerogatives: institutional privileges, power positions, or access to economic resources.

Perhaps the most threatening scenario is that of the proliferation of armed actors beyond the boundaries of legitimate institutions and formal politics, the perversion of the armed forces and the emergence of privatized forces of law and order. This private sector soldiering represents the dark side of the public service ethos within the armed forces. In situations where state disintegration is more marked, the infrastructure of the terror state is contracted out to the intelligence-cum-security apparatus, amplified with their more shadowy paramilitary and 'para-police' forces to create a climate of terror and fear.[49]

In short, present-day appreciations of political armies cannot be limited to the classical juxtaposition of military interventionism (ultimately leading to dictatorship) and civil supremacy (ideally in the form of democracy). The picture has grown more complex: we see the military adhering to democracy, but in an uneasy relationship towards civilian politics; we see them defining new missions geared to nation building and leading to political activism. Again, we find them defining new threats and enemies to national destiny, such as separatism, ethnic mobilization, religious fundamentalism, or maybe even 'Western' notions of pluralism and human rights. Finally, we come upon a military facing the ultimate doomsday scenario of imminent or factual state collapse, driven towards compliance with the proliferation of violence, the privatization of governance, and the criminalization of politics.

## Notes and References

1   We are grateful to Emanuel de Kadt for his valuable comments and editorial suggestions on the first (February 2000) draft of this chapter.
2   Quoted from *Pakistan Link Daily News*, consulted on 16 November 1999. We used their Internet Page (http://www.pakistanlink.com/headlines/Oct/12.html).

3 See Fitch (1998: xi–xv).
4 Brigadier General Helio Ibiapiana Lima (1999) 'Vivemos 1963?' *Revista do Clube Militar* 77 (381), pp. 4–5 (bold print and capital letters in the Portuguese original).
5 See Kruijt (1994) and González (1990).
6 Finer (1962: 4).
7 See Asprey (1993).
8 For the emergence of the German High Command and its relation to the Prussian state, see Fay (1937).
9 See Peukert (1992: 52 ff.). For details, see Shirer (1983: 167–210).
10 Toland (1970: 25 ff.).
11 General Kazushige Ugaki, a moderate and the emperor's choice as his new prime minister in February 1937, was unable to form a new government due to the open resistance of the army's leadership. He declined his political appointment and publicly declared:

> What I see is that only a few men in authoritative positions in the Army have formed a group and are forcing their views on the authorities, propagandizing as if their action represents the general will of the Army.... I believe that Japan stands at the crossroads between fascism and parliamentary politics. I am partly responsible for the present condition in the Army, which has become a political organization. (Toland, 1970: 46–7.)

12 See for details the memoirs of Beria's associate Sudoplatov (1994: 50 ff.).
13 See Bevor (1998).
14 Kinross (1999: 105–6).
15 See his excellent bibliography by Kinross (1999). For a general discussion on the emerging Turkish state, see Pettifer (1997) and Shaw & Shaw (2000).
16 See Garrido (1982). For the years thereafter, see Knight (1999: 105–24), and Pansters (1999: 235–63).
17 See Özbudun (1995).
18 The term comes from Janowitz (1964).
19 See Huntington (1957) for the conventional argument for civil–military relations under civilian supremacy and non-political military professionalism. Rial (1990: 17) summarizes the characteristics of this type of military under the label of 'advanced North Atlantic' armed forces.
20 If one takes for granted the weakness of the civil police force or its subordination to the military hierarchy (cf. Janowitz, 1964: 36 ff.).
21 See Finer (1962: Chapter 6).
22 See the various arguments presented by, among others, Finer (1962); Janowitz (1964); Pye (1962); Shils (1962).
23 See Huntington (1968: Chapter 4).
24 See Fernandes (1981).
25 See Kennedy (1974, especially Chapter 4).
26 See Nun (1967); O'Donnell (1973).
27 See the contributions to the volumes edited by Collier (1979) and by O'Brien and Cammack (1985).
28 See Koonings (1991, 1996) for a more detailed discussion.
29 See for instance the work done on Latin America by, among others, Rouquié (1989); Stepan (1971, 1988).
30 See Agüero and Stark (1998); Diamond, Linz and Lipset (1989); Domínguez and Lowenthal (1996); Fitch (1998); Goodman, Mendelson and Rial (1990); O'Donnell and Schmitter (1986); Zagorski (1992).
31 The military role expansion, analysed by Stepan (1976); or the establishment of professional militarism through military professionalism in the view of Nunn (1978); see also Rouquié (1989: Chapter 4).
32 In many cases, a political party can take on partly or fully this role, sometimes in close harmony with the armed branch of the movement in question. To the extent that, as we noted above, totalitarian parties come to dominate their military in such a situation, Finer's

(1962: 10) reference to these parties as 'lay armied' is still to the point.

33 See Janowitz (1964: 8–12) for a similar classification of the origins of armies in the new nations. He distinguishes between non-colonial (i.e., ex-imperial), ex-colonial, national liberation, and post-liberation origins of armies. In fact, Janowitz argues that this origin does not predetermine the political role of armies (or the absence of such role). We think, however, that different origins will give rise to differences in the way national foundational myths are developed by political armies.

34 See Fitch (1998); Loveman (1994); Rial (1990).

35 Chile's neo-liberal model under the Pinochet dictatorship was probably the major exception to this rule, alongside the less clear-cut and successful efforts of the Argentinean and Uruguayan military regimes in the 1970s and early 1980s.

36 See Perelli (1990) for a discussion of the Latin American Southern Cone countries in this respect.

37 See Kruijt (1996b).

38 Both a leading tank strategist and, as a retired general, a brilliant military historian. For his innovative technical thinking, see for instance Fuller (1943). His writings on military history (Fuller, 1933; 1954; 1961) influenced generations of scholars on military affairs.

39 This thesis, launched back in the 1930s as part of the Good Neighbour Policy, supposed mutual, Inter-American defence interests against the European fascist countries and Japan. At the start of the Cold War, its character changed to that of an anti-communist alliance. In the 1950s – with the Guatemalan and the Cuban revolutions – it became important to counteract 'internal enemies' as well.

40 For a more elaborate analysis we refer to Koonings and Kruijt (1999).

41 The most striking example of such a pact is perhaps the long-term military project in Guatemala between 1958 and 1996, eloquently described by Schirmer (1998) and Rosada-Granados (1999). The only apparently civilian interlude, the government period of Méndez Montenegro (1966–70), was based upon a formal, though secret agreement, signed between the civilian government and the higher military echelons. The complete text of the (then) secret pact can be found in Villagran Kramer (1993: 459–62).

42 In the case of Pinochet's Chile the president was also the senior member of the junta.

43 See Stepan (1976).

44 See Janowitz (1977).

45 See O'Donnell (1973).

46 We refer here to Koonings and Kruijt (1999).

47 See Rial (1990).

48 See Kruijt (1998; 2000).

49 For two exemplary studies, see Cleary (1999) and Pécaut (1999). See also Cilliers (1999) and Lock (1999).

# 2

# From Military Reformists to Civilian Dictatorship

## Peruvian Military Politics from the 1960s to the Present

### DIRK KRUIJT and MARIA DEL PILAR TELLO[1]

## Three Cycles of Civil-Military Relations

Peru has an established tradition of military involvement in national politics. Of the 72 presidents between 1821 – the year of Independence – and 2000, 51 were officers: eight field marshals, 34 generals, six colonels, two lieutenant colonels and one rear admiral. Between 1821 and 1872 the country was run by military presidents exclusively. By and large, Peru's political landscape between the 1830s and the 1950s was the theatre of an alternating government formula, where power was shared by a small oligarchic elite and a series of military presidents, generally acting as the guardians of the traditional order. A certain period, between 1895 and 1919, was even referred to by the Peruvian historian Basadre as that of the 'Aristocratic Republic'.[2] The traditional economy and social order remained largely intact during the first half of the twentieth century and in fact was not assailed until 1968. The subject of this chapter is the political role of the armed forces in the post–1968 period. Our analysis suggests that Peru's military politics from the 1960s to the present can be perceived as a succession of three cycles.

The first cycle comprises the 'Revolutionary Government of the Armed Forces', especially the period of Velasco. This leftist nationalist, reformist military government of the 'institutionalists' within the armed forces tried to modernize the Peruvian economy and society by putting into practice a *sui generis* military doctrine of national security and national development, formulated during the 1950s by intellectuals at the military study centre and in the intelligence service. The political-military projects of Velasco (1968–75) and Morales Bermúdez (1975–80) were basically efforts to break the power of the traditional elite, and to reduce the influence of foreign capital, in order to forge a strong Peruvian economy and national society. These projects were executed by the army's officer corps and a strong public sector, supported by 'participation' by organized labour, urban masses and peasant organization of the newly formed rural cooperatives.

The second cycle refers to the counter-insurgency years of the 1980s and the early 1990s, when the armed forces – reluctantly – were engaged in 'internal war' operations against the guerrilla columns of Shining Path (Sendero Luminoso) and other armed actors. The army, following the same military–development doctrines as during the Velasco years, and still recruiting the same social blend of officers and enlisted men,[3] found itself confronted by new and unexpected adversaries and an indifferent, maybe even hostile indigenous population in the 'emergency zones' where the war was fought out. After ten years of bitter counter-insurgency warfare, Shining Path was defeated when the armed forces made a strategic alliance with the indigenous self-defence organizations – the *rondas campesinas* – and brought these *rondas* as auxiliary and additional forces under military command.

The third cycle roughly coincides with the period of the Fujimori government, and was typified by the gradual subordination of the armed forces to a neo-populist regime. Supported by the special legislation of the counter-insurgency campaigns, and having eliminated most of the 'institutionalist' higher echelons of the officer corps, Fujimori managed to transform the armed forces into his political executive arm. In this new civil–military alliance, the head of the government was an elected, civilian president. In comparison with the former governments of Velasco and Bermúdez, when a sequence of military governments came to power to execute a 'national development project', this time no one within the Peruvian military had designs on the country's destiny. The military obeyed Fujimori, not vice versa.[4] This was the case, at least, until September 2000.

In this chapter we analyse these changes in military politics and civil–military relations in more detail. The key problem will be the question of what happened to the reformist tradition within the armed forces. First we examine the Revolutionary Government of the Armed Forces (1968–80); second, the period of the internal war under civilian presidents Belaúnde and García; third, the making of new civil–military alliance at the end of the internal war and before Fujimori's self-coup (1989–92); and, finally, the mechanisms of control of the Fujimori regime (1990–2000). The final section is concerned with the prospects and perspectives of Peru's armed forces: there we resume our analysis of the political demise of the Peruvian Army and the decline of its national development projects, followed by the unexpected eclipse of the political regime of Fujimori.

## The Revolutionary Government of the Armed Forces (1968-80)[5]

As a consequence of the humiliating defeat in the Pacifico War,[6] Peru tried to modernize the armed forces. Instructors from the French Army were engaged from 1896 onwards. French influence on the Peruvian armed forces, the army especially, was not confined to uniforms, badges and jargon. The structure of the armed forces, of the officer corps and the training schools, bears a French stamp. Alongside this, one encounters US military conceptions, procedures and organizational schemes. The presence of the US has been felt more keenly since the Second World War, not only by way of military missions, but also through programmes of military and civilian development aid, complemented by training in the US. Peru and Brazil were privileged to receive the largest share of such missions and assistance in all of Latin America, at least up to the mid-1960s.

During the 1950s and even more so during the 1960s military missions and military aid were standard practice in every Latin American country. Cooperative networks were formed, more or less openly, with US military and intelligence services. The CIA gradually strengthened its hold in Peru via a liaison with naval intelligence. The number of US officers acting as advisers in Peru was not large, and certainly modest compared with the former French hegemony. Consequently, influence in the national programme of training remained limited. The army reserved for itself the training and immersion in military thinking of its national cadre. Initially, the weaponry obtained consisted mostly of US material, but this changed in the early 1960s when repeated Pentagon refusals to provide the army and the air force with the latest defensive weapons led the Peruvian high command to shake off dependency on US military deliveries.

During the Cold War, US-related concepts of national security were diffused all over Latin America. In Peru, however, the 'normal' overwhelming anti-communism of the Latin American security thesis was felt much less strongly. When the Centre of Advanced Military Studies (Centro de Altos Estudios Militares, CAEM) was established in 1953, the leadership infused a markedly nationalistic orientation into army training and staff. The instructors – soon to become the first generation of 'military intellectuals' – drew upon the Latin American theorists in Santiago who were associated with the newly created UN Economic Committee for Latin America (ECLAC). The ECLAC theorists had launched new concepts such as 'underdevelopment', and 'centre–periphery' to explain Latin America's lag as compared with its powerful northern neighbour. These views accorded well with the nationalistic notions nurtured by the military scholars at the CAEM. CAEM officers not only fleshed out their Peruvian doctrine of 'National Progress and Integral Development', but also engaged in the study of the nation's economic, social and political potential.

One of the new priorities within the modernizing armed forces was to create the intelligence services and relevant training programmes. General Rodríguez Martinez, a late-1950s reformer of the armed forces, brought together a group of 35–40-year-old officers to execute his task. The members of this group were also the founders of army intelligence, national intelligence and the training schools for intelligence officers.[7] Most officers were strongly influenced by nationalistic authors and literature. Anti-imperialism and an anti-oligarchic political attitude were common traits. These were the same officers who in the late 1960s designed the national reform plans of the Revolutionary Government of the Armed Forces. In 1962 and 1963, however, their first efforts were directed at military reform.

In 1962, by means of an 'institutional coup' – planned and executed by the high command of the armed forces and the first of its kind in Latin America – two successive military juntas assumed government after national elections in which the APRA party (Alianza Popular Revolucionaria Americana, Popular Revolutionary American Alliance) had obtained a parliamentary majority. The concerns of these juntas can be related to the demands of the military intellectuals at the CAEM. In the Andes region guerrilla movements were biding their time. Peasant movements, which had confiscated property from the landowners, had announced their presence since the beginning of the 1960s. A limited land reform was announced for southern Peru, where Trotskyite leaders had instigated the occupation of lands. The modernizing military mind was also reflected in the founding of a National Planning Institute, explicitly charged with planning for development and reform. Cabinet posts went to reputedly progressive officers. The armed forces provided the infrastructure for new elections which took place in 1963. Belaúnde, a new popular politician with a reputation for moderate reformism and a middle-class party background, was elected president. When he was sworn in the armed forces pledged unstinting support for this reform-minded president. Belaúnde was invited to appoint three high-ranking officers to cabinet posts.[8]

The reform plans of Belaúnde's government, however, did not survive the continuous united opposition of APRA and the right-wing parties. The opposition in parliament made it impossible for the president to rule: the majority parties caused his successive cabinets to fall every few months or so. Cotler has calculated that in his four years in office Belaúnde went through 178 ministers.[9] Belaúnde's last years in office were characterized by one national strike after another. Devaluation of the national currency, a foreign debt rising fourfold in as many years, deployment of the army against the guerrillas, rural and urban social rumblings and eruptions, recurrent checkmates in parliament and concomitantly indecisive government, an endless parade of ministers coming and going ... it all contributed to the erosion of national political stability. Corruption scandals undermined the reputations of ruling ministers and cast their shadow on the occupant of the presidential palace, elected less than a handful of years before for his reasonableness, progressiveness and reform-mindedness.

In the 1960s, three guerrilla movements, headed by intellectuals from Lima but operating without a coordinating structure, tried to launch a 'Popular and Peasant's Revolution' in the indigenous highlands.[10] The Peruvian Army – its intelligence service had infiltrated these movements – crushed the three incipient guerrilla forces in the northern, central and southern Andes in surprisingly short campaigns, and without great bloodshed. Nevertheless, the anti-guerrilla campaign left its mark on the army officers, who had to fight adversaries who were not really enemies. It was felt that what caused the development of guerrilla movements had deep roots in the underdeveloped Peruvian economy and society; that the political system had failed; and that it was just a matter of time before a new wave of guerrilla-led rebellion would sweep the country.

Meanwhile, a study group consisting of a number of military officers had come into being around the commander of the army, General Velasco. The group convinced their commander of the necessity of a politico-military project of 'national development and structural reforms'. A military government should include reforms that went a great deal further than anything Belaúnde had even dared to think of. A few months later a coup plan was designed. The government plan for structural reforms did not drop from heaven, and the fact that soldiers rather than civilians conceived it can be explained. It is immediately related to the establishment of a nationalistic army, led by a group of officers sympathetic to reform.

In 1968, Velasco staged his coup. The reform programme of the Revolutionary Government of the Armed Forces was drafted by the officers and military intellectuals mentioned above, who had also played a leading role in the anti-guerrilla campaigns in the early 1960s. In fact, the reform programme carried out during the Velasco years (1968–75), was conceptualized as a coherent national development and anti-poverty strategy to prevent another guerrilla uprising in the near future. From 1975 to 1980, a second military government under general Morales Bermúdez implemented the second phase of the revolution. In those years, most of the reformist programme stagnated or was 'restructured to real proportions'. It has to be said, however, that during the benevolent Velasco years and the more authoritarian period of Morales Bermúdez, the public sector was visible everywhere in the country. Indeed, the last major military reform, in 1978, was even concerned with the creation of regional development ministries, established in the provincial capitals, with control over local and regional development projects in the underdeveloped regions.

In the light of what followed, we mainly emphasize here the strong points of the military reform programme: nation building through 'development', guerrilla prevention through good governance, and property and management reforms. Building up a strong 'Peruvianized' economy through expropriations and nationalizations, the Velasco military governed via an extended public sector, the instrument for their 'revolution from above', wielded with an authoritarian and paternalistic hand. The economic base of the old 'Aristocratic Republic', the *hacienda* estates of rural and agro-exporting landowners, virtually disappeared by means of far-reaching land reform. The exclusive private-sector hold on mining, industry and fishing was reformed by a complicated structure providing for worker participation in management and capital. The public sector was reshaped into a command structure for 'development' and for 'people's participation'. Through the public sector the military brought security to the capital and other cities, and to the provinces; it provided water and sewerage in the urban slums; it sent the peace judges to the indigenous communities; it launched the national literacy campaigns; it paid the salaries of nurses in the highland villages; and it supervised community workers in the jungle. In addition, the military utilized the public sector to enforce the law and established order for every citizen. It treated the labour unions with sympathy, the poor with compassion, the indigenous peoples with reverence; Quechua was recognized as the second official language of the country.

The government officials were anxious to 'reassociate the already organized and to organize the marginalized'.[11] They assisted in the creation of mass organizations for the indigenous peasants, deeply influencing the formation of a national peasant federation, which at the end of the 1970s had unified 160 peasant leagues with 4,500 local unions and a total of 675,000 members. The government officials also helped to set up workers' communities in industry, trade, and the mining and fishing industries, organized 'federations for landless peasants', and unified local squatter movements in the urban and metropolitan slums. The years of the military government probably formed the only decade of the twentieth century in which the public sector was present in the most remote regions of Peru, the most forgotten villages of the country.

However, Velasco's military project was a 'revolution by decree'. He governed by laws decreed at an average of at least two per working day. The stream of edicts and resolutions which the military poured out over the nation tells a story of nation building and development imposed from above. The presidential regime which shaped the reforms characteristically emphasized steering and control by way of military power and the political order, extending to every nook and cranny of Peruvian economy and society. The hard core of the reform programme in the early 1970s aimed at enhancement of national autonomy. Velasco's control over the armed forces and the state apparatus provided him with the leeway needed to implement his domestic reforms. Some of these, like the institution of workers' self-management, were patently utopian: a new, morally improved humanity would be the outcome of the great process of structural change. Meanwhile, all planning and steering to that end bore the indelible stamp of law and order, of hierarchy and control.

The members of Velasco's team and Velasco himself harboured a profound distrust of the existing party structures, especially of APRA. Their most outspoken sympathy – where there was sympathy at all – was reserved for the Communist Party and its associated trade unions. Containment of the influence of parties was sought in the expedient of not allowing them to take initiatives. Parliament was not disbanded but neither did it meet. Law giving was prepared by a Committee of Presidential Advisers (Comité de Asesoramiento a la Presidencia, COAP),[12] all members of which were trusted, high-ranking military men. Political parties were not outlawed, but for meetings and mass conventions permission was needed from the prefect of Lima, a general. Such permission was granted selectively. By and by prefects and mayors of the larger cities were replaced by military officers in active service or in retirement.

The problem of the regime's constitutional legitimacy continued to haunt the military. In day-to-day practice the constitution – of 1933 – was painfully observed whenever possible. The Statute of the Revolutionary Government stated that it would act in conformity with the constitution and existing law 'insofar as these are in harmony with the objectives of the Revolutionary Government'.[13] Reform of the state bureaucracy was predicated on a division of the public sector into sectors and systems. The sectors were headed by cabinet ministers with voice and vote; systems were presided over by ministers of state with voice only. The relative prestige and power was not primarily based on the importance of a ministry or department. A minister's seniority, his prestige in the military and his degree of intimacy with the president carried a great deal more weight.

Militarization of the state bureaucracy's top rank was initially meant 'to enhance the ethics of the state apparatus'. In the reform plans this body was described as 'inefficient, sluggish and dishonest'. Academic research even prior to 1968 confirmed this diagnosis completely. At first each ministry was given one or more colonels to keep tabs on the civil servants and to encourage their devotion to duty. Some of them kept lengthy surveillance in the corridors, pouncing on lazy civil servants and giving them a public dressing down for 'anti-patriotic behaviour'. Once the first nationalizations occurred, the number of state-run companies was mushrooming and many of the banks were appropriated as well, there was a need for reliable management. Recourse was had to officers in active service, retired colonels, generals, naval captains and admirals. The habit of appointing military officers became entrenched. In each part of the armed forces certain captains, majors, lieutenant colonels and retired officers were singled out for positions of trust. Under Velasco the number of military appointments and double appointments[14] was to a degree kept within bounds. It was estimated, however, that during the Morales Bermúdez period some 40 to 50 per cent of the senior officers were political or administrative executives.

The reform programme was not restricted to changes in the property structure and the modernizing of the state. The new property structures, new sectors and systems, new forms of control and new labour organizations came under the prime responsibility of the ministers of these newly created departments. The sectorization of the economy and the state apparatus also meant a sectorization of society. The military worked at the 'reorganization of the organized' and the 'organization of the hardly organized'. The land reform evoked reactions which in part were translated spontaneously into local forms of association. The population established a number of local Comités de Defensa de la Revolucíon. The military Cabinet understood that incisive reforms could not be accomplished without popular support; to achieve social change one needs planned action and a central organization. Why not let the state coordinate popular support?

The newly created National System for Social Mobilization (Sistema Nacional de Movilazación Social, SINAMOS) would prove an original and highly controversial institution. Velasco's team – the military men as well as the civilian advisers incorporated in SINAMOS – did not have much sympathy with party organization anyway, fearing a population radicalized beyond control. The choice of a bureaucratic alternative seemed even more attractive. One of Velasco's most radical team members was made minister of state and head of this new administrative entity.[15] His civilian advisers recruited progressive technocrats, ex-guerrilla leaders, university professors, etcetera.[16] Throughout its existence SINAMOS was never dull or grey. To right-wingers the organization was a gathering place for communists; among those of the left it became known as 'crypto-fascist'. Both groups of critics were right. SINAMOS proved to be an assembly of all kinds of control people and control freaks. After cabinet discussions, it was decided that the military regional commanders would be directors of the regional bureaux. Military personnel were even stationed at some sensitive local offices. Gradually, more intelligence service officers[17] reinforced the ranks of SINAMOS. Members of cabinet took to recruiting functionaries for additional tasks when a start was made with state-created trade unions in the fishing, industrial and educational sectors. The Ministry of the Interior placed policemen and special force members into the ranks of the civilian functionaries. The organization became gradually more manipulative and distrusted by the autonomous mass organizations. Most founding civilian cadres retired. Once Morales Bermúdez came to power he appointed an iron-willed general, Cisneros, as the new minister. He removed the last of the 'communists and infiltrators'. The organization was dismantled in 1978.

The Revolutionary Government of the Armed Forces was, first and foremost, a military government, undertaking a 'military revolution'. This was both its evident strength and its weakness. The strength of this military revolution was that it was able to implement change and execute reform in the course of just a few years and without significant opposition. All reforms, all experiments, even the participation of the people, were implemented by decree. And here we have the Achilles heel of this military revolution: the failure to integrate the anonymous masses in political structures. Unlike the military governments of Brazil and Chile, the Peruvian military did not bond with business elites of traditional bourgeoises. Velasco's alliance was based upon the loyal, progressive officer corps of the army, upon personal ties with other military commanders, upon the loyalty of progressive intellectuals and civilian technocrats, and upon the popular masses in varying degrees of organization. Morales Bermúdez's support came form the more conservative officers within the armed forces. Was it fear of possibly uncontrollable popular mobilization which caused the military cabinet to decide to channel the participation of the urban working classes, peasants and slum dwellers via SINAMOS, a civil service which soon received specific orders from a number of ministers and was carefully staffed with military cadres and intelligence personnel? The ultimate inability to fuse the military and civic cadres politically, the repeated postponement of a popular party or at least a popular support movement with real political participation, has been – as we see it – the single most important reason why Velasco's fall also meant the stagnation of the reform programme.

During the Morales Bermúdez years, popular unrest and national strikes paralysed the country. The military government ultimately turned to APRA for support. A tight control, exercised by the army intelligence service, was felt within the public sector and by the trade unions, the leftist parties and popular movements. However, the government certainly did not make use of paramilitary forces or death squads. In comparison with the situation in the 1990s, the regime was mild. In comparison with the Velasco period, however, Morales's last years were rather oppressive. An open alliance with its traditional antagonist – the old party system – was the military establishment's only hope of moving out with dignity. The armed forces felt tired, somewhat ashamed: they were responsible for the management of a revolution that nobody wanted anymore.[18] In 1976 a concord was established with the APRA leadership, first as a gentleman's agreement and later, during the election campaign for the Constitutional Congress in 1978, as a barely camouflaged pact. The constitution of 1978 opened the way to a negotiated transference of power to 'civilians', with presidential and parliamentary elections in 1980. Belaúnde, the president removed from office by the Velasco team, was elected for a second presidential term. The junta attended the last mass, marching along an indifferent audience; the civilian cabinet took over power with a solemn *Te Deum*.

## The Civilian Presidents and the Internal War (1980-90)[19]

During the last months of the military government, the three junta members decided to maintain the continuity of military command. By mutual consent with the president-elect, Belaúnde, they nominated themselves the new commanders general of the army, the navy and the air force, leaving the appointment of the three military ministers to the new civilian government. So Belaúnde lived the first year of his presidency in peaceful coexistence with his former adversaries. Even worse: General Hoyos, one of the co-authors of Velasco's government plan and his trusted intelligence chief, had been appointed as the army's chief of staff. After his death in 1981, another Velasquista, General Miranda, also co-author of the final reform programme, took office as his successor. It became a standard presidential policy to keep the military at a distance and to look to others for support. However, the military had lost their interest in 'national projects'. The army hierarchy had retired from national politics and licked their wounds.

Neither of the two civilian presidents during the decade of the 1980s – Belaúnde (1980–5, his second presidential term) and García (1985–90) – thought of 'national projects'. During the Belaúnde years a kind of restorative 'old party and old cronies' government was established. García's presidency at last brought APRA into office. APRA government, however, would spiral away in a political debacle. Conflict with the international and multilateral financial system about debt service and the repayment of the foreign debt in general brought Peru the status of an international credit pariah. The debt crisis was, in fact, a legacy of the Morales Bermúdez years. Much of the unpopularity of his government was due to the harsh adjustment policies introduced in 1977 to confront the crisis, which lingered on through the 1980s. During this decade, the country was plagued by two major problems: the worsening economic crisis, unprecedented in the country's history, and the threat to the state's stability posed by guerrilla movements – of which Shining Path was the most powerful and terrifying – and other armed actors.

The continuing economic crisis brought pauperization, mass poverty, informality and unparalleled social exclusion as its consequences. As in most Latin American countries, the phenomenon became increasingly intense during the aftermath of the military dictatorships in the early 1980s. Poverty became identified largely with the urban informal sector, a social and economic complex within the national economy and society. The social and political consequence of this long-term process of 'informalization' and social exclusion was the growing erosion of the legitimacy of the formal civil, political and public order. It contributed to the emergence of parallel institutions and the privatization of the public sector. Matos Mar described the decline of the organizations that make up civil society and sketched the timid emergence of a variety of micro-entrepreneurial organizations: local and regional chambers of artisans, the institutionalized soup kitchen and other organizations which provide cheap food in the metropolitan slums, all of them bound by dependency to private development organizations, churches, donor agencies, and welfare institutions funded externally rather than by the local or national authorities.[20] This phenomenon became particularly clear during the García years.

During the 1980s, the traditional political parties in Peru lost the confidence of the voters. In view of the social and economic crisis, and in response to the erosion of the traditional political parties, the public turned its attention to 'politicians without a party', who entered on the scene offering to form hard-working governments. The first electoral manifestation of this change was the election of the mayor of Lima, a TV company owner. He replaced the ex-mayor of Lima, Barrantes, leader of a left-wing and neo-Marxist coalition, who surprisingly had won the municipal elections of the country's capital in the mid-1980s. The newly elected mayor was soon accompanied by provincial mayors with a similar past. 'Coming in from the real world' of private business, without any explicit ties to political parties or political programmes, became a strong indicator for electoral success. One could argue that it was a coincidence. At the end of the 1980s, however, the phenomenon repeated itself at the national level. Suddenly the political background of a new candidate appeared to be insignificant: worse, a political past seemed to speak of incompetence and fraud. Of course, most Peruvian political parties were loose institutions, organized around one well-known, more or less charismatic person. The only political party with strong popular roots and rank-and-file discipline was APRA. And at the end of García's presidential term it was indeed APRA that stood discredited as the vehicle of ineffective economic policy, ineffective adjustment attempts – the third package policy after the efforts of Morales Bermúdez and Belaúnde – and ineffective answers to the spreading violence and guerrilla warfare. With the bankruptcy of APRA during the presidential elections in 1990 and thereafter, the national political edifice of right-wing, centre, and left-wing political parties also became insolvent.[21]

In order to understand the repercussions of the climate of violence and fear, we need a short commentary on Shining Path and other armed actors. Whereas the military left their 'national project' with their negotiated return to the barracks, an organization of a completely different order appeared with its own 'national utopia': Shining Path. Emerging as an obscure, shadowy ultra-leftist splinter party in Ayacucho, it acquired in two years, between 1980 and 1982, the status of Peru's principal problem, and, at the end of the 1980s, the position of its principal disintegrating force. The Belaúnde government did not trust the armed forces and thought it better to keep them quiet. *Velasquista* generals commanded the army, and the army intelligence service was considered to be the heir of the Velasco team. Instead of the army, the police force from the capital Lima, untrained and unfit for guerrilla fighting, was mobilized. When finally, in 1982, the armed forces were sent in to take over the initiative from the frightened police force, they did it reluctantly and without a coherent anti-subversive vision. Obando relates that the leading ideas behind the campaigns against Shining Path in the 1980s consisted of two anti-subversive manuals of the US army, dating back to the 1950s and translated into Spanish.[22]

The strategic framework used by the armed forces was attuned to geopolitical contingencies and external enemies. Even the contingency plans for the 'home defence of the territory'[23] exclusively concerned a situation in which an external enemy had penetrated Peruvian borders. Until the late 1980s – one of the most bitter phases of the war against Shining Path – only 20 per cent of the military forces was directly dedicated to the containment of the guerrillas and other 'sources of terrorism'.[24] The military chiefs in the war regions or 'emergency zones' – first Ayacucho, then most of the Andean departments – acted on their own in the absence of a coherent strategic concept. Consequently, most of the local and regional activities were carried out in the absence of the slightest coordination with other military chiefs in other regions. Most military anti-subversive activities were bluntly repressive and based upon the simple idea of terror against subversive elements and possible allies. If the government explicitly required action, it asked for military manifestations, indiscriminate military operations, bullets instead of a targeted combination of local development, local confidence building and tactical military counter-insurgency. An early counter-insurgency strategist, the Quechua-speaking general Huamán, made chief of the emergency zone of Ayacucho in 1984, opted for a paternalistic treatment of the peasant population. He asked for more political power, more local development projects, and more rational use of the *rondas campesinas*, the self-defence peasant organizations that had emerged all over Peru.[25] When he also complained in the national press, that the anti-guerrilla strategy should in the first place be a political and not a military one, he was substituted by a new regional commander.

Until the late 1980s, the internal war affected mainly the emergency zones with their indigenous populations. With the extension of Shining Path's realm to the metropolitan areas of Arequipa, Trujillo and Lima, the ingredients of the cocktail changed. The first areas of infiltration to be selected were the urban slums and the industrial cordons. The first category of persons to be intimidated were the independent or leftist union leaders, slum leaders, local mayors and councillors, and the directorate of the local development organizations. Sometimes they were 'persuaded' to retire, sometimes a 'popular tribunal' had to be organized to condemn the obstinate representatives and execute them with dynamite after trial. With the appointment of a more cooperative leadership, Shining Path then left selected supervisors behind. Public sector officials, NGO officers, lawyers, doctors and journalists were paid warning visits at home or in the office. The 'thousand eyes and thousand ears' of the movement were rumoured to be omnipresent. And to demonstrate their potential for public control, Shining Path periodically organized 'armed strikes' in metropolitan areas – organizing selective punishing by killing disobedient taxi-drivers and shopkeepers.

A second guerrilla organization, the Tupac Amaru Revolutionary Movement

(Movimiento Revolucionaria Tupac Amaru, MRTA), started its operations in 1984, in some respects as a competitor to Shining Path. If there is officialdom in guerrilla warfare, the MRTA belonged to the 'formal sector' of uniforms, military-style command and 'normal' behaviour, including public appearances and the bravado of its leadership. Both Shining Path and the MRTA tried to acquire control of the Alto Huallaga, with the former emerging as the major force and ultimate winner in the region. 'Normal' urban criminality, visible through spectacular raids, kidnapping and hijacking became chronic during the García presidency. Suspected criminal police officers, turned loose in mass discharges, mingled with unemployed ex-conscripts of the armed forces and petty criminals in the metropolitan areas.[26] The drugs economy also contributed to the process of informalization and violence. Originally mainly a Peruvian affair, with its local drugs aristocracy laundering money through the Banco Amazónico and establishing fragile ties with the regional military, it became a matter of 'Colombianization' and a division of labour between foreign and Peruvian involvement in the early 1980s. Ten years later, coca production in the Alto Huallaga valley alone provided the source of income of some 300,000 people. Nobody tried to analyse too deeply the interactions between the drugs lords, the drugs traffickers, Shining Path, the MRTA, the regular police, the army, the navy, the air force and the government.[27]

Peru's cocktail of violence also resulted in the emergence of new armed actors. One example has been the semi-institutionalization of the *rondas campesinas* as the extended arm of the police and armed forces. In their transformation into private armies in the late 1980s and early 1990s they went down the same road as the armed bands of workers in the popular districts or attached to the unions of the legal left: armed first with sticks, then with home-made arms, and finally with conventional weapons. The slum population invented home-made defence instruments like staves, sticks and bicycle chains. In the mine encampments and the industrial cordons the workers took up self-defence, virtually transforming themselves into local private armies. Alongside these popular self-defence and peace-keeping groups, private organizations of a similar type began to be formed. These are private sector security and vigilance institutions, companies with personnel recruited from formal and informal institutions, from retired, discharged officers and from ex-personnel of the army or the police. These private vigilantes find employment and income guarding banks, houses, districts, supermarkets, even ministries and public buildings. The coca peasantry in the Huallaga valley took up arms and formed a self-proclaimed militia.

During the García years, the governing APRA Party also created paramilitary units. The APRA-inspired Comando Rodrigo Franco earned a reputation as a 'political death squad' among its terrified adversaries.[28] Mention must be made, too, of the paramilitary bands, sometimes belonging to the complicated networks of the narco-economy. Finally, one must consider the consequences of the introduction in Lima of the *serenazgo*, the district police made up of self-armed metropolitan inhabitants: these are the armed members of the middle classes, protecting their belongings, functioning as a complement to the capital's police force.

## The Making of a New Alliance (1990-2)[29]

Against all odds, a political novice, Alberto Fujimori, won the presidential campaign of 1990. The new president-elect, without a list of cabinet members or a coherent government plan, looked for political allies. He had to face a situation of immense hyperinflation amidst a profound economic crisis, an inheritance from the former APRA government. He had to confront a situation of worsening guerrilla violence. Nearly half the country had been transformed into military emergency zones. He had to fight a variety of armed actors. He had to challenge a parliament in which he did not command a majority. The high command of the armed forces had supported the candidacy of Vargas Llosa.[30] Fujimori dismissed the members of the military general command on the first day of his presidency, 28 July 1990.[31]

Fujimori had to find trusted friends, a dependable support organization, and a programme of action. He found a friend and a politico-military mentor in Vladimiro Montesinos; he found his support organization in both the intelligence services and – last but not least – the armed forces.[32] The action plan was formulated when his presidency was already under way. The president-elect received warm hospitality from the Círculo Militar during the transition period and the first week of his presidency. There he was extensively briefed by military intelligence about anti-guerrilla tactics and human rights, development strategies and long-term economic and political priorities. Fujimori's political guide and intelligence mentor, Montesinos, president of the newly created Strategic Council of State, then became and remained the virtual president of the National Intelligence System (Sistema de Inteligencia Nacional, SIN).[33] General Nicolás Hermoza Ríos, an uninspiring officer selected for promotion by Montesinos, was made general commander of the army in 1991. He remained at his post from the early to the late 1990s. This triumvirate – Fujimori, Montesinos and Hermoza – would characterize most of the Fujimori era.

The economic crisis was to be attacked. Fujimori's economic team, headed by Minister of Economy Boloña, applied a merciless shock therapy without social anaesthesia. The adjustment policies affected the already poor, the new poor, the urban labour classes and the middle classes. However, they decelerated, then halted, the hyperinflation. The population accepted the results of this Fuji shock, as well as the harsh anti-insurgency policy somewhat later, as a matter of state security. In the process of the adjustment policies the last remains of the *Velasquista* property and management reforms were disposed of as well.[34] The president, when offered the possibility to redraft the constitution, tailoring it to his economic policies and political aspirations, designed a constitution in neo-liberal style, that eliminated many of the social security, trade union and labour codes.[35] Labour contracts and trade union arrangements were now easy to change, or to do without. The once-powerful trade unions, who could organize national strikes at the end of the 1970s and who held national significance until the late 1980s, suffered spectacular membership losses in the early 1990s from which they never recovered. The dismantling of the trade union structure is to be seen as a partial consequence of the same process that a couple of years before had announced itself in the decline of the political parties. An additional factor was the loss of employment in the formal economy, the traditional recruitment base of union affiliation. The informalization of Peru removed one of the pillars of socio-political stability: the trade unions and the political parties of the 'formal system'.[36] The enormous reduction of autonomous labour and of the political institutional context during the first years of Fujimori's two presidential terms (1990–5 and 1995–2000) contributed significantly to the unchallenged social and political control of his later years (see next section).

Fujimori's most acclaimed achievement was the demolition of Shining Path.[37] The movement's overall strategic concept had been 'to separate the cities from the rural hinterland'. At the end of the 1980s, Shining Path had developed – or so it was assumed – a formidable support organization of 'popular committees': 1,140 of them, controlling 211,500 individuals, generally in the indigenous departments of Ayacucho, Huancavelica and Apurímac. The control was based upon a barren, totalitarian regime of terror and fear, exercised by a 'total institution' with fundamentalist traits and devotion. 'Selective annihilation' was the strategy employed against enemies and adversaries. The cruelty of the war, the indiscriminate assassination of rural leadership and the horror felt among the peasant population had considerably diminished the local support required for the organizational stability of a guerrilla movement.[38] When Shining Path, in order to cut off Lima and other metropolitan areas from its 'food-producing hinterland', started to terrorize the peasants and consequently organized a killing campaign in order to establish the obedience of the indigenous Indian population, the local population started to revolt. *Rondas campesinas* confronted Shining Path's columns. In a kind of 'flight forward' Shining Path's leadership decided on an 'encirclement of Lima'. The organizational infrastructure for such an endeavour, however, was very weak. Certainly, the movement established some bases in the Ate-Vitarte and other metropolitan slums. However, when Shining Path launched direct attacks on slum leaders and trade union representatives, it quickly lost its already shaky reputation as a 'rebel' movement. Car bombs, 'armed strikes' and random assassinations of recalcitrant taxi drivers contributed even more to their infamy as desperate killers.

This switched the initiative. The armed forces, reflecting on the errors of the past and conceptualizing a more coherent anti-guerrilla strategy at the end of the 1980s, launched new ideas about central command, adequate intelligence, popular support, and protection of the peasantry.[39] The key principles of the new antisubversive doctrine were to try to obtain the sympathy and confidence of the population; to provide local development programmes; to provide local protection; and to re-establish law and order locally. At the end of 1988, the anti-terrorist police branches were reorganized in the National Institute against Terrorism (DINCOTE, Dirección Nacional contra el Terrorismo), with special intelligence groups, from 1991 on, under the competent command of (police) General Antonio Ketín Vidal. The new president, Fujimori, was quickly convinced by his intelligence mentor and the high command that bringing the war to an end required a special pacification strategy and special legislation. In 1990 and 1991, parliament approved a series of anti-subversive measures[40] providing the armed forces with much more freedom and special jurisdiction in the war zones; supporting the *rondas campesinas* with arms and training, and placing them under military command;[41] and expanding considerably the reach of the intelligence community. Shining Path – and the MRTA – were forced into much more defensive tactics. The military, supported by the *rondas campesinas*, had taken the initiative in the emergency zones, hunting the Senderistas down. In Lima, DINCOTE twice almost captured Guzmán, the Shining Path leader, arresting collaborators and capturing large quantities of documents. And then, suddenly, in September 1992, Guzmán and other Shining Path leaders were arrested by Vidal. Following the arrest of Guzmán, the character and the intensity of the war has changed substantially.

Sixty per cent of the national leadership – sixteen individuals – were captured with him. At the regional level, however, most of the organizational infrastructure remained intact. It was estimated by DINCOTE in February 1994 that the number of *guerrilleros* totalled three thousand, mostly organized in small columns and cells. Shining Path, as a coherent clandestine political organization, broke into smaller components. Its ambition of mounting a 'revolutionary project' shattered. As a military organization at the national level, Shining Path has been reduced to an organization of regional significance, although some of its columns, under new names, have displayed the same violence and surprise tactics as before. The most important group, under Guzmán's successor Feliciano, operated in the mid-1990s in the Huallaga Valley with an estimated total of four hundred Senderistas. Feliciano was arrested in July 1999.[42] A couple of small guerrilla columns are still present in Ayacucho and Ancash.[43]

In April 1992, five months before Guzmán's arrest, Fujimori had carried out a self-coup. Frustrated and apparently obstructed by a recalcitrant parliament,[44] the president in his function as supreme commander of the armed forces, with the support of the army, navy, air force and police leaders,[45] took over direct power. Parliament was dissolved. Public opinion strongly supported the man who was now 'civilian dictator'. The new 'Emergency and National Reconstruction Government' immediately sent the military in to the 'Sendero-infested' universities of San Marcos, Ingeniería and La Cantuta,[46] and into the penitentiaries, where Shining Path exerted a parallel administration. DINCOTE's successful round-ups, and in particular the final capture of Guzmán, seemed to justify the presidential coup. About 80 per cent of the population supported the self-coup after Guzmán's arrest in September 1992. The president convoked a new constitutional congress, but it was international pressure rather than local protests that forced Fujimori to call elections in November 1992. He obtained a majority – albeit with a very small margin – and in 1993 could proclaim a new constitution, fitted to his wishes and ambitions. In the presidential elections of 1995 he obtained, finally, a formidable 64 per cent of the national vote. Now he could count on a political majority party in parliament. However, as we shall see below, the president's *de facto* preponderance in politics was obtained by the subservience of the armed forces, and through the 'thousand eyes and thousand ears' of SIN.

## The Mechanisms of Control under Fujimori I: control over the armed forces

Fujimori could not have accomplished his achievements without the support of the armed forces. In fact, they functioned and still function as the strong right arm of his political machinery. Fujimori's control over the armed forces was established through co-option mechanisms, in the first place; by new legislation on military status and career paths; and by a keen system of internal espionage executed by SIN. Montesinos, now a presidential adviser and in charge of anti-insurgency intelligence, offered his who-is-who knowledge of the officer corps and recommended a far-reaching co-option of the higher army, navy and air force echelons.[47] In 1990, Fujimori, afraid of a possible coup attempt,[48] used promotions-cum-retirement tactics to eliminate disloyal anti-Fujimori commanders from the officer corps. Then, in 1991, a new *Ley de la situación militar* was approved, by which the president acquired the right to appoint the important commanding officers personally. The law also stipulated that commanding officers had to be retired after 35 years of duty.[49] That was how General Hermoza was appointed as general commander in December 1991. That was also how most of the 'institutionalists' – army officers espousing the military virtues of the uncorrupted, competent officer corps of the past – were forced into retirement in 1991–3.[50] As a *quid pro quo*, military counter-insurgency powers were expanded considerably. Military commanders of the emergency zones were bequeathed much more power: direct control over the military, police and civilian administrations. Legal impediments were removed. Military justice was meted out in insurgency and counter-insurgency affairs. A far-reaching Amnesty Law in 1995 established impunity from prosecution for human rights violations in war situations. In this way the loyalty of a manageable military hierarchy was consolidated.

Of course, even such suave subordination did not succeed without protest. Montesinos's influence in army affairs was resented. Internal SIN surveillance within the army was criticized, even by former right-wing military commanders, as 'a Gestapo within the Armed Forces'.[51] Two clandestine opposition groups, 'Sleeping Lion' and 'Commanders, Majors and Captains' (COMACA), ventilated criticism and leaked a series of human rights violations and SIN cover-ups to the national press throughout the 1990s. Retired generals and colonels did the same. In November 1992 SIN infiltrated an officers' group engaged in the preparation of a counter-coup. Nineteen officers were arrested of an estimated forty officers, from captains to generals, involved.[52] At the end of 1992, Fujimori, in a victorious mood, retired more 'disloyal' officers: the numbers two and three of the armed forces, generals José Valdivia and Rodolfo Robles. In 1992 and 1993, special commandos of the army and a SIN death squad appeared to be involved in two sinister killings in Barrios Altos, very close to the presidential palace, and at the La Cantuta University. General Robles made the involvement public and sought political asylum in Argentina. Unable to cover up the complete story, and afraid of a parliamentary enquiry, the loyal General Hermoza, in defence of his president, sent tanks out on the streets of Lima.[53] For weeks, photocopied documents of the instructions given to the special commandos circulated in diplomatic and journalistic circles. During the violent first years of Fujimori's first presidential term, it required a sharp eye to distinguish between the actions of the regular armed forces, the police, the paramilitary units and the death squads. Sometimes nobody knew who killed whom. Was it Shining Path? Tupac Amaru? A frightened *serenazgo* member? Did the drugs Mafia give the order? Or was it a political settlement? Was a presidential adviser involved?

Hermoza and Montesinos were both regularly accused of drugs trafficking. In 1993, under US pressure, Fujimori authorized the deployment of the armed forces in the drugs war. Fairly modest officers' salaries turned working in the narco-zones into a good opportunity to earn an alternative, lucrative income.[54] When the accusations in the national press could no longer be ignored, an internal inquiry was organized and more than a hundred officers were sanctioned – but Hermoza and his closest allies were not among them. In 1993 the president offered Hermoza the office of Minister of Defence. The general refused, knowing where the real power in the army was centred. Montesinos's former ties with the narco-economy made him even more vulnerable to critics. On at least two occasions, his complicity with the cartels embroiled him in distressing scandal: during the legal proceedings against Vaticano, one of Peru's most notorious drugs dealers;[55] and in 2000, when the opposition press published photocopies of Montesinos's hidden bank account in Lima.[56] Both times, his complicity was suppressed.

Hermoza, in professional military matters, did not perform very well.[57] In the old and everlasting frontier conflict with Ecuador, the Peruvian armed forces habitually overran the Ecuadorian military. They had had the upper hand in several frontier incidents during the twentieth century, most recently in the early 1980s. In 1995, however, another frontier incident caused a military conflict, and this time the war with Ecuador was lost. Hermoza, accused of military failure, forced all the generals who criticized him into retirement. It was clear that Hermoza had become a liability to the president, but it turned out to be difficult to get rid of him. The general controlled a strong network of submissive officers, tied together by mutual favours and mutual blackmail. In spite of tight internal control, the officer corps started leaking again. In 1996 and 1997, a series of planned operations came to light: Plan Bermuda, against a well-known journalist; Plan Naval, against the owner of a TV channel; and Plan Pino, to cover up the killings at the La Molina University. In October 1996, Hermoza ordered the arrest of general Robles. The confinement of this very respected retired general met with an angry reception both inside the armed forces and in the press. This time Fujimori intervened personally.

When in December 1996 a MRTA commando captured the residence of the Japanese Ambassador to Peru, together with the *crème* of the Peruvian political elite inside it – ministers, generals, diplomats, politicians, entrepreneurs, Fujimori's mother and his brother Santiago – the armed forces succeeded in liberating all the hostages while killing, together with the MRTA members, only one civilian: Chief Justice Giusti.[58] After the military operation – codenamed Chavín de Huantar – Fujimori claimed all the credit for himself and Montesinos.[59] A kind of public debate arose between the president, his intelligence adviser and his army commander. In an interview in December 1997, Fujimori diminished Hermoza's role during operation Chavín de Huantar. When the general called his regional commanders to Lima for a ceremony to honour their chief, Fujimori immediately ordered the military back to their posts. A couple of months later, Hermoza was publicly dismissed before a national TV audience. Thereafter Fujimori could count on even more ductile commanders in the high command and in the army, navy and air force.[60] Subordination to presidential patronage had now become a standard practice.[61] Fujimori was given a free hand. Because of the fact that none of the emergency laws had been withdrawn, the president and supreme chief of the armed forces was not hindered by parliament: control over military and defence budgets was legally non-existent.

## The Mechanisms of Control under Fujimori II: control over the intelligence community

SIN, the strong left arm of the government, embraces both the armed forces and the police. A rather modest service until the end of the 1980s, mainly confined to military and counter-insurgency matters, it saw its reach as well as its budget and personnel expand under the new management of Montesinos. What before had been a low-key, discreet activity – obtaining information on the whereabouts and activities of political opponents, spying on officers of the armed forces and the police, keeping tabs on academics, journalists, union leaders, TV directors and owners of the mass media, now became the core activity of the intelligence community. Montesinos quickly acquired Fouché-like ambitions and diversified

---

**Box 2.1    Portrait of an intelligence chief: Vladimiro Montesinos**

An army captain during the Revolutionary Government of the Armed Forces, and a member of the intelligence secretariat of the First Minister, he was dismissed from the army, accused of trafficking state secrets – the purchases of Soviet equipment – to US adviser Luigi Enaudi and the CIA. Condemned to prison, he emerged as a qualified lawyer. On his release he established a legal *estudio*, his clients being prominent drugs traffickers and military officers accused of violating human rights in the emergency zones. He came to be known as a reliable source in situations where a legal argument could be twisted or a judge could be 'convinced'. Well-informed and familiar with who was who in army circles, he proved to be an extremely useful ally for law-skirting manoeuvres in and about the armed forces. In 1989 one of the old Velasco generals brought him back to office in SIN. As a lawyer, he assisted Fujimori in his legal problems when the future president was accused of tax evasion and of violating a woman student at the La Molina University. He rapidly became the presidential adviser on appointments within the military, and on intelligence and security affairs. After his rise to power, he was always referred to as 'the Doctor'. Acclaimed as highly intelligent, his very rare public appearances showed him to be a mediocre and confused speaker.

---

the duties and activities of SIN into wide new arenas. Under Velasco, and more clearly under Morales Bermúdez, the public sector had been monitored by the intelligence services. From the early 1990s on, SIN expanded, broadened and pro-liferated. Its special informants now provided reliable reports on 'subversive activities' by politicians, political parties, communications media, and opposition organizations. Fortnightly evaluations of Shining Path and the MRTA also appraised the opposition, seeking damaging information on all elements not subscribing to *Fujimorismo*. SIN also provided access to ongoing rumours, criticism, plots, leaks, and treason in army, navy, air force and police circles, and even within its own ranks.[62]

It was not only SIN personnel who were engaged in surveillance and – when necessary – paramilitary activities. As in the case of the STASI in the former German Democratic Republic and of the state security organizations in other former Eastern bloc countries, an enormous network of petty betrayers, cash-paid village informants, office agents, and informers-by-blackmail provided the intelli-gence community with detailed information. At the top of its list of snoops were some cabinet ministers, such as ex-Minister of Labour and Social Affairs, Agusto Antonioli, for the time being appointed as president of the Constitutional Tribunal.[63] The president of the Corte Superior was an intelligence member. The president of the Electoral Tribunal, an ex-priest and a former member of Montesinos's legal office, was a SIN contact. Blanca Melida Colán, the nation's attorney, was an ex-SIN member. Martha Chavez, president of the Congress,[64] belonged to the SIN family. Oscar Medelios, *abogado-notario* and member of parliament, belonged to the extended SIN family.[65]

The public sector was extensively watched. Civil servants were closely checked by security people, vigilantes and colleague-informers. The directors were controlled by regular intelligence officers. Whoever was a member of the still existing trade unions – in the bank, telephone, transport, construction, public health or educational sectors – was sure to be under surveillance by professional intelligence people and a network of informers. The Fiscal Intelligence Branch (*Sistema Unitario Nacional Tributaria*, SUNAT) was used in financial affairs. The *comités de defensa* and the *rondas campesinas* provided information in rural areas. The zonal and local development committees, the *comités transitorios rurales*, the *cajas rurales* – the rural saving and credit cooperatives – and even the local NGOs provided additional details and pieces of information. The *clubes de madres* contributed their tales from the urban slums. The *serenazgo* members made an inventory of suspects in their *barrios*. Then there were the five thousand odd *arrepentidos*.[66] These were the ex-Senderistas who surrendered, came in with their arms, and betrayed their fellow *guerrilleros*. They obtained their conditional liberty and, of course, were eligible for 'special services': dirty jobs, wet jobs, an assault commando, participation in a death squad.

At the bottom of the pile the network of petty informers provided the information for local blackmail, local control and local promotion. This was the speciality of another of Fujimori's political and labour advisers, Absolón Vasquez.[67] He built an informers' edifice around the state- and donor-sponsored poverty alleviation and rural development programmes. The structure had a remote resemblance to the ugliest traits of SINAMOS during the Velasco years: control from above, parallel organizations, paid informers, hired opponents ... but now on a massive scale and unhindered by influential trade unions. They disappeared, as we mentioned, in the early 1990s. Peru's poverty and social exclusion indicators oscillated, from 1985 to 1995, around 55 per cent.[68] Indexed real salaries in the private sector dropped from 100 in 1985 to 59 in 1995. In 1995, the percentage of underemployment of the economically active population in Lima was estimated at nearly 80 per cent. Two thirds of the population older than 65 years had to live without any benefit from the national social security system.[69] Government and donor programmes against poverty – a national fund for (employment-oriented) development (FONCODE, the *Fondo de Cooperación al Desarrollo*), the *Vaso de Leche* programme (milk for school children), the national food assistance programme (*Programa Nacional Alimenticia* – PRONAA), school breakfasts, rural anti-poverty programmes and small rural village road-building schemes provided relief to between 30 and 40 per cent of Peru's population.[70] At least three million Peruvians received a government or donor food package every day. The anti-poverty programmes served a double objective: to provide food and food *bonos* in return for votes, income in exchange for electoral support, work as a reward for information about friends and foes. Work in the government or private sectors was provided, via the anti-poverty programmes, on 60–90 day contracts. Work was always a short-term favour. Work and income was never sure. It all depended on your votes, your willingness, your loyalty, your information.

## The Mechanisms of Control under Fujimori III: control over the justice system and the communications media[71]

Justice was partially militarized. Under the emergency laws of the early 1990s, civilian justice was in part transferred to military courts. All 'terrorist' and 'subversive' cases, all 'presumable terrorist' and all 'presumable subversive' processes, in principle belonged to the jurisdiction of military judges.[72] The implementation of all penitentiary and related legislation was delegated to military justice. Accepted as an emergency measure, a highly criticized system of anonymous tribunals, or *jueces sin rosto*, functioned from 1992 to 1997.[73] By and large, all cases related to 'high treason', 'terrorism', 'drugs trafficking', 'murder' and 'extortion' could be treated by military magistrates, recruited under military lawyers, advocates, solicitors, attorneys, prosecutors, even medical experts. One supposes that the majority of those who were condemned by the faceless tribunals were Shining Path and MRTA members. Nevertheless, nobody knew how many of the convicted were really perpetrators, and how many were innocent bystanders, or even victims of juridical aberrances. The militarization of justice, even in emergency situations, gradually led to the transference of all sensitive matters to military courts.[74] Peruvian justice in the Fujimori years was criticized for its arbitrariness; for the fact that political appointments were involved; for its sloppy handling of human right violations;[75] for the intimidation of civilian judges and magistrates who dared to act independently in matters that involved the interests of government representatives;[76] for interference by SIN members;[77] and for sanctioning the immunity and impunity of government advisers, death squad commanders and drugs traffickers.

There are several illustrative cases of abuse, intimidation and utter confusion. There was, for instance, the cover-up of the La Cantuta affair, when the cadavers of nine students and a university professor were discovered and the leaders of the Colina group, the executing death squad, stood to be condemned. Ultimately, and despite vigorous national and international protests, a parliamentary debate, and US diplomatic intervention, the case was transferred from a civilian to a military court by the Supreme Court. However, the accused – condemned by the Supreme Court of Military Justice to severe penalties – were amnestied in 1995 by the general *Ley de Amnestía*. Several narcotics proceedings received national and international attention. We have already mentioned the Vaticano case: detained by Colombian security forces, and not by the Peruvian police, he not only confessed his financial ties with Montesinos, but also delivered a detailed list of names and money transfers.[78] However, most higher military commanders involved escaped or were paid off with missions abroad.[79] Ultimately, Vaticano signed several documents invalidating his charges against the most senior officers, and saw his pending life sentence changed into a 30-year penalty. Even high-ranking magistrates could be intimidated. In 1997, when the president contemplated a third re-election campaign, the members of the Constitutional Tribunal who objected to his electoral interpretation of the Constitution of 1993 were removed.[80] Finally, we should mention the series of surprising and mysterious fires in 1993, all involving government buildings where sensitive data were preserved.[81]

Most television and radio stations are private property, as well as most journals and weekly magazines. Thus one would expect an open debate about political problems, drug scandals, corruption, bribes and paramilitary activities. However, most journals and radio and TV stations guarded a decent silence. This can partially be explained by the fact that the state exercised a tight control. Officially, there was no censorship, only self-censorship. There were, however, some remarkable examples of 'reprimands' and 'punishment' of directors and owners who crossed a boundary, or who displeased the president, his advisory team or the high command. The Channel Two political programme *Contrapunto*, for instance,

---

**Box 2.2** Portrait of a civilian dictator

Fujimori was elected President of Peru in 1990 and in 1995. After ten years in the presidential office, Fujimori was no longer the political novice of the early 1990s. He was an experienced Machiavellian, imposing his ideas as the reality others were forced to endure. Ambitious, cold, a formidable pragmatist with an inclination to amorality, he quickly learned how to exploit the deficiencies and weaknesses of opponents and adversaries, and how to capitalize on the talents and dedication of good people and short-term friends. A solitary man, he did not have many friends. He divorced his wife, Suzana Higushi, who financed his first, austere, presidential campaign when he was still a nobody. His only soft spot was his daughter, Kenyi. He discarded his former allies, his former political mentors and advisers: Juan Carlos Hurtado Miller, Hernando de Soto, Antonio Ketín Vidal, Alberto Arciniega. In politics, he preferred to be surrounded by newcomers and sycophants.

The president was a brilliant *ad hoc* tactician. His government style was one of *ad hoc* manoeuvring. During the 1990s he four times created a new political platform, substituting old political allies and spokesmen for younger, anonymous believers. Nearly nobody knew the names of his cabinet members. His old cronies and inmates were, on a regular basis, substituted by others. He attacked – while carefully maintaining the support of the armed forces and the intelligence machinery – all other political parties and movements, the Catholic Church, the human rights organizations, the trade unions and the organized workers, the military 'institutionalists', the intellectuals, the diplomats and journalists, etcetera.

Fujimori was streetwise in the extreme. Growing up in popular *barrios* like La Victoria – where his father had a tyre repair shop very close to the Red Light district of that time – he learned the hard way how to be unscrupulous. In his early years as president he described himself as the *mandoncito*, the 'boss' of his government. A *mandoncito*, a *matón*, is the boss of a street gang, a football team, the harsh, authoritarian leader whose judgement is not to be disputed, whose will is law. About good governance practice – to value fairness, to show respect for institutions and legal procedures – Fujimori commented during his first presidential term:

> I do not firmly believe in institutions that go by the book, in strict legal articles, because the important complementary part is the human person. If he does not exercise command, it does not make sense to institutionalize everything by the book.... Institutionalization is realized by long and tedious exercises. Exercises that can be traumatic, however effective.... I believe, false modesty apart, that I have management capacities.... I feel very close to the military, I've got a military mind. That's the reason that I do what I do. Within the armed forces, of course, I use the hierarchy principle. Outside, I apply the authority principle, that is another thing.[82]

Past master in *divide et impera* tactics, he was the eternal candidate, the eternal president, in the tradition of the great Latin American *pater familias* dictators. For most of the 1990s he co-governed via a triumvirate: the president, his intelligence chief Montesinos and General Hermoza. Over the last two years he monitored his Peru through an advisory body headed by the ➡

➡️ unapproachable Vladimiro Ilyich Montesinos, and composed of the equally taciturn Segisfredo Luza, Santiago Fujimori (his brother and political secretary), Rafael Merino and Absalón Vasquez. They supervised the ongoing corruption, the management of the hate campaigns, the segmentation of the adversaries, the dissolution of autonomous institutions, the manipulation of public opinion, the gathering of all those scraps of information on personal weaknesses, sexual preferences and unfulfilled ambitions that make people manageable.

The president governed through the mass media. There he appeared as the strong but fair father of his Peru. There he appeared as the schoolmaster of the nation, cracking a joke or two, being *criollo*, affectionate, eloquent, modest, honourable and dignified. Whenever the president attended meetings, officers and military men distributed his almanacs and his photographs. His intelligence service provided the latest results of his fortnightly popularity polls. His magistrates kept terrorists and subversives, and sometimes simply people considered to be undesirable, at bay. His adversaries were generally bypassed or controlled. Time and time again he emerged as the only possible political alternative.

was closed after its exposure of telephone espionage by SIN and the surprisingly high taxable income of Montesinos. Its owner, Baruch Ivcher, lost his company as well as his nationality.[83] Of the printed media, only *El Comercio*, *La Republica* and *Carretas* maintained an independent position.[84] In the popular press – the amply headlined journals that are read in the *kioskos* by most Peruvians – Fujimori was portrayed as the *macho*, the political boss, severe but fair. His adversaries and political opponents, on the other hand, were unanimously depicted as feminine, helpless, or gay.[85] The rest of the pages were filled with provocative nudes and monstrous scandals. Control over the mass media was such that, during the presidential election campaign in 2000, the announcements submitted and paid for by opposition politicians were 'voluntarily' refused. The opposition itself was – until the last moment – divided, distracted by petty scandals, the glamour of power and sullen pastimes.[86]

## Postscript: the downfall of the Fujimori regime and the transition period

This chapter was written at the end of February 2000, when Fujimori, although accused of fraudulent actions and intimidation of political adversaries during his third election campaign, seemed to face a divided opposition, splintered into more than ten *ad hoc* constituent movements. None of the opposition candidates looked like a possible winner. None of them chose to step down in favour of a unifying opposition candidate. However, one of the opposition leaders, Toledo, a professor at Lima's business university, ESAN, and a former consultant within the multilateral banking community, opted publicly for a place as deputy behind the best opposition leader. This show of political generosity was rewarded with a sudden rise in popularity in the polls. In a startling campaign finale that evoked some elements of Fujimori's successful run for his first presidential term in 1990, Toledo emerged as a serious electoral alternative during the last weeks of the presidential contest. Members of the Organization of American States (OAS) observation and verification mission, headed by Guatemala's former Minister of Foreign Affairs Eduardo Stein, openly expressed their mistrust of the fairness of the Peruvian electoral system. After a very long and much-disputed count of the final vote in the slums and the provincial hamlets, Fujimori was declared the official winner of the first round with 49.89 per cent of the national vote. Most analysts, however, thought there had been manipulation of the result in the remote areas where the armed forces exercised control. It seemed that the president's political friends had hesitated between declaring him winner by an absolute majority or opting for a second round. That was certainly the viewpoint of a fistful of army colonels who, immediately before the election, published a pseudonymous letter accusing the presidential entourage of electoral fraud. Immediately after the election result was officially published, thousands of angry men and women filled the streets of Lima and other urban centres protesting against the supposed manipulation of the vote.

The Electoral Tribunal ordered a second round between Fujimori and Toledo. Amidst waves of hitherto unheard popular protest and occupations of public places, the two candidates prepared for the coming contest. Then Toledo withdrew because of continuous intimidation and preparations for massive fraud. After an unprecedented one-party, one-candidate presidential campaign that recalled the guided elections in the former Warsaw Pact countries, Fujimori was declared winner of the second round. But Fujimori, inaugurated for a third term as elected president, had obtained a Pyrrhic victory, clouded by imminent popular protest. Although his newly formed political party, Peru 2000 (the fourth successive party he had founded) was the largest one in Congress, the number of opposition members was nearly equal. The government opted for a 'business as usual' approach: fraud, intimidation and bribery. However, the changed political scenario complicated this typical Fujimori–Montesinos manoeuvre. On 15 September 2000 a surprised Peruvian TV audience watched a video – apparently released by military opponents of the duo – in which Montesinos tried to bribe a reluctant opposition member in parliament by a cash payment in dollars to cross over to the Fujimori camp. Popular and international protests hit the roof and the following day Fujimori publicly announced his voluntary resignation as president within a year, with new elections in April 2001.

This public statement was the official confirmation of the political disintegration of the Fujimori regime. Soon afterwards an operetta-like downfall pattern materialized. Montesinos, blamed as the Rasputin of the regime, had to be sacrificed, notwithstanding his support in army circles.[87] Rumours of a possible coup surfaced in gossip- and scandal-prone Lima. Fujimori, apparently supported by a willing US government, then successfully obtained a safe conduct to Panama for his disgraced partner. Montesinos, flying in by private plane, stayed there half-hidden in a fine mansion, surrounded by hired bodyguards and a battery of lawyers. Then he suddenly returned to Lima, however, where he disappeared. The president himself, acting as a kind of Sherlock Holmes and leading a taskforce of policemen with dogs and all-terrain vehicles, was shown on TV personally looking after his once-so-trusted brother-in-politics, now wanted by the law. Fujimori's public image – now that of a broken president, uncertain and sleepless

– suffered a marked deterioration. Was the president ultimately at the mercy of the armed forces who protected Montesinos? Was he perhaps the puppet of a political machinery that by and large he failed to control? The political farce became even murkier when a group of middle-ranking army officers took some senior officers as hostages and escaped to the southern departments of Peru before finally surrendering.

The president's support ruptured: his own first vice-president Francisco Tudela stepped down, refusing to bear responsibility for Montesinos's return.[88] In the meantime, the united opposition in Congress obtained a tiny majority. Opposition leader Valentin Paniagua was elected congressional president. Thereupon the opposition announced the beginning of an impeachment procedure against Fujimori on the grounds that he was morally unfit to perform as president. The president himself took a final surprise initiative: utilizing a trip to Brunei, where he was scheduled to pay a short visit to the Sultan, he suddenly flew to Japan, announcing there that he would give up the presidency within 48 hours. The possibility that he would be succeeded by his second vice-president, Ricardo Marquez,[89] was swiftly blocked by Congress members: they immediately appointed their recently chosen president, Valentin Paniagua, as interim president for the already-agreed period to July 2001.[90]

Former UN secretary-general and defeated presidential opposition candidate (1995), Javier Pérez de Cuellar, was invited to act as the minister president in the new transition cabinet. Another expatriate opposition leader of undoubted prestige, General Rodolfo Robles, returned from exile in Guatemala.[91]

At the time we drafted this postscript – 31 December 2000 – the transition government was trying to reestablish a situation of normalcy. Apart from economic, social and political reforms, one of the most urgent priorities is the clean-up of SIN and of the armed forces, until the very end of the Fujimori regime an extremely dominant political player. The government style of Fujimori, like that of the other Peruvian civilian dictator Leguía in the decade of the 1920s, was based upon the control *and* the co-option of the armed forces. Both authors of this chapter had published on the Peruvian armed forces since the Velasco years, and periodically we both interviewed general officers in retirement. We could perceive the unchanged profile of recruitment and promotion within the ranks of the officer corps, and we noticed both a certain pride within the circles of retired officers about the years of the Revolutionary Government of the Armed Forces, when they had been invested with management responsibilities in the public sector or with government assignments and cabinet posts. When our interviewees alluded to 'the General', they referred – and this was far into the 1990s – to the military virtues of Velasco and his team: patriotism, honesty, discipline and respect for the common people.

The triumvirate of Fujimori, Montesinos and Hermoza purged this kind officer from the higher echelons. The subtle promotion of corruption-prone, backbone-lacking officers to the commanding ranks and the rough removal of the 'institutionalist' members of the officer corps, followed by the resented surveillance by SIN members, deprived the armed forces of its social conscience and its standing. Periodically, the younger members of the army's officer corps leaked information to the press: a certain evidence of feelings of frustration and humiliation. A new kind of officer, more subservient, albeit also more alienated from society, was moulded into the prescribed career pattern under Fujimori. Transforming the armed forces into a more professional support of elected governments, and reorienting, reducing, and cleaning up the staff and associates of the sinister SIN and its allied security forces and institutions, poses a definite challenge to Peru in the twenty-first century.

## Notes and References

1 The first draft of this chapter, written in February 2000, was reviewed in December 2000.

2 The subject of an entire chapter in Klarén's superb history of Peru (Klarén, 2000: 203–40). During the decade of the 1930s two new parties with popular and working-class support were founded: the left-wing APRA or Alianza Popular Revolucionaria Americana (for a detailed history of the APRA, see Klarén (1973) and Stein (1980)) and the PCP or Partido Communisata de Perú, both with their own trade union confederations (Sulmont: 1981). A series of incidents – revolts, intended coup, attempted infiltration of the military rank and file and, above all, the lynching of army officers by the APRA populace in 1932 – set the tone between the army and APRA. A set of 'political house rules' was developed between the armed forces' leadership and the political ruling classes that remained intact until the 1960s (the extended dispute between the military establishment and APRA is documented most exhaustively by the military historian Villanueva (1962, 1972, 1973, 1975, 1977a)). As the military saw it, every strike, uprising or incipient revolt was being masterminded by APRA plotters. The officer corps would rather have had the communists than opt for APRA, and the mere threat of an APRA election victory would suffice to stage a coup. The social elite and the military establishment were united in their anti-APRA sentiments: anything, even the status quo, was better than an APRA president.

3 See Kruijt (1991: 119–20).

4 As is the conclusion of 'The *de facto* powers behind Fujimori's regime' (1996: 21).

5 For this section we consulted Tello (1983), Masterson (1991) and Kruijt (1994).

6 The prosperity of Peru and Bolivia in the 1860s was based on the export of guano and, later, nitrate, situated in their southern desert departments. A dispute between Bolivia and Chile about the mutual exploitation of the guano and nitrate stocks led to a war. Peru felt constrained to honour a mutual aid treaty with Bolivia and participated in the conflict as a belligerent, with disastrous results. Within a few days Chilean forces overran the Bolivian coast. The southern Peruvian departments were conquered in six months. Thereupon, an expeditionary force of the Chilean army and navy encircled Lima from the north, the south and the sea. A spearhead force of 30,000 troops took the capital city. After three years of peace negotiations the two countries signed a treaty in terms of which most of the occupied southern departments would come under Chilean sovereignty. See Klarén (2000: 158–202).

7 Given the affinity with French military ideas, France was asked to help build up these institutions. The United States provided the technology, the ideas came from France. A third partner was Argentina, geopolitical ally in the never-ending antagonism to Chile.

8 The cabinet posts were Economy, Public Education and National Planning.

9 Cotler (1978: 358).

10 For an overview, see Béjar (1973).

11 Coined by Stepan (1978).

12 The committee was headed by a general with the rank of minister of state. The first COAP was completely made up by the members of Velasco's political team. Later, when promoted to generals, they were transferred to cabinet posts or appointed as directors of intelligence or regional army commanders.

13 The preambles of virtually every decree up to 1980 contained a lengthy legal reference to pre-1968 legislation and to the constitution.

14 Such as military commander/regional head of a ministry.

15 And military commander of Region II (Lima).

16 Brazilian anthropologist and populist politician Darcy Ribeiro, exiled from his country by

the military regime, eventually became director of the scientific bureau of SINAMOS.

17 In the 1970s army, navy and air force intelligence merged with comparable police and civil services into the System of National Intelligence (Sistema de Inteligencia Nacional, SIN). In each ministry, in all branches of the public sector, an intelligence sector was created, headed by a colonel who reported directly to the office of the prime minister, who was both army minister and army commander. In 1975 the Escuela de Inteligencia Estrategica was created, serving the whole national system of intelligence and security. The post of intelligence chief was always given to a trusted army general. The three branches of the armed forces maintained, in fact, a relative control over 'their' army, navy and air force intelligence until the Fujimori years.

18 No doubt the armed forces themselves, and especially the army, felt exhausted after ten years of government and politics. And it was not in the interest of that institution to continue confronting a substantive part of civil society, the former supporters of the revolutionary process. The mood in the armed forces was to transfer the government as soon as possible. It is certain that Morales Bermúdez grasped the hidden sentiments of the majority of the army officers, says General Ramón Miranda, the army's chief of staff in 1981–2. See Kruijt (1991: 83).

19 For this section we consulted Tello (1989, 1994); Degregori (1990, 1996); Kruijt (1991, 1996a); Cameron (1994); and Tapia (1995, 1997).

20 Matos Mar (1984).

21 At the presidential elections in 1980, APRA, Popular Action (AP, Acción Popular, Belaúnde's party) and the right-wing Popular Christian Party (PPC, Partido Popular Cristiano) acquired 80 per cent of the national vote. In 1985, APRA and left-wing United Left (IU, *Izquierda Unida*) alone were good for 75 per cent of the electorate. By 1995, APRA, AP, PPC and IU together could hardly score 10 per cent of the national vote! See Rochabrun (1996: 23).

22 Obando (1993).

23 See Tapia (1997: 29–30).

24 See Tapia (1997: 29–30).

25 Stern (1993) provides the following statistics for the situation in about 1990: 300 *rondas campesinas* and armed committees of civil defence in the department of Ayacucho, 200 in the department of Apurímac, 350 in the department of Junín, 150 in the department of Huancavelica, and 20 in the department of Cerro de Pasco.

26 The problem became so acute that the National Chamber of Industry and Commerce, in 1986, during collective negotiations with the government, formulated an 'effective protection against kidnapping' as the most important priority on behalf of the private sector. See Kruijt (1996a: 280).

27 *Caretas*, 6 October 1986, published the names of five high-ranking police officers (four generals and a colonel) and a retired army general as employed by Mafia boss Reynaldo Rodriguez Lopez. His legal adviser was later to become presidential adviser Vladimiro Montesinos.

28 The García government tried to establish a paramilitary force within the regular police forces. Specialized police troops received war equipment, and the well-armed Comando Rodrigo Franco was managed from inside the Ministry of Interior. Finally, the armed forces asked for their equipment back. See Obando (2000: 360–1).

29 For this section we consulted Bowen (2000); Cameron and Mauceri (1997); Crabtree and Thomas (2000); Grompone (1999); Mauceri (1996); and *Privilege and Power in Fujimori's Peru* (1996).

30 The armed forces supposedly had been working on a government plan, Plan Verde. This plan reflects the making of a 'directed and protected democracy', under the guidance of the armed forces who intended to manage the state for a period of twenty years. In 1993, excerpts of this Plan Verde were published in *Oiga*.

31 He also retired around 150 higher police officers in the first two weeks of his presidency.

32 Who had quickly changed their preference from Vargas Llosa to the winner, Fujimori.

33 See note 18.

34 See Inguiñiz (2000: 24).

35 In an interview, 30 October 1998, with Carlos Torres y Torres Lara, president of the Constitutional Committee and then president of Congress, he dryly admitted: 'The new Constitution was maybe not as elegant as the former one, but we had to adjust to the new economic situation.'

36 In an interview, 31 May 1995, with the Minister of Labour and Social Affairs, Agusto Antonioli, he cheerfully remarked: 'No my friends, poverty is only to be resolved by increasing productivity. One has to produce first, then we can speak out whatever we want. And with whom should I speak? The old trade union leaders? Or ... the old politicians of before? They only start complaining....'

37 We follow here Tapia (1997). He quotes extensively from an unpublished manuscript, written by the Shining Path's leader, Guzmán (1990).

38 See the regional analyses in Degregori (1996).

39 Tapia (1997: 45–55) quotes from a manual – *Guerra no convencional. Contrasubversion* – approved by the high command on 9 August 1999.

40 See Vidal (1993). We refer here to the most important issues and only in passing mention other measures: the interventions in universities, the restoration of order in the penitentiary institutions, reform of the Sistema de Defensa Nacional.

41 In 1990 there were already more than one thousand *rondas*. At the end of 1992, the Ministry of Defence had registered 1,730 *rondas* with 93,000 *ronderos*. In May 1994, the number of *rondas* – now named Comités de AutoDefensa or CADs – totalled 6,750 with 400,500 *ronderos*. See Tapia (1997: 73–4).

42 By a combined operation – Operation 'Siege' – of intelligence service and army. See *In Huancayo. Testimony of Pacification* (1999).

43 In September 1999, 6 per cent of the national territory remained under a 'state of emergency', compared with 40 per cent in September 1991. The number of 'dead terrorists' decreased from 891 in 1991, 723 in 1992 and 481 in 1993, to 57 in 1997, 11 in 1998 and 10 in 1999. The number of 'captured terrorists' dropped from 5,413 in 1993, 4,662 in 1994 and 2,582 in 1995, to 681 in 1997, 378 in 1998 and 240 in 1999. See *An Approach to the Pacification Strategy* (1999: 49–51).

44 There are other versions of Fujimori's motives. In January 1992 the president's then influential adviser, Hernando de Soto, publicly resigned with a bitter letter, accusing the Fujimori administration of leniency towards the drugs trade. Two weeks before the coup Fujimori's wife, Susana, the director of a private consultancy enterprise, publicly accused her husband and his brother Santiago of corruption. Parliament had already formed an *ad hoc* commission to investigate the denunciation. See Bowen (2000: 111 ff.). In an interview, 30 October 1998, with Fujimori's former first vice-president, Máximo San Roman, he confirmed the allegations and added that arrangements had already been made for an impeachment procedure.

45 An 'Official Communication' on 6 April 1994, signed by the four commanders of the army, the navy, the air force and the police, stated that:

the president's decision was correct, opportune and necessary. We are solidly convinced by the objective reality of a country that, then being in a situation of crisis and institutional chaos, now steps forward to a well-wished national pacification, a country where already reign the conditions of development of productive activities.... All these conditions are the basis and guarantee for the existence of a stable and indestructible democracy.

46 Tapia (1997: 77 ff.).

47 See Villanueva (1977b).

48 Rumours circulated of a plot, a quiet disposal of the unexpected winner. During the last year of the Garcías government, army intelligence had apparently prepared a plan for a coup against the disgraced president. The execution of this Plan Omega was postponed, but perhaps it could have been reactivated.

49 Until then, a service record of 35 years automatically implied an officer's retirement.

50 See Degregori (1994) and, more specifically, Obando (1996: 26, 32–3).

51 General Luis Cisneros, Minister of Interior during the governments of Morales Bermúdez and Belaúnde, wrote in an open letter (*Expreso*, 2 February 1994): 'The Armed Forces, especially the Army are performing the role of the political party of president Fujimori … Fujimori destroyed the professionalism of the Armed Forces…. The problem is the presence of the Gestapo within the Armed Forces…. An officer can not express his opinions anymore, not even to his colleagues….' Cisneros was given 90 days' house arrest by military justice.

52 Leader of the intended coup was General Jaime Salinas, the expected chief of the army's high command in 1992, but forced to retire by Hermoza; and General José Pastor, retired in 1992 and the expected general commander of the army, replaced by Hermoza. Salinas had been one of Velasco's *aides-de-camp*.

53 Obando (2000: 309).

54 US$250–350 a month in the early 1990s. When we interviewed the retired army generals at that time, we noticed that they had to live on US$300 a month. You could meet army captains in active service, commanders of anti-terrorist units in the emergency zones, on leave in Lima, and working as freelance taxi drivers to buy their children a Christmas present.

55 Vaticano, an alias for Demetrio Chavez Peñaherrera, confessed under interrogation that he had paid Montesinos US$50,000 a month for being given a free hand. Even before the judge could order Montesinos to testify, a suddenly confused Vaticano withdrew his statement, speaking very incoherently. His lawyer told the press that he had been treated with electric shocks. A medical test was denied, for security reasons, because Vaticano had been transferred to the Base Naval in Callao, where the captured leaders of Shining Path and the MRTA are imprisoned. Until 2024, Peñaherrera will enjoy the exclusive company of Abimael Guzmán and Victor Polay.

56 With a balance of more than US$2,600,000, an amount that could not be explained by savings from his adviser's salary. In 1997, a TV programme published SUNAT documents indicating that, in 1995, Montesinos – in his free time – had earned US$670,000 as a lawyer and legal adviser. See Rospigliosi (1997: 58).

57 Here we follow Obando (2000: 371–6).

58 An opponent of Fujimori, refusing to transfer civilian processes to military courts (see below).

59 See *Chavin de Huantar* (1997), a publication by the government. A very rare, recent photograph of Montesinos was published in the document (*Chavin de Huantar*, 1997: 31).

60 Already in 1995, at the beginning of Fujimori's second presidential term, the president had appointed Admiral Antonio Ibárcena and Lieutenant General Elsevan Bello as general commanders of the navy and the air force. Both had intelligence service backgrounds.

61 An example of the army generals' docility is the fact that General Howard Rodríguez, commander of the I Military Region, to the surprise of a TV audience in September 1994, was shown distributing almanacs with the president's photographs at secondary schools in Piura. Fujimori commended the general.

62 In 1997, when the cover-up at La Cantuta University was made public in the opposition press, Leonor La Rosa, a member of the army intelligence service (Servicio de Inteligencia del Ejército – SIE) was questioned and tortured. La Rosa escaped and accused her tormentors. She asked to be treated in a private clinic, whose director was the brother of General Robles. The government thereupon ordered SUNAT, the tax intelligence service, to pay a visit to the clinic. A couple of months before, the dismembered cadaver was found of Mariela Barreto, another member of the SIE and formerly the lover of Major Santiago Marin Rivas, chief of the Colina group, a death squad within SIN. Another member of the SIE and the Colina, Pedro Pretell Dramasso, was mysteriously killed as well. It should be mentioned that leaking is considered to be high treason. In 1992, when two SIN agents, Mesmer Carles Talledo and Clemente Ayalo publicly complained about mismanagement of intelligence funds, they were accused of being undercover Senderistas and received life

sentences. See Obando (1996: 374) and Rospigliosi (1997: 58).
63 Antonioli was with the intelligence service even in the Velasco years. Before Fujimori's downfall, two members of the Constitutional Tribunal were intelligence service officers.
64 March 2000.
65 In February 2000 he proved to be the key person in the scandal of the million falsified signatures on the presidential electoral lists. See *El Comercio* (29 February 2000).
66 Called after the counter-insurgency inspired *Ley de arrepentimiento* of May 1992. See Tapia (2000: 80–1).
67 Son of working-class APRA parents in Laredo, an impregnable APRA fortress since the 1930s, and himself an ex-worker of Laredo, familiar with dirty tricks in rural Peru.
68 Figueroa, Altamirano and Sulmont (1996), and Figueroa (2000).
69 Figueroa (2000: 232–48).
70 US$287 million in 1993, US$503 million in 1994, US$984 million in 1995 and US$1,055 million in 1996. See Figueroa (2000: 249).
71 For this section we consulted Grompone (1999: Chapter 6).
72 See Gamarra (1996a, 1996b).
73 Adapted from the system of 'regional justice' in Colombia. For an evaluation, see Gamarra (1997).
74 'When you start with judges *sin rostro*, you will end with a legislation *sin rostro*. And when you systematically transfer politically sensitive cases to a military tribunal, you start legalizing human rights violations and torture.' Supreme Court Justice Carlos Giusti told us this in an interview, 17 February 1994. As mentioned above, Giusti was the only hostage who was killed during Operation Chavín de Huantar.
75 America's Watch declared that 'Fujimori's government is based upon a military institution with unlimited power and a civilian bureaucracy willing to cover all violations of human rights by uniformed people' (*El Comercio*, 10 May 1994, translated from the Spanish). When Fujimori, also in 1994, accused a Peruvian human rights organization of 'complicity with subversion', Amnesty International demanded a retraction. The answer was never received (*Expreso*, 16 February 1994).
76 'A paso lento' (1999: 47).
77 'Democracia en la encrucijada' (2000: 28).
78 US$5,000 per flight that arrived at Campanilla airport. US$10,000 for 'airport taxes'. US$5,000 for the civilian authorities. *Cupos*, or taxes paid to Shining Path in Uchiza. US$1,000,- to each of the four SIN members who arrived to make arrests, but who offered protection to the Juanjuí village after payment.
79 Like General Eduardo Bellido Mora, military commander of the Alto Huallaga region and brother-in-law of General Hermoza. Three officers, Captain Gilmar Valdivieso Rejas, Captain Falconí Alvarez and Major Evaristo Castillo Aste, who testified against their commanding officers, were charged with 'insults towards superior officers' and other military offences. They had to seek refuge abroad.
80 See Obando (2000: 374–5). Ricardo Nugent, director of the Constitutional Tribunal, was the victim of an assault involving police and unknown 'delinquents'. Two of his marshals died.
81 The Constitutional Congress (self-coup and electoral archives, April 1993), the Banco de la Nación (debt archive, March 1993), again the Banco de la Nación (June 1993), PETRO-PERÚ (petroleum contracts archive), the Palace of Justice (drugs archives, September 1993), the Office of the High Command (documents unknown, September 1993), and – twice – the building of the Ministerio Público (disciplinary archives, October and Decmber 1993).
82 *Expreso*, 16 January 1994.
83 Treating the matter as a grave threat to national security, the high command issued a special *comunicado*.
84 The weekly *Sí*, highly critical in the 1980s and the early 1990s, was silenced after the rape of the fourteen-year-old daughter of the owner, presumably by two SIN officers.

85 An observation made by Carlos Iván Degregori who has written an essay about the political significance of the popular press.

86 Such as the appearance of a weeping Virgin Mary, a sex scandal in which a rival candidate is immersed, a special trip by the president, a sudden outbreak of violence in the penitentiaries, etcetera. The issues were probably provided by Segisfredo Luza, another presidential adviser. Luza, a psychiatrist who murdered the husband of his lover and who was sentenced for manslaughter, was the conceptual brain behind the besmirch and hate campaigns.

87 He enjoyed especially warm support from the army commander and from the commander of the tank division in Lima, his brother-in-law. Both generals were discharged by Fujimori in the last week of October 2000.

88 Presumably Montesinos lived quietly in Lima, negotiating by telephone with his army friends. When Fujimori finally discharged his most-favoured army generals, the former SIN chief escaped by private yacht on Sunday morning, 29 October, accompanied by bodyguards and call girls, via the Galapagos Islands, Costa Rica and Aruba to Venezuela, where he – by now known as Manuel Antonio Rodriguez – underwent plastic surgery. Meanwhile, the Swiss authorities were expected to block around US$70 million in his personal accounts.

89 A trusted first vice-president during his second presidential term (1995–2000).

90 28 July, Fiestas Patrias, is the normal government transition date.

91 The former third-in-command of the army, exiled to Argentina, he was expelled from the armed forces as a retired general and deprived of his military pension. Two of his children, both army officers, were also expelled from the armed forces. Robles, while living in Costa Rica before his return to Peru, acted as consultant in a FLACSO research project on war-torn societies.

# 3

# The Guatemalan Politico-Military Project

## Whose Ship of State?

JENNIFER SCHIRMER

Discussions of political armies often entail a description of the relations between political regimes and armies. But in the case of Guatemala, one needs to focus such a discussion on the shifts in the internal ideology of the military itself and the manner in which it has been responsible for the creation of a set of political outcomes at particular historical moments. In short, it is the military that has been the pilot navigating the stormy political waves, often navigating alongside of or shipwrecking political regimes. It never has been merely a member of the crew working cooperatively to service the ship of state. Thus, to understand how and why these changes have occurred, one needs to focus more on the military's internal cultural and institutional logics rather than on the formal relations and structures between a political regime and the armed institution. By tracing the military's ascendance to power by way of state violence through the eyes of the officers themselves, this chapter is based on an ethnographic approach in which research is conducted with the primary purpose of capturing the perceptions, categories of thought and systems of meanings of those interviewed, rather than an approach that imposes an outside frame of reference.[1]

After decades of naked military rule, the Guatemalan military had a political awakening in 1982: it needed to conduct its counter-insurgency war within the political parameters of civilian and nominally democratic governance. With the March 1982 coup staged by younger officers fearful of losing the counter-insurgency war to the guerrillas because of old guard-caudillist corruption, a politico-military project was launched that shifted from a massacre campaign to an election campaign in a matter of three years. This was a project overseen by institutionalist officers who learned to loot the vocabulary of human rights and democracy for the purposes of crafting a unique state of civil–military co-governance.... Now, fast forward seventeen years to a moment when two political events throw into relief the persistence of the army's role as helmsman of the state: the anti-military findings of the truth commission in February 1999 and the election of a right-wing populist/*Riosmonttista* regime (of Alfonso Portillo) in January 2000.

Three stages of political-military thinking in Guatemala will be delineated here: (1) from its institutional beginnings in 1873 until the 1960s the army was an instrument of elite power; (2) in the 1970s the army became its own government; and (3) in 1982 and on into the 1990s the army created its own political-military project of co-governance. At the core of this political-military project was the replacement of the personalistic *caudillo* model of military command with the military-as-institution. The military learned that to maintain power it had to recast the state in its own image and reformulate its identification as an institution within that state. With the UN-directed peace process and the Commission for Historical Clarification under way in the late 1990s, hopes for the military's compliance with the peace accords and collaboration with the commission ran high. Today the military utilizes a vocabulary of 'strategic peace' by insisting on its intention to comply with the peace accords while relying on the civilian government's panic over public order and security to justify its continued control over internal defence and intelligence matters. This chapter will focus mainly on the shift in military thinking and strategy in the years 1982–2000, and end with the question of how sustainable peace accords can be when military thinking has not been transformed to meet the needs of a democracy.

I shall argue that the Guatemalan politico-military project forces us to rethink several of the traditional assumptions about a military's accommodation to civilian rule and international pressures for truth and justice. Perhaps we need to ask whether demilitarization has been accomplished when a military 'prepares the environment' for elections by way of massacre and 'pacification', and embeds state security in both the constitution and the presidency, with few protections for human rights. It is not a question of when the military can be made to return to the barracks, retreat from power or even be made accountable to civilian rule. Rather it is one of the extent to which the military has been able to merge civil and military relations, and to adopt the vocabulary of human rights and democracy with the full collaboration of the civilian presidents. In addition, it raises the larger question for many of these fragile democracies of which institution, military or civilian, is in the end being strengthened by democratic processes.

Concomitantly, we need to ask whether peace processes and truth commissions change attitudes and practices (or at least inspire debate) within Latin American militaries, or achieve the opposite by further marginalizing and alienating military institutions from democratizing efforts. We should also consider whether to read internal 'technical coups' within the armed forces once the peace process is under way as a sign of the unstable identity of the military under the new circumstances or as an ideological split among officers over compliance with the accords – or possibly both. Focusing on Guatemala, this chapter will evaluate the extent to which the military have been willing and able to comply with the conditions set forth in the peace accords, and to what extent there has been a change in the way the military relates to civil governance and civil society. We will evaluate these issues on a number of levels – constitutional, doctrinal, institutional and attitudinal.

## A Brief History of the Guatemalan Military's Political Ascendancy

The paradoxical legacy of the 1944 liberal revolution was to provide, on the one hand, a firm, constitutional basis for the army's political ascendancy and, on the other, to have produced an officer-led guerrilla insurgency as the vanguard of social and economic justice. As 'the army of the revolution', it was converted between 1944 and 1954 from a provisional and rather unformed instrument of force to a state institution with its own political characteristics and ideological direction. And the direction it took – or, as some officers state angrily, that it was forced to conform to – with the US-financed invasion and 'counter-revolution' of 1954, was fiercely anti-communist and responsive to the Cold War fears of both Guatemala's elite and Big Brother to the north.

It was an army that began, at this point, to intervene in electoral contests, impeding the voting for candidates other than their own (as occurred with the 'election' of General Miguel Ydigoras Fuentes in 1958). In the years after the failed coup by rebel officers in 1960 (the culmination of the contradictions in an army that had directly participated in a revolutionary project for social and economic transformation), the army experimented with state governance. On 30 March 1963, Ydigoras's Defence Minister, Colonel Enrique Peralta Azurdia, staged a coup in the name of the armed forces, resulting in a state of siege and a 'calvary of terror'.[2] The regime of Peralta Azurdia (1963–6) established a political strategy that effectively prevented opposition reformist parties from participating in politics for the next fifteen years by waging counter-terror campaigns through clandestine groups 'designed to prevent any alteration – however minor – of the social and economic structure of the country'[3]. The Institutional Democratic Party (Partido Institucional Democrático, PID) was established at this time, dominated by the military. In 1970, Colonel Carlos Arana Osorio (who had directed the massacre campaign of 1966–7) reclaimed the presidency for the PID in the *electoral folklorico* of this period from civilian Julio Cesar Mendez Montenegro (who had had to sign an agreement 'to give the military a free hand in counterinsurgency and autonomy in…[the appointment] of the defence minister, chief of staff, budgets, etc.' before taking office).[4] A political matrix, described by officers in interviews as 'elected-but-appointed', *electos pero mandados*, was firmly established, with 'tacit under-standings among the military institution, the private sector and the political parties to create a façade of democratic politics, marked by periodic elections'.[5] Each military *cupula* distanced itself further and further from the army's constitutional mandate and closer to the defence of the oligarchic class between the years of 1970 and 1982.[6]

The counter-insurgency campaigns of the 1970s also permitted the military to deepen its control over state and civilian institutions, and to strengthen and make permanent its presence in the western highlands where traditionally it had been weak and absent. A new wave of repression began to be used selectively in 1975 under President-General Kjell Laugerud Garcia (1974–8), but it had little success in stemming either guerrilla activity or popular organizing. Hence, repression became increasingly blind, random and massive under President-General Lucas Garcia (1978–82), which, in turn, swelled the ranks of the guerrillas. The regime did not 'distinguish [in] its targeting of state authorities, the army's hierarchy, the political leaders [or] an entrenched bureaucracy'.[7] 'It's everyone for himself,' remarked Interior Minister Donaldo Alvarez in 1979.[8]

This pattern of explicit military elections and governance eviscerated political institutions and political life throughout the 1970s and into the 1980s. But it was during the Lucas Garcia regime that repression by state-controlled death squads and counter-insurgency patrols rapidly began to have a negative effect on the military as an institution. Counter-insurgency doctrine had been implanted internally in the institution in the mid-1960s, and added to an increasing ideological polarization between the army and ruling elites, on the one hand, and the armed insurgency movement on the other. But it also created deep divisions within the army itself. Arbitrary slaughter – paramilitary activity, summary executions, kidnappings and forced disappearances, leaving eight hundred bodies a month on the streets – was becoming increasingly counter-productive. It was during this period that the army had a political awakening: it began to realize that strictly military solutions and international denunciations would lead them into a 'Salvador-type of war', as one colonel of the 1982 junta admitted. 'The fact is, we were without power during this period and deteriorating rapidly internationally.'[9]

By February 1982, when the counter-insurgency campaign had effectively run out of money and fatalities were on the rise among soldiers and junior officers from a growing guerrilla threat, internal allegations of massive corruption against a group of civilians and soldiers whom Lucas Garcia treated as favourites produced a crisis within the military that threatened its hierarchical structure of command. An appraisal of the national situation by the high command and general staff in 1980, presented unofficially to President Lucas, read: 'To convince the citizen to vote, it is necessary to guarantee him that his will, articulated in ballot form, is a powerful democratic tool that will be respected. This would be much easier if a military officer did not participate as a presidential candidate in the next elections.'[10] Despite this advice, Lucas's final candidate was his own Defence Minister, General Angel Anibal Guevara. He was declared winner in March 1982, and when the three opposing civilian candidates staged a public protest at electoral fraud, they were beaten and thrown in jail. It was at this time that younger military officers began to conspire with the landed and business elite to depose the government.

With the March 1982 coup, a state of siege was proclaimed that suspended all constitutional guarantees and made it a capital offence 'to betray the nation [or to] act against the integrity of the state'. Special secret tribunals were set up to try a variety of crimes, and Congress and political parties were banned. The military set about to construct a more explicitly integral, long-term politico-military strategy:

> The first thing we did was very valuable: to recognize that the problem was the army's participation in political and economic decisions or in the social organization of the country. This was bad; it helped to maintain the status quo and didn't help to develop the country.... It was not precisely this that inspired the 1982 coup; nonetheless the system that existed exploded in 1982 and the army came to its rescue and had the opportunity to implement revision.... Without announcing that we were creating political space for everyone, we only said that there were economic, social and political problems that we must prevent. We said, 'We're going to pacify the country so that the political sectors act with legitimacy in order to make economic decisions and resolve social problems.' And the strategy of pacification was 30 per cent of bullets and 70 per cent of beans in order to adjust the economic problems.... We made an analysis about how to combat a terrorist insurgency within a democracy, and used a less costly, more humanitarian strategy, to be more compatible with the democratic system.[11]

This long-term, multiple-stage National Plan of Security and Development called for nothing less than the reorganization of the state to make it more 'efficient' and to create a climate of 'political stability'. With the plan in hand, the army proceeded to penetrate the executive, juridical, administrative and economic branches of government: it suspended the National Assembly and established a

Council of State; suspended the constitution and promulgated a Fundamental Statute of Government; imposed a state of siege to prevent political activities (Decree-Law 24-82), with Article 4 militarizing transport and education; set up Special Tribunals (Decree-Law 46-82) to supplant the Supreme Court; and placed the national police under the control of the Defence Ministry, thus militarizing the Interior Ministry. The plan recognized, as one colonel stated bluntly, that 'the army can no longer win with only guns'.[12]

While a reaction to the old order, the plan was not a progressive statement; it was designed to effect a 'return to constitutionality' while diligently and brutally pursuing the guerrilla through pacification and scorched earth techniques. The plan called for reorganizing the state to resolve the country's economic, political and military crises. Yet it sought to maintain existing state structures by introducing only certain kinds of reforms, such as reversing the economic recession but without tax reform (at this early period), and restoring a regime of electoral and constitutional legality (but without land reform). In this way, the army attempted to remain in full control of the reorganization of government, the armed forces and police, as well as the political life of civil society.

The 1984 National Assembly and 1985 presidential elections were 'ordered' by way of an army bulletin by Chief of State Mejía Victores (after General Rios Montt was relieved of his position in an internal coup in August 1983). The period 1984–5 was when, according to one Guatemalan intellectual,

> the military's strategies were consolidated with respect to civilian participation in terms of a Constitution, Congress, Constitutional Court and a civilian President. If these institutions exist, it is only because the military want them to exist. There is no political terrain gained by the civilians. This is not a democratizing process for participation; it is a … political space for civilians. But if it is a space, it is [one] granted by the military.[13]

This political transition has been referred to as the beginnings of a 'construction of a democratic institutionality' by Rosada Granados and Cruz Salazar, even though it neither implemented nor allowed for structural transformation. Nevertheless, they argue that this shift was the most important in the history of the army as it not only generated a return to the structures of civilian governance but also abandoned the principles of the doctrine of national security, thus establishing the foundations for a pro-democratic army.[14] Yet, as Rosada Granados also makes clear, this counter-insurgent army accepted the role of a pro-democratic army only because they were assured of their victory: 'In short, they supported the process of democratic transition if and only if the interests of the army were assured.'[15]

It was to be a formal electoral democracy in which security and development were integrated on the military's terms. On the first day of President Cerezo's term, 16 January 1986, he established the Council of National Security (Consejo de Seguridad Nacional). He was summarily told, according to one intelligence analyst, '"No, señor, you have been given the freedom to act, but to act only within the Plan." If civilians occupy their assigned places [los lugares asignados], then the success of [el proyecto] is assured.' [16]

## Civilian Presidents and 'Co-Governance'

Nevertheless, the policy of concerted collaboration with all civilian presidents since 1986 – collaboration so close that it is referred to by officers as 'co-governance'

– indicates that civilian presidents are not mere window-dressing. This new montage of political–military thinking assured officers that the counter-insurgency war would continue no matter who won the first civilian presidential elections in 1985. As the imagery of democratic constitutionalism was being forged, the armed forces began to disengage from government administration to guard against being blamed for civilian incompetence or human rights abuses in the future (indicating extraordinary foresight at the time, though it would prove inadequate in a different climate fourteen years later, when the overwhelming blame for violations was placed upon the army's shoulders in the truth commission's findings).

Rather than seek a transitional democratic model based on the assumed separation of civilian and military spheres, in which military involvement in politics is reduced and the armed forces are relegated to the barracks, the Christian Democrats and other similar centre–right parties – faced with a political climate in which few of the functioning (and by definition, these would be extreme right-wing) political elites were open to any kind of idea of *apertura* – had decided by the mid-1970s to collaborate with the 'less intransigent *linea*' within the military. This *linea* would themselves come to recognize by the early 1980s that their own institutional survival depended on such a civilian–military formula. While the electoral solution of unequal 'co-governance' by civilians and military would prove politically useful to both sides, it completely begged the question of civilian control over the military. Indeed, access to intelligence files and operations raises the possibility that presidents were not only compliant but complicitious in the militarization of the presidency (in contrast to the utterly marginalized civilian regime of Mendez Montenegro). Thus, the Cerezo years, and the other regimes since, should be seen as a collaborative project in which the Christian Democrats were not forced to participate, but chose to do so after having prepared the political groundwork for more than a decade.

And yet we should not forget, either, that it was the military institution that prepared the groundwork for just such a democratic *apertura* – strong enough to make civilian rule seem to count while ensuring that it remains irrelevant. Precisely how this co-governance sets the boundaries of civilian controls over military prerogatives is best illustrated a decade later, at the end of the counter-insurgency war, and with the signing of the peace accords.

The September 1996 Accord on the 'Strengthening of Civilian Power and the Role of the Army in a Democratic Society', part of the peace accords and constitutional reforms package later signed on 29 December 1996, requires that the army be limited to defending the constitution and providing external defence.[17] And yet, 'when the ordinary means for the maintenance of public order and domestic peace are exhausted, the President of the Republic may make exceptional use of the armed forces for this purpose', according to another constitutional reform.[18]

Unfortunately, these constitutional reforms became enmeshed in political party battles waged as part of the 1999 presidential elections. The Rios Montt party, the Guatemalan Republic Front (*Frente Republicano Guatemalteco*, FRG), which held a majority of seats in the Congress, refused to cooperate in the passing of any of the constitutional reforms without the revision of Article 186, which forbids any *caudillo* or *jefes* of a *golpe de estado*, or any of their relatives 'of fourth degree of consanguinity and second degree of affinity' from running for president. To make things more complicated, Article 183 (on the president's discretion over the use of force) could not be revised until Article 281, which includes Article 183 among those that cannot be reformed under any circumstances, was itself reformed. As we'll see, the referendum on a package of some fifty constitutional reforms designed to institutionalize the 1996 peace accords was made so unwieldy by these Congressional battles, and was so poorly planned by the Arzú government of 1996–2000, that it was roundly defeated on 16 May 1999, seriously placing in question fundamental army reform, and the final compliance of the army's *proyecto* with a democracy.

## The Army's Timetable and Compliance

In its 'Timetable: Transition Towards Peace 97', the national defence staff (the commanding officers of each of the institution's component parts: civil affairs, intelligence, operations, logistics and chief of staff of national defence) referred to its 'constitutional mission of maintaining the integrity of the peace and internal and external security'. It gave the assurance that the army 'in conformity with the peace accords, will carry out the reorganization, reduction and readaptation of its forces'. [19] The document lays out several phases of compliance.

*Personnel*

The 'first phase' is the 'reorganization and reduction' of troops, specialists, zones, bases, garrisons, recruiting centres, and so on, by 33 per cent. Three years into the process, it is safe to say that progress towards reducing these personnel and installations has been uneven at best, especially since the July 1997 changes in the high command. While eight battalions (with a total of an estimated six thousand soldiers) were demobilized, for example, others were simply redeployed to other military zones. [20]

A major problem with reduction is the lack of clarity as to precisely what the baseline force figures really are: for example, 33 per cent reduction of what? The army's proposed reductions rest on its own Table of Organization and Equipment. But differing figures have been proffered in both army documents and the author's interviews as to the Table of Organization and Equipment's estimation of force strength. According to a November 1997 army briefing, armed forces personnel reached a putative high of 54,326 in the 1980s; according to the army's public relations office and army documents, this force was reduced to 50,600 in September 1996. In contrast, in interviews with the author in 1996, 1997 and 1998, several army officers (many of whom were among the 29 forced out of the high command) consistently used and insisted upon the Table of Organization and Equipment figure of 41,100 overall personnel (troops, officers and special forces), dating back to 1974. What accounts for this disparity?

The inflated Table of Organization and Equipment figure of 50,600, according to a number of officers, includes reservists, retired officers and civilians (such as specialists, doctors and engineers employed by the military). Information provided by the army's public relations office indicates that of the 7,872 demobilized between January and April 1997, only 42 were officers.[21] By swelling the overall Table of Organization and Equipment, the army achieved its 33 per cent by reducing primarily civilian recruiters, administrative staff and low-level troops, while the number of officers and specialists remained at basically the same level. The officer corps was thus not reduced systematically. In fact, according to a number of interviews, there now exist three branches (*ramas*) for the rank of colonel for every military zone, as one analyst of Guatemala averred, 'to keep them out of trouble'. As Defence Minister Barrios Celada explained, 'We don't want to be a large or super-equipped army, but one that has the necessary force to defend the country.... But all transitions are complicated and difficult.'[22]

The accords clearly reiterate, by way of reform of Article 244, that the army is limited to defending the constitution and providing external defence. This means dismantling counter-insurgent security forces: 1) the network of 33,000 military commissioners first established in the 1960s and decreed dismantled by President de Leon Carpio in September 1995 (there is no mention of disarming the commissioners); 2) the 1.3 million-strong Civil Self-Defence Patrols (the *Patrullas de Autodefensa Civil* or PACs began to be disarmed and demobilized throughout the countryside in 1996, even though the agreement calls only for their demobilization thirty days after Congressional dissolution of the 1983 decree); and 3) the Mobile Military Police forces (Policia Militar Ambulante, PMA) (both the elite-trained PMA Ordinaria and the lesser trained PMA Extraordinaria) stationed throughout the country were to be 'dissolved' and 'demobilized' by the end of 1997 (as with the commissioners, there is no mention of their disarmament).[23]

However, 1996 and 1997 army documents contradict these statements. A March 1996 document, for example, calls for 'maintaining relations with the personnel of the demobilized military commissioners with the objective of organizing whatever type of group to be allied with the army in order to develop all classes of activities that promote the integration of this personnel and its unrestricted support of the armed institution'.[24] The failure to mention disarmament of the commissioners in the September 1996 agreement is thus very significant. As noted in the 1995 and 1996 United Nations Verification Commission for Guatemala (MINUGUA) reports, PACs are being converted into other kinds of groups, with the intelligence web shifting from officially recognized bodies to unofficially recognized ones. In 1999, MINUGUA reported that soldiers dressed as civilians took part in a mob attack on a provincial jail in which twelve former PAC members serving 25-year sentences for murder were helped to escape – underscoring the army's continuing interference in internal defence.

Similarly, although the PMA was dismantled, at least 40 of its former members entered the National Civilian Police (Policia Nacional Civil, PNC) and the Special Police Forces (Fuerza Especial Policial, FEP) illegally, where no screening was carried out to exclude those with records of criminality or histories of human rights violations, despite strong objections by MINUGUA.[25]

This maintenance of military and social intelligence networks in the countryside is especially worrisome in the rural areas where Civil Affairs Units maintain 'a close relationship with the rural population', as officers proudly point out, apparently oblivious of how this presence contradicts the 'strictly external defence' clause of the agreement. The longer the army's presence and meddling is maintained in these areas, the greater the potential for repressive action.

*Installations*
The second phase of the army's timetable is *readecuacion*, or the redrawing of the lines of jurisdiction of the 19 military zones and the PMA. Although the location of the eight major military commands is not affected by either of these phases, there is a disparity between the projections and the realities. While technically closing one military base, the army attempted to convert it into a school for

military cadets. This conversion was strenuously opposed by local residents, who insisted that the base be demilitarized and used for a new branch of the National University – as, on 31 December 1998, it was.

Another eight installations that had been closed have been reopened and six new ones established along the Mexican and Belizean borders to 'be able to collaborate with the civilian forces of security against delinquency', according to the army.[26] As MINUGUA's second report concerning compliance with the peace accords states,

> The Mission believes that the maintenance of fifteen military zones perpetuates the clearly territorial pattern of deployment adopted by the Guatemalan armed forces in the 1980s in the context of counter-insurgency activities and contrasts with their deployment in 1961, when the armed conflict first began.... Although current legislation permits [the deployment of military squads to combat organized crime], it must be strictly regulated according to the spirit of strengthening civilian power embodied in the Agreements. [27]

Slated in the peace accords to be decreased incrementally,[28] the military budget estimates appear to meet the minimum reduction targets agreed upon. This reduction is offset, however, by requests made by Defence Minister Barrios Celada to Congress. General Barrios, to ensure modernization of the armed forces, aims to increase soldiers' monthly salaries by Q100 (about US$16), improve their rations and upgrade production capabilities (to produce 9 mm bullets, for example) at the army's munitions factory.[29]

In summary, the army is still far from making the cuts stipulated. It appears that only two out of a total of 19 military zones have actually been closed to military use; eight detachment garrisons have been reopened and six new ones established. While an estimated ten battalions (of 300–450 soldiers each) have been demobilized or transferred, the largest military installations still remain open and fully (indeed doubly and triply) staffed. And the budget, which was to be reduced by 33 per cent, has instead been increased.

At his first press conference as Defence Minister, General Espinosa ignored these criticisms in proclaiming that the military had fully complied with the peace accords. According to his figures, 22 army battalions out of 43 had been deactivated, along with the PMA and the Guardia de Seguridad of the National Palace, and a demobilization had occurred at military bases such as Solola, Jalapa, Chiquimula, Salama, La Aurora, and the Capitania of the Airport.[30]

## The Issue of Military Intelligence and Public Security

What are the prospects for reducing military power and establishing civilian supervision? To what extent is the notorious military intelligence being brought under civilian control and held accountable for its operations? A restructuring of intelligence has begun to take place, but it needs to be understood in the context of public security concerns – the primary justification for enlarging the very institution slated for reduction.

The peace accords seek to establish greater civilian input into and supervision of intelligence activities through three civilian bodies (a presidential secretariat, a ministerial department and a Congressional commission). The civilian government also 'assumes the right to prevent the rise of networks or groups that are not part of the above intelligence and analysis units'. The Civilian Intelligence and Information Analysis Unit that was to be created within the Interior Ministry 'to combat organized crime and common delinquency' by means of a civilian national police force has, as of this writing, yet to be established. Moreover, the degree of independence of the police from the army was seriously weakened in the subsequent legislation on the military's role in a democracy. In addition, a (presidential) Secretariat of Strategic Affairs, reduced from three to one military adviser and headed by a civilian with the entrance of the new (January 2000) Portillo government, serves to 'inform and advise the president regarding the anticipation, prevention and resolution of situations of risk or threats of a distinct nature to the democratic state'. All three organisms – military intelligence, civilian intelligence and the secretariat – 'will strictly respect the separation of functions of intelligence and operations'.[31]

Nonetheless, when 'the ordinary means of maintaining internal peace' are inadequate, Presidential Accord No. 90-96 of March 1996 – which, as we've seen, is reflected in the constitutional reform of Article 183 – officially established a direct link between the secretariat, the government ministry (with its Anti-Kidnapping Commando operating directly out of the chief of staff's office) and military intelligence 'in order to combat organized crime and common delinquency'. 'In the future,' one intelligence colonel remarked, 'we will be regularly loaned out to the civilian intelligence service as advisers, just as FBI and CIA agents are loaned out to the US Army, and German army intelligence officers are loaned out to the German government.'[32] Here we see the legacy of the politico-military project of co-governance, in this instance in the form of a presidential accord that allows for 'integrated security' measures of 'logistical' and 'operational' support.

This integrated support was manifested daily on the streets of Guatemala City, especially between 1997 and 1999, in the form of 'combined forces' and joint patrols, completely under the logistical and operational control of the army chief of staff's office. These FEP units are two-thirds soldiers and have a sergeant-major in command, 24 drivers and jeeps; each of the three military garrisons is assigned a sector of the city to patrol. Military patrols in the rural areas 'have been requested by the population for protection in their communities', while special commandos (*kaibiles*) 'are supporting the Civilian National Police in the Peten', Defence Minister Hector Barrios told me in October 1997. (Although the FEP was temporarily dismantled in April 1999 in response to criticisms, a new FEP/PNC Reaction Unit Against Popular Protests was announced just two months later.)[33]

According to the army's own Plan de Operaciones 'Transicion Hacia la Paz '97', 'ex-*comisionados militares*, ex-soldiers, ex-PMA, ex-officers, ex-*patrulleros* and ex-combatants (groups previously involved in the internal armed conflict' (along with smaller bands and organized crime) are responsible for the spate of kidnappings, bank robberies, car thefts and prison escapes that is provoking fear throughout the country. This 'wave of criminality' has prompted demands for a hard line on crime, for swift justice and revenge by whatever means necessary – demands that would key-note the FRG's election campaigns throughout this period. And the Guatemalan military, encouraged by a reinforced presidential decree, is, as it has been in the past, ever at the ready to serve as guarantor of peace and order.[34]

*The Presidential General Staff: President Arzú strengthens the army's hand*
As in the earlier civilian regimes of Serrano and De Leon Carpio, a military officer who enjoyed the confidence of the president was placed in charge of the Presidential General Staff (Estado Mayor Presidencial, EMP) under President Arzú (1996–2000), with responsibility for the president's personal security. But the EMP has been more than a presidential security service; it has also served as an important nexus for the gathering of information and analysis on the national scene, and as a nerve centre for operations against those critical of the government. It is for this reason that dissolution of the EMP has long been a goal of many human rights groups. And that is why the peace accords mandated the demobilization of the EMP – including its notorious Archivos intelligence unit – and the reassignment of its functions to the civilian Ministry of Governance. But in direct violation of the accords, the Arzú government was intent during its four years on keeping these functions within the military, with the EMP remaining intact. Military officers in interviews between 1997 and 1999 argued that the EMP should remain in place as the president's security cannot easily be transferred to civilians. One high-ranking intelligence officer, after the defeat of the May 1999 referendum, was adamant that the 'No' vote was a vote of vindication *against* the dissolution of the EMP. President Arzú announced that the EMP would be dissolved in July 1999,[35] later retreating to a position that it would disappear with the inauguration of the next president in January 2000 – a statement reconfirmed by his new Defence Minister Espinosa.[36]

Why did President Arzú insist upon retaining the EMP, despite continual criticism from the international community? With the rise in rapid kidnappings of prominent Guatemalans and their families in 1995 and 1996, Arzú turned to his trusted EMP chief General Marco Tulio Espinosa to secretly form and operate an elite anti-kidnapping commando unit. Months before the signing of the peace accords, an office to investigate criminal activity was opened through the chief of staff's office. More significantly, according to several intelligence officers, the EMP's anti-kidnapping commando was relocated within the Intelligence Directorate of National Defence (Direccion de Inteligencia del Estado Mayor de la Defensa Nacional, EMDM). It is now increasingly apparent that the chief of staff has served as the leading protagonist in Guatemala's anti-crime drama, especially regarding these anti-kidnapping operations. In an October 1997 interview with me, General Espinosa stated:

> They are bands who we [military intelligence] had been surveilling, and our work produced good results. You may have the impression that these bands didn't do much harm because there wasn't much press coverage, but they operated freely. But when President Arzú came into office, he wanted to combat these bands, so then our work became publicly known. You see, with the kidnappings, we tried to keep [our work] quiet because we didn't want to make any more difficulties for the victims.... But this government said ... that we had to attack delinquency *frontalmente*, head-on, and logically, when we began to bring down these kidnapping rings, the press was there.... And [as you can see], the number of kidnappings has decreased dramatically.

The general confirmed the report that there were 'three hundred kidnappers in jail ... who can give names [of those involved in the organized bands] to whomever, thereby signing their death warrant. This is something very delicate.' In another interview with an intelligence officer, 'double agents' were mentioned as being on the payroll of both military intelligence/EMP and 'drug-trafficking bands'. These agents provide the bands with information on the EMP's anti-kidnapping squad activities, among other things. 'They pay very well for this information,' he stated. 'A price we cannot compete with.'[37]

While General Espinosa insisted that the EMP had no anti-kidnapping commando, that it is 'within the Government Ministry', Government Minister Rodolfo Mendoza, rather than playing down the Government Ministry's dependence on military intelligence, has admitted that its police are not capable of controlling prisons, dislocating squatters or patrolling streets without the military's help.[38] This militarization of internal security has not gone unnoticed. In MINUGUA's September 1997 progress report on compliance with the accords, the verification mission charged the EMP with 'illegal participation in anti-kidnapping operations'. In response, General Espinosa insisted that 'the kidnapping task force' remains located where it has always been: within the Government Ministry.[39] When asked to explain the discrepancy between what the government says and what MINUGUA says, Espinosa referred to Decree 90-96, 'Well, in reality, the government is making its official position clear, and demanding that MINUGUA remain within its mandate. The law of the state, the Decree 90-96, stands above all things.'

Similarly, the government, in response to MINUGUA's claims, has sought to articulate a legal basis for the army unit's participation in internal security matters. The Foreign Minister announced that reforms to Presidential Accord 90-96 were prepared

> so that there is no doubt about the legitimacy of the army's participation in anti-kidnapping operations, and so there will be no misunderstandings with MINUGUA. There exists a juridical space that allows for the participation of the army in the control of delinquency if the Executive so requests. But [with the legalization of the army's participation], we believe it is necessary that it be made more explicit and transparent.

With no time limit or specific delineation as to how or whether civilian supervision is to function, it seems appropriate to ask, what precisely is being made 'explicit and transparent'? Was the commando activity legalized with not only the acquiescence but the explicit legal authority and recognition of the executive office? What did such acquiescence indicate to a military high command that was only minimally complying with its other responsibilities under the peace accords? Whether the anti-kidnapping commando is located within the EMP, the EMDN or the Government Ministry, military intelligence is not only integrated into these operations, but it is very much 'on the front line', according to Defence Minister General Barrios, because of government pressures. As such, these operations (and the decree-law that formalizes them) are very much in contravention of the accords, which state that military intelligence is not to involve itself in matters of internal defence.

There may be a number of reasons for this overlap between President Arzú and Chief of Staff of National Defence Espinosa (appointed Defence Minister in June 1999): (1) necessity: the civilian government was then and is still today ill-equipped to deal with the public security problem (a serious problem faced by many civilian regimes during fragile transitional periods; (2) choice: Arzú preferred to keep his hands clean but needed to appear to be 'hard on crime', and let the military do the dirty work; (3) a desire on the part of the military high command to move back to being on the front line in the control of delinquency and intelligence matters overall; and/or (4) the coincidence of the personal and professional agendas of the president and his chief of staff/Defence Minister. [40]

This 'coincidence' may be a direct result of co-governance, underlining a president's complete dependence upon the EMP for much of his information, for arranging his agenda, for briefing him on issues, and even controlling discretionary presidential funds. [41] For example, President Arzú's relations with the armed forces changed over time: initially, they were rocky, with the army disliking losing its prerogatives before the signing of the peace accords. With time, and after he had survived an assassination attempt, [42] President Arzú and his main associates identified themselves increasingly with the army's high command. [43] Whatever the case, it means that direct violations of the accords were occurring with the legal authority and blessing of the civilian president – a key element in the maintenance of the politico-military project.

## The Army's View of the After-Peace Crime Wave

The wave of violence has been foreseen by the military high command over the last several years in two ways. First, since the late 1980s, officers have cautioned that while the peace process politically was right on track, economically the country remained in a dismal state. The wave of crime is, according to the army high command's document, 'the cost of transition', especially when 'the government does not fulfil its own promises and agreements, particularly with regard to economic and social demands'. [44] They consider the high unemployment rate and the devastating poverty rate not so much as morally unconscionable but as potential threats to stability. This instability, they argue (rather as many NGOs do), is primarily due to poverty.

Some officers, such as Defence Minister Barrios in 1997, suggested in the press that it would be only three years before the National Civilian Police could take over; other officers scoff at the notion that police can be trained in less than five. [45] The question arises, if the army has been perfectly aware that the police remain untrained and incapable of maintaining order, why agree to peace accords that demanded the withdrawal of the army from internal defence? [46] Did they, along with everyone else, have high expectations of real social and economic distribution? Or was this vacuum of authority allowed to occur in order to give the military a golden opportunity to tout the usefulness of its intelligence apparatus – for so long under attack for its repressive uses – and to shore up its public image?

The second irony is that, commenting on who is responsible for much of this crime, this same army document, like several active-duty and retired high-ranking officers in both interviews and the press, remarks that most of these kidnappings and assaults are so well-planned by well-armed and well-trained men that they did not doubt they were carried out by demobilized soldiers, military commissioners, the PMA (Ordinaria and Extraordinaria), and PAC members – who constitute an estimated 20 per cent of the adult male population. [47] One might ask why this problem was not addressed by all the parties involved at the time of the signing of the accords? Why were retraining and employment programmes not established alongside demobilization to alleviate the swelling of the criminal ranks?

Yet, knowing such crime would occur, the military was entirely prepared for it, despite General Espinosa's earlier remarks. The 315 PMA officers who were transferred into FEP commandos with their riot gear are only a small part of the re-equipping and retraining of officers for police activities that has been going on for a number of years. The author witnessed an exercise in 'mob control' by a squadron of such riot police at PMA headquarters in Guatemala in the early 1990s. I was informed at that time by an officer that the FEP was preparing for future 'street demonstrations'. It is not only common and organized crime that constitutes the threatening element.

Army documents continue to reflect the military's threat mentality. The National Defence Staff's *National Strategic Analysis for 1996*, for example, speaks of 'eliminating and/or neutralizing adverse factors for the Guatemalan State', including 'the repatriated'. Their poor living conditions allow them to 'maintain their connection to terrorist groups, providing human resources and materials for their survival, and from there, the logic is to continue organizing groups to re-establish themselves in the areas of armed skirmishes'. Non-governmental organizations (NGOs) are seen, moreover, as 'supporting the cause of the armed opponent in the areas of armed skirmishes' and 'supporting the absence of governmental authorities in areas of re-settlement'.[48] Other adverse factors from the army's perspective include the emergence of a Pan-Mayan movement which 'for the next five to six years will be run only by Mayan intellectuals and academics'. Officers voiced concerns that the movement could easily be taken over by former *guerrilleros* being reincorporated into political life with the peace accords: 'Now, everyone's Mayan, or ethnic, or whatever they call themselves.' Apparently, the assumptions underlying these categories continue to form part of the military's new arsenal of subjugation into the twenty-first century.[49]

## Army Corruption

Related to the failure of the military to change its attitudes, to reduce its number of officers, and to allow for more civilian accountability over military interests is the issue of rampant corruption within the army. Thousands of dollars in weekly bribery and extortion payments are provided to high-ranking officers by actions carried out by their military and civilian subordinates. Commanders of each military zone have their system of 'Paid Absent' (*Ausentes Pagados*, AP). This refers to positions that exist only on paper and serve as extra income for commanding officers. For each section at each military base, a percentage of the proceeds and budget automatically are provided to the 'AP' of the commander. For example, the G-4 is in charge of funds for the zone. If the zone receives Q150,000 (approximately $21,430) monthly for its operations, and Q40,000 (approx. $5,700) is left over at the end of the year, it is normal for the commander to buy expensive gifts for his family at Christmas, at the troops' expense. Moreover, a percentage of those earnings of the G-1, in charge of all stores and clubs in the zone, are automatically diverted to the commander's 'AP'. The infirmary is also beholden to provide a percentage of its funds to the commander, even if it means a soldier does not receive medical treatment. Soldiers, too, are made to work for the commanding officer's 'AP': a soldier stands in line to receive his monthly salary, goes to the end of the line, changes his name tag and receives another salary that he must give to his commander. Another commander has five people on the list for salaries – one washes his car, another cleans his house and yet another serves as his chauffeur. The colonel then takes half of each of their salaries. 'What does it matter that these people don't receive enough to eat? What can they do? They don't dare speak out,' one officer complained. Each military zone commander, along with the commanders of the military bank and pension system, military industries and the military finance office pays, in turn, a percentage of his take to the Defence Minister. After 25 years in the army, officers earn Q2700 a month (approximately US$445), with take-home pay, after pension, medical, rent, and other deductions, of Q1,799 (approximately US$300). They are perfectly aware that a percentage of their automatic deductions for military pension and medical payments goes directly into the pockets of the Defence Minister. Several officers argued for the need to create the position of an army ombudsman to ensure a fairer distribution of income within the armed forces.

These corrupt activities and payments are assumed to be part and parcel of officers' salaries, as one former Defence Minister explained in an interview – something officers believe they deserve once they reach a higher rank. Given the short amount of time an officer serves as either a member of the high command or a military zone commander, it is an unspoken rule that the colonel or general is expected to 'earn' as much as possible before he retires. One defence minister is known to have amassed eighty million quetzales (or approximately US$13 million); under threat of being exposed by counter-intelligence for 'doing business' over official phone lines, he was forced to retire (on a hefty pension). One chief of the presidential general staff, and later of the national defence staff, in charge of an anti-kidnapping squad, was rumoured to have been handsomely rewarded by the national elite for saving prominent family members.

Extortion (beyond the legal entry tax) from truckers, tourists and others at the custom house at each border crossing is another way to 'extend' one's salary as a member of the high command, with a typical weekly intake estimated at 200,000 quetzales, or approximately US$35,000. Corruption can also be more random, with some officers involved in car theft, import–export, weapons theft and sales, and drugs trafficking, among others. 'A colonel over here is stealing cars, a general over there is stealing timber, another one is killing', one officer explained. 'These officers are shifted around in their posts but *everyone knows what's going on*, and the cases never get resolved.' It's a question of adapting to *la fibra*, the subculture of the Escuela Politecnica based on intense loyalty, discipline and the keeping of secrets. In one prominent weapons-theft case in 1998–9, one officer was apparently sentenced to fifty years in prison.[50] One colonel, disheartened by the corruption-based income disparities in the army, shrugged aside this 'advance' in punishment for officers:

> These criminal activities are due to the low wages of lower-ranking officers. It's easy to point the finger at these officers and say you're cleaning up the army. But these lower-ranking officers who stole the weapons are small potatoes compared to what they see their commanding officers at army general headquarters, in the army department of finances, in the army weapons factory, etc., earning by way of their APs and percentages and other corrupt practices.

How does corruption affect the military's compliance with the peace accords? With the resulting serious imbalance of salary distribution among the lower and upper ranks of officers, and an even more serious one between soldiers and officers, officers commit themselves to a career based on both economic and political power – that is, they identify with the traditional vision of the military-as-protagonist. Even among the institutionalist officers, 'a little personal gain' is expected to flourish alongside careerism. Under the peace accords, military life, including intelligence and operations, is to be brought under civilian control and scrutiny. But with corruption so often tied to human rights violations, the military is reluctant to allow civilian scrutiny of the military's 'public secrets'.

## A Post-War Crisis of Identity

Interviews with a number of officers indicate that the armed forces are suffering a crisis of identity, with fears about what the Peace Process and the constitutional reforms entail for doctrine, doubts about serving as policemen on patrol, and anger about the lack of balance in the Historical Clarification Commission's report on the 36-year conflict. In all aspects, there is an increasingly ambivalent response by officers to the process. Some officers are more willing than others to encourage civilian knowledge and accountability over more and more aspects of military doctrine and actions in both the present and the past.

Concerning constitutional reforms, the most significant for the army are those reforms that change the function of the armed forces. According to one officer,

> The army is divided now not on political matters but on the elemental crisis of identity. In this transition from war to peace, obviously after having fought an enemy, we are now spread out everywhere [as policemen in the fight against crime] and we figure here in the political scene as well, and suddenly, there are people who say to us, 'Look, you guys are doing your job very well.' All of these kinds of pressures.... But above all, the fact that the army will have nothing to do with internal security which the accords are obligating us [to drop], just like any other armed forces, implies a reformulation of everything [the army has stood for]. It is now a concept that has been abandoned. That presents a problem of identity, and has become an internal crisis [within the armed forces].[51]

Moreover, as the military become more involved in crime prevention, there appears to be on the part of many officers a reluctance to participate in police activities. *'Hay sus dudas, hay sus dudas*, officers have their doubts,' Defence Minister Barrios admitted:

> There may be some who don't value the effort that the army is now providing, because police work is hard. It's easier, though, than when we were in combat against the guerrilla, when one had to sleep on the ground in the rain under very difficult conditions. Now they don't fear for their lives, their companions don't come back dead. It's a positive change when the national police take over the tasks that correspond to them.[52]

The technical distinction being drawn by the public and government ministries regarding 'logistical support' that is being provided by the anti-kidnapping commando to the national police who, at least publicly, make the arrests – as a way of keeping these operations within legal bounds – does not inspire much confidence among officers. As one intelligence colonel explained, as to why the *patrullas conjuntas* patrol only certain hours a day and not during the night (8 am to 5 pm and 8 pm to 10 pm), 'No officer wants to be doing this, coordinating police work; we don't want to be individually blamed for an operation that gets out of hand.'[53] Another intelligence colonel stated angrily, 'The army is trained to kill, not to police. And now by way of these *patrullas conjuntas* and *fuerzas combinadas*, we are merely training the police in such methods....'[54] The consequences of using militarized police in messy police activities, such as removing squatters from land invasions or policing the streets, he is saying, is only asking for trouble.

*The Historical Clarification Commission (Comisión del Esclaremiento de la Historia, CEH)*
There were also deep suspicions and fears among officers about the role of the UN-appointed Clarification Commission, and the consequences of its report for individual officers who participated in the 'dirty war'. And so it was in 1999, when the politico-military project withstood its strongest test. The commission established on 31 July 1997 to clarify past human rights violations and acts of violence against the Guatemalan people investigated a number of representative cases of human rights violations between the 1960s and 1990s, requesting information and documents from the Guatemalan National Revolutionary Union (Unidad Revolucionaria Nacional de Guatemala, URNG), the Arzú government and the armed forces. While the URNG provided materials apparently without much delay,[55] the army high command's replies were slow and incomplete, access was restricted, and the documents provided were marginal to military operations. As the MINUGUA report of February 1998 states, 'It is in the armed forces' own interest to help shed light on the years of the "dirty war" and show just how it operated ... in order to avoid a recurrence of such events. State bodies or entities must give the commission whatever assistance it requires to that end.'[56]

The commission's final report of February 1999 concluded that more than 200,000 people had been killed or had disappeared during the 36 years of the armed conflict, and that between 1981 and 1983 a deliberate policy of genocide against the Mayan (indigenous) population was carried out by the Guatemalan state. Nearly all – 93 per cent – of all cases investigated were attributed to the armed forces and their paramilitary agents, and of 658 documented massacres, 626 were carried out by the armed forces and its agents and 32 by the URNG guerrillas. A call to establish an *ad hoc* commission to purge military and police officers implicated in human rights violations evoked a government statement that it did 'not consider it necessary or convenient to establish new entities' as the army is 'at present a renovated institution whose internal transformation has provided it with a decisive role in the conquest of peace and in the compliance of the accords'. President Arzú asked the nation for 'forgiveness for our actions or omissions, for what we did or did not do'.[57] On 30 June, Army Day, the president directly contradicted the CEH's finding: 'Genocide represents the extermination of an ethnic group, and I do not believe this was the case in Guatemala [as the CEH had stated] because this was not the motive for the brutal conflict that we lived through.'

Suspicion, anger and disdain were uppermost in the response of most officers to the commission's report. But for three officers who voluntarily, as individuals, provided the CEH with testimony, the military refused to collaborate in any manner with the commission. In refusing to provide documents, the high command argued that there was no written evidence, or what written evidence there was had been destroyed. According to a number of officers, a small commission of intelligence officers was established by the high command in 1985 (a few months before civilian President Cerezo was inaugurated) to travel to each military zone to purge all documents concerning the 'dirty war' and the pacification campaign. Army documents continued to be destroyed by the high command in the early 1990s, but especially after July 1997 and during the entire period of the Catholic Church's Truth Commission investigation.[58]

Although a handful of officers admit to excesses and abuses, even they reject the notion that a policy of genocide was followed. 'It was a war against ideological groups that converted part of the indigenous population into combatants, particularly against the EGP [Ejército Guatemalteco de los Pobres, Guatemalan Army of the Poor] which was successful in this regard.' Another officer angrily described the CEH report, together with the Truth Commission report (Recuperación de la Memoria Historia, REMHI), as 'public punishment and revenge against the armed forces during the war. I believe that the army has always had fears with regard to everything about the process [of peace, of transition]. But if there is something the army really fears, it is [these truth commissions]'.[59] Several officers admitted that they would not provide testimony to either commission because they

> are not investigating legitimate armed actions. They are investigating the excesses, the aberrations, and the damage to the non-combatant civilian population. Thus, it isn't against the struggle that the URNG [guerrillas] evoked, because who would have been able to avoid it? It's a lie, a sordid game. At times, there are people who fall into extreme pacifism, an unrealistic pacifism.[60]

On 16 July 1998, Colonel Otto Noack Sierra, the loquacious army spokesperson for the Department of Military Information and Disclosure (Departamento de Informacion y Divulgacion del Ejercito, DIDE) from mid-1996 to July 1997, gave an informal interview to Radio Netherlands in which he acknowledged that the army should recognize the excesses it committed during the armed confrontation and ask the population's forgiveness. He suggested that all should testify before the CEH, and if necessary apply to the Guatemalan court for amnesty.

Noack has since stated that he didn't think the European broadcast would be broadcast in Guatemala. Despite his rather bland appeal for forgiveness and amnesty, and failure to break new ground as regards impunity, Noack was first suspended and then charged with breach of military discipline for speaking with the press without prior consent from his military superiors. He was arrested and jailed for thirty days (he had been put on standby status in July 1997 and could no longer speak publicly for the army). Many human rights organizations protested: Amnesty International sent a message to the Guatemalan government, expressing its concern and its view that Colonel Noack was a 'prisoner of conscience'. Christian Tomuschat, head of the CEH, after visiting Noack in detention, publicly stated that he did not deserve such punishment, and called on other officers to follow his example of admitting past abuses. The government accused Tomuschat of meddling in internal politics and announced it would file a complaint with the UN Secretary-General requesting Tomuschat's resignation.[61]

Noack's detention exemplifies the recalcitrance of the military high command and the government in cooperating with the CEH. But does Noack's action indicate the beginnings of a change of attitude in the officer corps – a recognition of the need for the army to face up to its behaviour regarding the armed confrontation of the early 1980s in order to be able to accommodate itself to the democratic transition? Or was this merely a reconciliatory gesture without any attempt to dismantle the army's impunity?

We need to ask, in this connection, if the high command in 1996–7 was serious about compliance, why did its 1996 strategy call for demobilizing the Civil Self-Defence Patrols and then regrouping them, demobilizing military commissioners but retaining them as informants, and maintaining a threat mentality with regard to non-governmental organizations, returning refugees, and the Mayan movement? Similarly, we must ask why the high command under President Arzú failed to cooperate with the CEH and fully comply with the accords, and why it jailed Colonel Noack and announced it would admit any 'errors' only after the commission had issued its report (failing, in the end, to make any such admission). Given the intense rancour with which high-ranking officers responded to Noack's statements to the press (at a meeting of military zone commanders at the time, he was called a 'traitor'), internal dissent seems to reveal that the glacial belief system of the army, based on decades of threat mentality, contempt for civilian scrutiny, and a stalwart culture of impunity, has melted to a depth of only a few centimetres in the climate of international global warming of human rights advocacy. This shows how little substance there is to the semantics of the army's disinformation campaigns of the last decade.

But the civilian government of Arzú, too, played a central role in defending the military against human rights criticism.[62] It stated unequivocally that it would not follow up the truth commission's recommendations regarding the military during the remainder of its tenure; this would be left to the next government. At a meeting of military zone commanders a few days after the release of the CEH report, the president's personal secretary and foreign minister described the report as the 'last bitter drop' the military had to swallow. They assured the commanders that the government would not follow the CEH's recommendations because it went beyond the Oslo mandate in two respects: finding for genocide and calling for the establishment of an *ad hoc* commission to review the individual histories of military officers. At this same meeting, there was discussion of providing housing and better retirement packages as a way of avoiding *disturbios*.

When several officers asked how much the army would be willing to back them financially at trials, and would they have to pay the price alone for having followed orders, one colonel at the meeting responded that they had entered the military voluntarily, and knew the consequences of breaching the law. Some middle-ranking officers, in private conversations, admitted they feared upcoming trials, and are not prepared to 'pay the bill alone'. 'We are willing to recognize that mistakes were made, but we aren't willing to just line up [at the courtroom door] and say, "Okay, here we are, ready to be sentenced!"'[63] These officers say that if it comes to that, they are prepared to name those commanding officers who gave the orders. As one officer stated, 'I can place that general there, that colonel over there, and I will do so publicly if I need to save my own skin.' In the months following the release of the CEH report, officers were extremely wary of speaking to journalists, even scholars, worried they could lose their pension, housing and health benefits if reprimanded by the high command.

In two separate interviews, two officers offered the same advice to the high command as to how to deal with the CEH report: 'They must admit that these things went on in the past, that it was a dirty war, but at the same time announce that things are different now.' For now, the majority of officers still retain a visceral reaction to the process and to the CEH, which has, without a doubt, polarized the social environment.

*The referendum, the 'No' vote and the Portillo government*
On 16 May 1999, a package of fifty constitutional reforms designed to institutionalize and provide legal authority to the key elements of the December 1996 peace agreement was defeated by an overwhelming 'No' vote in a public referendum *(consulta popular)*. The twelve original reforms grew to fifty within the Guatemalan Congress (only to be challenged for months in the courts); they were voted on in 4 categories: (1) the nation and social rights; (2) legislative; (3) executive; and (4) judicial reforms to the constitution. The key elements were indigenous rights, intelligence and strictly internal defence reform of the armed forces and reform of the justice system. This complexity appears to have been the major barrier to their passage in a country of high illiteracy and political manipulation. It was, in short, a serious blow to the Guatemalan peace process and a grave setback to institutionalizing reforms in the near future. The defeat throws into doubt the process of military reform, including key changes in the army's role in internal security and intelligence.

The 'No' vote shocked and angered some of the officers who had been part of the peace process, leading them to place the blame on the Arzú government for not informing the population about the reforms until the referendum was no more than a fortnight away. Other officers, though, tended to be unable to disentangle their bitterness about the Clarification Commission from the original commitments made by the army in the peace accords, interpreting the 'No' vote as a vindication of their position of partial compliance with the accords. They viewed it as the population giving its democratic seal of approval to their continuing power and political influence. A few days before President Arzú announced that the EMP would be dismantled, inspite of the defeat of the referendum, one high-ranking officer stated in an interview that the 'No' vote indicated to the army that the population rejected the findings of the truth commission in placing institutional responsibility on the armed forces for the vast majority of grave human rights violations, and in demanding the restructuring of intelligence, voluntary recruitment and the withdrawal of the army from internal defence in the peace agreement. In brief, the 'No' vote, in the minds of some officers, served as vindication that the population neither believed the CEH report nor accepted its challenge to the army's impunity. As one high-ranking intelligence officer stated in a 1999 interview: 'The "No" vote means that the people stand by their army, that they understand that the army does not have to comply with the truth commission's recommendations or the peace accords. We do not need to dismantle the presidential chief of staff, as both the CEH and MINUGUA are demanding.' From this perspective, the 'No' vote thus places in jeopardy long-term reform of the military, and the establishment of unconditional civilian scrutiny.

Arzú's successor, FRG President Alfonso Portillo, was installed in January 2000 and immediately began to make changes. He gave every indication that he would appoint a general who had been central in the signing the peace accords, General Perez Molina, to be Defence Minister. Instead, he appointed an unknown colonel, thereby forcing nineteen generals into retirement or 'exile' abroad. When asked why he took this step, Portillo stated in a March 2000 interview that he had wanted to appoint a civilian Defence Minister, but the law needed to be changed. Meanwhile, all the generals were '*politicizados*, connected to political parties'. Besides, he said, ex-dictator Rios Montt, who founded the FRG and is now the president of the Congress, objected to the appointment of Perez Molina because of his participation in the 1983 palace coup which ended Montt's military career. On the basis of these comments, one might conclude that civilian presidents have been held hostage to the military's web of impunity. And yet if we keep in mind the collaborationist character of the politico-military project, Portillo may not be that different from his predecessors. While he is seeking to investigate human rights cases, he is not too hopeful that the Gerardi investigation[64] will result in indictments against military officers. While he has appointed a leftist academic to head the Secretariat of Strategic Affairs and oversee the dismantling of the EMP, he has failed to demilitarize the EMP (which currently employs 35 officers), at least for the moment. More significantly, Portillo is dependent upon ex-military officers who were sacked from the army for drugs trafficking and/or involvement in the explicitly anti-democratic 'self-coup' of President Serrano in 1993 for his security both during his campaign and as president. The left/right populist under-pinnings of Portillo's regime thus make it difficult at this time to know how far civilian supervision and military accountability – and the implicit collaborationism of the politico-military project – will be tested.

## Conclusions

Since the 1944 Revolution, and most especially throughout the 1980s and 1990s, the Guatemalan military has continued to learn to reconstitute itself for a variety of political contingencies. It displayed its versatility in utilizing the vocabulary of human rights to create a 'repressive humanitarianism' during the 1982–3 massacre campaign. Today, it employs a vocabulary of a 'strategic peace', insisting upon its intention to comply with the peace accords while relying on the civilian government's panic to maintain public order and security. It retains its control over internal defence and intelligence matters, and as a result refuses to comply fully with the peace accords. This brief history of the military's project reveals an ominous lack of effective subordination of military power to civilian authority. There is a strong possibility that the military, once entrenched in crime pre-vention, will not entirely withdraw from internal defence once the civilian police are in place. It raises the question: will giving presidential legitimacy to the military coordination of internal defence activities undermine the potential for democratic governance in the name of the public good?

The negative reaction within the army to the truth commission report (and individual officers' declarations of 'excesses') indicates that the high command has not been moving to accommodate its officers to human rights and democratic forces but instead has been utilizing the political battle over constitutional reforms and the resultant 'No' vote as a vindication of the army's maintenance of its hegemony over security issues – thereby entirely undercutting the peace process and weakening any prospects for democratizing the heart of the state. Thus, the question remains whether the peace accords can make military intelligence account-able and subject to civilian control. This is the major challenge for the attainment of sustainable democracy in Guatemala.

Yet, there is internal dissension within the institution. On the one hand, we find a high command that has been very reluctant to comply fully with the peace accords; on the other hand, the democratic opening of civil society has begun to have an impact on the ability and willingness of officers (particularly those who ensured the finalization of the accords) to speak publicly and critically about this chequered compliance. It is ironic that the Guatemalan military, so successful in co-opting the language of human rights and democracy to serve in its crafting of an *apertura* of co-governance in the 1980s, should find itself ensnared in internal dissension over making good on its agreement to comply fully with the peace accords in the 1990s. In the end, such dissension is about how the institution can maintain its institutional identity and come to accommodate itself unconditionally to the demands of a democratic civilian regime. The visceral reaction by the majority of officers to the process, to the Clarification Commission and to Colonel Noack, however, indicates how far ahead the path to full compliance may wind.

As former President Vinicio Cerezo stated in a 1991 interview, the army has to pass through three stages in the 'historical process of democratic consolidation':

> The first stage is that in which the army ceases to be an instrument of the economic oligarchs who want to maintain the status quo and who oppose [any kind of] change. The second stage is that in which the army considers itself part of the institutionality and not the only institution – as the soul of the nation, and not as the most important institution of the nation – around which everything must revolve, and they have advanced to this stage. And the third stage is when the army converts itself into an instrument of the institutionality, it is at the orders of the institutionality.

> We are currently at the second stage. This is precisely where the discussion is at the moment between civilians and the military: either the national objective [of stability for security's sake] above all else or stability and economic development, with security as only one element. The thesis of national stability is in fact about institutional stability for economic development: it assumes that without economic development there is no security, and without security, there is no economic development. If we consolidate that [stage], the next stage is only a matter of years, if the politicians maintain a clear perspective during this process and do not want to make the army an instrument at the service of their own interests.

It is imperative to understand the internal logics and mentality of militaries in the world. In the interesting case of Guatemala there is not only a long history of a strong and independent armed institution but a current attempt to find an electoral solution based on unequal co-governance between civilians and military. This is a relationship that can only beg the question of whether civilian control over the military is possible in Guatemala.

## Notes and References

1 See Schirmer (1998: Chapter 1) for details.
2 Cruz Salazar (1970: 96).
3 Handy (1984: 394).
4 Trudeau (1989: 94).
5 Gonzalez, quoted in Rosenthal (1992: 32).
6 Rosada Granados (1999: 23).
7 Gramajo (1991b: 6).
8 Black with Milton Jamail and Norma Stolz Chuchilla (1984: 41).
9 Colonel Gordillo (1988 interview).
10 Gramajo (1991a: 7).
11 1990 interview.
12 1986 interview.
13 1988 interview.
14 Rosada Granados (1999: 22–3).

15 Cardona Recinos (1999).

16 1990 interview.

17 Article 244 *Constitution, organization and functions of the armed forces*. The last sentence in italics will serve as a replacement: 'The Guatemalan armed forces are a permanent institution in the service of the nation. They are unique and indivisible, essentially professional, apolitical, loyal and nondeliberative. *Their function is to protect the sovereignty of the State and its territorial integrity*'.

Article 246 *Duties and powers of the President over the armed forces*. The first paragraph will be replaced with the following: 'The President of the Republic is the Commander-in-Chief of the armed forces and shall issue his orders through the Minister of Defence, whether he is a civilian or a member of the military.'

Article 219 *Military courts*. 'The military courts shall take cognisance of the crimes and misdemeanours specified in the military code and in the corresponding regulations. Ordinary crimes and misdemeanours committed by military personnel shall be tried and judged by the ordinary courts. No civilian may be judged by military courts.' (Constitución Política de la República de Guatemala, 1998).

18 Article 183 *Functions of the President of the Republic*:

The deployment of the armed forces shall always be temporary, shall be conducted under civilian authority and shall not involve any limitation on the exercise of the constitutional rights of citizens.... The operations of the armed forces shall be limited to the time and modalities which are strictly necessary, and shall end as soon as the purpose has been achieved. The President of the Republic shall keep Congress informed about the operations of the armed forces, and Congress may at any time decide that such operations should cease. At all events, within fifteen days of the end of such operations, the President of the Republic shall submit to Congress a detailed report on the operations of the armed forces (Constitución Política de la República de Guatemala, 1998).

19 *Siglo Veintiuno*, 8 May 1999.

20 According to the eigth and ninth reports of the United Nations Verification Mission for Guatemala (MINUGUA) of June 1998 and March 1999, approximately 180 former members of the Mobile Military Police (Policia Militar Ambulante, PMA) illegally entered the first course of 'recycling' in the police academy. These reports also document the illegal entry of 40 ex-members of the army, including 22 ex-army sergeant-majors, into the Civilian National Police force (Policia Nacional Civil, PNC); they were admitted into the police academy with false Treasury Police documents and promoted as PNC officers. Moreover, a group of agents who had provided security services to the US embassy were incorporated into the PNC with only one month (instead of the required three months) of training. Additionally, MINUGUA identified members of the former police structures, cited for human rights violations, who were participating in the PNC courses; these individuals were retained, and graduated as PNC agents. This constitutes, according to MINUGUA, 'a serious inattention to the agreement to purge the security forces of the state' (MINUGUA 1998/9: A/53/853, Anexo: p. 12).

21 *DIDE Comunicado de Prensa*, No. 58–97.

22 April 1997 interview. According to 1996 army documents, the final figure of 33,607 troops and officers was scheduled to be reached by December 1997. Yet the final Table of Organization and Equipment figure of 45,000 officially presented by the Minister of Defence to MINUGUA and the Arzú government in late 1997 implied a post-accord figure of 31,423 (MINUGUA 1998d). This 'represents 81.04 per cent of the total forces ... a sufficient percentage for compliance with this accord', concludes a 1998 MINUGUA report (1998e). However, this final Table of Organization and Equipment did not include the national defence general staff, the Ministry of Defence, the Military Academy, the cadet schools, the army public relations office, the army bank and pension system, or the administrative offices of finance, law and computation, among others (anonymous interview: 1998).

23 In March 1997, a little over half of the elite 'Ordinary Mobile Military Police' (Policia Militar Ambulante Ordinaria, PMAO) were demobilized (699); the rest took advantage of programmes for placing them in other jobs: 315 were integrated into the new National Civilian Police, 136 entered the Directorate-General of Prisons, a hundred were hired by private security firms and 33 took FONAPAZ (Fondo Nacional de la Paz, National Peace Fund) training courses (Holiday and Stanley: 1999)

24 Ejército de Guatemala (1996b: 7–8).

25 MINUGUA (1998c: 22); Holiday and Stanley (1999: 49).

26 *El Periodico*, 24 October 1997.

27 A/52/57, pp. 13 and 12 respectively. New mobile units of 40 soldiers, with a lower-ranking officer (e.g., sergeant-majors) staffing these detachments, highlights the army's new emphasis on creating more compact, rapid-deployment elite army commandos (similar to those used during the 1982–3 counter-insurgency campaign).

28 Eleven per cent in 1997, 22 per cent in 1998 and 33 per cent in 1999 in relation to the gross domestic product (GDP)

29 Stanley and Holiday (1999: 2).

30 *Boletin, Agregado Militar de la Embajada de Guatemala*, 19 July 1999.

31 MINUGUA (1998e).

32 1997 interview.

33 *Prensa Libre*, 12 June 1999.

34 This Decree-Law 90–96 established that the 'Government Ministry, through the forces of civilian security, will elaborate, execute and supervise the plans of public security which they judge to be necessary', and that 'the Defence Ministry, by way of its National Defence Staff, will collaborate and support in combating organized crime and common delinquency' (*Presidencia de la Republica*).

35 *Siglo Veintiuno*, 21 May 1999.

36 *Prensa Libre*, 30 June 1999, 19 July 1999.

37 High-ranking officers have been adamant over the years of the author's interviews that 'no guerrillas' have been involved in the kidnappings, bank robberies or drugs trafficking, as one officer clarifies:

'They are all the same people: organized crime.'

Q: *But who is organizing them?*

'Many are poor Guatemalans, Hondurans and Salvadorans.'

Q: *Ex-soldiers?*

'Yes, and also officers…. We have some elements [within G-2/EMP] who continue to kidnap.'

38 *La Hora*, 21 October 1997.

39 Personal communication, 27 January 1998. As the military attaché further explained, 'General Espinosa insists that operationally and legally [the commando] is under the control of the Interior Ministry. It has never been under the EMP or the Defence Ministry. Now, at times, it has been logistically [under the EMP] with combined forces, the National Police come from the Cuartel General. That is the practice.'

40 Major changes in the army high command were made in early July 1997 which worked in favour of Arzú's principal military adviser, General Espinosa. Defence Minister Julio Balconi Turcios, National Defence Chief of Staff General Sergio Camargo Muralles, National Defence Deputy Chief of Staff Victor Manuel Ventura Arellano, and Inspector General General Otto Perez Molina, all of whom had been central military figures in negotiating and signing the peace accords, were suddenly retired, made *disponible* (whereby an officer remains unassigned to any task but still receives pay and benefits), or assigned abroad. President Arzú designated General Hector Barrios Celada as Minister of Defence and assigned his principal military adviser, General Marco Tulio Espinosa, to the position of Chief of Staff for National Defence. In a number of interviews with the officers who were replaced, there was no clear understanding of why the president agreed to these changes, although many believe that it was primarily because of his close relationship with General

Espinosa. Many of these officers also raised the possibility that the signing of the peace accords was one thing but complying with them would have been quite another, both for a sector within the army and for an influential civilian sector in government and within the business community. Whatever the case, these officers all expressed complete surprise and dismay over the July 1997 changes in the high command.

41 Stanley and Holiday (1999).

42 Like civilian presidents before him, Arzú believes he is beholden to the EMP for saving his life. On more than one occasion he has been known to say, 'They [the army] want to kill me!' Curiously, every civilian president has encountered – and survived – an attempt against his life, usually at the beginning of his administration, as one prominent Guatemalan lawyer pointed out.

43 Examples of this close relationship are: (1) When MINUGUA issued a report indicating the responsibility of General Espinosa in the forced disappearance of 'Mincho', a URNG militant, President Arzú responded by promoting Espinosa to second in the chain of command. (2) When the army presented a counter-report to the Catholic Church's REMHI report, soon after the assassination of Bishop Gerardi in April 1997, Arzú took the army's side, publicly praising the army: '[T]his report counterbalances the REMHI report' (Molina Mejía 1998: 25).

44 Ejército de Guatemala (1997).

45 When asked if it was in fact possible to train ten thousand more policemen in only a matter of three years, however, Barrios added, 'Don't ask me, ask the Government Minister. But I would respond for my people [that] we have 124 years of developing a professional army by way of our military academy, and that is what they must do to develop a national police' (22 October 1997).

46 Foreign Minister Eduardo Stein has stated that 'within two years', once the Civilian Police were capable of such work, military support would be dispensed with (*La Hora*, 21 October 1997: 9).

47 October 1997 interviews.

48 Ejercito de Guatemala (1996a: 79, 99).

49 It should be duly noted that pressure from the US intelligence and military community is a significant factor in maintaining this culture that breeds contempt for accountability. The tremendous pressure by the DEA (US Drug Enforcement Agency) to combat drugs trafficking continues to pull G-2, navy intelligence and operations and the Treasury Police dangerously back into the quagmire the peace accords are trying to draw them out of.

50 26 M-16s, a Mauser rifle and one grenade-launcher were stolen from the General Head-quarters in Guatemala City by three captains (one of whom was vice-chief of decommissioning of the army), a major and a lieutenant in October 1998. They had also privately contracted the manufacture of mini-Galils at the army munitions factory to sell to private citizens, including organized crime. (Drugs raids by the Department of Anti-Narcotic Operations (Departamento de Operaciones Antinarcoticos, DOAN) in February and March 1999 would recover some of these same weapons.) What has happened to these officers is rather unclear: according to the press, one of the officers, the major, was sentenced by the military court to fifty years in prison for stealing weapons; while the other officers were detained at army general headquarters. Another officer contended that three of the major's collaborators were put to death by injection.

51 April 1998 interview.

52 Interview, 22 October 1997.

53 October 1997 interview.

54 April 1998 interview.

55 Unidad Revolucionaria Nacional Guatemalteca (URNG) (1998: 18).

56 MINUGUA (1998e: 4). Article 10 of the National Reconciliation Act (Decree No. 145–96) instructs the Clarification Commission to devise means whereby the historical truth about the period of internal armed conflict might be uncovered and acknowledged (MINUGUA 1998e: 4).

57 'Posicion inicial del Gobierno de la Republica ante el informe y las recomendaciones de la Comision de Esclarecimiento Historico' (*Siglo Veintiuno*, 16 March 1999).

58 Officers have admitted that in 1985 a G-2 commission was established; its members visited all military bases in the country with the mandate to purge and destroy all intelligence files concerning the counter-insurgency campaign and operations in the years 1982–5.

59 1999 interview.

60 1999 interview.

61 Cf. Molina Mejia (1998: 25–6).

62 The Alliance Against Impunity has charged the Arzú government with 'obstructing justice in cases in which military personnel are involved, such as the murder cases of Mack, Carpio, Gerardi and the massacre of Xaman.... We are convinced that this concerns a policy in which judges, magistrates and the attorney general's office take part but for rare exceptions' (Alliance spokesperson, *Prensa Libre*, 16 October 1998; see also 'Caso Xaman: MP Prestara' Apoyo', *Prensa Libre*, 14 October 1998).

63 1999 and 2000 interviews.

64 Bishop Gerardi, coordinator of the REMHI publications, was murdered a day after the publication of these reports. Intelligence members and the army officers tied to the presidential advisory body are being accused of serious involvement in the murder.

# 4

# The Military and Politics in Brazil

## 1964-2000

## CELSO CASTRO

Brazil spent the 21 years between 1964 and 1985 under military rule. The military came into power when they overthrew the legally constituted government of João Goulart. By 1964, episodes of military intervention in Brazilian republican history were far from unusual. Actually, the republican regime in Brazil was inaugurated in 1889 through a coup executed by a group of military officers. This 'capital sin' of the Brazilian republican regime happened again and again in the following decades, by means of several military interventions: in 1930, with the deposal of President Washington Luís; in 1945, with the deposal of Getúlio Vargas; in 1954, in the crisis that pushed Vargas to suicide; and in 1955, with General Lott's 'coup in defence of legality'. For some analysts, such interventions have been the manifestation of a 'moderating power' exercised by the armed forces. According to this way of seeing military interventions, the armed forces, going above and beyond the roles of the three traditional branches of government, have exercised the power of intervening in the political scene when they judged necessary, representing the nation, in order to solve institutional crises and serious political deadlocks. However, an important pattern distinguished these interventions: political power was invariably and rapidly returned to civilians.

The coup of 1964 broke with this pattern: a genuine military regime was established, during which the military institution remained in power for 21 years. In stating matters in these terms, I am not suggesting that the military ruled alone. Powerful civilian groups – political, business, religious and even popular – stimulated, supported and collaborated with the successive military governments. However, we can consider the regime to be military because during the entire period the higher echelons of the armed forces were clearly the actors who kept political participation under strict control. When they were confronted by or became unsatisfied with even the limited political interplay that they allowed, the military governments acted several times in a highly authoritarian manner (through the infamous 'Institutional Acts'): shutting down Congress, amending the constitution, disrespecting the judicial branch, deposing elected congressmen, mayors and governors from their offices, forcibly retiring public servants, revoking political rights, applying censorship, and exerting the most extreme forms of political repression (such as exile, prison, torture and even the outright assassination of members of the opposition).

Throughout this period the military institution was united against the civilian opposition in defence of its role in 1964 and of the military regime as a whole. It is important to emphasize, however, that in no way was the military regime homogeneous and uniform, neither in the intensiveness of its repressive measures, nor in the composition and ideological orientation of the military officers in power. A good way of grasping how the military regime changed over time is to divide its 21-year life span into three phases – even though any such procedure is arbitrary and open to debate.

The first phase extends from the 1964 coup to the Institutional Act No. 5 of December 1968, encompassing the entire term of General Castelo Branco and the beginning of General Costa e Silva's term. In these years, officers with a more radical orientation ('hard-liners') gradually gained power and pushed for the continuation of the military regime and for the adoption of more repressive measures, eventually out-competing the politically more moderate officers ('soft-liners'). This does not mean that the moderate-oriented officers were political 'liberals'. They were authoritarians as well, but in comparison with the hard-liners they were less radical, defending a shorter stay in power and a less profound intervention in Brazilian society. The second phase covers what came to be known as the *anos de chumbo* ('years of lead') of contemporary Brazilian history, from 1968 to 1974. This period includes the end of Costa e Silva's term, the three months of the Junta Militar, the military triumvirate that ruled the country after Costa e Silva's removal (on grounds of 'health') and the whole of General Médici's term. Repression was at its most aggressive. 'Hard-liners' exercised power in a virtually uncontested fashion. Finally, the third phase was opened by the inauguration of General Ernesto Geisel, who rose to power with the project of liberalizing the regime, in a 'slow, gradual and safe' (*'lenta, gradual e segura'* ) manner, to quote his own words. Although Geisel employed authoritarian measures against the opposition many times, he controlled 'hard-liners' inside the armed forces and was the only president who managed to choose his own successor – João Figueiredo, who concluded the political transition and transferred power to a civilian president in 1985.

In this chapter I intend to highlight how the military lived through this experience of political power during these distinct phases. My basic sources will be the data obtained through a research project conducted between 1992 and 1995 at the Centre of Documentation of Brazilian History (Centro de Pesquisa e Documentação de História Contemporânea do Brasil, CPDOC) of the Fundação Getulio Vargas, including two hundred hours of taped interviews with military officers.[1] Among the interviewees, were Ex-President Geisel and an important group of officers who in 1964 were in the middle echelons and supported the coup. During the 1968–74 phase, in which the highest degree of authoritarianism occurred, several officers from this group held important posts precisely in the new intelligence and repression agencies of the armed forces. When military rule came to an end in 1985 most of these officers had already retired, having occupied highly important posts and key positions in military institutions. When we started the project, several books with the depositions and memoirs of the 'generals of 1964' were already available. However, the generations of military officers who reached the summit of their careers during the military regime had remained silent until then about this long experience in exercising political power. Obviously, as our project explored military memory, the views given by the interviewees cannot be considered as expressions of the 'historical truth', but as subjective and retrospective interpretations of their experiences. However, our research helped reveal how the military did not hold a homogeneous set of ideals, nor a shared political project, between 1964 and 1985. We found also that there is not a 'military memory' about the period, but different military memories that compete with each other over several aspects. The results of this research project therefore proved again the problems that arise when one speaks of the armed forces or 'the military' in general, without taking into account the differences of political opinion and thought which co-exist in military institutions. These differences must be carefully considered, especially if we want to understand the critical junctures of the military regime.

In the chapter that follows, I adopt the above-mentioned division of the military regime into three phases and then examine the role of the military during the 'New Republic'. However, before we move on to the subject of the major internal cleavages that emerged among the military, let us examine some of the general characteristics of the military regime in Brazil.

## 21 Years in Power: a very brief overview

The military officers involved in the 1964 coup justified their action by stating that their goals were to restore discipline and hierarchy in the armed forces and to put an end to the 'communist menace' that they believed was threatening Brazil. A basic idea among the participants in the coup was that the major threat to the capitalist order and to the security of the country would not come from abroad, by means of a traditional war to be fought against foreign armies; it would come from within the country itself, by means of Brazilians who acted as 'internal enemies', a quite common expression at the time. These 'internal enemies' would pursue their objective – to subvert the existing order and install communism in Brazil – by means of a revolution. This is why the military called them 'subversives'. This line of reasoning was reinforced by several international examples, such as the revolutionary wars in Asia, Africa and, above all, in Cuba, where Fidel Castro had risen to power after a successful guerrilla campaign. This way of looking at the world was at the base of the so-called 'Doctrine of National Security' and of the theories of 'counter-insurgency war' or 'anti-revolutionary war' taught in the higher-learning institutions of the armed forces.

The military who rose to power in 1964 believed that the democratic regime installed in Brazil after the Second World War had proved unable to block the advance of the communist threat. Therefore, on the one hand, they started to build a political regime characterized by authoritarianism, giving a strong hand to the state in its dealings with individual rights, and to the executive branch in its interaction with the legislative and judiciary branches; on the other hand, the regime always had a hybrid nature, seeking the support of conservative political forces, despite the clear supremacy of the military. The most remarkable result of this second trait was that, despite several temporary interruptions and purges, the regime always kept the constitution working and with it the federal legislative branch and its counterparts in the states and municipalities. It also held periodical direct elections for all legislative posts. When taking oath, all military presidents promised, as a matter of course, to take the country back to 'democratic normality' and to stimulate the return of economic growth.

In the economic arena, the military governments wavered between hard-line anti-inflationary phases (as in the Castelo Branco term, which featured 'The Government Programme of Economic Growth' – Programa de Ação Econômica do Governo, PAEG), phases of speedy economic growth (as in the years of the 'Brazilian miracle', during the terms of Costa e Silva and Médici), and periods of economic crisis (such as the one that followed the international oil crisis that started in late 1973). In order to step up the country's development, the military governments invested heavily in several large construction projects, such as the Transamazon highway, the Itaipu hydroelectric dam, and a nuclear reactor pro-gramme. The military regime took advantage of spells of economic success and used them for propaganda, promoting hyper-nationalist feelings and behaviours. This propaganda bragged about national riches and accomplishments, appealing to an overblown sense of patriotism. When the Brazilian national soccer team won its third World Cup in 1970 in Mexico, this feat was specifically exploited by the military government to build an image of a 'Great Brazil'.

For 21 years the military had direct control of Brazilian national politics. The Brazil of 1985 was very different from that of 1964. It is true that there was a significant development of the national economic infrastructure, a fact always mentioned by defenders of the military regime. Despite this, however, in 1985 the Brazilian economy was going through very serious difficulties. After two decades, income distribution had become worse, and the gap between the poor and the rich had grown. And when the military regime came to an end the country was suffering from record levels of inflation, unemployment and foreign indebtedness.

Besides economic problems, the lack of democracy and the violent repression waged against all those who had opposed the military regime disorganized the country's political life and left bad feelings that would take a long time to soothe in the national political memory. To go beyond this legacy became a great challenge to Brazil's young democracy. Now, however, let us examine the major cleavages that emerged in the ranks of the Brazilian armed forces during their tour of duty in power, considering also how they help us to understanding the dynamics of the military regime.

## From the 1964 Coup to Institutional Act No. 5

The military who took power always emphasize – and are certainly justified in doing so – that the 1964 coup was not the result of a plan that they made up on their own, because important segments of civil society, intimidated by the possibility of leftist currents gaining power in Brazil, also participated in the coup or supported it. There is a consensus about this point among the officers we inter-viewed. The participation of civil society in the 1964 coup – or 'the Revolution', as the officers like to refer to the military regime – is nowadays frequently forgotten. According to General Leônidas Pires Gonçalves, in an interview in 1992:

> The revolution came about as a result of the pressures exerted by civil society. We cannot forget this. I have the habit of repeating this and, if you have not heard it from somebody else, you will hear it from me: I believe that the armed forces until this day

have reasons to be resentful in relation to Brazilian society. This is so because Brazilian society impelled us, it was one of the forces responsible for the 1964 Revolution, and nowadays the media constantly point the finger at us and calls us torturers, killers ....[2]

This excerpt illustrates well the resentment of these military officers, motivated by the 'historical conniving' (*'safadeza histórica'* in the words of General Leônidas) that occurred after the military regime was over. In the end the long period of military rule was credited solely to the initiative of the armed forces, and many people have forgotten that important civilian groups agreed with and stimulated military intervention. There is a recurrent argument among our interviewees that there were ardent civilian appeals for military intervention, and this argument works as a tool that provides legitimacy to the coup.

However, right from the beginning there was an all-important division among the military involved in the 1964 coup. On one side were those who called for more radical measures against 'subversion' and supported a longer military tenure in power. On the other, there were the officers who followed the historical tradition of the 'moderating' interventions and defended a swift return to 'normal' political and judicial conditions (for example, after a 'corrective intervention'). This included giving political power back to civilians after a short span of time. The first, more radical element came to be known as the hard-liners and gravitated around the Minister of the Army, General Costa e Silva. The other, more moderate element gathered around President Castelo Branco and included officers who held important positions in government such as Ernesto Geisel, Osvaldo Cordeiro de Farias and Golbery do Couto e Silva. This should be seen as a division between two different institutional and political orientations inside an encompassing authoritarian common view, and not as two organized and homogeneous 'groups'.

In the early days of his government Castelo Branco gave out clear indications that he was willing to honour – at least in part – his promise of returning Brazil to political 'normality'. The exceptional powers given to him by the 1964 Institutional Act, such as the nullification of the terms of elected congressmen, or the revoking of political rights, or the firing of civil servants, should last only a few months. Castelo Branco accepted the time limitation placed on his exceptional powers, while 'hard-line' officers defended their expansion. Furthermore, Castelo Branco allowed scheduled elections (on 3 October 1965) for the selection of the governors of eleven Brazilian states to happen, despite hard-line opposition.

In these elections, opposition candidates won in the most important states, particularly in Guanabara, with Negrão de Lima, and Minas Gerais, with Israel Pinheiro. Considering these victories of the opposition to be a threat to the military government, hard-line officers increased their pressure on President Castelo Branco to make the military regime even more restrictive. Costa e Silva, the Minister of the Army, became the spokesman of the more radical officers and even criticized the elections in public. On 6 October 1965 younger officers threatened to lead an armed rising of Vila Militar, the army barracks in Rio de Janeiro, in a protest against the election results and a government they deemed 'not revolutionary enough'. Costa e Silva spoke to them and guaranteed that 'we shall not turn back to the past'. He asked them not to be concerned about the fact that a few 'worthless men' (*'homúnculos'*) would come to occupy the posts they had just gained in what he emphasized was 'an authorized election, a knowingly authorized election'.

It is interesting to note that in this same speech Costa e Silva was strongly applauded when he stated that, after a year, the 'Revolution' was having problems only

> in containing those who are excessively revolutionary. *(Applause)* We do not fear counter-revolutions…. *(Applause)* What concerns us is actually the enthusiasm and eagerness of this younger generation that yearns for more revolution. But I guarantee you, my friends, I guarantee you, my young officers, that we know where we stand. Our current commanders, as I said yesterday and repeat today, are as revolutionary as the young revolutionary officers. *(Applause)* I guarantee you that we will not return to the past. *(Ovation).*[3]

To better understand the differences between hard-line and soft-line officers, it is also important to pay attention to their generational differences. In this case, I am using generation not in its biological sense, or as a simple indicator of difference in ages, but as a cultural fact related to basic experiences that shape the social and professional identities of individuals. In general, the more moderate officers were older and held higher posts in the military hierarchy when compared with the radical officers, who were usually young, as can be inferred from Costa e Silva's speech cited above. The younger officers had started their careers after the traumatic communist revolt of 1935 (which involved army personnel and even today is considered by the military as a prime example of 'treachery') and went through a long process of indoctrination during the Cold War years. They learned that the role that the armed forces of peripheral nations had to play was the containment of 'internal enemies'. For them the '1964 revolution' meant not a short intervention aimed at correcting the route of the Brazilian polity, but a radical reform of the country, a 'clean-up' of the country's institutions and political life. Some even believed in the utopia of the elimination of all politics. In this sense, the pressure of hard-liners inside the armed forces was directed towards radical changes in the political process, because these officers were convinced that the true enemies were at home and were still very strong.

The reaction of hard-liners to the 1965 elections led to the issuing of a new Institutional Act, No. 2. This new act established indirect elections to the post of president, reopened the process of nullification of the terms of lawmakers and elected officials, and again allowed suspension of the political rights of any citizen. Furthermore, existing political parties were dissolved. Instead of the multi-party system formed in 1946, Brazilian politics was now moulded into a two-party system. The National Renovative Alliance (Aliança Renovadora Nacional, ARENA) supported government; the Brazilian Democratic Movement (Movimiento Democrático Brasil, MDB) was the opposition. Thus the return to 'democratic normality', as promised by Castelo Branco, became a vanishing reality.

The process that lead up to the issuing of the Institutional Act No. 2 was a victory for the hard-liners and expanded their influence in the military regime. One of the consequences of this was the successful candidacy of Costa e Silva as president of the Republic, even if he was not the choice of Castelo Branco and his supporting officers. Costa e Silva was inaugurated on 15 March 1967, after being indirectly elected by Congress.

The years 1967 and 1968 were marked by intensive political radicalization. Government, on its side, increased its repressive apparatus. Military leaders considered that the police were not sufficiently prepared to deal with 'subversion'. Thus the armed forces started to take over functions formerly exercised by the police. Intelligence and repression agencies were created in the army (Centro de Informações do Exército, CIE) and in the air force (Centro de Informações e Segurança da Aeronáutica, CISA); the navy reorganized its Centro de Informações da Marinha (CENIMAR) so it, too, could function as a repressive force. As the expression of opposing points of view inside the political system became quite limited, effective opposition to the regime started to shift to several social movements. There was an attempt to revive the workers' movement, with serious strikes in the industrial cities of Contagem and Osasco. These were the first strikes recorded since the beginning of the military regime. A 'progressive' group of Catholic clergy also formed an increasingly visible opposition group. This part of the clergy, although a minority inside the Catholic Church, used non-violent demonstrations and exposed the lack of political liberty in Brazil. The strongest strain of opposition came, however, from student movements. Even though they had to operate illegally, students organized several street demonstrations and rallies, protesting against the military regime. Government reacted by increasing repression. This process reached a climax with the issuing of the Institutional Act No. 5, aptly dated Friday, 13 December 1968. This was the harshest institutional act of the entire military regime; it gave almost absolute powers to the president of the Republic.

## From Institutional Act No. 5 to Geisel's Inauguration: the *anos de chumbo*

Institutional Act No. 5 was a benchmark in the process of the increasing authoritarianism of the military regime, on the one hand, and the radicalization of the opposition on the other. After it was issued, several leftist groups engaged in armed struggle against the dictatorship, mainly through urban guerrilla actions. Repression was violent and after little more than two years all urban guerrilla groups had been destroyed or disbanded. One last guerrilla attempt was made later in the rural area of the Araguaia River region, but by early 1974 this, too, had been defeated. The harshest phase of the military regime, initiated during the Costa e Silva government, lasted throughout the entire tenure of his successor, General Emílio Garrastazu Médici.

The military think that, although they won the war against the organizations of the revolutionary left, they lost the battle over the historical memory of this struggle. Many officers complain precisely about the fact that a distinct, military version generated by the armed forces about the repression of guerrilla warfare – a version that could have become socially legitimate – was never publicized. In the matter of fighting the guerrilla actions, the history of the vanquished therefore prevailed over that of the winners.

In our interviews we find implicit and explicit references to internal problems experienced by Brazilian military institutions during this phase of repression, and because of the dynamics of this repression. These problems can prompt us to identify the reasons why no official armed forces version of this experience in repression ever became established, not even 25 years after the defeat of the leftist organizations engaged in armed struggle. We have seen that there is a consensus among the military in evaluating the political situation that preceded the 1964 coup, and about the reasons that led to military intervention. On the issue of military repression of armed political opponents, however, opinions are divided. This is seen in the ways that some interviewees linked to intelligence and repression agencies refer to colleagues who criticized or disagreed with the methods adopted. General Leônidas calls them 'theorizers', General Coelho Neto says that they are 'cowards in disguise', and to Colonel Cyro Etchegoyen they are no less than 'traitors'. These acrimonious expressions indicate that the degree of internal conflict over the matter was strong.

In the books that we published to draw attention to these interviews, there are depositions that indicate the existence of internal tensions created by the operation of the new repressive agencies established inside the armed forces. The armed forces had a well-established and traditional command structure, based on clearly defined geographical units, but this structure was often undermined by the new operational intelligence network, which recognized no geographical boundaries and was controlled directly by the office of each military minister. Generals Otávio Costa and Moraes Rego, for example, had problems with army intelligence officers in the military regions under their command. These officers tried to execute operations involving the military structure commanded by the two generals without informing them about the matter.

The operational intelligence network had a strong degree of autonomy in the planning and execution of its actions. Besides this, the coordination between the new repressive agencies themselves was very weak. Officers directly engaged in repression gained a *de facto* power that was not in proportion with their hierarchical rankings. In some cases – in the Air Force, for example – officers not engaged in political repression actually came to feel threatened by their own colleagues engaged in the intelligence sector. Despite these differences, the need to preserve the *esprit de corps* of the armed forces in the face of civil society prevailed, and the existence of such internal tensions was not acknowledged. They became more visible only when the main political issue became the 'opening' of the military regime in General Geisel's term as president.

## The 'Opening' of the Military Regime and the Difficult Return to the Barracks

The third and last phase of the military regime starts with the inauguration of President Ernesto Geisel in March 1974. Its basic traits were a lower intensity of repression and an increased hostility in the conflicts between more radical and more moderate sectors within the armed forces. Geisel's presidency brought back into power several officers who, immediately after 1964, had been part of the so-called 'Castelista group' in the armed forces. Geisel himself had been Castelo Branco's chief military aide. However, the fact that he became president should not be taken to mean that the more moderate officers composed a majority in the military institution, or even the strongest group inside it. On the contrary, the hard-liners were at the peak of their power and were suspicious of the choice that made Geisel the successor of Médici. This was so despite the fact that Geisel had developed a good image as an administrator during his term as president of Petrobras (the state oil monopoly) during the Médici government. Ernesto Geisel had the all-important support of his brother, General Orlando Geisel, Médici's Minister of the Army, who had a good reputation among the ranks of hard-liners as the strong man behind the repression of subversive organizations. The two brothers had taken separate political paths years earlier, but Orlando Geisel negotiated with President Médici and vouched for his brother as future president.

Geisel started out his term with a clearly defined project of political liberalization, although he proposed, as we have seen, a 'slow, gradual and safe' transition that would have to live side by side with authoritarian instruments such as the powers given to the president by Institutional Act No. 5. Geisel's project was more about liberalization than democratization. He wanted to take the military institution out of the centre of political power, but he wanted to control the rhythm and define the limits of this political transition. He also planned to restore the pre-eminence and the control of the traditional military chain of command, breaking up the autonomy of the military agencies dedicated to political repression. However, as this political project turned into a political process, Geisel found himself facing the opposition both of the MDB, which wanted to hasten the pace and expand the range of political liberalization, and of the more radical military sectors, who were opposed to any political liberalization. Geisel thus had to fight simultaneously on two fronts:[4]

> There were people in the army, in the armed Forces as a whole, who had this obsession with conspiracy, with communism, with the left. And the situation became more complex because the opposition, particularly in Congress, instead of understanding what I was doing, my attempts to gradually solve this problem, once in a while took aggressive and hostile stands. Every time that the opposition took radical stances and attacked the armed forces, by means of speeches, manifestos, public statements, obviously there was a reaction on the other side, and this created great difficulties for me....[5] I was pressed from both sides; by the opposition and by the military sector, unsatisfied with the criticism and with the expressions used by the opposition.... I spent my entire term in the middle of this game. This is what caused the delay of the final solution, the extinction of the Institutional Act No. 5. While the opposition was so aggressive, it was not possible to liberalize the regime and satisfy it. I could not turn my back on the military, who, despite the cooperation of ARENA, were the main supporters of the revolutionary government....[6] The acts of the opposition exacerbated [my difficulties with] the hard-liners, who, to a certain degree, were on the side of my government, but who were the other sector that I needed to control. In other words, I had to fight on two fronts: against the communists and against those who fought the communists. That is the truth, indeed.[7]

The process of political liberalization led to irresolvable disagreements between the military who were in favour of it and the hard-liners who opposed it. This was indeed one of the critical moments of Brazilian contemporary history. Two episodes decided the conflict in favour of Geisel. The first came about after the death by torture (the official version called it a suicide) of Manuel Fiel Filho, a worker in a military unit of the city of São Paulo, in January 1976. Less than three months before that, a ranking journalist, Vladimir Herzog, had been 'suicided' in the same unit, and Geisel warned the four-star general Ednardo D'Ávila Melo, commander of the Second Army, that he would not tolerate any more deaths under the same circumstances. With Fiel Filho's death, Geisel reacted immediately, shocking many officers: he summarily relieved the general of his command.

This was intended to be a clear sign that the commanders would now be responsible for all repressive actions that occurred in areas and units under their command, even if such actions were executed without their knowledge or consent. In this manner, the traditional hierarchical chain of command was reinstated above the 'operational' network of intelligence and repression. In making this decision, Geisel was not concerned mainly with human rights violations. In fact, in his interview, Geisel made it clear (and shocked many people by doing so) that he considered torture to be necessary under certain conditions, as in the more critical confrontations with the leftists engaged in armed struggle. Geisel was really concerned with controlling the military agencies dedicated to intelligence and repression, in order to restore the institutional principles that he thought were jeopardized by the autonomy attained by these agencies.

Geisel's second crucial moment in his confrontation with the military radicals came about when the hard-liners started to raise the name of the Minister of the Army, General Sílvio Frota, as a candidate to succeed Geisel in the presidency. Frota had endorsed the standard hard-line critiques of Geisel's liberalization measures and had thus entered on a collision course with the president. In October 1977 Geisel fired Frota from his post as minister, in an unexpected but carefully planned manoeuvre designed to neutralize possible reactions in favour of Frota.

It is interesting to notice that this moment is structurally similar to the crisis experienced during the term of Castelo Branco, the first in the military cycle. The Minister of the Army, the government's 'strong man', again rose to the position of spokesman for the unrest among the more radical officers who felt uneasy with a politically more moderate president. Geisel, however, did what Castelo Branco could not do, or did not wish to do: he fired his Minister of the Army, Sílvio Frota. Besides the differences between the personal styles of Castelo Branco and Geisel, we must keep in mind that the upper echelons of the armed forces in 1977 were significantly different from those of 1965. Castelo Branco had adopted a law by which military promotions created much shorter and strictly limited terms of active duty for generals. Because of this, ten years later all generals with careers stretching back to 1964 had passed to the reserves; the armed forces no longer had those long-lasting generals who surround themselves with entourages of officers in the course of their long reigns in command posts. Although the two junctures both pitted a president against the Minister of the Army, the hierarchical distance between President Geisel and Frota was much greater than the distance between President Castelo Branco and Costa e Silva.[8]

Once Frota had been fired, Geisel was free to pursue his goal of liberalizing the regime. He was also free enough to become the first and only military president to select his preferred successor, General João Figueiredo, sworn into office in March 1979. Before leaving government, Geisel had already revoked Institutional Act No. 5. One of Figueiredo's first measures was to send an amnesty bill to Congress. It became law before 1979 was over. Proceeding with the politics of liberalization, in 1982 Figueiredo presided over elections for state governors in all Brazilian states. These elections were clean and based on direct ballots. However, Figueiredo's attitude in relation to the so-called 'Riocentro case' tarnished the image of the armed forces. In 1981, an army captain was seriously injured and a sergeant died when a bomb exploded accidentally inside the car that they were using. They were wearing civilian clothing and had just arrived at the scene of a large musical concert being held to celebrate Labour Day at a convention centre called Riocentro in the city of Rio de Janeiro. The episode made it clear that there still were groups of military officers linked to the repressive and intelligence military units who wanted to destabilize the process of political liberalization. The military investigation that followed defended the ridiculous fiction that the captain and the sergeant had been the victims of a terrorist act, denying that they themselves were the terrorists. Figueiredo thought he could protect the military institution by accepting the result of this investigation and decided not to punish any military personnel, not even the surviving captain-terrorist. Only in 1999 was this captain officially deemed to be a suspect, as the Riocentro case was reopened.

The Riocentro episode demoralized Figueiredo's government and spread a deep aversion among almost all circles of Brazilian society. It also marked the end of the deeds of military or paramilitary groups against political liberalization. It was also decisive in stamping a negative public image on the entire experience of military rule. All military officers that we interviewed agree in their feeling that, once the military cycle was over, they lacked credibility to engage in any sort of political interplay with other actors. They also felt that their biographies were in many cases reduced to a stigma, the stigma of having participated in the military regime. Accusations of torture and complicity in the fate of persons missing since the phase of more intensive repression remain at the heart of the criticism directed at the military until this day. The recovery of the public image and of the professional identity of the armed forces thus became one of the major problems that all military commanders had to face during the New Republic.

Therefore, the legacy of the military regime for the armed forces and for the new generations of officers has been very heavy. This refers both to the external image of the military institution and to the internal strife caused by the 21-year experience of direct participation in political power. In 1992, General Moraes Rego summarized this heavy legacy in his interview: 'Nobody can help us recover – and no one even acknowledges – the losses that we experienced: friendships that were torn apart, camaraderie that was lost. This revolution cost us much, very much indeed.'

## The Military under Civilian Rule — the 'New Republic' (1985-)

The transition to civilian rule in 1985 nevertheless occurred under norms that pertained to that authoritarian period. The first civilian president, Tancredo Neves, was elected indirectly by an Electoral College, despite the huge civic and popular mobilization in favour of the popular and direct vote (the campaign for the *Diretas Já*). Tancredo, however, fell ill before his inauguration and was replaced by the elected vice-president, José Sarney, a conservative politician who had always supported the military regime. A few weeks later, Tancredo died. What happened in the ranks of the military after they retired from the strongholds of political power? Did they return to the barracks and just watch as their influence shrank? Or did they remain politically powerful and behave as a sort of 'tutor' of Brazilian democracy? There is a clear a lack of consensus among the analysts of this matter: the question is still open to debate.

Let us examine the arguments presented by two opposing and mutually exclusive points of view. Jorge Zaverucha[9] argues that democratic civilian control over the military in Brazil is denied by the continuing existence of military 'prerogatives'. These 'prerogatives' are defined by him as areas in which the military institution is presumed to have 'gained the right or privilege, formal or informal, to govern over these areas, to exercise roles in extra-military affairs within the state apparatus, and even to shape the structure of the relationships between the state and civil or political society'.[10]

He calls this situation a 'tutelary democracy' (*democracia tutelada*), characterized by the institutional and political autonomy of the military, who would thus be acting as the 'guardians' of democracy. In this situation, half-way between dictatorship and democracy, the military institution, by threatening with coups, explicitly or not, has set limits to the range of behaviours of civilian politicians.

Zaverucha lists the survival of seventeen distinct military prerogatives throughout the governments of Sarney, Collor and Franco, and Cardoso's first term (until 1998). These prerogatives are: (1) the armed forces are still charged with the role of guaranteeing constitutional powers, law and order; (2) the military retain control over the major intelligence agencies, in charge of surveillance over lawmakers; (3) active-duty and reserve military officers have been present in the higher echelons of the executive branch; (4) the lack of a Defence Ministry; (5) the lack of routine legislation and detailed examination by Congress of matters pertaining to national defence; (6) absence of Congressional influence over the promotions of generals; (7) state military police corps continues under the control of the armed forces; (8) fire-fighter corps also remain under partial control of the armed forces; (9) small probability of military officers going on trial in civilian courts; (10) strong probability of civilians going on trial in military courts, even for political or common violations; (11) military officers retain the right to arrest civilians or military personnel without court orders or without them being caught on the scene; (12) the military may exercise extra-judicial and legislative authority; (13) the military can become an independent executive force in the case of internal turmoil; (14) the armed forces have major responsibility for the security of the president and the vice-president; (15) military presence in areas of civilian economic activity (space, naval transportation, aviation, etc.); (16) the armed forces are allowed to sell military property without being fully accountable to the national treasury; and (17) wage policies for military personnel are similar to those that were adopted during the military regime.[11]

Zaverucha considers that the civilian governments of the New Republic varied only in the degree of their stance *vis-à-vis* the military, and not in the nature of their behaviour. Thus, what we have is a tutelary democracy, with military prerogatives remaining strong and with a low degree of military resistance to civilian orders. This means not that the military have returned to the barracks, but that there is 'evidence of their significant participation in the political decision-making process'.[12] This non-democratic and 'unstable' balance in civilian–military relations can, according to Zaverucha, be broken as soon as a civilian government tries to put an end to military prerogatives, a fact which would detonate 'a praetorian reaction that will threaten the ruling government'.[13] In this sense, the Brazilian transition would therefore be an incomplete one and, as Zaverucha argues, 'there are no promising indicators that we will be able to pass from a democratic government to a democratic regime, in both short and medium terms. In the long term, as Keynes reminds us, we will all be dead.'[14]

On the other hand, Wendy Hunter, in a much more optimist view,[15] disagrees with authors who see Brazilian democracy as designed to suffer the influence of the military because of the negotiated nature of the transition – 'a transition from above', as it is commonly called. In this type of transition – very distinct from the one that happened in Argentina, for example, which was a 'transition by collapse' – the Brazilian military would hold on to a tutorial role, thus creating barriers to the consolidation of democracy. Hunter believes, on the contrary, that civilian–

military relations in Brazil have displayed a much stronger dynamism and that, 'rather than creating a static framework, democracy unleashes a competitive dynamic conducive to change'. Her research 'suggests that countries that return to civilian rule through elite-led negotiations need not be constrained indefinitely by the balance of forces that prevailed in the transition and immediate post-transition period'. Thus the operation of democratic rules and the political competition associated with them allow for changes in the conservative pact that rules over the transition. As to the matter of military prerogatives, so strongly emphasized by Zaverucha, she believes that, although they may continue to exist, 'leading officers appeared increasingly unable to use them to wield actual political influence'. Therefore, there would not be a deep contradiction between the persistence of some prerogatives and a limited degree of political influence of the military.

Hunter believes that the military lost their political influence in the New Republic because of 'the unfolding of the rules and norms of democracy'. She argues that the military lose their muscle in democratic scenarios. Electoral competition entices civilian politicians to reduce the political influence of the military, and electoral victories reinforce the ability of these politicians to do so. Therefore, what results is a trend for the erosion of military influence. Hunter wrote – in a phrase that is becoming famous (it has been cited in a number of subsequent academic texts) – that, 'at the risk of exaggeration, conditions of the 1980s and 1990s have rendered the Brazilian military somewhat of a paper tiger'.[16]

Other analysts have sided with one or the other of these two positions. Tollefson,[17] for example, strongly defends Hunter's theses, criticizing Zaverucha and what he calls 'the myth of tutelary democracy'. Martins Filho and Zirker,[18] on the other hand, reach conclusions that are opposite to those reached by Hunter, stating that the political drive of the military was not reduced, and even pointing to 'the rise of a new kind of military influence', in a perspective that they consider to complement the outlook presented by Zaverucha.[19]

In order to understand two perspectives that are so different – one very optimistic, the other so pessimistic – we must appreciate the difficulty of the topic. The major events are still too recent; inertia clings to the interpretative schemes, strongly influenced by the historical role of the military in recent Brazilian affairs; and the available sources are meagre, despite the information stemming from the press and military statements. What follows, therefore, is based on ongoing research about the military in Brazil's New Republic.[20] As such, this research should be considered provisional and subject to changes. My perspective is closer to Hunter's than to Zaverucha's. I believe that the military have in fact lost a significant degree of power and influence in the Brazilian democracy.[21] I must make two preliminary points, though.

First, we must distinguish the first years of the transition from the ones that followed. In the beginning of the New Republic, during the Sarney government (1985–90), the military still exercised a significant degree of political power. As mentioned, Sarney was the vice-president of Tancredo Neves, elected by an indirect ballot and deceased before his inauguration. He sought support from the armed forces because of the weakness of his position, shattered by the failure of the Plano Cruzado, his economic stabilization plan, in late 1986. The Army Minister, Leônidas Pires Gonçalves, was particularly visible, because of his constant political statements about non-military matters. Also, through efficient lobbying, the military got the 1988 National Constitutional Assembly to approve the agenda that they thought to be central: the military conserved their constitutional role of intervening in the case of serious political crises, if requested to do so by any of the three branches of government; banned military officers and non-commissioned officers were not to be accepted back by the armed forces; a separate wage and benefit policy was maintained for the military; mandatory conscription for military service was preserved, and a planned Defence Ministry was not created. For this phase of the Sarney government, it makes sense to defend the notion that the military exercised some sort of tutelary role. The situation changed considerably, however, under the governments of Collor and, above all, Fernando Henrique Cardoso, both of whom exercised a strong degree of political direction over the armed forces.[22]

Second, I agree with Hunter on the general point that military influence in Brazil has been decreasing since 1985 and will probably continue to decrease as the democratic process becomes stronger and stronger. However, a wider historical perspective on the role of the military in Brazilian republican history, associated with the perception of the enormous social problems and inequalities that persist in Brazilian society, should make us stop short of characterizing the Brazilian military as 'paper tigers'. It should be kept in mind that the Brazilian political culture also carries an ancient authoritarian tradition, one that existed well before the military regime itself. Nothing stands in the way of a reversal of military subordination in the case, for example, of deeper social or economic crises.

Having made these points, I will now focus on four issues or moments of the New Republic which are important for the understanding of the changes experienced by the relationships between the armed forces, the state and society during the 1990s.

## Critical Moments

*Actions during Collor's impeachment*
It would have been hard for any political analyst to predict that the Brazilian armed forces would voluntarily keep a safe distance from political matters in the case of the serious political unrest that caused the impeachment of a president accused of grave deeds of corruption, and in the middle of a strenuous economic crisis, especially given a long-term perspective of Brazilian republican history. However, this is exactly what happened. Resisting their historical 'messianic calling', the military held on to a strictly institutional stance, avoiding statements or threats of coups or intervention aimed at 'saving' the president, or the nation, for that matter. This was the military's 'baptism of fire' in the New Republic. Despite being prompted by the press, by politicians and even by Collor himself, the armed forces insisted that their role was to respect the constitution and the legal political process. It is important to recall, in assessing the institutional context of that decision, that during the entire New Republic there has not been a single day of alert in military barracks.[23]

*The creation of the Ministry of Defence*
Historically, Brazil did not have a Ministry of Defence. Traditionally the commander of each service has also been a government minister. During the entire military regime, these posts were filled by military officers and not by civilians. As the joint chief-of-staff of the armed forces and the top presidential military aide

(*Chefe da Casa Militar*) held ministerial status, Brazil always had at least five military ministries. With a Ministry of Defence, this situation was to change considerably. The commanders of the three services were to lose their status as ministers and fall under the Minister of Defence (and, ultimately, the president, who constitutionally is the supreme commander of the armed forces). The joint chief-of-staff was to disappear. The president's top military aide would also lose the status of minister, as his duties were to be incorporated into an Institutional Security Office (Gabinete de Segurança Institucional, GSI), a civilian agency.[24]

The creation of a Ministry of Defence was an objective that could already be found in the electoral platform of Cardoso's first term. However, it took four years for such a ministry to be created through an executive provisional decree at the end of 1998, a few days before Cardoso started his second term. This delay in the creation of the new ministry should not be interpreted as the result of tensions in the relations between civilians and military, because it is explained by deep divergences to be found among the military themselves. Each service had its own view about the institutional design of the new ministry. Tensions were particularly visible between the navy, on the one side, and the army and the air force, on the other. During the military regime such disagreements were minimized and the army held a clear hegemonic position. Besides that, the existence of a military president worked as a decisive component in the control or resolution of these disagreements. This changed during the New Republic. The end of military rule also brought about more competition between the three armed forces, and this weakened the ability of the military services to act together. The Ministry of Defence surely has a long way to go before it effectively becomes the agency responsible for military matters, but one cannot ignore the changes introduced in the relations between civilians and military in Brazil by the sheer force of its creation.

The first Minister of Defence was Élcio Álvares, a politician lacking any national importance. He was a senator from the small state of Espírito Santo, and was not re-elected. His name was chosen after a number of important politicians were invited to stand. They all declined. On 18 January 2000, however, a little over a year after the creation of the Defence Ministry, President Cardoso fired Álvares. This followed a crisis that started in December 1999, when a Congressional sub-committee investigating drugs trafficking decided to probe the possible involvement of Álvares's top aide of activity over more than twenty years in money-laundering in favour of organized crime in the state of Espírito Santo. A few days after this decision, the air force commander, Brigadier-General Walter Bräuer, when asked about the episode, answered that all persons in public office should have a clean record. On 17 December, the minister fired the commander, considering his words a breach of discipline. He also fired the aide who had been singled out by the Congressional sub-committee. In an attempt to defuse a tense situation, Cardoso invited the retired Brigadier-General Carlos Almeida Batista to be air force commander. He was the president of the Supreme Military Court and a highly respected officer in the service.

In fact, the disagreement between the minister and the air force commander involved other delicate matters, such as the privatization of Brazil's airports and the creation of a National Civilian Aviation Agency, unlinked to the air force, that until now controlled the sector and employed quite a number of reserve officers.[25] A luncheon to honour the fired Brigadier-General Bräuer, on 28 December 2000, brought together more than seven hundred people and prompted radical speeches, but the vast majority of those who attended were retired officers.

Álvares's position became untenable after he gave an interview to the weekly *Época*, defending himself and his aide and criticizing two fellow ministers (José Serra, Health, and José Carlos Dias, Justice). He was fired only a few days later. Geraldo Quintão, the advocate-general of the federal government, who took over the office on 24 January 2000, replaced him. Speaking at his inauguration, Quintão supported two of the major military demands: more money for re-equipment of the armed forces and higher wages. According the to air force commander, in doing so he started at the right pace....

This episode does not reflect a 'military crisis', as diagnosed by some eager journalists and analysts. This was a political crisis, caused mainly by the lack of political refinement on the part of the ex-minister Álvares in dealing with the accusations against his aide. It is also remarkable – and a good sign – that during this period the commanders of the army and the navy stood aside and said nothing about the accusations against the aide nor about the dismissal of the air force commander.

*The Committee on Missing Persons (Comissão dos Desaparecidos) and the reopening of the Riocentro case*
This committee set to work after a law was issued to solve the legal situation of the families of people who disappeared during the military regime, none of whom were officially declared dead. The enforcement of this law means that the Brazilian state recognizes its responsibility for the death and disappearance of these people. Most of more than three hundred predicted financial reparations have been paid.

On 22 January 1996 the first practical result of the committee's work was the issuing of a death certificate, received by his widow, in the name of the ex-representative Rubens Paiva, arrested at home in 1971 and officially 'missing' since then. During the ceremony, held at the presidential palace, there was a moment when the president's chief military aide, General Alberto Cardoso, hugged the widow of Paiva. The photos of this moment were posted on the front pages of the nation's newspapers and the officer's attitude was interpreted as a new stance of the military in relation to the political past. The gesture was criticized, however, by a number of reserve officers, especially those in charge of the Clube Militar and those belonging to about ten small right-wing groups, always willing to criticize any attitude perceived by them as part of a 'campaign to demoralize' the armed forces.

It is true that most active military officers, including military commanders, were deeply annoyed by some of the financial reparations awarded by the com-mittee, even more so because they amounted to admitting that the state – in this instance represented by the armed forces – had failed in its duty to protect the lives of prisoners under its guard. The two most sensitive cases were those of the ex-congressman and guerrilla leader Carlos Marighella, killed in an ambush in 1969, and, above all, of Carlos Lamarca, an ex-captain of the army who deserted in 1969 and became one of the major leaders of the armed struggle against the military regime until he was killed in 1971.

Despite the bad feelings among the military, clearly stated in an internal message written by the Minister of the Army stating that Lamarca would continue to be considered a traitor according to the military code, the work of the committee as a whole was not contested by the military. Among the officers, the view that the matter was about the relationship between the Brazilian state and these families prevailed over the notion that it might imply a moral judgement of the institution.

In much the same way, there have been no major incidents following the reopening in 1981 (after the Amnesty Law) of the investigation of the Riocentro episode which had been so damaging to the institutional image of the Brazilian military. For the first time the army captain of 1981, now an active colonel, was treated as a suspect. For almost twenty years everybody had thought that this would not be accepted by the military under any circumstances, but what is happening is exactly the opposite.

*Changes in important military celebrations*
Another striking aspect that has escaped the attention of researchers is that an entire set of symbolic elements that characterized the Brazilian armed forces – in some cases, going back to the 1920s and 1930s – have also undergone important changes since the military left the nucleus of political power in 1985. These changes, in my view, follow the same course as the changes in the political behaviour of the military.

With the end of the military regime, two once important celebrations have experienced a decline so strong that it is reasonable to suppose that they will disappear from the official calendar. One is the commemoration of victory over the 1935 communist revolt, staged each 27 November at the Praia Vermelha in Rio de Janeiro. The other is the commemoration of the 31 March 1964 coup (or 'revolution', as it is called by the military), held in all military barracks and units. In 1990, for the first time since the 1930s, the president of the Republic failed to attend the 27 November ceremony. A few years later the armed forces decided to put an end to the traditional public ritual held at the Praia Vermelha. Similarly, the usual joint statement of the military commanders of the three services, issued every 31 March, has not been made in recent years.

When the communist revolt was defeated in 1935, the aftermath was an intense process of institutionally driven affirmation of anti-communist ideology among all services of the Brazilian armed forces. Although most sectors of the military services were opposed to communism even before the rebellion, it was only after the event that the communists were clearly identified as the public enemy. An important part of this process of instituting anti-communism was the yearly celebration of the victory over the 27 November revolt.

From 1936 until 1996, the Brazilian armed forces doggedly paid their respects to the victims of the revolt. This occurred in Rio, first at the São João Batista cemetery, in which a mausoleum was built in 1940, and later, starting in 1968, at the Praia Vermelha, near the site of the rebellion, where a monument that still exists was built for this purpose. The idea of transferring the yearly ceremony from the cemetery to the newly built monument, according to the proclamation of Army Minister Aurélio de Lyra Tavares, was to 'allow a more effective participation of the general population in the ceremonies'.[26] The celebration, in which the presidents of the Republic had always participated, included the reading of proclamations written by the three military ministers. This was a hallmark of the strongly anti-communist institutional culture into which the military generations that took power in 1964 were bred.

This celebration gained strength with the new military regime of 1964. The most important rationale used in the more recent run of 27 November speeches was that in 1964, the communists had attacked again, and this attack, as in 1935, was again thwarted by the armed forces. In other words, thirty years later the enemy was the same, and it still required armed repression. Comparing 1935 and 1964 became a mandatory piece of rhetoric. Besides, a new commemoration was created, with the reading of the proclamations of service commanders in all military barracks and units on each anniversary of the coup of 31 March. The two celebrations mutually reinforced each other, ritualizing the anti-communist spirit of the armed forces.

After 1985, with the end of the military regime and the re-establishment of political democracy, both celebrations started to lose importance. At first, the proclamations read in the 27 November celebrations fell from three to one, amounting to a joint statement by the commanders of the three services. Even the content of the statement was gradually watered down. The old, vehement anti-communist symbology lost its drive. In 1990, the absence of the president of the Republic, Fernando Collor de Mello, marked the first time that the ceremony was conducted without a president in attendance. According to Collor's Minister of the Army, General Carlos Tinoco, the president informed his military ministries ahead of time that he would not go to the ceremony.[27] Collor simply announced his decision: as he did not ask the opinion of his military ministries, there was nothing to discuss. He did not oppose the celebration, however. Nonetheless, his stance significantly aided in the ceremony's loss of importance, and it never again managed to secure the attendance of the president of the republic, dwindling to an exclusively military affair.

Finally, in 1996 the military ministries attended the ceremony at the Praia Vermelha for the last time. Their joint proclamation stated that communism had come to an end. The heroes who had been an example and had inspired the perpetual anti-communist feeling among the military for sixty years had also concluded their struggle. At its closing, the proclamation warned that, in case there was not a celebration in the following years, the prevailing regime of liberty and democracy would be the best way to pay reverence to those heroes, a living proof that their deaths in defence of democratic institutions had not been in vain.[28]

It is worth highlighting that the Clube Militar – whose directors are usually army reserve officers, all of whom made their active careers during the military regime – has been speaking out against the withering of these ceremonies. Actually, over the last few years the Clube has been trying to play the role of promoter of these two rituals, in a posture that is explicitly critical of active military commanders. At the closing of the 1998 ceremony, the cultural director of the Clube, Colonel Sodré, a reserve officer, told two of my research assistants, present at the occasion that the Clube took the initiative of organizing the celebration after the army 'watered down' the event, since the Collor government, and that the situation had become serious after 'the communists reached power' – with the Fernando Henrique Cardoso government! According to the same colonel, the lack of interest in the ceremony (reflected in the low turn-out) was explained by an alleged campaign against the armed forces, conducted above all by the media.[29]

The 1999 events with which the same Clube Militar commemorated 31 March also combined radicalism and slim attendance. The audience at a 'debate' conducted on 29 March 1999 were mostly from the club's board of directors, joined

> **Box 4.1** General Gleuber Vieira speaks on the communist revolt of 1935[30]
>
> The commander of the army, General Gleuber Vieira, stated in the official newsletter of the army, published 27 November 1999, that it was important to understand 'that everything flows, nothing persists, nothing remains the same', and that this was the perspective of the army in relation to the episode. In the same conciliatory and Heraclitan spirit, he continues:
>
> > We are not tied to the past, we look into the future – after all, each time we wade into the historical river of time, we touch new waters. And therefore, despite the fact that we are the winners, we do not scoff at the losers.... When we erect monuments, we do so only to think deeply about History, never to demean opponents or to stir up disagreement. We know that to build the foundations of tomorrow means bringing seed to fertile soils, never waking up ghosts. This is what keeps us above ideologies, above discord, above resentment.

by a few reserve military officers, less than thirty people in all.[31] It is clearly wrong, therefore, to state that the Clube Militar is the mouthpiece of active military officers on matters pertaining to politics.

## Conclusion

Other points could be cited as examples of the much-lessened presence of the military on the political scene and of the acceptance, by the military, of a new pattern of civilian–military relations during the last decade. However, in order to conclude, I will now deal with the matter of how and why these changes were possible.

First, as emphasized by Hunter, one of the major factors in the decrease of the political influence of the military was the operation of democracy itself – and the manner in which the military themselves perceived the situation. Other factors should be mentioned, such as the external influences of the international scene, and a certain 'trauma' that was part of the heritage of the military regime.

The end of the Cold War and the new international scene in which bipolar ideological opposition vanished, together with heightened regional integration through MERCOSUR, put an end to strategic scenarios and ideological cleavages that had prevailed for four decades. Memories of the internal divisions and tensions inside the armed forces during the military regime also played a role. I also believe that the effects of the 'defeat' suffered by the military in the matter of the historical memory of the military regime were an important factor, leading to lack of political support and credibility. One thing is quite clear when we examine Brazil's recent history: the military never made any political move without the support of important social groups. In the absence of societal support and in the absence of civilian allies for the execution of coups or barracks uprisings, the risk of such actions is even higher for the military. Consensus about democracy is today higher than in the past. Finally, as time goes on there is a natural replacement of the military generation that lived through the military regime by another generation that is emotionally unattached to this period. Measures targeted to make the military more professional – issued paradoxically by a military government (Castelo Branco) – and a promotion law that restricts the time that officers can spend as active generals, are working to transform into history the experiences of the generation that lived under the military regime.

Of course one can always think that the change in the attitudes of the military during the New Republic is actually no more than a 'disguise' for a new 'serpent's egg'. It is true that several 'prerogatives' are preserved in the constitution and laws, and Zaverucha's list can be seen as a good agenda for what has yet to be changed (some of these prerogatives have already been dropped without any significant resistance on the part of the military). It is also true that ten years is a short period of time, and that Brazilian democracy is still fragile, still under construction. Finally, the Congress, the political parties, the universities and other civilian institutions have so far failed to acquire expertise in defence matters, thus leaving the military with more autonomy. But is a mistake not to consider the significant changes that have occurred. The attitudes of Brazilian military commanders over the last decade have not run counter to the path of democracy. It seems that for them it is a matter of re-establishing a socially valued and positive image, washing away the stigma left by the military regime. There is still a long way to go – and, as with all long paths, there is uncertainty – but the process that I have described may help lessen the burden of the negative heritage left by its recent political involvement to the military as an institution.

## Notes and References

1  This project was conducted by Maria Celina D'Araujo, Gláucio Soares and myself, resulting so far in five published books: Soares and D'Araujo (1994); Castro, D'Araujo and Soares (1994a, 1994b); Soares, D'Araujo and Castro (1995); Castro and D'Araujo (1997).
2  General Leônidas Pires Gonçalves, 1992 interview.
3  Speech at the Vila Militar, 6 October 1965, Rio de Janeiro (Costa e Silva Archive, Getulio Vargas Foundation/CPDOC).
4  See Castro and D'Araujo (1997).
5  Castro and D'Araujo (1997: 377).
6  Castro and D'Araujo (1997: 391).
7  Castro and D'Araujo (1997: 420).
8  Actually, Castelo Branco and Costa e Silva graduated from the army academy in the same year, and Costa e Silva pulled rank on the president.
9  See Zaverucha (1994; 1998).
10 Zaverucha (1994: 93).
11 Zaverucha (1998: 2–3).
12 Zaverucha (1998: 2).
13 Zaverucha (1998: 33).
14 Zaverucha (1998: 34).
15 Hunter (1997).
16 Hunter (1997: 23).
17 See Tollefson (1995).
18 See Martins Filho and Zirker (1998).
19 See Zaverucha (1998: 2). A distinct perspective is contained in the text of Oliveira and Soares (forthcoming in 2001), emphasizing the inability of Brazilian society to deal with the

topic, but not falling into either camp. In other words, these authors are pessimistic in relation to the civilians, and not the military. My own view on the matter is closer to the one voiced by these authors.

20 This research is funded by the Brazilian Funding Agency for Studies and Projects (Fianancia-dora de Estudos e Projetos, FINEP) and by the Brazilian Programme to Support Research Centres of Excellence (Programa de Apoio a Núcleos de Excelência – PRONEX), and has been executed at the CPDOC of the Fundação Getulio Vargas by Maria Celina D'Araujo and myself. We conducted open interviews with all the military ministers of the period, besides some armed forces chiefs-of-staff commanders and top presidential military aides.

21 I am convinced, of course, that there is a political democracy in Brazil, as the eight conditions proposed by Robert Dahl (1971) are fulfilled: (1) the freedom to form and join organizations; (2) freedom of expression; (3) right to vote; (4) eligibility for public office; (5) right of political leaders to compete for support/votes; (6) alternative sources of information; (7) free and fair elections and; (8) institutions for making government policies depend on votes and other expressions of preference.

22 For the concept of 'political direction', see Oliveira and Soares (forthcoming in 2001). Itamar Franco's government managed to stay between Sarney and Collor/Cardoso in the matter of political direction of the armed forces. Franco was afflicted, to some degree, by the same political weakness as Sarney, because he rose to the presidency as a consequence of the impeachment of Collor. Franco was more hesitant than Collor to increase civilian control over the military.

23 There were some isolated interventions, but they happened always at the request of one of the three branches of government, as predicted by the constitution, and never by military initiative.

24 This office is currently under the command of a general, but this can be seen as the choice of President Fernando Henrique Cardoso, not a military prerogative. General Alberto Cardoso also had to retire from active duty following the creation of the GSI. It is also important to note that the new intelligence agency created after the extinction of the Serviço Nacional de Informações (SNI) by Collor is a demilitarized one.

25 Notice that the previous ministry was called Air Transportation (*Aeronáutica*) – and not Air Force – precisely because of its control over civilian aviation.

26 Carvalho (1981: 428).

27 Tinoco was interviewed by Maria Celina D'Araujo and myself in July and August of 1998, at the CPDOC.

28 I thank my assistant Dulcimar Dantas de Albuquerque, who helped research the history of the 27 November celebrations and attended the 1996 ceremony.

29 In the ceremony of 27 November 1999, three senior officers representing the armed forces and the military units of Rio de Janeiro were present, but they abstained from speeches or statements. The attendance was minimal and the ceremony was highly formal. The proclamation issued by General Gleuber, mentioned above, was read. Since 1995, no military ministries have attended the event.

30 I thank my research assistants Aline Marinho, Carlos Sávio, Carolina von der Wied and Priscila Brandão Antunes for the information that helped me describe these events.

31 Noticiário do Exército 27 November 1999, issue no. 9,626.

# 5

# A Political Army in Chile

## Historical Assessment and Prospects for the New Democracy

FELIPE AGÜERO

The notion of political army as developed by the editors of this book may be usefully applied to the Chilean military, especially in the light of the recent 17-year period of military-authoritarian rule (1973–90). The foundational attempt to establish a new political regime, beginning with the 1973 *coup d'état*, led the Chilean military to their highest historical expression as a political army. In ways quite unintended, however, this political role has significantly diminished in the post-authoritarian period inaugurated in 1990. The extent to which there remains an overtly political role, and, especially, the prospects of this role for the future, require careful examination in the context of the military's situation in the post-authoritarian regime. This context demands the analytical inclusion of the set of differing views and policies held and pursued by political elites about the army's role. With the inauguration of democracy a decade ago, the formal and real responsibilities of actual military roles depend on the views and policies of civilian political elites and not on the military alone. Civilian views and perspectives must therefore be brought squarely into the analysis.

Understanding future prospects, however, necessitates an historical perspective, and one that goes well beyond the analysis of the recent military-authoritarian period. The size of the political hump interjected by the Pinochet regime in the history of the military's integration into the (previously often democratic) political process needs to be evaluated from such a perspective. How political will the Chilean military remain, even with a full return to 'normalcy?' In other words, how political would a 'normal' Chilean army be? What lessons can be drawn from history about the current period of relative depoliticization of the Chilean military? The historical perspective needed to answer these questions must address the manner and extent to which the military have been political in the past, and must shed light on previous critical junctures of military politicization and depoliticization for comparison with the present one.

This chapter deals with these questions by starting with a brief historical overview of the contradictory manner of insertion of the Chilean military in the political process at the start of the twentieth century. It then addresses the main issues observable in the democratic period which preceded the Pinochet regime, where one finds clues to the seemingly unexpected force with which the military rose to political prominence in the 1970s. The next section deals briefly with the nature of the military dictatorship that ruled between 1973 and 1990. Finally, the manner of transition from authoritarianism and its consequences for the ensuing democratic period is analysed with a view to ascertaining trends toward the future.

## The First One Hundred Years: state formation, professionalization and military intervention

Peculiar circumstances made possible the early emergence of a competitive political regime in the 1830s and 1840s, not long after the period of internal political chaos that followed the war of independence (1814–18). In part these circumstances were shaped by the attitude adopted by victorious generals of the early, post-independence wars of the 1830s, who stepped down and relinquished otherwise tempting political roles.[1] During this period, and all through the nineteenth century, the Chilean army actively participated in the formation of the state.[2] In fact, the early foundations of democracy in Chile were partly laid by a very active army, prominent in the country's conscience as the main fighter for independence. The army's active role was clearly expressed in the war against the Peru–Bolivian Confederation in 1836–9; in the centralist defeat of regional rebellions in the southern and northern parts of the territory in 1851 and 1859, respectively; in the armed conflict with Spain in 1865–6, and in the dramatic, long and consequential War of the Pacific against Peru and Bolivia in 1879–83. The consolidation and expansion of territory in these wars led to an important role for the army in the colonization of the frontier, both north and south, and in the war against indigenous resistance that continued from colonial times.[3]

Modern professionalization of the Chilean army, however, did not begin in earnest until after the performance of those crucial roles in Chilean state formation. Following the victorious conclusion of the War of the Pacific, and after hearing reports from top army leaders, the government decided to initiate a profound professionalization of the army. Aware of the flaws displayed by the military in the war, Chilean leaders intended military professionalization to deal with the defence needs of a vastly expanded territory containing large mineral riches, and to overcome the chaotic organization that had resulted from an overstretched army that for several years occupied a large part of Peru. Falling prey to the allure of the prestigious Prussian army, the government contracted in 1885 the services of Colonel Emil Körner, who came with more than twenty officers to initiate changes in organization, structure, procedures and training. The most important features and organs of the modern Chilean army, such as the War Academy, the Revista Militar and the general staff, were set in place in this period. The work of the German mission continued until 1914, at which time important reorganization had been accomplished along with significant importation of modern weaponry from Germany and Europe.[4] Chilean military academies played host to Latin American military officers, and Chilean officers travelled to Germany for training and to other Latin American countries to provide instruction.[5] An important consequence of military professionalization and modernization was that soon the army acquired a new corporate identity and a distinct view of its role as a modern army.

As a result of its professionalization process, the Chilean army began to experience an intense contradiction as it entered the early decades of the twentieth century. On the one hand, it was strongly influenced by the outlook of a foreign army which based its clout and prestige on the central role played in German national unification. The Chilean army acquired the self-image of an entity central to the nation's development. It was, at the same time, socialized in modern notions of 'total war': the war effort belonged to the nation as a whole, supported by all its constituting 'fronts', all coexisting in harmony, with the military playing a central role. Just as in the European countries from which it borrowed its outlook, the Chilean military understood that modern total war required the development of a strong national industry. Army officers were, in the first two decades of the twentieth century, strong proponents of industrialization, more so than any other elite group in Chilean society. The self-image of a strong army at the centre of the nation's development – an army prepared, with its advanced modern training and weaponry, to advance the nation's interests militarily – required, however, a sound economic and military foundation standing on a strong industrial sector. The possibility of actualizing such a self-image could be entertained on the basis of the impressive economic growth which territorial expansion had made possible by allowing the development of the nitrate industry.[6] On the other hand, however, despite the illusion fostered by the bonanza of nitrate exports, this image collided with the sour reality of an economically and socially backward country that had no industry, and in which social conflict emerged rampantly to claim a repressive role for its army.[7]

This contradiction came to a head as a result of the gradual collapse of the nitrate export economy following the end of the First World War. This decline of the export economy occurred at a time in which the social structure was undergoing deep changes. The country's rate of urbanization had expanded dramatically during this time and new social layers from the middle sectors – teachers, professionals, public employees – and an expanding working class added to the complexity of the social structure, which resulted in increased social demands.[8] Social mobilization combined with expanded union activism to create a dangerous scenario for the ruling oligarchy. The changing social context, and the resistance of the oligarchy to opening the political system to the new groups, inevitably engulfed the military in a coercive role at odds with its self-image as the backbone of a grand nation in need of a strong national defence.

A widening gap had developed between the military's self-image and a ruling class which utilized the state through the parliamentaristic form it had given it to share in the spoils of the booming export economy. The social strains created by this growth and, particularly, by the subsequent economic decline, put the military between the imagined country and the real one. The real country was one in which the ruling elites assigned it repressive roles against workers' mobilization and neglected the military's demand for a continuous increase in professionalization, modernization, and expansion. The military began to show signs of discontent with the repressive uses assigned it and the lack of government leadership to promote the desired industrialization.[9]

The military's discontent was channelled through a discourse of anti-politics and anti-parliamentarism.[10] They criticized the particularistic concerns of politicians which led, in their view, to short-sighted responses to crisis. The military, instead, saw themselves as concerned with big-issue politics, a concern thwarted by the short-sighted and repressive views of politicians. In this context, in the midst of the so-called 'social question', fragments of the military began to plot against parliament's opposition to social reforms. Finally, in 1924, the military intervened to oust President Alessandri after his failure to overcome parliamentary opposition to his platform of social reforms.[11] In a rather chaotic and unstable period, during which power resided more or less directly with the army's reformist echelon, many important reforms were passed. The military, led by middle-level officers, did away with a Congress controlled by conservative oligarchic forces and passed social legislation, incorporated labour organizations into the political system, expanded public services, created the national police, and significantly advanced the promotion of national industry. Through different degrees of participation in government, the military did not end its intervention until democratic politics fully resumed in 1932.

In sum, during the nineteenth century, Chile's military had a central role in the formation of the state that ranged from foreign wars through defeating regional rebellions and colonizing frontier territories. During that century, the military integrated itself within an oligarchic democratic regime that became gradually consolidated, and played a central role in the constitutional crisis and civil war of 1891. The nature of the military's political role was significantly affected, however, by the drive towards modernization and professionalization begun after the War of the Pacific. While the military modernized and grew stronger, social tensions emerged from the strains of development and the travails of a fluctuating export economy. These tensions led the elite to intensify the repressive uses of the military while ignoring its professional demands and remaining ignorant of its expanded corporate views. The military had in fact acquired features which set it in conflict with the oligarchy and its attempts to resolve social tension arising from a changing social structure. The military distanced itself from oligarchic political leadership and developed a growing critique of this leadership and its political practices through parliamentarianism. Providing early historical material to refute Huntington's thesis on the connection between military professionalism and political abstention,[12] the newly professionalized Chilean military intervened to help quell social conflict by passing weighty social and political reforms. The military, in fact, crowned one hundred years of development, and especially the modernization and professionalization drive initiated in the 1880s, by setting itself up as a fully fledged political army.

## From Insulation to Inter-Americanism, National Security and Military Coup

Despite the social reforms it promoted, and its leading role in reshaping the political system toward a more inclusive regime,[13] the military came out of that period badly wounded. Having alienated much of the political class, and weakened by factionalism, it could count on little support when the government, headed by Colonel Ibáñez, was hit by the world economic crisis of 1930. The military left in defeat, despised by an angry civilian reaction that empowered itself through civilian-led militias.[14] This reaction had two basic consequences. The first was that civilian administrations ignored the military and kept the armed forces weak and poorly funded. The second was that the military ducked and did not contest the civilian reaction. A newly appointed military leadership strongly supported and enforced military subordination. At the same time, military officers desperately tried to give the services legitimacy in the eyes of civilian elites by attuning the armed forces to the new ethos of industrialization and expansion of the public sector.[15] For fifteen years following the resumption of democracy in 1932, through three administrations (Alessandri, Aguirre Cerda and Montero), the military lived in isolation, neglected by the political elite.

The outbreak of the Second World War, but especially the new (Cold War) order that emerged after it, came to rouse the Chilean military from its state of enforced lethargy and isolation. The start of the Cold War, the 1947 Inter-American (Rio) Treaty and the Mutual Aid Pacts with the US gradually helped bring the military back closer to centre stage. By giving it a new sense of mission – the defence of the West from its enemies within and without – the military felt it now had a consistent justification to promote its institutional importance in the domestic arena. The military profession slowly began to gain in prestige again or, at least, to lose the feeling of social ostracism with which it had been identified after the civilian reaction of the 1930s.

The anti-communist ideological tenets that quickly began to permeate the inter-American scene struck a chord with the military's old and new doctrinal definitions. The old definitions combined the teachings of nineteenth-century geopolitics schools with various notions of total war. The new definitions, which could easily be integrated with the preceding ones, were received from US versions of international relations theory and its materialization in state policy and organization, captured in the notion of national security.[16] In many Latin American countries, Chile included, the concept of national security became the military's *leitmotiv* for claiming a stronger participation in national affairs. The old conceptual architecture of societies and nations as harmonious bio-organisms was coupled with the meaty anti-communist substance brought in by the inter-American alliance, all cemented in the national security doctrine.[17]

By the 1950s – during the civilian, democratically-elected administration of Colonel Ibáñez – the military's doctrinal views around the concept of national security had cohered to the point of conceiving and submitting national security and national mobilization bills to the Ministry of Defence, which submitted them to Congress. These bills contemplated the organization of the state sector – and its leadership of society – in ways which facilitated the logistics and control of information for war-preparation purposes. They envisioned national security capacities at all levels of the Chilean state, with the military playing a crucial role in their central coordination. The bills were severely criticized by the opposition and the media, and the executive withdrew them from Congress once it became convinced that they would not be legislated upon.[18] However, despite the fact that the initiatives had no immediate practical consequences, they did reflect the new professional-political mindset which had gained ascendancy in the military. The notions inspiring the bills elaborated on previous views of total war, and added the more contemporary views of national security and a national security system.

This episode – the formulation, presentation and withdrawal of the bills – was quite indicative of underlying processes in civil-military relations of the time. At bottom, it reflected the diverging paths taken by the civilian political elite and the military. The latter had reawakened from its lethargic period, empowered with new doctrines and a new international scenario that highlighted its hemispheric and domestic political importance. But the civilian elite continued to undervalue the military institution and pay little attention to it, despite the fact that the hemispheric dynamics unleashed by the Cold War had influenced significant elements in the political elite. Thus ideological trends inspired in the military by the Cold War found a parallel in the domestic political process: President Gabriel González Videla (1946–52), extricating himself from the centre-left coalition that had brought him (and two previous presidents) to power, expelled the communists from cabinet posts, outlawed their party and exiled its leaders. The next administration, headed by Colonel Ibáñez, maintained this partial realignment of Chilean politics.

The entire civilian elite, however, including the element that shared anti-communist stances with the military, abdicated leadership responsibilities in the military and defence fields. By embracing the inter-American alliance in 1947 and its accompanying military institutions, the political elite in effect transferred leadership responsibility in this area to US-dominated international agencies. The gap between the civilian political world and the military appeared clearly in the contrast between a pluralistic political system, which included a strong leftist pole well represented in Congress and occasionally in the executive, and a military that was now totally enmeshed in the ideological dynamics of the Cold War. While the democratic features of the Chilean political process maintained the military's formal subordination to political authority, an actual gap widened between civilian and military officials. For all practical purposes, the military stood behind a veil of irrelevance for most sectors in the political elite, who remained ignorant of doctrinal developments in the armed forces. Behind this veil the military nurtured a deep resentment of the political elite, aggravated by the harsh economic conditions under which the services and their personnel lived.

The first visible and dramatic manifestations of this gap surfaced in 1968, when the whole class of graduates of the military academy simultaneously submitted individual letters of resignation, arguing harsh economic and professional conditions. This situation led to the removal of the Minister of Defence and the army chief, and the unusual appointment of a retired general to the post in the ministry, with promises of alleviating the economic hardships cited in the letters of resignation. This first overt act of discontent was taken a stage further a year later, towards the end of the Frei administration, when one of the top army generals, Roberto Viaux, and a group of officers rebelled, staging not a coup attempt but a 'protest demonstration' from within the powerful Tacna garrison close to downtown Santiago. This was a forceful expression of resentment by a large group within an institution that felt ill-treated and abandoned by the political elite. The underlying message, strongly supported within the army, was the military's claim to have its status upgraded to the level of its own self-image as the institutional backbone of national security. The negotiations that led to a settlement, including the removal and retirement of General Viaux, were a long-overdue attempt to bridge the gap now so wide that it could only be tackled under duress.[19]

The civilian–military gap had been growing against a background of rising political tension and polarization. The political process initiated with the resumption of democracy in 1932 had organized around multi-party polarized competition, with strong parties on the right, centre and left of the political spectrum. While this process functioned smoothly around coalitions organized by the major centre party (the Radical Party), at least until the González Videla administration banned the Communist Party, it became much more rigid and competitive in the 1950s and 1960s. The administration of Colonel Ibáñez (1952–8) was succeeded by that of Jorge Alessandri, who, with the support of the right, had defeated the candidate of the left, Salvador Allende, by a mere few thousand votes. The reformist policies of the Christian Democratic administration that followed, led by President E. Frei Montalva (1964–70), further animated social mobilization and political polarization. An ideologically reformist and rigid centre, now monopolized by the Christian Democratic Party, added to the institutional difficulties of a presidential system in a multi-party context.[20] Alone in government, the Christian Democrats were aggressively flanked by Marxist parties to the left, while the new National Party on the right assumed a far more authoritarian stance than the traditional conservative parties it had come to replace. A politicized and polarized scenario, in the context of sluggish economic growth that reflected the loss of dynamism of the inward-oriented development model, served as the background for the expanding gap between the political elite and the military.

The election of the socialist–communist coalition led by Salvador Allende to the presidency in 1970 greatly heightened political tensions. As with the earlier contest between Alessandri and Allende in 1958, in 1970 the tallies also gave the winner (this time Allende over Alessandri) a very slight majority. Because the winner was a Marxist, the possibility that Congress might exercise its prerogative of selecting the runner-up as president became very real. All kinds of political manoeuvrings developed thereafter, and in the short two-months transition period between Frei and Allende, the army was brought even closer to the centre of the political stage.

This was the result of at least three important developments. First was the attempt by a small group of disenchanted elements ousted from the military, led by General Viaux, jointly with emerging extreme right-wing organizations, and supported by US intelligence agencies, to prevent the ascent of Salvador Allende to the presidency. The plan consisted of kidnapping the army's chief, General Schneider, in the hope that this would unleash the army's intervention and stop the constitutional process. The plot failed because Schneider was killed in the kidnapping attempt.

Second was the army's advancement of the so-called Schneider doctrine, named after this same General René Schneider, who had assumed the top army post following the shake-up after General Viaux's rebellion the previous year. Schneider had simply restated explicitly the role that the constitution mandated in the case of a presidential election with no candidate obtaining an absolute majority. The constitution affirmed that in such a case a plenary session of Congress would elect the winner from the two largest pluralities. The Schneider doctrine was presented as a democratic military doctrine because it reaffirmed the constitutional route, which signalled that the army would not interfere with Congress should it ratify Allende's majority. But the Schneider doctrine contained another part, which added an ominous afterthought to this constitutional reaffirmation. General Schneider had made it clear that the army owed obedience to the permanent institutions of the nation, while governments were only transitory. The Schneider doctrine contained, then, these two elements: a restatement of a part of the constitution, and a statement on the difference between nation, or state, and government, which made explicit a specific way of operationalizing 'national security' views that had been developing in the military.[21]

Third was the set of pressures on the army exerted by political groups from various quarters. The very fact that the army had to brandish the constitution to signal its position meant that political polarization had already advanced to the point where significant segments of the civilian elite sought to break the rules of the game. In the face of an undesired electoral outcome, these elites overtly reached out to the army. These attempts came from various quarters, not only from small extremist right-wing groups or the US government agencies. They came from the mainstream political right, which had been reorganized around nationalist-authoritarian tenets. They came also from influential circles within the Christian Democratic administration, close to the president himself, which helped in creating situations designed to urge action from the military. The military, in turn, resisted these situations with the shield of the constitution, and counter-argued that they demanded political and not military decisions.[22]

These trends signalled that the gap between civilian and military elites that had developed through the previous decades would be bridged via the convergence of the military following the path of its 'national security' doctrine, on the one hand, and the right, reorganized under a nationalist-authoritarian leadership, on the other. The political polarization which developed to extreme levels under Allende's presidency further advanced this process. Allende's policy of bringing military officers into his cabinet at several points to weaken right-wing offensives aimed at disrupting public order was based on mistaken assumptions. He thought that the civilian–military gap could be bridged in a national-popular direction that countered the authoritarian route pursued by right-wing elites and struck a chord with military chiefs. But the assumptions behind the president's policies ignored the aforementioned ideological developments within the military, and helped to increase the speed at which the military politicized and came closer to the positions of the coup-plotting right.

The military's decision to oust President Allende was not made until it had determined that several ingredients for a successful coup were in place, a fact that points to the high threshold of intervention by a professional military. These ingredients were, first, the unification of all the opposition under the actual leadership of its most right-wing segment, the National Party. Second, the statement declaring the illegitimacy of the Allende government issued by Congress's opposition majority. Third, the social turmoil, accompanied by economic disarray and near ungovernability, promoted by the opposition and US agencies under President Nixon's leadership, and worsened by the government coalition's fractious and ineffective policies. Last, the resignation of chief army commander General Prats and a few of his fellow generals, all Allende supporters, at the behest of the majority of the generals. Allende's appointment of General Pinochet to the top army post opened the way to an institutional military coup. Rather than letting the most active conspirators in the army lead the coup, the military waited until its legitimate top leadership was ready to make the move to intervene. Only at this point did the military, propelled by the navy's leadership, decide to unleash the coup with massive force. Imbued with the 'politics of anti-politics',[23] the military moved to become the most formidable political army ever to emerge in Chilean history.

# The Pinochet Regime: a military government with a foundational intent

The anti-liberal and anti-democratic inspiration of the forces that gave rise and sustenance to the Pinochet regime had one main aim: to completely reorganize Chilean society in such a way that what they saw as corrosive, divisive forces, namely political parties, never surfaced again. The military's goal was to eradicate political parties and their leaderships in order to create an organically integrated society. This goal would be accomplished by promoting economic growth under neo-liberal conditions, which, in their view, would end up rendering parties unnecessary. At the centre of a future of harmonious institutions, the military would carve out for itself a permanent monitoring position as a guarantee of the politics of anti-politics. Herein lies the foundational intent of the military government.[24]

The regime relied primarily upon the support of the armed forces, which participated actively in governmental activity. The full inclusion of the military in government inaugurated a completely new form of politicization that broke with a long-standing tradition of subordination and exclusion. The 1973 coup catapulted the military-as-institution into a position of absolute power, controlling the core and the helm of the new regime. The Chilean regime thus became part of the new wave of military-authoritarianism that had pervaded the region since the 1964 coup in Brazil. To varying extents and in different forms, the authoritarian regimes that sprang up in the 1960s and 1970s in South America were all military in nature. In all of them, the military played the key role in the selection of the head of government and other major government officers, and in the definition of major policy orientations.[25] The Chilean regime under Pinochet was no different. It fully was a military regime; ultimate decision-making powers lay with the military.

Despite views of the Chilean military regime as the personalistic regime of General Augusto Pinochet, often compared with the likes of Stroessner in Paraguay or Franco in Spain, this was a military regime *tout court*. It is true that General Pinochet acquired extraordinary powers as head of the army, head of state, and president of the republic. The head of the feared central intelligence agency utilized for repression and state terrorism – first called DINA (Dirección de Intelligencia Nacional or National Intelligence Directorate), then CNI (Central Nacional de Informaciones or National Information Centre) – responded directly to Pinochet. The constitution passed in 1980 assigned him high and exclusive temporary powers, and charged him with the control of executive power for the duration of the transitional constitutional period. This feature of individual power centralization distinguished the Chilean regime from those of neighbouring countries, where government control was subject to the whim of councils of generals.[26] Nonetheless, Pinochet's was first and foremost a military and not a personalistic regime. Constitutional and legislative power always remained with the military junta, until the very last day. The junta was formed by the chiefs of the navy, air force, police, and the second in command in the army. These individuals could draft legislation and approve and change the constitution. According to the constitution which they approved in 1980, they had the power to nominate the single candidate for the presidency that would be submitted to referendum in 1988. Very importantly, the junta functioned under the rule of unanimity, requiring the consent of all top military chiefs. All legislatively enacted policy orientations were the result of the consensus of the armed forces' leadership. This collective military body fully made the Pinochet regime an institutional government of the armed forces.[27]

The military participated widely at all levels of government.[28] Although only a few general officers were members of the cabinet, military officers exclusively ran the critical presidential staff and the presidential advisory committee, which later merged with the presidency's general secretariat. These offices coordinated policy, filtered the relations between the ministries and the president, and conducted legislative liaison with the junta. Other important government agencies, such as the National Commission on Administrative Reform, were run by the military. In addition, a large number of military officers joined civilians to staff the various legislative advisory committees of the junta. All chiefs of Chile's administrative regions were military officers, who were also the officers in command of military units in those regions. The military was thus actively involved in the conduct of government policy.[29]

However, in practice the regime carefully followed a division of labour between the military-as-government and the military-as-institution.[30] While a large number of officers were assigned to government tasks, the bulk of the military remained concerned with its traditional national defence duties. These separate parts of the military found cohesion in a single leadership at the top: the commander-in-chief led the army while the president led the government.[31] Pinochet, who kept both positions, unfolded himself into this dual role, aided in the army by a deputy commander who also served in the junta. Both the military in government, who followed and applied government policy, and the military in the barracks abstained from deliberation. Only the top chiefs of the armed services, who constituted the military junta, overtly deliberated on policy and the delineation of the regime's future. This organization of military participation was expressly conceived to prevent military factionalism of the kind which had been so pervasive in neighbouring countries. In his presidential address of 11 September 1979 Pinochet, for instance, pointed to the 'absence of politicization which has allowed us to maintain the forces of national defence in an optimal state of professionalism and preparedness'.[32] This division of labour for the most part succeeded in maintaining discipline, hierarchy, and non-deliberation through the ranks, and in keeping a well-trained military in shape. The military knew it would confront threats from neighbouring countries, and it was prepared to handle them efficiently when they indeed emerged.[33]

However, despite such a pervasive and protracted military presence in government, the regime did not always succeed in forestalling severe internal political dissent. For instance, General Leigh, the head of the air force, persistently opposed the market-oriented policy orientations which the government imposed on the economy and social sectors. Dissent became so disturbing that, with the support of the other junta members, Pinochet decided in 1978 to oust him and all but one of the air force generals. On the other hand, full political involvement of the military was occasionally activated, although always in a centrally controlled manner, as occurred with the pro-Pinochet campaign during the 1988 referendum.[34]

But however militarized the regime, the armed forces did not rule alone. The military assumed government in 1973 with foundational interests of its own and, as such, remained the primary force sustaining the regime. However, the regime was also the expression of all social and political forces that had for some time been cherishing an authoritarian restructuring of the Chilean polity. Just as the military brought to the coup coalition strong views about the wrongs that had to be righted, so did leading sectors of business and the political class on the right, organized in the National Party.[35] From their own distinctive paths these forces converged to give birth to an authoritarian re-foundation of Chilean politics and society. The military government relied on the support and participation of a vast number of civilian leaders, who came primarily from the former National Party and techno-cratic groups. However, no organized civilian political party support was allowed to emerge, and civilian participation was structured around individuals. Parties, whatever their origin, were perceived as fractious, and would have carried the threat of undermining Pinochet's and the military's well-established autonomy. Many existing, although substantially reorganized, civilian organizations – pro-fessional associations (lawyers, doctors), some unions, business organizations – provided the regime with organized support, at least during its early phases, and so did other state institutions, namely the obsequious Supreme Court of Justice.

In terms of policy and regime orientations, two elements stood out as the most important civilian participants in the coalition. One was the very cohesive and like-minded group of economists – the Chicago boys – who imbued the regime with a radical plan of economic reorganization. Their plan aimed at modernization and internationalization by full integration into the world economy. It broke radically with the decades-old strategy of inward-oriented industrialization, and instead liberalized and privatized the economy, stripping it of state controls. This group provided the regime with persistent policy implementation and a universal-istic policy rationale that buffered the regime from particularistic pressure groups. It also provided it with a broad market orientation that pervaded all sectors of the economy, state and society.[36] During Pinochet's tenure, the group suffered occasional setbacks in tandem with periods of recession or economic decline. On the whole, however, it succeeded both in irreversibly revamping the economy in a neo-liberal direction and in granting the military regime significant domestic and international legitimacy.

The other group was much less cohesive; in fact, it was more a collection of individuals than a group. They were individuals trained in law, university professors and lawyers with or without experience in the public sector. They helped furbish the regime with rules and procedures that would substitute for the old constitution and previous legislation. Its ultimate grand contribution was the 1980 constitution, originated in a small drafting committee appointed by Pinochet in the early years of his rule. Debated by small circles close to power, then by the Council of State appointed by Pinochet and by the military junta, which finally approved it, it was successfully (albeit not in a fraud-free process) approved by referendum in 1980.

Besides those very important contributions to the regime, these groups also provided the government with an ample pool of functionaries with which to staff state agencies. Amalgamated within these groups there existed another identifiable group, formed by young professionals ideologically trained in conservative Catholic doctrines combined with modern technocratic views. This group – the former *gremialistas* – occupied positions in the executive and a number of state agencies, and were scattered throughout the regional and local administrative centres and municipalities to promote the regime's social policies.

The coalition cemented during the authoritarian regime brought together all those institutions and groups that contributed to its success: the military, business, and civilian leaders from the former National Party and the technocratic groups that led the economy and the regime's institutionalization process. From these civilian groups would spring the parties that would inherit the authoritarian legacy: the National Renovation Party and the Independent Democratic Union. On the opposite side lay the groups and organizations that fought the regime and promoted a return to democracy: the former parties at the centre and the left of the political spectrum, the Catholic Church, most of the remaining labour unions, and some of the professional associations which had shifted sides in the course of the struggle for democratization.[37] The dynamics of civil–military relations for the ensuing post-authoritarian period sprang from the opposition and interaction of these different groups, and developed in the context of the democratization process, against the new institutional background advanced by the transition.

Despite the electoral defeat that pushed it out of government, the military exited the authoritarian regime in good standing, and with significant social and political support. In contrast to many other cases in the region and elsewhere, the military did not alienate its original social and political allies. It left government surrounded by the recognition of having successfully overhauled the economy and forged a new era in the nation's development. To the social and economic bases of success, the constitution added institutional protection and monitoring roles. Compared to the previous transition of 1932, this was a vastly more successful exit.

It was an exit nonetheless, and an undesired one at that. The immediate cause for exit was the defeat of Pinochet in the 1988 referendum. The constitution approved in the 1980 referendum envisioned a transitional period of eight years, after which the constitution would enter into full effect. It would inaugurate a reinforced presidential system, with vast monitoring powers for the military, and a much diminished Congress. It was, in fact, tailor-made for the continuity of Pinochet's rule. However, a transitional clause contemplated a referendum to be held in 1988 to decide on the person who would assume the presidency for a renewable eight-year period. When Pinochet reluctantly agreed to accept this clause in 1980, he anticipated no problems for a referendum that would be held way into the future. He felt confident that the economy would continue to perform, and that he would have no difficulty adding one more to the series of plebiscites that had already been successfully held to reject the United Nations' condemnation of Chile's human rights situation. Defeat in 1988 came as a big surprise for him. The 'No' vote against the military junta's proposal of Pinochet for president obtained 57 per cent of the total. Pinochet attempted to invalidate the referendum the very night the results came out, but the junta members decided otherwise and the outcome held.[38] This led, as contemplated in the transitional clauses of the constitution, to competitive elections in 1999, which allowed the centre–left coalition candidate, Patricio Aylwin, to assume power in 1990.

Military exit, determined by defeat at the ballot box, was evidently and inescapably the result of failure. The clearest expression of failure was the full resumption of party activity that negated the anti-party goal of the coup's foundational intent. Opposition parties resumed in full force to organize the 'No' campaign for the referendum, and right-wing parties organized to prepare for elections. Although affected by the new electoral system defined by the departing regime, the new parties significantly resembled those existing prior to the coup, and many of their leaders, those that had survived the brutal years of repression, came from the previous democracy. Opposition party activity re-emerged, after a decade of intense repression, as a consequence of the opportunities created by the 1982–3 economic crisis, during which GNP declined precipitously by 12 per cent. Massive protests and mobilization against the regime overcame the repression-imposed fear and apathy in the population, and gave sustenance to the rebirth of overt party-led opposition. The crucial component of the politics of anti-politics had failed. The military would have to contend, once again, with the politics of parties and politicians.[39]

Failure was also evident in the dark side of economic restructuring: enormous social costs and inequality, and a significant expansion in the proportion of the population living below the poverty line.[40] Perhaps the most enduring expression of failure was the legacy of massive human rights violations and state terrorism.[41] The military's exit thus combined elements of success and failure that simultaneously strengthened and confined its power. These features determined the contradictory nature of the Chilean transition to democracy and influenced the dynamics of civil–military relations in the successor regime.

## Military Exit, Confined Transition and Civil Military Dynamics

The comparatively high level of institutionalization attained through the constitution allowed the regime to set the terms of the transition (even if its outcome was not fully the one it had envisioned). The opposition had in fact wanted an earlier transition than allowed by the constitution, and an entirely different set of institutional rules to those the constitution bestowed.[42] While it succeeded in contesting the referendum that determined the exit of Pinochet from government, the opposition could not do away with the institutional edifice created by the military. A successor government would have to coexist with Pinochet at the helm of the army for eight more years, with a National Security Council (NSC) that included military members holding the same voting powers as the president, and with several other institutional legacies.

The institutional edifice arranged for the successor regime left things 'tied up and tied up tightly' in much stronger terms than Franco's dictum for his own legacy had in Spain. Whereas in Spain it took only a law to set in motion the institutional and electoral machinery for the demolition of Franco's institutional legacy, in Chile the Pinochet regime had tied its knots more effectively.[43] Non-elected senators, an electoral system that initially granted a disproportionate power to Pinochet allies in Congress, and very high requirements for constitutional reforms made it impossible to reform the constitution without the consent of the parties of the right.[44] These parties, in the decade following democratization, refused to allow their votes for a reform of the constitution. However, in spite of its authoritarian origins and many features strongly disliked by the anti-Pinochet forces, the constitution turned out to be no major obstacle to the effective functioning of democracy in most areas after 1990. The one exception was the powers of elected officials over the military and the prerogatives reserved for the latter, where significant restrictions on democracy prevailed. If democratization remains incomplete in Chile it is primarily due to the permanence of these features in the constitution.

Among those features, two are of utmost importance: one is the existence of the NSC, composed, on the civilian side, by the president, the president of the Supreme Court, the president of the Senate, and the Comptroller General, and, on the military side, by the commanders-in-chief of each one of the four armed services.[45] The council has the power to 'state its views to the President of the Republic, Congress or the Constitutional Court with regard to events, acts or matters which severely undermine the institutional bases or compromise national security'.[46] The council may be convoked by the president or by two of its members, requires a quorum of five of its members, and takes its resolutions by absolute majority. It appoints four members of the Senate from among former commanders-in-chief of each of the armed services, and two of the seven members of the Constitutional Court. The other important feature is the restriction of the president's power to appoint the commanders-in-chief: he must choose from among the five most senior generals or admirals only, and appointments are for a fixed four-year term. The president may dismiss them only in extraordinary circumstances, and then only with the consent of the NSC.[47] In addition, the organic law of the armed forces restricts presidential powers of appointment and dismissal of general officers in the armed forces, and subjects these powers to the initiative of the relevant commander-in-chief. This law also grants a fixed floor to the military budget, and supplements it with a fixed percentage of profits from copper exports.[48]

Within this legal framework, the top military chiefs may challenge the civilian leadership, as they have done on several occasions, without fear of punitive action from elected officials. Furthermore, they may convoke the NSC and censure these elected officials, and they may overpower the president in the selection of senators and court members. The NSC has been convoked several times and numerous episodes of contestation provoked by the military have developed with impunity.[49] It is these powers that have largely determined the dynamics of civil–military relations since 1990. The military has mostly used those powers defensively, to protect itself from attempts to assert civilian power and from judicial investigations of crimes of various sorts, primarily human rights cases. This means that the military no longer carries a societal or political project of its own. Its goals have mostly returned to professional concerns, and to organizational protection from what it perceives as outside interference.

The resumption of democracy makes those constitutionally established powers subject to reform, leaving it up to civilian political forces in Congress. If these forces were to decide on constitutional reform and substantial reduction in prerogatives, the military would have no choice but to accept. Thus, a substantial part of military politics must be understood in the context of cleavages existing within the political elite. There clearly has existed a substantial regime cleavage among the political elite and in the electorate – an authoritarian/democracy cleavage – that expresses itself in differing views on constitutional reform, which up to now have prevented all change. This cleavage relates specifically to different views about what the role of the military ought to be.[50] Reforming the military clauses of the constitution amounts to completing the democratization of the political system; opposing those reforms amounts to fully supporting the Pinochet-imposed constitution and a tutelary role for the armed forces.

Clearly civil–military relations in the post-authoritarian period have been caught within the dynamics of the interaction of the government, the military, and the opposition. Other very important players have been civil society groups such as the organizations defending human rights and advocating justice for crimes committed during the dictatorship, the Catholic Church, and youth organizations advocating reform of the draft system. Significant players have been the courts, both domestic and international, particularly since the detention of Pinochet in London in 1998.

## Confrontation, Appeasement and Catharsis in the New Democracy

In the decade since democratization, civil–military relations have gone through roughly three stages. The first stage (1990–4) overlaps with the first successor administration of Patricio Aylwin and may be characterized as one of confrontation. The second stage, of appeasement or accommodation, starts with the Frei administration in 1994.[51] The third stage – catharsis – starts in October 1998 with Pinochet's arrest in London and is reinforced with the assumption of the presidency by socialist Ricardo Lagos (2000–). Whether or not this stage may lead to a fourth stage of settlement is very much an open question.

Government has been, during the whole decade, in the hands of a centre–left coalition – the Coalition of Parties for Democracy – made up of political forces that had converged earlier to oppose the military regime. Paramount in all three stages has been the question of accountability for past human rights crimes. This and factors that arose in the judiciary and from electoral dynamics account for the main features of civil–military relations during the 1990s.

The first administration's stated goal was to make possible the affirmation of democracy; it was thus termed a transition administration. This feature was reinforced by a reform passed by the coalition, which established a four-year tenure for the first administration, half the regular duration of the presidential term established in the constitution.[52] A primary goal of Aylwin's government was the reform of the most restrictive features of the constitution. In addition, this government faced the former dictator as commander-in-chief of the army, a position that Pinochet fully resumed for eight years according to the legal framework he had imposed. Pinochet had clearly stated that he would stay on 'so that my men are not touched'. These elements clearly set the tone for the confrontational mode of civil–military relations during the early years of post-authoritarianism.

During the first period, the new institutions combining elected officials with authoritarian enclaves had to be tested. The grey areas left in laws and regulations created for another scenario had to be clarified in practice. An important occasion arose with Pinochet's first proposal of the list of generals for promotion that had to be signed by President Aylwin. The president refused to authorize the promotion of a general who carried an especially negative background on human rights. Pinochet took the dispute to the Constitutional Court, arguing that the president had no choice but to promulgate the respective decree. The court ruled in favour of the president. This then clearly established limits to the enormous power of the commander-in-chiefs of the armed services, and restored a minimum bargaining resource for the president.

Against the army's views, the president also succeeded in creating a Commission on Truth and Reconciliation that would investigate the most egregious crimes committed under Pinochet's rule.[53] The commission, made up of public figures and lawyers from all quarters of the political spectrum, produced a lengthy and detailed report after months of investigations during which statements by thousands of individuals were taken privately. With no collaboration from the military, the commission was nonetheless able to report thousands of killings and disappearances. It did not delve, however, into other violations such as illegal detentions, torture and exile. The report, with no necessary judicial consequence, was an attempt to acknowledge the atrocities publicly. The president, in a public address to the nation in March 1991, used the report to apologize on behalf of the state for crimes committed during the Pinochet regime.[54]

Several other areas of confrontation opened on the investigation of past abuses. The new democracy inherited an amnesty law passed by the junta in 1978, which cleared the military of responsibility for crimes up to that date. The law expressly left out, however, anything related to the assassination of former Allende minister Orlando Letelier in Washington DC by DINA agents. Investigations of this case and of other pre-1978 as well as post-1978 crimes began to hit the military. Investigation of the former proceeded under the interpretation upheld by the government and many judges who argued that a crime had to be established before amnesty could be applied. Investigations initiated in Congress on corruption cases affecting the military, and particularly one affecting Pinochet's son, further muddied the waters for the military. Lashed by congress and the judiciary, the military also felt overt hostility from the administration. However powerful, the military needed the government to clear their budget requests, the administrative flow of their programmes, and the continuation or activation of international connections for training or weapons maintenance and acquisition. The top military leadership felt the government was not very cooperative, as the latter dragged its feet for bargaining purposes. In addition, in the face of all the problems confronting the army, Aylwin's tough Minister of Defence was correctly perceived as applying pressure for Pinochet's resignation.[55] The army reacted to this perceived hostile environment by staging acts of protest in defiance of civilian authority, forcing concessions from the government. These acts, supported by the other armed services, consisted of unannounced military exercises, with full billeting of the forces, publicly displaying defiance.[56] The government negotiated, bypassing the Minister of Defence, reassuring the military on budgetary and other concerns, and definitely shelving investigations into the dubious financial connections of Pinochet's son with the army.[57]

During this period the opposition did not consent to any of the major constitutional reforms proposed by the executive. The government could not rid itself of Pinochet and little progress could be shown on the assertion of civilian–political supremacy. Nevertheless, the government did assert its powers, however feeble, on military promotions and kept alive the possibility of furthering human rights investigations. Importantly, it made much progress in solving most of the remaining border disputes with Argentina, taking away from the military an important source of empowerment. The ruling coalition came out of the first administration solidified by the excellent management of the market economy inherited from the previous regime, taking it to higher levels of growth, while attempting to confront the extreme legacy of inequality.

Benefiting from this solidity, Eduardo Frei came to government in 1994 empowered by a strong electoral mandate of 58 per cent (with another 10 per cent for candidates of the left), against a combined 30 per cent obtained by the two right-wing candidates. However, his administration tried to distinguish itself from the previous transition administration by adopting a post-transition platform focused on new modernization tasks. Even if the tasks of transition had not been accomplished, the administration operated as if the transition was over, granting itself freedom to focus on the future. Accordingly, in regard to the military, the government sought appeasement by not confronting Pinochet, while de-emphasizing the human rights issues and all other controversial investigations. Constitutional reforms were only symbolically pursued, since there were not enough votes in Congress to overcome the high approval threshold required. As a result, during its first five years the administration did not face the pseudo-revolts by the armed forces that had troubled its predecessor.

Nonetheless, a difficult episode was presented by the initial refusal of General Contreras, former DINA chief, to comply with the seven-year sentence issued in 1995 by the Supreme Court for his intellectual authorship of the assassination of Orlando Letelier in Washington DC. For a week, with the support of army and navy units, Contreras remained in hiding before turning himself in, but then only to a special, comfortable prison built for him, under the surveillance of army guards. This episode was followed by a public demonstration of support outside the prison facility by army officers dressed in civilian clothes.[58] Despite these episodes, Frei's Minister of Defence, Edmundo Pérez Yoma, developed excellent relations with Pinochet, so much so that Pinochet rated him the best minister in the cabinet and awarded him an official army decoration in a special ceremony. The cost of the policy of appeasement, however, was the maintenance of the status quo on practically all civil–military fronts. Contentment with the policy of appeasement began to fade, however, when Pinochet decided to take up the Senate seat, which the constitution assured him at the end of his career in the army in March 1998. Pinochet appeared well placed to assume the leadership of the right in the new Congress elected in 1997. The elections yielded an invigorated right, with a significant number of former hard-line officials from the days of the Pinochet regime, and higher levels of abstention that expressed disappointment with the government.[59] Not long after the swearing-in ceremony, in which Pinochet was greeted by pictures of the disappeared carried by centre–left senators, a group of deputies presented a constitutional accusation against the former dictator. However, the period of appeasement was not over, and the majority of the centre–left coalition did not allow the accusation to succeed.

In many ways, Pinochet began to thrive in the Senate, and was able to agree with its president on a motion to abandon the 11 September holiday commemorating the coup of 1973. But Pinochet's blooming image, developed among many in the country and abroad, of a respectable, elderly, former statesman crumbled precipitously with his arrest in London in October 1998. His arrest signalled the start of the phase of catharsis in civil–military relations. The atrocities committed under Pinochet's rule were reiterated via international denunciation in the House of Lords and respectable foreign tribunals. This helped to reopen the channels for expression inside the country of a long-suppressed frustration with the impunity conferred on those responsible for these crimes. Language that had been suppressed by the 'political psychology' of transition – requiring cooperation between supporters of the powerful former dictator and the opposing elected officials – now fully resurfaced to remember crimes, torture, assassination, and so on.[60] The event in London had several repercussions in Chile. It manifestly revived the authoritarian–democracy cleavage pervading the political elite and the electorate, which so clearly arises around the figure of Pinochet. It also led to diverse views on the legal position to adopt on the detention.[61] The government rejected the right of foreign courts to handle a domestic issue involving a former head of state and senator. The military and the right, who nonetheless wanted stronger and quicker action, supported it on this. The left in the centre–left coalition only gave lukewarm support to its government on this, and emphasized the need to prosecute him effectively in Chile should he return. Meanwhile, lawsuits against Pinochet piled up on top of the ones a judge was already investigating.[62]

The arrest intensified a divisive scenario, but at the same time it generated an unprecedented recognition by many across the political spectrum of the atrocities committed under military rule. For the first time representatives of the right uttered unthinkable words such as 'disappeared' in a respectful manner, and gave thought to ways of addressing the pending human rights issues. In addition, the courts' view that all crimes should be investigated before applying the amnesty gained momentum. Most importantly, the Supreme Court validated the view that crimes connected with disappearances could not fall under the amnesty law; that they should be viewed as ongoing crimes at least until the remains appeared. Even then, amnesty was not immediately applicable because it could not be determined that they resulted from pre-1978 actions.

Debate over Pinochet's situation in London began to fall behind the greater immediacy of cases before the Chilean courts. At the same time, the electoral dynamics for the presidential election scheduled for December 1999 began to take centre stage, with great influence over the course of civil–military relations. The main impact came from the candidate of the right, Joaquín Lavín, a successful mayor of a Santiago municipality, who had acquired enormous personal popularity and could thus gain autonomy from the more hard-line leadership of his own party, the Independent Democratic Union. Lavín, contrary to the previous presidential candidacies of the right, saw the possibility of capitalizing on his popularity to stage a confident electoral assault on the presidency. His electoral strategy aimed at the centre voter and planned to reach out to supporters of the Christian Democratic party in the centre–left coalition, exploiting the trepidation of some of these voters when it came to supporting the coalition's socialist nominee. This strategy demanded that Lavín distance himself from the right's more hard-line pro-Pinochet positions, a feat that Lavín ultimately accomplished thanks to the actual physical remoteness of Pinochet. Lavín, for instance, met with the organization of relatives of the disappeared and refrained during his campaign from any mention of connections with the Pinochet regime. His buoyant, successful campaign left him only a few decimal points short of a plurality, and he was defeated by only a few percentage points in the second round in January 2000.

The cumulative effect of Pinochet's detention in London was a radically changed situation for the army. Two of the solid bases of support that had accompanied the military during the transition were no longer there: the judiciary and the right. The judiciary, which had obsequiously consented to endless violations during the dictatorship, gradually began in the 1990s to take a more assertive role in the prosecution of those crimes. The courts grew more sensitive to democratically expressed public mood on the subject. At the same time the new presidents began to alter the composition of the courts, promoting more democratically-minded judges. On the other hand, influential sectors on the right, swayed by electoral considerations, moved away from the overt, staunch and homogeneous defence of Pinochet which had been its distinguishing mark. Moreover, the centre–left now felt confident enough to push more assertively for the solution to human rights cases, and so did individuals who began to use the courts for the same purpose. Facing more investigations affecting active-duty officers, and without its previous supports, the army felt isolated. New commander-in-chief General Ricardo Izurieta sought to lead the army out of situations of isolation and to rid it as quickly as possible of the pernicious human rights legacy of the military regime so as to focus on modernization plans. Izurieta, appointed by President Frei in March 1998, belonged to a generation entirely different from the coup clique. He had no history of involvement in any of the atrocities, and came from a family of distinguished army officers. But his attempt to concentrate on a programme of modernization for the army was derailed by the Pinochet affair. He was thus eager to snatch the army out of its cornered position by pursuing a more cooperative attitude regarding human rights cases.

An important sign of this new attitude was General Izurieta's willingness to provide the courts with the names of all army officers working in the former CNI. But perhaps the most important shift in the military's position came from their acceptance of minister Pérez Yoma's proposal to join human rights lawyers and other public figures at a *mesa de diálogo* (literally, a dialogue table) with the goal of producing information on the fate of the disappeared. This acceptance entailed the unprecedented recognition of the validity of the claims of the human rights lobby, which had heretofore been permanently derided by the top military chiefs. The *mesa* was able to survive despite the domestic fallout from the Pinochet case, and it succeeded in laboriously producing a joint statement on the circumstances leading to the human rights violations. Ultimately, the military committed itself to seeking information about the fate of the disappeared, guaranteeing secrecy to informants. The results of this effort were expected for January 2001, although much of the earlier optimism had faded as a result of the deterrent effects on potential informants of progress by the courts in prosecuting human rights cases. Another signal of army cooperation came with the army's instructions to General Ramírez Hald to resign his commission upon his indictment for responsibility in the assassination of a major union leader in 1982.

Cooperation has been tested on many occasions related to the evolution of the Pinochet case. So far, the military has accepted President Lagos's firm stance on letting the judiciary work without interference. It accepted, reluctantly, the Supreme Court's decision to relieve Pinochet of immunity from prosecution. However, the indictment and order for the arrest of Pinochet on charges of kidnapping and homicide, issued by an investigating judge on 1 December 2000, was the cause of great dissatisfaction. The four commanders-in-chief urged the president to call a meeting of the NSC, with the clear implication that they would call it if the president didn't. The president did call the meeting, albeit voicing disagreement with the existence of the NSC and insisting that discussion of decisions of the judiciary should not be part of the NSC's agenda. As of this writing, the meeting had not taken place as the president delayed it until the Supreme Court decided on an appeal of Pinochet's order of arrest.

The cathartic impact of Pinochet's arrest in London affected all major players in the Chilean political process. The army, in particular, was impelled to shift its position significantly to start seeking accommodation and cooperation. Despite the ups and downs in the relations between the military and the executive resulting from Pinochet's arrest and other legal cases, the military have seemed eager to cancel the human rights debt and to concentrate on professional modernization plans.[63] It is a possibility that the cooperation attained in the context of the catharsis phase may lead to a final settlement.[64] This, however, would entail a widely agreed solution for most of the pending and most pressing human rights cases and the co-operation of the right in the reform of those aspects of the constitution dealing with military and presidential powers. These conditions are not easy to obtain and neither are they short-term. But their possibility should not be ruled out.

## Settlement, Engagement and Prospects for Civilian Democratic Control

The military interventions of 1924 and 1973 were preceded by long historical periods during which military and civilian elites went in different directions. Modernization and professionalization in the late nineteenth and early twentieth centuries sent the military in unsupervised directions that led it to criticize political elites, parties and parliamentarianism. The military's criticism was simultaneously an expression of the crisis of oligarchic rule and one of the causes of its demise. The 1924 coup and the military-influenced period that followed were a perverse way of closing the civilian–military gap. The end of that period of military rule left the military isolated and chastised by the resurgent conservative forces of demo-cratic restoration, and ignored by the political leadership of the emergent popular sectors. The military and the elite of the post-oligarchic state developed in quite different directions, the former ignored by the latter. This disconnection was reinforced by the elite's abandonment of the Chilean military to the unmonitored influence of the inter-American system inspired by the Cold War. This again resulted in military criticism of politics, democracy and, this time specifically, of contest-governed parties. The threshold for intervention had risen, having to await the convergence of deep political and military crisis. Once it occurred, it unleashed a violent and long-lasting repressive reaction. The military interventions of 1924 and 1973 were crude ways of closing the breach between the state and its military.

It is pertinent to ask, in the light of that experience, if the military's exit in 1990 bears any resemblance to that of the 1930s or to the previous historical juncture that initiated civil–military separation. Will the recent military exit lead to another cycle of separation that may need a future resolution? The decade-long experience of the post-authoritarian period yields decidedly no significant similarities. Paradoxically, the harshness of the period of military rule left too many conse-quences for the post-military period. These have basically maintained the military and the new ruling elites, actively engaged in dealing with the post-authoritarian legacy, preventing any early disconnection.

The depth and breadth of the legacy of human rights violations have forced military and civilian elites to confront each other continuously through the stages described above. The debate on the memory and the future of human rights realities and policies is likely to continue for a long time. Legacies are not always negative, and it is unlikely that the painful experience under military rule and the transition will be lost on future generations.[65] At the same time, civilian and military elites have remained focused on the pending constitutional issues that affect their relationship. If the debate on constitutional reforms is brought, sooner or later, to fruition, a broader and more in-depth debate about the proper ways of integrating the military into the democratic state, and of asserting civilian political supremacy, is likely to ensue. It will, of course, be necessary that, if and when these reforms are passed, they be followed by a period of consolidation rather than civilian lethargy and contentment. Engaging the military actively in the democratic state, from the angle of its own professional mission and under continuous and effective civilian leadership through well-established institutions and mechanisms, is of the essence.

The possibilities just outlined stand on rather optimistic premises. There are, however, reasons to support them. Most players in the Chilean polity have an interest in solving the human rights issues. The government and its supporting coalition is interested because of its views on society and democracy, and because of its constituency. The judiciary is interested because it allows it to make up for its previous obsequious behaviour under the dictatorship. And the military is interested as well, because solving the human rights question presents it with the opportunity to restore links to all of society and concentrate on professional modernization. The right may remain determined to block constitutional reforms, particularly on the military clauses. However, its recent electoral successes were based on moderation in these areas and it is hard to believe that the right would benefit from a tutelary military should it gain electoral access to government again. And, in contrast with previous historical junctures, there are no threats from any political quarter to the dominant social and economic order that would, in the right's view, necessitate a tutelary military.

Moreover, the dynamically changing political and economic regional and international scenarios demand a greater cohesiveness in state policies and outlooks. Economic expansion and regional integration, under the prevailing market economy, demand greater cooperation of all sectors, including the state, societal organizations and business.[66] If the military, under civilian political supervision, are made a part of this integrated outlook, separation between civilians and the military would not develop. By integration and cooperation I do not mean that the military should get involved in developmental tasks. I mean, rather, that the political and economic scenarios in a globalized world demand coherent state responses that take the military into consideration, unlike the kind of state policies of the previous periods analysed in this chapter, in which the military were allowed to drift autonomously.

The modes of civil–military relations that prevailed during the military modernization of the late nineteenth and early twentieth centuries, and during the democratic period stretching between 1932 and 1973, may be said to conform to Huntington's model of objective civilian control. Just as in the model, too much military autonomy was allowed to develop, which in this case turned into a civil–military chasm. And civil–military relations had, as in the model, too much objectivity but very little in the way of actual control.[67] The new circumstances of the recent transition are different from the previous ones. They start out from a deep gap between the democratizing elite and the military. But because these opposing forces have not had the choice of ignoring each other, remaining instead deeply engaged, there is a chance that the gap that in previous historical periods developed over time may be diminished. This will require settlement, as described above, and the development of assertive control policies.[68]

# Notes and References

1 See Valenzuela (1999).

2 For a pioneering study of the military's role in state formation in Latin America, see López-Alves (2000). This work, however, does not include the case of Chile. For other work in this field see also Centeno (1998).

3 See Castedo and Encina (1985); Encina (1984); Ramirez (1885); Loveman (1988); Collier (1993); Villalobos *et al.* (1974).

4 Joxe (1970: 48–51).

5 See Loveman (1988: 80–1); Nunn (1970, 1976). The navy also acquired great strength with the purchase of powerful battleships and the organizational development of the service, which followed British rather than German inspiration. The navy reached its strongest point right at the turn of the century. See Urrutia Lópea (1969).

6 On the powerful impact of the mining sector on the growth of the export-based economy, see Hurtado (1966); Muñoz (1977).

7 See Varas, Agüero and Bustamante (1980). In Joxe's words: 'With its spiked helmets, its monocles and its moustaches, but without heavy industry and without foreign markets to conquer, the military could no more than mimic Prussia.' Joxe (1970: 50–1) (author's translation).

8 Geisse (1989).

9 Geisse (1989: 42–6); Loveman (1988: 191–3); Loveman (1999: 80–5); Joxe (1970).

10 See Bicheno (1972); Loveman and Davis (1997).

11 Orrego *et al.* (1979).

12 Huntington (1957); Fitch (1986).

13 Nun (1986).

14 The *milicias republicanas*. See García and Montes (1994). The republican militias, supported by the right and centre parties, maintained fully fledged organization and a mass of volunteers that reached about eighty thousand people, far more than the army. They were finally dissolved in 1937.

15 For instance, the new Labour Military Corps offered to provide training and help enhance skills for the labour force in industry and agriculture. See Varas, Agüero and Bustamante (1980). In the 1930s and especially in the 1940s the Chilean state turned decisively towards the promotion of industrialization, with the active support of expanding public agencies. This development model – known as inward-oriented industrialization – was adopted by many of the South American countries and Mexico during this time.

16 Latin American countries had far less institutional experience in and capability for subjecting the military to civilian control; hence, the importation of notions of national security to domestic contexts in turmoil would naturally have very different, and detrimental, consequences. Latin American versions of national security were also influenced by French doctrines. See Comblin (1979).

17 Varas and Agüero (1984). See also Arriagada (1986).

18 Varas, Agüero and Bustamante (1980: 108–11). The Ibáñez second administration represented a reaction against party dominance, and the enhancement of military roles made sense in it.

19 Varas, Agüero and Bustamante (1980: 171–7); García and Montes (1994: 331–42).

20 Valenzuela (1994).

21 Agüero (1988).

22 These situations were very well documented by, among others, General Carlos Prats, who at the time headed the army's general staff and succeeded Schneider at the army's helm following his assassination, and Nathaniel Davis, at the time the US ambassador in Chile. See Prats (1985) and Davis (1985).

23 Loveman and Davies (1997).

24 Garretón (1982).

25 In this sense they were militarized as opposed to civilianized regimes, such as those of Franco in Spain and Salazar in Portugal. Agüero (1995).

26 The Brazilian regime (1964–85) was the only other regime that, halfway through its tenure, arranged for fixed terms for the general presidents. The Chilean and the Brazilian were the only two regimes that institutionalized military rule with a constitution of their own (Agüero 1998). For a different view of Pinochet's regime, see Remmer (1989).

27 Barros (forthcoming in Spring 2001). See also Valenzuela (1991).

28 This was especially true for army officers. Participation of navy and air force officers in government tasks decreased significantly over time. See Huneeus and Olave (1987).

29 Agüero (1988).

30 Stepan (1989). A third component identified by Stepan – the military-as-information community or the intelligence sector – was clearly present in the Chilean case, with the powerful and feared DINA, later turned CNI. Many officers were recruited to serve in this section, which responded directly to Pinochet. See the chapter on 'Army of the Shadows' in Constable and Valenzuela (1991).

31 Similarly, the top regional commanders also assumed the top state administrative positions of their assigned regions.

32 Quoted in Arriagada (1965). See also Arriagada (1985) and Varas (1987).

33 Towards the end of the 1970s the military government faced a difficult national defence situation. On one hand, the Peruvian military government had escalated weapons acquisitions from the Soviet Union right on time for the centennial of the War of the Pacific, and relations with Bolivia had soured considerably after failure to negotiate on territorial demands. On the other hand, tensions with Argentina climaxed when the military government there rejected Great Britain's arbitration decision over the border demarcation in the Beagle Channel south of Patagonia. The initiation of armed hostilities was imminent when the Vatican stepped in as a mediator.

34 Varas (1991).

35 O'Donnell (1973) generalized the notion of coup coalition to all cases of bureaucratic-authoritarian installation. In the Chilean case, the coalition was actually established once in government, after the coup, even though all its members were knowingly moving in the direction of a coup.

36 See Valdés (1995); Huneeus (1998); Martínez and Díaz (1996).

37 Garretón (1987).

38 Constable and Valenzuela (1991: 309).

39 See e.g. Agüero et al. (1998).

40 Tironi (1988).

41 Roniger and Sznajder (1999).

42 In 'Legacies of Transitions' I have offered a comparative analysis the level of institutionalization of Pinochet's regime and the consequences this had for the transition. It was fortunate for the regime that the constitution had been passed when the political-economic crisis of 1982–3 opened the way for the mobilization of the opposition. The level of institutionalization which the constitution gave the regime empowered it with enough bargaining strength to resist political pressures for rapid democratization. See also Garretón (1987).

43 In Spain, it was the Law for Political Reform passed by Prime Minister Adolfo Suárez during the government of the monarchy. See Agüero (1995).

44 Government and opposition, in the interim period between Pinochet's defeat and the competitive elections a year later, did agree, however, partially to reform the constitution in order to make the transition viable. Important reforms were made, although very partial, which softened somewhat the more extreme authoritarian controls originally envisioned, and allowed for total pluralism by eliminating the prohibition on the Communist Party. This constitutional reform, as mandated by law, was approved by referendum with the support of government and opposition.

45 Originally, the military had a majority. A constitutional reform later balanced the number of civilian and military members. A few of the government ministers may attend the meetings, but without voting powers.

46 Geisse and Ramírez (1989) (author's translation).

47 *Constitución Política de la República de Chile*.

48 It should be noted that the constitution retains that traditional clause, shared by most constitutions in Latin America, that assigns the military the role of guarantors of the constitution and the political order. See Loveman (1995).

49 Never has the National Security Council met as a result of the military calling the meeting. However, many times the president has had to call a meeting in order to pre-empt the military from calling it first and forcing the president to attend. A recent meeting had to be called by President Ricardo Lagos only to anticipate a military move in that direction. The military wanted to discuss the indictment of General Pinochet by a local judge in December 2000.

50 On the authoritarian/democracy cleavage see Tironi and Agüero (1999) and specifically on the cleavages on the military question see Agüero.

51 For a similar approach to this period see Fuentes (1997).

52 A constitutional reform passed towards the end of Aylwin's administration adopted a six-year presidential term.

53 Barahona de Brito (1997); O'Shaughnessy (2000).

54 See *Report of the Chilean National Commission* (1993).

55 Fuentes (2000).

56 See Agüero (1993).

57 See Agüero (1993).

58 Fuentes (2000).

59 Agüero (1998).

60 Silva (1999).

61 Garretón (1982).

62 As of this writing 197 lawsuits had been filed against Pinochet.

63 On military modernization plans in this period see Rojas and Fuentes (1998); Fuentes (1997); and Varas and Fuentes (1994).

64 Burton, Gunther and Higley (1992).

65 Already, for instance, the military has inaugurated courses on human rights in its academies.

66 Rojas and Fuentes (1998).

67 For a critique of the model, see Feaver (1996); and Agüero (1997).

68 Agüero (1995); Feaver (1996); and Fitch (1998).

# 6

# The Janus Face
# of the Indonesian Armed Forces

NICO SCHULTE NORDHOLT

Recently Indonesian society has found itself in a turbulent, multi-dimensional transformation process in which the role of the Indonesian armed forces[1] is particularly crucial. The final outcome of this process is far from certain. The real issues at stake are so complex and paradoxical, and sometimes even contradictory, that it would be far too optimistic to conclude, at this point, that the transformation process will bring greater democracy. What is more certain is that the outcome will be significantly shaped by forces within the military.

The tragic contradiction in the position of the Indonesian armed forces is that on the one hand they were essential for the process of nation building within the unitary state of the Republic of Indonesia in the years 1945–59. The archipelago, in size equalling the distance between Seattle, Washington and Washington DC, or, in Europe, having the same range as that between Belfast and the Ural Mountains, is at the moment of writing still a unitary state. This in itself is a miracle, for on both flanks, in Aceh in the west and in Papua in the east, separation movements are active, and since the second half of 1997 Indonesian society has found itself in a deep crisis. On the other hand, however, very influential groups within the army now pose a major threat to attempts to maintain unity within the richly populated but extremely heterogeneous Indonesian society. In Indonesia these forces are also referred to as 'dark forces', because they attempt to maintain their old privileged positions by committing sheer acts of terror. Such acts reinforce opposition to central government or Java/Jakarta, and support the call for independence in those regions that suffer most from repression.

Therefore, in all periods since the proclamation of independence on 17 August 1945, the military have played a crucial role, albeit with the two faces of Janus. At present the main challenge for the armed forces is to contribute constructively to the two fundamental issues that Indonesian society as a whole has to resolve. The first of these is the quest for a new national consensus: what does being Indonesian mean to the inhabitants of the thousands of islands of this large archipelago, including the inhabitants of Aceh and West Papua? The second issue is the restructuring of the economy, including the abolition of the dual function of the armed forces. Emphasizing Indonesia's contemporary dilemmas, the analysis will focus on these two fundamental issues. First, though, it is necessary to recall some important events determining the 'collective memory' of the armed forces. The particular aim in the first section is to explain the doctrine of the unitary state and the political–ideological view of the military.

Developments within the armed forces over the 32 years of Suharto's New Order, and the role they played during the seventeen months' interregnum of President Habibie, are dealt with in the second and third third sections. The fourth considers the consequences of the principle of 'dual function' in relation to the present socio-economic restructuring of Indonesian society, and to organizational aspects within the military itself, emphasizing the development of the Special Forces and intelligence agencies, and their relations with a number of militia groups. The secretive role of certain forces of the New Order that are still active in the present military is underlined, clearing the way for an assessment of the role of the armed forces within the present struggle for power and the attempt to democratize Indonesian society.

## The Armed Forces' Ideological Position and 'Collective Memory'

The debate with regard to the position of the armed forces in transforming Indonesian society is largely dominated by different interpretations regarding the role of those forces at the time of important episodes in the history of the young republic. Briefly sketched, the debate pits the 'collective memory' of the military against that of the democratic forces within society.

First we see the forming of myths around the struggle for independence between 1945 and 1950. The military consider themselves to be the protectors of the revolution. This means unconditionally holding on to the state ideology, the *pancasila*, as the basis of state and society, and unconditionally holding on to the constitution of 1945. Two important documents, 'Soldier's Oath' and 'Seven Pledges', became the basis for this stand. Both documents are sacred in the eyes of the armed forces, and not a single jot or title may be altered. Apart from that, especially during the Suharto era, the military made themselves more and more the sole keepers of the nation's well-being.

All this was based on a self-imputed heroic part in casting off the colonial yoke.[2] Especially during the Suharto years contributions from politicians and in particular those from diplomats at the international front in that same battle were systematically ignored and diminished, and those of the army put on an ever-higher pedestal. Suharto's own role in particular, as commander of a battalion during a six-hour raid in Yogyakarta on 1 March 1949, was blown up out of all proportion.[3]

Now, in the present post-Suharto era, in which ample room has become available for a more critical judgement of the past, those dogmatic interpretations by the military are being attacked by the democratic forces. But within the army itself some officers look back on their own role and place within society with a surprisingly critical attitude. Thus, not only are the supposed heroics of Suharto reduced to a minor performing part,[4] but in a recent publication a high-ranking group of officers called for a deconstruction of the official interpretation of the past by the armed forces themselves.[5] Later in this analysis, the new critical voice from within the ranks will be assessed, and we shall try to find out how it compares with the forces of restoration boasted by Suharto's New Order, with or without Suharto's family empire.

Until very recently the armed forces, boosted by that official interpretation, considered themselves a unique army and became more and more immune to criticism from outside. Their position during the recent *dénouement* of the East Timor tragedy (September 1999) provides a dramatic example. Although the Indonesian army likes to compare itself to the heroic Vietnamese army in its battle against French colonial rule, a completely different ideological orientation lay behind its claim to be the agent of national unity. Already in the 1950s that claim had been elaborated with the formulation of the *dwi fungsi* (dual function) doctrine.

In those years the unity of the republic was threatened by regional,[6] in some instances religious[7] separatist movements. At the end of the 1950s the commander-in-chief at that time, General A. H. Nasution, was able to convince the first president of the republic, Sukarno, that for the sake of national unity the armed forces, in addition to their normal defensive duties, should be entrusted with the political-administrative care of the country and its people. After 1957 martial law and a state of war had been proclaimed in a number of regions, so that when Sukarno on 5 July 1959 issued the decree by which parliament was dissolved, society had already been militarized for a number of years, especially the economy.

In those final years of the 1950s the republic fought a fierce diplomatic battle against the Netherlands over West New Guinea (Irian Jaya).[8] To increase the pressure on the Dutch their property was nationalized. As national possessions, these new state-owned enterprises came under the rule of the armed forces. For daily management they appealed to Chinese business people.[9] From that moment on the symbiosis between the military and the Chinese business class was further institutionalized. Such a symbiosis had already developed during the struggle for independence,[10] but the scale and intensity of the cooperation was magnified by the nationalization of Dutch companies at the end of the 1950s. Some years later (1963–5), during the *Konfrontasi* with the Malayan Federation[11] – seen by Jakarta as a British imperialistic construction – British and American companies were also nationalized. This further strengthened the bond between the military and Chinese businessmen, and this involvement in 'doing business' was seen as legitimate by the armed forces themselves on the basis of the dual function doctrine.

By granting them authority over local companies under the condition that central government in Jakarta was fully recognized, that formula offered a splendid way to lure rebellious officers, military unit and all, back into the 'womb' of the republic. In this way the positions of many regional warlords were strengthened, without increasing the threat of separatism. This form of 'incorporating' regional rebels not only saved lengthy and costly military operations, but also neutralized their positions in a rather peaceful way. Moreover, this arrangement met the direct material needs of the troops, who, because of the declining economy of the period, were under the constant threat of being further underpaid – an important pressure on regional commanders to rebel against the centre, Jakarta. This 'legitimate' incorporation of business within the military sphere of influence in those years actually came in the nick of time because the army leadership, under General Nasution, was having to demobilize large parts of the army after the Dutch finally recognized Indonesia's independence on 27 December 1949. This demobilization initially met with heavy protest and increasing support for separatist movements.

The nationalization of the Dutch companies, from December 1956 onwards, was also in this respect a part of the solution.

A purely pragmatic (in that it met material needs) and a more tactical-strategic consideration (in that it incorporated potential rebels) were disguised under the pretext of an ideological argument: the battle for the unitary state (incorporating Irian Jaya and preventing separatism elsewhere in the archipelago). It was precisely under this ideological cover-up that the interests of the army and those of the civil president, Sukarno, met. With the introduction of the Preliminary Constitution of 1950, the latter had been forced to accept the reduction of his presidential position to a mere ceremonial function for several years. But with the full support of the commander-in-chief, General A. H. Nasution, on 5 July 1959 President Sukarno was able to dissolve parliament by decree and at the same time reintroduce the constitution of 1945. In that constitution the president's position of power is more dominant.

Therefore, it is more correct to see 1959 as the end of the 'democratic experience'[12] and from that year on to label the Indonesian political system as repressive-authoritarian. In fact, from a political point of view, Suharto's New Order was the continuation of the 'guided democracy' introduced in 1959 by Sukarno with the help of the armed forces. So when Suharto 'stepped aside' on 21 May 1998 the democratic forces were able to organize freely for the first time in no less than forty years. This history has far-reaching consequences for the relative strengths and weaknesses of these forces *vis-à-vis* the authoritarian forces nurtured during the New Order.

It means, for instance, that the proportion of the present population who consciously experienced the parliamentary-democratic period in the 1950s is very small. This has led to a remarkable paradox. On the one hand few of the political parties that sprouted from the ground like mushrooms in the year prior to the national elections of 7 June 1999 had anything resembling a programme. This can be explained partly by the short period of time they were given to found themselves and register for the elections. On the other hand, however, nearly three quarters of the 48 parties admittedly referred in name or symbolically to one of the political parties from the 1950s, although political answers to present problems within Indonesian society seemed to matter less than 'holding on' to a period from the political past that after four decades of repression had suddenly re-emerged as a democratic paradise. The Democracy Party for Struggle (*Partai Demokrasi Indonesia – Perjuangan*, PDI–P), with Megawati Sukarnoputri as its leader, may be considered the prototype of this unconditional falling back on the past. Her political charisma was (and is) based almost completely on her family connection (daughter of) and strong resemblance to the first president of the republic, Sukarno.

Oddly enough, in the present Indonesia hardly anyone wishes to remember the repressive period under Sukarno, whilst his role as Proclamator of independence is emphasized.[13] Next to that incorruptible Sukarno, and in his wake, just or unjust, his daughter Megawati is in shining contrast to the completely corrupted Suharto family – the difference between the family of the first and that of the second president of the republic turning out in favour of the first.

The military's involvement in the economic sector at the end of the 1950s put them directly into the position of 'employer' within the economic framework. It also put them in opposition to the labour movement, which was mainly controlled by the Communist Party (PKI). This anti-communist attitude dated back to September 1948. Then, just after the start of the Cold War, army units loyal to the Hatta administration crushed a rebellious movement within the army to gain support from the United States in their battle for independence against the Dutch. This internal revolt is known as the Madiun affair, and forms one of the most important events in the collective memory of the armed forces.

Renewed confrontation with the communist ideology, this time at the end of the 1950s and the beginning of the 1960s, and in the economic field, further exacerbated relations between the armed forces and the most important socio-economic actors, such as the trade unions and the left-wing political parties. Eventually this was to culminate in the bloody reckoning of the years 1965–8, with the introduction of Suharto's New Order, when approximately between 500,000 and a million people were killed because of their (assumed) communist sympathies.[14] This anti-communist attitude gave Suharto's New Order much credit in the West – so much so that, until the end of the Cold War, the West looked the other way when the army committed human rights violations. In fact, it was not until the massacre in the Santa Cruz cemetery in Dili, East Timor on 11 November 1991 that the first outburst of criticism was heard from the West.[15] And when it came to labour issues, Western entrepreneurs found the army on their side.

Two other characteristics of the army in relation to society during these first twenty years of the republic, still of influence today, claim their place in the discourse on the role of the armed forces in the current transformation of Indonesian society. The first is the army's relation to politics – not only to the political parties, but especially also to their ideologies. The second, a direct result of the experience of guerrilla warfare (1945–50), is the tactical and strategical application of (political) violence to destabilize or maintain the political regime.

The well-known Indonesian priest, writer, architect and human rights activist Y. B. Mangunwijaya saw a direct line between the fascist character of Suharto's New Order with its predilection for the Indonesia Raya (Great Indonesia) idea and the fascist Japanese regime during the Second World War.[16] The constitution of 1945, drawn up by Professor Supomo, a customary law specialist, is indeed strongly based on the integral view of the state of the Meji era. In this view the nation is considered an organic entity, in which the president, as head of state, is at the same time regarded as the 'wise father of the nation'.[17] In article 31 of the constitution of 1945 the so-called *azas kekeluargaan*, or family principle, is mentioned. On the basis of a particularistic interpretation of this article by Suharto, from the mid-1980s Indonesian society was seen as 'owned' by the Suharto family, the so-called 'Cendana empire'. Loveard refers to Suharto as Indonesia's last Sultan: as in a traditional sultanate Suharto and his children considered the national resources as private property: *l'état c'est moi*.[18] To put this interpretation into reality Suharto relied on some crack troops within the army – Strategic Command, or KOSTRAD, and Special Forces, or KOPASSUS – to enforce and safeguard the business interests of his family and those of his cronies. Although within the army the actions of these troops regularly led to tensions with regular, territorial commanders, the ideological indoctrination obviously had so deeply penetrated all ranks that it was only after Suharto had resigned in May 1998 that open criticism of this far-reaching form of 'privatization' was heard within the army.

In 1978 this indoctrination was officially introduced as the P-4 programme, a course on the *pancasila* as the official state moral and life doctrine, with the aim of turning the Indonesian citizen into a true *pancasilais*, a *pancasila* man. To start with all civil servants and military had to take this P-4 course; later it was extended to other segments of society. In his dissertation Ingo Wandelt[19] points out how this indoctrination through the curriculum of the military academy succeeded in straitjacketing all officers in Suharto's particularistic interpretation of the state ideology. This makes it remarkable that so soon after Suharto left the political stage such fundamental criticism of the New Order as a political-economic system came from the ranks of the army itself – notably expressed by the then Major-General Agus Wirahadikusumah in 1999.

This ideological orientation of the armed forces also explains its attitude towards the political parties. Oddly enough, it was during the years of the revolution that the political parties had major influence. Within the civil administration democratic rules were applied. The Founding Fathers of the republic, who all happened to be civilians, did not regard the military a socio-political force. In fact, the constitution of 1945 does not mention such a provision either.[20] Although because of the struggle for independence no elections could be held, a vast committee, consisting of representatives of the then-existing political parties, functioned as a sort of parliament. The government was politically accountable to these representatives, and in case of a motion of confidence a new (coalition) cabinet was formed. Despite the war situation the army fought under political direction, albeit with conflicts, sometimes even open ones. In December 1948 the then very popular Commander-in-Chief General Sudirman refused to obey President Sukarno's order to surrender to the Dutch troops in Yogyakarta. Later, in October 1952, there was a 'near coup' by high-ranking officers who opposed the demobilization of large parts of the guerrilla army. In the collective memory of the armed forces Sudirman's refusal forms the evidence that it was they who brought about independence, while the second incident (17 October 1952) is registered as proof for the fact that the Indonesian armed forces, unlike those in South-American 'banana republics', do not resolve their political differences by using the tactics of a 'coup'.

Two processes in the 1950s crucially influenced the military's collective memory and its relation to the state and society: (1) professionalization within the armed forces (reorganization and demobilization); and (2) the growing political-economic influence of the armed forces, especially of the army, on administration and political parties. In both processes General Nasution, as was stated earlier, played a decisive role. In the course of the republic's history other individual generals appear to have played remarkably important roles. To later generations of officers they in turn became important role models. Next to Sudirman and Nasution, in the years of the revolution and the 1950s, we might mention Lieutenant-General T. B. Simatupang.[21] During the New Order other generals functioned as role models – this time, however, in a negative sense. General Suharto's right-hand man, Lieutenant-General Ali Murtopo, and his successor, General Benny Murdani, are Rasputin-like characters. They both had immense influence on the ambitious high-ranking officers who in the 1990s had been waiting to replace the old Suharto (born 1921). Imitating their 'gurus', these officers did not hesitate to play off those ambitions against each other, as the bloody chain of events starting in the middle of 1996 shows.

To the armed forces the end of parliamentary democracy in 1959 was the convincing evidence that 'civil politicians' were incapable of governing the country. That the foreign economic influence, which, in fact, still exploited Indonesia, had a crucial impact on that proven incapacity of parliamentary democracy was conveniently excluded from the collective memory of the armed forces. But from 1959 onwards the armed forces had to endure President Sukarno's political game. His formula – 'Nationalism, Religion, Communism' (*Nasionalis–Agama–Komunis*, NASAKOM), connecting nationalism (for instance the political aspirations of the army) to religion (Islam) and communism – was in fact unacceptable to Nasution and the military. However, the armed forces were not strong enough politically and economically to openly and broadly defy the enormous charisma of President Sukarno. Before that could happen, first the economy had to worsen; above all, the Cold War witch hunt against communism, allegedly an atheist ideology affronting the religious character of Indonesian society, had to be played out more fiercely and in the political–ideological sense. That in doing so the anti-communist element in the army received strong support from the West, especially from the United States (itself sinking more and more deeply in the swamp of the Vietnam War), was deliberately excluded from the collective memory.

Within the military, meanwhile, the favoured principle of 'no (direct) coup' was maintained, and because of that there was a steady process of political manipulation and infiltration. Sukarno tried to resist military manipulation by leaning more and more to the left.[22] This further raised tensions between large parts of the armed forces and the communists. In reaction to this they looked for the political support of Islam, despite their deep loathing for *politik-islam* as it had been presented by the Darul Islam movement. When in 1965, with the introduction of the New Order, anything 'leftist' was silenced, both in the literal and figurative sense, the army could count on active Cupertino from certain sections of Islam. ANSOR, the youth organization of the Nahdlatul Ulama, the largest Muslim organization in the country, played a particularly important role in this. But despite Islam's contribution to setting up the New Order, the forces of *politik-islam* were denied political space by Suharto and his generals.

This was the third time in the history of the republic that Islam, although the faith of an enormous majority (85 per cent) of society, was forced to accept a minority position in politics. The first time was during the proclamation of independence, when the Jakarta Charter[23] was stricken from the preamble of the constitution; the second time was an attempt to set up an Islamic state by force, through the Darul Islam movement. Once again in 1965 Islamic expectations were fruitless: they had hoped that their support for the army in its battle against the communists would lead to the Islamization of society under Suharto. *Politik-islam* had to wait until 1990 for Suharto to call on Islam again, this time in an attempt to protect himself from forces within the army.[24] In doing so, Suharto left behind the old armed forces dogma of unconditionally upholding the *pancasila* as the basis for the republic. Later we will see how this change in Suharto's course not only led to considerable differences of opinion within the armed forces, but also took the entire Indonesian society to the brink of civil war along religious lines.

Finally, looking forward to the installation of the New Order and back at the guerrilla war period, which is still of great importance in the present power struggle in Indonesia, we ought to mention the phenomenon of *preman*-ism, the relation between gangs of thugs and the army. The general who is the role model in this area is Lieutenant-General Ali Murtopo.[25] As a young officer during the guerrilla war he was already involved in a number of intelligence operations. He was able to develop the qualities he showed then to such a level, that at his death in 1984 the future president, K. H. Abdurrahman Wahid, then still working as a commentator with *Kompas*, one of the most important Indonesian daily newspapers, wrote that he hoped that with Murtopo's death 'the psychology of fear' had come to an end.

This *preman*-ism is anchored in old sociological structures of Javanese society especially: groups of youngsters, before they have settled down, wander around looking for adventure, and making themselves available to do all sorts of odd (dirty) jobs. In modern Indonesia drop-outs and young people with informal jobs are easy to recruit for such 'adventures'. Without any doubt this was also a continuation of the operational style of the so-called warlords and their troops during the guerrilla war and within regional separatist movements afterwards. In providing a future for warlords within the republic, in the use of intelligence actions and in holding out the prospect of economic rewards the culture of *preman*-ism became a part of the army. Especially during the Suharto era this was shown in the formation of Pemuda Pancasila (Pancasila Youth). This organization, with its formal and ideal goal of rehabilitating juvenile delinquents and recidivists, in practice appeared to consist of a pool of around two million members from which the intelligence services could select agents to do all sorts of 'odd jobs', such as intimidating political opponents of Suharto's New Order.

In a related development, retired military were put to work in such *preman*-like organizations. Almost all private security services, especially area and company services, but also nearly all car-park services, were made up of retired military under the command of a *preman*. During the occupation of East Timor, however, this phenomenon deepened: an East Timorese orphan, adopted by an officer who was often a member of the Special Forces, as an *anak angkat* (adopted child) could be used as a militiaman in later years. This mechanism, developed in East Timor, was later much used in other regions of the archipelago where elite forces were involved in intelligence actions, such as in Aceh and Papua. In the recent fratricide in the Moluccas the various sections of the armed forces also fought each other with the help of such militia.

## The Armed Forces during Suharto's New Order

The New Order as a political-economic system can be regarded as a mere product of the Cold War period. Its geographical position has ensured that political developments within the archipelago have always been strongly influenced by international forces. Five out of seven global sea trade routes are situated within the territorial waters of Indonesia. There was interference from outside during the struggle for independence, as we have noted before, and in the 1950s, when the US endorsed anti-Sukarno regional officers. Some years later, during the liberation of Irian Jaya, the Kennedy administration put heavy pressure on the Netherlands to give in to the demands of the republic, hoping to stop the leaders of this young state from moving any further into the sphere of influence of the socialist hemisphere. In 1965, after President Sukarno had already embraced the Beijing–Hanoi axis, Washington supported those powers within the army able to stop Sukarno and the communists. When subsequently the then 44-year-old Major-General Suharto and his military supporters also appealed to a group of Western-trained and educated economists[26] who had mastered the language of developmentalism, Suharto could count on the full financial-economic support of the West to get his country out of the deep economic chaos it had got itself into at the start of the 1960s.

One of the most influential architects of the political-economic development model that was to be applied within the New Order was the above-mentioned Lieutenant-General Ali Murtopo. Entirely according to Rostow's model of five stages of (economic) growth and the socio-political strategy of Samuel Huntington, in which political stability had to be ensured for the sake of economic growth, Murtopo and his people put together a 25-year development model. The remarkable thing about the New Order is that this long-term strategy was consistently applied, albeit with some pragmatism when this was required by developments within the world economy, such as a sharp fall in oil prices. Because of this, Indonesia could soon be regarded as a genuine developmental state, having implemented three five-year development plans by the mid-1980s.

To bring about the necessary political stability, existing political parties were further muzzled, the press and other public organizations, such as the intellectuals and the student organizations, effectively put under legal restraint, and organized labour completely curbed. To enforce all this the armed forces acted as the 'stick', using the threat of force or actual force where they saw fit. In a more subtle way, based on the dual function principle, the policy of *kekaryawan* was applied: 'employing' the military in civilian functions within the administration as well as within the economic sector. In this way civil servants were directly confronted with the discipline and hierarchy of the armed forces. This raised the managerial force of the state departments considerably and resulted in greater effectiveness in realizing the five-year plans. Further, all civil servants were forced to join Golkar, the government party which, certainly during the first 25 years of the New Order, was heavily influenced by the military. This 'party' – in fact a cluster of corporatist organizations of functional groups of professionals such as civil servants, farmers, fishermen and labourers – had already been set up from within army groups in 1964 as a counter-force to the then-increasing influence of the communist PKI.

Because of this direct and indirect interference by the armed forces, the set goals were met in nearly all sectors – not only in terms of physical infrastructure but especially as regards social infrastructure such as public health, education and credit programmes. In that sense Suharto's New Order certainly also provided the 'carrot'. Especially prior to the five-yearly elections, government programmes were promised to the inhabitants of politically sensitive areas provided they would help Golkar, the government party, to a majority. This proved to be a successful policy, for from the first five-yearly national elections in 1971 until the sixth in 1997, during Suharto's reign Golkar was always able to gain between 64 and 74 per cent of the votes. In some regions, especially where Islam was politically deeply rooted in the local community, the military openly intimidated the population, but the tactics of the 'carrot' proved to be enough in most areas to secure victory.

The international donor community was, of course, aware of the role intimidation and blackmail practices played in such victories. Above all, it was well understood that the legislative foundation of political participation by the contestants and voters was all but democratic. But the official view of the West was that the Indonesian population, on the basis of its own legislation, had re-elected the government in office. Whether that legislation had come about in a legitimate way was a question the donor institutions and Western governments preferred not to answer publicly, merely for the sake of good economic relations with the Suharto regime.

The policy was not always carried out efficiently. On the contrary, because social and political accountability was lacking within this system, corruption became more and more prevalent.[27] According to Transparency International, of all Asian countries Indonesia scored highest on the list of corrupt countries. Several estimates mention a 30 per cent corruption rate in the national economy.[28] Later we will see that the themes of corruption and nepotism became the spearheads of protest against President Suharto and his successor Habibie.

To put it briefly, as long as Suharto was able to deploy the armed forces, the bureaucracy and the technocrats, and was assured of financial aid from the big Chinese capitalists (cukong) to support his power base, he appeared to be able to create impressive economic growth (7 per cent as an annual average over a period of thirty years). With a legitimacy within the population based on this performance, he did not meet with much systematic criticism, except with regard to mismanagement – the so-called KKN practices (korupsi, kolusi dan nepotism: corruption, collusion and nepotism). This lack of systematic criticism is one of the most important reasons why the forces of civil society within Indonesia appeared to be so poorly developed.[29] It also needs to be mentioned that the figurative and literal silencing of critical intellectuals meant that the capacity to create a more analytical-critical opposition was hardly present.[30] And the brainwash effect of the P-4 indoctrination course could be felt in all layers of society.

In the scope of this analysis it is not necessary to go into all the political-economic aspects of Suharto's New Order and the developments during his 32-year rule in great detail. Many excellent and accessible major publications on these issues have been written.[31] The present analysis will focus more on relations between the armed forces and the state, and between this complex (armed forces/state) and society.[32] Publications in this area form an established frame of reference for Indonesian analysts, but owing to the relatively low circulation of these (foreign) studies, the relevant information has not spread beyond a small group of specialists. Because of the strong repressive character of the New Order, until recently hardly any critical studies on the armed forces by Indonesians and in Bahasa Indonesia were available. Therefore the internal debate on the role of the armed forces was, on the one hand, relatively shallow from an analytical point of view, and, on the other hand, it was strongly influenced by the official version coming from the armed forces themselves. The present analysis looks especially at these recent Indonesian studies with regard to the two dimensions or inherent fundamental issues of the present transformation process summarized in the introduction. The aim is a better assessment of the present power struggle in Indonesia.

However, in order to do this properly some structural points need to be mentioned first. One is the role legislation has been assigned within the New Order to legitimize the socio-political role of the armed forces. As stated before, in 1958 General A. H. Nasution introduced the 'middle road' concept, subsequently translated into the dual function principle. Right after the emergence of Suharto, and under the scrutiny of his right-hand man (then) Colonel Ali Murtopo, this principle was further refined through some regime-sponsored seminars (1965, 1966 and 1967). Subsequently it was implemented in policy. Finally, in 1982, this dual function principle was made law by the government as Act No. 20.[33]

Based on this principle, military personnel could be employed in all sorts of strategic positions (the so-called *kekaryawan* principle). This was not limited to the national level, where between 30 and 50 per cent of all ministers' posts and high civil service functions (from permanent secretaries to heads of department) were taken by military officers, but had also reached village level. At least 70 per cent of all provincial governors and 50 per cent of all district officers had a military background. Besides, in most cases regional judicial functions were taken by (former) military, as was the case with the position of chairman in regional parliaments. Although all these officers had handed in their military uniforms, they still operated within the lines of command of their former military superiors.[34]

Next to this 'civil' government structure a military territorial organizational structure to the level of villages was set up; there was thus a double check on development programmes as well as on the political orientation of the population and of social organizations such as the press, religious associations and educational bodies. Moreover, the armed forces, using a Special Forces unit, Opsus (*Operasi Khusus*), were able to supervise the permitted political parties.[35] By 1974 the existing parties had been forced to merge into two pseudo-parties which were supervised by government: the Islamic 'Unity and Development Party' (*(Partai Persatuan Pembangunan*, PPP), and the secular-nationalistic Indonesian Democracy Party (*Partai Demokrasi Indonesia*, PDI), into which also two small Christian parties were forced to merge. In its relations with the international donor community this gave the New Order an alibi of democracy, but in practice led to a situation in which political energy was spent in fighting intra-party conflicts instead of challenging the government party, Golkar, which during election times, using government money, was able to monopolise the support of the population.

In recent studies[36] a wealth of detailed information is presented on the deep involvement of the military in the economic sector. The business connections of many well-known (ex-)generals and their family members have been traced. It has been shown, for example, that a single province of the business empire of the Suharto family – in relation to the state-owned oil company Pertamina – is divided into more than 124 companies.[37] The fact is that since the middle of the 1980s the six children of the former president have 'gone into business'. Years later their interests have fanned out so wide that, according to popular opinion in Jakarta, any company that might seem to make a profit is immediately bought up by 'the Family'.

As well as all these direct business connections another system of economic activity developed under the Suharto regime, that of the *yayasan* foundations which continue to wield considerable influence. These so-called non-profit organizations with supposedly charitable aims were able to withdraw vast sums of money from the regular economy without giving any account or paying any tax, simply by using the political-economic connections of the board members. George Adicondro, an Indonesian researcher of corruption cases who fled to Australia in 1994, has calculated that the Suharto family had established more than 46 such foundations with a total estimated capital of fifteen billion dollars.[38]

Various sections of the military, down to regimental level, established foundations of their own. Formally these constructions were meant to provide additional income enabling routine expenditure, since the regular budget for the armed forces was indeed very poor (see note 1). But since the accounts of such foundations were completely opaque, it was very easy to withdraw 'extra' income, which would subsequently disappear into the pockets of high officers. It was generally well-known which foundation belonged to which military section. Businessmen, especially Chinese business partners (*cukong*) of military commanders, could very easily use the foundation name with the rest of their business contacts, thus enabling them to profit on a private basis from their *koneksi* (connections) outside their activities for the military. Whether this in fact was the case was of hardly any relevance to the general perception among the population. In any case these *koneksi* practices were quite intimidating, creating a situation in which businessmen who were not able to make use of them nearly always got the worst of it.

Over the years such practices deepened the anti-Chinese sentiments within society, especially amongst Islamic entrepreneurs and tradesmen, who almost until the end of the New Order had been deliberately discouraged by the government out of fear of increasing *politik-islam* forces. But just because of these sentiments the military knew that the Chinese depended for support and protection on the armed forces, thus making them vulnerable to blackmail. In this way the already vulnerable position of the Chinese community as a whole doubled. And it even tripled because many of the leading Chinese businessmen belonged to the Christian minority as well.

## Rivalries, Conflicts, Regime Transition

Because of the hierarchical structure of society and the lack of any form of effective social-political control, abuse of power at the top had its influence on lower levels, where the 'potentates' were merely smaller in size. But because of the vast number of smaller power holders at those lower levels of administration, the cumulative effect was as astonishing in size. Here we should mention a policy instrument which turned out to be fatal to the process of developing a civil society. This instrument is known by the acronym SARA (*Suku, Agama, Ras, Antar-golongan*: ethnic, religious, racial and socio-economic differences). Suharto's New Order issued a ban on naming social conflicts by referring to any one of these characteristics as such. It was, of course, inevitable that within a fast-transforming society like the one experiencing the 'construction model' of the New Order many conflicts had to occur. But through *denying* those 'horizontal' conflicts as such, the New Order, the bureaucracy and the armed forces reserved the right to create top–down solutions to them. Because of this social dependence on the government was enlarged, while at the same time the still-existing social mechanisms for conflict management were further eroded or even entirely silenced – and the New Order as political-economic system rotted away from the inside. Social cohesion was hard to find, resulting in a situation in which society had become extremely vulnerable to rumours and inflammable as soon as hatred, revenge and retaliation got the upper hand.

But as long as the economic growth figures rose, this internal decaying process stayed unnoticed. It was not until the 'Asian Flu' financial epidemic in the middle of 1997 that it became apparent. At that time sharp contrasts showed that the entire economy was nothing more than a giant with feet of clay. During that crisis it also became clear in which way a second factor – the rivalry between the pretenders to Suharto's throne within the armed forces – in all its intensity brought this very decaying process to the surface. They did not flinch from using social violence, even along religious lines, to fight their internal battles. After Suharto had stepped aside, these conflicts brought society to the brink of civil war.

The first time such rivalry became visible was during the Malari affair in January 1974. This was a conflict between the then commander-in-chief, General Sumitro, and Suharto, in which Ali Murtopo, using his base in the intelligence service, backed the latter. The conflict resulted in four direct consequences for the armed forces: (1) the police were added to the three sections of the armed forces, and central command over the four sections was tightened; (2) the territorial units were reorganized in order to prevent incidents such as the Malari affair from happening again; for example, lines of command to the territorial units were better centralized; (3) Suharto speeded up the building of KOSTRAD, in which KOPASSUS held their own position as elite troops (thus creating, far ahead of Saddam Hussein, his own Republican Guards) – in the 1980s he had put his brother-in-law at the head of it, and in the 1990s his son-in-law, Lieutenant-General Prabowo, was to play a dominant role within KOPASSUS; and (4) the Malari affair resulted in a reorganization within the intelligence agencies: from now on there were three, and they were not only meant to keep an eye on the potential rivals of Suharto, but also and especially on each other.

The second time the rivalry between the candidates for succession violently came to the fore was in March 1982. During a Golkar election rally in Jakarta agitators created a situation in which passions mounted, resulting in a large part of the (Chinese) shopping mall, Pasar Senin, going up in flames. There are strong indications that Lieutenant-General Murtopo was behind this action. In any event the result was that he fell into disgrace and his disciple in the intelligence service, General Benny Murdani, became the new strong man. Immediately after his appointment he was connected to the summary shooting of some thousands of semi-criminals, all of whom, in some way or another, had been under the influence of Ali Murtopo. Many of these *preman* were members of Pemuda Pancasila, Golkar's youth organization, from which gangs were recruited. According to public opinion in those days it was General Murdani himself who had ordered the shootings, hence his nickname Benny the Killer.[39] For most of the 1980s Murdani was seen as Suharto's second-in-command, although he was not vice-president. Through regular reorganizations Murdani, as new commander-in-chief, succeeded in increasing his influence over the territorial commanders and the intelligence services. Suharto allowed this for some time because Murdani, a Catholic by religion, seemed to lack the social credentials to pose an immediate threat to him. This situation changed at the end of the 1980s when Murdani revealed himself as leader of a group of malcontents within the army.

At the start this feeling of dissatisfaction was expressed in purely material terms. Half-way through the 1980s the six children of the president had all gone into business on a scale which aroused the jealousy of some generals. Prior to Suharto's re-election for a fifth term in March 1988 Murdani urged him to select a vice-president, who would be nominated by the army chiefs. This would not only allow the succession in 1993 to run smoothly, but would also guarantee a wider spread of privileges. Suharto, however, rejected this request and appointed one of Murdani's opponents as his vice-president. From that moment on, though, he knew he had to deal with a strong opposition within the armed forces. Murdani was removed as commander-in-chief, but his position was still so strong that Suharto had to endure him as secretary for defence and security.

To be better armed against his opponents in the military Suharto ordered his confidant Habibie to found the Indonesian Association of Muslim Intellectuals (Ikatan Cendekiawan Muslim Indonesia, ICMI) in December 1990. The members of this new organization predominantly came from Muhammadyiah, the oldest and largest Muslim organization in the country but one, with 28 million members according to own sources. Now for the third time it was evident that there was serious rivalry within the New Order; in the end this would lead to Suharto stepping aside in 1998.

With the foundation of ICMI Suharto had given that rivalry a religious-ideological dimension. It turned out that within this ICMI there was a hard core of Muslims who had not given up their ideal of a *politik-islam*. Now they aimed to realize that ideal gradually. Under Habibie's wings they started a process of Islamizing the peaks of the military and of the bureaucracy, hoping that 'if Allah would call Suharto onto Him' they would hold all major positions. They spoke of the *hijau* (green) wing within the armed forces, referring to green as the colour of Islam. Because Murdani had disappeared, Suharto's son-in-law Prabowo was given ample space for a rocket-like career within the Special Forces. Thus Prabowo was in close contact with groups inside and outside ICMI striving for *politik-islam*.

In reaction two counter-movements arose. Abdurrahman Wahid, then chairman of the largest Muslim organization, Nahdlatul Ulama (a claimed membership of 30–40 million), drew to him some non-Muslim intellectuals and opponents of Suharto to found Forum Demokrasi in 1992. The Forum wished to stick uncon-ditionally to the *pancasila* as the sole basis of society. For that reason it was given silent support by Suharto's opponents within the armed forces. Hence this wing was called *merah–putih* (red–white), the colours of the national flag and therefore the symbolic colours of the *pancasila*. A second counter-movement appeared with the political launch of a civilian opponent to Suharto for the 1997 elections. Regional commanders still under the influence of Benny Murdani supported his choice of Megawati, the daughter of the first president, Sukarno. Megawati, in appearance resembling her popular father, would on that basis alone be able to mobilize the masses. With her political inexperience and unproven personal qualities she seemed to pose no direct threat to military ambitions to maintain the dual function.

Against Suharto's wish Megawati was elected president of the PDI in 1994, and the popularity of this small quasi-party rose. It seemed to provide an outlet for all the political frustration which had been bottled up in society. Internal polls, conducted by Suharto's intelligence services in 1995, pointed to the possibility of Megawati winning up to 40 per cent of the votes in the 1997 elections. This would considerably weaken the position of the aging Suharto, forcing him to negotiate on his succession. He and his supporters within the armed forces, foremost among them the then commander-in-chief General Feisal, did not want that to happen under any circumstances. Through political dirty tricks they succeeded in dethroning Megawati as party president and eventually forcibly cleared her office on Saturday, 27 July 1996. Immediately, that day became *Sabtu Kelabu*, Grey Saturday, with reference to other days of infamy such as Bloody Sunday in Derry, Northern Ireland, in 1972.

From this incident onwards the battle between the two wings in the New Order, the greens and the red–whites, was violently joined. Not much later, in October 1996, churches were set on fire in the eastern corner of Java, Situbondo.

This region was the cradle of Wahid's Nahdlatul Ulama (NU), and the intention was to undermine his position. Should people believe that NU members had committed these acts of violence, the credibility of Wahid as a tolerant person with whom minorities could seek refuge would have been seriously damaged. In this way, with the political dethroning of Megawati already accomplished, the second potential civilian political challenger, Abdurrahman Wahid, would have been silenced. But Wahid was resolute enough to know how to prevent that.

The contradictions within the armed forces cannot be reduced entirely to a form of rivalry between the greens and the red–whites. This was interwoven with another form of rivalry: the battle for the top positions within the armed forces. In any military organization there are tensions because of promotion policy. In Indonesia this had already led to fierce collisions and 'near-coup' situations in the 1950s. Such tensions came to be resolved by using a professional method for promotion, based on performance. Over a long period of time this worked quite well until in the 1990s three phenomena occurred simultaneously to exert serious pressure on the system.

First, a Human Resource Programme emanating from ICMI was aiming at occupying as many strategic posts as possible with officers favouring the ideals of *politik-islam*. Second, for political-strategic reasons President Suharto gave preferential treatment to his son-in-law Lieutenant-General Prabowo and his 'buddies', causing the careers of their former classmates to get jammed. Third, and possibly of most importance, at the end of the 1960s and the beginning of the 1970s the inflow of cadets had become very unbalanced. Some 25 years later this had grave consequences with regard to the opportunities of those high-ranking officers who, considering their careers, were eligible for promotion to the rank of colonel, brigadier and higher. From the mid-1990s on the armed forces tried to solve this institutional problem by speeding up the lead time between promotional transfers, which in some cases came down to six months.[40] The direct consequence of this measure was that commanders of field troops had too short a period in their new posts to become acquainted with their own troops and with the situation in the field. This offered ample opportunities for infiltration through intelligence operations, which were focused on political issues. An indirect consequence of this situation was that in the eyes of the population the authority of the armed forces declined steeply because of increased civil violence and uncertainty with regard to the real perpetrators, and the obvious inability of the regular territorial troops to track down and arrest those perpetrators.

Yet another consequence of this convoluted situation was that every rival had several agendas, or at least could have. Alongside political-ideological contrasts within the armed forces, 'day-to-day' rivalry for the highest posts created a sort of personal agenda. Given the political constellation of that time, when everyone knew that age must soon bring the presidency of Suharto to an end, these complex motives led to the formation of several shifting alliances. Therefore, certainly while Suharto was still in power, one could not speak with confidence of 'wings' or 'camps' within the armed forces; certainly one could not point unambiguously to any leaders. This in itself increased the number of rumours regarding conspiracies.

In the scope of this analysis it is impossible to mention all the political entanglements that arose as reactions to these often bloody incidents.[41] The upshot, though, was that Suharto and his followers succeeded in winning the May 1997 elections with yet another landslide victory – but, of all elections held during

Suharto's New Order, these were the most violent: more than four hundred people were killed.

Shortly after that, in August 1997, the Asian financial-economic crisis hit Indonesia hard. The final outcome is well known. In March 1998 Suharto succeeded in having himself appointed president by the People's Congress for a seventh five-year term, with B. J. Habibie as vice-president. But only two months later, on 21 May, and after some days of violence in Jakarta and a number of other cities resulting in thousands of victims, he felt forced to hand over the presidency to his confidant Habibie and his former adjutant and commander-in-chief, General Wiranto. The fact that he completely directed the scenes of that day was an indication that the opposition had not won the race outright. The battle continued, but new actors had appeared on stage.

From January 1998 students had demonstrated in masses against KKN, the acronym for corruption, collusion and nepotism. In the first place they targeted the Suharto regime, but at the same time it was an expression of such a general nature that it lacked a clear political alternative. The slogan used was: *reformasi*. Islamic critics of Suharto had sided with groups within the armed forces which had realized that the New Order as political-economic system under Suharto had gone bankrupt. Thus a broad opposition against the Suharto government was created, although lacking unity in its vision of the future. Both wings within the armed forces had connections to the protesting students. And both wings had taken measures to put armed civil units into action in case of open violence. These militia groups were called 'reds' and 'whites' according to their different headbands. The 'reds' were associated with the secular-nationalistic wing, and the 'whites' with the *politik-islam* wing in the armed forces.

Instructed by the military in their protests, students restricted themselves to actions on campus, but from the beginning of May they turned to the streets after some of them had become the victims of snipers, probably belonging to KOPASSUS. Already, before these actions started, a few dozen student leaders had been kidnapped by these elite forces; few of them survived.[42] Subsequently these demonstrations were infiltrated by gangs of *preman* under the direct command of elite forces; this would lead to the bloody and violent actions of 14–15 May 1998. In reaction, the students occupied the parliament building for a week, without this leading to resistance by the armed forces. This occupation made Suharto realize that he was no longer capable of controlling the crisis, hence his decision to step aside and leave the crisis to his confidants. By the time Habibie had lost the elections seventeen months later, the failure of these tactics had been amply demonstrated.

In relation to the political role of the armed forces after Suharto had handed over power four important points can be mentioned. First, although when the Habibie government came to power, with General Wiranto as the strong man, the New Order as a political-economic system had not directly changed, possibilities for fundamental change had been created, albeit in opposite directions. On the one hand, the chances for the *politik-islam* movement had improved considerably. This became clear shortly after when Amien Rais, then president of Muhammadyiah, and one of Suharto's most important opponents, gave the Habibie government the benefit of the doubt on its first day in office. With Habibie, then still chairman of ICMI, as president, the possibility of realizing the ideals of *politik-islam* was generally believed to be much higher. And, with this support, Amien Rais simultaneously caused a schism within the student front. Part of it wished to refuse to compromise and to continue the battle against the KKN and for *reformasi*. Another part, following Rais, supported the Habibie government. On the other hand, after Habibie's coming to power there were possibilities for real change that could be considered a part of the *reformasi* momentum. The Habibie government, under pressure from the economic crisis, themselves spoke out in favour of *reformasi*. This meant that through new legislation the position of political parties and the whole conduct of the national elections were improved considerably, although one could not yet speak of complete democracy. The military, having played a very important role in drawing up this new legislation, still had an influential role in political questions. To balance that, Habibie did not tamper with the freedom of the press, gained by the media on their own account.

Second, during this transition of power the forces of civil society had very little influence on the final direction of events. For instance, it became clear that the students occupying the parliament building abandoned their actions without demur when instructed by the military to do so. We can therefore conclude that deals between students and certain groups of military had been made with regard to the occupation. This indicates that the student protest movement, as one of the elements making up civil society, did not act entirely autonomously.

Third, during the first months of the crisis one could hardly speak of organized resistance from within the political parties. Of course this was understandable, since under Suharto organized politics had been completely fettered. This meant that the visible opposition came down to a relatively small group of intellectuals and independent political figures operating from within temporary networks.[43] The role of NGOs during these transition months also appeared to be of no more than a supportive nature. Politically speaking they were not prepared for this crisis, either.[44] Only from within the press was there a consistent flow of criticism and disclosures on corruption and human rights violations by the armed forces. In particular the atrocities committed by KOPASSUS during the ten years of virtual martial law in the most westerly province, Aceh, were revealed in all their aspects.

The fourth, and possibly most important factor for the final position of the armed forces, is the conflict in East Timor. In an attempt to gain international (economic) support, made quite unexpectedly and initially without consulting with the armed forces, Habibie, on 27 January 1999, launched a plan offering a solution to the East Timor conflict. The entire tragedy regarding East Timor can be considered a formal example of Cold War imperatives in action. The annexation of the eastern part of the island of Timor took place in December 1975, just after Saigon had fallen into the hands of North Vietnam in April of that year. It was not until the Cold War had come to an end in 1989 that the West started to show concern with regard to the violations of human rights.[45] As long as Suharto was able to allocate economic revenues to Western investors, though, that criticism was largely muted. The Habibie government, however, did experience the full blast of Western disapproval over the way in which this 'province' was occupied by the military. Civilian advisers in particular pointed out to Habibie that the East Timor question was a 'millstone round his neck', postponing any form of rapid economic recovery through international support. And such a recovery was needed to win the elections of June 1999.

We know how Habibie's plan ended. Contrary to what civil advisers expected, and despite frantic attempts by certain groups within the armed forces to intimidate them by using militia groups, on 30 August 1999 almost 80 per cent of the East Timorese population voted for independence. The frustration on the Indonesian side over this result led to such violent reactions by the military and their militia that the international community, using a United Nations military force, had to intervene. The direct result of this was that the Indonesian armed forces, and their commander-in-chief General Wiranto in particular, were bound to end up in the dock. The process of decolonization of East Timor was completed under Habibie's successor, Kiai Haji Abdurrahman Wahid, leader of the Nahdlatul Ulama, who on 20 October 1999 became Indonesia's first democratically elected president.

During Habibie's interregnum the relationship between the armed forces and politics was rather ambiguous. Habibie and Wiranto had both been appointed as caretakers by Suharto. As a civilian president, after the 32 years of Suharto's reign, Habibie did not know how to prevent pressure and manipulation by the military. It is said that within the presidential palace more than 24 high-ranking officers were in charge of the president's daily schedule. It was also decided that, until the elections planned for June 1999, no vice-president would be appointed. This meant that General Wiranto was able to function as such. So, on the one hand, the armed forces gained more power in political matters, such as drawing up new legislation; on the other hand, though, exposed to the growing freedom of the press, the image of the armed forces grew worse by the day. The reformers within the armed forces used this worsening image to convince the hard-liners to make concessions with regard to new legislation. Yet, protected by their powerful positions, many high-ranking officers did not stop their corrupt practices. This, in its turn, harmed the position and the prestige of the Habibie government, and adversely influenced the way in which the international donor and business community regarded it.

## The Dual Function and the Restructuring of Indonesian Society

On Armed Forces Day, 5 October 1998, a new paradigm for the Indonesian armed forces was published: *Redefinition, Repositioning, and Reactualization of the Role of the Armed Forces in the Life of the Nation.* The basic ideas of this paradigm came from a group of reformers who, after the 1999 elections, also published a book with a more detailed vision: *New Indonesia and the Challenges of the Armed Forces.* That such a critical group should manifest itself so soon after Suharto's downfall is less surprising if the tradition of the armed forces is considered. The Sukarno–Suharto transfer also saw a new paradigm, formulated in a series of critical seminars. The dual function doctrine itself allowed the emergence of an intellectual wing within the military. Many officers went to foreign universities to receive academic educations, and a tradition of analysis of societal trends has existed throughout the New Order. Only when Suharto punished public expression with transfers, back in the 1970s, did this movement go underground. These networks were vulnerable, of course, to intelligence operations and personal feuds.

The group that recently surfaced in the military is the generation of the early 1970s. In those years, elite sons went to military academy rather than university. At least three of the most outspoken figures are relatives of retired generals. For example, Lieutenant-General Susilo Bambang Yudhoyono is the son-in-law of the late General Sarwo Edhie, who was involved in the coming to power of Suharto and responsible for mass killings in the 1960s, and who was later liquidated, probably by Suharto followers. Susilo Bambang Yudhoyono became Coordinating Minister for Politics, Security and Social Affairs in President Wahid's second cabinet (formed in August 2000). A second prominent figure, Lieutenant-General Agus Widjojo, is the son of a general murdered during the alleged 'leftist' failed coup of 1965, so he also has unfinished business with Suharto. He married the daughter of an influential politician in Megawati's PDI–P. A third figure is the editor of *New Indonesia and Challenges for the Armed Forces*, Lieutenant-General Agus Wirahadikusumah. He is a cousin of retired general Umar Wirahadikusumah who, as military commander of Jakarta, assisted Suharto's rise at a crucial moment in 1965. General Umar was rewarded with one term as vice-president, but subsequently he has not dealt with the New Order as a political–economic system. These three generals draw great prestige from their backgrounds, and have been less dependent on Suharto in their careers. That relative independence was used to develop critical visions which, on the basis of Wirahadikusuma's book, can be summarized as follows:

Instead of 'back to the barracks', as proposed by democratic forces in Indonesia, the intellectual generals talk about 'back to the basics'. The basics are hard to define, but call for a variety of ingredients. First of all, there is the critical assessment and redefinition of the dual function doctrine. This also means reinterpreting other doctrines and the historical role of the military. The view now is that dual function, as interpreted under Nasution and especially under Suharto, supports a regime rather than the sovereignty of the people. Here one may quote General Sudirman, the founder of the original people's armed forces. Sudirman told the military on 5 October 1949, in the midst of the fight for independence, that they should never allow themselves to submit to the power of a political party or group because the armed forces belong to the people as a whole. The 'basics', in this context, means a high degree of professionalism and a non–partisan stance 'above any political party or interest'. The concept of 'people' gets a sacred meaning here. One of the authors of the book states that: 'The armed forces ought to be an instrument of the people, because the voice of the people is the voice of the Lord.'[46]

Furthermore, the 'basics' means the military focus on the core business of defence and security, and that no active serviceman is a member of the (regional or national) parliament. On the other hand, the book maintains that a political role remains in guarding essential national interests. It is not very concrete on this point, except in the case of national unity. Quite probably, this means the unitary nature of the Indonesian state, effectively banning a federative structure. But then the possibility of changing the 1945 constitution is acknowledged. In order to safeguard the essential national interest, the armed forces would retain seats in the People's Consultative Assembly (Majelis Permusyawaratan Rakyat, MPR), though the authors do not give any indication of how many seats would be required. (In December 2000 the armed forces and the police had 10 per cent of the MPR seats, which had proved crucial in Wahid's election to the presidency in October 1999).

On other issues, like democracy, law enforcement, corruption and restructuring of the economy, the authors remain vague. No mention is made of a need to divest the army of its interests in business, or even of a gradual scaling-down of these and a concurrent rise in the regular budget, making the financial management of the armed force more transparent. Some generals did make public statements on this point.[47] Also, the first civilian Minister of Defence, Dr Juwono Sudarsono, had pronounced ideas on the need for a gradual approach with a time horizon of ten years to achieve the required transparency and professionalism.[48] The point of contention within *reformasi* is the speed of the scaling-down and concurrent budgetary rise. These differences of opinion are partially caused by different perceptions of the causes of economic crisis and the possible remedies. To what degree should Indonesia accept lectures from the IMF? In other words, to what degree should national sacrifices be made and for which or whose interests? The differences make moderate reformers susceptible to the arguments of hard-liners, who denounce the interventions of the West, especially the IMF, as an intrusion on the sovereignty and integrity of the state and the nation; an intrusion on the basics.

The results of the national elections of 7 June 1999, however, did not bring about a clear winner who could claim the presidency outright. Therefore, the reformers within the armed forces were faced with a crucial question: who to support? Habibie, who would mean a form of continuity with the New Order, albeit with some openness towards the functioning of a free press but also with strong *politik-islam* influences? Or Megawati, with the chance of the armed forces openly opposing Islamic forces? Or Abdurrahman Wahid, half-blind and physically weakened by two strokes, but convincingly democratic? Or, finally, the commander-in-chief, General Wiranto, a candidate from within their own ranks? Initially it seemed that General Wiranto himself was inclined to back Habibie, but then, by the end of September 2000, it turned out that he had decided to endorse the candidacy of Abuddurahman Wahid. When he made this choice, it was generally believed that the reformers within the armed forces had the upper hand and had thus been able to convince General Wiranto to side with Wahid instead of Habibie, or trying to become president himself. A year later, in October 2000, the conclusion had to be much bleaker: the 'dark forces', steered by the cronies of former president Suharto, were working hard to restore the New Order as a political economic system. In that perspective, even the possibility of a political comeback by General Wiranto could not be ruled out.

Because of the stalemate position that had arisen, Amien Rais, the big loser in the elections, was able to suggest a compromise: that of the 'axe in between', meaning a third candidate, one to represent the united Islamic parties, including those parties which had sided with *reformasi*, such as his own National Party (Partai Amanat National, PAN) and Wahid's People's Awakening Party (Partai Kebangkitan Bangsa, PKB). Amien Rais's candidate was, surprisingly, his rival, Abdurrahman Wahid, but Rais made a conditional claim to be elected as chairman of the MPR, the third-highest position within the Indonesian constitutional setting.

On 24 September 1999 society was on the brink of civil war. Due to the passing by the old parliament, at its last gasp, of a very controversial Act on National Security, giving far-reaching authority to the armed forces, there was an outburst of violent protest. 'Reds' opposed 'whites' (Muslims), each backed by military support. Wahid then knew he had to convince General Wiranto to postpone the date of commencement, and in that way the pressure was taken off. The session of the People's Assembly was then able to take place in relative quiet in October. The outcome of that session was that on 20 October Wahid was elected as president and, one day later, Megawati as vice-president. Obviously Wahid had succeeded in getting political support from Wiranto − in exchange, it is said, for the guarantee that once elected President Wahid would not permit an international tribunal to investigate the role of the Indonesian armed forces in East Timor, since that would be considered a violation of sovereignty. Wahid, however, had not promised there wouldn't be an internal investigation, the results of which turned out to be so negative that eventually Wiranto was forced to give up his ministerial position. The critical findings of the investigation owed much not only to the courageous attitude of some of the committee's members, but also to the international threat of setting up a UN tribunal should the internal result turn out to be unsatisfactory.

On 14 February 2000, after months of political tug-of-war, in the course of which he was supported by *reformasi* elements within the armed forces at crucial moments, and by helpful international pressure throughout, Wahid succeeded in manoeuvring Wiranto out of what was then still a politically strong position. He thought he would be able to consolidate this success by appointing his close associate Major-General Agus Wirahadikusumah as commander of KOSTRAD. But support for the 'Wiranto line' within the armed forces appeared to be stronger than Wahid had suspected, so strong that by the end of July – within four months – President Wahid was forced to remove Wirahadikusumah from his post. The president was forced to accept this blow just a few days before the first meeting of the annual session of the MPR. Criticism of his policy had by that time grown so fierce that the chairman of the MPR, Amien Rais (his support for Wahid as candidate for the presidency in October 1999 notwithstanding) had announced a special session to start an impeachment procedure against the president. But a clever political response, in which he played off opposing forces against one another, enabled Wahid to prevent this. He was forced, however, to make deep concessions to the hard-liners within the armed forces.[49] This was in itself a very important setback for the democratic *reformasi* forces. Hence, whether the *reformasi* can be asserted against a restoration of the status quo (in effect, the New Order without the Suharto family) seemed very doubtful one year after President Wahid took power.

*The first fundamental issue: the quest for a new national consensus*
The armed forces maintained a complex pattern of relations with the already-existing and also with the new political parties. In particular, the ties between certain groups within the army – whose alignment could be traced back to now-retired General Benny Murdani – with Megawati's PDI–P were of great importance. This was not only because no less than 48 out of 153 members of her party belonged to Christian minorities, but also because at the regional level many important party functions were occupied by members of these minorities. Hence, Megawati could easily be accused by *politik-islam* forces of being a 'hostage' of the Christian members who allegedly dominated the PDI–P.

Against the background of decade-long discord between the green (Muslim) and the red–white wings within the armed forces, this meant that those tensions were still present. Megawati, given President Wahid's allegedly weak physical condition, was very literally 'just a heartbeat away' from the presidency. Above all it had become clear that, should she be called to the presidency for that reason, she and her party would no longer support the *reformasi* movement. The PDI–P party congress (end of March 2000) in Semarang showed that its internal party politics could hardly be distinguished from those of Golkar during Suharto's reign. Without others being able to step forward as candidates, Megawati was 'unanimously' appointed new party president, leaving all important party functions to the cronies of her husband, businessman Kiemas. Similarly, the party congress of the third *reformasi* party, Amien Rais's PAN, in February 2000 appeared to move away from its original open and secular character by installing a committee, mandated to answer within a year the question whether the party should turn into a religious party based on Islam rather than *pancasila*.

Wahid's opponents within the armed forces and the Islamic parties needed, as it were, simply to wait until the battle for the presidency, and with it the nature of the state, would be opened again. The short-term political and economic success of the Wahid government was no concern of theirs. One can hardly wonder that they failed to cooperate wholeheartedly inside and outside the cabinet. For that reason Wahid drastically changed his cabinet after the outcome of the annual session of the MPR in August 2000. By appointing only those ministers who were loyal to or dependent on him he reckoned to be able to control them better. In doing so, however, he left the formula of a widely supported coalition and hence reduced his political support in the People's Representative Council (Dewan Perwakilan Rakyat, DPR) to a very small minority government. But since the constitution still prescribed a presidential system, this did not necessarily signal the end of his political life. Undeniably, though, he had placed his fate even more securely in the hands of the military, who now had to support him politically. And the military in question had at their command the former anti-terror specialists of KOPASSUS, trained in the United States, ready at any time to be used as 'managers of violence'. The threat did not come from the armed forces as the legitimate instrument of the state, with a monopoly of the use of power, but from provocateurs able to create 'violence' at any moment. As far as that is concerned one may rightly say that the arch-intriguers Ali Murtopo and Benny Murdani had set a standard. By appointing the already retired Lieutenant-General Susilo Bambang Yudhoyono ('SBY') as Coordinating Minister for Security, Politics and Social Affairs, President Wahid hoped to be able to neutralize those 'dark forces' within the armed forces. But the question had to be asked how far 'SBY', known in 1998–9 as a *reformasi* general, would be able in his new function to discipline the hard-liners. The violent events continued after his appointment and there was not much reason to be optimistic.

It was clear that should this form of obstruction last for any length of time the country would be heading towards complete chaos. A military junta, perhaps behind the façade of the 'civil face' of Megawati's PDI–P but bent on the restoration of the New Order, would then be the likely outcome. As an alibi the hard-liners within the armed forces would prior to that accuse the civil forces of administrative incompetence and inability to lead the Indonesian archipelago, just as they had at the end of the 1950s. The omnipresence of created chaos and regional tensions seemed to form the perfect terrain across which the armed forces could regain access to their old positions. If the first fundamental issue the Indonesian society was facing was the quest for a genuine form of national consensus, that had to seem further away than ever after the first 55 years of the republic.

*The second fundamental issue: restructuring the Indonesian economy to end the dual function*
As was suggested at the beginning of this chapter, eliminating the dual function doctrine will require more than a withdrawal of the armed forces from the political

and administrative sectors. This is because a complex military network is woven into the very structure of the economy. It is therefore important to ask whether the new government will be able to track and control the shifting economic roles of high military ranks, and will be capable of removing the corporate and individual military interests from the numerous companies and foundations in which high-ranking military interests especially have been able to nestle over a period of forty years.

A first clue to this can be found in the formation of Wahid's cabinets, and more specifically by asking how much influence the military still have within their most important ministries. The conclusion has to be that the most important departments in this respect, Transport and Communications, and Mining and Energy, in which the military have built up lucrative business interests, were and are still headed by retired generals or someone very close to the military. A third ministry where many and vast military interests are concentrated is that of Forestry and Plantations. Since October it has been headed by a young civilian minister, Dr Nur Mahmudi Ismail, leader of one of the smaller Islamic parties, the Party of Justice (Partai Keadilan). Initially he seemed to live up to the goals of his party, for within a number of months he had reorganized the top echelons of the ministry and had sidelined many high-ranking and corrupt civil servants. But while a former intelligence general remains Permanent Secretary it is doubtful whether the armed forces will ever be separated from their material interests in plantations and forests. Therefore we must conclude, in respect of the second fundamental issue, that one year after the shift in political power the economy remained under the control of the forces that made up the New Order.

The outcome of a transformation process as penetrating as that in Indonesia can never be judged after a period of just one year. One reason for a more optimistic conclusion is that the vast network of civil society organizations – such as the critical press, students and intellectuals, and the many NGOs that have been active since the beginning of 1998[50] – cannot be silenced as easily as in the 1960s. Besides, the geopolitical context in the year 2000 completely differs from that of the Cold War period. To these factors must be added the profoundly damaged image of the Indonesian armed forces, due to their involvement in a vast range of human rights violations, particularly in East Timor. Internationally this now prevents any too-open return to the New Order if financial and economic support from the West is to be expected. However, it would be unwise to place too much confidence in pro-democratic Western sanctions. The international community – the Western countries, but also Indonesia's ASEAN neighbours – holds great stakes in political stability in the region. And if the armed forces were able to guarantee such stability, it is likely that sanctions against human rights violations would be set aside in favour of this priority. And as long as the military continue to be involved on both sides – *reformasi* and status quo – the Janus mask will be the true face of the Indonesian armed forces.

## Notes and References

1 From 1974 till 1999 the Indonesian armed forces were called ABRI (Angkatan Bersenjata Republik Indonesia or Armed Forces of the Republic of Indonesia), and included army, navy, air force and the police; in 1999 the police were separated from the other three forces, and thenceforth referred to as TNI (Tentara Nasional Indonesia); as an administrative unit,

though, the police force still falls under the jurisdiction of the Minister of Defence. Some crucial indicators for the armed forces in Indonesia are as follows:

**Table 6.1.** The armed forces in Indonesia

| | | | |
|---|---|---|---|
| Population (million) | 203.5 | Army main battle tanks | 0 |
| Military expenditure (US$ million) | 2.767 | Navy submarines | 2 |
| Military expenditure/population | 13.6 | Destroyers | 0 |
| Armed forces (1000s) | 298 | Frigates | 17 |
| Armed forces/1000 population | 1.464 | Air Force fighters | 91 |
| Arms exports (US$ million) | 10 | | |
| Arms imports/total imports (%) | 0.14 | | |
| Military expenditure/GNP (%) | 1.5 | | |
| Military expenditure/Central govt. | | | |
| expenditure (%) | 8.9 | | |

Source: *Military Balance, 1999/2000; Sipri Yearbook 1999; UN Statistical Yearbook 1998.*

2 Notosusanto, Nugroho (1984), and many (auto)biographies, including that of Suharto himself, 1989.
3 For instance in a film production in which Suharto's role was the central one.
4 *Daily Kompas*, 1 March 2000.
5 Wirahadikusumah (1999).
6 Permesta, a movement especially active in Sumatra and Sulawesi (Celebes).
7 Darul Islam, especially active in West Java, cf. van Dijk (1981).
8 The slogan 'From Sabang to Merauke' had in fact been copied from the glorious days of colonial rule, when the Dutch were proud of having such a large archipelago under their rule; the revolutionary rhetoric of President Sukarno, in the framework of his nation-building policy, exploited that slogan in his struggle to bring Irian Jaya (West New Guinea) into the Indonesian nation-state.
9 Already in the Dutch colonial period the Chinese had been manoeuvred into a buffer position, in which they were allowed to take up strong economic positions without political rights; at first this was intended to prevent rising nationalism, initially developing along Islamic organizational lines, from establishing a strong economic basis.
10 The collaboration between the Chinese businessman Liem Sioe Liong and then Lieutenant-Colonel Suharto dates from the years of the revolution; as Suharto climbed the military ladder so the economic influence of Liem increased; eventually this would culminate in a huge business empire during Suharto's presidency, with Liem, better known by his Indonesian name Salim, already ranking among the world's ten wealthiest persons according to *Fortune* magazine in the 1980s.
11 Until 1965 Singapore was part of this federation, as were Serawak and Northwest Kalimantan (Borneo).
12 Feith (1962).
13 Next to Sukarno stands Hatta, as second Proclamator, also present at the birth of the republic.
14 Cribb (1991).
15 Peter Carey, British historian and respected commentator on the East Timor issue, compared the historical meaning of this bloodbath in Santa Cruz held for the independence of East Timor with the brutally suppressed uprising at Amritsar in 1919 and its meaning for the final independence of India in 1947; in Carey (1996: 16).
16 Mangunwijaya (1994).
17 Simanjuntak (1989).
18 Loveard (1999).
19 Wandelt (1989).
20 Moreover, the armed forces as such were not even mentioned. Only very recently, during

the annual session of the People's Consultative Council (MPR), held in August 2000, in a new article added as an amendment to the constitution, were the roles and positions of the armed forces and the police elaborated in detail. In particular one provision – in which the role and function of the armed forces in relation to the society is formulated as *Sistem Keamanan dan Pertahanan Rakyat Semesta* (a security and defence system including the total population) – proves that in 2000 the dual function of the armed forces has received even stronger legal reinforcement than it had before (albeit against the wish of the democratically elected president, Abdurrahman Wahid).

21 As an army intellectual he resigned from active duty as a result of the '17 October incident', and until his death at the end of the 1980s played a very important role within the Protestant Christian minority.

22 This also happened in the international field, which in 1964 finally led to Sukarno taking Indonesia out of the United Nations under the slogan 'To hell with your aid'.

23 Before amendment the preamble of the constitution of 1945 stated that it was expected of Muslims that they would live in accordance with the *Shari'a*, a requirement which in fact would turn Indonesia into an Islamic state. Under pressure from some Christian leaders, especially from Eastern Indonesia, where Christians in many islands formed local majority positions, Sukarno and Hatta succeeded in convincing the rest of the Islamic leaders to strike out this phrase.

24 This interpretation of Suharto's position is challenged by Dr Salim Said, a well-known Indonesian analyst of the military (1998). He is an active member of the *ICMI*, however, and his argument may be rather biased in this respect.

25 In Schulte Nordholt (forthcoming) I have given a detailed description of this phenomenon of *preman*-ism and in particular of the role of Ali Murtopo in relation to it.

26 This group of technocrats were to become known as the 'Berkeley Mafia' because of the fact that some of them had studied at that university; this group, however, also consisted of economists trained elsewhere in the United States, or even in Europe (in Rotterdam's Erasmus University, for instance).

27 Schulte Nordholt (1996, 2000: 65–94).

28 See for example Jeffrey Winters (1999), who also mentions a 30 per cent corruption rate in projects financed by the World Bank.

29 Billah (1995).

30 Schulte Nordholt (1999).

31 Without seeking comprehensiveness we will mention: Robison (1986), Bourchier and Legge (1994), Ramage (1995), Schwarz (1999) and Vatikiotis (1999). These are not only very relevant to the theme of this chapter, but they all offer a general narrative overview. It should be noted, though, that, with the exception of the publication by Schwarz (issued in 1999 in a third edition and updated with an account of recent developments until the beginning of that year), nearly all these studies describe the New Order as a stable system.

32 On these themes also some major publications exist. We will mention Sundhausen (1982), Jenkins (1984), Crough (1988), Singh (1994), MacFarling (1994), and Lowry (1996). Further, the regularly updated overviews of appointments and transfers of high officers within the armed forces, issued in the bimonthly journal *Indonesia* (published by Cornell University), are a valuable source to all wishing to stay informed on developments within the Indonesian armed forces as an institute.

33 During the seminars mentioned, there still existed a different interpretation of the objectives of the New Order. But after Suharto had managed to purge his military opponents, such as Lieutenant-General Dharsono, Ali Murtopo's views were implemented.

34 These five functions were collectively referred to as *MUSPIDA* ('consensus of regional leadership'): governor or district officer; regional military commander; regional police commander; regional prosecutor; chairperson of regional parliament (provincial or district).

35 Recently a research report by a group of Indonesian social scientists was published in which the relation between the armed forces and the political parties is thoroughly analysed. In a graph a detailed picture is given of the military–Golkar relationship (p. 111). The

intelligence service interventions within political parties, especially those during the New Order, are described in detail. It is made clear that under the command of Ali Murtopo a special force, Opsus, had been set up to influence and supervise the actions of political parties (*Tentara Mendamba Mitra* [The Military in Search for Partnership], 1999).

36 See, e.g., Iswandi (1998).

37 Iswandi (1998: Table 3.29, pp. 219–29).

38 *Time Magazine*, 14 February 1999.

39 In popular speech those killings were referred to using the acronym *Petrus* (*Penembak misterius*, the mysterious killings), referring at the same time to the Catholic background of General Murdani. In his semi-autobiography of 1989, however, Suharto claims to have given the order for these shootings himself, as a sort of shock therapy. His argument was that the shootings were aimed against growing criminality in those years, but it was generally thought that that statement was particularly meant to make it clear that it was not Benny Murdani, but Suharto personally, the super-*jago*, the game-cock, who should be feared. It is interesting that this book was published just after Murdani had visited Suharto with his 'request' to appoint as vice-president a candidate from 'his' wing within the armed forces.

40 Kammen (1999).

41 In total more than 700 churches and many dozens of Chinese temples were burnt in more than 25 violent incidents between 10 June 1996 and 20 October 1999, when Abdurrahman Wahid became president. The violent actions in the Moluccas, which erupted on 19 January 1999 and have continued, and the incidents in East Timor related to the referendum of 30 August 1999 and its bloody aftermath, are not included in these figures.

42 During an internal military investigation later that year Lieutenant-General Prabowo admitted that his troops were responsible for those kidnappings. This led to his honourable discharge from the army.

43 Estimates differ in the range of 3,000–7,000 individuals, mainly living in the capital, Jakarta.

44 Schulte Nordholt (1999).

45 This evoked international criticism regarding the Santa Cruz cemetery massacre in Dili on 11 November 1991.

46 Wirahadikusumah (1999: 275–92).

47 Most notably, Lieutenant-General Agus Wirahadikusumah himself – since March 2000 acting as commander of KOSTRAD – in July 2000 exposed a case of fraud, allegedly conducted under his predecessor, Lieutenant-General Djaja Suparman. This outspokenness, however, evoked such resistance within the military at large, that President Wahid was forced to replace Wirahadikusumah immediately after his disclosure of the fraud case. This was a severe blow for the president, who had appointed this general with the specific aim of clearing up fraud and misconduct in the military.

48 This minister, though a civilian and professor of international politics, has in-depth knowledge of and extensive contacts within the armed forces due to a previous function as vice-governor of the armed forces' Strategic Institute (Lemhannas). He suffered a stroke in January 2000, however, and was therefore replaced in August by another civilian, also a professor but in the field of state legislature, and lacking Dr Juwono Sudarsonoany's insights and contacts.

49 In an amendment to the constitution they had an article added through which the position of the armed forces and the police was much more securely embedded (see also note 20); but he also had to give in with regard to his tolerant attitude towards the protesting forces in Aceh and Irian Jaya. Using a policy based on dialogue, Wahid thought to appease these forces in order to avoid violence, but after the come-back of the hard-liners within the armed forces increasing violence within these provinces came to seem unavoidable.

50 Ever since the second half of 1998 a vast network of civil society organizations, Indonesia Masa Depan (Future Indonesia), has been active. Within this network thousands of people spread all over the archipelago talk about different scenarios for the year 2010. The objectives of these groups are to stimulate public awareness and debate on which consensus can be based. Broadly speaking four scenarios are used, all four labelled with fairly poetic

names, although three of them are rather negatively charged: (1) 'Scattered Emerald', in which the archipelago falls apart and anarchy rules; (2) 'Waves in the Islands of Peace', in which one can speak of a return to a situation comparable to that of the New Order: a closed society with a high amount of government intervention; (3) 'Roaring Volcano', a scenario in which society is relatively open, but in which, due to the high degree of government intervention, natural resources are rapidly being exhausted, increasing social problems that society is unable to solve; and finally (4) 'Early Morning Sun Clearing the Fog Away', being the most desirable one.

# 7

# The Military, Politics
# and Post-Cold War Dilemmas
# in Turkey

AYLİN GÜNEY

During the last four decades the Turkish military intervened in politics three times (in 1960, 1971 and 1980). Today the high-profile role of the Turkish armed forces as a political army and guardian of the nation is regarded as a major impediment to democratic consolidation. This perception of the negative implications of the military role has been revived especially by the rise of political Islam in the second half of the 1990s, challenging the principle of secularism on which the republic was founded. The role performed by the military wing of the National Security Council (NSC) during this crisis and the attitude it adopted after the crisis was a major issue of contention both within and outside the country. This crisis, together with the pressure for more democratization from the European Union to which Turkey is aspiring to become a member, put the political role of the Turkish military under scrutiny and posed a challenge to its traditional 'guardianship' role.

This chapter aims to explain these challenges, which left the Turkish military with a dilemma. First, the origins of the guardianship role of the Turkish military will be explained with reference to the historical cultural legacies they inherited, which formed the backbone of their ideology, doctrine and principles. Second, the actual exercise of the guardianship role will be elaborated. Finally, the challenges to the perceived role of the Turkish military will be assessed with reference to the impact on the military–civilian relations of post-Cold War developments including the Torumtay affair, the challenge of political Islam in late 1990s, the Kurdish issue and Turkey's future membership of the European Union.

## The Origins of the 'Guardianship' Role of the Turkish Military

There are three important historical legacies that have had an impact upon the construction of the guardianship role of the Turkish military: the Ottoman legacy, the legacy of the independence war; and the legacy of Mustafa Kemal Atatürk and the Kemalist ideology.

It is important to note that the 77-year old Turkish Republic rests on a 600-year Ottoman legacy. This legacy contains two important traditions, one bureaucratic and statist, the other military. In the glorious times of the Ottoman Empire, the role of the army was identified with the state; in one author's words, 'the Ottoman government had been an army before anything else'.[1] From the nineteenth century on, the military became ardent supporters of Westernization and democratization as the rule of the Sultan descended into corruption and decline. Students at military staff colleges and particularly at the medical schools became the core membership of secret political organizations. Sultan Abdülhamit II's attempt to reverse Westernizing innovations in many fields while allowing them to continue in the army pushed the officers further toward the forefront of social change. Thus arose the conviction that the officer corps was the vanguard of a new enlightenment, to be based on the adoption of Western techniques and patterns of thought.[2]

With the demise of the Ottoman Empire and the foreign occupations of Anatolia, the army was the institution that first mobilized the population under the command of Mustafa Kemal Atatürk, a former Ottoman officer himself. The military's role was further strengthened by victory in the independence war and the consequent inception of the Turkish Republic. Thus, the military became identified with the republican Turkish population from the beginning and attained a high degree of legitimacy in the eyes of the public as the guardian of a national destiny preserved from the domination of foreign powers. At the end of the independence war the new state was left with the generals, lieutenants and other army officers, on one side, and a highly illiterate, leaderless, devastated and extremely poor society on the other. The challenges that faced the military were the lack of a democratic culture, the strong influence of Islamic tradition and regional upheavals, as in the case of Kurdish sheikhs. Thus the ideological roots of the nation-building process that would follow the independence war were shaped within the military corps and the military pioneered the project that would transform Ottoman identity to Turkish identity.

With the victory of the independence war and the proclamation of the Turkish Republic, the definition of the military's mission and role became even clearer. The founder of the republic, Atatürk, was aware of the important role of the military. Yet, he also saw it as an impediment to the development of a democratic regime. On the one hand, he enunciated a litany of exhortations to the military to be the bulwark of the state against all domestic and foreign enemies.[3] On the other hand, the most important principle of the young republic was that, while the army was not excluded entirely from the political scene, serving army officers were barred from exercising independent power in the central organs of the state. The military was even deprived of the right to vote and the number of retired officers was kept quite low in the lifetime of Atatürk. Thus Atatürk defined the Turkish military's role as the 'ultimate guardian of the republic especially between the years 1927–1938'.[4] The basic principles to be protected under the guardianship of the military were secularism, democracy and the integrity of the country. Deriving their legitimacy from these principles put forward by Atatürk, the Turkish military have perceived themselves ever since as the guardians of the Turkish Republic. This dedication to preserve the secular and democratic order makes the Turkish military different from other militaries in the world.

## From Guardianship to Decision Making: the three military interventions

The Young Turkish Republic started its experience with the multi-party regime in 1946; the three military interventions that followed the transition to multi-party politics in Turkey should be seen in this light. The army did not intend to get rid of democracy; on the contrary, in each case its professed purpose has been to further consolidate democracy. In neither of the three interventions have the military entered into an alliance with a political party, social group or class. On the contrary, they have demonstrated a deep-lying lack of trust towards the politicians, who are regarded as striving for political interests rather than the interests of the state and the nation.

The first intervention took place on 27 May 1960 when the Turkish army overthrew the Democrat Party (*Demokrat Parti*) government, mainly in reaction to the perceived threats to the democratic and secular functioning of the republic. The increased authoritarianism of the government, its ambivalence toward modernity and secularism and its ultra-conservative social and economic policies were the main reasons for the intervention. However, the transition to democracy took only one year and the 1961 constitution, prepared in the aftermath of this *coup d'état*, has been regarded as one of the most liberal constitutions by many students of Turkish politics. One of the central elements of the new system was the creation of the National Security Council as a legal mechanism to assure a voice for the military.[5] The second military intervention came about ten years later through a *pronunciamiento*. It was a reaction to the culmination of a deteriorating political situation marked by a rising tide of violence, the fragmentation of political parties and weak and ineffective government.[6] However, rather than a full intervention, it was a declaration stating that the generals would use the authority vested in them to protect the state and would take power directly only if the civilians refused to provide more effective rule.[7] As a result of this *pronunciamiento*, the military was satisfied with a promise from the leading parties to enact a series of constitutional amendments designed to strengthen the hand of the government in dealing with violent dissident groups.[8]

The next military intervention took place on 12 September 1980. The factors which compelled this intervention were

> the incapability of the governments to fight with infiltration and destructive effects of armed conflict which accumulated to a level that threatened the very existence of the State and nation, because of the political squabbles, petty party politics, capriciousness, fantasies, unreasonable demands and both overt and hidden aims which ran contrary to the characteristics of the Turkish state. [9]

This was regarded as the most profound crisis of the state ever to occur during the history of the Turkish Republic. Even though actual military rule lasted for only three years, the 1982 constitution – prepared under the supervision of the military and approved by the Turkish people through a referendum – envisaged an enlarged constitutional role for the Turkish military, a role which endures and continues to be contested today. The most important legacy of the 1982 constitution consists of the articles that laid down the institutional organization of the military's guardianship role through the National Security Council as established under Act No. 2945 of 9 November 1983 (see Box 7.1).

**Box 7.1** The Turkish military and the National Security Council in the 1982 constitution

Art. 118 of the 1982 constitution stipulated:

The National Security Council will consist of the president of the republic as presiding officer, the prime minister, the chief of the general staff, the ministers of Foreign Affairs, Interior and Defence and the commanders of land, air and naval forces and of gendarmerie. Depending on the issue discussed relevant persons can be called in to express their views. The Council of Ministers is obliged to 'consider with priority the decisions of the National Security Council concerning necessary measures for the protection of the existence and independence of the state, the unity and indivisibility of the country and the peace and security of society'.

The duties of the National Security Council under the Act No. 2945 include:[10]

1 The determination of policies concerning the planning and implementation of the state's national security policy decisions and the necessary co-ordination;
2 The determination of the measures relating to the implementation of national objective plans and programmes prepared in accordance with national security policy;
3 Following closely and evaluating the national elements of power that influence the state's national security policy and the social, economic, cultural and technological environment and developments;
4 The determination of the fundamental principles that will further the direction of national objectives;
5 The determination of the measures required to maintain the existence and independence of the state, the integrity and indivisibility of the country and to maintain public peace and security;
6 The determination of the measures to maintain constitutional order, to ensure national unity and integrity, to unite the Turkish nation around the ideology, principles and reforms of Atatürk and the national values and ideals, all of which will guide the nation towards the national objectives;
7 The determination of views for states of emergency, martial law, mobilization and state of war;
8 The determination of the necessary principles for the inclusion of measures and funds related to the following issues in the development of plans, programmes and annual budgets: general defence made by the public, private institutions, organizations and citizens in peacetime, wartime or in the post-war periods, national mobilization and other issues;
9 The determination of measures for the inclusion of programmes and annual budgets, services oriented to the society − financial, economic, social and cultural − and other issues required by the general defence services;
10 Proposing options regarding the past and future international treaties signed in the field of national security. The NSC notifies the Board of Ministers about the views, measures and principles of court decisions and fulfils other tasks as specified in the acts.

The definition of the concept of 'national security' is important in this respect, since it is the main reference point for the military. Threats to national security provide the basis for intervention in politics by the Turkish military. 'National security' is defined as the protection and maintenance of the state's constitutional order, the national image, integrity, and interests, and the contractual law that constitutes the legal parameters of the policy.[11] The potentially wide range of issues that could be covered by the National Security Council agenda constituted the source of future challenges to the 'guardianship' role of the military.

## Political Islam and the Military in Post-Cold War Turkey

The collapse of the Berlin Wall, the dismantling of the Eastern bloc and the disappearance of the immediate communist threat necessitated a restructuring in the armies of the Western Allies and the United States. NATO started to reconsider its priorities and the US closed down most of the bases that had been of crucial importance in containing the Soviet Union during the Cold War years. Despite these developments, however, the emerging ethnic and regional conflicts in the Balkans, the Caucasus and the Middle East, and the crisis that followed Iraq's invasion of Kuwait did not allow a reduction in the role of the Turkish military. The military continued to be very important in the problematic geo-political context that surrounded Turkey. In the context of the Paris Charter and the Conventional Forces in Europe Treaty (CFE) (Avrupa Kon Vansiyonel Kuv-vetler Anlasmasi) signed in 1990, the threat to national security was defined as the 'separatist movements of the terrorist organization the Kurdistan Workers Party (Partita Karkaren Kurdistan, PKK)'.[12]

The first challenge to the 'guardianship role' of the military came in 1991 when the Gulf crisis erupted. The crisis confirmed once again the perception that the military displays professional traits in dealing with matters of national security, whereas the civilians lack them. The then chief of the general staff, Necip Torumtay, had been critical of President Özal for frequently leaving the military out of the decision–making process on issues they deemed critical.[13] For example, when Turkish radio and television stations reported the closure of the pipeline along the border, this was how Torumtay became acquainted with the decision. He didn't approve of Özal's meddling in military matters and he complained that the military received no guidelines from the government on the basis of which to determine military strategy during the Gulf War.[14] Özal's persistence in making military suggestions and demands, including an operation against Iraq, was the last straw: it led to Torumtay's resignation on 3 December 1990. His statement of resignation read: 'The principles I believe in and my understanding of the way the state should function make it impossible for me to go on holding this office.'[15] It was the first time in Turkish history that a chief of the general staff had resigned as a result of a conflict of views with a civilian leader. The incident was also an important sign of the military's reluctance to take action and become directly involved in politics, even when they totally opposed a given course of action.

The military faced another serious challenge which they perceived as infringing the democratic and secular character of the republic: political Islam. This time the military did not refrain from involvement in politics. Yet the crisis was resolved not by resorting to arms, but through a 'civilian coup'. The military managed the crisis through the following steps.

*Step 1: The military as cautious observers*
The 1995 general elections in Turkey resulted in the emergence of the religion-oriented Welfare Party (Refah Partisi) as the most popular party. The military did not act immediately after this result: they observed the political process without intervening. On 28 June 1996 the Welfare Party and the True Path Party (Doğru Yol Partisi) formed a coalition government, generally referred to as Refahyol. The coalition was a major surprise inside and outside Turkey, since it was the first time in the history of the secular Turkish Republic that a religion-oriented party had emerged as the best-supported party in the elections, obtaining 21 per cent of the votes and finally coming to power in a coalition government. Nevertheless, the coalition government obtained a vote of confidence from parliament (278 to 265), even though it remained a question whether the Welfare Party would put its anti-secular projects into action immediately. The military did not lift a finger when the Welfare Party came to power in its coalition government through democratic means. The military did not appear to be lacking in confidence but at the same time remained cautious, not wanting to act with prejudice against the government. However, during the Supreme Military Council meeting on 1 August 1996 13 military officers who were involved in some kind of reactionary initiative were dismissed from the army: this was a first clear sign that the military were highly sensitive about the issue.[16]

*Step 2: The military warn civilians*
The military nevertheless expressed its concern to the government and the president about separatist and fundamentalist movements which were aiming to overthrow the Kemalist, secular and democratic order. For instance, in a briefing given by the chief of the general staff to President Demirel, the military informed him that 'reactionary activities' had become the primary internal threat, together with the separatist movements. Some neighbouring countries, especially Iran and Syria, provided support to the terrorist activities of the PKK and to some religious organizations in Turkey. The briefing was a clear sign that the military were considering intervention. The Turkish armed forces formulated the West Operation Concept and formed the West Working Group,[17] made up of intelligence experts who closely monitor radical Islamist activities and attempts to subvert the secular regime.

*Step 3: The military take steps*
However, the military was not satisfied with the role of the president, who was not really able to do much more than warn the government and attempt to solve the crisis through democratic means. On the basis of intelligence reports gathered from the National Intelligence Agency and the General Directorate of Security, the military had become extremely alarmed by the 'reactionary activities'[18] taking place within Turkey, aimed at initiating an Islamist revolution against the secular state by creating an alternative structure and joining forces with big business supporters.[19] The increasing number of religious orders (*tarikat*)[20] and religious associations (*dernek*) as well as their fundamentalist vision[21] and abuse of 'spiritual power' to get material benefits[22] from the poorer parts of the society revealed the intensity of the threat to the secular and democratic order. Meanwhile, Erbakan's invitation to the major religious order leaders to attend a dinner at the prime minister's palace in religious garb during the holy month of Ramadan was

intolerable for the military as well as for the secular elite of Turkey.[23] It was perceived as giving recognition to the religious orders at the state level, and so undermining the secular character of the Turkish Republic.

According to the military's own intelligence, the increasing number of prayer leader-preacher schools (*imam-hatip okullari*), the number of their graduates, the Koran courses and the number of students who enrolled in those courses, were alarming.[24] The political behaviour and preferences of the graduates of these schools and the Welfare Party voters showed similarities, and yet the values of the former were harsher and more extreme than those of the latter. The students are educated in conformity with Islamic values and principles. The increasing number, financial strength,[25] and illegal structuring[26] of private sector companies that gave support to these movements, and the support given by the government to these companies, were also perceived as alarming developments by the military.

Increasing numbers of Islamic cadres and practices in state organizations, and Welfare Party projects for restructuring some state institutions, were another problem for the military. There were also important projects directly aimed at the military itself, such as making the chief of the general staff accountable to the Ministry of Defence instead of the prime minister, revising the rules about dismissals of officers from the Turkish armed forces on the basis of their involvement in Islamist activities, and changing the regulations regarding entrance to the officers' clubs. The response of the military to these issues was harsh and immediate. First, the military stated that the attachment to the Ministry of Defence was an issue that concerned the whole system of military organization. In order to be able to make a slight change in the structure of the military organization, it might be necessary to change the whole system. Regarding the second issue, it was stated that military personnel were not permitted any involvement in political activities; nor were they allowed to enrol in political parties or associations. According to the Personnel Code, if they did so they were expelled from the army. With respect to the third issue it was stated that 'those who are dressed so that they reveal a certain political or religious tendency, which is against the dress code, may not enter the officers' clubs'.[27]

The increasing number of armed Islamic mlitants and their links with terrorist organizations was another problem. A report prepared by the security forces and submitted to the National Security Council stated that Hizbullah (The Party of God) and the Great Islamic Raiders' Front (Islami Büyük Akincilar Cephesi, IBDA-C) were among the most active and violent organizations in Turkey. These organizations perceived the democratic and secular republic as an enemy and they targeted it.[28] It was known that some civil society organizations including the National Youth Foundation (Milli Gençlik Vakfi) provided support to these groups.

Another alarming development for the military were the public speeches of some deputies and municipality leaders of the Welfare Party, which targeted openly the Atatürkian principles, the democratic and secular nature of the regime, and the unity and integrity of the country. Representative of these was one of Prime Minister Erbakan's public speeches:

> Jihad is the first precept and all of us will be included in this army and become soldiers.... This is the army of the Welfare Party. You have to work to strengthen this army. If you do not work then you are from the potato religion. The degree of Muslimness of a

person is measured by how much he/she donates money to jihad. You have to give your *zekaat* [religious donations] to the Welfare Party. Welfare means to work for the establishment of the Koranic order. If you support any other cause, your place is hell.[29]

The foreign visits paid by Prime Minister Erbakan to some Middle Eastern countries such as Iran, Libya, Egypt and Pakistan further aggravated the tensions between the Welfare Party and the military. Despite many warnings that Iran and Libya especially were the supporters of terrorism both in Turkey and in the world, Erbakan decided to visit the leaders of these countries with the purpose of establishing good relations between his and their governments. However, the Libya visit especially was regarded as a total failure; the Libyan leader Muammer Quaddafi put both Turkey and Erbakan in a difficult situation with some of the things he said. He criticized past governments, pointing at what he called their 'pro-American and pro-Israel attitudes', said that Kurds were being mistreated in Turkey and, last but not least, called for the establishment 'of an independent nation of Kurds under the Middle Eastern sun'.

Quadaffi stated that although Libya had some business connections with Turkey, Libya wasn't pleased with Turkish foreign policy. He also said that his sole consolation was that Erbakan had become the prime minister in Turkey: 'There is a Supreme Islam Commanders Council and Erbakan is a member of this council. I salute him as a commander of Islam.' The visit was considered as a great failure on the part of Erbakan and was subject to harsh criticisms in Turkey. However, the harsh criticisms directed against him by the opposition parties and the media did not seem to bother the prime minister at all. He calmly stated: 'These remarks are unfair and reflect negative propaganda. They will all disappear with one blow of our breath when we return to Turkey.'

The above-mentioned concerns of the military finally drove them to place the issues on the agenda for the first time at the National Security Council meeting held on 28 February 1997. It was certain that the military's perception of the internal threat had changed and that priority was now being given to the activities of political Islam. At the first meeting the military wing of the National Security Council listed the above-mentioned issues, which they considered as a threat to the democratic and secular order of the Turkish Republic, and suggested some measures that should be taken by the coalition government. They also mentioned that some 'sanctions' might be applied if these measures were not taken.

*Step 4: The military's wait-and-see policy*
All these points made by the military wing of the National Security Council revealed that the military was extremely sensitive regarding some basic principles. The most important four principles stated by the chief of general staff were: (1) Atatürk nationalism, seen as the source, foundation and infrastructure of Turkey's unity and integrity; (2) Atatürkian principles and revolutions, seen as the starting points of development and modernization, and their dynamic inner content; (3) secularism, seen as the essence of intellectual development and the freedom of religion, conscience and thought, and as the *sine qua non* of democracy; and (4) liberal democracy, seen as the way of life for free and civilized people and the natural path of development. These are the common denominators and essential considerations of the nation. 'We have to stick to these and we do not give any concessions to anyone under any conditions.' [30]

The measures put forward by the military in their declaration of 28 February were followed up at the other National Security Council meetings. The military wanted to give some time to the coalition leaders to start implementing the suggested measures. For this reason they did not pressure the government too much during the second meeting, which took place on 31 March 1997. However, after two months, at the third National Security Council meeting on 26 April 1997, military members of the National Security Council said that adequate steps had not been taken in the past month to check on fundamentalist activities; that such activities continued despite the internal memorandum the Interior Ministry had sent to the provincial officials. They displayed two videos, one called *An Enemy of God*, a controversial theatrical play performed in Erzurum (an Eastern province of Turkey) and the other depicting street scenes from Istanbul's Fatih district, teeming with people dressed in an anachronistic manner in violation of the dress code. The commanders also criticized the way the Welfare Party deputies had turned that year's pilgrimage into a political show.[31] The military continuously drew attention to the politically loaded speeches of Welfare Party deputies at the pilgrimage and in Turkey. Even though the military made its uneasiness public, Prime Minister Erbakan kept on saying that his government had very harmonious relations with the military and that no efforts to destroy this harmony would bear fruit. Finally the secretary-general of the chief of general staff, Erol Özkasnak, made the counter-statement: 'The Turkish Armed Forces are in harmony only with the ones who believe in the secular Republic that Atatürk founded and who work with this purpose. It can and will not be in harmony with any others.'[32]

On 26 May 1997 the military decided to convene a special meeting of the Supreme Military Council with the purpose of expelling officers who had engaged in 'reactionary activities'. The second purpose of this meeting was to get Erbakan to approve the prioritizing of 'reactionary activities' within the National Military Strategic Concept (Milli Askeri Strateji Konsepti). During the Supreme Military Council meeting the military also pointed out that they would not permit the infiltration of Islamist forces into the army, and that they had expelled 161 commissioned and non-commissioned officers who inclined towards 'fundamentalism'. This appeared to be a direct response by the upper ranks of the military to 'divisive efforts' by the Welfare Party to suggest that it had plenty of supporters within the armed forces who were in total disagreement with senior officers.[33] According to the vice-chief of general staff, Çevik Bir, 'if anybody can find someone who is involved in dirty business and has not been expelled from the army yet, we throw away our ranks'.[34] This revealed the determination of the military to stay away from political Islam and politics in general.

*Step 5: The military act as a pressure group*
It was obvious that after these National Security Council meetings, the military was not convinced that the measures it had called for were being implemented sufficiently by the coalition government. It then resorted to other means and started a series of briefings that were given to the media (29 April 1997), to the civil society organizations, to universities (2 May 1997), and to judges and public prosecutors (10 June 1997). This was another way to enlighten different sections of society about the perceived threat from the radical Islamist activities that had gained ground in Turkey. General Güven Erkaya, commander of the navy, later stated in a newspaper interview that 'they [the commanders] regarded their

mission as based on two pillars: first, they should make the Turkish people realize that reactionary activities were a threat and, second, this problem should be solved not by the armed forces, but by the civilians … civil society … organizations … i.e., the unarmed forces'.[35] These briefings, directed at society at large, were probably the best means the military could employ in aiming at a civilian solution.

In the briefings the military explained the perceived 'threat from the Islamic reactionary movement' in a very detailed and documented way. The aim of the briefings was stated by the chief of the general staff as 'to contribute to the civil society's struggle with the reactionary movements by exposing the situation'. The military also took care to establish the legal basis for its briefings by pointing to the relevant articles of the constitution and the Turkish armed forces internal service code. The military stated in the briefings that

> after 1984, against the threat perceived from the separatist terrorist organization, an internal security operation concept was formulated. Domestic developments in Turkey and the attitude of countries around Turkey required a rearrangement of the national defence concept. This rearrangement has been made, and first priority has been given to the internal threat, namely the reactionary activities of political Islam directed against the country's indivisible unity and against the basic characteristics of the republic defined by the constitution.[36]

The main issues presented in the briefings were not very different from the agendas of the National Security Council meetings. In addition, the military also revealed their complaints about insufficient implementation of the National Security Council decisions, even though the National Security Council document had been signed by the government.

*Step 6: The civilian coup*
All in all, the military concluded that, despite the National Security Council decisions, the 'reactionary forces' had been intensifying their activities in a coordinated way. The duty of the Turkish armed forces is defined clearly in article 35 of the Internal Service Code (*İç Hizmet Kanunu*) No. 211 as 'to defend and to protect the Turkish territory and the Turkish Republic that is defined by the Constitution', and in the Internal Service Bylaws, art. 85/1 as 'to defend the Turkish territory and the Republic against internal and external threats through arms if it is deemed necessary'. It was clear that the military were trying to justify to civil society their indirect involvement in politics through the National Security Council.

Meanwhile, two other initiatives strengthened the position of the military. First, the attorney-general of the Council of State, referring to article 68, paragraph 4 and article 69, paragraph 6 of the Turkish constitution, applied to the Constitutional Court with the allegation that 'the Welfare Party is leading Turkey into a civil war'. The allegation was primarily based on the speeches and statements of some members of the Welfare Party, including the prime minister.[37] The pressures on the Erbakan-led government augmented with the support of the politicians and the civil society organizations. Many politicians made statements supporting the reaction of the military. For instance, the leader of the Republican People's Party, Deniz Baykal, stated that

> the Turkish Armed Forces have worked like a democratic mass organization and contributed to the formation of a public opinion against the Welfare Party. The mask of

the Welfare Party has fallen without an interruption in the democratic life. This is totally a new strategy, and a new phase in the military–civilian relations from which everyone should derive a lesson.[38]

The joint declaration of some leading civil society organizations confirmed Baykal's observation: 'The Welfare Party has been trying to destroy democracy by using democracy.' They stated that they would do whatever they could to protect Atatürkism and called on the parliament to do its duty: a secular government, attached to Atatürkian principles, should be formed immediately.[39] The tension ended when the Erbakan government resigned as a result of the above-mentioned pressures from the military, civil society organizations and the media. President Demirel appointed Mesut Yılmaz, leader of the Motherland Party, to form the new government on 20 June 1997.[40] The decision created intense debate since some party leaders, including Erbakan and Çiller, thought this decision to be totally undemocratic. Çiller, who was expecting to be asked to form the new government, even called it a 'Çankaya [presidential] coup'.[41] President Demirel, on the other hand, defined his decision as a 'political rather than a numerical one'. Even though the second-largest party in parliament was the True Path Party, it was obvious that if Çiller had been asked to form a government, she would have reverted to the same coalition. What would change would only be the name of the coalition: Yolrefah instead of Refahyol. And the tension would continue.

The one-year period of the coalition government between the Welfare and the True Path parties (June 1996–June 1997) marked some very important changes in military–civilian relations in Turkey. Despite the anti-secular policies of the Welfare Party, who led the government, the military did not take power in its hands, but rather acted as an interlocutor by bringing the vitally important issues to the agenda. It is obvious that the Turkish military are a learning institution and have learned a lot from their past experiences. In the past the military have been criticized for intervening in the political life of the country. This did not mean, however, that the military kept silent when it perceived a threat from increasingly 'reactionary activities'. The military used two constitutional channels simultaneously to overcome this crisis. The first was the presidency which had been strengthened by the 1982 constitution. In this regard, President Demirel was a major constitutional channel through which the military could transmit its unease to the political elite and to society. Second, the military declared its unease several times through another democratic and constitutional channel, the National Security Council. It gave briefings concerning the external but especially the internal threats that Turkey was facing. In this way, the military tried to do whatever it could without resorting to arms.

The military continued to perform its 'guardianship' role, however, even after the new government was established. On 31 October 1997 the National Security Council approved the *National Security Political Document*, which encompassed the list of principled measures considered vital by the National Security Council and submitted to the Council of Ministers. The principles, in summary, included the following points: (1) the 'separatist and reactionary' activities are equally important threats and should be given priority; (2) political Islam continues to be a threat for Turkey; (3) there are tendencies within Turkish nationalism to revert to racism and the radical right-wing Mafia want to take advantage of the situation; (4) the extreme left is still a threat, if somewhat diminished; (5) relations with the Turkic republics should be strengthened and their governments should be supported; (6) attention should be paid to the perceived threat from Greece. Even though Turkey does not desire one, it should not overlook the possibility of a conflict; (7) structures should be created to develop local and cultural traits without imposing them in the public sphere; (8) the objective of Turkey's full membership to the EU should be maintained, but the negative attitudes of some member states should not be disregarded; and (9) economic efforts, including privatization, should be increased in integrating Turkey within a globalized world.[42]

## The Military and the Kurdish Question

Another important challenge to the 'guardianship' role of the Turkish military in the 1990s was the so-called Kurdish question. The direct involvement of the army since 1984 in a sort of guerrilla warfare with the extremely violent organization PKK was a focal point of critical debate on Turkish issues, especially internationally. By many the situation was perceived as a war against the Kurdish population in south-east Anatolia, who wanted to establish their own state. However, the military enjoyed considerable legitimacy among the people living there. They often supported military operations against the PKK insurgents, who threatened their lives. The head of the PKK was finally arrested on the initiative of the military, who threatened a declaration of war to gain the dismissal of Öcalan from Syria. Öcalan was finally arrested in Kenya and brought to Turkey, together with other PKK leaders. Since then their activities have been kept under control. Regarding the death sentence on Öcalan, the military stated that 'first the judiciary and then the parliament could decide about the issue according to the constitution'.[43] The arrest of Öcalan increased the credibility of the army in the eyes of the Turkish public: an opinion poll showed that it was considered the most important entity behind the successful arrest.[44]

The decreasing intensity of the armed conflict in south-east Anatolia left the military to review its mission there. At present the military is involved in a campaign called 'Citizen and Soldier Hand in Hand'. In the context of this campaign the military spent 3.4 billion Turkish Lira in 1999 to support social programmes aiming to rehabilitate the region. These activities involved

> providing electric lines to 77 villages, building water pipelines to 112 villages, paving roads in 1,028 villages, providing health services in 9,368 villages. The aid also included the repair and maintenance of schools, providing clothing and school equipment to children, and giving assistance to the students taking university exams, forestation, maintenance of the health centres, building carpentry establishments.[45]

This kind of civil–military development effort is apparently appreciated by the local population, as it is elsewhere. It even places the state's efforts under scrutiny. When, for example, the national government put a budget ceiling on development in the region, the regional chamber of commerce was not satisfied with the amount of aid. They stated that they would submit a report to the office of the chief of the general staff who they saw as one who knew the situation in the south-east much better than the civilians, and therefore would guard their interests.[46]

## The Military and EU Membership

The Helsinki European Council held on 10–11 December 1999 produced a breakthrough in EU–Turkey relations since the Presidency Conclusions of the European Council stated that

> Turkey is a candidate state destined to join the Union on the basis of the same criteria as applied to the other candidate states. Building on the existing European Strategy, Turkey, like other candidate states, will benefit from a pre-accession strategy to stimulate and support its reforms. This would include enhanced political dialogue, with emphasis on progressing towards fulfilling the political criteria for accession with particular reference to the issue of human rights, as well as on the issues referred to in paragraphs 4 and 9a.[47]

The military's attitude towards this decision of the EU was positive and they stated that 'they supported the EU decision in this respect'.[48] The military also stated repeatedly that it is the responsibility of the politicians to meet the criteria of the EU and that Turkey should develop its legal system and democracy.[49]

However, the developing relations between Turkey and the EU had some important repercussions for the 'guardianship' role played by the military in a couple of ways. First, the EU made known its concern over the enhanced role of the army in Turkish political life and criticized the National Security Council as an undemocratic institution. The autonomous role of the National Security Council was contentious if Turkey was to meet the political requirements of the Copenhagen Criteria[50] and was even regarded as an 'obstacle' to full Turkish membership of the EU.[51] The most recent EU document, 'Progress Report on Turkey for the year 2000', only restated the EU's disquiet about the role the National Security Council played in the political life of Turkey. The report stated that there was no change in the role of the National Security Council and that its presence seemed to place serious limitations on the functioning of the government. In addition, the report stated that there seemed to be a clear lack of parliamentary control on issues related to defence and security. To counter this criticism, recently it was proposed to increase the number of civilians in the National Security Council from five to eight. The military response was ultimately positive to this proposal.[52] Under the new arrangements, the representatives of the Human Rights Coordinating High Council, the Ministry of Finance and the Ministry of Justice, together with the vice-prime ministers, would be present at National Security Council meetings.[53]

Another issue is the status of the office of the chief of the general staff. The chief of the general staff is appointed by the president and is responsible to the prime minister. The basic argument of the EU is that in developed democratic regimes the chief of the general staff is responsible to the Ministry of Defence, and that this should also be the case in Turkey. However, the Turkish military oppose this proposal, arguing that the present arrangement is due to the *sui generis* status of the military in Turkey, and that there is no necessity to change it. A second issue of contention between civilians and the military is the report the secretariat of the Human Rights Coordination High Council prepared in the light of the EU's Copenhagen Criteria. The report sets out the changes Turkey needs to make regarding human rights issues. The representative of the National Security Council secretariat had some reservations on the changes that would be made in articles 13, 14, 26, 27 and 28, which stipulate 'limitations' on fundamental rights and freedom of thought.[54]

Despite officially stating their firm attitude on the maintenance of the integrity, secularity and democratic character of the Turkish Republic, the Turkish military seem aware of the necessity of making changes in their strategies and policies to integrate more with civilians. One example of such an initiative are preparations for 'brainstorming or brown-bag meetings' to be held between the chief of the general staff and the press. The basic aim of these meetings is 'to avoid incomplete and misinformation of the people inside and outside Turkey on important issues concerning Turkey'.[55] The hosts at the recent cocktail-hour invitation issued by the military to leading journalists were in civilian clothes, a symbolic sign of the will to overcome differences. The invitation to the journalists Mehmet Ali Birand and Cengiz Çandar was another sign of goodwill, since before this journalists were banned from entering the officers' clubs.[56]

## Concluding Remarks

The post-Cold War role of the Turkish military in politics revealed some important changes. Even though the Turkish military continue their 'guardianship' role, its scope seems to have changed depending on the circumstances and especially when it is compared to the period when the three direct military interventions took place in Turkey. The military seems to be learning from their past mistakes and are making an effort not to repeat them. The resignation of the chief of the general staff during the Gulf crisis and the constitutional role that the military tried to play in tackling the challenge of political Islam were the two main indicators of this learning process. A second aspect of this change is the will to cooperate with civil society in spreading awareness of threats to national security. The publication of the memoirs of Torumtay in the aftermath of his resignation from office and the briefings given to the civilian sectors of society by the military during the crisis stemming from the rise of political Islam constitute two example of this will.

It is obvious that the Turkish military want people to realize that their ultimate aim, like that of all professional armies, is to remain in the barracks. They never tire of stating this. Yet the weakness of the political system in Turkey – undermined by petty party politics, high levels of corruption, the threat of political Islam and perceived threats to the unity and integrity of Turkey – will provide the military with arguments to continue their 'guardianship' role. Challenges to the role of the military in the post-Cold War period have revealed the fact that the scope of the 'guardianship' role may remain limited and less 'political'. Even in such a case, this will be the result not of increasing domestic and international pressures, but of self-evaluation by the military.

## Notes and References

1 Hale (1994: 2).
2 Hale (1994: 2), Rustow (1957: 515).
3 Harris (1988: 181).
4 Özdag (19: 43).
5 Harris (1988: 182).
6 Heper and Tachau (1983: 23).
7 Harris (1988: 187).
8 Heper and Tachau (1983: 23).
9 Birand (1991).

10 İba (1998: 185–6).
11 İba (1998: 185).
12 İba (1998: 106).
13 Heper and Güney (1996: 628).
14 Heper and Güney (1996: 628).
15 Torumtay (1993: 130).
16 İba (1998: 221).
17 *Sabah*, 12 June 1997, *Turkish Daily News*, 14 June 1997. The name of the group comes from Turkey's secular, democratic structure which it perceives as Western-oriented, and which aims to send the message that they are combating fundamentalist threats backed by neighbouring eastern countries. The intelligence department chiefs of land, navy and ground forces, the operational bureau chief of the gendarmerie and two major-generals of the general staff are the key figures who determine the agenda of the West Working Group. West Working Group investigators probe many different spheres, including various levels of government, the local administrations of provinces and towns, alleged radical Islamist infiltration of the army, outlawed fundamentalist organizations such as Hizbullah, pro-Islamist businessmen who allegedly back the fundamentalists, pro-Islamist media outlets, certain parties' youth branches, and pro-Islamist private schools and universities. The West Working Group is authorized to demand directly any information from all military headquarters and intelligence departments, and from other state intelligence institutions such as the National Intelligence Agency.
18 For a detailed account of the reactionary activities perceived as a threat by the military, see Heper and Güney (2000).
19 This is stated in the 'Report on Reactionary Movements' submitted to the military. See *Milliyet*, 1 March 1997.
20 The dictionary definition of *tarikat* is 'small brotherly groupings of mystics living in communities'. *Tarikat*s are traditional Islamic organizations which have responded to various cultural, social and political needs. After the establishment of the Turkish Republic the networks of secret mystic brotherhoods were pushed underground when the *tarikat*s were outlawed by a law that banned *tekke*s and *zaviye*s in 1925 during one-party rule. In this period they provided a semi-secret platform for conducting covert Islamic activities. After the easing of the rigid secularist measures during the period of the Democratic Party rule (1950–60) and the provision of civil liberties by the 1961 constitution, *tarikat*s began to operate on a semi-legal basis and they forged alliances with political parties.
21 An interview with the leader of the Aczmendi *tarikat* in one of the leading newspapers confirmed this concern of the military. The leader stated that:
> even if the regime today does not want to go, it will have to go. If the leaders themselves do not choose *Shariat*, the people will bring it. And God forbid, there will be a lot of bloodshed then. Now we are at the third stage of this struggle. And many other organizations that want to bring the *Shariat* order are moving underground.... We are peaceful people. However, we do not remain silent if we are insulted regarding religion. If we are forced to, we do not listen to any rules and regulations. And what we can do in this case cannot be compared with either DHKP–C [Devrimici Halk Kurtulus Partisi Cephesi – Front of the Revolutionary People's Independence Party, a radical leftist terrorist organization] or with the PKK.

The leader also answers the question, 'What if the army does not let *Shariat* come?'
> We believe that the army will become wiser. There comes such a point that the army will be weakened. It kills one, a thousand and then remains helpless. As in the case of Iran, when the nation revolts, the only thing that the army can do is either to join them, or to leave the country with the red passports (*Milliyet*, 5 October 1996).

22 The illegal commercial activities of the religious order leaders and their sexual abuse of their disciples were the main issues that attracted the attention of the military. The main example of such a scandal was revealed by the wife of such a leader, who made confessions about the inner organization of the religious order that she was in and the sexual abuses of her husband

towards his disciples. In addition she confessed that her husband had some illegal links with the municipal leaders of the three major metropoles (Istanbul, Ankara and Turkey) who were members of the Welfare Party. This issue occupied the headlines of the newspapers in Turkey for weeks. *Hürriyet*, 20 January 1997.

23 Prime Minister Erbakan made some statements to the leaders of the religious orders such as 'We are waiting for your prayers. Maintain your unity and togetherness. Everybody should refrain from activities that would harm the government.' One of the religious order leaders stated after the dinner that 'we all prayed to God and we talked about the orders of God. We always help [the party], we gather votes [even] from others (*Hürriyet*, 12 January 1997).

24 For instance, even though the yearly need for imams is 2,288, the number of graduates from these schools every year reaches 53,553. The rest of the graduates (51,265) are oriented towards the faculties of political science, law and police academies. The main objective is to form the cadres of political Islam. (*Hürriyet*, 12 June 1997). These numbers were then presented by the military in the briefing that was given to the media on 11 June 1997.

25 Of the six companies that support reactionary activities each has a capital accumulation of more than a hundred trillion Turkish Lira (*Milliyet*, 11 June 1997).

26 They have enlarged themselves through the money that is collected from the Turkish workers in foreign countries by the European National Vision Organization (a religious organization), through hundreds of foundations they have established in Turkey, and through the income obtained from the collection of sacrificial skins (*Milliyet*, 11 June 1997).

27 *Milliyet*, 19 November 1996.

28 It is also stated in the report that the aim of these organizations is to establish a state based on *Shariat* in three stages. The first stage is called *teblii* (communication), in which all the people are invited to fight for the acceptance of Islam by all the people. The second stage is called *cemaat* (community), in which the community fit for the communication is formed. The third stage is *jihad* (holy war), in which there is a call for armed struggle for the establishment of an Islamic state.

29 *Milliyet*, 2 May 1997.

30 *Sabah*, 25 December 1996.

31 *Turkish Daily News*, 28 April 1997.

32 *Hürriyet*, 3 March 1997. Also see *Yeni Yüzyil*, 2 February 1997.

33 *Turkish Daily News*, 15 May 1997.

34 *Hürriyet*, 25 December 1997.

35 Interview with journalist Yavuz Donat, *Milliyet*, 13 August 1997.

36 *Turkish Daily News*, 30 April 1997.

37 *Milliyet*, 22 May 1997.

38 *Yeni Yüzyıl*, 18 June 1997.

39 *Sabah*, 22 May 1997.

40 *Yeni Yüzyıl*, 21 June 1997.

41 Çankaya is the presidential palace.

42 *Hürriyet*, 4 November 1997.

43 *Milliyet*, 18 December 1999.

44 *Milliyet*, 2 February 2000.

45 *Milliyet*, 14 April 2000.

46 *Milliyet*, 6 April 2000.

47 Presidency Conclusions, Helsinki European Council, 10–11 December 1999, paragraph 12.

48 *Milliyet*, 18 December 1999.

49 *Radikal*, 12 April 2000.

50 The Copenhagen Criteria contain three main requirements: (1) to provide the stability of institutions that secure democracy, the supremacy of the rule of law, human rights and respect for minorities; (2) to have a functioning market economy and to be able to cope with the competitive pressures and market forces in the European Union; (3) to be able to meet the responsibilities that would stem from full membership as well as from the political, economic and monetary union.

51 *Hürriyet*, 19 February 2000.

52 The chief of general staff stated that 'the number of the civilians can even be increased to a hundred. It does not matter. The National Security Council takes decisions by consensus under the chairmanship of the president, not by lifting fingers' (*Milliyet*, 25 July 2000).

53 *Milliyet*, 25 July 2000.

54 *Milliyet*, 18 June 2000.

55 *Milliyet*, 23 September 2000.

56 *Milliyet*, 15 November 2000.

# 8
# Army, State and Nation in Algeria

LAHOUARI ADDI

Ever since independence in 1962, the army has played a critical role in the political life of Algeria. The army's prominence is based on three factors: its historical legitimacy, the personal popularity and charisma of Colonel Houari Boumédiène, and the army's populist discourse, which offered the prospect of a form of social and economic development oriented towards poverty alleviation. By the start of the crisis in the 1980s, the historical legitimacy of the army had declined with the renewal of succeeding generations. Having failed to deliver on its promises, the populist discourse had also lost its credibility and influence.[1] From being based on the charismatic leadership of a popular figure, the Algerian regime evolved into a military oligarchy after the death of Boumédiène in 1978. The appointment of the notably uncharismatic and politically unambitious officer, Colonel Chadli Bendjedid, as president in 1978 was to lead the regime into a particularly violent period of crisis. In an effort to escape from this dead-end, the same regime that had appointed Bendjedid then nominated Abdelaziz Bouteflika as president. By doing so, the regime expressed the desire to turn back the clock and return to the successes of the past, by choosing in Bouteflika a former 'brother in arms' of Boumédiène.

Among what are commonly known as 'political armies', Algeria is a case in point. As a country of the Third World where independence was obtained through a war of national liberation, the army had acquired a considerable degree of historical legitimacy as a result of this experience. The army came to be identified as the main source of political power in the new state. During the 1960s and 1970s, the popularity of the regime was bolstered by its leader, the charismatic Colonel Houari Boumédiène (1965–78). What undermined the confidence of the ruled in their rulers was the failure of the whole development project, promised by official policy statements but undermined by demographic changes (the population tripled in forty years). The result was a profound sense of social malaise and discontent. During the 1980s, the regime was buffeted by pressures caused by internal and external changes and tried to break free of its past policies. However, there were serious and undeniable political obstacles in its way, which resulted in a dangerous lack of political reform, and a tendency towards stagnation.

These obstacles will be analyzed in relation to the army's political role, making it possible for us to understand the nature of the violent crisis that has beset the country since 1992. Nevertheless, it is first necessary to define a key notion that will be much used in this research; namely the notion of a political army. Basically, an army can be said to be 'political' when it is itself the main source of state power, and presents itself as the key holder of political legitimacy. In Algeria, there is a political army in this sense, since the army itself appoints the president and the members of the government. The army also intervenes in the political domain, under the supervision of a special service, La Sécurité Militaire (Military Security), which is under the control of the Ministry of Defence.

The regime in Algeria has always sought to minimize the importance of the army in the construction of state power, but in the violent confrontation with the Islamists the real picture emerged, through the use of the Military Security forces. In general, both researchers and public opinion have had a tendency to ignore the army's supremacy in Algeria, even though this is clearly a central dimension of the country's overall political sociology. Nevertheless, the serious crisis which shook Algeria in 1992 unavoidably focused public and media attention on the military hierarchy, which now appeared openly as the single main actor in the political arena. To get a better understanding of the role of the army, it is important to bear in mind its pivotal place at the origin of the present Algerian political system, and to grasp the strength of the army's connection to the very idea of the Algerian nation. When Boumédiène, then Minister of Defence, deposed the elected president, Ben Bella, in June 1965, despite the latter's election two years previously, this coup was carried out in the name of historical legitimacy.[2] It was also in the name of restoring historical legitimacy that Boumédiène then appointed Chadli Bendjedid as president in 1979, and in 1992 proceeded to oust him on the same grounds. Even the decision to annul the elections of December 1991, in which the Islamists won the majority of the vote, was taken in the name of historical legitimacy. This time Mohamed Boudiaf, who was a co-founder of the National Liberation Front (Front de Libération Nationale, FLN) and in exile since independence, was the chosen one. In all these cases, the army's position in Algerian political life is closely tied in with the whole question of historical legitimacy, which is itself a critical issue for any political system, whatever its complexion.

## The Bipolar Nature of Power: a contradiction in motion

The main contradiction within the Algerian political regime is the bipolar nature of power relations. On the basis of this bipolarity, opposing 'clans' are formed, each of which seeks to control the state administration. Even seeking to discover who really controls political power in Algeria is not a neutral exercise, since it involves unveiling the mechanisms for the reproduction and distribution of political power, as well as the inner contradictions of the regime itself, and the violent crisis it is experiencing. The two-sided structure of state power frames the whole field of political life. For this reason, it is necessary to examine this bipolarity in more detail, so as to integrate the nature of the Algerian power structure into the whole history of the nationalist movement in the post-independence era. The bipolarization of the regime is not recognized in the official discourse because the legitimate power of the army is neither institutionalized nor constitutional. There thus arises a gap between rhetoric and reality, between the officially sanctioned lines of authority within state institutions and the influence of informal networks on decision making at different levels of the state bureaucracy. At an individual level, military personnel are among those most critical of the inefficiency and incompetence of state administrative personnel. Yet they do not see the connection between this lack of competence and their own controlling role over the powers of state. Any senior military officer finds it perfectly normal, for example, that it is the military that give the go-ahead for forming a new government, and issue detailed advice on which civilians are to be selected to form part of such a government.[3]

For the military, such privileges are justified by their role of providing historical legitimacy to the political leadership, given the army's place in the foundation of the state. Nonetheless, the military have generally veered away from installing a military regime as such, given the legacies of the anti-colonial struggle. This is why, despite the importance of the army, the Algerian regime is not a military regime, let alone a military dictatorship of the Latin American type. It is, instead, an authoritarian regime which in large part derives its legitimacy from the armed forces. The army, in turn, expects the regime in power to prevent any independent civil society forces from emerging, and thus to avoid the public institutionalization of conflict.[4] The roots of the authoritarianism of the Algerian state are not found in its military origins, but rather in the populist ideology which the army upholds. It is as if the latter has consistently demanded, since 1962, that the state administration should create a new society based on equal citizenship, and underpinned by state guarantees, with everyone depending on the state for their subsistence.

From this point of view, one can interpret the historical legitimacy of the army as a potent political resource, which allows the army itself to intervene in politics – both directly and indirectly – in order to bring about the desired adjustments in government policies and to carry out the role entrusted to it. Thus, for example, stressing the uniqueness of the party, and placing the economy under state control in the name of socialism, were measures to control society and prevent the emergence of autonomous and potentially rival political, economic and cultural elites. This explains why economic reforms, required since the mid-1980s, have never been applied. If such reforms ever were implemented, the inevitable result would be the withdrawal of the state from the economic sphere. The political cost would be that the state was obliged to abandon its capacity to use material resources for political ends, in order to control Algerian society. Privatization policies do not fit in with the established order, in which the army controls the state, which in turn controls society.

An absolutist and authoritarian understanding of power underpins the military's ideological outlook, in which power is seen as an end in itself, and a necessary means of dominating society in order to deny or stifle political conflict. This form of power has been perpetuated at the cost of the weakening of civil society, particularly in the economic and cultural spheres. In this way, state power has undermined itself too, since the limits of political power depend on what society as a whole can provide. At the same time, the army's 'political culture' is historically speaking one legacy of a colonial system that consistently refused to make any concessions that might improve the lot of Algerian people, or enable them to participate in the political affairs of their own country. After the Second World War, independence through armed struggle was the only way out of this anachronistic position. Legitimately engaged in revolutionary violence, the FLN was born out of the very rigidity of the colonial system to which it was opposed. Having been submitted to a brutal form of domination under French colonialism, Algerians adopted violence as a means of resolving political conflicts. Independence was achieved only after seven and a half years of war, and at the cost of several hundred thousand lives. As independence was seized through revolutionary violence, an Algerian state was established under the overall control of the army. This remains the situation today, with the armed forces acting rather like a single party regime that cannot tolerate any opposition to its own monopoly position. The dominant culture of violence remains deeply ingrained among the ruling class, and largely accounts for their persistent intolerance towards any kind of freedom of expression.

It should not be forgotten that the FLN itself disintegrated shortly after independence. The movement was in a sense reintegrated, or absorbed into the army in the form of a populist ideology which preserved the FLN's role symbolically; the army thereby came to embody the historical heritage of the FLN. In portraying itself as the soul of the nation and the conscience of the state, the army drew on this legacy and on the collective memory of what the FLN represented. The regime's populism was expressed most starkly by Colonel Boumédiène, and in particular in his opposition to multipartism, which he regarded as divisive of the general national interest. As Algeria's political leaders were fond of reminding everyone, the old political parties had not been able to bring about the downfall of the colonial regime, and had done no more than create divisions among the general mass of the population. In addition, more recently created political parties are accused of recreating the inequalities of the colonial system through sanctioning private property. The army therefore presents itself as the champion of the whole nation, opposed to the legalization of political parties and devoted to the defence of the nation from all its internal and external enemies.

## Houari Boumédiène: a charismatic military leader

During the war of 1954–62 political instability arose out of the numerous conflicts that emerged between the leadership of the nationalist movement and the local authorities in the *maquis* (the regional leaders of the revolutionary movement). Boumédiène became chief of staff in 1959, and was assigned the task of disciplining these *maquis* and imposing political and military order among them. From the time of independence, the classical army structure that Boumédiène started to organize in Tunisia and Morocco was designed to neutralize any moves towards insubordination among leaders of *maquis* in the interior. In the meantime, Boumédiène refused to take over the reins of power himself, and instead invited Ahmed Ben Bella to act as head of state. Whilst the head of the armed forces nominated the head of state, the latter formally appointed the former as Minister of Defence. Boumédiène was able to unify the army and reintegrated former combatants from the interior of the country; as Minister of Defence, he subsequently emerged as the dispenser of political authority, and no major political decision could be taken without his agreement.

From 1962 onwards, state power in Algeria was divided into two distinct forms; the legitimate power of the army, and the 'executive power' of the president and government. The constant battle between these two forms of power for control over the state has affected Algerian political life since independence. In seeking to assert his relative independence from Boumédiène, President Ben Bella relied on Colonel Tahar Zbiri, whom he appointed as major-general without consulting his own Minister of Defence. Ultimately, the friction between Ben Bella and Boumédiène found expression in the *coup d'etat* of 19 June 1965, which some referred to as a simple 'readjustment', given that the number of people removed from office was fairly small.[5] In fact, within the terms of the logic of the regime, the contest between 'legitimate power' and 'executive power' now resolved itself fatally in favour of the former.

In seizing executive power himself, Boumédiène took the precaution of not appointing a head of the army, in order to avoid falling victim himself to the same deadly logic that had afflicted his predecessor. He therefore retained the post of Minister of Defence for himself, and created a 'Revolutionary Council'. He himself presided over this collective body, which was declared the ultimate repository of national sovereignty and historical legitimacy. In creating this public institution, Boumédiène was able to avoid accusations of personal ambition, whilst using the council as a cover behind which important decisions could be made. The subtle fiction of collectivism was doubly advantageous: it institutionalized historical legitimacy by detaching it from the military hierarchy, and on the other hand, it allowed Boumédiène, as president of the Revolutionary Council and head of state, to keep a firm hold simultaneously on legitimate and executive power.[6] In this way, he was conforming to the logic of a political system which, whilst tending to concentrate power in the hands of a single individual, was also opposed to personalistic forms of political leadership. Even the fiction of collective decision making, behind which Boumédiène hid, could not protect him from a near-successful attempt in December 1967 by the chief of staff, Colonel Zbiri, to overthrow the regime by military force.

After this coup attempt ended in failure, and in order to guard against any further disturbances of the military machinery, Boumédiène initiated a wide-ranging programme of economic and social reform, and sought to associate these changes with his own persona. Further feeble attempts by the military to oust Boumédiène were hopeless, given the degree of popular attachment to him as a political leader, and given his own close identification with the national liberation movement – out of which the army itself had arisen. The president was able to undermine his potential rivals in the armed forces by keeping himself somewhat aloof from his original power base within the army, and by advocating a more populist set of economic and social policies. These included plans for mass industrialization, an agrarian revolution, public enterprises run along socialist lines, and free state services for all, including health care. All this went hand in hand with a more overtly charismatic and personalistic style of leadership, which was eventually rejected by the Algerians.[7]

This programme, incorporating economic modernization, radical agricultural reform, social justice through universal education, free health care and the creation of employment, did reflect many Algerians' popular aspirations after independence. In giving priority to these goals, Boumédiène transformed himself into a charismatic leader who inspired the confidence of local communities. For the most part, the Algerian public trusted him as a leader whose personal legitimacy was based on the personal qualities he placed at the service of the society's shared goals and visions (material progress, the equitable distribution of resources, and the achievement of other utopian aims buried within the collective unconscious of the Algerian populace). After several years of turbulence during the 1960s, state power was consolidated around Boumédiène himself, who came to be regarded as the repository of legitimacy, in large part because in his speeches and pronouncements he forcefully expressed the aspirations and hopes of ordinary Algerians, giving the 'people' the feeling that they were taking a more direct part in political life through his own intervention and personality.

Boumédiène was able to mobilize popular political energies for the benefit of the state public administration, to which the specific task of developing Algeria's economy was allocated. However, personal charisma is neither a stable base for rule nor an inexhaustible source of legitimacy. Maintaining charisma depends on the constant juggling act of matching public expectations and demands with the resources available to satisfy such demands, both materially and symbolically. In this particular political climate, the cult of the leader produces the illusion that injustices can be redressed. It must be said also that Boumédiène was certainly a skilled leader, who resorted to the use of force only when there was no other option available. Under his presidency, Algeria experienced a period of relative peace and stability which was unusual in its history. Although he knew how to exercise control over people, Boumédiène nonetheless did not have much understanding of modern economic and political culture. He had a quasi-mystical belief in the ability of the state, provided it was run by well-trained, able and committed officials and bureaucrats. His vision was one where politics was rooted in the individual psychology of policy makers. If his conception of the ideal Algerian society had not been so utopian and unrealistic and led the country into crisis, Boumédiène might have been a twentieth-century Massinissa or Abdel-moumen.[8]

Generally speaking, for the Algerian elite the underlying problem that emerged from the war of liberation was the question of how to construct a non-partisan state capable of controlling a conflict-free society; in achieving this, the option of establishing particular institutions to deal with problems of legitimacy and sovereignty has not even been considered. Algerian society has tended both to naturalize the whole question of state legitimacy and to fetishize sovereignty, through a political discourse that formally denied yet simultaneously mythologized these qualities. Whether applied to the nationalist discourse of the army or to the Islamic discourse, this political dilemma had to be resolved one way or the other. It is useful to remind ourselves of the meaning of such terms as legitimacy and sovereignty, both in theory and in relation to practice. We will now consider some of the ways in which such questions of legitimacy and sovereignty have arisen in the context of Algeria.

## Political Legitimacy and Sovereign Power

It is possible to distinguish sovereign power from executive power within the dominant structure of the state. Sovereign power is held in the name of legitimacy, and executive power is exercised by the government and distributed among the various administrative levels, from the minister to the administrator. Sovereign power is delegated to the authority of the government in place, which is responsible for administrative affairs and the management of the mainly oil-based revenues. In organic terms, state power is a form of hierarchy, in which each level has the prerogative to be obeyed by the level below. At various levels of the administrative ladder, a subtle pecking order distributes power so that each successive rank has progressively more power than that below it, and less than the rank above.

There is, however, a difference in the nature of power allocated to the top tiers of the state administration, compared with power at other levels. The upper echelons derive their power from outside the hierarchy, and on the basis of a form of legitimacy that created the hierarchical structure of the state in the first place. The external source of this elite's power is the constituent legitimacy of the state itself, which ensures the general consent of the governed. The state bureaucracy functions as an administration which passes on orders through delegation. Within this structure, the head of state is delegated by sovereign power (the king or queen in a monarchy, the electorate in a democracy, and the army in Algeria's case). It is this that gives the leader the ability to take advantage of his authority to direct the state administration and to obtain the general compliance of the governed.

Legitimacy establishes the basis for administrative authority, and makes it possible for such authority to be accepted without excessive use of physical force or coercion. Legitimacy is also expressed through the shared consent of the popular majority, who agree to obey those in authority and state power.[9] Legitimacy – in other words the internalized belief of the governed, whether subjects or citizens, which leads them to voluntarily obey without being physically forced to do so – is an essential basis of state power, and for that matter of any other form of power relationship. This form of power enables those who govern to secure the obedience of the majority of those over whom they rule. If necessary, force will also be used to gain the compliance of a minority to the norms of the established order. Legitimacy, in this sense, is the mechanism by which a majority of the population supports a political regime, and recognizes it as operating in the people's general interest.

The operational efficacy of legitimacy in this sense depends on the belief among the majority that the regime is well-intentioned, and that it is committed to protecting and promoting the general interest, whatever difficulties it may face in doing so. The power of the state to impose itself is derived from the mobilization of the energies of this majority; what matters in this context is not the ability of the state to exercise physical force in order to gain compliance, but rather its ability to derive legitimacy from popular beliefs. If political authority is regarded as legitimate, then those in power can mobilize the potential energies of all those who hold this view – in order, for example, to use it in confrontation with any minority that might not acknowledge the legitimacy of the regime. This mobilization of the majority makes it possible to defend the existing political system. In Algeria, the legitimacy of the political system, as in any other case, is historically rooted; in this case it is indissolubly linked with the national liberation struggle that was waged in order to bring an end to colonial domination. Legitimacy is first and foremost the product of historical processes which may combine to lend it great efficacy or alternatively may serve to remove its capacity to function effectively. To put it another way, legitimacy always has a historical dimension, and unless it is actively renewed and reconfirmed, can lose its ability to underpin state power and effectively integrate the masses.

For reasons to do with the country's history, the Algerian regime established itself as an administrative state (the state being reduced to the bare bones of its administrative structure). Within such a framework, sovereignty is neither officially declared nor located within particular institutions, as it would be in an ideal legal-rational state structure. Legitimate power, in this context, is hidden behind institutions which have no basis in political reality, and in this sense prevents the national community from becoming aware of its own ability to exercise powers of sovereignty. This fear of public exposure arises out of neither cynicism nor machiavellianism, but out of the fact that the political sphere is not clearly distinguished from the religious and social spheres. The military hierarchy, from which such legitimacy is derived, is not even aware that it displaces the electorate by exercising sovereignty in its place. The electorate in turn does not ask for this sovereignty back, so long as it considers that it is being used wisely.

Patriarchal communal structures of authority are not aware of themselves as autonomous from the great meta-social forms of security, as Alain Touraine calls them, of God, Nature, History and Morality.[10] Members of such a society do not seek to exercise their sovereignty, or at least not in the institutional forms usual in a parliamentary democracy.[11] At this point, it can be emphasized that the problem of sovereignty only arises in a society where there is functional differentiation, but not in a context where political, psychological, religious and moral spheres lack autonomy from each other.[12] In the few ideological texts that exist, the army refers to national sovereignty as something which it protects from external attack. No reference is made to popular sovereignty, as expressed through universal suffrage. The army identifies itself with the collectivism of the Algerian nation, but not with the electorate as such. The electorate is ignored since it is assumed that there are no political conflicts among Algerian citizens, and therefore no need to go through the periodic process of sorting out a majority and minority in terms of public opinion.

The only conflicts which are acknowledged openly are those between Algerians and foreigners, and between patriots and traitors. The latter conflict is not to be formalized in any case, since the only solution is to exterminate the traitors. This approach accounts for the bloody nature of the present crisis, since for one side traitors include all those opposed to the national community, and for the other side the traitors are all those opposed to Islam, which is taken to define the political community. In neither of these forms of antagonistic political discourse does the notion emerge of an electoral body, or of popular political sovereignty. This is because such notions presuppose the sense of a neutral public space in which individuals can exercise their civil and political freedoms, and in which a minority has the recognized right to oppose the majority.

In such a context, the rule of law, in the sense of a system of modern law based on popular sovereignty, is simply not possible. This is because the political leadership does not consider itself sovereign and allows the army, or – in the case of the Islamists if they ever came to power – would allow an Islamic army to control the process of legitimation. This situation can account for the laziness or the zeal with which those in power violate the juridical regulations they themselves put in place, and which in theory have the force of law for every citizen. Various competing clans and their followers even go so far as to parade their ability to break existing regulations with impunity, in order to demonstrate their powerful position. In short, laws which are put into force by the state administration are ignored or respected according to the relative dominance of various political clans. Without a clan, the individual is delivered to the arbitrariness of the Hobbesian state. He or she must pay in order to benefit from any law that accords some civil rights, and must also pay if he or she wants to escape from the constraints imposed by a particular piece of legislation. This double-bind means that public officials have exorbitant powers, since they are in a position to interpret the law, and also to decide whether to apply it or not in a particular situation, depending on the relative advantage they can draw from either option. The growing gap between the population and the state arises out of this form of administrative power and the tendency for officials to abuse the public and submit them to corruption and arbitrary governance. The reforms instituted in the early 1980s in Algeria were intended to close this gap between the state and the people, and to stabilize the regime in power. It was the ambiguity of reforms intended to consolidate the status quo which helped to provoke the violent crisis now facing the country.

## The Ambiguity of Political Reform under Chadli Bendjedid

When Boumédiène died in 1978, the army was opposed to the idea of reviving the Revolutionary Council, believing that this body had worked against its interests. It therefore appointed as Boumédiène's successor the regional military commander Chadli Bendjedid, who lacked his predecessor's dominant personality. The newly appointed president was unable to impose himself on his peers, and lacked the charisma needed to embody legitimacy. The regime thus entered a period of crisis and paralysis which would work to the benefit of the Islamists. When they appointed Benjedid as president, the military undermined the foundation on which the regime was constructed, and created a political vacuum that the Islamists would come to fill. Across different societies, experience suggests that legitimacy is expressed either through particular persons (in the form of charismatic domination) or in the more depersonalized form of institutional power (in the form of the modern state and legal–rational authority).[13] So long as the political sphere is not separate from forms of mystical nationalist and religious ideology, power will tend to be identified with a particular human being, namely a charismatic personality in whom the members of the national community recognize themselves. This charismatic personality is expected to ensure the unity and cohesion of the nation by defending it, or rather by organizing the nation to defend itself against external threats.[14] The fatal mistake of the army has been to refuse both charismatic leadership and free elections, instead preferring to install as presidents political leaders with limited abilities. Examples include Chadli Bendjedid, Ali Kafi, Liamine Zéroual and Abdelaziz Bouteflika. One of the few exceptions was Boudiaf, who was assassinated.

The charismatic authority of the leader is essential to the ability of the patriarchally structured regime to reproduce itself. This regime needs the leader whose legitimacy is based on a populist form of political discourse, which translates symbolic values and images into political terms. The personal qualities of the leader are essential to the regime's continued survival; he must be an arbiter, and must be strongly committed to his office, devoting many hours per day to his work. Such qualities certainly distinguished Boumédiène from his successor, although it is also true that Chadli Bendjedid's term of office was during a difficult time, the model put in place by his predecessor having reached the end of its useful life, and the period being marked by the collapse of world oil prices in 1985–6. His government initiated reforms which were intended to improve the productivity of the economy, but their reforms were thrown out by the army, which considered them too liberal and feared that the free market would undermine the political capacity of the populist project.

The regime in power in Algeria provoked a crisis that was potentially fatal for its future survival. It did this by failing to put in power a leader with whom the public could identify, and by failing to create institutions with the capacity to regulate power relations between the state and the public. The lack of clear leadership created a vacuum which the Islamists were to exploit by taking power, whether through the ballot box or by force. Chadli Bendjedid tried to give a constitutional basis to the single party system, and thus to institutionalize power. When the Revolutionary Council was abolished, it was replaced by an elected Assembly, which became the official holder of national sovereignty. In reality, however, control over national sovereignty remained firmly in the control of the army through the office of the president, who was elected through universal suffrage at the end of an electoral campaign run by a single party in support of a single candidate. The constitution allows the president to derive his power from the electorate, and this enables him to form the government and outline to the government the political and social policies that he has promised to implement. But this constitutional image is illusory, given that the president himself is chosen by the military elite; the electorate is asked to ratify the military's choice, and the president is as a result highly dependent on the military elite that has selected him. The president can play off one faction or clan against another. Within limits, he can also choose who his collaborators will be, but his room for manoeuvre is strictly limited since he cannot himself take over the legitimate power of the army. With such dependency on the army, a special relationship is maintained between the presidency and the Ministry of Defence, which influences the presidency politically and in personal terms. Formally speaking, these kinds of influences should be coming from the FLN, the single party.

Officially, the FLN controlled the country and was the basis of political authority. Observing the real workings of the institutions of power, and the relative weight of the party *vis-à-vis* public officials and the army, suggests that the official supremacy of the party was a myth.[15] Both under Boumédiène and his successor, Bendjedid (1979–92), the FLN was organized as an administrative arm of the state, with its own hierarchy and budget, under the control of the president's office. The party never played any major political role, and never took part in any important decisions. Instead it operated as an outer garment for a regime where the army played the role of a dominant single party, and was thus the main source of political power. Under the cover of the FLN, any political debate that did not take place within the party structure was prohibited, so as to neutralize any local challenges to the dominant political order. In particular, the goal was to prevent the emergence of new elites, and to prevent them from gaining any autonomy. As living conditions deteriorated and corruption became an increasing problem, the flaws in this system were exposed, and this provoked various internal and external challenges to the system. After the riots of October 1988 (which caused the death of dozens of young protesters), the regime was obliged to introduce a number of institutional reforms in order to ensure its own survival.

As a leader, Chadli Bendjedid believed in the importance of formal institutional structures inherited by his regime. The system he inherited lacked flexibility, and the changes he introduced created additional obstacles to effective decision making. Bendjedid gave the party an importance that it lacked under Boumédiène, and he expected the National Assembly to play its proper part within a parliamentary system. He also created the post of prime minister, under the control of the assembly. At the same time, he introduced some notable changes in the organization of the army, including the creation of the rank of general. The greatest change in the organization of the army, however, was the decision to marginalize the Military Security forces, having restricted these forces and having limited their powers to those directly attributed by official regulations. All these reforms appeared obvious enough to Chadli Benjedid, but having introduced them his regime lost much of its coherence in the 1980s. Ministers were used to implementing the orders of Boumédiène and hesitated to take any decisions, preferring to wait – as in Boumédiène's time – for instructions from the president himself. As the system became blocked, and was confronted with the collapse of world petroleum prices, paralysis resulted as clan competition for shrinking resources intensified. The regime was organizationally incapable of being reformed. The only options were either to reinforce the existing logic in order to restore some coherence and hence some effectiveness to the regime, or alternatively to create a completely new regime in which the army would cease to hold the reins of power. Lacking the breadth of vision required, unable to master the subtleties of politics, and above all incapable of intellectual insight, Chadli Bendjedid was unable to manage the transition which he wished to see through following the riots of October 1988.

Democratic reforms were introduced through the constitution of February 1989, but the binary nature of state power, which the military hoped to preserve intact, proved a stumbling block to genuine democratization. The military agreed to open up the political system and allow the operation of a multi-party system, electoral competition, freedom of the press to restrain corruption and to improve the overall credibility and effectiveness to the regime. They believed that multi-partyism would revive the fortunes of the FLN through electoral competition. The purpose of the democratization process was thus to bring about an institutional reshuffle, by deriving executive power from the ballot box without undermining the unwritten, underlying constitution of the regime that the army is the basis of state power. The military did not fear the outcome of the elections, since they expected the FLN to reach a compromise with the Islamic Salvation Front (FIS) within the National Assembly, and form a government which would continue to recognize the overall legitimate power of the army. What resulted, namely the outright victory of the FIS, threatened the political hegemony of the army. There was the distinct danger that a single party, not the FLN, would form a government without any reference to the army, and might even impose its own Minister of Defence. This would have meant the installation of a new regime, the end of the bipolar structure of state power, and the end of the army's legitimate power.

The paradox of democratization in Algeria was that the existing political leadership sought to bring electoral legitimacy, which sanctioned the government, in line with historical legitimacy, which was embodied in the army. The military authorities expected these two forms of legitimacy to coincide, and thus to restore to the regime its popularity and to reduce the level of corruption and inefficiency in the public administration of the country. In its attempt to resolve the problem of corruption, the military exposed a fatal flaw in the underpinnings of their own position. They ignored the principle that any system rests on a single power base, with only one ultimate source of legitimacy. Far from strengthening the regime, the constitutional reforms of February 1989 hastened its liquidation, bringing about a violent crisis. The regime sought to escape from this crisis by reverting to the strategies of the 1960s, and this was symbolized in the return of Bouteflika, a former minister under Boumédiène. The current regime's composition is incompatible with multi-party politics, since its leaders accept neither the independence of the judicial system, nor the principle of freedom of expression, nor the outcome of free elections.

## The Presidency of Abdelaziz Bouteflika

The appointment of Bouteflika as the army's preferred candidate in the presidential elections of April 1999 was a sign of changes the military wanted to usher in. By choosing a civilian who had been one of Boumédiène's close and faithful comrades they suggested a desire to reinforce the message that the regime was not a military regime, whilst also suggesting the desire for a return to the past and the era of Boumédiène, although under a president who lacked the authority of a more charismatic head of state. His selection also served another purpose; Bouteflika was Minister of Foreign Affairs for some time, and was selected for his knowledge of international institutions, which would be of use in defusing external pressure from international NGOs objecting to Algeria's abuses of human rights. At first the army gave Bouteflika some room for manoeuvre, and was prepared to forego their usual role of selecting the government, even though the negative consequences of the government's economic and social policies would reflect back on the army. A clear line was traced, nonetheless, separating the civilian regime from the domain controlled by the army (this included the appointment of the Minister of Defence, selection for promotion within the armed forces, the military budget, overall charge of the FIS affair, and the question of the Western Sahara). The president was entitled to appoint other ministers for Housing, Health, Tourism and so on.

Following the underlying premise that the civilian president would not stray into the army's 'private domain', the presidential election of 15 April 1999 fitted into the logic of restoring a central role to the armed forces. It is worth pointing out that the usual 'conclave' of generals did not meet in order to select Bouteflika as presidential candidate. Instead, General Mohamed Lamari, chief of staff of the armed forces, decided against such a meeting, leaving the head of Military Security, General Tewfik Médiène, free to oversee the security operation known as 'presidential election', which was to replace the outgoing Zéroual.[16] Military Security was in charge of organizing the elections, and ruled out any candidates who could not be controlled or were thought capable of winning the election and using their power against the army and Military Security. However for the elections to be credible, opposition candidates had to be encouraged to present themselves. A non-violent and loyal opposition which, whilst not necessarily accepting the supremacy of the army, did not wish to take over power itself, was essential to the regime. This loyal opposition would be rewarded by being allocated a few ministerial positions.

The military's aversion to a strong president has been a constant feature of Algerian politics since the death of Boumédiène. Given this aversion, those who have been appointed have lacked the broad appeal of a popular leader. Bouteflika is no exception, even though some statements which he made during his first few months in office caused concern, since they reflected a wider critique of the state by ordinary Algerians. Bouteflika has undermined himself by talking too much, sometimes in an incoherent and brash manner – and above all by not taking any action which would suggest his overall control of the army. His main aim seemed to be to recreate the political system of the 1970s, based on external respect and on fear in the domestic arena. In trying to achieve this objective, he relied on out-dated and weak modes of populist and Third Worldist rhetoric. The only way that Bouteflika could succeed in his goals, is if he were able to combine in his own person both the real and formal powers of state. This is highly unlikely, however, in view of the present fracture between the regime and society, which has tended to give the army an even greater political role than before.

Although they have clearly indicated that there is a line over which he must not stray, the military distrust Bouteflika because of his unpredictability and his lack of coherence. In order to protect themselves against any unpleasant surprises, they have appointed General Larbi Belkheir – who previously held the same post under Bendjedid, as principal private secretary. Bouteflika was not able to refuse this nomination, but in accepting it he compounded the incoherence of his own position; having blamed the ongoing crisis on the policies of Bendjedid, he now accepted into his government Larbi Belkheir, who had been the main architect of those very policies.

To overcome his loss of legitimacy since being designated by the military, the newly elected president has been doing whatever he can to gain popularity. He has been seeking to initiate a peace process which can bring an end to the violent crisis Algeria is facing, and which has already claimed 150,000 lives since the national elections of December 1991, which were won by the Islamists, were cancelled. The government introduced a new law, known as the 'law of civil concord', which was intended to release all imprisoned Islamists who had taken part in the uprising against the regime, provided that they had not been not involved in violent crimes. The project was discussed and adopted by the National Assembly and then subjected to a referendum in September 1999, when the majority of Algerians voted to accept the new law. President Bouteflika is aware that the majority of Algerians want peace, and seeks to promote an image of himself as a peacemaker. The task is a difficult one, however, and there are many obstacles in the way.

There are two possible scenarios. Either Bouteflika may submit to the conventional logic of the Algerian political system, in which the president obeys the informal power of the army, even though he has formal authority over the army.[17] Or he refuses to accept this logic, since it makes him a puppet of the army, and insists on exercising authority over all the institutions of state, including the army itself. If he adopts the latter approach, Bouteflika will be confronted with fierce opposition, as was Chadli Bendjedid when he was forced to resign in January 1992. After this, Mohamed Boudiaf was publicly assassinated in June 1992, and Liamine Zéroual's presidential mandate was prematurely brought to end.[18] The golden rule in politics since at least the time of Machiavelli is that there is no room for both the king and the king maker. If Bouteflika wishes to control the army, he needs to appoint new high-ranking officers so as to ensure their support, given that they owe their promotion to him. But any such appointment would raise suspicion among those in control of the president's security. If they felt threatened, they might somehow remove him from office altogether. Bouteflika's main problem is that he cannot wield power as extensively as those who designated him as president. The army is still in control; and either Bouteflika gets rid of high-ranking officers, or he agrees to be a puppet in their hands. Can he remove the high-ranking officers who selected him as president? Only time can tell.

Bouteflika not only has to be concerned about the military; he also has to worry about what the Islamists are doing. In his relationship with them, he is mainly concerned if he will be recognized as the legitimate president. He also has the credentials needed to initiate a dialogue with the Islamists. He took part in the liberation war against France, which in itself gives him historical legitimacy. One of the accusations of the Islamists is that many high-ranking officers in the Algerian army formerly fought on the French side when Algeria was still a colony. According to them, France is still fighting Algeria indirectly through these officers. In other words, the Islamists claim that the liberation war did not end with formal independence, but continued through other means. Another advantage that Bouteflika has is that he was not in power when the election won by the FIS was cancelled. In one of his speeches, he surprised many by stating explicitly that this cancellation itself was a form of violence. The president has attempted to gain the confidence of the Islamists, and has asked them to renounce violence and to respect the formal institutions of state in which he says they will one day have their place. Prior to any agreement or discussion, however, the Islamists demand the removal of a number of high-ranking army officers. This is the line that Bouteflika cannot cross, and it is unlikely that time will give him the opportunity to do so. If he is to have any success in his negotiations with the Islamists, he will need to demonstrate his autonomy *vis-à-vis* the army. Yet this is very difficult to achieve. If Bouteflika is able to convince the Islamic groups to give up violence and accept the regime in power, he will be able to gain the trust and support of the army. But if he fails to achieve this, then the political stalemate will continue for some time.

Bouteflika knows that no settlement can be reached with the Islamists unless high-ranking army officers who were involved in the decision to cancel the December 1991 election results are first removed from their posts. Yet these officers will put up fierce resistance if Bouteflika attempts to cross the thin red line that separates civilian from military power. The president is thus caught between two sets of irreconcilable demands: the army on the one side; the Islamists on the other. The very same officers who designated him president, in order to improve the regime's image abroad, are the ones the Islamists would most wish him to remove from office.

The only concrete outcome so far of the negotiations that have been taking place since October 1997 between the intelligence services and Military Security has been the 'law of civil concord'.[19] This only extends the law to introduce a general amnesty for imprisoned Islamists who have not committed any violent offences. Negotiations have remained highly secretive, and even well-informed journalists do not know who is taking part in the discussions on either side. Neither does anyone know exactly what the Islamists are officially demanding. All the Islamic leaders are under surveillance, and none of them is permitted to give an interview to the press. Some observers are even questioning whether the negotiations that are claimed to have taken place did indeed occur. There is speculation that the talks may be a fiction invented by the intelligence services in order to further confuse the public about the current reality. It is believed that only the release of the two Islamic leaders, Abbassi Madani and Ali Belhadj, would prove that a settlement had been reached between both sides. The logic of this peace process, which is controlled and overseen by the intelligence services, totally ignores the political aspects of the conflict in Algeria, and tries to resolve this conflict by legal means alone. The logic behind this seems to be that, if a peace is brokered, the Islamists will give back their weapons and will be forgiven for what they have done. The peace process has little chance of succeeding on either of these two grounds.

Bouteflika also has to deal with the non-Islamist opposition, which will similarly judge him on the basis of his actions rather than his words. These groups are asking for a negotiated peace reached through a political settlement, and with a transparent negotiating process. To achieve this, the non-Islamist opposition is calling for a national meeting which would bring together all political parties, including the FIS, to discuss ways of ending the crisis. Another goal of a national meeting would be to establish clear guidelines regarding the need to respect the outcome of elections, guarantees of freedom of speech, equality between the sexes and other related issues currently emerging as essential components of development.

An open and broad-based meeting did take place in Rome in January 1995. This meeting was hosted by the Sant' Egidio Community and attended by the FIS, the FLN and the Socialist Forces Front (FFS). However, the document produced by the participants[20] was violently rejected by the military, who accused Italy and the Catholic Church of supporting terrorists and interfering in matters of national sovereignty. In order to understand this reaction, we need to appreciate that many high-ranking officers in Algeria believe that in general political parties are useless and can even be harmful to civil society. They also believe political parties should have no claim on the state or on sovereignty, which continues to be embodied by the army itself.[21] With officers trained within the confines of such a narrow political culture, there is little chance that Algeria will be able to put an end to the bloody crisis that it has been experiencing for many years.

The path towards peace is both very long and very fraught since each side in the conflict has its own interpretation of what peace means, according to their respective interests. The army wants peace on condition, first, that the Islamists forget what has happened in Algeria since 1992, and, second, that the opposition agrees to conform with the unwritten law of the Algerian political system, namely that the ultimate source of all political power lies in the army.[22] The Islamists want peace as well, but only on condition that the high-ranking military officials involved in the crackdown on Islamists since the cancellation of the December 1991 election results are removed from their posts. President Bouteflika himself also wants to secure a peaceful settlement between the two sides, but he is confronted by two apparently insurmountable obstacles in the attitudes of both the army and the Islamists.

## The Army as a Political Party

After the October 1988 riots, the military hierarchy became convinced that political reforms were necessary. These reforms were only apparently democratic; the main aim was to appoint civilians from a wider range of backgrounds.

Previously, the military had mainly drafted militants from the FLN into office. Political pluralism was legalized but the parties were not to put into question the prerogative of the army in the matter of choosing the president. Elections were intended to lend legitimacy to decisions that had already been made, and the military hierarchy hoped the Islamists would accept this framework. From an ideological perspective, it is possible to envisage a compromise between the army and the Islamists, particularly because one of the main sources of Algerian nationalism lies in Islam. Historically speaking, Algeria's particular brand of nationalism has been heavily influenced by the teachings of Islam, and the role Islam played in resistance to France is emphasized in the official history taught to children at school.

However, it is important to remind ourselves that the army and the Islamists are not fighting over ideological issues. What is at stake is who controls the state. The regime in power, defended as always by the army, is exhausted and has lost much of its legitimacy due to its unpopularity and corruption. It is now also challenged by the Islamists who believe their own legitimacy is derived from their support among the most destitute parts of the population. The extreme violence of the conflict reflects that fact that what is at stake is sovereignty itself. Sovereignty is something which the army clearly does not want to give up, and something which the Islamists wish to seize, whether by the ballot or the bullet. The Islamists' desire to gain sovereignty was clearly reinforced by the decision of the army to cancel the electoral victory of the FIS in January 1992. Yet, it is interesting to note that the military and the Islamists are similar in several ways. Both conceive the body politic as conflict-free, and therefore with no need for political parties. The military have sought to achieve an egalitarian society run by civil servants appointed by themselves and not by politicians. For the Islamists, too, the aim is to create a society that abides by a single set of religious laws and thereby avoids open conflict. The kind of equality sought in such a society would be the equality of all believers, united by their religious convictions into a quasi-family.

Having prevented political conflict from being expressed through an institutional framework, the military is now faced with an armed opposition that is supported by the most destitute among the Algerian population. This opposition is eager for radical change and expresses the concerns of the marginalized through religious discourse and demands for cultural identity. The military's monopoly over politics has led to a politicization of the whole society, with political actions being judged according to religious standards.

There has been a major shift in political discourse, with more radical terms being used by new actors emerging with their own conception of what the state should be and how it should relate to society. Basically, the Islamists wish to reform the former in order to improve the condition of the latter. Within the world view of the new Islamist actors, and according to their utopian vision, the Algerian state has consistently betrayed the hopes of the erstwhile popular liberation movement. There is an overwhelming feeling of deception and disappointment, since it was the state that was to have met the Algerian people's needs and hopes for social justice. On the whole, the new political actors do not expect anything from a democracy that they regard as out of line with the precepts of Islam. Indeed they despise this democracy with the same contempt that the military have reserved for civilian pluralist politics, seen as an invention of competing elites who wish to conquer the state from the legitimate authority of the army. The military appear to believe that if they lose control of the state then the nation itself will be in danger.

Since the military and the Islamists are unable to reach a compromise without one side or the other betraying their own political principles, there is a stalemate in Algerian political life. This is a game in which there can be only one winner; it is a zero-sum conflict. Sovereignty is not regarded as something that can be shared or be the object of a political compromise. The Islamists insist that high-ranking officers must be brought to trial for their part in previous injustices involving, among other things, bribery and political assassinations. It is unlikely that the military would allow this to take place, and impeding the opposition from coming to power through the ballot box has been part of this defensive strategy on the part of the military. Democratic transition cannot take place until the army and the Islamic opposition can somehow be convinced that it is in their mutual interests to reach some sort of political agreement or compromise.

The Algerian experience shows that where the major protagonists feel that their lives, families and wealth are at stake and all their basic interests threatened, a shift in regime through democratic transition from authoritarian rule can fail completely. When electoral victory is seen only as an opportunity to crush the regime's opponents who have shown themselves openly, the losers who remain in office will stop at nothing to prevent the electoral transition from taking place. This leads to an atmosphere where the settling of scores is the main game. This is what accounted for the cancellation of the election results of December 1991, when the Islamists won. Some Islamist opponents of the government publicly threatened members of the ruling elite, demanding openly that they change their way of life, and accusing them of living in a manner that was contrary to Islamic values. Rumours spread immediately following the elections about people being arrested following accusations that they were living a lifestyle contrary to Islam; this gave rise to widespread fear. Taking advantage of this situation of panic, the army pushed the president to resign, cancelled the elections in January, and then in turn arrested and jailed many of the Islamists who had been elected. A cycle of violence and repression, followed by more violence, was set in motion and this cycle continues. After eight years of fighting, the civil war has now claimed an estimated 150,000 lives, causing huge human suffering.

Some of those who consider themselves democrats supported the army crackdown on the Islamists, and supported the cancellation of the election results, all in the name of democracy. The culture of the party system is so deep-rooted in Algeria that the so-called democratic parties did not acknowledge the basic need for political pluralism. To have some chance of succeeding, electoral democracy and democratic transition require that the major protagonists in the political contest share the conviction that electoral victory does not mean the right to defeat the opposition through violence and the gun. If the stakes are about living or dying, rather than simply winning or losing office, the electoral process may take place but transition will be frozen by the political stand-off likely to result. As in Algeria, this stand-off is likely to unleash a dynamic of violence as other avenues of political expression become blocked off. In these conditions, the intervention of the army is seen as unavoidable if order is to be defended and if those in power are to be protected from attack and danger. Elections in Algeria may only be able to result in a transition if they are prefaced by a national contract or a civic pact. The purpose of such a contract or pact would be to establish that all the parties involved in the electoral process agreed to commit themselves to respecting the rules of democracy and to renouncing violence and the settling of accounts through killings after the outcome of a fair electoral process. A contract of this kind had indeed been reached in January 1995 in Rome, but was later rejected by the army as meaningless and non-binding. Clearly, a spirit of agreement is needed as well as a paper contract. The army's control over the institutions of state confirms its status as a quasi-political party, operating as a single party system, somewhat reminiscent of other authoritarian single-party regimes, including the former supremacy of the Communist Party in the Soviet Union. In Algeria the main difference is that this supremacy exists *de facto*, but is nowhere written down in law or in the country's constitution. Nonetheless, the actions of the armed forces illustrate the way in which it works as a dominant political party on the national and international scene.

In January 1992, for example, no longer trusting the elected president, the military asked him to resign. Again in September 1998 the chief of staff of the army asked President Liamine Zéroual to stop negotiating with the Islamists and asked him, too, to resign. The chief of staff was acting like the leader of a dominant political party. His disagreement with the president was shared by the majority of high-ranking officers, who meet regularly in a 'conclave'. This is a kind of central committee or sovereign assembly which decides the military's position on a range of sensitive issues, from selecting candidates for the presidency to deciding on the virtues and drawbacks of negotiations with the Islamist opposition. In a real sense, the army emerges from this process as a sovereign body which controls the presidency and the civilian regime, rather than as an institution which serves the civilian regime, as formally stipulated by the constitution.

Relations between the army and the government – which does not control the Ministry of Defence – express the subordination of an executive institution to a sovereign authority which claims historically derived legitimacy. The army entrusts to civilian elites the task of running the state and implementing social and economic programmes (industrialization during the 1970s, agrarian reforms and health care policies). Such policies were inspired by the army's populist goal of improving the living conditions of the poor peasants and the unemployed in the major cities. From the 1960s onwards, the army considered itself to be pursuing the programme it had been bequeathed by the liberation movement, and upon which its own legitimacy rested. This link ostensibly allowed and entitled the army to claim to embody the interests of the nation as a whole, and to be the only source of power.

Both under the one-party system (1962–89) and under the multi-party system introduced by the 1989 constitution, the Algerian political arena is characterized by the supremacy of the army. The military wields sovereignty in non-institutional forms and seeks to shape the opposition according to this peculiarity. Indeed, the military desires that parties which compete to be in government do so on the basis of tasks of a technical nature, and do not concern themselves with issues of sovereignty. Political parties are allowed to criticize the government, and even the president, but never the army itself. The National Assembly is a framework for formal debates and criticisms but the representatives cannot bring into question the prerogatives of the army. As a consequence, the National Assembly deals only with the formal power of the president and the government, and never with the real, but informal, power of the army. This situation results in two different kinds of political opposition; those who accept the underlying rationale of the regime and another opposition which challenges the assumption that the army should remain unchallenged as the backbone of any political regime. The operation and rationale of the Algerian political system in the last decade have confirmed the view that in reality there is only one political party allowed – namely, the army. Making constant and implicit references to its position as a source of historical legitimacy for any civilian regime, the army claims for itself the ultimate right to control the civilian regime in power, and to retain for itself a monopoly of 'legitimate violence' under the cover of the state. The army has agreed that reform of Algeria's political system is needed, but does so only on condition that the military itself does not have to give up the privileged position it has enjoyed since independence in 1962. The outcome of this situation is a multi-party system in which various competing political parties are forever insulting each other and criticizing the government. Yet at the same time, they are obliged to turn to the army, asking it to grant civilian rulers the power to run the institutions of state, whether by appointment or through recognizing the outcome of elections (whether rigged or fair).

The dualistic structure of power within the operation of the state introduces relations of rivalry between the Ministry of Defence and the presidency. State power is undermined in so far as the president seeks autonomy from the army, but is appointed to office by the army in the first place. Clientilistic political clans become powerful in this context where parties are delegitimized, some supporting the president, others supporting his opponents. When a civilian or journalist criticizes a high-ranking officer, he or she almost always has been given the green light to do so by another high-ranking officer, usually from among those in a more powerful position than the officer(s) being criticized. High-ranking officers may seek to settle their own accounts among themselves by using civilian institutions, including political parties and the media. Within such a system, the civilian individual does not have the means to challenge an officer or to play a political role. The civilian concerned can only mount such a challenge if he or she is assured of the protection of officers better placed in the military hierarchy. In such a system it is fair to say that, in order to be taken seriously, the opposition may find itself obliged to resort to violence as a means of expressing its opposition to the status quo. The Islamists certainly understood their position in this way; they were explicitly seen as opponents by the army, and any kind of settled agreement was only possible once they had resorted to violence. However, unlike isolated civilian opponents of the regime, the Islamists were able to confront the army effectively, being more deeply rooted in society than any other political parties or movements. Many more of their members were also ready to fight, and if necessary to die in resorting to violent opposition to the regime and the army.

From time to time, the Algerian army intervenes openly in military operations, but it intervenes covertly on a more permanent basis, through La Sécurité Militaire (Military Security), whose very name arouses a sense of fear. Military Security is under the control of the Ministry of Defence and has the responsibility of watching over the political arena in order to guarantee the safety of the regime. It is organized rather like an underground party and operates as if it were above the law, unregulated by state authorities, police or judicial system.

The role of Military Security has certainly not facilitated the process of democratic transition from authoritarian rule, which was formally initiated by the

1989 constitution. On the contrary, Military Security has eagerly encouraged violence by itself infiltrating the ranks of the Islamist movement and parties. The army's intolerance of the Islamist position, and the verbal violence against the FIS of many so-called democrats, were part and parcel of the military's strategy of discrediting freedom of speech and multi-partisan, pluralist political processes. The main aim was to demonstrate to the Algerian public that pluralist democracy represented a danger to civil order and to social peace. There was widespread infiltration of civilian political parties, the sowing of dissent and crises within and between the parties, and routine manipulation of the media, blackmail of journalists, threats against party militants and other 'dirty tricks' in Military Security's toolkit. All these means were used to prevent civil society from developing in the direction of genuinely autonomous associations. Any association not under the control of the army is seen as *per se* a threat to the regime. All these observations serve to confirm the main argument in this chapter: that, despite the occasional appearance of pluralism, the Algerian regime consistently operates as if it were a one-party system.

That anyone who is suspected of being involved in a subversive network can be arrested at any time by Military Security provides us with further evidence that in Algeria there is no rule of law. Military Security has been taken aback, however, by the popular support for FIS and the Islamists, since the military personnel involved were mainly trained to guard against the emergence of rival elites, rather than to police the popular masses. The military were not prepared for a popular upsurge of violence on the present scale. In response to the widespread violent opposition to the regime, Military Security has resorted to ever more blatant violations of human rights. The army also uses all the means at its disposal to resist the proposal coming from many human rights organizations that there is a need for an international commission of inquiry into human rights abuses in Algeria.

The main reason the army is so keen to keep a tight control over the political arena by means of Military Security is to undermine the credibility of the civilian opposition and the autonomy of civil society. The goal is to be able to point to the (created) havoc caused by 'free expression' of various conflicting interests, in contrast to the harmony arising from the single voice of a unified Algerian nation. The army fears the emergence of a competing competent and autonomous political elite emerging from the ranks of civil society. The military want to continue choosing which civilians are to run the state administration; they suspect civilians of being less patriotic than themselves, since the army embodies the nation. Fully forty years after independence, Algerian political culture is still pervaded by this notion of historical legitimacy. The military still regards itself as the only channel through which state authority can be passed to civilian politicians, on the condition that these civilians respect the unwritten law that the army is to remain the sole source of power in the Algerian political system.

## The Army as Embodiment of the Nation and Master of the State

We need to bear in mind that the army still regards itself as the most unswervingly patriotic element of the Algerian population. The military elite considers that its own commitment to the Algerian nation has been fully tested over time. Higher-ranking officers in particular believe that their promotion places them closer to the origin of historical legitimacy, and believe that they are uniquely placed to set the ideal standards of nationalist behaviour and policy. Not only are they ready to die for their country (like the Islamists, ironically enough). They have also deliberately chosen the harshness of barracks life over the comfort and ease of a family and community. Their daily lives thereby symbolize the sacrifices that first liberated Algeria from foreign domination. Since he deters external (and internal) aggression against the state, the soldier can be regarded as the 'shield' of the nation. As such, the soldier can be considered to hold the historical legitimacy from which any administrative authority must necessarily be derived. All this is of course no more than an ideological representation, the purpose of which is to justify the political supremacy of the army. By monopolizing legitimacy to the detriment of the general development and refinement of state institutions, the army has in fact prevented the integration of conflicting movements into the institutional structures of power. Its dominance has driven all those who seek reform or change into the arms of the Islamists, both by hampering the emergence of any real sense of citizenship and by completely smothering the emergence of an autonomous civil society. The political interest of military elites is to destroy and undermine the formation of any kind of public sphere for political debate and expression. The military make frequent reference to the legacy of a national liberation struggle, but rarely invoke respect for the rule of law. This is not surprising, since the rule of law would imply that the army is just one institution among many, and should not be in overall control of state power.

## Conclusion

This chapter has tried to show that, in Algeria's case, state power is divided into two elements: the element of sovereign power, which is not regarded as accountable to any institution, and another element of power, which is detained by the government and informally accountable to the army. Executive power held by the state civilian power holders is conceived as a tool for implementing policies rather than deciding on matters of national sovereignty or security. The policies implemented by the executive power mainly concern the basic needs of the population. Sovereign power embodies the nation itself, and is concerned with defending the nation against both its internal and external enemies. Of these two forms of state power, the first pertains to the nation, the second to the state.

Algerian history has not created a nation–state; it has created a nation and a separate state, linked by relations of subordination. A crisis has been generated, whose origins are to be found in the conception of the nation and also in the limits imposed on the state. As in so many other countries, the nation in Algeria is a mythical notion. But in Algeria the myth is exaggerated to the extent that the citizens are united in the nation not in their existing form, but in an idealized form derived from the ideological beliefs of the army on the one hand, and the Islamists on the other. The competing images of the Algerian nation are so much in conflict that it is fair to say that the very idea of an Algerian nation is in question. In a sense there are many Algerian nations which serve to divide the people against each other.

There have been at least three historically distinct concepts of the nation in the past: the first was that of Messali Hadj, the populist; the second that of Abdelhamid Ben Badis, the early Islamist; and finally, that of Ferhat Abbas, the national modernist. At independence the competing foundations of these three forms of nationalism were not reconciled. On the contrary, independence divided them more than ever and their followers are still fighting one another today. Each political current within the nationalist movement has sought to take over the state and to eliminate its rivals. Each has its own idea of what the nation should be, and seeks to impose these ideas by force on society. In this ideological environment, a multi-party system does not lead smoothly or automatically to democratic transition or consolidation. Instead, it tends to arouse further intolerance and generate cycles of violence that are difficult to end. Whereas the nation generally is seen as a unifying element of political life, in Algeria the idea of the nation divides the population further. This in part accounts for the army's own monopoly of legitimate violence, and explains why it is almost impossible for any civilian leader or movement to claim to speak on behalf of the nation as a whole. The army cannot but be involved with different political movements and parties, each with their different agendas and priorities. However, political rivalry also exists within the army itself, and can become more of a threat to civil peace than conflicts within civil society. Until recently, such divisions within the army have been well hidden; it is impossible to say, however, whether this will continue to be the case, and whether the army will continue to appear as a relatively stable and united force.

One of the most distinctive features of Algeria's political system has been that the state has rarely embroiled itself in the ideological divisions that have split the society. Whereas in most democratic countries, the non-military institutions of state have a political character, in Algeria their role is almost purely technical; they have been confined to the role of administrative tools specialized for management of economic resources and geared as far as possible towards meeting people's daily needs. The state is not directly linked to the electorate; it is simply an instrument at the disposal of the civilian elites for obtaining civil peace through the redistribution of resources. Relations between the sovereign nation – embodied by the army and not by the electorate – and the state administration shape the political realm in which institutions find their function in the hierarchy formed by the mythical nation and the administrative state.

In all representations of Algerian political life, there is a major difference between the nation and the state. The nation is an ideological construct, and cannot be concerned with political opposition, popular unrest or daily concerns. The state, on the other hand, is an administrative instrument of control, assessed on its ability to ensure satisfaction for the people in material terms. Rightly or wrongly, the main criticisms of the state are framed in terms of misdemeanours, the incompetence of civil servants and official corruption. The mythical nation is thus in no way debased by such criticisms, which are almost uniquely directed at the institutions of the civilian state. Such criticisms, of course, are bound to intensify as the executive institutions of the civilian state are less and less able to manage the deepening crisis which Algerian society is undergoing.

There are many opportunities to make money when in public office in the state sector. In the public view, this tends to attract less honest people who serve themselves more readily than they serve the public. The resulting rejection of the state administrative institutions by the public fuels social tensions and violent unrest, leading on some occasions to riots and killing. It could be said that Algerian people love their nation but dislike their state. Accordingly, even when the state comes under the fiercest criticism, this is on behalf of the nation. Political parties compete for power, and when they are prevented from doing so, may claim that the nation which they represent is in danger of disintegration. The army, however, will not allow anyone but its own leaders to speak on behalf of the nation as a whole, and will accuse any civilian who does so of divisiveness and disloyalty, or worse.

The Algerian state is not a 'modern' state as political scientists would define it. It is certainly not an institutional framework able to balance the autonomous judicial, legislative and executive arms of state power. As is the case in many Third World countries, the Algerian state does not provide a framework for supporting individual citizenship and neither does it allow or enable the free expression of competing political views through political parties, popular participation and a respect for civil rights. In order for citizenship to be a meaningful term, political legitimacy should stem primarily from the electorate, through some process of elections perceived as free and fair, and resulting in the election of representatives who are involved in the formation of the government. This is the ruling idea within most democratic regimes, and is more or less the norm in most parliamentary democracies.

To draw an analogy, in Algeria it is the army rather than the electorate which provides the basis for political legitimacy within the system as it stands. This source of legitimacy is, by its nature, based on force and the threat of force. Since the civilian state administration draws its authority from the army and not from the electorate, the state is weak compared to the army and powerful in relation to society, which is crushed by the lack of autonomous leverage over power holders, civil servants and the armed forces. This results in a generalized tendency for corruption and clientelism which pervade public life. For this reason, the state administration has all but lost its credibility among the majority of the Algerian populace, and particularly among the most destitute and marginalized elements of the population.

Being fully embroiled in the conflicts of civil society and the state administration, the army is not as impartial as it ideally should be within a 'modern' political system. Instead, it is used instrumentally by those who control its upper echelons for their own purposes, including the purpose of getting rid of adversaries and critics, and those merely considered as potential adversaries. The army's strategy is to distribute the offices of state to more than one civilian political grouping, in order to hold each 'clan' and its divisions in check. The state thus finds itself under the double demands of the military, who continue to keep a close eye on whatever is done by the state administration, and the society, which expects the state administration to meet the social needs and political aspirations of the people. The military can see that their control over the state administration may have to be loosened somewhat. It seems they may be prepared to loosen their grip on the government, and give political parties more room for manoeuvre, on condition that they can keep a tight rein on the process of appointing the president.

So long as Algerian political culture continues to be shaped by the legacy of the liberation struggle and national liberation movement, the army will remain the single most important actor in the political field. Algeria gained its independence through violence, and the consequence of this historical reality can be seen as twofold. In the first place, violence underpins most forms of civilian and administrative politics. Second, political conflict is defined primarily in terms of opposition to foreigners and their domestic allies, who are regarded as traitors to the nation. Within the context of this particular political culture, democracy generally entails conflict and even war.

In the end, the failure of the Algerian regime has been mainly a political failure. The army has suffocated the state which was itself created through revolutionary violence. Throughout the world, the 1980s and 1990s were decades of post-populism and of a rapid transition from authoritarian rule towards more democratic forms of politics, and from state control towards the free market. The Algerian army has been out of step with this global trend, and has seemed to ignore the implications of the fall of the Berlin wall. Instead of giving the nation statesmen of the ability of Colonel Boumédiène from within its own ranks, the army has preferred to hide behind the blunderings of a state run by incompetent civil servants. It is this politically created power vacuum that has encouraged the Islamists to try and take over the institutions of the state and claim historical legitimacy from the army, using both the ballot and the bullet.

## Notes and References

1 Cf. Addi (1990).
2 In the declaration of 19 June 1965, the various charges against Ben Bella, which were used to justify the coup against him, are listed in some detail.
3 There is no reference in any public document to the army's role in forming the government. On the contrary, the various constitutions (1963, 1976, 1989) stipulate that the president is the supreme commander of the armed forces, which in turn have the duty to obey his government.
4 This hypothesis is developed in Addi (1994).
5 In the Proclamation of 19 June 1965, the expression used was 'revolutionary readjustment'. This was not simply propaganda. In practice, military power, which incarnated political legitimacy, was therefore entitled to put an end to the mandate it had extended even to the head of state, the president himself. The president was thus accountable to the army and not to the people. Cf. *Annuaire de l'Afrique du Nord* (1966).
6 Cf. Leca and Vatin (1976).
7 Stability is of course also obtained through the use of compromise, alliances, allocation of jobs, exclusion and other forms of more or less overt pressure and persuasion.
8 Massinissa was a Berber chief during classical times, and under his rule Numidie became a prosperous state. Abdelmoumem was one of the Almohad emperors who promoted the expansion of Arab and Islamic civilization in North Africa and in Spain.
9 The present crisis in Algeria is precisely this: a crisis of legitimacy, which shakes the very foundations of state power in the country. See Addi (1993).
10 Cf. Touraine (1974).
11 See Addi (1999b) on the patriarchal structures of Algerian society.
12 I use the classical sociological distinction between society and community as employed by Marx, Tönnies, Durkheim and Weber, in order to analyse the process of social differentiation, including the growing awareness of members of a particular society that they constitute a sovereign political body and the ultimate repository of legal authority. This process results in the separation of the political sphere from the spheres of religion, morality and psychology.
13 Cf. Weber (1947).
14 Algeria has had two major charismatic figures with which the nation identified, and whose political legitimacy was acknowledged. The first was Messali Hadj, leader of the nationalist movement until 1954, who incarnated the national community forged out of the idealism of

the independence struggle, and Houari Boumédiène in the 1970s, who incarnated the popular goal of economic development.

15 This is the crucial difference between the Algerian regime and the Soviet regime, where the Communist Party was in control of both the army and the KGB.

16 There were many indicators that Military Security had instructed the government to lend all support needed for the election campaign of Bouteflika.

17 See Addi (1996).

18 See Addi (1998, 1999a).

19 For more information on La Sécurité Militaire as a political police force above the judiciary, see Reporters Sans Frontières (1996).

20 See La Plate-forme de Rome (1995).

21 See Addi (1994).

22 See Addi (1998).

# 9

# Entrenched Militarism and the Future of Democracy in Nigeria

## J'KAYODE FAYEMI

The conventional wisdom today is that the Nigerian military is in retreat after almost four decades at the centre stage of politics. The decisive, albeit disputed, victory of the dominant People's Democratic Party in the 1999 presidential polls which produced an ex-military leader, General Obasanjo, as elected president, and the subsequent actions undertaken by the government, are seen as concrete evidence for this. Without a doubt, President Obasanjo has surprised many people by the bold steps he has taken to break the grip of the military elite, to attack corruption and to espouse an agenda for transparency and accountability in the polity.

Nevertheless, there is little evidence of the political institutionalization of these steps and it may be misleading to overemphasize the scale and intensity of the military retreat. In the light of the numerous false starts that Nigeria has witnessed in her past democratic experiments, there ought to be a growing realization of the need to think less teleologically about democratic transitions brought about by a combination of military fracturing and incoherent civil society agitation. After all, if the experience of post-Cold War Africa is anything to go by, it seems clear enough that, while democratic transitions may lead to democratic development in stages or 'in parts',[1] pact-based transitions have not necessarily led to consolidated democracies nor stemmed the tide of democratic reversals, especially in places where militarism influences and penetrates the fabric, ethos, language and character of public discourse and action.

The above underscores the need to temper euphoric and triumphal outbursts with a cautious optimism. This encourages an investigation into the prospects for democratic control over military and security establishments. In that spirit, this chapter focuses on the role of the military in Nigeria's democratization project. Without an in-depth look at how military control has developed, nourished and coursed through the system, we run the risk of either underestimating the rather convoluted network of military influence or inflating the importance of a 'democratic moment' in the quest to deconstruct the military 'problem' in fluid and pluriform societies.

An accurate assessment the role of Nigeria's military in the democratization process and its impact on the future of the fledgling democratic dispensation would benefit, therefore, from a nuanced approach which does not treat the institution as a monolith. Neither should it be defined simply by the excesses of its aberrant officer corps, nor seen through the prism of the distinction often made in the literature between reformers and hard-liners, moderates and radicals. Consequently, it is important to trace the sociological and institutional underpinnings of the military's role in Nigeria's chequered history of democratic transition, to enable us to assess (1) the conditions, ingredients and consequences of military projects for nation-building (political institutionalization and economic development through democratic transition); (2) the impact of the post-civil war 'democratic pressure' on the political role of the military and their nation-building agenda, and the impact of the post-Cold War pressure on the military and the state; and (3) the likely impact of the manifold legacies of Nigeria's authoritarian past on the consolidation of civil politics and democratic governance. Approached this way, it is possible to review the political role of the military project in the future, amid the emerging realities of post-military politics in Nigeria.

## Background to Military Involvement in Nigerian Politics

Understanding the colonial character of the military is a crucial factor in explaining the rise of the praetorian instincts in post-colonial militaries in Africa. As Gutteridge observed: 'the armies of Africa … are the direct descendants of the colonial forces raised in the territories of the imperial rulers to sustain the old order'.[2] What emerged as the Nigerian armed forces in 1963 had a long history as a product of British colonialism. Established as a small constabulary force at the beginning of the century, just before the Second World War it became part of the Royal West African Frontier Force, made up of soldiers from all the satellite states of Nigeria, Gold Coast, Sierra Leone and Gambia.

In its recruitment policy for the colonial army, the British government promoted the concept of 'martial and non-martial tribes' in West Africa. Some ethnic groups were found to be more loyal and cooperative than others. Besides, they happened to be less literate in Western education than their southern counterparts and therefore more amenable to orders. Given the long history of interaction with the metropolitan force and the crucial role of the dependent territories in the victory of the allied powers in the Second World War, Africans in the colonial armies developed a more confident political and social outlook that did not exclude direct involvement in political affairs. As Crowder argued:

> Africans had fought alongside white men, killed white men, seen brave Africans and white cowards … met white soldiers who treated them as equals, or who were like themselves, hardly educated.… Above all, *having fought in the defence of freedom, they considered it their right that they should share in the government of the land.*[3]

After independence the new political leadership was ambivalent – both concerned and indifferent – about the growth of the military institution; they saw the military as an extension of the colonial authority. This ambivalence rested partly on concern over the constitution of the military and its likely impact on the regional politics of the period. The concerned ambivalence of the post-independence political leaders about the armed forces was understandable but somewhat exaggerated, given their own close connection to the metropolitan power. Whereas they distrusted the local military institution put together at the instance of the metropolitan power, the ruling elite still trusted the colonial power sufficiently to accede to an Anglo–Nigerian Defence Pact at independence. Even after the abrogation of the Anglo–Nigerian Defence Pact, the dependence on the colonial power by the ruling government was still ingrained in the leadership, hence the absence of a locally codified or articulated defence policy, broadly outlining military objectives as well as identifying internal and external threats based on emergent developments, and not as a proxy in the superpower rivalry of the period.

In this context, the relationship between the military and the political leadership of the country was understandably fraught and this multi-layered colonial hangover defined the development (or lack of it) of the military political doctrine – especially considering 'development' and 'security'. Indeed, since the post-colonial state inherited, and in most cases expanded, the hegemonic tendencies of the colonial period, the post-independence army remained essentially colonial in character. The nationalist leaders thought the most logical way out of this dependence was an accelerated Nigerianization policy. While this showed evidence of direction and purpose on the part of the leadership, the Nigerianization policy undermined the professionalism of the military as loyalty among the fighting men became divided along regional and political lines. According to Dudley, the 1962 law that sanctioned a quota system in the army recruitment process created a significant impression:

> Whereas before the system was introduced, recruitment and mobility were thought to be dependent on the individual's ability, with the [new] system the suspicion grew that this mattered less than who were one's patrons. The 'unintended consequence' of the political decision to introduce a quota system was the politicization of the military.[4]

Yet, in spite of the notion that the military had become an extension of the dominant political elite, as Dudley suggested, it is equally arguable that the Nigerianization agenda merely reproduced and expanded the colonial armed forces' recruitment pattern. Representativeness was never an issue for the colonial army and the bulk of the recruits came from northern ethnic groups. Nonetheless, in the officer material where the forces needed fairly well-educated men, most men originated from the southern ethnic groups. This early pattern of recruitment was replicated in the post-independence armed forces. Clearly, the political elite of the immediate post-independence era was very sensitive to the fact that two thirds of the officers by 1962 were from the South (and mainly Ibo), hence the 1962 quota policy aimed at redressing the imbalance already dominant in the officer ranks.[5]

The decision to adopt a quota system for recruitment of the armed forces was seen as an innovative mechanism in dealing with diversity and a genuine effort to ensure representativeness in an important national institution. Nonetheless the political-military doctrine at the time denied the very existence of that diversity. In a very significant way, the doctrine upheld the old order bequeathed by the British: national security assumed a military and external character. Indeed, the leadership's description of the nation-state – as co-extensive with the ethnic and individual boundaries – followed closely the tradition of classical realists. To legitimize this view, the constitution that regulated the affairs of the state at independence institutionalized the towering of the 'idealized' state over the 'real' society. Just as had happened during the colonial era, the military soon became the most visible face of this forced notion of unity.

Additionally, given the historical circumstances in which African countries emerged and guaranteed the primacy of the state and the monopoly of coercive instruments by the anointed ruler, threats to national security did not include domestic threats to national stability. Instead, domestic threats were seen as 'little local difficulties' among competing political interest groups for state control. In consequence, the pre-1966 political violence in the country hardly provided any lessons for innovative conflict management in the interest of the nation-building project. Indeed, it soon became a political-military doctrine that resonated in the decision-making process of successive regimes, in that any challenge to the 'idealized national community' was often interpreted as a direct challenge to the legitimacy of the government in power. In consequence, internal dimensions of threat often needed to assume the cloak of matters of regime security to receive the attention of political leaders, and it was in this context that the existing military force was seen to have a political role. For example, the near-total dependence of the first republican government in Nigeria on the army to quell the political turmoil in Western Nigeria and the Middle Belt region has been cited as a major factor in the eventual overthrow of the regime, given the manner in which the military was encouraged to become a pliant instrument of the ruling elite in dealing with opponents.

As a result of the growing influence of the military, those who felt excluded from the competition for political power also courted the institution. Having discovered its own indispensability to the political elite, the place of the military was enhanced and, at the same time, undermined by the politicization of its post-independence recruitment. Many who entered via the political route owed allegiance to political forces external to the military institution. Additionally, some politically minded officers, genuinely frustrated by the venality of the political leadership, began to see the institution as a genuine alternative power centre for social change. The consolidation of the army's place in society was facilitated by the fact that it controlled the instruments of violence and radiated order amid disorder and chaos.

The local conditions were reinforced by the intensity of power rivalry which characterized Cold War politics and the impact of this on the development of post-colonial states in Africa. Violent overthrows of elected governments started to find political and intellectual justification, from the action of the Free Officers in Egypt to the coup against President Olympio in neighbouring Togo, following the ideological and intellectual arguments that military rule correlated to nationalism, and therefore modernity. The pattern continued throughout the Cold War era. Leading intellectuals of the era promoted praetorianism based on the alleged modernizing characteristics of the military. Imbued with this intellectual justification of 'nationalism' and 'modernity', Major Nzeogwu, the leader of Nigeria's first coup, could claim that 'the men and officers who carried out the 1966 operation in Kaduna were a truly Nigerian gathering, and only in the army do you get true Nigerianism'.[6]

Notwithstanding, it would be wrong to assume there were no structural problems that encouraged the involvement of the armed forces in politics. Indeed, military involvement in politics has often been seen as the result of chronic societal disequilibrium, exemplified by the corruption of politicians.[7] In effect, it has always been consistent with military organizations involved in 'role expansion' from its 'satrapic'[8] orientation to active praetorianism in Africa to explain its intervention in politics as resulting from the 'corruption' of the political elite. Nzeogwu's coup speech of January 1966 provided a template for subsequent military coups in Nigeria. According to him:

> Our enemies are the political profiteers, the swindlers, the men in high and low places that seek bribes and demand ten per cent; those that seek to keep the country divided permanently so that they can remain in office as ministers or VIPs at least; the tribalists, the nepotists, those that make the country big for nothing before international circles; those that have corrupted our society and put the Nigerian calendar back by their words and deeds.[9]

Certainly, praetorianism grows faster in situations of structural disorientation and national identity crisis. It is also true that coups have a greater chance of success in moments of overwhelming national frustration with irresponsible political leadership. The Nigerian experience confirms that insufficient weight is given to the personal motives of ambitious, discontented officers, who find legitimate cover in periods of structural fragility and prebendal politics.[10]

In this context, the next section examines the role of the military during the transition and nation-building project. How did the military become compliant in the consolidation of the old order, be it colonialism or patrimonialism, even when the rhetoric was one of reform? It will be argued that the political-military doctrine, the reference point of successive military regimes, was one in which internal threats were relegated to the status of a dependent variable, whilst the primary focus was on external threats in the pursuit of the 'idealized nation', always likely to result in a 'permanent transition'.

This chapter aims to show that all military regimes allowed this to happen deliberately by exaggerating foreign threats, as a way of diverting attention away from seemingly irresolvable domestic problems. In effect, the search for grandeur and institutional aggrandizement tended to underemphasize the unsettled nationality questions in the country, the damaging effects of military involvement in politics and the personalized nature of rule. This in turn underemphasized the extent to which the Nigerian public disapproved of military rule, and obviated public exposure of the extent to which the nationality question, which had led to civil war, had been left unresolved. This became a consistent, dependable political-military doctrine: the few military regimes that deviated from it did not last.

## Transition to Militarism:[11] military politics and the nation-building project

When the Nigerian military first intervened in politics in January 1966, their action was claimed as a nation-building project aimed at eradicating corruption and reordering the state. Six months later, the Nigerian army had become the catalyst for national disintegration as it broke into ethnic and regional factions and exacerbated the pre-existing primordial cleavages which had earlier undermined professionalism, eventually leading to a three-year civil war.

For those who had acclaimed the attributes of the military in terms of its *espirit de corps*, cohesiveness and unified outlook, this sudden turn of events was difficult to explain. It was only within the military, as a truly authoritarian structure of control preoccupied with regime security, that the colonial authorities encouraged and fostered the interaction of Nigeria's segmented elite in any common fora, a feature which seemed logical given their role as agents of imperial power for the limitation of militant political activity by nationalist politicians. In this manner, the tradition of cross-sectional consociational elitism seemed better developed within the military than in any other professional group. Their training and orientation in foreign and local institutions may have been crucial in their socialization process.

The training and orientation of the military thus promoted a socialization process that fostered inter-ethnic interaction among the country's elite. The fact that the ethnicized nature of politics and personalized form of rule later consumed the military elite, and made it possible for it to serve as the vanguard of interests that were neither institutional nor majoritarian, underscores the failure of a nation-building project that was not derived from consensus. While the inter-ethnic interaction was likely to predispose military officers to the nationalist project as a result of this socialization process, the enemy was no longer as clear-cut as it had been under colonialism, blurred by other cross-cutting links that went beyond the institutional. As Luckham explained, in addition to a unified outlook,

> such an organization … requires a higher degree of goal consensus than those in which relationships are more segmentary. Brotherhood creates genuine integration of officers and men only if they show self-discipline and if the system of command and control is itself adequately institutionalized. Otherwise it may be disruptive.[12]

In Nigeria it was disruptive in the early days and continued to be disruptive as officers carved up their own niches and groomed protégés using the same authoritarian structures of control that allowed for the 'layering of fraternities' prevalent in satrapic military organizations. Consequently, the military could no longer lay claim to being cohesive, a condition often attributed to their sound training and collective military honour. Neither could the Nigerian military trust in the collegial links that had served other militaries in good stead, especially in Latin America. Not even the supposedly collegial ruling councils served this purpose beyond the interim periods that punctuated military administrations. It was for this reason that Luckham observed that the disruption of the professional cohesion

> goes to suggest that we need to seek for other factors than common training which might generate solidarity among military equals; that the officer corps was held together by something more than the mere agglomeration of different brotherhoods and course mates ….[13]

What has become even clearer since Luckham's work on the Nigerian military is the prevalence of sectional loyalties within the military hierarchy and the way this has been used to advance the ruling elite's prebendal proclivities. Although the military caste consistently maintained the professional and solidaristic strategy that kept it in power for three decades, the nature of that strategy would appear to have assumed a far more segmental edge after Nigeria's second republic. At that stage, professional camaraderie and institutional cohesion seemed relatively less important in the alliance used to sustain the military in power. On the one hand, it was possible for successive military regimes to retain power with some measure of authority in areas where the personal projects of the military ruling elite coincided with group or corporate interests. On the other hand, in areas where rulers did not respect institutional interests or restraints, they hung on by the strength of coercive capabilities and co-optive strategies which depended on alternative power centres outside the military: civilian bureaucracy, the business sector and intellectual circles. Successive military regimes adopted this strategy, from General Yakubu Gowon to the recently departed General Abdul-Salami Abubakar. The regimes of Generals Ibrahim Babangida and Sani Abacha represented two extremes in this continuum.

## The Gowon Years (1966–75)

Strengthened by the favourable aftermath of the Nigerian civil war, General Yakubu Gowon utilized the legitimacy provided by the successful 'resolution' of the civil war to incorporate the military in the nation-building project. Consequently the civil war, although it had fragmented the military as an institution, now provided it with an opportunity to redeem its image. Yet, this was not necessarily on account of its professionalism in the conduct of the war. Although the civil war is not the focus of this chapter, it is important to highlight the degree to which it influenced the actions of the military regime, especially its claim to a nation-building role.

In 1976 the post-civil war agenda of reconstruction, which was meant to culminate in political disengagement by the armed forces, elicited a high level of consensus within the military and political society. Yet this meant more continuity with the old order than change. Indeed, Gowon personified the legitimacy of the era and his name soon became an acronym for 'one Nigeria' in popular culture. His support from civil and political society was derived from the underlying acceptance that power belonged to the people. This was demonstrated by Gowon's specific announcement of a timetable for military disengagement from politics. Although it was evident that the military had now become politicized, Gowon was able to involve credible politicians in the work of the administration by maintaining a political order within their purview, to be controlled by them. Even those who were concerned about the growing concentration of power saw its possible benefits. What destroyed the overwhelming support from both the military and political constituencies was the inability of the Gowon administration to consolidate the nation-building project in the aftermath of civil war.

First, while state power was enhanced by the civil war, the improvement in the country's economy through oil wealth sharpened the predatory instincts of the military ruling elite and their consociational allies in the civil service and business sector. This undermined the military's institutional capacity for independent action and in turn for the nation-building project. Even though corruption was rampant during the civil war, it was the rapacity of the regime functionaries in the aftermath of the war that focused attention on General Gowon's weak leadership qualities in a situation where state governors behaved as 'provincial chiefs in a decentralized patrimonial order', charged with plundering the new-found oil resources.

Second, while state military power was potentially enhanced by the post-civil war 'no victor, no vanquished' reconciliation policy (especially given the fact that the federal forces merely muddled through), the Gowon administration failed to concentrate on reorganizing the internal workings of the military institution. Although military planners sought to improve service coordination and came up with suggestions for demobilizing and mechanizing a military which was now spending 90 per cent of its budget on salaries for the 250,000-strong force (from a pre-war strength of 10,000), there was no doctrinal principle that guided defence management. Indeed, as his official biographer noted, 'as Gowon settled to issues of state governance after the war, his contacts with the military gradually decreased as his relationship with the civilian bureaucracy grew'.[14] It was a failure to seize the opportunity provided at the end of the civil war to reorganize the institution that laid the basis for the contest for dominance between praetorians and professionals which eventually led the military down its slippery slope.

The above situation was exacerbated by the growing dependence on the civilian bureaucracy; some personnel had become powerful and indispensable to General Gowon. This long-term dependence on the civilian bureaucracy manifested itself in various ways in the post-war years. The political involvement inevitably acquired economic imperatives after the Nigerian civil war with Nigeria's new-found wealth in the oil sector. The origins of Nigeria's 'bureaucratic-economic militariat' could indeed be traced back to the central role played by the military in the control and management of this new-found wealth, especially after its promulgation of the Nigerian Enterprises Decrees of 1972 and 1977. What became apparent at this stage was the personalized pattern of private capital accumulation which prevailed, even if this was sometimes held in proxy by the military officers' fronts. This generated a crisis of confidence in the military. Within an authoritarian structure preoccupied with its own institutional survival, there was a growing perception that Gowon was isolating himself from the institution – a situation his colleagues in the military found disconcerting and which eventually led to his overthrow. As his successor, General Murtala Mohammed, noted in his maiden speech: 'After the civil war, the affairs of the state, hitherto a collective responsibility, became characterized by a lack of consultation. Things got to a stage when the head of the administration became inaccessible even to official advisers.'[15]

Notwithstanding the failed national development agenda and the evident lack of the military's much-acclaimed modernizing characteristics, General Gowon might still have survived if he had not reneged on the transition timetable. As aptly captured by the late social critic, Tai Solarin, the regime's tattered credibility came crashing down and it was the 'beginning of the end' for the Gowon administration. The refusal to keep the transition agenda in view provided a base of unity for all his opponents, both within the military and in civil society.

## The Mohammed–Obasanjo Years (1975–9)

Based on the experience of the Gowon administration, one of the first lessons the new administration, the Mohammed–Obasanjo regime, might logically have learned was the need to diffuse the power concentrated by the head of state. Indeed, it was thought at first that the original intention was to constitute the three most senior members of the military junta into a ruling triumvirate with a rotational leadership – a style common to Latin American military juntas. When the junta finally settled for what was essentially the mode of rulership under General Gowon, with the Supreme Military Council intact, power was to be shared between the head of state, Brigadier (later General) Murtala Mohammed and the chief of staff, Brigadier (later General) Olusegun Obasanjo.

In spite of this attempt to diffuse power, the strong leadership exhibited by General Murtala Mohammed not only demanded but also received a variety of alternative options from his intellectual circle and the military itself. It also precluded the structure from working in a delegatory manner. As the regime's chief of staff, General Obasanjo, later revealed in his memoirs, the relative ease with which service chiefs and corps commanders established links with the head of state and the chief of staff created the impression that the regime did not need a Minister of Defence. This perceived neglect was raised repeatedly by the Minister of Defence, Brigadier Iliya Bisalla, especially after the military promotion exercise which saw the army chief raised higher in rank. This was adduced as a reason for his involvement in the abortive coup which resulted in the assassination of the head of state, General Mohammed.[16]

Undoubtedly, Brigadier Mohammed also assumed a creative role in the defence planning process himself.[17] As a result, the first steps towards the systematic realignment of the ends of security policy to the means of achieving policy goals began under the regime. However, the regime still failed to resolve the problem of coordination of structure, the bane of the armed forces since the civil war days, probably complicated further when General Obasanjo assumed office as head of state, commander-in-chief and Minister of Defence. Although this was informed more by the development leading to the assassination of the former head of state, the combination of the defence portfolio with his primary duty as head of state heralded once again the issue of concentrated power.

First came the renewed ascendancy of the civilian bureaucracy in defence policy making and implementation, a feature the regime leaders had relentlessly criticized under the Gowon administration. For a government that demanded more discipline from the civilian bureaucracy by sacking over eleven thousand public officials all over the country, the fact that the government resorted to the same bureaucracy exposed the superficiality of that populist move. It also meant that nothing was done to resolve the structural problems that had plagued previous administrations in terms of ensuring an effective synergy amongst different aspects of governance.

To its credit, the regime made a determined effort to address substantive issues relating to the reorganization of the armed forces and the renewal of the political transition programme. However, the implication of this was the huge capital outlay that accompanied this effort, and this further deepened the centralization of authority and increased the dependence on the civilian bureaucracy. This had its own implications for the eradication of corruption, in spite of their best efforts. As Richard Joseph correctly argued, 'the transitional military regime of Mohammed and Obasanjo ... by dint of enhancing the state's omnipresence and omni-competence in the devising and implementing of national projects, added even more fuel to prebendal politics in Nigeria'.[18]

Although the regime was clearly more reformist in character and orientation than the previous military leadership, its onslaught on corruption was largely superficial and unsustained. Unsurprisingly, many of the military officers who ruled the country between 1975 and 1979 soon found themselves in business and politics courtesy of their contacts with the civilian bureaucracy and the business sector. Indeed, if one traces the personal, political and financial links of a number of individuals associated with the military prior to their exit from government and in the immediate aftermath of the return to civilian politics in 1979, there is clear evidence of a network including the military, the civilian bureaucracy and business moguls.[19] At this stage though, it would appear that the acquisitions were largely in pursuit of personal wealth, rather than a conscious institutional programme of neo-militarism.

The proclivity of the ex-generals to wield financial control was not limited to their top brass. Others who retired before them, and several who did so after, entered the boardroom game too. As one observer of the retired military phenomenon noted,

> an increasing number of retired senior military officers … combine chairmanships/directorships of their own private businesses, with part-time appointments to key governmental posts and parastatals relating to agriculture, commerce, and industry, in addition to interlocking directorships of many foreign companies incorporated in Nigeria.[20]

Yet, in spite of the growing tendency towards personal accumulation that had become noticeable in the post-1979 transition phase, and which certainly continued under the post-1983 Buhari–Idiagbon junta, a distinguishing feature of these pre-Babangida military regimes was that they were less directly subservient to foreign capital and less inclined to flaunt political influence, although an insignificant number of military officers went into politics in the second republic. While there were officers committed fully to the market orthodoxy of privatizing the state on the economic front, those who advocated economic nationalism and greater state control won these internal struggles. Several government institutions in the oil, energy, water and telecommunications sectors remained under government control.

On threat analysis, the Mohammed–Obasanjo regime acknowledged that Nigeria confronted both external and internal threats, although priority was still assigned to the foreign arena. However, this regime shifted from Gowon's whimsical determination of defence, foreign and security policies to a more rationally ordered identification and prioritization of the objectives guiding foreign and defence policies. The ideas underlying these objectives had a significant impact on policy formulation and fashioning of doctrine. The Adedeji panel set up to review state objectives broadened the foreign policy goals to include continental security, making Africa the centrepiece of Nigeria's foreign and defence policies. Simultaneously with the new regime's pursuit of Gowon's nine-point domestic programme, its stance on the continental scene set out an offensive doctrine and an expansion of the previous regime's concentration on regional integration efforts, especially on questions of decolonization of the continent. This was not done to the detriment of domestic issues: indeed, the external agenda dovetailed nicely with the regime's internal agenda in many areas. For example, demobilization was identified in the immediate aftermath of the civil war as an issue that required urgent attention. Equally, the military leadership was aware that the battle readiness of the armed forces was inextricably linked to the uncertainty surrounding the demobilization programme, especially given the neglect of this issue by the previous regime. By the time it was leaving government, the regime had reduced the size of the military by 100,000, easily the most ambitious reduction ever conducted by any government in Nigeria.[21]

Other issues given priority by the Mohammed–Obasanjo regime in the pursuit of foreign and defence policies included barracks reconstruction, weapons procurement, training, defence production and cohesion – all aimed at the institutionalization of military professionalism.[22] The perspicacity of its actions not only provided implementing agents with a clear policy guideline to the country's military mission, but also gave decision makers a logical sequence to frame the employment, deployment and acquisition policies making up the military organization.

In spite of their unflinching commitment to the transition project, the regime left an inoperable political system, which made it impossible for the new government to transform itself into a truly democratic dispensation. The military was so influential that, even after its formal disengagement, the civilian president conceded that there were only two parties in the country: the ruling National Party and the Nigerian army.

## The Civilian Era (1979—83)

After thirteen years of military administration, a civilian democracy returned to power in Nigeria on 1 October 1979 and the civilians were in government until 31 December 1983. The period witnessed a different defence structure which, for the first time, placed all services under a single chief of defence staff, who also doubled as principal adviser to the president on defence through the Minister of Defence. Two key advantages of this development were thought to be better co-ordination of the political and military ends of policy and standardization. It would bring clear employment, deployment and acquisition policies to the entire armed forces. The lesson of the previous years had been that services embarked on different, often conflicting and sometimes overlapping programmes which exacerbated rather than healing national contradictions. Inter-service coordination was also thought to be the key to enhancing the doctrinal position of defence in line with governmental objectives and national interests.

As a result the civilian administration continued with the continental pro-gramme of the erstwhile regime with little or no modification, although the rhetoric had become less anti-West. On the doctrinal question, the government essentially reverted to the days of reactive doctrinal postures. While most security problems the regime experienced were within predictable range and manageable limit, the administration's reactions to them were neither planned nor situated within the ambit of articulated doctrinal principle. The relatively high incidence of threats to the country's territorial integrity and the eventual (mis)management of the threats during this period pointed to a government in which the military still had influence outside the normal institutional channels. The effect was the low level of complementarity between foreign and defence policies, resulting in a doctrinal standpoint dictated by occasional exigencies and prestige considerations rather than requirements of long-term survival in the country's strategic environ-ment.[23] In the end, military officers closest to the civilian administration were the leading figures in the coup that engineered its overthrow, and there are many who still hold the view that the coup leaders acted in concert with some politicians to save the country from a bloodier resolution of the crisis that had plagued it in the 1960s. Some members of the ruling party, however, felt sure that the coup plotters had acted for themselves.

## The Buhari—Idiagbon Regime (1984—5)

What distinguished the Buhari—Idiagbon military junta from other military regimes was its refusal to even pretend that it had a transition programme for the country.

Although it came into office with support from a public fed up with the venality of its politicians, this refusal to adopt an agenda for civilian transformation was seen by various interest groups, both within and outside the military, as in itself a carefully articulated political agenda. Indeed, their authoritarian administration was largely resented by Nigerians, and some have traced their ouster in a palace coup, after twenty months in government, to their single-minded pursuit of an isolation-ist foreign and defence policy and their intransigent political stand that gave no indication of a plan for the return of the country to civilian rule.

The Buhari regime, for instance, acknowledged Nigeria's security problems as mainly internal, reduced the rhetorical continental agenda hitherto pursued by previous regimes, and looked inwards.[24] For this policy, the regime received criticism as well as pressure from external powers and neighbouring countries whose interests were in conflict with this policy; local opprobrium was minimal.[25] In terms of transition politics and military doctrine, one can conclude that their period in office was too short for a clear direction to emerge; they operated a more collegial rule but suffered seriously from the public perception of their regime as 'nasty and brutish'. The fact that they ruled at a time of wide-ranging economic problems may also have precluded effective monitoring of defence spending in terms of direction and agreed policy. Their short stay in office saw a reversal in patterns of military spending, although they emphasized traditional service prefer-ences over an integrated national security package. Funds allocated were not necessarily used for enhancing the non-military dimensions of security: the regime, like others before it, still perceived security through the narrow prism of power and prestige.

## The Babangida Years (1985–93)

With the arrival of General Babangida at the helm of affairs in 1985, for the first time Nigerians had a military ruler who opted for the all-encompassing title of president, hitherto thought to be restricted to democratically elected rulers, rather than the low-profile 'head of state' that had become the norm for military rulers. Indeed, the situation began to resemble closely the institutional and personalistic agenda of control pioneered in countries like Thailand and Chile. As the country faced an economic crunch, which resulted in a structural adjustment programme, the elevation of speculative finance over industrial capital became the defining characteristic of economic policy. Short-term monetarist policies – exchange rate devaluation, removal of subsidies, sale of state enterprises, freeing of prices and generalized deflationary policies – took precedence over the structural reform of a debilitating economy which the national consensus favoured at that time. The deregulation of the financial market ensured that the financial sector became the only growth sector, with interest rates determined by speculators as agriculture, manufacturing and industry floundered.

Not even the mini-boom engendered by the Persian Gulf oil crisis of 1990–1, in the latter years of the Babangida regime, brought any respite to the generality of the population. Instead, the extra funds gained were regarded as discretionary income by the regime. The windfall was used to fuel a massive spending binge that diverted revenues into corruption, funded patronage, sharply expanded extra-budgetary expenditure and bloated an already inflation-ridden economy. Between September 1988 and 30 June 1994, according to the devastating summary presented in Dr Pius Okigbo's official inquiry into the finances of the Central Bank of Nigeria,

> US$12.2 billion of the $12.4 billion (in the dedicated and special accounts) was liquidated in less than six years ... spent on what could neither be adjudged genuine high priority nor truly regenerative investment; neither the president nor the Central Bank governor accounted to anyone for these massive extra-budgetary expenditures ... clandestinely undertaken while the country was openly reeling with a crushing external debt overhang.[26]

Little wonder, then, that the economic reform programme started by the military regime in 1986 (under General Babangida) finally collapsed under the weight of the 1993 annulled election and the massive capital flight that followed. By 1993, Nigeria, according to the World Bank, was among the twenty poorest countries in the world. The situation worsened under the Abacha regime: GNP grew only 2.8 per cent in 1994; inflation ran at over 60 per cent just as the country experienced an exponential unemployment growth rate; and the Nigerian naira virtually collapsed.[27]

But it was not just the economy that suffered in this state retrenchment exercise. The prospects for democratization also dimmed. Given the diffused level of autonomy exercised by the military institution, the result of parcelling out the state to private military interests, the class and group project engendered by previous military rule was exchanged for the personal rule of the 'benevolent dictator'. Through his benefaction, many, including his superiors, had become beholden to Babangida as direct beneficiaries of his generosity. While it may be stretching credulity to assume that all of those involved were aware of their role in class terms, especially given the linkage between finance capital and the state apparatus, they would have known that the conjuncture of a shared-out state and personal rule had been responsible for their financial success. They would also have realized that supporting General Babangida's rule in one way or another would be the price to pay for their financial benefits.

In the larger society, privatization exacerbated the prebendal politics, with its attendant pressure on ethnic relations as many who lost out in the scheme of things concluded that the overwhelming power of the centre was responsible for their fate. But if these tendencies were simply limited to the government, it would be less disturbing. By institutionalizing favouritism and bribery as legitimate instruments of governance, the military regime headed by Babangida succeeded in culturing a miasma of anti-democratic practices reproduced regularly in the world view of the ordinary Nigerian, either in the form of the common belief that everyone had a price, or in the disappearance of loyalty to the state, as militarism became embedded in the psyche of the average individual.

The restructuring of the economy along monetarist lines represented an ambitious attempt by the 'techno-military' authoritarian state under General Babangida to generate a new hegemonic bloc. This was carried out on two broad levels: economic and political.[28] First, as a result of the government's privatization agenda, several of the state-owned industrial and commercial ventures were sold directly to ex-military generals or to conglomerates linked to them. In addition, the new merchant banks that emerged to take advantage of the liberalization of the financial sector featured several retired military officers on their boards. In fact, it was common knowledge in the late 1980s and early 1990s that, no matter how solid one's capital base was, the likelihood of gaining a bank licence was dependent on having at least one ex-military figurehead listed on the board. The fact that many of these banks eventually collapsed under the weight of bad management was not unconnected to the excesses of bank executives who concluded that military presence on their boards was a licence to steal as long as the military board members were kept happy. Indeed, many military generals were prominent beneficiaries of the bad loans allocated by these failed banks.[29]

Second, General Babangida went beyond the personal pecuniary motives of erstwhile military rulers by ensuring that the stratification of the military from the rest of society did not exist only at the level of retired officers, but also at an institutional level. Hence, by adopting a practice common to Latin American and some South-east Asian military institutions, he announced the formation of an Army Bank (which never took off), an industrial armaments city (which also did not see daylight) and the Nigerian Army Welfare Insurance Scheme. To ensure that every military officer considered the stratification project an institutional agenda, the government spent N550 million (US$60 million in 1992), advertised to a hapless public as loans, to purchase cars for serving military officers of and above the rank of captain. This was later extended to the non-commissioned officers in the form of motorcycles, while the rank and file got bicycles.

By now, a paradigmatic shift had occurred in the mindset of the military cabal intent on remaining in power. Before, it was an anathema for serving officers to flaunt their involvement in the economic sector and to claim permanent political control. Now, many became closely identified with oil, financial and shipping interests, whilst justifying their new role as political actors. Serving officers declared in several public fora that they were the ones to take Nigeria to political and economic heights because of their military training and the advantage of a liberal university education. This tendency became more pronounced under General Abacha, when military officers began to threaten Nigerians that they would return by hook or by crook, even if they were removed from a direct political role.[30] The idea of a military party took firm root and some of the officers and civilian intellectuals involved in the project were assigned to study the Nasserist/Baathist models in Egypt, Syria and Iraq as well as the foundational regimes in Latin America and South-east Asia.[31] In the end, though, Babangida had to vacate the seat of power unceremoniously because he failed to realize the transition project.

## The Abacha and Abubakar Years (1993–9)

Knowing how weakened the military had become on assuming power, the military return under General Abacha was widely portrayed as a reluctant comeback and the 'only alternative' to save the nation from disintegration. On the political front, General Abacha won respect by his deft assemblage of a broad-based civilian 'diarchic' coalition of prominent politicians. As with the political militaries before him, Abacha's promise of a 'brief tenure' and the announcement of a National Constitutional Conference with 'full constituent powers' were presented to their constituents as their main reason for service by politicians. The fact that General Abacha adopted the characteristic rhetoric of his predecessors – promises to 'clean house', free the nation's economy from corruption and ruin, reduce dependence on the fluctuating international market and return the economy to ordinary Nigerians – was unconvincing. Not lost on them was the fact that this 'cleaner' of the stable was not untainted, having been in the corridors of power for the last decade: he had announced three *coups d'état* and was rumoured to be the most corrupt general, leaving aside his role in the annulment of the 1993 presidential election. The crucial point here was that General Abacha succeeded in gaining the benefit of the doubt, which he needed for initial legitimation.

Within the military, this was also a favoured strategy. On coming to office, the 'professional' wing were left in charge as they controlled the army in the dying days of the Babangida regime, especially after the purge of the so called 'IBB Boys' – hence Major-General Chris Ali, a 'pro-democracy' officer, was put in charge of the army, Rear-Admiral Alison Madueke in charge of the navy and Air Vice Marshal Femi John Femi in charge of the air force. What gave these officers more confidence was the presence of General Oladipo Diya, the main fixer of the political class during the early days of the coup and one of the few officers who openly challenged Babangida's continued presence in the military during the days of the 1993 national crisis.

All this was soon to change. By mid-1994, revelations by a disaffected participant in the November 1993 coup (Brigadier-General David Mark) that the regime did not in fact intend to limit itself to a brief stay in power strongly supported the view that the Constitutional Conference was, after all, only part of the government's attempt to create a veneer of legitimacy. Outside of the military, the public had woken from its battle-wearied slumber, and national strikes, coordinated by the labour unions and a newly formed broad coalition of civil society organizations, ethnic pressure groups and political alliances, paralysed the government for ten weeks with a seriously negative impact on an already parlous economy. Chief Abiola, winner of the annulled elections, used the opportunity to reclaim his mandate as the elected president of Nigeria. In desperation, the regime jettisoned its collegial facade and adopted a repressive edge which gave Nigeria its pariah status and led to her suspension from the Commonwealth in 1995, after the regime murdered environmental rights activist Ken Saro Wiwa and his fellow minority/environmental rights activists.

Inside the military, however, dissension was also growing. When two of the outspoken service chiefs, Major-General Chris Ali and Rear-Admiral Alison Madueke, urged the release of political prisoners from jail, General Abacha simply sacked them and replaced them with officers he considered more supportive of a permanent transition agenda. Further repressive measures were soon to follow, including the convictions obtained against several retired and serving officers. Among them were an ex-head of state and his deputy, General Olusegun Obasanjo and Major-General Shehu Musa Yar'adua, now in the vanguard of opposition activities. Leading democracy activists and journalists like Dr Beko Ransome Kuti, Malam Shehu Sani, Chris Anyanwu and Kunle Ajibade were also jailed on trumped-up charges of plotting to overthrow the regime.

Abacha, like previous rulers, was concerned about how this internal attack on civil society and the military institution would appear to the outside world. In preparing his external dimension he also displayed method. Having rid himself, albeit temporarily, of the main threats to his rule within civil society, the military and the political elite, and in order to sustain a public image of seriousness, he sought legitimacy as the champion of Nigeria's bourgeois technocracy. Yet this image-boosting alliance offered only a temporary reprieve rather than a long-standing nation-building strategy. The contradictions within the Nigerian state and the failure of government cannot be dealt with without addressing questions of democratic governance and the accountability of state structures as part of the quest for an enduring nation-building project.

Drawing significant inspiration from the neo-militarist credo in Latin America and South-east Asia, General Abacha and his advisers believed it was possible to engineer a succession plan as long as he could convince the West and the international financial institutions of a commitment to deregulation and market reform. There were two planks to this agenda. The first was a version of Mohammed Mahatir's Vision 2020 agenda in Malaysia, called Vision 2010. This liberal economic policy agenda was co-coordinated by the deposed interim government leader, Chief Ernest Shonekan. Abacha was principally encouraged to introduce this agenda by the dramatic fall-off in the international campaign for sanctions against the regime barely months after the execution of Ken Saro Wiwa, and by the apparent lack of any internationally coordinated policy to expedite democratic reform in Nigeria. The regime's contention was that a significant section of the international community accepted the idea that individual freedom and democratic reform should sometimes be sacrificed to economic growth and structural reform – a view seemingly confirmed by the feeble response of world powers to the campaign for international sanctions against the regime.

The second plank, advanced simultaneously with this bid for technocratic support to reassure the international community, consisted of seeking regional legitimacy by promoting (and where necesary inventing) a West African tradition of military-turned-civilian presidents, aiming to establish a conducive climate for General Abacha's role transformation. There is evidence that resources were provided by the Abacha regime for military-led political parties in Niger and Gambia,[32] while the president of Ghana received pecuniary benefits for his unwavering support of the Abacha dictatorship. All the while, in spite of his heavy-handed treatment of the opposition, General Abacha kept the political transition project in full view, just as his predecessors had. He concluded, perhaps consistently with other military rulers before him, that participating in such a political project mattered less than being seen to have one.

Although it was General Babangida who put in motion the idea of constructing a disguised military party, it was General Abacha, his military successor, who dusted off the blueprint and successfully implemented it through the brazen creation of artificial political parties. At the time of his death, all the five parties in his democratic transition project had 'unanimously' adopted General Abacha as the presidential candidate. Notwithstanding the strong opposition in civil society to this undisguised manipulation, many interested observers, including leading figures in the international community, had resigned themselves to an Abacha civilian presidency.[33] The official pretence of a collegial façade which military rulers always projected had been wholly discarded by the time General Abacha died in June 1997. Unlike General Babangida, who parcelled out the state to friends and mentors within the military, General Abacha kept the spoils of office for himself and his family, the coterie of his security apparatus and a small circle of foreign friends. He made a point of ignoring the military institution; the ruling military council hardly met. An alternative power centre, loyal to the person of General Abacha, was set up in the security/intelligence units, which undermined the institutional legitimacy of the military. Credible but unconfirmed information shows, however, that it was this failure to pay sufficient attention to the military constituency that eventually paved the way for his unexpected demise.

The nature of General Abacha's exit and the arrival of General Abubakar on the scene arguably determined the outcome of the democratization project. However one may view the eventual outcome of the rushed transition programme, the fact that General Abubakar was not responding to a full defeat of the military could hardly be discounted in understanding the push for a graceful exit and elections by what was thought to be the closest party to the military hierarchy. The compromised nature of the political settlement was therefore a product of democratic pressure on the military's political agenda. The fact that military influence is still very strong in the country – albeit in a disguised form – is an indication of the huge challenge the country faces in the post-military era. It also underlines why the democratic experience remains fragile, under threat from various unresolved issues traceable to the influence of the political army.

## Impact of Transition Politics on Military Professionalism

Given the extent of military involvement in politics for over thirty of forty years of independence, it is hardly surprising that the institution was riven by a variety of corporate, ethnic and personal grievances developed over time in the prolonged years of military government. The negative impact on military professionalism and operational effectiveness had become noticeable in the confusion and lack of direction of the Nigerian armed forces in the immediate aftermath of the civil war. Unfortunately, the euphoria of federal victory and the immediate pressures of rehabilitation, reconciliation and reconstruction of the political terrain fostered the creeping organizational inertia in which the armed forces had become embroiled. Military planners were not sanguine enough to believe that the war had been won by effective organization of the military,[34] and honest enough to admit that peacetime deterrence would be harder to achieve without renewed attention to professional and organizational issues sich as doctrine, force posture, force levels, combat operational command, resource allocation and weapons procurement.[35]

In spite of this recognition, Nigeria's immediate post-war defence organization did not clearly abolish pre-war circumstances, mainly because the preference for incremental change was overwhelming. A wide gap existed between defence organization and strategic purpose. Although a few cosmetic attempts were made to reorganize the defence organization, subordinating the service viewpoint became the main problem in the promotion of a defence review. Service interests, service needs and service power have dominated the Nigerian military structure, frustrating all efforts to establish a rational system of strategic planning, force development, resource allocation and collective military coordination. Successive military regimes inherited the weaknesses of the service-dependent structure without much hope of central coordination. And successful separation of the office of the Minister of Defence and the head of state by the military ensured that the incumbent minister lacked a clear picture of his role, which in turn threatened regime security.

Yet the implications of the military's transition politics transcend defective defence organization and management. One aspect that deserves particular examination is the impact of military coups on corporate professionalism. By their very nature, coups are high-risk ventures, which in their success or failure almost always result in the loss of perpetrators, or their targets, or both. The persistence of coups and the decimation of the officer corps had a negative impact on the profession and, invariably, national security. For example, the 1966 coups saw the loss of at least two thirds of the officer corps; the abortive 1976 coups led to the execution of 116 military men, police officers and civilians; the 1986 abortive coup resulted in the deaths of some of the country's best pilots, and this in part led to the near-total decimation of the air force under General Babangida, a situation which further resulted in the avoidable deaths of 150 military officers in a defective C-130 Transport plane crash in 1991. The April 1990 coup led to the deaths of at least 50 military officers. Altogether no fewer than four hundred officers have lost their lives in or as a result of *coup d'états*.

In addition to the loss through executions, the scale and intensity of premature retirements, dismissals and promotions that resulted from abortive or successful coups were high. Ordinarily, retirements and promotions in the military establishment are a routine thing. Yet despite the surface plausibility of 'routine exercise', 'natural attrition' or 'declining productivity' that accompanied the dismissals and promotions in this period, the overwhelming consensus was one of an exercise overtly politically motivated. Under the regimes of Babangida and Sani Abacha, however, the Nigerian armed forces became an organization where 'anything was possible', to paraphrase the anguish of a former army chief, given the nature of the dismissals and promotions that took place. In the quest for total personalization of power, there was a desperate need to abandon the collegial and institutional agenda and subject the group project to the personal wishes of the individual autocrat, with little regard for the general wishes of the military constituency and its corporate interests. Consequently, the strategy required the neutralization of all real or imagined opposition, leaving no one in doubt about who was in control of the military establishment and of the country. By the time General Abacha died in June 1998, the military institution had suffered seriously from this blatant disregard for its structures and no fewer than three hundred members of the officer corps had lost their commissions in the course of these haphazard retirements and dismissals.

The flip side of the above situation was excessively rapid promotion, which tended to create false expectations through rank inflation. This had other implications for the country's security as commanders kept changing and there was not enough time to get used to command and staff posts, the overall consequence of which was acute disorientation and organizational dysfunction among the rank and file. At another level, the political careerism resulting from successful coups also engendered resentment, rivalry and disunity amongst military officers. Thus, organizational dysfunction in the Nigerian military apparatus resulted primarily from this political involvement. Both played a mutually reinforcing role in their impact on professionalism; the military was unable to govern the civil society directly or effectively without losing its professional attributes and without ceasing to be an army.

Apart from the threat the political military constituted to its profession, the increasing personalization of power also led to the loss of morale and the ascendancy of policies and processes which did not emerge from the military constituency. This breakdown of institutional cohesion and *esprit de corps* in the context of the personalized nature of rule over the last decade, especially under Babangida and Abacha, witnessed the rise of alternative power centres in shadowy security and intelligence outfits, which inevitably became the anchor for regime security. Consequently, the growing influence of the intellectual architects of military politics and the overwhelming influence of military intelligence and associated bodies became directly proportional to the loss of influence by the military as a corporate institution. The policy of *divide et impera*, which had sidelined the best professionals within the military and reduced talented individuals to the status of mere purveyors within the personalized autocratic project, served to mask the growing mutinous tendencies within the military establishment. In this way the alternative power centre undermined military professionalism and the role that it played in hampering the nation-building project.

## Role Expansion and the Security and Intelligence Services

Although political leadership might address the internal crisis within the armed forces through a redefinition of its role and mission – a rethink of force design, posture and structure, weapons acquisition, political reorientation, retraining and demobilization – any serious quest for military reform has to address the alternative power centre, developed around the security and intelligence networks, that has been used by successive rulers to undermine the military institution in order to remain in power.

As in every post-independence sovereign country in Anglophone Africa, Nigeria's intelligence activities were largely conducted under the auspices of the Special Branch of the Nigerian police force, except for military intelligence work. Military intelligence was blamed for failing to read accurately the strengths and weaknesses of the breakaway republic of Biafra, contributing to the failure of the Nigerian armed forces to complete the civil war operation in 48 hours as envisaged by military planners. It was also blamed for not articulating correctly the role played by Nigeria's neighbours in the crisis. Although the post-war regime considered reorganizing the structure of 'collection, collation, evaluation, analysis, integration and interpretation of all collected information', this only resulted in a strengthened internal covert operation by the Special Branch.[36] Besides, since the weakness of the military intelligence branch was neither articulated nor seen as a threat to regime security, its contribution was more likely to be ignored in the prioritization of national security needs.

The Special Branch, modelled after the metropolitan arrangement in Britain, was responsible for domestic security intelligence but lost its pre-eminent role in this regard after its failure to uncover the 1976 abortive *coup d'état* in which the head of state, General Mohammed, was assassinated. Thus only when harm came to the single individual heading the government did the institution as a whole come to the realization that something had to be done about the intelligence aspect of national security. Even so, as Major-General James Oluleye observed, 'one cannot fully blame the Special Branch of the Nigeria police for non-detection of the plot ... the army or the services have intelligence organizations that could detect the planning of a coup, but regrettably, the plan (Dimka's) never leaked'.[37] Add to this the fact that the Special Branch had been dissuaded from doing anything about the coup plot it had uncovered the previous year.[38]

The organization created after the abortive *coup d'état* that killed General Mohammed, the Nigerian Security Organization (NSO), assumed wider powers in intelligence duties, including responsibility for external intelligence. The decree setting up the NSO incorporated the External Affairs Ministry's research department as the NSO's external wing. While administrative supervision of the section remained with the ministry, operational control was with the NSO. This affected relations between the two bodies later. The other complication arose from the fact that a military intelligence officer was drafted to head the new all-encompassing security organization. The officer, Colonel Abdullahi Mohammed, who had served as the general staff officer for intelligence work at the planning headquarters during the civil war, was at the time military governor in the then Benue-Plateau State. Colonel (later Major-General) Mohammed headed the security agency until the civilian government assumed office in October 1979. General Obasanjo was concerned about the role played by the Military Intelligence Directorate in the July 1975 coup plot which brought their government to office, a concern which convinced him of the need to curb military intelligence involvement in national security policy making.[39] This was reflected in the prominence under Obasanjo of civilian intelligence officers in the organization's operations. In spite of this balancing act, a participant observer still noted that the organization could easily have become a witch-hunting Gestapo unit.[40] The discovery of a secret government detention camp by the human rights body Civil Liberties Organization confirmed the view that the NSO was not only a product of regime security, but also performed its duties in a manner liable to create the impression that it was not driven by national security concerns if these were not couched in regime security terms.

The succeeding civilian government expanded the powers of the NSO while its director, Alhaji Umaru Shinkafi, also doubled as the president's principal adviser on intelligence matters. While the nature of the democratic set-up made the organization more accountable, its public image as a gestapo for hounding private citizens equally gathered pace. By the time the military overthrew the civilians in December 1983, the tension between the NSO and the External Affairs Ministry's 'research department' had reached a high point. Simultaneously, the competition for dominance in the intelligence service between military intelligence and the NSO had become intense. The change of leadership at the NSO seemed to have worsened relations between the head of military intelligence, Brigadier Aliyu Mohammed, and the NSO director-general, Ambassador Rafindadi, a career diplomat with a wide-ranging background in intelligence. As if to exacerbate the tension, the head of the NSO was made a member of the Supreme Military Council, the highest policy-making body, alongside the director of military intelligence, who had always been a member.

On the other hand, the personal animosities between the NSO director and the administration's Minister of External Affairs affected the smooth running of the external aspect of the intelligence services. According to the minister, since the director of the NSO was a member of the ruling council and he was not, 'he appeared to have seen himself as the member of the Supreme Military Council with the supervisory role over the ministry'.[41] Having contributed to major decisions affecting the ministry prior to the minister's appointment, including the selection of new ambassadors and the reduction of ministerial staff, the NSO head was widely respected by the military leadership as a professional intelligence officer whose experience was invaluable. Apparently, that much confidence was not reposed in the minister, an academic without practical experience of government. Equally, the leadership did not place much trust in military intelligence at that time.[42]

To regain its frontline status, military intelligence resorted to a portrayal of the other services as uncouth and brutal, with no regard for human rights. So effective was this campaign (the treatment meted out to politicians and journalists by the NSO under the Buhari–Idiagbon regime helped its cause) that the public perceived the NSO as an organization completely out of control. Equally, the Military Intelligence Directorate continued to agitate, albeit unsuccessfully, for its own prominence. Perhaps this was responsible for its deep involvement in the palace coup that ousted General Buhari in 1985. As the former head of state later revealed in a rare interview, 'I realized it was one of the master plans of the fifth columnist to embarrass and discredit my administration.... I knew it was the military intelligence, not the police, not the NSO.'[43]

Even though the Babangida regime made a much-publicized attempt to expose the 'excesses' of the NSO under the previous administration and to 'reinstate professional credibility to the intelligence service', the attempt appeared superficial and directed toward regime security. The ultimate beneficiary of the move by the new administration was the Military Intelligence Directorate, which had lost much ground in the Buhari administration. Babangida not only reinstated its head, Brigadier Aliyu Mohammed Gusau, who had been threatened with dismissal by the previous government, but also disbanded the NSO.[44] As with previous regimes, however, General Babangida's determination to restructure the intelligence service only gathered pace after the abortive coup of April 1990. As he informed the Command and Staff College graduates two months after the abortive coup:

> We must in the light of the April (aborted) coup also review and re-conceptualize the responsibilities of the security and intelligence services.... The leadership must evolve a professional rigour of threat identification which enables it to respond to early warnings against all forces of destabilization as well as develop the capacity to differentiate categories of threats.[45]

The new regime centralized the intelligence services by creating the post of a Coordinator for National Security in 1988 to superintend the activities of three bodies created earlier: State Security Services, responsible for internal security; the National Intelligence Agency, responsible for external intelligence; and the Defence Intelligence Agency, charged with responsibility for coordinating intelligence among the armed services. Yet units like the Military Intelligence Directorate remained in place and still appeared more powerful than the Defence Intelligence Agency and State Security Services in matters relating to perceived and real military threats to regime security. Clearly, the in-bred tension did not curb inter-agency rivalry fully, but the intelligence services became more powerful in the institutional hierarchy of national security policy making, particularly in ensuring regime security and the determination of internal and external threats.

However, there is a non-institutional side to the rise of the intelligence services under the Babangida regime. The creation of these parallel structures by military leaders assumes far greater importance in the context of their distaste for institutional arrangements that could moderate the excesses of the head of government – a role which had made the Supreme Military Council very central to previous episodes of military rule in Nigeria. With the ascendancy of the security and intelligence units, however, the associational and corporatist character of the regimes at inception took on an authoritarian hue as they attempted to consolidate a more personalized power base.

Although this practice had started with the creation of NSO in 1976, it was institutionalized under General Babangida when he set up a plethora of security networks culminating in the creation of an alternative paramilitary service – the National Guard – to undercut the military institution. By this time the role of private military companies in the activities of the intelligence services and in the overall arrangement of regime security had become a source of concern within the military as an institution.[46] Equally, a regime that had come into office touting respect for fundamental freedoms and human rights had lost all credibility with civil society, and agitation had increased exponentially by 1989. Through their responsibility for discovering and nipping 'undue radicalism' and civilian versions of *coup d'état* in the bud, the role expansion of the security and intelligence services guaranteed them an autonomy and influence they had not hitherto enjoyed.

This growing influence took on pernicious proportions under the late General Abacha, with the formation of the Libyan- and Korean-trained Special Bodyguard Services for the personal protection of the dictator, as well as the Strike Force and K Squad – responsible for carrying out state-sponsored assassinations of political enemies. That this alternative power bloc around General Abacha completely made a nonsense of the military institution and destroyed the hierarchy that is so central to it became obvious in the subsequent trials of the junior officers who ran the complex.[47] Credible military intelligence sources claim that at least five thousand members of these services were trained and that the short period of General Abubakar's regime, which concentrated on the military handover to civilians, failed to address military reform in any significant manner.

The more things change, the more they remain the same. Even under the new dispensation, President Obasanjo resorted to employing some of those who had set up these shadowy security agencies, responsible for serious human rights abuses in the past.[48] While this may help the government in achieving a better under-standing of the strengths and weaknesses of the intelligence services, it has reinforced the personality-driven style of power at the expense of a structured and institutional approach aimed at professionalism in an atmosphere of accountability. Ultimately, the key to ensuring that intelligence services act within the rule of law is an institutional strategy that demands accountability through an ethical code, legislative oversight and executive control. Clearly, democratic control over the activities of the armed forces is central to curbing the excesses and restoring the military to its pride of place and legitimacy among the people; equally clearly, the intelligence services remain unaccountable under the democratic dispensation, although they are more sensitive to criticism. Whatever professional difficulties the military had experienced in the past, the shocking revelations of military excesses after just one year of civilians in power support the idea that the organizational inertia can only be arrested through concerted efforts that centre on redefining the role, mission and ethos of the military institution.

## Farewell to Political Armies or Transition to Neo-Militarism?

Military disengagement from politics represents an important first step towards democracy, even if it does not equate with or immediately translate to civilian democratic control. From the evidence available in Nigeria so far, the formal demilitarization of politics has widened the space within which concrete and sustainable democratic reform is possible. But it has also opened up various fissures which on previous occasions have invited military intervention. Even with the new start, a complete disentanglement of politics from its military roots – especially in a body politic that has become so atomized and in which the symbols, values and ethos of the military are replicated throughout civil society – is still far away.

Yet if the country is to attain stable civil–military relations and consolidate Nigeria's fragile democracy, a critical task is reclaiming the militarized mind which has enthralled the entire society, fed by deep-seated feelings of social exclusion under military rule. Given the prevailing political culture, bred by three decades of militarism and authoritarian control in Nigeria, the current political transition only represents a reconfiguration of the political, economic and military elite, rather than an opening up of the political system and a broadening of participation. What we have witnessed is the creation of a 'shadow' military and security hierarchy. One indication of this feature is the influence of the retired military serving in the affairs of state. Another is the rise of militant political activity in various parts of the country, believed to have been fuelled by those closely connected with the erstwhile military leadership who seem dissatisfied with the direction of the state. After years of repression and control under military rule, many communities are now adopting military strategies in responding to any form of domination in their lives.

The greatest challenge in combating the scourge of political militarism, therefore, is addressing the psychology of militarism that has become reified in the context of an exclusionary politics. Herein lies the paradox of democratization and demilitari-zation not just in Nigeria but also across the rest of post-Cold War Africa. Dominant theories of civil–military relations contend that all that is required to correct the above anomaly is to ensure that the authority to use and control military power resides fully with the elected authorities, and completely outside the realm of professional soldiers. This Huntingtonian model of civil–military relations assumed a level playing field in which 'autonomous military professionalism' can be predicated on 'objective civilian control' which encourages an 'independent military sphere' that does not 'interfere in political matters'. In reality, this per-spective treats civilian control as an event, a fact of political life which exists along a continuum, and not as a process.[49]

In our view, civilian control should not be seen as a set of technical and administrative arrangements that automatically flow from every post-military transition, but as part of complex political processes which must address the root causes of militarism in society, beyond the formal removal of the military from political power. There is a need to redefine our notion of the apolitical military – a notion which has been central to the dominant civil–military discourse. In Nigeria, where the military have become entrenched in all facets of civic and economic life and where politics have just featured a reconfiguration rather than a transformation of power, simply anchoring the need for objective civilian control to the notion of an apolitical military underestimates the seriousness of the issues at stake. While formal mechanisms of control are not wrong in themselves, the reality underpinning Nigeria's crisis of governance underscores the fact that sub-ordination of the armed forces to civil control can only be achieved when civil control is seen as part of a complex democratic struggle that goes beyond elections.[50] These processes are expressions of relationships that are inherently political, subjective and psychological.[51]

Only when the political and psychological issues arising out of military involvement in politics are grasped, can we begin to look at objective control mechanisms. Therefore, the areas that need serious policy attention if there is to be real change in Nigeria are the constitutional dimensions of democratic control; the redefinition of the role and mission of the military; the development of civilian, democratic defence policy expertise; the confirmation of professional autonomy; and the creation of the necessary opportunities for networking and dialogue between military representatives and civil society workers. But work in these areas must be prefaced by a careful review of the cumulative, protean nature of the military crisis.

Nor can a true resolution allow the isolation of the domestic arena from the international. This becomes a central issue given the increasingly important role private, external military companies are playing in setting the agenda of military reform in Nigeria. Indeed, viewed within the context of globalization, ownership of the processes of change and military reform in a manner that is process-led and people-driven is being sacrificed to another top-down security agenda driven by external players who are promoting their own interests. The fact that all of this is taking place with no discussion by the people underlines the need to locate change within a constitutional framework.

## Constitutional Dimensions of Civil–Military Relations and the Future of Democratic Consolidation in Nigeria

The location of the military in terms of its accountability to the executive, the legislature and the wider society needs to be clarified in constitutional terms. This is important for a number of reasons. First, accountability, transparency and openness have become fundamental constitutional tenets and the current administration is leading the way in this respect. Second, as a national institution, the military rely on the public for support and sustenance in order to fulfil their constitutional mandate. Third, the idea that military matters are exclusive to the military constituency can no longer be tolerated. Issues relating to the armed forces must be subjected to public discourse and the executive branch of government. If the state is to resolve the problem of accountability and address the lacunae of its post-colonial legacy and prolonged military dictatorship, popular participation and organizational coherence, not exclusivity, are the crucial elements needed to counter military control and widen national security perspectives.

Unfortunately, previous constitutions have tended to be silent about the armed forces and their role in society. The same is true of the 1999 constitution. Although Section 217 (2) defines the purpose of the armed forces, this inadequate formulation was lifted from the 1979 constitution with no reflection on the problems that arose from prolonged military rule in the intervening two decades. Although it is arguable that this general conception gives the political authority enough flexibility to define what it seeks, this lack of clarity can also be the problem. Civilians frequently lack knowledge and understanding of military affairs, and the apportioning of civilian and military responsibilities often depends on the military, or on a small coterie of elected civilian officials. This situation, obviously, can often lead to a further lack of accountability, as is the case in Nigeria currently. Given the burden of its authoritarian past and the loss of credibility by the military, it was thought that elected civilians would be allowed to play a key role in military restructuring and the redefinition of its roles and missions. Yet there is a conflict between a section of the populace who feel that legislative scrutiny should be central to democratic control and others who feel that the president and his Defence Minister, as ex-military men, should have ultimate powers to restructure the military without obligatory recourse to other checks and balances within the system.

In fact, the legislature has largely functioned as a rubber stamp as far as military matters are concerned. Often unaware of developments, it has been short-changed by an overbearing executive branch in terms of determining policy on the size and character of the armed forces, overseeing the armed forces' activities and approving actions taken by the executive branch.[52] It had been expected that the review of the country's constitution would provide an opportunity to re-examine the constitutional dimension of military matters and to clarify the roles of the executive, the legislative branch and the wider society in ensuring stable civil–military relations.

*Quest for a military mission*
In ensuring civilian supremacy and a democratic pattern of civil–military relations, the civilian leadership in any post-authoritarian state must define the role of the military in a clear and precise manner. A 'missionless' military poses a serious threat in relation to its primary role as defender of the nation's territorial integrity. In the past, the political usurpation of military talents has proved dangerous in areas where the military was needed to function professionally. While the Nigerian military has acquired a reputation for its commitment to and participation in international peacekeeping duties, for example, involvement in regional security is not a role clearly specified in Section 217 of the 1999 constitution, nor in any post-independence constitution. This gives the impression that it is not seen as a primary feature of the country's defence arrangements and inadequate attention is therefore paid to it. In several instances, the professionalism of Nigerian soldiers on peacekeeping missions has been found wanting. Yet it is a fact of civil–military relations that in countries where the military has a clearly defined external role and mission, the military increases its apolitical profile, partly due to the external focus of its mission. Within reason, therefore, it is useful to restrict the military mission to its traditional external combat role as a means of strengthening civil–military relations and reorientating it toward a more professional outlook. If it must get involved in internal security operations, proper criteria need to be developed for evaluating the involvement of armed forces in such non–combat operations.

This is an issue that Nigeria has to address urgently given the government's tendency to use the military to suppress civil insurrection, as was witnessed when the new authorities sent soldiers to the Niger Delta and the president declared a 'shoot at sight' order on prime television, even threatening a state of emergency in Lagos. Again, while Section 217 (2)c of the 1999 constitution indicates that 'suppressing insurrection and acting in aid of civil authorities to restore order when called upon to do so by the President' may be necessary, the constitution is very clear that 'this is subject to such conditions as may be prescribed by an Act of the National Assembly'. Even so, there was no indication that the National Assembly prescribed any such conditions before the military was dispatched into the Delta. This clearly remains a slippery slope which must be addressed if Nigeria's fragile democracy is not to fall prey to an authoritarian mindset.

If militarization is to become less significant as a means of managing conflict and enhancing the nation-building project, then the military mission has to be redefined by the political leadership with input from civil society. Within the context of the identified challenges, the entrenchment of the military in all aspects of civic and economic life makes their eventual permanent removal a task that will demand considerable skills in a country like Nigeria. This will have to be done by assuaging their fears about their future in a post-military dispensation and finding an appropriate role and mission for those left behind in the institution, in terms of maintaining their professional autonomy. Up to now, the unifying theme in all negotiations within the political elite has been the determination to assert civilian (not necessarily democratic) supremacy and supervision and the subordination of the military to objective civilian control.

While concentration on civil control is understandable, given the kind of Faustian bargains struck to ensure that the military suffers no great loss of influence as an institution, suffice it to say that such pacts will only lead to democratic consolidation when they guarantee the complete subordination of the armed forces to the democratic authority, and not to either individual officers or influential military cabals, even if the need to assuage legitimate fears and concerns within the military is recognized. In situations where pacts have been engineered for the consolidation of personal autocracies in exchange for military privileges, which precludes the accountability of the military to democratic institutions, it is reasonable to predict that such democracies will either be rendered inoperable or subverted in no time at all.

Finally, without being prescriptive about this, any attempt to redefine the role and mission of the Nigerian military, given the declining external security threats faced by the country, must consider security in its holistic human security dimension. To achieve legitimacy and democratic accountability, the future of civil–military relations must be predicated on a broader perspective of security that is no longer restricted to military and internal policing. For democratic control of the military and security services to happen, security policy must be broadened to see stability as the flip side of development in its political, economic, social and environmental dimensions. In doing this, particular attention must be paid to the protection of offshore interests and the promotion of a professional peacekeeping command. Even the military aspect must pay particular attention to peace support operations as the primary external role of the Nigerian military. By achieving a consensus around these issues within both the military and wider civil society, a clear strategy governing conditions for involvement in military missions – extent of commitment, conditions for withdrawal of troops, rotation of soldiers, training and doctrine, and due legislative supervision – can be developed in a policy-oriented rather than an *ad hoc* manner.

*Developing civilian expertise for legislative scrutiny*
The point has been made earlier about how the lack of any expertise on the part of elected civilian authorities has prevented effective scrutiny of the various branches of the armed forces. Any redirection of the defence policy process will inevitably require a different kind of expertise, which must be supplied by a mixture of civilians and military professionals. To sustain this, there is a need for a significant thawing process through changes in relationships between the military and civilian political elite, and a significant increase in contacts between opinion

moulders and the outside world. The process of agreeing an appropriate role for the military can only be successfully completed in a climate of sustained dialogue. Presently, contact is virtually non-existent, or is on an unstructured social basis. In introducing civilian expertise, however, care must be taken not to substitute military incompetence in a political setting with civilian inexperience, neither should power be given to technocrats who are not wholly accountable to the electorate through the National Assembly. If civilian control is to be democratic, it must empower those who have political platforms to lead the confidence-building relationship. This is not to suggest, however, that professional civilian expertise is unnecessary. In fact, a possibility worth exploring is the creation of a 'strategic cell' that may serve in an advisory capacity between a civilian presidency and the military professionals. At no time should the military be left to conduct its affairs on the principle of 'no interference', although the political elite should leave the military to design and direct wholly operational matters in areas where the broad policy questions have been settled.

*Ensuring professional autonomy over military matters*
The second major issue for consideration is the separation of broad policy decisions over matters such as size, shape, organization, force structure, equipment, weapons acquisition and conditions of military service, on the one hand, and operational control over these issues, on the other. The professional military love a civilian head who understands their predicament, and value unrestricted access to the president as well as autonomy over their internal organization and operations. Any redirection of the defence policy process will inevitably require a different kind of expertise, which must be composed of a mixture of civilians and military professionals. There should be constant exchange and redistribution of knowledge between the military and civilian political elite and a significant increase in contact between the military and the larger civil society. The process of agreeing an appropriate role for the military can only be successful in a climate of sustained dialogue and full consultation with the larger population. Once again, this level of contact is either non-existent or exists only at an unstructured social level.

Equally, the incoming leadership must respect the professional autonomy of the military in spite of the temptation to want to display superior knowledge of the institution. Respecting the professional autonomy of the military should not mean abdication of responsibility on the part of the political leadership. This is one of the paradoxes of the arguments for objective civilian control. While objective civilian control might allow the military to concentrate on military matters and minimize its involvement in political issues, its logic also delimits civilian control over military matters. The experience of Nigeria's second republic under President Shagari showed this phenomenon very clearly. Instead of maintaining political leadership, it resorted to completely arbitrary control by strengthening the police and paramilitary forces as an alternative to the military institution, even after admitting that the military was the other political party, outside of the ruling National Party of Nigeria.

The immediate challenge, therefore, is for the civilian, democratic leadership, not just the presidency, to have an understanding of the sociological underpinnings of the military. Measures that combine emphasis on unequivocal change with some elements of continuity will be necessary. However, whilst the government must work with the military hierarchy, recommendations from them on who gets what job in the military should be handled with dignified scepticism if the danger of military politicization in the ranks of serving officers is to be avoided. It would certainly bode ill for genuine reform if some of those influencing change under the new administration had any remote connection to the problems of the past. Even if this were to be avoided, the incoming government has to address the pervasive influence of politics among very junior officers, many of whom joined the armed forces primarily for the fast route military service offers to political control.

*Resolving the challenge of ethno-nationalism in recruitment*
The resolution of the highly volatile question of recruitment is only possible to the extent that the nationality question is resolved in Nigeria. Although Section 217 (3) of the Nigerian constitution states that 'the composition of the officer corps and other ranks of the armed forces of the Federation shall reflect the Federal character of Nigeria', the fact that this clause has been in every Nigerian constitution has not assuaged the perception of ethnic favouritism in military recruitment.

Various military regimes in the world have used the strategy of ethnic favouritism as a safety valve for survival in office. While this is a political problem that cannot be resolved on a rational basis, military professionalism requires that the issue of recruitment pattern be debated on three central questions: Should the armed forces in a democratic dispensation be equal opportunities institutions? Should they be combat-effective, battle-ready forces recruited from the most able in the most rigorous and competitive manner? And should the manner of recruitment matter – if the training is standardized and geared towards bringing out the best in every recruit? Although these are the questions to which answers must be found, they are not necessarily more important that the structural issues. And political issues are structural.

If good personnel are at the core of any effective military organization, the concern about representation is a legitimate one, especially in ethnically diverse societies where the armed forces are seen as key instruments of national integration. If the military are not inclusively and broadly representative of the religious, ethnic and geographical configurations, the process of confidence building and nation building will be significantly hampered. Getting recruitment wrong from the outset has implications for the level of discipline, attrition rate and the organization's institutional cohesion in the long run, all of which must be situated within the context of the perceptions and misperceptions bred by ethnic, religious and geographic domination. Therefore, attempts at demilitarization and stable military relations must ensure a balance between merit and equal opportunity. This can only be done in a situation where the armed forces are not seen as the fastest route to political power but as professional institutions serving the interests of all citizens.

What becomes of utmost importance within this context is what the military mission is. What objective threats does the nation face? What are the necessary force levels, rather than manpower levels, necessary for the accomplishment of the missions arising from the threats envisaged? Are the personnel procured for and retained in the armed forces suitable for the types of missions the military may be called upon to perform? Are the manpower levels cost-effective? And, most importantly, does the institutional recruitment process procure individuals who are wholly dedicated to their military duties in a democracy?

Another way this has been addressed is through compulsory military service. The 1999 constitution made a passing reference to compulsory military service in Section 220 (1), but only in terms 'of establishing and maintaining adequate facilities for carrying into effect any Act of the National Assembly providing for compulsory military training or military service for citizens of Nigeria'. In countries like Tanzania and Senegal that have experienced long years of stable civil–military relations compulsory military service as an integral part of their armed forces demystifies the military and undermines their exceptionalist tendencies. Besides, this can also complement the task of demilitarization and demobilization because armies in this mould tend to be political in orientation, even when they refrain from partisan politics. A much-reduced but highly mobile deployment force within a streamlined recruitment process can still achieve a credible deterrent doctrine in many countries in West Africa whilst addressing the huge concerns about ethnic monopoly with the democratization of military training and discipline. These are crucial issues that must be addressed in trying to deal with the question of demilitarization in a holistic and democratic manner.

Yet if we are to resolve the problem of recruitment, especially at a time of declining national resources, the size of the armed forces itself must come up for scrutiny. These are political issues that can only be resolved through a process of confidence building and conflict management mechanisms. There is no accurate figure on the size of the Nigerian armed forces, but most estimates range between 70,000 and 80,000 men; this makes an accurate headcount of Nigerian soldiers an immediate necessity. There is also a consensus that given the level of threats faced by the nation, Nigeria can make do with significantly reduced armed forces, although it must be said that traditional assessment would consider the current size inadequate to the country's population and its regional responsibilities. To buttress the demand for reduction in size, even the much-discredited Constitutional Conference that produced the 1995 constitution agreed that the size of the military should be cut to 50,000.

The challenge that will necessarily arise out of an objective assessment is the need for demobilization and rationalization of the forces currently in place. What to do with the demobilized soldiers in terms of retraining and job opportunities in their civilian future will necessarily pose a danger to the stability of a consolidating democracy, especially within the context of militant non-state actors whose ranks they could easily swell. Ultimately, a 'jobs for guns' strategy to ensure that violent crimes that might further threaten civil–military relations do not increase exponentially in the course of the demobilization effort would be necessary. The most important point at this stage is to take a principled stand to address the crisis posed by a huge, bloated army that has become unprofessional in terms of objective threats, national security demands and affordability.

Scholars of democratic transition in countries emerging from a prolonged authoritarian past have often stressed the virtues of sequencing and argued that any opening for democracy can, at best, be a means to an end, an instrumental response to a multi-faceted crisis. Yet this position sometimes assumes that democratic transition is irreversible and would ultimately lead to consolidation, as long as it was incremental in nature.

Given the several false starts in Nigeria's democratic journey and the controversial nature of the outcome of the last elections, there is an increasing need to think less teleologically about the current process producing a settled democracy eventually. While democratic transition may lead to democratic development, pacted transitions have not necessarily led to consolidated democracies nor stemmed the tide of democratic reversals. Based on the evidence so far, the current administration has convinced Nigerians and detached observers that it is not a cloak for continued military rule. However, we have also witnessed the resort to other means of fomenting crisis in the country, given the fact that a coup has now become unlikely under present circumstances. No one would rule out democratic reversal in Nigeria's fragile new state. Yet, even if reversal were the intention of military praetorians, the ascendancy of military constitutionalists in the current re-organization, coupled with an 'active' civil society, may well develop a logic of its own – strong enough, perhaps, to challenge the overwhelming likelihood of military manipulation or democratic reversal. Militarism and militarization will still pose a major problem for the democratization project in Nigeria: we are not about to see the demise of political armies.

## Notes and References

1 Sklar (1992).
2 Gutteridge (1969: 6).
3 Crowder (1970: 505) (my emphasis).
4 Dudley (1971: 171).
5 See *Tempo Magazine* (Lagos), 28 August 1997.
6 Interview with *New Nigerian* (Kaduna), 18 January 1966.
7 Huntington (1968: 194). On Nigeria, see the view espoused by Larry Diamond that the character of the armed forces cannot be identified as a significant factor in the failure of democracy. See Diamond (1990: 392).
8 Perlmutter defines satrapism as aping a superior, usually an external culture. Psychologically, it results from colonial and patrimonial rule. See Perlmutter (1977: 177).
9 Cited in Omotoso (1989).
10 Decalo (1976); Joseph (1987).
11 Defined here as the process whereby the civilian sphere is increasingly militarized in both the psychological and political senses.
12 Luckham (1971b: 108).
13 Luckham (1971b).
14 Elaigwu (1986: 77).
15 Mohammed (1975: 23).
16 See Obasanjo (1990).
17 The post-July 1975 military leadership included the radicals of the previous regime who had insisted on the reorganization of the armed forces and the maintenance of professionalism through the exit of the military class from political power.
18 Joseph (1991: 75).
19 At least three of the Gowon's era 'super-perm-secs', Phillip Asiodu, Ibrahim Damcida and Ahmed Joda, are now leading figures in the People's Democratic Party. It is interesting to note that General Danjuma and Alhaji Ahmed Joda were on the board of the French trading company, SCOA and ex-board members of Chagouri and Chagouri Construction Company. General Danjuma, who is well respected in several circles and might have earned these business links completely unimpeachably, has resigned several board positions since he assumed office as Defence Minister. This, however, cannot palliate the convoluted nature of these networks and their perceived impact on probity, transparency and accountability in governance.
20 Adekanye (1993:30).
21 I have written this advisedly, aware of the contention by Professor Bayo Adekanye that

Babangida's demobilization programme was the most far-reaching. I have come across no evidence to confirm this contention. See Adekanye (1997).

22 See the revised Second National Development Plan for evidence. Also see Fayemi (1994: especially Chapter 4).

23 The debate on Nigeria's nuclear option typifies the preference for the prestige factor rather than the need basis in defence policy. The prestige component in defence policy is elaborately treated in Kamanu (1977/8: 35).

24 For details of the period's international involvement, see Gambari (1989).

25 The fact that they shut Nigeria's borders, a means of livelihood in many of the contiguous countries, and succeeded in forcing these countries to sign an agreement banning the smuggling of Nigerian exports through their territories did not endear them to neighbouring leaders. Also, the government's refusal to allow American planes to refuel in Nigeria at the time of President Reagan's Chad involvement irked the Americans. At the same time, its policy of 'mutual reciprocity' with the British, Nigeria's erstwhile colonial masters, marked a departure from Britain's easy ride with Nigeria's ruling elite. Ironically, save for the regime's high-handedness, all these policies were praised at home as Nigerians saw in the two leaders protective messianic tendencies and the ability to stand up to world powers.

26 See Address by Dr Pius Okigbo at the submission of the report of the inquiry into the finances of the Central Bank of Nigeria between September 1988 to June 1994.

27 World Bank (1994).

28 For a fuller discussion of this twin strategy, see Fayemi (1999).

29 For an elaboration of this point, see Fayemi (1996: 20–4).

30 A former military administrator in Oyo State, Colonel Usman, made it clear to a public gathering that the military was here to stay. According to him, even if the masses managed to remove them from direct political control, they would scale the fence and get involved.

31 See my interview with Colonel Tony Nyiam in *The News Magazine*, May 1994. Colonel Nyiam, a former staff officer to General Babangida, was one of the leaders of the 1990 *coup d'état*.

32 *Newswatch Magazine*, 2 October 1996.

33 Speaking in Cape Town, South Africa, in this period, President Clinton went as far as suggesting that the United States had no objection to Abacha's involvement in politics as long as he made his position clear.

34 Oluleye (1985).

35 Obasanjo (1990).

36 Obasanjo (1990).

37 Oluleye (1985: 178)

38 Even when the head of the special branch, Alhaji M.D. Yusuf, uncovered the July 1975 coup plot and tried to confront the plotters, he was dissuaded by the head of state, General Gowon. See Elaigwu (1986: 228).

39 Obasanjo, personal interview.

40 Oluleye (1985: 68).

41 Gambari (1989: 25). Gambari was the foreign minster during the period.

42 For details, see 'Why I Was Toppled', exclusive interview with General Mohammadu Buhari (5 July 1993). This was the first interview granted by the former head of state since his overthrow in a palace coup in 1985. He details how his colleagues used military intelligence to undermine his administration. In the interview he referred to the head of military intelligence as a fifth columnist.

43 *Ibid.*

44 As now confirmed by one top military aide to General Babangida, 'the coup itself was not a nationalistic one. He [General Babangida] was trying to protect his interest by protecting Aliyu Mohammed [head of the Military Intelligence Directorate] among other things.' See my interview with Major Debo Bashorun, former public relations officer to General Babangida in *The News Magazine* (Lagos), 24 January 1994.

45 General Babangida (29 June 1990: 3).

46 Ex-Israeli agents were already in charge of training the intelligence outfits and the presidential guard.

47 There is a plethora of primary documents now covering this period. Among many others, see *The News Magazine*, 4 October 1999; *The Week Magazine*, 4 October 1999; *Tell Magazine*, 4 October 1999, 8 November 1999; and *The Week Magazine*, 6 December 1999. Also, a lot of the petitions submitted to the Human Rights Violation Investigations Commission cover the state-sponsored assassinations that took place under General Abacha.

48 For example, his current chief of staff, Major-General Abdulai Mohammed, was the first Director-General of the National Security Organization and his National Security Adviser, Major-General Aliyu Mohamed Gusau, was formerly Director of Military Intelligence and Coordinator for National Security under the Buhari and Babangida regimes.

49 Kohn (1997).

50 Williams (1998); Fayemi (1998).

51 Unfortunately, the external military agency – Military Professionals Resources Incorporated – assisting the government with its military reform programme is still steeped in the Western tradition of objective control mechanisms.

52 In the course of researching this chapter, the writer was told that even direct access to serving military members by members of the Defence Committee has been blocked. Equally, the executive decision to hire an American private military company to assist with the restructuring process in the military was not subjected to parliamentary scrutiny or approval. This pattern of executive fiat is not limited to armed forces matters. It would appear generally that the executive branch has no confidence in the legislative branch and resorts to extra-constitutional means to attend to some issues.

**Table 9.1** A profile of Nigeria's governments since independence

| Dates | Type | Main protagonists | Control of the military |
|---|---|---|---|
| January 1960–6 | Elected, civilian, with strong regional bias | Prime Minister Balewa, Alhaji Ahmadu Bello (Premier, North), Chief Awolowo (Premier, West) Dr Okpara (Premier, East), President Azikiwe | Small military (10,000), colonial in orientation but professional in character, increasingly drawn into internal security by rising political tension |
| January–July 1966 | Military junta after first coup | Major Nzeogwu, General Ironsi | Assassination of prominent political leaders – especially in the north – destroyed military *esprit de corps* and threatened professionalism |
| July 1966 –July 1975 | Collegial military junta, weak at inception, but strengthened by civil war victory | General Gowon and members of the Supreme Military Council | Broad-based support of all armed forces for military junta, in spite of earlier problems partly due to lack of commitment to political timetable |
| July 1975– September 1979 | Military junta | Generals Mohammed Obasanjo, Danjuma and middle-level officers who overthrew previous junta | As above, but with more credibility and more emphasis on professionalism and political change |
| October 1979– December 1983 | Elected civil rule under 1979 constitution | President Shagari of National Party of Nigeria; multi-party political structure, presidential style of government | Limited control of the military; creation of alternative base in police force as well as patronage to ensure loyalty to government |
| December 1983– August 1985 | Popular military junta | Generals Buhari, Babangida Idiagbon and Abacha | Professional-political prerogative; increasing authoritarian tendency in a largely internally oriented policy agenda |

**Table 9.1**  (cont.)

| Dates | Type | Main protagonists | Control of the military |
|---|---|---|---|
| August 1985 —August 1993 | Transition from junta to personalized - dictatorship in a palace coup | General Babangida was the main player, with 'bit parts' to close civilians and military 'politicians' | Co-option of the military in the ruler's personal project via patronage and deft political manoeuvrings |
| August 1993— November 1993 | Interim government representing interregnum after annulled elections and exit of Babangida | Chief E. Shonekan, head of interim government and General Abacha, Defence Minister | Clear military control of government that lacks legitimacy and popular support in a period of high political tension |
| November 1993—June 1998 | Full-blown military dictatorship | General Abacha | Undermined military professionalism, increased use of intelligence and security outfits (especially death squads) against political and military opponents |
| June 1998— May 1999 | Military dictatorship with a human face — under pressure to reform politically and exit gracefully | General Abubakar Abdul-Salaam | Focus on political transition and preparation for withdrawal from government |
| May 1999—? | Elected civilian government | General Obasanjo, presidential style a non-ideological centrist | Increasing presidential control of military, rather than democratic control; commitment to military professionalism, and has diminished the likelihood of full-blown military coup |

# 10

# Radical Soldiers, New Model Armies and the Nation-State in Ethiopia and Eritrea

ROBIN LUCKHAM[1]

What is a political army? Are not all armies, even those of Western liberal democracies, 'political' in that they are instruments of state power, being deployed to defend a particular political, economic and social order? Yet clearly some are more political, or differently political than others. Arguably, being non-political is a different kind of politics.[2] Thus the best way of thinking about the politics of political armies, may be to draw a contrast with the politics of 'non-political' armies.

The idea of a non-political military is closely associated with the idea of 'civilian control' over the military. And both arise from a particular historical environment in Western Europe and North America, created by the formation of the modern nation-state, industrial capitalism, the industrialization of war and differentiated professional military establishments.[3] The industrialization of war, along with the wars and colonial conquests of the nineteenth and early twentieth centuries, greatly increased the cost of permanent military establishments. To pay for them two related bargains were struck. The first of these was between ruling classes and emergent bourgeoisies (and also the ordinary citizens who made up the bulk of conscript armies), under which the latter agreed to fund war by raising taxes, and rulers in exchange became accountable to parliaments and electorates. The second was between the armed forces and the state, under which military establishments accepted their subordination to elected governments, but in exchange were conceded considerable professional autonomy.

These bargains – and the idea of a non-political army – presupposed two further distinctions. First there was a differentiation between the state on the one hand and the capitalist economy on the other, together with the class structure and civil and political society. The second was between the state as a permanent structure, set of institutions or 'rules of rule', and 'politics' as a process of contestation for state power and for the collective (and sometimes private) goods accessible through the state.

Armies are non-political, to the extent that their loyalty is primarily to the state, and that they do not participate in the contest for state power, or seek to define the ideological, political or economic goals of the state. That is, they are non-partisan and subordinate to political authority, but not necessarily politically indifferent, for instance to threats to the survival of the state itself. However, loyalty to the state is a necessary but not sufficient condition of being non-political. For political armies as well commonly profess their loyalty to an overarching state. Indeed the 'politics of being above politics' is a common ideological device of soldiers seeking to justify their intervention to sweep away allegedly venal and disputatious politicians. In contrast non-political armies are subordinate to legitimate public authority, as constituted by democratic institutions under the constitution and the rule of law. In other words, non-political armies have a political engagement – not to particular ruling groups or power holders, but to democratic institutions, which in turn presupposes a commitment not just to the constitution, but in addition to the practice of democratic politics.[4] This is not a purely theoretical point. For, as I shall argue later, it is central to present-day debates about whether and how far the armed forces in post-1991 Ethiopia and Eritrea are committed to democratic institutions and legitimate public authority – or remain political armies in the mould of those of the Ethiopian imperial system or of the revolutionary Derg.

In contrast, political armies are directly involved in political contestation itself. One may distinguish five main forms of military politics. First, there is the corporate politics of professional military establishments intervening behind an ideological curtain of state interest or national security, of which Latin American military establishments furnish many classic examples. Second, the armed forces may be the partisan instruments of state elites or other groups controlling or competing for state power. For example, in civilian autocracies like the Philippines under Marcos or Côte d'Ivoire before the 1999 military coup or pre-revolutionary Ethiopia, the armed forces were subordinate but far from politically neutral. Third, the armed forces or factions within them (for one should not assume their cohesion or political homogeneity) may be partisan contestants for power with an explicit political or ideological agenda of their own. In effect they may be a 'military party' (or parties) in their own right, like the Derg in Ethiopia.[5] Fourth, in periods of acute crisis, the armed forces may become an arena or site for political contestation in which struggles for power are fought out between the various contestants for state power, allying themselves to different military factions within a fractured military establishment, as in the early months of the Ethiopian revolution. Finally, a fifth form of military politics is that of non-state military formations. This has become increasingly important in 'new conflicts' in sub-Saharan Africa, the Balkans, the Caucasus and other regions,[6] where these non-state formations challenge the state's monopoly of violence, and at the same time state military establishments fragment or become privatized.

Ethiopia furnishes examples of all these forms of military politics, except arguably the first. It is of particular interest to students of military politics for four main reasons. First, uniquely among sub-Saharan Africa states, it has an impressive continuity of more than two thousand years of statehood, in which military force and standing armies were defining elements of the state. It was the only African state not colonized by European powers, and in which modern statehood was not shaped by colonial governance.[7] Yet, second, Ethiopia also experienced sharp historical discontinuities in its history, upon which other historians focus: for instance, between the shifting political formations of the early Ethiopian empires; the fledgling nation-state consolidated by the emperors Menilek and Haile Selassie during the late nineteenth and the twentieth centuries; revolutionary Ethiopia under the military rule of the Derg; and the present 'democratic' governments established after the defeat of the Derg in 1991 by the former revolutionary fronts in Ethiopia and Eritrea. The transitions between each of these mutations of statehood involved immense, traumatic upheavals – and each of these gave rise to its own distinctive political–military relationships, considered below. Third, Ethiopia is distinctive because the more recent of these upheavals produced different variants of left-wing military politics, revolutionary militarism or garrison socialism. These have not been completely unique in Africa, in that there have been subaltern military revolts, left-wing regimes and revolutionary armies elsewhere in the continent[8] – in marked contrast, say, to the conservative forms of politics more usually associated with military interventions in Latin America or Asia. Yet soldiers and revolutionaries in Ethiopia and Eritrea have certainly been the most advanced exponents of left-wing military politics anywhere outside of China, Cuba or Vietnam. Their revolutionary legacies continue to shape civil–military relations in both countries, despite the waning of the original revolutionary project. Fourth, moreover, the politics of non-state military formations has been of cardinal importance in both Eritrea and Ethiopia, especially in the form of the two armed liberation movements, the Eritrean People's Liberation Front (EPLF) and Tigray People's Liberation Front (TPLF)/Ethiopian People's Revolutionary Democratic Front (EPRDF), which defeated and destroyed Ethiopia's massive conventional army, brought down its military regime and reconstructed the state and armed forces (partly) in their own image.

Hence this chapter tells the tale of four revolutions and of the various forms of military politics which arose out of them. The first was a slow (and politically conservative) revolution from above, started under Emperor Menilek and carried through by Emperor Haile Selassie, which took on the contradictory task of reconfiguring the Ethiopian empire as a state-nation, along with a modern army, bureaucracy and other instruments of a developmental state, whilst at the same time trying to conserve an autocratic monarchy and a quasi-feudal system of surplus extraction. The armed forces were political not only because they upheld an imperial autocracy, but also because they enforced central imperial control over peripheral regions like Eritrea or the Ogaden.[9]

The second revolution, the Ethiopian Revolution of 1974, arose out of the contradictions of the first. It was initiated through an uprising by subaltern groups in the army, as well as in the urban areas, who overthrew the imperial system and laid claim to the mantle of revolutionary socialism. The armed forces became an arena in which different groups contested for power within the revolutionary state. The triumphant military faction or 'party' imposed 'garrison socialism' from above,[10] with military radicals standing in for a vanguard party. A centralized and repressive revolutionary military regime waged war against armed liberation movements in Eritrea and Tigray, in order to hold together a fracturing state-nation; only for the massive and well-armed military machine it had created with Soviet and Cuban assistance to disintegrate before the advancing insurgents in 1991.

The third revolution began in Eritrea, and took the form of a protracted national liberation struggle waged by armed movements, particularly the EPLF, initially against the imperial state of Haile Selassie, later against the military regime of the Derg. In alliance with the TPLF, the EPLF comprehensively defeated the Derg by 1991. Eritrea withdrew from Ethiopia after holding a referendum on independence. The EPLF was reconstituted as the core both of the 'new model' national army and of the new ruling party of a unitary nation-state, which was very much the product of the armed struggle.

The fourth revolution was the parallel armed struggle of the TPLF in Tigray against the Derg military government. Unlike the EPLF, however, the TPLF reconfigured itself as a broad coalition of opposition groups – EPRDF – shortly before the defeat and collapse of the military regime. Thus reconfigured, it began reorganizing the Ethiopian state as a federation of Ethiopia's main nationalities or ethnic groups, as well as rebuilding the national army around the core of the liberation army, incorporating elements of the Derg's army which possessed needed technical skills. In both cases it drew upon a seemingly contradictory combination of its own paradigm of revolutionary war and political mobilization, and the dominant donor rhetoric of liberal democracy and of democratic control of the armed forces.

We shall see later, however, that in both countries the legacies of societal militarization and revolutionary war were difficult to shake off, and were compounded, especially in the Ethiopian case, by deep insecurities about the political identity and national composition of the state. In 1998 a seemingly minor conflict between the two former allies over national currencies and borders turned into a large-scale conventional war. Although hostilities have been brought to an end through the mediation efforts of other African countries, the underlying issues are far from being resolved.

## Military Modernization and the Contradictions of the Imperial State

A major reason the shift to the left during the 1974 Ethiopian Revolution was so violent and extreme was the incomplete and contradictory nature of the modernization process undertaken under the previous imperial regime. Historians differ significantly in their assessments of the latter. Some emphasize modern Ethiopia's antecedents in several centuries 'of continuous large-scale political organization found in few if any other parts of Sub-Saharan Africa'.[11] Others hold that 'shorn of its mythical origins, the Ethiopian state was formed historically through a long, protacted and conflict-ridden process',[12] marked by historical discontinuities as well continuities. In particular, the modernizing autocracies of emperors Menilek and Haile Selassie initiated a major 'mutation of historic Ethiopian statehood', starting from the late nineteenth century, which transformed Ethiopia into a multi-national imperial state held together by military force.[13] Indeed, whether or not the Ethiopian state existed in anything like its present form prior to this century is also a profoundly political question, with implications for the political identity of the modern state and for its relationships with its national and ethnic minorities.

What does seem clear, however, is that the first states in the Ethiopian region date back to the Aksumite kingdom which flourished from the first to the seventh century AD. During the following centuries state systems were built up and disintegrated in a series of hegemonic cycles.[14] To simplify drastically, most of these states were built upon three pillars:[15] the extraction of agrarian surpluses from plough-based peasant agriculture; long-distance trade based on the exchange of these surpluses for luxuries and weapons; and military power: as one Ethiopian historian puts it, they were 'fiscal-military states'.[16] Usually they were organized around relatively centralized rule within the core political kingdom, combined with loose (but often harsh) dominance over peripheral regions from which tribute was extracted. The core shifted from one region to another over the centuries – for instance, from Tigray in the North to Shewa in the South following the assumption of power by the Shewan Emperor Menilek in 1889. Yet the spread of orthodox Christianity into the region from the fifth century brought an important element of continuity; and Ethiopian kingdoms were organized to a greater or lesser extent around the defence of a common Christian Abyssinian identity.[17]

In all these states military force was a key constitutive feature of the state itself. Military and civilian administrations were so closely intertwined as to be almost indistinguishable: royal officials were administrators and judges in times of peace and commanders in times of war.[18] There was a dual structure of standing military forces, made up of royal regiments commanded by officers directly under the emperor, combined with larger regional levies raised by feudal lords for particular military campaigns. From the mid-nineteenth century the standing forces became increasingly specialized, received training from foreign military advisers, and were armed with imported firearms. In 1896 they were able to inflict a major military defeat on the invading Italian colonial army at the battle of Adowa, which became a defining moment in the history of the modern Ethiopian state. Elite units also developed a capacity and taste for political intervention; in the early twentieth century the Mahal Safari ('those who are deployed at the centre') made three decisive interventions in political affairs – and paved the way for the elevation to the imperial throne in 1930 of the future Emperor Haile Selassie.

The changes introduced by the emperors Menilek and above all Haile Selassie amounted to a qualitative transformation in the entire basis of state power, in four major respects. First, the process of centralized state building was put on a more systematic footing than before, in order to create a state which could stand up against the colonial empires. Second, the Ethiopian state was expanded by military conquests which incorporated many peripheral areas, especially in the South and East, which had never been fully part of the previous empires, and were politically and culturally distinct. The Ethiopian state-nation thus 'contained a myriad of diverse and religious groups with economies, polities, ideologies and kinship systems that radically differed from each other ... held together by an imperial state itself heavily dependent on foreign resources'[19] – and subjected to a process of cultural and linguistic assimilation by the dominant Amharic core.

Third, the extractive capacity of the state was enhanced through an expansion of commercial agriculture, especially in the large-scale quasi-feudal estates of the newly assimilated regions – a process which reinforced the relative decline of peasant farming in the Northern highlands, including regions like Tigray, which were also marginalized by the shift in the political centre of the empire to Addis Ababa under Menilek and Haile Selassie. Linked to this, fourth, were a series of peasants revolts,[20] which some see as the precursors of the liberation wars of the late twentieth century.

Fourth, modern bureaucratic apparatuses – such as a civil service, a professional army, a police force – were created, along with an educational system to supply trained personnel. From the 1930s, the professionalization of the armed forces was accelerated: military academies were established at Holata and (after the Second World War) Harar; military and police training was supplied by a series of foreign powers (Britain, Sweden, Norway initially, and the US, Germany and Israel from the 1950s); the army was re-equipped and a modern air force and navy were created. By the 1960s Ethiopia had the largest and best-equipped military force in sub-Saharan Africa (apart from South Africa).[21]

This process of state building, however, hastened the demise of the imperial autocracy. The latter seemed increasingly archaic and lacked political channels through which grievances and the new interests brought into being by the modernization could be expressed. Despite the emperor's espousal of 'development',[22] the latter was conceived mainly as an extension of imperial power, contrasting sharply with the alienation of large groups of people brought into the economy by the development process itself. The government's failure to get a grip on the real issues of development, notably in the 1973–4 famine, and its inflexible and repressive response to demands for greater regional autonomy, especially in Eritrea, ultimately corroded the emperor's own legitimacy, as well as that of his government.

The armed forces' strategic position as the last line of defence of imperial rule made them a nodal point for political unrest. Their professionalism came into conflict with the Emperor's vast patronage system and his use of personal surveillance networks to assure their loyalty. There was a growing gap between the military elite, who could secure personal advancement from the court, and the bulk of the lower-ranking officers and men in the ranks, who were increasingly frustrated by poor pay, inadequate barracks, promotion barriers and, above all, the unresponsiveness of their seniors and of the government to their grievances.[23] The first major manifestation of military discontent was the failed coup attempt of 1960. This was organized by well-connected reformers in the elite Imperial Guard and the civilian bureaucracy, and aimed to reform rather than replace the imperial system. However, the subaltern military uprisings from the ranks, which initiated the Ethiopian Revolution of 1974, were completely different, challenging the entire structure of imperial domination, together with the military hierarchy.

## The Revolution of 1974 and the Contradictions of Garrison Socialism

The Ethiopian Revolution has sometimes been described as a 'creeping coup', taking almost nine months during 1974 to dismantle the imperial regime – though it could hardly have been more unlike a conventional coup.[24] It started with a series of barracks revolts by NCOs and junior officers in regional garrisons during January and February 1974. Their initial demands were mainly for improved conditions, although it was not long before limited political demands, for instance for the right to form parties, anti-corruption measures and land reform, were presented. There was no group of military radicals orchestrating events from the outset. Instead these emerged from the process of agitation and organization itself. A series of military committees sprang up based on different military units and factions. These were consolidated through the formation in June of the Co-ordinating Committee of the Armed Forces, Police and Territorial Army, known to the public as the Derg ('the committee'). This was made up of 125 representatives elected by the men in the ranks and junior officers in all military units; the majority were from the ranks, though they included some officers up to the level of major and lieutenant-colonel.

Step by step the Derg took charge of the revolution, acting, according to its own proclamations, 'in response to the mood of the people',[25] steadily radicalizing its demands. In September 1974 it deposed the emperor, suspended the constitution, formed a provisional military government (the PMAC), and proclaimed its nationalistic guiding principles of *Ethiopia Tikdem* ('Ethiopia First') as the basis of state policy. It initially elevated a popular military commander, Lieutenant-General Andom, to chair the Derg and PMAC (the two were in practice the same thing, and below the two terms will be used more or less interchangeably) and to head the armed forces. But when he proved too independent, he was killed resisting arrest in November 1974; this precipitated the summary trial and execution of most of Ethiopia's generals (eighteen of them, along with some other senior officers), two ex-prime ministers and many other leading figures of the former aristocracy and political class.

The broad consensus among scholars, at least until recently, was that the Ethiopian Revolution of 1974 was genuinely a revolution, despite being appropriated by the military, being at least partially comparable to the classic revolutions against agrarian absolutisms, including the French and Russian revolutions.[26] The subsequent contradictions of military socialism, the Derg's military campaigns in Eritrea and Tigray, and its inglorious collapse in 1991, may seem to demand a reassessment.

Yet the argument that this was a revolution and not simply a creeping coup remains cogent for three main reasons. First, it comprehensively dismantled the political and social structures of the previous imperial system. Second, the subaltern upheaval in the armed forces was part of a much more broadly based popular revolt against the imperial system. Barracks mutinies coincided with a series of strikes and demonstrations by civilian groups, including teachers, students, taxi drivers and urban workers, during the crucial months of 1974. Third, as we shall see, there was a systematic and at the beginning fairly successful attempt to implement major redistributive programmes, especially under the Derg's urban and rural land reforms, as well as to consolidate the revolution politically on classic Marxist-Leninist principles.[27] The revolution's ultimate ignominy does not mean it was not a revolution – any more than one could argue that the French Revolution was not a revolution because was displaced in turn by Thermidor, Napoleon and a restored Bourbon monarchy.

In the course of time, however, the revolution became more and more militarized. What started as a more or less equal partnership between military radicals, left intellectuals, trade unions and other civilian groups was quickly taken over by the Derg, starting with a major break with the trade unions in the autumn of 1974. It was almost as if soviets of mutinous soldiers and sailors had assumed control of the Russian revolution, rather than the Bolsheviks.

On the one hand, the Derg formed a series of alliances with factions within a deeply divided left intelligentsia. In 1976 an ideological charter for Ethiopian socialism was proclaimed under the National Democratic Revolution Programme of Ethiopia. At the same time the Provisional Office for Mass Organizational Affairs (POMOA) was set up to formalize the Derg's relationship with left-wing organizations, and to form the urban residents' associations (*kebeles*) and peasant associations as the basis of the PMAC's mass mobilization programme. On the other hand it liquidated the various left factions one by one, culminating in the Red Terror of 1977–8, when members of the different radical groups were drawn into urban guerrilla war with each other and with the Derg, and were hunted down with the help of revolutionary defence squads from the *kebeles*. Thousands were killed, and the remnants of the student movement and left intelligentsia fled into exile or joined the insurgencies in the North.

These conflicts interlocked with a series of power struggles within the Derg itself, starting with the killing of General Andom and two members of the Derg in November 1974. Four further Derg members were purged for 'intrigues against the revolution' in July 1976. Colonel Haile-Mariam Mengistu, the first vice-chairman of the Derg, and his supporters staged a palace coup in February 1977, when the then chairman of the PMAC,[28] its secretary-general, the head of its security guard and four other leading Derg members were assassinated by Mengistu supporters who burst into a central committee meeting. This was followed in November 1977 by the execution of Mengistu's last remaining rival, Colonel Atnafu Abate, the second vice-chairman of the Derg, after he had publicly questioned the wisdom of the killings at a PMAC congress in November 1977. By the close of 1977 Mengistu and the extremist elements in the Derg had out-manoeuvred their rivals and gained undisputed control of the revolution and of the state.

More was at issue, however, than just factional rivalries. There was a simultaneous consolidation of the revolutionary government's political control structures. This followed classic Marxist-Leninist lines although, instead of a vanguard party, the Derg and the armed forces themselves formed the nucleus of the revolutionary vanguard. Marxism-Leninism, together with democratic centralism, provided an attractive organizational blueprint, offering a ready-made way of filling the organizational vacuum left by the destruction of the pre-revolutionary state and military hierarchies. It was all the more seductive to the soldiers of the Derg because of its emphasis on the centralization of power and on secretive, conspiratorial governance. Furthermore, it facilitated the formation, soon after Mengistu's palace coup, of a strategic alliance with the Soviet Union and Cuba – made all the more necessary by the more or less simultaneous expulsion of the US military mission and ending of American arms supplies.

There was a reciprocal militarization of the revolution and politicization of the military. The Derg/PMAC itself was restructured in 1977 on a standard socialist organizational pattern, with a congress, central committee and standing committee. Meanwhile the military radicals had formed their own political organization, Abiyotawe Seded ('Revolutionary Flame'): its secretary-general was Mengistu, who in turn ran it through his hatchet-man Sergeant Legessie Asfaw, also a leading figure in the Derg. Initially Seded worked with the civilian radicals in POMOA but, after the latter were purged, it formed the nucleus of the working groups which planned the formation of the Commission for Organizing the Party of the Working People of Ethiopia (COPWE) in 1979. The latter in turn paved the way for the establishment of the Workers Party of Ethiopia (WPE) in 1984. Both COPWE and WPE were heavily dominated by the armed forces and, at the very top, by members of the Derg. Of the 123 founding members and alternates of the COPWE central committee, 64 per cent were present or former members of the armed forces and police; 22 per cent were members of the Derg; in 1984 the corresponding proportions for the WPE were only slightly lower, at 48 and 18 per cent respectively. Seven of the WPE political bureau's 11 full members were drawn from the surviving top leadership of the Derg, although by now only one, the Minister of Defence, still made use of his military title.[29] In 1987 a new constitution was introduced establishing the People's Democratic Republic of Ethiopia (PDRE) and transferring power to an elected legislature guided by the WPE, which was confirmed in its political monopoly as a vanguard party guided by Marxism–Leninism – although in reality the constitution made virtually no difference to the way power was exercised.

In practice all pretence of collective leadership had by now vanished. Mengistu's personal dominance of the government, the military and the revolution was unquestioned. In this respect there was little difference from any other military dictatorship, although the regime's control structures were perhaps more elaborate, and penetrated more deeply both at grassroots, and (as we shall see) within the armed forces themselves. The Red Terror had initiated a process of political demobilization, involving the harsh repression of all forms of political dissent by both legal and non-legal methods.[30] An extensive surveillance network co-opted the grassroots organizations which had sprung up to mobilize popular support for the Derg in the early years of the revolution – the *kebeles* in urban areas and the peasant associations in the countryside – and converted them, alongside the WPE, into instruments for political control, made all the more necessary by the failure to deliver the promised benefits of the revolution.

The first of these promised benefits was the liberation of the mass of the country's peasantry from the exploitation and poverty it had suffered under the imperial system. The Derg's land reform programme (announced in 1975 under the slogan 'land to the tiller'), rural mobilization campaign and creation of peasant associations (to which an estimated 5.5 million peasant families belonged by the 1980s) initially enjoyed considerable popular support. Moreover, they seemed to deliver tangible benefits to the peasantry during the early years of the revolution, though more in the former feudal estates in the South and East than in the smallholdings of the Northern highlands. But as the wars in Eritrea and Tigray ground on, the Derg's relationships with the rural areas became increasingly extractive. The peasantry became alienated, as the Minister for Land Reform in the Derg's early years put it, 'by the extraction of their grain and their sons'.[31] Peasant associations were used to collect taxes and other impositions and to purchase grain at deflated prices, as well as to draft recruits into peasant militias and the army. The rural surpluses extracted to pay for the war amounted to an estimated third of total disposable peasant incomes.[32]

The precise cost of the war is hard to determine, as is the level of Soviet, Cuban and Eastern European subsidies.[33] What we do know, however, is that the size of the armed forces increased to not far short of half a million men by the late 1980s. The defence budget greatly aggravated the country's economic imbalances. It increased by 19 per cent annually in nominal terms between 1974 and 1988.[34] By the final three years of the war it consumed 46 per cent of the recurrent budget, 52 per cent of imports and 9.7 per cent of GDP.[35] Agricultural output began falling behind population growth in the early years of the revolution, but by the 1980s it was declining in absolute terms too (2.1 per cent annually from 1980 to 1987). A corresponding stagnation of GDP growth left it well behind population growth.

Rural poverty was aggravated not only by the conflicts, but also by the military regime's own commandist approach to economic decision making, including draconian price, marketing and foreign exchange controls. Large-scale rural collectivization, villagization and resettlement programmes were begun during the late 1970s and greatly expanded following the 1983–5 famine. The Derg's response to the latter was inadequate and subordinated to its own political priorities. It downplayed the famine until after the founding congress of the WPE in late 1984. It shamelessly manipulated the donors and emergency NGOs to divert famine assistance into the war effort.[36] And it used the rural resettlement programme to depopulate areas suspected of giving sustenance to rebel movements, especially in Tigray.

The Derg's failure to deliver the economic benefits of revolution was thus complexly linked to its failure to manage the conflicts stemming from the imposition of a centralized state upon a multi-national society. The collapse of the empire and the 1974 revolution had opened political spaces in which minorities could reassert themselves and challenge the existing form and boundaries of the state itself. The EPLF launched a major offensive in 1975, bringing large parts of Eritrea under its direct control; and this coincided with the first manifestations of armed opposition in Tigray. Somalia invaded the Ogaden region in July 1977, calculating that Ethiopia's political disarray, and its break with the USA, opened a window of opportunity in which it could advance its ambition to assimilate the Ogaden's Somali-speaking population into a Greater Somalia.

These were genuine threats to the integrity of the state and, so the military revolutionaries believed, to the revolution as well. The Derg responded with a remarkably effective military mobilization, in conditions of considerable national-istic fervour. This mobilization included both a major expansion of the armed forces themselves and the training of a large peasant militia.[37] It defeated Somalia and expelled it from the Ogaden by March 1978; and it forced the EPLF to retreat back into its base areas in the mountains and deserts of the far North by mid-1979. Neither would have been possible, however, without massive Soviet and Cuban arms supplies, as well as the direct deployment of Soviet and Cuban military advisers and some 16,000 Cuban troops, which served to lock the conflicts in the Horn into the Cold War system.[38]

Yet even with Soviet and Cuban support, a series of military campaigns failed to dislodge either the EPLF in Eritrea or the TPLF in Tigray. The failure to resolve the conflict in both places was as much political as military. The Derg's promise in the National Democratic Revolution Programme of 1976 that it would recognize 'the right to self-determination of all nationalities' proved largely theoretical; and was subordinated to the overwhelming emphasis on democratic centralism. From the early days of the revolution the Derg refused to contemplate any serious devolution of power in Eritrea (the mere discussion of which was one of the reasons General Andom was liquidated). An effort to negotiate a settlement under a nine-point peace plan in 1976 failed, largely because the plan had little to offer. The suppression of the student left and the Red Terror drove many former militants into supporting the TPLF and other opposition movements. The Red Star Campaign launched at the start of 1982 – perhaps the most ambitious of all the Derg's campaigns in Eritrea – combined military operations with classic counter-insurgency methods of 'winning hearts and minds' under a development campaign spearheaded by a newly organized Eritrean branch of COPWE. But it refused to engage with any of the Eritrean movements, which it lumped together as 'anti-freedom, anti-unity, anti-people and anti-peace bandit gangs'.[39] Indeed it was not until the final stages of the war in 1990–1, when it faced imminent defeat on the battlefield, that the military regime was prepared to offer serious concessions in negotiations with the EPLF, TPLF and other opposition movements.

In sum, the revolutionary project was slowly and inexorably turned on his head by the centralizing logic of the political and military processes initiated by the Derg. The same processes began to undermine the military establishment itself. The sustained assault by junior officers and men upon the hierarchy during the early days of the revolution undermined discipline and made the settling of accounts between the various military factions (see above) especially vicious. Although the Derg was remarkably effective in coordinating across different military units, its emergence meant that there were two competing authority structures: the regular military command and the shadow command of the Derg. The solution was to establish a political administration of the armed forces – originally set up by Sergeant Legesse Asfaw before the formation of COPWE and the WPE[40] – with political commissars who maintained surveillance over the professional hierarchy, while remaining (like the latter) subservient to the military government.

At the same time the military as regime – including most members of the Derg who were allocated posts in the government and/or party – became differentiated from the professional officers holding regular military command positions. However, there was a degree of overlap, with some Derg members being promoted to military command positions, and many senior commanders becoming *ex officio* members of the WPE central committee. At the apex of both the military as regime and the military as institution was Colonel Mengistu, who maintained his tight personal control over both.

During the military campaigns of the late 1970s, the politicization of the armed forces had little discernible impact on their combat effectiveness; perhaps the reverse. The assessment of one of the EPLF's leading commanders is that the Ethiopian forces were strong and well-organized militarily. In his view it was the Derg's frustrations in the field and inability to break the EPLF'S defences which ultimately undermined it, losing it the support the Ethiopian population and facing it with escalating costs.[41] The introduction of national service in 1983, replacing the mass mobilizations of the peasant militias, swelled the ranks of the forces with several batches of recruits delivered by the peasant associations and urban *kebeles*. But recruitment targets proved increasingly difficult to meet, desertions increased, and morale and discipline suffered.

The demoralization of the officer corps[42] was particularly striking. The triumvirate command – of commander, commissar and inspector – at each level of the hierarchy 'was effective in checking dissension in the army, but killed the initiative of the officers and encouraged insubordination and indiscipline'.[43] On several occasions senior officers pressed for the restoration of a single command at WPE Central Committee meetings. The situation was made worse by the direct involvement of Mengistu and his close associates in the conduct of the war. In one notorious incident in 1987, Mengistu ordered the summary execution of the divisional commander of the Afabet front, and the dismissal of several other senior officers, for their temerity in informing him of weaknesses in his force. Not long after, the division was overrun and Afabet was captured by the EPLF in one of the most decisive military engagements of the war.

Festering discontent in the military elite culminated in May 1989, when the chief of staff of the armed forces, the air force commander and many senior officers attempted a coup during Mengistu's absence abroad, only to be frustrated by their own woeful planning and the swift intervention of the elite Presidential Guard. One hundred and sixty senior officers took part in the plot, of whom 39 were generals; 27, including ten generals, were slaughtered during the attempt; 14 were executed; two escaped and the rest were jailed for life. In one blow most of the armed forces' experienced commanders were swept away, and were replaced for the most part by politically loyal ex-officers in party and administrative positions. This accelerated the disintegration of Ethiopia's large and well-equipped military machine and, with it, the entire edifice of military rule. The Second Revolutionary Army in Eritrea suffered a series of military reversals during 1988 and 1989. Ex-Sergeant Legessie Asfaw was appointed supreme commander of the Third Revolutionary Army and chief administrator of Tigray, which was placed under martial law administration. But twice in 1988 and 1989 the main garrison in Endaselassie was besieged and overrun by the TPLF – allied with the EPLF on the second occasion. Large numbers of tanks and other hardware were captured, and the Ethiopian army carried out a forced retreat from Tigray.

Meanwhile under donor pressure the regime began to jettison its socialist programme, trying to reinvent itself, without much success, as a reforming government committed to sweeping market-oriented economic reforms.[44] But neither this, nor sporadic peace talks with the EPLF, TPLF and other opposition movements, initially chaired by US ex-president Jimmy Carter, could save it. The liberation movements were by now meeting little resistance from a disintegrating Ethiopian army, and pressed forward toward Addis Ababa. They entered the capital in May 1991, soon after Mengistu had fled the country.

The Ethiopian armed forces had lost the war against the two guerrilla movements despite its considerable advantages in size, professional training, external military support and stockpiles of advanced military hardware. This was partly because of the prowess of the two movements on the battlefield, but it was also the product of the gradual delegitimization of the socialist military regime, particularly among the impoverished peasantry, but also among all groups in Ethiopian society. This delegitimization became reflected in the demoralization of the military's peasant conscripts, and in its own disarray and disintegration as an institution.

## National Liberation Struggle and its Political–Military Legacies: the EPLF and TPLF/EPRDF

Transition from military government under the Derg came about through the latter's defeat on the battlefield and the dismantling of its entire military and security apparatus. Thus it was very different from the standard transitions from military/authoritarian to civilian/democratic governance considered in the civil–military relations literature. Initially, moreover, the reins of power were taken over, not by formally elected politicians, but by the leaders of the two liberation movements that fought against the Derg, the EPLF and the TPLF/EPRDF.

In both cases the new governments reshaped the state and the armed forces upon lines that differed significantly from their original national liberation project, dropping Marxism-Leninism; and instead claiming to embrace liberal democracy, a market economy, military professionalism and non-political armed forces. Yet I shall argue later that all was not quite what it seemed. The political, cultural and organizational legacies of national liberation and armed struggle remained enormously important, and had a palpable impact upon the transition, the democratization process, military restructuring and civil–military relations, as well as influencing the major military confrontation which later broke out between Eritrea and Ethiopia in 1998. In this section I shall briefly review these legacies, before considering their impact on political transition and military politics in post-1991 Eritrea and Ethiopia. There were both major similarities and significant differences in the EPLF's and the TPLF/EPRDF's origins, military organization and approach to politics.[45] The rebellions in Eritrea and Tigray were geographically linked, in the northern corner of the former Ethiopian empire, which had been peripheralized through consolidation of Shewan Amharic dominance under Emperors Menilek and Haile Selassie. Yet each had a different relationship to the Ethiopian state, each developed its own historiography and each had a completely different approach to the nationalities question.

Eritrea had become an Italian colony in the late nineteenth century, merging the Tigrinya-speaking Coptic Christian kingdoms of the Northern highlands with the mainly Muslim and ethnically diverse coastal lowlands, which over the centuries had shifted between Ethiopian, Ottoman and Egyptian hegemony. It was placed under British military administration before being federated with Ethiopia by the UN in 1952. Resentment against Ethiopia was fuelled by the imperial government's replacement of Arabic and Tigrinya with Amharic as the language of government business, the ending of Eritrea's federal status in 1962 and savage repression of resistance against Ethiopian hegemony. Armed resistance was initiated in the late 1950s. To begin with it was led by by the Eritrean Liberation Front (ELF), with support mainly in the Muslim community and aided by neighbouring Arab states. However, a rival movement, the EPLF, emerged in the early 1970s from splits in the ELF over the latter's alleged sectarianism. Civil war broke out between the two movements in the early 1970s and again in the early 1980s, from which the EPLF emerged as the sole credible military opposition to the Derg.[46] These antecedents shaped the EPLF's strong territorial Eritrean nationalism, constructed around the 'artificial' boundaries of the former colony, and its rejection of ethnic or religious identities as the basis of military and political organization.

In contrast, the TPLF originated as a movement which from the start embraced a radicalized version of Tigrayan ethnic nationalism – emphasizing the centrality of national over class contradictions, and in particular Shewan Amharic domination over other Ethiopian nationalities, both in the empire and under the Derg. It was one of a number of groups that began organizing armed resistance in Tigray during 1974–5 after the Derg's purges of the civilian left, and sprang from an earlier organization formed to link Tigrayan students with militants in Tigray itself. It faced a number of rivals, including the Ethiopian Democratic Union (EDU), led by anti-Derg nobility, and the EPRP (Ethiopian People's Revolutionary Party), the largest organization of the Marxist revolutionary left, which stressed class over national contradictions. But unlike the latter it harnessed the long-standing resentments of Tigrayans against their perceived marginalization, and well as securing a broad base of support among the Tigrayan peasantry. The latter feared that the Derg's land reform programme would deliver their land into the control of the government – rather than saving them from the landlords, who had a less oppressive presence in Tigray than in other regions.

The TPLF fought simultaneously against the rival guerrilla fronts and against the government. By late 1979, however, it was in more or less undisputed control of the armed struggle in the whole of Tigray. In contrast to the EPLF, however, it never committed itself outright to secession. Instead it wavered between this course and Tigrayan self-determination within a multi-ethnic state, the course it ultimately chose during the final stages of the campaign against the Derg. Despite the differences in their political goals the EPLF and TPLF were remarkably similar in organizational structure. In both there was a fusion of military and political leadership in a small founding group, with continuity of leadership throughout the armed struggle and indeed after it (President Issayas Afeworki of Eritrea and Prime Minister Meles Zenawi of Ethiopia were members of the EPLF's and TPLF's founding groups). The fronts had separate military and political wings, which in the TPLF's case had equal representation in the TPLF Congress. They also established shadow administrations in liberated areas – the EPLF's Department of Public Administration was set up in 1977 – and their own judicial institutions. They were in many respects integrated party-armies with additional state and development functions, rather than politicized (but organizationally distinct) armies. Leaders were 'expected to be anywhere and everywhere. One could be military commamnder, diplomat, agronomist, economist or political militant'.[47]

Their political organization followed the classic Marxist-Leninist paradigm of democratic centralism with congress, central committee and executive committee/ politburo, and decision making concentrated in the latter. Both fronts had a secret inner party organization, the Socialist Party in the EPLF and the Marxist-Leninist League of Tigray in the TPLF. Both maintained powerful security organizations, which kept a close watch for signs of dissent. Both gave considerable emphasis to adherence to 'a clear, consistent and nationalist political line', as one former EPLF commander put it,[48] in order to avoid the factional disputes by which they had been plagued in their formative years. As another put it 'we could not afford any difference of opinion. If we were divided we could not have achieved anything.... To fight we required active political understanding, as well as active military participation from all our fighters.'[49]

Although the fronts' formal organization had a certain similarity to that of the Ethiopian WPE, how they functioned was completely different. Their democratic centralism had a genuinely democratic or participatory content, which was never extinguished by central control. Both fronts had significant numbers of women militants and indeed fighters. Both worked closely with mass organizations and organized a systems of *baitos* or representative councils. Both extended these as far as they could into areas still under Ethiopian occupation, where the EPLF created *bdho* ('challenge') committees, armed for self-defence and linked to a system of militias. The TPLF evolved an institution of public debate and self-criticism (*gim gima*) in its military wing, which was later extended to the mass associations and *baitos*. These organizations not only solidified their popular support, but also contributed to their military success.

Both fronts could call on the assistance of substantial diaspora communities of Eritrean and Tigrayan refugees in Europe and North America, which funded arms, food and medical supplies. Each established relief organizations – the Eritrean Relief Association (ERA) and the Relief Society of Tigray (REST) – which proved extremely effective in channelling diaspora and external NGO assistance to relief and development activities, in contrast to mainstream donors, which were reluctant to by-pass official Ethiopian channels. REST in particular played a crucial role in offsetting the Derg's attempts to manipulate the 1983–5 famine to increase its political and military control in Tigray. In sum, as Prendergast and Duffield argue, the two fronts 'were able to establish a political economy of liberation capable of simultaneously providing effective famine relief, engendering political support, and pressing the war'.[50]

Military organization in both fronts was based on a similar mixture of central direction and bottom-up initiative. Both had well-developed lines of command, but no fixed system of ranks separating commanders from ordinary fighters. In both there were political commissars who attended to the political education and morale of fighters, maintained security and kept a watch on dissent. In the TPLF, more-over, the commissars were integrated into the command structure – commanders at each level being having to consult both their deputy and the political commissar before taking major decisions.[51] Former EPLF and TPLF commanders interviewed by the author concur that a relatively flat hierarchy and consultative decision-making did not confuse lines of command, as in the Ethiopian revolutionary army. Instead it improved morale, increased upward flow of information, facilitated coordination of the political and military dimensions of the guerrilla campaigns, and helped mobilize popular support.

A much-noted feature of both fronts[52] was their self-reliance and pragmatism, perhaps increased because Soviet, Cuban and Eastern European support for the Derg after 1977 cut them off from the most obvious potential sources of external arms and military assistance.[53] Hence they had to adopt the principle of 'killing the enemy with his own gun':[54] capturing and repairing considerable quantities of Ethiopian military hardware, including in the later stages of the war large artillery pieces and tanks. Some of the EPLF's leaders received military training in socialist countries, but very few of the TPLF's command had any form of foreign military training, although some trained with and indeed fought for the EPLF in the late 1970s and early 1980s.

But there were also crucial differences between the two fronts.[55] These were serious enough to result in rupture between them during some phases of the armed struggle. The EPLF was not only formed earlier than the TPLF, before the Ethiopian Revolution, but also developed conventional military capabilities sooner, after falling back on its 'circle of steel' in the Sahel during the Ethiopian military campaigns of the late 1970s. From then on it fought a war of position behind strong defensive positions, moving forward from these in a series of flanking movements after 1986, although there was also some guerrilla activity behind enemy lines. The TPLF in contrast remained a mainly guerrilla force until 1988, controlling increasing areas of the countryside and raiding Ethiopian positions, but falling back when under attack. Differences over strategy and tactics, including TPLF criticism of EPLF inflexibility and the EPLF's assertion of its primacy as the senior revolutionary movement, were among the reasons for a serious split between them in 1985 at the height of the famine. Cooperation was not resumed until the TPLF had demonstrated its military credentials through a series of success-ful attacks on Ethiopian military positions during its counter-offensives of 1988.

The political disputes between the two fronts were put on hold in 1988, when they agreed to differ over the boundaries between Eritrea and Tigray, in order to pursue the war against the Derg, leaving the issue to be settled by negotiation later. But behind the territorial dispute was a fundamental difference in their approach to the nationality question. As we have seen, the EPLF developed a strong secular nationalism, deepened by the war of independence, in which territorial boundaries became the principal markers of national identity for the new multi-ethnic state-in-formation.[56] The TPLF, in contrast, gave far more importance to cultural and linguistic markers of national identity, to some extent justifying Adekson's categorization of it as an ethnic guerrilla movement.[57]

However, it was not until the final stages of the military campaign against the Derg in 1989–91, when it moved southwards out of Tigray towards Addis Ababa, that the TPLF finally committed itself to transforming the Ethiopian state by giving its various nationalities more autonomy within a federation, rather than limiting itself to Tigrayan self-government. Initially there was a crisis after many of Tigray's peasant fighters defected to their farms when asked to carry the war into other regions. This was resolved in characteristic participatory manner, not by disciplining defectors, but through a region-wide debate in which fighters had to be convinced of the case for continuing. Moreover the TPLF was well aware of the political dangers of moving into Ethiopia as an apparently sectarian or ethnic guerrilla movement. Hence in 1989 it formed a broad front of federated movements, the EPRDF. And it was as the EPRDF that it advanced into Addis Ababa in May 1991 following the disintegration of the Ethiopian army and Mengistu's flight into exile.

## New Model Armies and the Reconstruction of the State in Ethiopia and Eritrea

The EPLF and EPRDF administrations which took control of Eritrea and Ethiopia in 1991 faced a Herculean task. They had to reinvent a collapsed state, in Eritrea's case more or less from scratch. They had to turn insurgent armies into national military forces, at the same time (in Ethiopia's case) as demobilizing the immense military machine of the ousted regime. They had to restore law and order in a situation which was growing more lawless and chaotic by the day, fed by the explosion of previously submerged peasant resistance to the former Ethiopian state.[58] They had to cope with mass movements of refugees and displaced persons. And they had to begin the process of economic reconstruction, following years of economic decline under the war economy of the Derg.

That they could do so, and in an exemplary manner, without falling into state collapse and generalized violence as in Somalia or the Congo, was due to the strength of the political, military and administrative structures created by the two fronts during the period of armed struggle, and to the care with which the fronts planned the reconstruction of the state.[59] Despite their Marxist–Leninist ideological legacy, they did not follow the example of the post-revolutionary regimes of the Cold War era, such as Cuba, Vietnam or Mozambique. Instead they demonstrated their pragmatism, awareness of how the world had changed since the fall of the Berlin Wall, and appreciation of the strength of donor orthodoxies by committing themselves – at least on the surface – to market-oriented development and democratic constitutional governance. Indeed they had little alternative, because Ethiopia's command economy had failed to deliver, and there was simply no question of reviving it, given the disappearance of socialist assistance and the power and resources of Western donors. Both fronts were swift to recognize these realities, and had a Machiavellian ability to turn them to their own advantage. Both Eritrea and Ethiopia – until the eruption of war between them in 1998 – became adjusted states or donor-recognized development success stories, taking their place in the donor pantheon alongside countries like Ghana and Uganda.

As in the two latter countries the political will was supplied by populist (and originally left-wing) armed struggles or military revolutions from below. These brought to power governments with a significant capital of popular legitimacy, able to embark on major economic and political reforms. Yet the EPLF's and EPRDF's historical legacy as former insurrectionary armies deeply conditioned how they attempted to build democratic states and create new model national armies. Democracy would have to be reconstructed in a manner that was consistent with their traditions of popular participation, and did not seriously challenge their 'ownership'[60] of the new democratic state. Moreover, the habits of power the two fronts acquired during the struggle – their democratic centralism, secrecy and intolerance of dissent – have, as we will see, proved difficult to reconcile with the open, pluralist politics of liberal democracy. Indeed, some analyses of the post-liberation Eritrean and Ethiopian regimes debate whether their new democratic constitutions conceal new forms of autocracy.[61]

A cardinal feature of the transformations in both countries has been the manner in which the military–political leadership of the two fronts assumed control of the political, administrative and military hierarchies of the state. Their capture of the state derived from their control of the gun, and in this respect they may be compared to military governments. But unlike the latter they had broad popular legitimacy, mass organizations and a leadership whose skills were at least as much political as military. This leadership, moreover, was well equipped to move into other roles. In both countries former commanders and political commissars of the liberation forces were swiftly parachuted into leading positions in ministries, in the new ruling party hierarchies and even in business organizations, as well as continuing to supply the top leadership of the new national armies. This has had its dangers. Indeed it has been suggested that the growing involvement of the fronts and their members in the business sector, as well as their autocratic tendencies, began seamlessly to 'fit them into a model of neo-patrimonial politics'.[62]

The reconstruction of the two liberation forces as national armies posed a particular dilemma for the new leaderships. As the chief of staff of the new Ethiopian armed forces put it during debates on the constitution, 'the approach of building a barracks army has led Ethiopia into disorder in the past and we should not repeat that failed experiment'.[63] To create an effective state army, however, seemed to require professionalization, the introduction of a hierarchy of military ranks and the insulation of the armed forces from partisan politics, including dismantling of the system of political commissars and the resignation of senior officers from party positions. The problem was how to create a non-political army that would support the institutions of the new democratic state without falling back into the praetorianism that has been the curse of so many other African military establishments.

However, the EPLF in Eritrea and the EPRDF in Ethiopia took somewhat different approaches to these issues, dictated by their history and approaches to the national question and state building, which require separate examination.

# Eritrea: the problems of professionalizing a political army

The EPLF entered Asmara and established the provisional government of Eritrea in 1991, although the country did not acquire international recognition as an independent state until a UN-supervised referendum in 1993. The problems it faced were in some respects more difficult and in some respects easier than those faced by the EPRDF in Ethiopia. The state had to be rebuilt from scratch around the EPLF's political administration and shadow state apparatus, transferred whole-sale to Asmara in an 'unruly, unplanned and uncoordinated ... rushed move'.[64] Most of the former provincial government infrastructure had been destroyed by the retreating Derg – not to speak of the immense devastation caused by the war. However, the EPLF enjoyed considerable popular legitimacy; it had more or less undisputed control of the whole country; both its own cadres and those of its army were broadly representative of the whole country; and there was little questioning, for the present, of its discourse of secular, territorial nationalism.

Its approach was gradual – a deliberate tortoise's pace in a favourite metaphor[65] – emphasized self-reliance, and remained suspicious of donor and external NGO prescriptions for reform, all the more since the donor assistance committed to the country's reconstruction was relatively meagre. Military and political restructuring went hand in hand, and were both shaped by the strong concern with develop-ment and social justice which had emerged during the struggle.[66] Initially the EPLF's central committee became the legislature, though it was replaced in 1993 by the National Assembly, in which central committee members sat alongside representatives of the provinces and nominees chosen to represent citizen groups, including women. Most ministers – especially those holding key portfolios like foreign affairs, finance and defence – had been corps or divisional commanders, or former heads of the front's intelligence organization or political administration; though there were also some technocrats in the more technical ministries. Political, military, administrative and judicial functions began to be separated, although there remained considerable overlap, especially at the top.

An immediate priority was the demobilization of many of the 95–100,000 fighters who had fought against the Derg, in order to form a slimmed-down, more professional force and to release resources for reconstruction and development. In all some 54,000 ex-fighters were demobilized in three phases.[67] In the first, most of those who had joined the struggle in 1990–1 were released; in the second, more experienced fighters who were old or wounded, or lacked the requisite skills, were demobilized; in the third, a number who had been transferred to duties in the civilian administration were released, as part of a slimming-down exercise in the swollen bureaucracy. In 1993 there was a mutiny of first-stage demobilized fighters and in 1994 a strike of wounded veterans, revealing some weaknesses in planning and insensitivity to the plight of both groups – though this was remedied by the creation of Mitias,[68] an efficient organization for the demobilization and resettle-ment of veterans. At the same time a National Service Corps was established, reflecting Eritrea's unique blend of militarism and popular participation, to 'shape young people ... especially those who did not take part in the struggle', and as 'a means of reducing the size of the army and to have a defensive capability that extends beyond the army'.[69] Not only did large numbers of young people receive training in military and developmental skills; they would be available in emergencies like the war which broke out with Ethiopia in 1998.

The EPLF committed itself in principle to democracy, political pluralism and a multi-party system as early as its second congress in 1987. At its third congress in 1994, it transformed itself into a purely political organization, in theory distinct from the government, the People's Front for Democracy and Justice (PFDJ), and proclaimed a national charter, which listed political democracy as one of six goals for Eritrea's future (listed second after national harmony, and above economic and social development). In 1995 a constitution-making exercise began, culminating in the ratification of a new constitution in 1997. This provided protections for civil liberties and social rights, an independent judiciary and an elected legislature, though it tended to favour the executive under a semi-presidential system.[70]

The Constitutional Commission was representative of the country's cultural and social diversity – about half its members were women – and held consultations throughout the country. These included discussions in all military units, which raised more or less the same issues as in consultations with civilians. For, as the chairman of the commission put it, 'the army regards itself as the advance guard of everything in this society, so it doesn't limit itself just to things military'.[71] Two linked issues raised in the constitutional discussions were only partly resolved, however, and, owing to the outbreak of war against Ethiopia in 1998, remain unresolved: first, the nature of the party system, and second, the relationship of the armed forces to the PFDJ and the political process. The PFDJ has remained part-way between a single ruling party and a national movement, and the legislation needed to establish a multi-party system has yet to be prepared.[72] Some members of the political and military elite remain sceptical about multi-party democracy, partly because of the latter's perceived limitations, but also reflecting their own approach to governance honed during the armed struggle.

As a senior PFJD cadre put it, 'in terms of the Western restrictive, procedural meaning of democracy, we feel that doesn't do justice to the concept of democracy. We really don't like what we see, if you talk of democracy in the USA, and we don't think it should be our goal.' Democracy should be participatory, foster the 'accountability that was the EPLF's great strength in the struggle', give priority to social justice, be inclusive of 'everyone, all ethnic groups, women, rural areas, pastoralists', and yet 'recognize and respect their differences, but not [as in Western democracies] in order to concentrate on these differences, but to concentrate on overcoming them'.[73] As a senior minister and ex-commander put it, 'whatever the provisions of the constitution, where is the social and political basis for multi-partyism? Who would form an opposition party? Anyone who tried to challenge the PFJD would be asked, "Where have you been during these thirty years of armed struggle, what have you contributed to this nation?"'[74] Political parties of the conventional kind and multi-party politics 'are alien to our people, especially in rural areas'.[75]

However, this residual mistrust of open debate creates problems for democracy and for democratic control of the military and security establishments. As one of the experts drafting the constitution emphasized: 'The EPLF had to keep secrets, this was very useful and necessary during the struggle, but the question now is what to do with a habit and practice that has kept on repeating itself over thirty years.' The answer in his view was strong parliamentary government, since 'if it were left to the executive the tendency would be to foster a strong police, strong military forces and unaccountable intelligence bureaucracies'.[76]

The politicization of the armed forces and their relationship to the PFJD is another thorny issue. The consensus seemed to be that they 'cannot be divorced from politics'.[77] Indeed

the whole idea of an apolitical army is misplaced.... The army *must* be political, not in the sense of being partisan, but in upholding the constitution, in knowing its duty to serve society and not be an elite force that asks for privileges.... As for those in the army now, even if one were to cancel their membership of the front, or say they cannot hold office, they will still be very influential, after all up to now most of them have been leading the front.[78]

The nub of the problem for the government was 'how to make our armed forces professional without diluting their political commitment'.[79] At the front's 1994 third congress it was decided that in future uniformed commanders could neither be ministers nor members of the National Assembly; nor could they be politically active. Yet as of early 1996 senior army commanders still belonged to the central committee and the executive committee of the PFDJ. The army had operated outside the cash economy,[80] there had been no formal structure of ranks, nor were there any higher-level staff and command training courses – although the top echelons of the EPLF and army were very much military intellectuals.[81] Formal rank and pay structures were introduced in 1996 following consultations in the army – including the promotion of the Minister of Defence as a general and the promotion of eight division commanders as major-generals – when officers were also supposed to resign positions in the front. Professionalism involved relatively little external input, as it was felt that 'we will be taking a major risk by becoming a regular army. So we must not simply go and copy from other armies, but work out what is best for Eritrea.'[82] And in so far as any foreign model was mentioned it was that of Israel's citizen force.

The constitution made the president the commander-in-chief of the armed forces, but was not explicit on their organization, control and relationship to parties.[83] Nor was there yet a clear separation between the Ministry of Defence and the general staff. As the then Minister of Defence put it,

I'm not a civilian trying to pay lip service to civilian control, I share the same experience as my people [in the armed forces]. As Defence Minister it may be contradictory, but I don't understand the need for a sharp demarcation. It may be that in nations like us and Israel, that are the products of war, the relationships are bound to be different.[84]

## Ethiopia: military professionalism and ethnic federalism

When the EPRDF swept into Addis Ababa in 1991 it faced many of the same problems as the EPLF in Eritrea, of rebuilding both the state and the liberation forces as a national, professional army. In contrast to Eritrea, there was at least a partly functioning central state structure, with a civil service and a tax adminis-tration, to be taken over. Yet the EPRDF had to rebuild authoritative government in a larger, more complex country which was still in a state of ferment, and where its own legitimacy still had to be established. Four crucial dilemmas had to be overcome.

First, there was widespread insecurity and unrest, especially in the regions that had not previously been liberated by the incoming EPRDF. The collapse of the military government brought the latent rural discontents of the Derg's agrarian socialism into the open.[85] Rural disturbances were increased by the expulsion, harassment and killing of one ethnic group by another, for which the ethnic policy of the new regime (see below) must take some responsibility. Insecurity was also aggravated by the breakdown of regular policing, since the police force had been closely tied into the military structures of the Derg and like the latter was demobilized. Second, although the Derg regime had become deeply unpopular throughout Ethiopia, the EPRDF was not universally seen as a liberating force. Indeed in many regions of the country it faced competition from other armed groups, including the Oromo Liberation Front (OLF). It still had to establish both its own legitimacy as a government and its monopoly of organized force. Third, although the EPRDF presented itself, with a degree of justification, as a broad multi-national front of groups opposing the Derg, in reality Tigrayans constituted the core of the new national government and army, owing to the TPLF's leading role in the armed struggle. This could not but affect how it was perceived in the rest of the country, especially since Tigrayans formed only a small part of Ethiopia's 56 million people. Fourth, the entire armed forces of the Derg, that is to say not far short of half a million men in uniform, were in captivity in their barracks, were wandering around leaderless in the countryside, or had fled to neighbouring countries. They added to the prevailing insecurity, and had to be disarmed and demobilized with minimum delay.

The strategy partly mapped out by the new leadership even before it moved into the capital, and partly improvised after it formed the Transitional Government of Ethiopia (TGE) in July 1991 with US encouragement,[86] was multi-pronged. It derived from its own approach to the nationalities question described earlier, which was adapted in order to transform a minority liberation movement and its fighters into the core of a more broadly based Ethiopian government and army.[87]

The first step, indeed, had been the formation of the EPRDF itself in 1989. It had two key characteristics. First, it was a federation of ethnically (or nationally, to use its own discourse) constituted movements, of which the TPLF was primus inter pares. Second, rather than federating existing movements, new ones were created: besides the TPLF, the founding members of the front were the Ethiopian People's Democratic Movement (renamed the Amhara People's Democratic Movement in 1991), the Oromo People's Democratic Organization (OPDO), and the later-disbanded Ethiopian Democratic Officers Revolutionary Movement (EDORM), made up of ex-prisoners of war or defectors from the Derg's army. Important movements like the OLF, the Afar Liberation Front (ALF) and the Western Somali Liberation Front (WSLF) were not included, either because they were regarded as militarily and politically unreliable, or because they declined to join. The next step was to constitutionalize the front's authority, and bring in the democratic institutions being promoted by the donor community – without, however, permitting any serious challenge to its political control. A national conference was held in July 1991, which formed the TGE, confirmed the chairman of the EPRDF, Meles Zenawi, as its chairman, and approved the charter under which the country was to be governed until the implementation of the new democratic constitution in 1995.

Most members of the national conference and of the new legislature (the Council of Representatives) were representatives of nationality-based organizations. Some had a pre-existing history of political and military organization, like the OLF, ALF and WSLF, but others did not. There were significant omissions, including the leading parties of the old student left. The EPRDF had the largest bloc of delegates in the Council of Representatives and together with the representatives of smaller minorities dominated its proceedings and controlled most of the key ministries – although careful attention was paid to ensuring ethnic balance in the latter and in other government appointments.[88] In 1993–4 a constitution was drafted and ratified by an elected Constituent Assembly and came into force with the establishment of the Federal Democratic Republic of Ethiopia in 1995.[89] In parallel with the constitution-making process there had been a devolution of power to eight federal regions (plus three urban municipalities), reconstituted on the basis of the country's major nationalities, in accordance with 'the EPRDF's core ideological assumption that democracy can only be established though ethnicity, through regionally defined rights'.[90] This formal process of democratizing and federalizing state power was qualified by informal processes that shifted the real balance of political forces ever more decisively in favour of the EPRDF. A number of key potential rivals, including the OLF, the main move-ment of Ethiopia's largest nationality, the Oromo, were outmanoeuvred and left the TGE. At the same time the EPLF's own network of 'nationality' organizations was extended, and took control in nearly all the new regions. Initially this unleashed a series of regional power struggles in which the armed wings of the contending movements fought against each other and against government forces, and in which large numbers of Amhara and other 'settlers' in the regions were forced to flee. But slowly new political facts on the ground were created through the EPRDF's and its member organizations' control of such instruments as local government machinery, rural credit facilities and the restructured peasant associations – not to speak of its superior coercive resources. On this far from level political playing field, the EPRDF and allies won massive majorities in 1992 local and regional elections, 1994 Constituent Assembly elections and 1995 national and regional elections, made all the larger by poll boycotts by the main opposition organizations. As Lyons notes in a study of the 1995 elections, 'what had begun with a noisy diversity of views among a broad array of political organizations ended quietly with the clear hegemony of the EPRDF'.[91]

None of this would have been possible, however, had the EPRDF not moved decisively to ensure its monopoly of organized force. It took over responsibility for security in the TGE, and in January 1992 its army was reconstituted as the state defence force for the transitional period. In contrast, the military wings of other movements experienced varying fates. Some were initially encamped, including the largest, the OLF, with 20,000 men under arms (although 15,000 of these, including some demobilized soldiers had joined up since the defeat of the Derg). The OLF was disbanded in June 1992 after it attempted to break out of its camp and launch an insurrection; all of its men were demobilized, and none joined the national army. Other military formations, including the principal Somali movements, evaded encampment, and resumed irregular military activities. Small numbers of fighters from a few of the smaller movements, however, were recruited into the police and armed forces.

Most important of all, the remnants of the Derg's immense army were swiftly and efficiently disarmed and demobilized. 'Integration' of the latter with the liberation forces, as in some other post-conflict situations, was never a serious option, given its involvement in repression and its officers' lack of political commitment. As one of those responsible for the military reorganization put it, 'appointing officers of the Derg army to command positions would have been a recipe for disaster.... Our objective was to create a totally new army, in contrast to South Africa [after apartheid] where what you have is a kind of half-breed army in which the old army still influences the new.'[92]

Demobilization and disarmament began almost immediately in June 1991, when the Commission for the Rehabilitation of the Members of the Former Army and Disabled War Veterans was established, although planning had begun earlier, being modelled on the EPRDF's structures for demobilizing prisoners of war. The Commission processed 455,000 former soldiers, of whom 38,000 were disabled. Most surrendered and were sent to camps and collection areas where they were disarmed and 'reoriented' through discussion and self-criticism, before being demobilized. The UN High Commissioner for Refugees (UNHCR) and the International Commission for Refugees assisted in the repatriation of 130,000 from Sudan and Kenya, where they had fled. Others demobilized themselves and returned to their home areas, where they registered with *kebele* 'peace and stability committees' and handed in their weapons (although the country was awash with arms, which 'were planted like cabbages in people's backyards'.)[93] The commission also demobilized 21,000 ex-OLF combatants, as well as 30,000 of the EPRDF's own forces in 1995. This was the largest demobilization exercise anywhere in Africa, and by any standards was an impressive achievement, as a World Bank assessment recognizes.[94] The commission could take most of the credit[95] – although roughly half the funding was provided by external donors. Above all, demobilization prevented the insecurity of the unquiet countryside from getting worse. There was some banditry by demobilized combatants, especially at the start; but this was insignificant in proportion to the large numbers demobilized.[96]

At the same time the TGE began to restructure the EPRDF military forces as a national army. The process had already begun during the latter stages of the war, when the TPLF began to shift from guerrilla to conventional operations, recruited Derg defectors or prisoners of war with professional skills, and broadened the ethnic composition of their forces by forming the EPRDF. Now, however, military restructuring was put on a much more systematic footing and linked to the EPRDF's constitutional and political programme. The chief of staff, Tsadkan Gebre Tensae, spelled out his own vision for the new armed forces in a remarkable contribution to a symposium on the constitution. The ideas summarized in Box 10.1 contain profound insights, even if the practice did not fully match his aspirations.

Military restructuring had begun soon after the establishment of the TGE in 1991. It had four main components: military cuts, including demobilization of part of the EPRDF's own force; broadening the national composition of the armed forces; introducing pay and rank structures; and separating the armed forces from the EPRDF's political structures.

Military cuts reflected the official view that 'peace and stability should be provided by the people themselves and not by big budget military defence'.[97] The peace dividend was indeed substantial. Defence spending was reduced dramatically, to 12.5 per cent of the government recurrent spending and 2.3 per cent of GDP by 1993–4, compared with 46 per cent and 9.7 per cent in the final three years of the Derg[98] – and the reductions were maintained until the outbreak of war with Eritrea in 1998. Arms imports were minimal, partly because the armed forces could draw on the large stockpiles abandoned by the former military government. Demobilization contributed significantly to the cuts. It was also extended to the

**Box 10.1  The chief of staff, Tsadkan Gebre Tensae, spells out his vision for the new Ethiopian armed forces[99]**

- The national army should 'be guided by and loyal to the constitution', which should in turn inform 'the social and political consciousness of the armed forces'. The military 'cannot be an instrument to suppress internal political dissent or to resolve political problems within Ethiopia, that should be resolved politically and democratically'.

- Without violating the needs of discipline 'if the army is not run internally as a democratic institution, it cannot maintain democratic relations with the civil society. Members of the armed forces will lose their commitment to defend the democratic rights of the population because they themselves are being denied those rights within the army.'

- Close ties should be forged between 'the army and the people. I mean that … the army as an institution must be designed so as to make it very difficult to operate without the full backing and support of the population.'

- Command 'must rest with the elected civilian authorities'. But for these 'to effectively control the military it is necessary that there be greater political understanding. Legislative authorities must understand the inner workings of the army…. The military must understand the political and legislative processes.'

- The national army 'must be accountable at several levels': to the civilian authorities, to the legislature and under the law of the land, in order to 'demonstrate to the civil society that the military is not above the rule of law and thus cannot abuse its power'.

- The armed forces should be 'of a size that is realistic and affordable'. As Ethiopia faced no serious external threats, internal conflicts were diminishing and local police forces were being improved, it had 'no need for a big army…. Reducing the size of the army to the minimum necessary level is not only a matter of conserving economic resources, but also of making sure that the army is not big enough to impose its will on the people of this large and diverse country.'

- 'The national army of Ethiopia must be broadly representative of the society. This does not mean that its composition should be based on an ethnic quota system, but that it should be truly national in character and of sufficient diversity to allow the people of Ethiopia to feel ownership.' But at the same time 'to function as a national army, the military must be under central command and cannot be composed of various ethnic armies'. It would only be possible to address internal conflicts 'effectively and fairly if the army is truly national in character and thus cannot be assumed to have a local or ethnic agenda'.

EPRDF's own personnel in 1984–5, and 30,000 of its fighters either left the armed forces of their own accord, or were resettled under the official demobilization programme, reducing the army's size to around 90–100,000.

Broadening the national composition of the armed forces was an urgent priority because at least 60–70 per cent of the EPRDF's forces, and thus initially of the new national army, were of Tigrayan origin,[100] and the proportions were probably higher in the upper ranks. As the chief of staff readily admitted,[101] the military was 'not, for historical reasons, as representative as it should be', and had to be reshaped 'to reflect the participation of all nationalities'.

It would not prove easy to fulfil the requirements of article 87 of the new constitution that 'the national defence forces shall reflect the equitable representation of the nations, nationalities and peoples of Ethiopia'. A start had been made during the demobilization exercise, when the armed forces absorbed 6–7,000 former officers and NCOs from the Derg's armed forces, who had needed technical or administrative skills – although none were above the rank of colonel and all were vetted to ensure they had not been involved in human rights abuses. Added to these were some recruits from smaller armed movements, which had fought against the Derg – but not the OLF, all of whose personnel were demobilized. There was no further recruitment during the transition period.

But when regular recruitment resumed in 1995–6 a major effort was made to secure recruits from under-represented regions. Ensuring balance in the higher levels of the hierarchy was more difficult. It seems ethnic and regional origins were taken into account when ranks were allocated under the new rank structure in 1996. Of eight senior military appointments made public following the ranking exercise (corps commanders and above, in the ranks of brigadier or major-general), three, including the chief of staff, Major-General Tsadkan, were of Tigrayan origin, three were Oromo and two were Amhara.[102] Balancing the officer corps may have been facilitated by the transfers of several TPLF/EPRDF war-time commanders into political, bureaucratic, developmental or business positions in Tigray or in the federal government structure. Planning for the introduction of pay and rank structures began in 1991–2, and involved extensive consultations within all military units about differentials – in principle the pay of those at the very top of the hierarchy was to be no more than ten times that of the most junior soldiers. Soldiers even had a say on where individual commanders were placed on the salary scale and which ranks they were allocated.[103]

There remained some anxiety about the conversion of a liberation or guerrilla army to a regular professional force. The danger was that 'if you kill the guerrilla mentality, you may create not a good professional army, but a bad professional one'. Yet professional skills were considered essential, 'a good people's army must be a good professional army at the same time, or it cannot accomplish its mission of defending the people'.[104] Hence the goal was to professionalize, whilst preserving elements of the guerrilla tradition such as closeness of soldiers to the people, a sense of commitment based on soldiers' understanding of their orders rather than blind obedience, 'normal, free, democratic relations between officers and the lower ranks'[105] and a consultative command structure, based so far as possible upon the committee decision-making practices the army had inherited from the TPLF. How far in practice it was possible to conserve these elements of the guerrilla tradition – and whether they survived the remobilization of the armed forces in 1998 for the war against Eritrea – is hard at present to judge.

The system of political commissars was abolished during the transition period. The EPRDF's fourth congress discussed the separation of the front from the army, and in January 1995 all officers resigned their positions in the front and its member organizations, shortly before the new constitution came into force. Article 78 of the constitution declared that the Ethiopian national defence force should be 'free of any political partisanship to any political party or political organization' and that 'the Minister of Defence shall be a civilian'. This formalized a differentiation between front, bureaucratic and military positions, which had been continuing since 1991. A leading example was Ato Seye Abraha, the former commander of the EPRDF's forces, who was Minister of Defence during the key 1991–5 transition period, before returning to Tigray to head EFFORT (Endowment Fund for the Rehabilitatuin of Tigray), a Tigrayan development organization, become a member of the national legislature and chair the national airline. Even so, as one of those who had helped plan the restructuring of the armed forces put it, 'whether one likes it or not, we were a political army, and still are to a certain extent.... You can't expect things to change in a day. For the time being [the top military leaders] have their political connections, just as they are still a democratic army.'[106]

This separation required adequate civilian control structures to replace the party–army links which had assured the control of the liberation forces. The first ministers of defence were prominent ex-fighters, although some were more active in supervising the armed forces than others. However, it was the cabinet defence committee, presided over by the prime minister, Meles Zenawi (who took a close personal interest in military matters), which decided all major policy issues, and the Military Council, chaired by the chief of staff, which made implementing plans, decided operational issues, and passed requests for budget appropriations, equipment and reorganization up to cabinet level. The Ministry of Defence and general staff were in theory separate, but still to a considerable extent fused. Both reported to the minister through the chief of staff, who headed the entire Ministry of Defence establishment, including its 'civilian' departments (themselves mostly headed by ex-fighters).[107] The new legislature, the Council of Representatives, had powers to legislate on national defence and security matters, approve budgets and exercise oversight through parliamentary committees, including a committee on defence, security and the police – although the latter still lacked the capacity and expertise to ensure effective supervision.

But how these formal control structures would operate, and whether they would ensure democratic control of a military insulated from politics, depended not just on the new constitution, but upon how far it opened spaces for democratic politics. The problem was that the constitution was to some extent the victim of the EPRDF's political success in consolidating its hegemony after the displacement of the Derg. The constitution itself – though reflecting a fairly broad public debate – had been formulated without serious participation by opposition groups. Although it provided for free elections, the right to participate in political parties and other organizations, freedom of the media and other fundamental rights and freedoms, together with many other attributes of a liberal democracy, the reality was rather different.

A single-party dominant system emerged from the 1995 elections, in which there was little room for organized opposition, in part because of the failings of the latter, but also due to the EPRDF's model of ethnic federalism and its ingrained suspicion of political competition. As the speaker of the legislature reflected, when asked if Ethiopia's new democratic framework differed significantly from Western democratic models, it did so

> most of all [because] it's an attempt to bring relevant government to the people ... to have local government responsible to local people. In our estimation the only way to do this was through an ethnically-based government, and that is why the issue of nationality is so crucial. Democracy, then, is creating local, regional and federal governments that are genuinely responsible and responsive to the people. If this is so we don't expect much opposition. When the bottom line is development, and we're all in favour of development, then there's nothing to oppose, so one will get no opposition except that which is based on alien forces. [In contrast to Western democracy] our democracy is not adversarial; it is based on discussion to allow the correct adjustment of interests. And because it is based on a coalition of different nationalities, differing national interests can be adjusted in a harmonious way. Under the EPRDF, the Oromos, the Tigrayans and the Amharas and all the other nationalities are most of all interested in bringing development to their regions.[108]

How far Ethiopia is a functioning democracy and whether human and political rights are adequately protected has been much debated.[109] Certainly the political system is much more open than under the Derg, and violations of rights (though they occur) are much less egregious. But it would seem that it is at the regional, more than the federal level, that democratization is weakest and rights least well protected. The EPRDF's ancillary ethnic structures in the regions have been busy building *de facto* single-party governments,[110] based on the coercion of opponents and tight control of local patronage. The danger is that in the course of time the ethnic structures established under the EPRDF umbrella might break loose from the latter, and find themselves opposed to the federal government, putting severe stresses upon the federation itself.

Although the constitution in principle gives regions the right to secede, it seems more likely that the federal government would declare a state of emergency (which it can do in any part of the country under article 93 of the constitution, when there is 'a breakdown of law and order that regular law enforcement agencies and personnel cannot control'). The military is the sole national coercive structure capable of acting against secession, since the police (except for a small federal force) have been regionalized. Despite being in principle representative of all the country's nationalities and peoples, the armed forces have an integrated command. And rather than being composed of regionally based units, based on nationalities, all units, wherever they serve, are in principle ethnically mixed. In sum, Ethiopia has an integrated national army, rather than a multi-national force along the lines of the ethnic federalism, which is the guiding principle of the rest of the constitution. In any future emergency this would put the military at the eye of the storm, increase its political influence and make it the potential arbiter of state survival.

## Epilogue and Conclusion: the Eritrea–Ethiopia war

In May 1998 Eritrea and Ethiopia went to war with each other over an unresolved boundary dispute. In a major irony of history, the two new model armies that emerged from the EPLF and EPRDF liberation forces, which had fought side by side against the Derg, now fought a series of conventional campaigns against each other. Casualties on both sides ran into the tens of thousands, before fighting was halted after an agreement brokered by the Organization of African Unity (OAU).

This is not the place for a detailed discussion of the causes, course and consequences of this tragic and wasteful war.[111] But to most outside observers it seems that the territorial dispute, as well as the disagreements arising out of Eritrea's decision to create its own currency, which also poisoned relations between the two countries, could easily have been solved through negotiation. Indeed the war apparently took the governments and armed forces of both countries by surprise. Not until they were on the threshold of war did either consider the other to be a likely military threat.[112] That minor border incidents were allowed to escalate is symptomatic of the weakness of conflict-management mechanisms in the Horn[113] – but also suggests there were deeper contradictions behind the conflict. Some of these stemmed from the earlier history of the two liberation fronts, including the disputes between them during the armed struggle in the mid-1980s.[114]

At the same time the conflict reflected the profound differences in their approaches to the nationalities question, considered earlier. As Tronvall[115] has argued, the EPLF's discourse of secular, territorial nationalism has made Eritrea peculiarly insistent on its territorial boundaries; this is reflected in its boundary disputes with Yemen and Sudan, as well as with Ethiopia. The EPLF has also been suspicious of most forms of identity politics, and especially those that cut across national boundaries, such as the claims of Afars, who are divided between Eritrea, Ethiopia and Djibouti, to a nation of their own (claims which fit more easily into Ethiopia's multi-national vision of statehood).

For its part, the EPRDF has always been especially sensitive to markers of national identity in Tigray, which is immediately contiguous to the Tigrinya-speaking area in dispute with Eritrea. At the same time the EPRDF's critics outside Tigray have always blamed it for allowing the secession of Eritrea in 1993. Moreover Ethiopia's ethnic federalism, as argued earlier, has made both the government and armed forces potentially vulnerable to the rise of ethno-nationalism in the regions presently controlled by the EPRDF's affiliate nationality organizations. Although one could not in all fairness accuse the Ethiopian government of going to war to reunify the country and prolong its own hegemony, the conflict certainly produced major demonstrations of support for the war effort, and permitted a major mobilization of military manpower almost reminiscent of the early years of the Derg.

The war also serves as a reminder of the dangers as well as the advantages of the ideologies and forms of politics which arose from national liberation war tradition, in which 'nationalism became impregnated by the model of war, whose own specific culture and terminology it tended to assimilate into the language of nationalist militancy'.[116] Both the EPLF and the EPRDF had an impressive ability to mobilize popular support, motivate their fighters and combine political with military methods of warfare. The Janus face was a strong preference for consensus politics, mistrust of political pluralism, strong belief in the correctness of their own political line – and a predisposition to use force to defend it, conditioned by many years of armed struggle.

In Eritrea at least, it seems the war may have dented the EPLF's self-confidence and popular legitimacy, in part because of military reversals. The government was also criticized for allowing the conflict to delay the country's democratization process. In Ethiopia, however, it is arguable that the war for the time being enhanced the EPRDF's claims to be a broad national government, with popular support in most of the country and not just in Tigray. But in both countries the human and economic costs were enormous, and in both there was serious damage to the demilitarization and democratization processes which had begun so hopefully in 1991.

## Notes and References

1   The research on which this chapter is based was funded by grants from the US Institute for Peace and from the British Department for Overseas Development (ESCOR). The author is most grateful for their assistance and forbearance.

2   Of course this point is not new, being made in Finer's (1962) classic *Man on Horseback*. Finer, however, analysed the differences as a continuum from less to more political involvement, starting with influence (as in most Western democracies) and increasing in a number of steps ('blackmail', etc.) to open military intervention and government. Below I pay more attention to qualitative differences in the forms of military politics (for a much earlier attempt to tease out the qualitative differences see Luckham: 1971a).

3   Luckham (1996); Tilly (1985).

4   The interrelationship between democratic institutions and democratic politics is examined in more detail in Luckham, Goetz and Kaldor (2000).

5   See Luckham (1994) and Rouquié (1981), where the complexities of this concept are explored in greater detail.

6   Kaldor and Luckham (2001).

7   Although Eritrea was an Italian colony from the late nineteenth century, and there was a brief interlude of Italian over-rule over Ethiopia itself, following Italy's war of conquest shortly before the Second World War.

8   See Hutchful (1986) and Luckham (1994) for comparative analyses.

9   And it is in this sense that some commentators have stressed the similarities to as well as the differences from the colonial empires.

10   Markakis (1987: Chapter 9).

11   Clapham (1988: 20).

12   Gebru Tareke (1996: 27).

13   For a useful summary of these arguments, see Adhana (1994); a good general history is Bahru Zewde (1991).

14   Luckham and Bekele (1984): though it does not follow that these followed any single pattern.

15   Clapham (1988: 20–31).

16   Although Tegenu himself uses the term to characterize the more fully developed fiscal-military system which emerged in the late nineteenth century. See Tsegaye Tegenu (1996).

17   Adhana (1994) and Markakis (1974).

18   Details in this paragraph from Bahru Zewde (1998: 261–6); further details of military organization are in Pankhurst (1990).

19   Gebru Tareke (1996: 27).

20   Gebru Tareke (1996).

21   Even so, at some 40,000 men it was less than a tenth the size of the Derg's military machine in the 1980s.

22   See the brilliant satirical description of the emperor's 'Hour of Development' in Kapuscinski (1983: 85–8).

23   Erlich (1983).

24   The description below is based on Erlich (1983), Pliny the Middle Aged (1978–9), Clapham (1988: Chapter 3) and Haile Selassie (1997: chapters 3 and 4).

25   Haile Selassie (1997: 126).

26   See in particular Halliday and Molyneux (1981); Lefort (1983); Markakis and Ayele (1978).

27 Stressed in particular by Clapham (1988).
28 Brigadier-General Teferri Bente, a respected professional officer who had been appointed to head the PMAC after Andom's assassination, largely because he was neutral *vis-à-vis* the Derg's main factions.
29 Details in this paragraph from Clapham (1988: 77–92).
30 See De Waal (1991) for a well-documented account of the Derg's repressive measures and human rights violations.
31 Interview with Zegede Asfaw (January 1996).
32 Dessalegn Rahmato (1994: 246–7).
33 Probably not high, despite the immense transfers of military hardware, since most weapons were supplied on credit or through barter deals for coffee and other commodities: Henze (1990); Luckham and Bekelle (1984); Pateman (1991).
34 Hansson (1995).
35 Coletta *et al.* (1996: 109–15).
36 De Waal (1991 and 1997).
37 At its peak the militia numbered up to 300,000 men. Its initial deployment against the trained guerrillas of the EPLF in 1976–7 was disastrous; but, retrained, it was much more effective in the 1977–9 Ogaden and Eritrean campaigns.
38 Luckham and Bekele (1984).
39 Clapham (1988: 209)
40 Political commissars in the armed forces originally reported to the office for politico-military affairs under Asfaw; but later to the armed forces branches of COPWE and WPE. East German advisers played a major role in the introduction of military security procedures.
41 Interview January 1996 with Sebhat Ephrem, Eritrean Minister of Defence and former commander of the EPLF forces.
42 Described in some detail by Haile Selassie (1997: 284–300).
43 *Ibid.* (286).
44 Hansson (1995: chapters 6–8).
45 The analysis of this section draws on Alemseged Tesfai (1998); Cliffe (1994); Markakis (1987); Pool (1998), Young (1996a, 1996b and 1998) and De Waal (1991).
46 In part because the Ethiopian military took control of most of the ELF's base areas in the coastal lowlands, but could not dislodge the EPLF from its base areas in the mountainous Sahel.
47 Interview with Yemane 'Jamaica' Kidane (January 1996).
48 Interview January 1996 with Haile Woldensae, Eritrean Minister of Finance (now Minister of Foregn Affairs), former EPLF corps commander and ex-head of the front's political administration.
49 Interview with Sebhat Ephrem, January 1996.
50 Prendergast and Duffield (1999: 38).
51 The EPLF, according to Sebhat Ephrem (interview January 1996), did not have a similar system: 'if you have a committee it suggests you do not have full confidence in your commanders; it is better to have strong officers who enjoy the support of their men'.
52 Graphically conveyed in *Road to Eritrea* by the Australian novelist, Thomas Kenneally, written soon after a visit to the EPLF frontline.
53 Although self-reliance was also partly a deliberate choice. One of the reasons for the EPLF's original split with the ELF was the latter's excessive reliance on the support of Arab countries.
54 Interview with Haile Woldensae (January 1996).
55 Analysed in some depth by Young (1996).
56 See Tronvoll (1999).
57 Adekeson (1997).
58 Dessalegn Rahmato (1994).
59 In Ethiopia's case it was also because – despite the Derg's loss of political legitimacy and

military collapse – the basics of routine state administration, including a still functioning taxation system, had been maintained more or less throughout the war.

60  As Clapham terms it (1996).

61  See Ottaway (1995) and the debate between Henze (1998) and Harbeson (1998).

62  Abbink (1998: 557).

63  Tsadkan Gebre Tensae (1994).

64  Alemseged Tesfai (1998: 259).

65  Iyob (1997: 667–8).

66  The analysis in this section draws on Cliffe (1994), Makki (1996), Doornbos and Tesfai (1999), Iyob (1997).

67  Teclemichael W/Georgis (1998).

68  A term derived from the obligation of a community to help a newly married couple establish their home (Woldemichael and Iyob, 1998: 37).

69  Interview with Haile Woldensae (January 1996).

70  Makki (1996: 486–8).

71  Interview with Professor Bereket Habte Selassie (January 1996).

72  The constitution provides for freedom of political organization and association, but the constitution makers left the formalization of multi-party democracy for future legislation.

73  Interview with Yemane Gebreab, political secretary of PFDJ (February 1996).

74  Interview with Sebhat Ephrem (January 1996).

75  Interview with Haile Woldensae (January 1996).

76  Interview with Paulos Tesfagiorgios (February 1996).

77  *Ibid.*

78  Interview with Yemane Gebreab (February 1996).

79  Interview with Haile Woldensae (January 1996).

80  Soldiers were fed and housed and received allowances based on need and position.

81  Interview with Professor Bereket Habte Selassie (January 1996) and confirmed by my own interviews.

82  Interview with Sebhat Ephrem (January 1996).

83  It was the chairman of the Constitutional Commission's considered view that it would restrict the right of uniformed personnel to belong to party decision-making bodies, attend political meetings or openly agitate for parties – but would not necessarily rule out party membership: interview with Professor Bereket Habte Selassie (January 1996).

84  Interview with Sebhat Ephrem (January 1996).

85  Dessalegn Rahmato (1994).

86  America's role in pressing the EPRDF to take over and form the TGE – rather than forming a government on the basis of the negotiations being held in London between the military government and all the opposition groups – has been widely criticized by the EPRDF's critics. But given the military realities on the ground and the danger of the country dis-integrating into chaos, it may have been the only realistic alternative.

87  Besides the published studies cited in this section, the athor has been able to draw on two very useful unpublished studies by Adekson (1997) and Tucker (1998).

88  Adekson (1997: 8–14).

89  On the constitution and its background, see Brietzke (1995).

90  Abbink (1995: 152); Ehiopia's experiment in ethnic federalism is also analysed in Cohen (1997); Joireman (1997); Mengisteab (1997); and Young (1996).

91  Lyons (1996: 131).

92  Interview (January 1996) with Yemane 'Jamaica' Kidane, who was chief of personnel and administration in the Ministry of Defence during the reorganization period.

93  Interview with the Commissioner for Rehabilitation, Mulugeta Gebre Hiwot (January 1996).

94  Coletta *et al.* (1996).

95  Indeed, both commission staff and some donor representatives told me that in the initial stages demobilization had succeeded in spite of the donors – although donor funding and

some donor organizations like the German Agency for Technical Cooperation (GTZ) were crucial, especially during the rehabilitation phase.

96 *Ibid.*

97 Interview with head of the office of the chief of staff, Ministry of Defence (January 1996).

98 Coletta *et al.* (1996: 109–15).

99 Tsadkan Gebre Tensae (1994: 187–92).

100 This was the range of estimates provided in interviews with the director of training and personnel in the Ministry of Defence, with the Commissioner for Rehabilitation and with Yemane Kedane, January 1996.

101 Tsadkan Gebre Tensae (1994: 190).

102 *Seven Days Update*, Addis Ababa, 23 December 1996.

103 Interviews in the Ministry of Defence, and with Yemane Kedane (January 1996).

104 Interview with head of the office of the chief of staff (January 1996).

105 Interview with director of training and personnel in the Ministry of Defence (January 1996).

106 Interview with Yemane Kedane (January 1996).

107 Details above from interviews in the Ministry of Defence (January 1996), although there were some differences of opinion about the extent to which both the military and civilian components came under the control of the chief of staff.

108 Interview with Ato Dawit Yohannes, Speaker of the Council of Representatives (January 1996).

109 See the debates already cited above; Ethiopia's human rights record is discussed by Human Rights Watch (1997) and Tucker (1998).

110 The main exception is Region 5, the main Somali-speaking region, where the EPRDF's allies have had least success in establishing themselves.

111 See Abbink (1998); Gilkes and Plaut (1999).

112 Those whom I interviewed in both countries in early 1996 specifically said there was no serious possibility of the other being a threat, because of their fraternal relations. In a visit shortly before the conflict broke out in 1998, I received similar disclaimers from Ethiopian official (non-military) sources.

113 Cliffe (1999).

114 Young (1986).

115 Tronvoll (1999).

116 Makki (1996: 477).

# 11

# Army Politics as a Historical Legacy

## The Experience of Burma

MARTIN SMITH

Since the independence of Burma (Myanmar)[1] in 1948, armed politics and military government have become dominant features in the day-to-day landscape of the country. Indeed, the Burmese armed forces, known as the Tatmadaw, have been in control of the national government for over four decades. During this time, present-day officers argue that emergencies and other circumstances have forced the Tatmadaw to evolve from a government of last resort to a government of first resort. In contrast, pro-democracy supporters contend that the Tatmadaw has long since ceased to be an answer to the country's many problems, becoming instead the central problem in itself. Certainly, the political challenges that face Burma are immense, but the perpetuation of so many years of military rule has the most profound consequences. As a Rangoon diplomat told the author in 1991, 'There is no government in Burma. There is just the Burmese army.'

It is important, then, to acknowledge at the outset that the issue of the military in politics has remained critical during Burma's independence struggle and all three eras of government since the British departure. This includes both the short-lived parliamentary era (1948–62) and the isolationist 'Burmese Way to Socialism' (1962–88) that followed. However, it has only been since the rule of the State Law and Order Restoration Council (SLORC) and its successor, the State Peace and Development Council (SPDC), that the question of army politics in Burma has really come to international attention. In particular, the world was horrified in 1988, during the SLORC takeover, by international media images of the Tatmadaw's suppression of pro-democracy protests that swept the country that year.

Since that time Burma's political crisis has continued, but there have been few indicators as to how the impasse will be resolved. To understand the complexity of the malaise, many analysts have come to identify the modern deadlock as representing a three-cornered struggle between the main groups in contemporary Burmese politics: the military government; the re-emergent democracy movement headed by Daw Aung San Suu Kyi; and the country's diverse ethnic minority organizations, some of which have been under arms against the central government since independence. As a result, 'tripartite dialogue' has become the preferred solution of many concerned actors and parties, including the United Nations, where Burma's crisis has remained under constant review.[2] But, as to how such dialogue might be brought about, there has been little consensus. While Western governments supported boycott strategies that projected Burma as 'the South Africa of the 1990s', most Asian governments preferred a policy of 'constructive engagement' with the military authorities instead.[3]

By the beginning of the twenty-first century, however, there was little indication that dialogue in such tripartite shape was imminent. After years of conflict, a 'winner takes all' attitude appeared unfortunately pervasive in the different camps. Even more important, defying a decade of intensive opposition both at home and abroad, the military government had, almost paradoxically, been able to extend its control over a greater area of the country than ever before. Indeed, as officers took on the language of 'human resource development' and 'nation building', there were many indications that Tatmadaw leaders were reconnoitring the way for another generation of military-dominated rule in new guise.

Thus, although there are reasons to believe that dialogue will one day break the deadlock (and reports of secret talks between Aung San Suu Kyi and military leaders in January 2001 renewed many such hopes), there can be no doubt that the Burmese armed forces have long since become the controlling key. Whether initiating or accepting any process of reform, the Tatmadaw is the only functioning national organization at the political centre of power. And here the dilemma deepens. For while the aspirations of pro-democracy and ethnic nationality parties have generally become much better understood during a decade of international publicity, the Tatmadaw remains one of the least-known political armies in the world. Secrecy has long been its hallmark.[4]

To understand Burma's political crisis, then, it is necessary to look to the Tatmadaw. This, however, means turning the clock back to its foundation during the turbulent years that surrounded independence when many of the contemporary troubles first began. Burma's political crisis did not begin in 1988: in both national and military politics, there is a continuity that can be dated back significantly earlier. Indeed, in recent years, the continued predominance of the modern-day Tatmadaw has prompted growing research even further back into Burma's royal past, when the traditional Burmese state was strongly authoritarian in character.

## Background to Military Politics

Burma, a land with a population of fifty million in the year 2000, is one of the most ethnically diverse countries in Asia.[5] Concomitantly with this, it has suffered a legacy of insurgencies – political as much as ethnic – that began three months after independence when the Communist Party of Burma (CPB) took up arms against the elected government of Prime Minister U Nu. This state of confrontation has endured until the present day, with the result that the history of modern Burma is dominated by men in both government and opposition who have taken up arms, at some stage, in pursuit of their goals. Not only in government but in the opposition National League for Democracy (NLD), which won the 1990 general election, military veterans hold senior positions, while in many ethnic minority areas armed opposition has long been a virtual way of life.[6]

These different experiences mean that a diversity of views can be heard on military affairs, which generally contrast with the monolithic pronouncements that characterize military governments in Rangoon. Nevertheless, from such differing perceptions three main themes usually emerge: first, the difficulties of establishing a modern nation-state after the damaging interruptions of colonial rule; second, the background of armed struggle which has underpinned the rise of rule – and opposition – by gun; and, third, the overarching role played by Ne Win (born 1911) who, more than any other individual, has been the dominant force in shaping the present-day Tatmadaw. Whatever the aspirations of contemporary parties, all three influences are vital in understanding how the Tatmadaw emerged during the twentieth century to become the country's controlling force.

Burma's independence was born out of conflict, symbolized by the 1947 assassination of Aung San (along with most of his cabinet) by the gang of a political rival. As leader of the independence struggle and founder of the Tatmadaw, his name is still writ large in Burmese politics today. However, even before his death, there were many warnings of the issues and tensions that would later give rise to the centrality of military forces in politics. First, the formation of local militia or *tat(s)* was a tradition in the culture of Burmese politics that had not entirely been undone by British rule. This was graphically evidenced by the Saya San rebellion, led by a former Buddhist monk, which raged across the countryside during 1930–2.[7]

Moreover, the colonial division of Burma into two administrative territories – the ethnic minority 'Frontier Areas' and 'Ministerial Burma', where the Burman majority lived – was to further antagonisms that have had lasting impact. For although a degree of parliamentary home rule was introduced in Ministerial Burma, the British abolition of the monarchy in 1886 dealt a debilitating blow to the traditional structures of authority in Burmese society, especially among the Burman majority,[8] and this was never adequately replaced. In the Frontier Areas, by contrast, not only were the traditional rulers and chieftains largely maintained, but the British actively preferred recruits from minority backgrounds in the British Burma army. As late as 1939, there were only 472 Burmans in military service as compared with 1,448 Karens, 886 Chins and 881 Kachins.[9] All such issues offended the leaders of Burma's fledgling national independence movement, virtually all of whom were ethnic Burmans and who saw such tactics as classic 'divide and rule'. A divisive wedge was developing in the experiences of Burma's peoples, a third of whom are ethnic minorities, which has left a legacy of conflicting political and military traditions.

The protection of Buddhism and culture from alien influences were the first rallying cries for the young Burman nationalists in the early twentieth century. A major step forward was then taken in 1930 with the formation of the Dobama Asiayone ('We Burmans Association') during the advance from what Thakin Thein Pe Myint called the 'religious nationalism' to 'narrow nationalism' stages of anti-colonial organization.[10] However, as the Saya San rebellion warned, it was clear from the outset that the establishment of armed movements was also going to be an integral part of the coming struggle. Two pre-war prime ministers, U Saw and Dr Ba Maw, both formed *tats*. But it is from the military formations established by Aung San and the Thakins of the Dobama movement that the modern-day Tatmadaw claims its lineage.[11] Although largely tolerated by the British, most of these *tats* were formed in direct opposition to British rule.[12]

Inspired by the Saya San rebellion, the first such nationalist *tat* was formed in

1930, and in 1935–6 both the Dobama and the students' union established *tats* of their own. Although the young nationalists initially lacked any clear ideology, the influence of Marxism, socialism, communism and totalitarian ideas became highly important as the political agitations of the 1930s increased. For example, although he subsequently left, Aung San was a founder member of the CPB, established in 1939. 'One party, one blood, one voice and one command' became the war-time slogan of the Dobama movement, a motto which lives on in the Tatmadaw's 'One blood, once voice, one command'.

The entry of Japan into Burma during the Second World War marked a further stage in the Tatmadaw's genesis. Indeed, the Tatmadaw is probably the last army in Asia with uninterrupted traditions that can be dated back to imperial Japan. Initially, he had intended contacting the communists in China for military support, but eventually it was to Japan that Aung San turned, with Ne Win and the famed 'Thirty Comrades'. After training on Hainan Island, the Burma Independence Army (BIA) was inaugurated on 28 December 1941, and three days later the first BIA units entered Burma with the Japanese Fifteenth Army. The actual fighting role of the BIA against the British was relatively small and, even though Aung San and a number of others were given ministerial posts in government, the young nationalists quickly grew weary of the 'sham independence' granted under Japanese occupation.[13] The Japanese became equally doubtful about the BIA, described by Guyot as a 'political movement in military garb'.[14] As a result, in 1942 the BIA was reformed as the Burma Defence Army, and in 1943 this was superseded by the Burma National Army (BNA), with Ne Win as commander-in-chief. In the meantime, underground contacts had been resumed through the communist Thakin Thein Pe with the British in India, and eventually, on 27 March 1945, as the British Fourteenth Army advanced back into Burma, the BNA joined the uprising against the Japanese. This date has since been commemorated as Armed Forces Day in the country.

The war, however, had left a terrible burden of conflict and division, not least in the military field. Not only had there been a dramatic escalation in military capabilities, but the war had finally brought into open confrontation what Wiant termed the 'colonial tradition' of the British Burma Army, which was dependent on ethnic minorities, and the 'nationalist tradition' of the BIA, which was largely ethnic Burman.[15] There were serious outbreaks of inter-ethnic conflict during the war in which ethnic minority peoples, especially the Karen and Indian, were regarded as 'mercenaries' and 'collaborators' for staying loyal to the British; in consequence, they suffered especially badly.[16]

In institutional terms, the war further exacerbated these differences. For while minority troops continued to receive British training, a generation of young Burman officers, who were soon to lead the country to independence, had their first training from Japanese instructors. Nearly eight hundred cadets graduated from the officer training school set up by the Japanese at Mingaladon, while as many as 150 went for advanced training in Japan.[17] This experience was to become highly influential in the 1950s when the Tatmadaw War Office was reorganized.[18] Equally poignantly, the bitterness of these war-time divisions has lived on in the battlefields of Burma where prominent ethnic insurgent commanders, such as the Karen leaders Bo Mya and Tamla Baw, were formerly in the British army and have continued to run their forces along British lines. Often opposing them in the front line have been former BIA soldiers, and, even in the year 2000, there were still outbreaks of fighting in what is one of Asia's longest-running and most devastating conflicts.[19]

In an attempt to head off such differences, the British created a 'hybrid army' before their departure from Burma in 1948.[20] At the war's end, the BNA had been reformed into the Patriotic Burmese Forces (PBF), and Aung San worked hard to keep the PBF together as a 'nucleus' force, separate from the Karen and other minority units in the British Burma Army whom they regarded as 'mercenaries'.[21] Eventually, a compromise was found through the creation of 'class battalions', based largely on ethnicity. The PBF were reformed in to what became four battalions of 'Burma Rifles' and amalgamated with eight ethnic-based battalions of 'Karen', 'Kachin' and 'Chin' Rifles to create the new Tatmadaw at independence.[22] Partly to placate minority concerns (and throughout 1945–7 ethnic rights were a highly contentious issue), the Karen general Smith Dun, who was Sandhurst-trained, was appointed chief of staff, while another Karen, Shi Sho, was placed in charge of the air force. However, the composition of the Tatmadaw along such ethnic lines only heightened the contemporary equations of ethnicity with politics, while the preferment of ethnic minority officers hardly sat well with BIA veterans of the 'nationalist tradition'.

Whether Aung San could have controlled subsequent events can never be answered. Significantly, he had resigned from the army at the war's end to go into politics, which is the legacy pro-democracy supporters prefer to point to today. However, Aung San was nothing if not a pragmatist, and in 1945 he had also formed a new *tat*, known in English as the People's Volunteer Organization (PVO), for war-time veterans. Rapidly growing to a force over a hundred thousand strong, it not only put enormous pressures on the British to hurry their departure, but also became another major player in the military confusion that was now about to break out. The *tat* traditions of 'pocket armies' were certainly not dead.

It is equally important to recognize, as Callahan has argued, that the widely held notion of Burma's government of 1948–62 as 'democratic' in contrast to the military governments that followed is a simplification that does not tell the whole story.[23] Although the 1947 constitution was both federal and parliamentary in concept, the establishment of a liberal democratic system was not the guiding aim of Burma's leaders at independence. The ruling Anti-Fascist People's Freedom League (AFPFL) coalition which won the 1947 election was broadly socialist in composition, and, indeed, for the next 40 years Burma was to be something of a rarity in Asian politics as a 'leftist' government where principal opposition frequently came from the left (largely in the form of the CPB). As Aung San, a two-time CPB member, had written in his 'Blue Print for Burma': 'There shall be only one nation, one state, one party, one leader. There shall be no parliamentary opposition, no nonsense of individualism.'[24]

Speculation, then, could be endless. But, as a concluding comment on political armies in the colonial era, the claims and perceptions of Tatmadaw literature are revealing. Not only had its key founding aim of 'national independence' been achieved, but modern-day histories frequently assert that it was during this period that the Tatmadaw began to assert its 'leading role' in the political life of the country.[25] Both Aung San and Ne Win, the prominent first-hour generals of the Burmese army, made early references to the Tatmadaw's foundational role (see Box 11.1). Certainly, within a decade, both the British and Japanese had been

---

**Box 11.1**  General Ne Win and General Aung Sang on the Burmese armed forces

'The armed forces are meant for this nation and this people, and it should be such a force having the honour and respect of the people. If instead the armed forces should come to be hated by the people, then the aims with which this army has been built up would have been in vain.' General Aung San, Tatmadaw founder and late independence hero, undated.[26]

'The Burmese Army is not only the hope of the country but its very life and soul.' General Ne Win, on the liberation of Rangoon, May 1945.[27]

---

forced to leave under the pressure of armed resistance. The situation, however, was by no means straightforward. Indeed, there were several other organizations and political armies that were now about to dispute this very same 'leading role'.

## Civil War and the Emergence of Ne Win

The impact of the civil war that broke out in Burma in 1948 was absolutely devastating for a country that was still struggling to rebuild from the loss and destruction of the Second World War. 'A country goes underground', pronounced a newspaper headline as the CPB began armed insurrection, to be joined shortly afterwards by the 'White Band' PVO and pro-communist units in the Burma Rifles. Indeed, four of the former 'Thirty Comrades' were in the front line of the opposition offensive, leading the attempt by the CPB's People's Army to seize power.[28] In the analysis of the CPB, which considered itself the leading force behind wartime resistance, Burma's independence was as 'sham' under U Nu's AFPFL government as it had been under imperial Japan.[29]

The situation then deteriorated even further the following year when Karen units in the new Burma army, who until then had remained significantly loyal, joined the Karen National Union (KNU) in insurrection along with Mon, Karenni, Pao, Rakhine and other ethnic minority forces. At one stage the authority of U Nu's cabinet was reduced to what was known as the 'Six-Mile Rangoon government', since this was the only part of the country they controlled. Over one million internally displaced people and 60,000 deaths may well have been the human cost in the first two years of fighting alone, as vast areas of the country fell under insurgent control.[30]

The wonder is that the central government endured, and this, in no small measure, was down to General Ne Win and loyal troops from the Fourth Burma Rifles (his old battalion) around whom defence of the country was built.[31] As with the 'Thirty Comrades', another small group of friends was about to try and take charge of the country's destiny, only this time, on the whole, they would be fighting their own peoples. Equally important, although the Tatmadaw was desperately weak, the mutiny of both communist and ethnic minority officers had left the military stage open to Ne Win and officers from the 'nationalist tradition'. They, too, were mainly on the political left, and they were clearly smarting from what they called the 'Karenization of the Tatmadaw' and the prevailing influence of 'Rightists'.[32] But, always a bluff soldier, Ne Win also took the pro-communist mutinies from the Tatmadaw in his stride. His reaction to news of defections by former comrades to the CPB was reportedly: 'Good. Now we know who is black and who is white.'[33]

In January 1949, Ne Win made his move at the outbreak of the KNU insurrection, replacing Smith Dun as commander-in-chief and beginning the removal of troops regarded as rightists or from different military traditions from Tatmadaw ranks.[34] This was a goal Ne Win admitted to twenty years later. 'Our Tatmadaw emerged from the crucible of the independence struggle, through the BIA, BNA, and the BPF [PBF].... In the case of the Navy and Air Force, we had to make use of personnel left by the British as the nucleus for our forces. We had to reorientate such people to see our point of view.'[35] At this stage, however, Ne Win's Tatmadaw was heavily outnumbered, with as few as 2,000 troops, and the situation was further exacerbated in late 1949 when 12,000 armed Kuomintang remnants from China, who enjoyed clandestine American backing, invaded Shan state. The situation could not have been worse.

This new catastrophe was to have a profound impact for the fledgling nation in ways that few could have imagined during the countdown to independence. Not only did the fighting increasingly bring the Burmese armed forces into all regions of the country (including ethnic minority regions where they were often not welcome), but the continuing political chaos heightened the frustrations of Tatmadaw officers who were battling – and losing lives – in the field. The result was an increasing distrust of civilian parties and politicians, who were seen as self-interested and opportunistic, and a growing belief that it was only the unity of the Tatmadaw that was holding the union together.[36] Until the present day, no official Tatmadaw publication would be complete without criticisms of politicians and repeated pride in the 'unflinching' sacrifices made by the Burmese armed forces during these years.[37]

It would be wrong, however, to depict the parliamentary government of the 1950s as completely unsuccessful. Despite the country-wide insurgencies, by the early 1950s central authority had largely been restored. An independent judiciary existed, Burma enjoyed greater press freedom than most countries in Asia, and, by the time of the 1956 election, a semblance of democratic opposition was functioning. However, many of the actions taken by the government during these days did not bode well for the establishment of democratic institutions and practices.[38] Not only did the U Nu government have frequent recourse to security laws to silence political dissent (notably the 1947 Public Order Preservation Act), but it also went along with the formation of local *tats* by district leaders who, it was believed, would support its authority.[39] Known under such names as the Sitwundan and Pyusawhti, throughout the 1950s these paramilitary groups greatly added to the general climate of warlordism and political violence.[40] In a country of such diversity, a dangerous intolerance of opposing or different viewpoints was being allowed to develop.

It was to this volatile background that the Tatmadaw began to expand, frequently undertaking actions that were in advance of government authority in the field. The unifying influence was Ne Win, but, reflecting a pattern that still exists, a pragmatic autonomy was also allowed to trusted commanders at the front. In this way, the Tatmadaw began to develop both personal and institutional skills in dealing with local crises. It was not, however, a one-man show under Ne Win, and forward-looking officers, especially colonels Aung Gyi and Maung Maung, were key sources of planning and ideas.

An important step forward in the Tatmadaw's consolidation was the reorganization and centralization of the war office in 1951–2, which was hastened by the realization during the Kuomintang invasion that the Tatmadaw had to be prepared to fight international as well as internal wars. Armed forces' unity and the elimination of civilian influence were also the themes of Tatmadaw meetings in the early 1950s, which saw the navy and the air force placed under Ne Win's control as chief of staff.[41] As a result, by the mid-1950s the domination of Ne Win and former BIA–PBF officers was complete, and at the commanding officers' 1954 conference in Maymyo, Ne Win, perhaps still wary of communist infiltration, spoke for the first time of the need for a guiding ideology for the Tatmadaw.[42] Simultaneously with these discussions, moves were undertaken to secure the Tatmadaw's institutional basis. In 1951, a Defence Services Institute (DSI) was set up to provide troops with consumer goods at subsidized prices. Then, to advance educational standards, the Officer Training School (OTS) was revived and a Defence Services Academy (DSA) was established in 1955, both of which continue to produce annual batches of qualified officers and graduates. Since such training was frequently combined with battlefield experience, Tatmadaw officers quickly became regarded as among the most combat-ready in Asia.

Almost unnoticed, the Tatmadaw's growing experiences and capabilities were changing the political balance of government. This set the scene for Ne Win's emergency 'military caretaker administration' during 1958–60. How seriously the integrity of the union was threatened at this stage has been much debated. In 1958, the insurgencies were probably at their quietest pitch for years following an 'arms for democracy' initiative, introduced by U Nu, which had seen various Mon, Rakhine, PVO and communist forces renounce armed struggle. At the same time, the political factionalism of Rangoon had not abated, and the split of the governing AFPFL into 'Clean' and 'Stable' factions that year led to an uncertain situation which Ne Win feared might allow communists into government.[43] Whatever the truth, these political schisms were eventually used by Ne Win as the pretext for his military takeover. In his first speech to parliament as prime minister, he described the situation as 'closely approaching that sad spectacle of 1948–9'.[44]

In many ways, the caretaker administration acted as a trial run for Ne Win and his officers. As troops went about relocating squatter communities and cleaning the streets, there were many precedents for the subsequent takeovers in both 1962 and 1988. The Tatmadaw's achievements were publicized in a book – *Is Trust Vindicated?* – which drew attention to a further downturn in the insurgencies and an increase in rice production to post-war highs.[45] Significantly, too, it was during this time that the DSI expanded to become the country's largest commercial institution, with interests in transport, construction, banking and other businesses. On a more controversial note, however, there were also ominous signs of the Tatmadaw's growing involvement in politics, the most notable of which was the signing away of rights by the traditional *sawbwas* (princely rulers) in the Karenni (Kayah) and Shan states. Both of these territories had been granted the right of secession from the union after a ten-year period in the 1947 constitution. This was something Ne Win was determined to forestall.

In 1960 Burma was briefly returned to civilian government. However, for all the successes of the caretaker administration, few observers were surprised that the elections were again won by U Nu – and not the 'Stable' faction that Ne Win supported. Ethnic tensions (and insurgencies) were rising once again. U Nu then compounded the problem in 1961 by trying to make Buddhism the official state religion of Burma, which especially upset Christian sensibilities in the Kachin state where a new armed movement, the Kachin Independence Organization, was getting under way.

Finally, nearly four years after he had assumed control, ostensibly to prevent communists getting into government, it was over a very different issue – ethnic rights and 'federalism' – that Ne Win seized power in March 1962. 'Federalism is impossible; it will destroy the union,' he claimed.[46] U Nu, his cabinet and dozens of ethnic minority leaders, including Burma's first president, Sao Shwe Thaike, were arrested, and the era of parliamentary democracy was brought to an abrupt end. In 1962, however, the Tatmadaw that had now taken control was not the 'hybrid army' which the British had left at independence. From only 2,000 in the dark days of 1949, by 1962 it controlled over 100,000 troops, organized in five regional commands, and these forces had been established on the basis of a 'modern nation-state'.[47] In the process, senior leadership had been taken over exclusively by a small group of BIA/PBF veterans, virtually all of whom were ethnic Burmans with socialist ideas, and those with different viewpoints had either been purged, re-educated, gone underground or quit.

In effect, as Callahan has argued, the Burmese armed forces had already begun 'state building', almost by default, during the breakdown of civilian government in the 1950s.[48] Now, however, Ne Win and his officers were able to impose any vision they chose. Unity, conformity and loyalty to the state were the virtues they mostly believed in.

## The Burmese Way to Socialism

In *The National Ideology and the Role of the Defence Services*, published in 1960, three main objectives were set out: restoring peace and the rule of law, consolidating democracy, and the establishment of a 'socialist economy'.[49] Ne Win now manifestly dropped the second of these. For 26 years, Burma was to disappear behind a bamboo curtain as the country became one of the most isolated in the world. Indeed so isolated did the country become that, in 1979, Ne Win even took Burma out of the Non-Aligned Movement.

Upon seizing power, Ne Win declared a ruling 17-man Revolutionary Council of senior military officers. Such a radical self-description was an important attempt at legitimization. Their actions, Brigadier Sein Win claimed, were just the 'second half of a revolution' that had begun with the independence struggle; now the Tatmadaw's duty was to 'transform the society to socialism'.[50] Myoe has described this as a change from 'praetorian army' to 'revolutionary army', Wiant as the formation of a 'vanguard army'.[51] However, there can be little doubt that the underground CPB – and its still active People's Army – was the main ideological competitor that Ne Win had in his sights.

In terms of political armies, then, it is perhaps the most significant character of Ne Win's government that he set up a political party, the Burma Socialist Programme Party (BSPP), to sustain military rule. Almost uniquely in the world of the 1960s and 1970s, this was a military regime with a left-wing philosophy: the 'Burmese Way to Socialism'. The final inspiration for this, many believe, was a visit Ne Win made to China in 1960 where he had been impressed by the position of Chairman Mao. 'Chairman' Ne Win was soon to become his favoured appellation. For all the rhetoric, however, the socialist language of the BSPP never disguised the military character of Ne Win's rule. An idiosyncratic mix of Marxist, Buddhist and nationalist principles, the BSPP's guiding philosophy was outlined in a small volume, *The System of Correlation of Man and his Environment,* but it was never enlarged upon.[52] Indeed, it was not until 1974 that a new constitution was introduced – and after a much-disputed referendum.

Instead, freed of parliamentary controls, Ne Win's officers concentrated on a basic two-fold strategy for much of the BSPP era: launching constant offensives against insurgent forces in the rural countryside while instituting a one-party system of government that was planned to radiate out from Rangoon into the ethnic minority states. All national resources were co-opted to these ends and dissent was never tolerated, as the bloody suppression of student protests at Rangoon University in July 1962 had starkly warned.

The only apparent hesitation was at the very beginning, during 1962–4, when Ne Win briefly tried to win over insurgent groups to the new socialist cause. However, following abortive peace talks in 1963, the regime went into full swing.[53] In the following years, the arrest of political opponents continued, key sectors of the economy were nationalized, most foreigners expelled (including the substantial Indian and Chinese business communities), and the independent media and non-state sectors of education were abolished. Tight controls were also placed on students and Buddhist monks, historically the catalysts for political change in Burma, and the security blanket was further tightened by draconian new regulations, such as the 1962 Printers and Publishers Registration Law.

Perhaps the most telling indictment of the BSPP's failures was the inability of the party or government to bring in civilians. Initially ruling through local 'Security and Administrative Councils' led by serving or retired officers, the BSPP administration was slowly expanded around the country, but top positions were invariably taken by those with military backgrounds. Indeed, by 1972, over half the BSPP's 73,369 members were still from the armed forces,[54] and only one civilian of international reputation, Dr Maung Maung, ever served in its highest ranks. Supportive workers' and peasants' councils were also established, but, in many respects, the Tatmadaw continued to operate as a parallel system of administration throughout the country.

The fact that it was the Burmese armed forces undertaking this major expansion of state-building activities at this delicate stage in Burma's post-colonial history is very significant. The era of British rule, combined with the Second World War and the insurrections, had not only amplified divisions in society but created a vacuum in many local structures of authority which the military government was now seeking to fill. In an earlier era, there may have been greater societal resistance or competing institutions (such as the Buddhist clergy or professional groups), especially in Burman-majority areas where the government was largely centred. But after 1962, in the words of Steinberg, 'civil society was systematically eliminated'.[55]

However, a lack of societal resistance was certainly not the case in ethnic minority borderlands, vast areas of which had never been brought under the direct control of any centralized government, be it Burmese or British. And here armed opposition to Ne Win's Tatmadaw was continuing to grow. In consequence, as in the parliamentary era, combating the insurgencies was to remain a continuing preoccupation of the Tatmadaw leadership. But far from quelling rebellion, the *Burmese Way to Socialism* merely poured fuel on its flames. In particular, ethnic passions were enraged by what many regarded as a policy of outright 'Burmanization', imposed by a Burman military elite. Education in minority languages was downscaled, publication in minority languages restricted, and the preferment of ethnic Burmans to senior positions in the armed forces and government visibly increased. Indeed, all but three seats on the first Revolutionary Council were given to former BIA men, hardly encouraging minority feelings of inclusiveness. In effect, the BSPP was attempting to impose the model of an 'ethnocratic' state.[56] This marked a serious reversal of Aung San's 'unity in diversity' philosophy at independence.

Ne Win's problems, however, did not end here. For the BSPP government not only faced renewed insurgencies from ethnic minority forces but from ethnic Burman opponents as well, raising the real spectre of international intervention in Burma for the first time since the early 1950s. First, following anti-Chinese riots in Rangoon in 1967, the People's Republic of China provided a decade of full-scale military backing to the CPB, which launched a cross-border invasion into northeast Burma, establishing substantial 'liberated zones' in the Shan and Kachin states in the process. Then, in 1969, the deposed prime minister U Nu, along with three of the ex-'Thirty Comrades', also went underground in south-east Burma where, with quasi-CIA backing, they took up arms in short-lived alliance with the KNU and other former ethnic opponents.[57] Little reported in the world outside, tens of thousands of lives were lost in the pitched battles of these years, which again devastated many communities, as various communist, 'parliamentary' and ethnic federalist armies fought with the BSPP army of Ne Win.[58]

The Tatmadaw confronted such opposition in ever more ruthless style. Many of the trends had already been apparent in fighting during the 1950s, but it was under the BSPP government that many of the military practices for which Burma has become internationally notorious (notably forced labour and forced relocations) were first used systematically.[59] Especially criticized was the 'Four Cuts' strategy, which was first unveiled in the Irrawaddy Delta region in 1966. Similar in concept to the 'strategic hamlet' operation of the USA in Vietnam, it was described as the BSPP's version of 'people's war'. The Tatmadaw had just three tasks, illustrating the harsh priorities of the times: 'To liquidate insurgents, to organize the people, and to study the party's programme and policy'.[60] At the same time, the Tatmadaw high command often allowed a good deal of flexibility in the front line, especially in dealings with paramilitary or local armed bands which proliferated in many areas against the backdrop of war. In contrast to the perennial conflicts with the 'political armies' of the CPB or KNU, Tatmadaw officers were permitted to engage with such irregular self-defence forces on a 'soldier-to-soldier' basis. One particularly controversial tactic was the formation in the late 1960s of local home-guard militia, known as Ka Kwe Ye, to try and defuse the fast-growing insurrections in Shan state. Within a few years, however, the policy had to be abandoned because of international criticism of the open involvement of several of these local Ka Kwe Ye forces in narcotics trafficking.[61]

Nevertheless, if viewed purely in counter-insurgency terms, the Tatmadaw's tactics of these years met with some success, especially in the Delta, Pegu Yoma and central regions of Burma which had been virtually cleared of all armed opposition forces by the mid-1970s. By comparison, in the rugged ethnic minority borderlands, military operations were always likely to fail. Moreover, given the growing failures of the socialist economy, it was mainly the insurgent groups that were thriving from taxes on the country's lucrative black market trade in everything from teak and cattle to consumer goods and opium. By 1988, an unofficial World Bank estimate put the annual value of this trade at US$3 billion, or some 40 per cent of Burma's GNP.[62] The days of the BSPP were coming to a close.

In the 1960s and 1970s, the few anti-government protests in urban areas had been swiftly suppressed. Rare manifestations of discontent within the Tatmadaw were also quickly acted upon. The most notable were in 1976–7 when several officers were arrested for an alleged assassination plot against BSPP leaders. In 1976, the Tatmadaw commander-in-chief and Minister of Defence, General Tin Oo (the present-day NLD leader), was also dismissed and imprisoned for seven years.[63] The second time was in 1983 when Brigadier Tin Oo (no relation) was dismissed, along with his supporters, for trying to build up his own power base in the Military Intelligence Service (MIS or Directorate of Defence Services Intelligence, DDSI), which he headed. But, in many respects, this latter purge weakened the eyes and ears of the government at a critical moment. Protected by privileges, the Tatmadaw was growing into a class living apart within Burmese society. 'The Tatmadaw does not constitute a separate class. We are of the working people,' Brigadier Thaung Dan had claimed in 1965.[64] But popular protest was now to shake this complacency.

All the time, the country was heading towards the brink of international bankruptcy, signified in December 1987 when Burma was accredited with 'least developed country' status at the UN. One of the most potentially prosperous countries in Asia at independence had become one of the world's ten poorest, on a level with Ethiopia and Nepal. By most estimates, around 40 per cent of the annual national budget was being spent on the armed forces. It was these mounting pressures that led to Ne Win's unexpected resignation in July 1988. It is quite likely that, when he stepped down with General San Yu and a few veteran colleagues, Ne Win presumed that a reformed BSPP (and he left the door open to a referendum on multi-party change), would eventually continue a system of Tatmadaw dominance. Within two months, however, the BSPP had totally collapsed, raising the question as to how far the party had ever really existed. As a final legacy, Ne Win could probably claim to have preserved the integrity of Burma and kept it undamaged by international influence during an era when Cold War conflicts had ravaged many of its neighbours. But Ne Win's unique strategy, which was whimsically homespun and based largely on security perceptions, had come at an enormous price to the people.

Thus ended the second 'socialism-building' stage in the Tatmadaw's official histories. In international terms, the country was emerging from a 26-year sleep-walk. Among the people, expectations were high. A number of realities remained, however, not least the long-standing insurgencies. Over 20 armed opposition groups, including the CPB and KNU, were still active in the ethnic minority borderlands, despite a quarter century of one-party rule to try and destroy them.

But, above all, regardless of the BSPP's fate, there remained the Tatmadaw, which had not only doubled in size to around 180,000 regulars during the BSPP era, but had considerably extended its administration and infrastructure. The way its new leaders now moved would be critical.

## The Era of the SLORC–SPDC

Although often described as a 'coup', the assumption of power by the SLORC in September 1988 was more of a continuation of military-based government than any abrupt change from the BSPP. The SLORC were all Ne Win loyalists, and the first SLORC chairman, General Saw Maung, was both armed forces' chief and the last BSPP Minister of Defence. However, the sheer scale of pro-democracy protests that swept across the country during 1988 vividly demonstrated that, this time, the demand for change was going to run very deep. Not only were international pressures for reform rapidly mounting, but criticisms from Tatmadaw veterans were adding to the momentum. The most damaging of these were highly critical letters to General Ne Win from his former deputy, ex-Brigadier Aung Gyi, that were circulating among the crowds.

However, it was the words of Aung San Suu Kyi that captured the epoch-making spirit of the times when she called for Burma's 'second struggle for national independence' at a mass rally on the historic Shwe Dagon hill in August that year.[65] Coming from the daughter of the founder of the Tatmadaw, these were poignant words in the Burmese context, issuing a direct challenge to the military establishment.

The subsequent suppression of the pro-democracy movement has since been widely covered in the international media.[66] The legacy of the one-party system meant that there were no existing institutions for democratic change. Student activists wanted Aung San Suu Kyi and a committee of respected elders, including U Nu and the army veterans Aung Gyi and ex-General Tin Oo, to form an interim government to hold elections, but they fatefully hesitated. At the same time, there were a number of killings and outbreaks of violence, all of which left the door open to Tatmadaw hard-liners who were getting ready to strike. Still, Tin Oo upheld his belief in the possible coexistence of the military and democracy (Box 11.2).

---

**Box 11.2   Ex-General Tin Oo on the Burmese armed forces**

'We served in the defence services according to the teachings of General Aung San and the experiences we gained through our history. We were also guided by the principles of the defence services. Soldiers should stay clear of party politics. Military personnel should be engaged only in military affairs.... Achieving democracy will not hurt the defence services personnel, it will benefit them instead.'– Ex-General Tin Oo, NLD deputy chairman and former Tatmadaw commander-in-chief, August 1999.[67]

---

On 18 September 1988 the SLORC assumed power, declaring martial law and suspending the 1974 constitution. In the following weeks, the security forces relentlessly put down protests. Meanwhile, in the ethnic minority borderlands, where thousands of students and democracy activists had fled to take sanctuary, fierce fighting broke out with insurgent groups. A new cycle of insurgencies appeared imminent, with the tragic result that 1988 witnessed one of Burma's highest death tolls in many years. Estimates of the country-wide fatalities in 1988 run as high as ten thousand. But, as Ne Win had warned in his resignation speech, 'When the army shoots, it shoots to hit.'[68]

Analysing the subsequent course of events becomes difficult. Senior officers have privately told the author that they had no prepared plans for government at the time of the SLORC takeover but believed they were dutifully responding, as patriotic soldiers, to a situation of extreme emergency which, they say, threatened the survival of the union. 'I saved the country from an abyss,' General Saw Maung later claimed.[69] Certainly, many of the actions taken by the military government appear highly reactive. But, as the years went by, it is indisputable that the new military leadership prioritized steps to ensure continued Tatmadaw dominance from the outset. 'Only if the armed forces are strong will the nation be strong,' remains a much-repeated slogan of the post-1988 era.

Complicating the problems of analysis, the post-1988 government, unlike the BSPP, never published a blueprint philosophy or plan. Nevertheless, a number of trends quickly became salient, as the Tatmadaw moved from what official reports described as a 'socialist' to 'nation-building' role in the creation of a 'new democratic state'.[70] In line with these goals, upon assuming power, the SLORC declared the objectives of introducing a new era of 'open-door', 'market-oriented' and 'multi-party' democracy, once law and order had been restored. Claiming the rights of a *de facto* government, military leaders asserted that only the Tatmadaw was qualified by its history and experience to undertake this transitional role. In particular, it designated 'Our Three Main National Causes', which are printed in every newspaper and publication, as its exclusive prerogative: non-disintegration of the union, non-disintegration of national solidarity and the perpetuation of national sovereignty.[71] In addition, the SLORC declared 'national politics' a special preserve of the Tatmadaw, as distinct from the 'party politics' of civilian organizations. 'The SLORC is a military or public service government that stays clear of party politics,' explained Lieutenant-General Tin Oo, SLORC second secretary.[72]

On this basis, the SLORC moved towards the May 1990 general election. In reality, the situation was one of crisis and emergency. Indeed, many of the SLORC's early actions were more reminiscent of Ne Win's Revolutionary Council. Across the country, local Law and Order Restoration Councils were set up by the military, similar to the Security and Administrative Councils of the RC, and these were still essentially in operation a decade later. Meanwhile, although new political parties were permitted to form, the SLORC clamped down on any signs of public opposition. Ruling under existing security laws and new martial law decrees, the regime arrested or detained thousands of political prisoners, including Aung San Suu Kyi, ex-General Tin Oo and many other leaders of the newly formed NLD. 'Martial law means no law at all,' explained Lieutenant-General Khin Nyunt, the MIS chief and SLORC first secretary.[73]

By allowing the election to go ahead at this time, it is quite likely that the SLORC was acting on the presumption that its own favoured party, the National Unity Party (NUP), would win. The party had inherited much of the property and machinery of the defunct BSPP. In the event, the NUP won only ten seats as compared to 392 for the NLD, which, while a poor showing for 25 per cent of the vote, still marked a stunning electoral victory for the NLD. It was of equal importance that the result was widely recognized around the world, leading to increased international human rights' pressures on the military government over the following decade. However, it was not a result that the SLORC was likely to accept as a basis for the NLD forming a government. Aung San Suu Kyi and several other senior NLD leaders were not immediately released, and, when victorious candidates tried to meet to form a parliament, Tatmadaw hard-liners again cracked down, arresting over thirty NLD representatives on treason charges. Meanwhile, a dozen newly elected members of parliament joined the exodus into territory controlled by armed ethnic opposition groups, where they formed a rival 'National Coalition Government Union of Burma' headed by Aung San Suu Kyi's cousin, Dr Sein Win. In many respects, the political landscape was as dangerously polarized as at any time since independence, and each day the state-controlled media were full of allegations of both 'communist' and 'imperialist' conspiracies against the union which, they claimed, the international media were supporting.[74]

However, the SLORC did not cave in, and Tatmadaw leaders once again used their professional unity of purpose – and dominant position – to demonstrate their skills in surviving the minefield of Burmese politics. In the wake of the BSPP era, the Tatmadaw was the only organization that was functioning effectively in most parts of the country. In comparison, the NLD or armed opposition fronts, such as the 23-party Democratic Alliance of Burma (DAB), were institutionally very weak or localized.[75] At this critical moment, the SLORC was helped by the outbreak of ethnic mutinies during 1989 from the 15,000-strong People's Army of the CPB in north-east Burma, leading to the virtual collapse of the Tatmadaw's long-time opponent. Seizing the initiative, Lieutenant-General Khin Nyunt quickly agreed ceasefires with four breakaway forces, spearheaded by the United Wa State Party, instituting an unexpected ceasefire policy with ethnic opposition forces that steadily expanded over following years. By the mid-1990s, 15 of the 20 most important armed ethnic organizations had agreed military truces – although not political agreements – with the regime under a new 'peace through development' strategy.[76] The timing was important. The unexpected opportunity of ceasefires gave the beleaguered government time to strategize and regroup. Increasingly, the post-Ne Win generation was taking control and, from this point on, there were subtle changes. The pace of reform was slowed down and the new focus switched away from politics, where the government (especially General Saw Maung) was struggling, to issues such as development, narcotics control, economic progress and international relations, where its role was less challenged. The new priority was emphasizing the Tatmadaw's claimed 'nation-building' role.

The objective of multi-party democracy was never officially dropped, and in 2000, for example, Foreign Minister Win Aung again publicly pledged that the government was still committed to this goal.[77] But, in the meantime, there were increasing qualifications, which subtly redefined the Tatmadaw's objective as 'disciplined democracy' that had to be suitable for Burmese society and conditions. Simultaneously with this, the number of 'legal' political parties was steadily cut from over two hundred in 1988 to just ten (not including ceasefire groups) by the mid-1990s. Equally striking was the way the state-controlled media constantly returned to the themes of the 1958 and 1962 coups, warning of the failings of civilian parties in Burma. 'Politics is dead,' concluded one particularly severe commentary in the *Kyemon* newspaper.[78]

It should be stressed, however, that some members of the military government genuinely believed that the SLORC's new nation-building focus, especially the ethnic ceasefires, paved the way for solutions to be found. In defence of their strategies, they pointed to a number of initiatives undertaken by the government in the early 1990s. The SLORC's first attempt at change came in April 1992 when, following fierce fighting with the KNU in south-east Burma, General Than Shwe replaced General Saw Maung as the SLORC chairman, over two thousand political prisoners were released, martial law restrictions were lifted, and all offensives against ethnic armed forces were halted 'in the name of national unity'.

Following on from this, in January 1993 a hand-picked National Convention was introduced to draw up the principles for a new constitution.[79] From the outset, however, it was clear that the SLORC's vision of democracy was likely to be based on the model of Indonesia, which was then still in the Suharto era. Not only would the 'leading role of the Tatmadaw' have to be guaranteed in 'national political life' as a guiding principle, but 25 per cent of all seats in the new parliament must be reserved for military candidates; indeed, military experience would be a requirement in any future president. And comparisons with Indonesia continued to multiply after September 1993 with the formation of a new Union Solidarity and Development Association (USDA), under the patronage of the SLORC chairman. With the electoral failure of the NUP, it was clear that the SLORC was attempting to create a fresh civilian support base. Reaching an estimated ten million members by the end of the century, many observers believed it could be turned into an Indonesian-style Golkar Party at any time in the future.[80]

Meanwhile, the SLORC was actively seeking to entrench itself in other fields. In 1988, Burma was isolated and on the point of financial collapse, and all Western government aid had been cut off in protest at the SLORC's takeover. However, in line with its new 'open-door' policies, the regime was able to ward off the immediate threat to its financial survival by logging and fishery deals with military-backed interests in Thailand, and, subsequently, trading links with China and other Asian neighbours. In contrast to the Western policies of isolation and trade boycotts,[81] Asian countries were clearly more keen to establish government-to-government relations with an emergent but unpredictable neighbour. Given their own experiences of political transformation, they were also far more reluctant to pronounce on internal affairs, and this policy of 'constructive engagement' was eventually to see Burma join the Association of South East Asian Nations (ASEAN) in 1997. Respected Asian leaders, including Chinese premier Li Peng, Singapore's Goh Chok Tong and Dr Mahathir of Malaysia, all made state visits to Rangoon.

Inter-military links, however, became even closer, with Thailand, India and Pakistan. But, without doubt, the most important was a US$1,000 million arms deal agreed with China shortly after the CPB's collapse. The security of this deal, from such an overshadowing neighbour, gave an underlying assurance to the military government that would see it through many crises during the next decade[82] – even though it is a dependent relationship many officers, in private, admit they would not have wanted. Vital arms deals were also arranged through other Asian countries, including Pakistan and Singapore; buoyed by such agreements, the war office began a massive expansion of the Tatmadaw, which grew from around 200,000 troops in 1988 to 320,000 by 1995 with projections of between 400,000 and 500,000 in the twenty-first century. Equipment was also upgraded with the purchase of tanks, artillery, fighter aircraft and naval vessels, with the first steps being taken to develop a modern navy and air force.[83] Certainly, freed from the isolationist dogmas of the BSPP, the Tatmadaw was at last gaining important technological advances over its insurgent opponents.

A restructuring of the Tatmadaw was also undertaken: senior ranks were upgraded and the number of regional commands increased from nine to twelve, strengthening the army's presence in areas where it had previously been weak. New paramilitary groups and local police militia were also formed (including a new border unit), while relations were tightened with ceasefire groups and the various village defence forces in front-line areas. Many observers believed that the Tatmadaw leadership was, in effect, preparing for any future decentralization and civilian-based reforms by expanding its organization on the ground first.

In such planning, much of the discussion came from a new think-tank, the Office of Strategic Studies (OSS). Set up in 1994 under Lieutenant-General Khin Nyunt, it included colonels Kyaw Win, Kyaw Thein, Thein Swe, San Pwint and Hla Min, who had international experience and were seen by many diplomats as the military's intellectual wing of the future.[84] The scale of Tatmadaw long-term planning was further emphasized by the opening of new tertiary and medical colleges, hospitals and welfare foundations for soldiers and officers. With about four million family members or dependants of serving soldiers and veterans around the country, the armed forces had come to constitute a very sizeable group within Burmese society. Parallel with these moves, steps were undertaken to improve the financial base of the Tatmadaw through a new 'productive establishment' policy. In 1990 a military-backed company was set up, the Union of Myanmar Economic Holdings, and during the 1990s the Tatmadaw opened factories and took part in a variety of development projects, including the new international airports for Rangoon and Mandalay. This 'human resource development', Colonel Thein Swe asserted, was part of the Tatmadaw's contribution to the 'crucial task of nation-building': in small or developing countries where technology was lacking, he argued, the armed forces had a special duty to develop its skills for the nation.[85]

In another conspicuous development, senior officers began to unveil a new list of special duties, shared with other 'international armies', that they declared would still require the unique role of the Tatmadaw in the twenty-first century. These included: readiness for anti-insurgent or conventional warfare; maintaining law and order; the suppression of narcotics trafficking and transnational crime; immigration and border controls; protection of the environment; and peace and development programmes in war-affected areas.[86] SLORC chairman General Than Shwe summed up the military's new nation-building role as follows:

---

**Box 11.3  General Than Shwe on the Burmese armed forces**

'Today our armed forces are engaged not only in the task of defending the state, but as part of their historic duty, are performing other duties in the political, economic and social sectors. Since we have been given, through circumstance, the opportunity of shouldering the responsibilities of State at this time, we have pledged with pure good will to make every endeavour to build a modern developed nation where peace prevails.' General Than Shwe, SLORC chairman, Armed Forces Day, March 1996.[87]

It is, therefore, an important reflection of the military government's concept of nation building that a massive construction programme, instituted by the SLORC during the 1990s, was the main achievement most usually held up as evidence of the Tatmadaw's fulfilment of these patriotic tasks. Every day, photographs and news clips were shown in the state-controlled media of military leaders inspecting a sizeable array of new projects, including bridges, dams, canals, roads and railway lines, all of which were being built around the country. Much of the work was, in fact, carried out by civilians. It is no little irony that it was the widespread use of civilian workers, in conditions that were judged to be forced, which finally led the ILO to consider sanctions against Burma by member countries in 2000. This was the first time the ILO had ever taken such a drastic step.[88]

The fact is that the military government, like the country, was desperately poor and had few resources for the ambitious social or development projects it proclaimed. Throughout the 1990s, officers were assailed by difficulties. Economically, a brief mini-boom in the early 1990s had proved short-lived, especially after Western trade sanctions began to bite. International criticisms were also severe over drugs trafficking activities, especially by certain ceasefire groups (notably the Mong Tai Army of Khun Sa and the United Wa State Party in Shan state). Indeed, at one stage in the 1990s Burma was the world's largest producer of illicit opium and heroin. As a result, allegations were widespread that money laundering was fuelling many of the new business developments in Rangoon and other conurbations.[89]

As the 1990s progressed, however, rather than introducing the kind of basic reforms that the World Bank was advising, the military government appeared to be driven back into isolationist mode by constant international criticisms. Military hard-liners, led by the army chief of staff, General Maung Aye, grew increasingly suspicious of any foreign involvement or rebuke. Although international joint ventures continued, the virtues of 'self-reliance' were once again advocated and a new class of 'national entrepreneurs' promoted as the main means to boost the economy. In a return to BSPP priorities, agriculture and rice production were again singled out for expansion. Indeed, when the construction market collapsed in the late 1990s, 19 such 'national entrepreneur' companies, including Myanmar Billion and Yuzana, were given vast tracts of land to turn over to farming, even though they had no such experience.[90]

But perhaps the most curious feature of military government in the 1990s was that in much of its official propaganda, rather than face the future, it appeared to be delving ever deeper into the past. In 1995, a defence services museum was opened in Rangoon, while a seven-volume history of the Tatmadaw was commissioned and published. The new armed forces' leaders were clearly determined to try and cement their place – and legitimacy – in Burma's history. However, unlike the BSPP, the SLORC did not stop at the 'national independence' struggle, but routinely went much further back to the royal court era of pre-colonial times when famed military commanders, such as Bandoola, fought the British and other foreign enemies. The beginning of this policy was signified in 1989 when Burma was renamed Myanmar, an older version of the name for the country. In the following years, the royal palaces at Mandalay and Pegu were reconstructed, while royal regattas and equestrian pageants were revived. More remarkably, a particular focus of publicity were the Pondaung primate fossils, 40 million years old: Lieutenant-General Khin Nyunt asserted that they proved the 'ancient roots' of the people and culture in Burma where, he argued, history had been distorted by imperialism.[91] Since the government had so little legitimacy in the present, Houtman argued that they had no choice but to back themselves ever deeper into history in a policy he dubbed 'Myanmafication'.[92]

And, indeed, as the twenty-first century began, it was the issue of legitimacy which was undoubtedly the most challenging of the many crises the government faced. For while the SLORC had been busily entrenching, the political reform process had stagnated. Given the background of repression, how far the decisions of the National Convention or the regime's reform process would ever be accepted seemed questionable. During the 1990s, under the weight of international criticism, Burma was increasingly accorded pariah status with such countries as Iraq and Serbia. Western governments introduced sanctions, while the UN and various international human rights' bodies produced many damning reports.[93] In particular, the credibility of the constitutional National Convention was dealt a damaging blow in 1995 when, four months after Aung San Suu Kyi's release from house arrest, the NLD withdrew from further meetings in protest at restrictions on freedom of expression. From this point on, relations between the military government – and Aung San Suu Kyi especially – rapidly deteriorated. In 1998, they reached a new low after the NLD, in frustration at the lack of dialogue or political change, announced the calling of a 'people's parliament'. This resulted in another crackdown by the security services on NLD supporters, the closure of many party branches and, indeed, concerns that the government might eventually shut the party down forever. The universities, too, were again closed for over three years at the end of the 1990s because of government concerns over possible student protests.

In contrast, Tatmadaw leaders continued to hold peace talks with armed ethnic opposition groups as part of their 'peace through development' strategies, but, by the end of 2000, open dialogue with the NLD had not been forthcoming, although there were rumours, as in the mid-1990s, that negotiations might eventually begin. A stalemate thus existed, which periodically hit the international headlines when NLD activities were further curtailed. Moreover, as the impasse continued, it was clear that the military government was also facing its own internal problems. Governing Burma without reform was becoming ever harder, and many younger officers recognized that the energy of the past decade had not resolved the deep and underlying problems. The rapid expansion of personnel and technology was unsustainable, many units were under strength, fighting still continued in several border areas, and the array of social problems was immense. From refugees and internally displaced persons to illicit narcotics and HIV/AIDS, Burma faced some of the most serious humanitarian crises in Asia, as a steady stream of international surveys showed.[94]

Most importantly, the military government also faced problems within its own ranks. This became quickly apparent during the change from the SLORC to the SPDC in November 1997. The planning for this transformation had been some time in the making and was intended to mark another step forward. The new 19-man SPDC would bring together the senior leaders of the armed forces with all the regional commanders, who would no longer hold ministerial posts in the cabinet. This was intended to stream-line the government and reduce the confusion of military and national administrative powers.

The final impetus for this move, however, came from the surfacing of some very embarrassing corruption allegations, made to the aging Ne Win on a rare international trip to visit President Suharto of Indonesia in September 1997. As a result, in the change from SLORC to SPDC, 14 senior officials, including three ministers (generals Tun Kyi, Kyaw Ba and Myint Aung), were reportedly placed under partial house arrest. But this attempt to isolate the guilty and limit the damage failed. As the days passed, a contagious cloud of suspicion enfolded all government officials and the new SPDC was unexpectedly paralysed. It was another reminder of a continuing lesson in the Tatmadaw's history. While the leadership is united, its position is strong; but when there is tension within the ruling oligarchy, the entire governing apparatus can become unexpectedly cautious and hesitant. This, in the main, was the mood of the regime as it braced itself for the twenty-first century.

Perhaps the most significant aspect of this episode was the almost forgotten role of Ne Win. Almost ninety years old, he was indubitably retired, and a new generation was taking over – but he remained the father figure to them all. To an extraordinary degree, he personified the entire course of contemporary Tatmadaw history back to the first days of the BIA and the national independence struggle. This is why Aung San's daughter, Aung San Suu Kyi, was such a symbolic challenge to him, since by her very presence and democratic outlook she cast doubt on his 60-year Tatmadaw legacy. 'My father didn't build up the Burmese Army in order to oppress the people,' she once said.[95] Thus few Tatmadaw officers expected or planned dramatic changes while he was alive. Like a Tito, a Franco or a Castro, he has cast a long shadow over twentieth-century Burmese politics. What would his passing portend for both the Tatmadaw and country? On and off since 1962, people all over Burma have been discussing and awaiting that event.

## An Outlook to the Future

Predicting the future course of military or political developments in Burma is hazardous. The possible role of the Tatmadaw under a future democratic government is also beyond the scope of this chapter. In recent years there have been a number of analyses of both authoritarian and democratic future paradigms.[96] In addition, the scale of the problems the country now faces means that future volatility can never be ruled out. But whatever the scenario, the essential processes of transition require that every future government will have to deal with the nation-shaping legacies of military politics in Burma's recent past.

If the future remains uncertain, a number of brief conclusions can be drawn from the evolution of the modern Tatmadaw that give clear indications as to the thinking and characteristics of its leadership – at the beginning of the new century, at least. First, decades on the battlefield have entrenched the belief of senior officers that only the military institution of the Tatmadaw has united the country and preserved it from both internal and external threats. The armed forces, it is true, have suffered enormous casualties,[97] – and because of this the military believe they have earned the right to take unilateral and forcible action. Moreover, in the recent expansion of military strength and concentration on such new-century goals as border control, anti-terrorism and the suppression of narcotics trafficking, senior officers appear to see no diminution in the continued leading role of the Tatmadaw in Burmese political life.

Related to this is a second characteristic: the mental state of siege in which the leadership lives. Although there is a certain 'peace dividend' due to the ceasefires of the last decade, the bitterness of conflict is slow to dissipate, and the Tatmadaw has evolved over a 60-year period fighting threats, both real and perceived, to the union from parties of many different persuasions. As a result, the Tatmadaw has become, above all, a 'military intelligence' government that wants to know what is going on, perceiving Burma as the 'Yugoslavia of Asia' and arguing that politicians should never be entrusted with all the nation's affairs.

The third characteristic is the narrow exclusivity of command – both ethnically and politically – which has been fostered since the earliest days of the BIA. In a country of constant upheaval, there have been only seven commanders-in-chief since independence.[98] But in this narrowness of command lie the seeds of many problems in any modernizing process. The most obvious is the ethnic dilemma. By the year 2000, there was hardly an ethnic minority officer of even colonel's rank. Political pluralism, however, requires inclusiveness. This narrowness of command is just as conspicuous in the military's control of the state civilian apparatus. In the 1990s, for example, the SLORC first secretary, Lieutenant-General Khin Nyunt, simultaneously headed the government committees on education, health, tourism, foreign affairs and border development.

This leads to a fourth characteristic which should not be underestimated: the unity that has survived almost intact in the Tatmadaw during all the years since 1949. This stands in contrast to the factionalism and disunity that have been all too prevalent in other national movements in the country during the same period. Moreover, this unity has continued, to date, under a collective system of decision making after Ne Win stepped down, confounding many predictions of splits. In recent years, for example, there has been much speculation about differences between regional commanders and the SLORC/SPDC administration, or between the army and the Military Intelligence Service. In particular, this has been seen as rivalry between the army chief, General Maung Aye, and Lieutenant-General Khin Nyunt, the MIS chief. Certainly, there are different outlooks and styles, but, until now, although there are differences of opinion, such senior officers have worked hard to ensure that they do not develop into conflicts of interest.

This continuing stability and insularity of leadership relates to a fifth characteristic of the Tatmadaw government; although pledging new nation-building goals, in many ways it is still continuing the same centrist policies of state building that it inherited from its BSPP predecessor. Other than the market-oriented and open-door foreign policies, nothing much has changed dramatically in the political philosophy of government since 1988, and daily life in the country has remained strictly controlled by most international standards. The contrast between state building and nation building could be pivotal here. In essence, state building represents a concentration on the construction of the physical or administrative institutions of government from the political centre, while nation building is based more at the local or community levels where action, democracy and development are organized from the grassroots.[99] Thus, although the SLORC/SPDC has undoubtedly given attention to the notion of community-based programmes (and since 1994 as many as twenty international non-governmental organizations have been allowed into the country to begin locally run projects), its underlying instincts and behaviour remain those of centralized control.

This, in turn, has caused an ongoing debate between critics of the government, including the NLD and many international activists, who believe that little can change fundamentally in Burma without political reform first, and those who believe that an incremental and developmental approach on the ground is more likely to bring about real political change in the long term. In the ethnic ceasefire process, in particular, there are former opponents on both sides who believe that, given the legacy of conflict, special development and trust-building initiatives are needed which will take time and have to run parallel with the process of political reform. Only through such long-term measures, they argue, will the impasse be broken.[100]

This raises the whole question of the Tatmadaw's political vision and transitional strategy, since it is never fully elucidated. It is perhaps the most significant indication of the long-standing impact of insurgency and the regime's continuing security priorities that the SLORC/SPDC chairman, General Than Shwe, has described the ethnic ceasefire process as the most distinguishing characteristic of SLORC/SPDC rule.[101] Indeed, because of the ceasefires, SLORC/SPDC leaders have gone so far as to proclaim that their government, through a policy of 'national reconsolidation', marks nothing less than the fifth 'unified era' in Burma's history – the fourth being the independence government achieved under Aung San, and the first three associated with the great Burman monarchs, Anawrahta, Bayinnaung and Alaunghpaya, who lived 700 years apart between the eleventh and eighteenth centuries.

This unexpected regard for history is the final characteristic of the military government to be noted. It may well be significant. For although the turn back to history is surely – like the patronage of religions – a search for legitimacy, it might also say something much deeper about the culture of politics in one of the world's most isolated lands. Certainly, in recent years, the military's ambitious restoration of ancient buildings has drawn attention again to the authoritarian values, based on Indic cultural roots, of the traditional state in Burma's pre-colonial past. At this time, concepts of power were highly personalized and Buddhist monarchs, through both merit and patronage, were afforded semi-divine status. Therefore, analysing the SLORC/SPDC's preoccupation, Houtman has argued that much of the language of the current struggle between the military government and Aung San Suu Kyi has to be understood in the historic context of the interlinking Buddhist concepts of *ana* ('authority/power'), which the military government is said to possess, and *awza* ('influence'), which Aung San Suu Kyi and the NLD have earned by their words and deeds.[102] In other words, the contemporary impasse may not only be one of different political ideologies and visions, but, in the Burmese context, a divergence between democratic *awza* and military *ana* which, after four decades of military government, will also need to be reconciled.

Thus the dilemma of military and political transformation in Burma remains. Arguments can be put forward for change through a number of scenarios, all of which have potential: a breakdown that leads to an uprising; dialogue, which is the preferred solution of most; or an incremental process of both development and reform, where political transition is achieved in the longer term. In all three scenarios, the armed forces are likely to remain principally involved. However, for the moment, the continuing isolation of Burma may, ironically, be actually helping to sustain military rule while the country remains so poor and strife-torn. Isolation, internal dissent and the economics of survival under such conditions are all challenges that the military government has managed to learn to live with – so far. However, modernity, development, internationalism, civil society and the tasks of sustaining a transparent and equitable economy in one of the fastest-growing regions of the world may well be the greatest challenges to its ultimate rule. To succeed in such an integrated and competitive environment – with its powerful Asian neighbours of China, India and the ASEAN member states – will require radical and substantive socio-political reform. Indeed, these pressures for change are already starting to build.

There is no room for complacency. The challenges Burma faces are daunting. And here is perhaps the greatest room for hope. Generational change is under way, and, in private, younger leaders on all sides are aware of the overwhelming need for reform. The roots of the current deadlock, they know, lie in the legacies and failings of the past. To achieve lasting solutions, inclusive reform must lie ahead. But for the moment, the question of the military's future role, like that of democratic transition, is very far from settled. Precedent would certainly suggest caution.

## Notes and References

1   The official name of Burma was changed to Myanmar in June 1989 by the ruling State and Law Order Restoration Council. Although recognized by the United Nations, it has yet to become colloquial or widely accepted international usage. The name has also been rejected by a number of ethnic minority and opposition parties as a historic ethnic Burman name for their country.

2   Since 1993, the UN has published annual reports of a Special Reporter on Human Rights to Myanmar, while, since 1995, a special envoy of the UN Secretary-General has also undertaken frequent missions to the country in an attempt to facilitate dialogue.

3   The South African analogy was made by Archbishop Tutu (1993). For a discussion of policies, see Bray (1995).

4   Detailed studies on the Tatmadaw that are publicly available are in short supply. After 1962, few foreign academics or journalists were allowed into the country for any extended period. Since 1988, two important exceptions are the American academic Callahan, whose PhD thesis contains much unique information on the Tatmadaw's evolution from primary sources; see Callahan (1996). This is being revised into a book. The other is the Australian academic Selth. He is the author of *Transforming the Tatmadaw: the Burmese Armed Forces since 1988* (1996) and has also published a series of other informative working papers about different aspects of the Tatmadaw for the Strategic and Defence Studies Centre.

5   Over a hundred languages and dialects have been identified in Burma. The Burmans are the majority population. The largest minorities are the Shan, Karen, Karenni, Kachin, Chin, Mon and Rakhine.

6   In the 1990s, former Tatmadaw officers in the top NLD leadership included the party's chairman, ex-Brigadier Aung Shwe, and deputy chairpersons, ex-General Tin Oo and ex-Colonel Kyi Maung. The history of insurgencies is examined by Smith (1999).

7   For a discussion of the long-standing phenomena of *tats*, insurgent and rural-based rebellions in Burma, see Smith (1999: 88–101).

8   'Burman' is generally used to refer to the majority ethnic group and 'Burmese' to language or citizenship; for example, a person can be an ethnic Kachin or Shan but their citizenship is 'Burmese'.

9   Furnivall (1956: 184).

10   Thein Pe Myint (1956: 535–6). The Dobama slogan was: 'Burma is our country, Burmese literature is our literature, Burmese language is our language. Love our country, raise the standards of our literature, respect our language', as translated in Silverstein (1980: 39).

11   For a 'nationalist' history of the Tatmadaw's development, from pre-colonial history until Ne Win's 1962 Revolutionary Council, see U Ba Than (1962).

12 The *tats* were mostly unarmed, usually concentrating on drilling and training. The British seemed to accept them as a form of social organization. For a discussion, see Callahan (1996: 114–21).

13 U Ba Than (1962: 44). For a detailed account of these years, see Becka (1983). Those also appointed to Dr Ba Maw's cabinet included the future CPB leader, Thakin Than Tun, the future socialist leader Thakin Mya, and Burma's future prime minister, U Nu. Only Dr Ba Maw, who took on the title of *anashin* (dictator), showed openly fascist views or sympathies.

14 Guyot (1967).

15 Wiant (1986: 242–3).

16 See, for example, Smith (1999: 62–3). An estimated 500,000 Indians fled Burma during the war. Until 1937, Burma had been administered as a province of India, which had the dual effect of encouraging Indian immigration but increasing nationalist resentment among the majority Burman population.

17 Wiant (1986: 243).

18 Callahan (1996: 177).

19 Until the present, ethnic opposition forces are routinely accused by Tatmadaw spokesmen of 'craving colonial servitude', while insurgent commanders accuse the Burmese armed forces of having learned such human rights abuses as forced labour and torture from imperial Japan. In early 2001, there were over 100,000 Karen refugees in Thailand and around a third of the population of Karen state alone was internally displaced.

20 Wiant (1986: 243).

21 Callahan (1996: 264–7).

22 There were also two other Burma Rifles battalions, one from the Burma Military Police and one of mixed nationality. In addition, a Gurkha battalion was formed; see Maung Aung Maung Aung Myoe (1998: 42).

23 See Callahan (1998b: 10–11); Callahan (1998a: 49–67).

24 As quoted in Callahan (1998a: 53), from Aung San (1983: 20).

25 For example, *The Working People's Daily*, 9 October 1992: 'The Tatmadaw's traditional leading role in national politics emerged out of [the] struggle for independence.'

26 Quoted in Aung San Suu Kyi (1995: 195).

27 AFPFL, *From Fascist Bondage to New Democracy: the New Burma in the New World* (Nay Win Kyi Press, Rangoon, [1945?]), p. 30, as quoted in Silverstein (1977: 45).

28 Lieutenant-Colonel Bo Zeya, Tatmadaw general staff officer, Colonel Bo Ye Htut, commander 3rd Burma Rifles, and the trade union leader, Bo Yan Aung. Bo La Yaung led the White Band PVO, which was the strongest PVO faction with around 4,000 troops. Another ex-'Thirty Comrade' and communist sympathizer, Brigadier Kyaw Zaw, who became a hero of Tatmadaw campaigns in the 1950s, joined the CPB underground in 1976. Eight of the 'Thirty Comrades' had died or been killed in the Second World War. For three other 'Thirty Comrades' who later took up arms, see note 57.

29 Certainly CPB commanders and organizers were among the most influential in the BIA/BNA. See, for example, Smith (1999: 60–2). After the war, however, the CPB was weakened by the breakaway of a smaller 'Red Flag' faction, headed by Thakin Soe, from the main 'White Flag' group whose leader was Aung San's brother-in-law, Thakin Than Tun.

30 Smith (1999: 119).

31 For an eyewitness account of how close the government came to collapse, by a Tatmadaw officer who stayed crucially loyal, see 'In His Own Words' (1997: 10–24).

32 Maung Aung Myoe (1998: 2–3).

33 Colonel Chit Myaing, quoted in Callahan (1996: 348). Several times married, Ne Win remained an enigmatic and retiring character throughout his life, despite his political prominence. He was always happy in military company. Born into a Sino-Burmese family, he did not finish college and was a postal clerk in the 1930s when he joined the Dobama movement.

34 For Smith Dun's version of his removal, see General Smith Dun (1980: 53–4).

35 *Forward*, 15 October 1968.

36 Maung Aung Myoe (1998: 5).

37 See, for example, Colonel Thein Swe (1998: 155): 'The Myanmar Armed Forces had its hands full, but it unflinchingly tackled the armed insurgencies and other related problems at the cost of blood, sweat and toil right down through the years up until 1988 and the advent of the State Law and Order Restoration Council.'

38 Callahan (1998b: 12–13).

39 Callahan (1998b: 12–13).

40 In 1957, for example, Burma had the highest murder rate in the world; Smith (1999: 97).

41 Callahan (1996: 398–401); Maung Aung Myoe (1998: 6–7).

42 Maung Aung Myoe (1998: 7). These concerns came to a head in 1956 when captured documents linked Brigadier Kyaw Zaw, a former 'Thirty Comrade', with the CPB. He was dismissed.

43 For a contemporary description of these events, see Sein Win (1959).

44 *The Times*, 1 November 1958.

45 Government of the Union of Burma (1960).

46 *The Times*, 3 March 1962.

47 Callahan (1996: 444).

48 Callahan (1998b: 16).

49 Silverstein (1977: 77). This book is one of the few detailed studies of Ne Win's rule. For a different analysis, see Taylor (1987).

50 Silverstein (1977: 80). 'We are just Burmese revolutionaries and socialists who are keeping pace with history,' proclaimed the manifesto of the Burma Socialist Programme Party; quoted in *ibid*.

51 Maung Aung Myoe (1998: 13); Wiant (1986).

52 The main authors were five ex-CPB or communist sympathizers and three Tatmadaw officers, Brigadier Tin Pe, Colonel Kyaw Soe and Colonel Than Sein; see, for example, Smith (1999: 203–4), p.477: note 11.

53 Smith (1999: 206–13).

54 Silverstein (1977: 103).

55 Steinberg (2000: 112).

56 For a brief analysis of 'ethnocratic' states, both pre- and post-colonial, where political power is concentrated in the hands of a majority ethnic group, see, for example, Stavenhagen (1990: 11–12). For a detailed discussion of 'the ethnocratic state and ethnic separatism in Burma', see Brown (1994: 33–65).

57 The three were Bohmu Aung, Bo Yan Naing and Bo Let Ya. See, for example, Smith (1999: 273–93). U Nu called his new movement the Parliamentary Democracy Party and the armed wing the Patriotic Liberation Army.

58 By the late 1970s, U Nu's Parliamentary Democracy Party had failed, and he and several other senior officers returned to Rangoon under a 1980 amnesty. Remaining insurgent groups largely divided into two camps: one headed by the CPB and the other by the National Democratic Front, an 11–party alliance of ethnic minority forces set up in 1976 to seek the formation of a federal union of Burma.

59 For an analysis see, for example, Smith (1994). It is important to reflect that the culture of human rights abuses in Burma generally evolved against a backdrop of armed violence. Armed opposition groups, for example, have made particular use of child soldiers.

60 *Far Eastern Economic Review Yearbook* (1968: 121). For a description of the 'Four Cuts', see Smith (1999: 258–62).

61 See, for example, McCoy (1972: 332–6).

62 Smith (1999: 25).

63 For Tin Oo's own description of these events and personal reflections on army and political life, see Aung San Suu Kyi (1997: 206–39).

64 *Far Eastern Economic Review Yearbook* (1966).

65   Aung San Suu Kyi (1995: 193).
66   See, for example, Lintner (1990). For the view of Dr Maung Maung, the lawyer and writer who briefly became BSPP leader following a failed 18–day interregnum by Brigadier-General Sein Lwin, see Maung Maung (1999).
67   *BurmaNet News* (in Burmese), 9 August 1999, as quoted in Andrew Selth (2000: 73).
68   *The Guardian* (London), 26 July 1988.
69   *Asiaweek*, 27 January 1989. In addition to the breakdown of law and order and threat of insurgent groups, Tatmadaw officers have privately pointed to the entry of American naval vessels into Burmese territorial waters and also fears over a possible China border reaction.
70   See, for example, Thein Swe (1998: 153–61).
71   According to Maung Aung Myoe, the Tatmadaw dates this as the eighth stage in its ideological development since the 'national independence' era of the BIA during 1941–3, the seventh having been the Burmese Way to Socialism. See Maung Aung Myoe (1998: 11–14).
72   Rangoon Home Service, 8 September, in British Broadcasting Corporation, *Survey of World Broadcasts*, 11 September 1991.
73   Amnesty International (1992: 1). This report contains an analysis of human rights violations by the government and armed opposition groups during the early SLORC period.
74   For a book version of such allegations, see, for example, Brigadier-General Khin Nyunt (1989).
75   For an analysis, see Smith (1999: 434–50). The main components of the DAB were the 11-party National Democratic Front of ethnic minority forces and various student and pro-democracy groups.
76   As the 1990s progressed, the ceasefires also included important members of the National Democratic Front, such as the Shan State Army, Kachin Independence Organization and New Mon State Party. For a 1999 list of armed opposition groups and ceasefires, see *ibid.*, Chart 3.
77   *Reuters*, 12 December 2000.
78   *Kyemon* (in Burmese), 4 July 1996.
79   The convention consisted of 702 selected delegates representing eight social groups: MPs-elect (including the NLD), other legal parties, ethnic nationalities (including some of the ceasefire groups), workers, peasants, civil servants, intellectuals and other specially invited guests.
80   For a discussion, see Steinberg (1997: 4–11).
81   The only major exception was the construction of two gas pipelines in southern Burma during the 1990s by two oil company consortiums, one including Unocal (USA) and Total (France), and the other Premier (UK).
82   For discussion of the military impact of arms deals with China, see Selth (1997: 6–8). In return for these deals, there were many rumours that China was allowed naval and intelligence listening facilities along the Andaman Sea coast.
83   For an assessment, see Selth (2000: 56–67). For an analysis of the Tatmadaw shortly after the SLORC takeover, see Tin Maung Maung Than (1989: 40–55).
84   For an OSS analysis, see Colonel Hla Min (1999).
85   Colonel Thein Swe (1998: 161).
86   See for example *ibid.*: 159–61, and Lieutenant-Colonel Thein Han (1998: 215–26).
87   Quoted in Colonel Thein Swe (1998: 158).
88   *Kyodo*, 9 December 2000.
89   For reports of these issues, see, for example, Kean and Bernstein (1998); Davis and Hawke (1998: 26–34). For the government's response, see Central Committee for Drug Abuse Control (1999).
90   *Living Colour Magazine* (in Burmese), February 1999. The government later claimed that the number of hectares under cultivation in Burma had increased from 8.10 million in 1988 to 9.72 million in 2000; *The New Light of Myanmar*, 23 December 2000.
91   Quoted in Houtman (1999: 144).

92 Quoted in Houtman (1999: 37–156).

93 See, for example, Commission on Human Rights (1998).

94 See, for example, Carriere (1997); Smith (1996); and UN Working Group (1998).

95 *Christian Science Monitor*, 15 June 1989, as quoted in Aung San Suu Kyi (1983: 308).

96 See, for example, Selth (2000: 67–87); Taylor (1998: 3–12); and Carey (1997: 3–11).

97 In early 1990, General Saw Maung revealed that 28,000 families in Burma were receiving pensions for soldiers killed in action since 1953 and 40,000 for disabled veterans; *The Working People's Daily*, 10 January 1990. In this rare public statement of recognition, he also gave the first-ever estimate of the possible national scale of casualties, including civilians, since 1948: it might, he said, run as 'high as millions'.

98 Generals Smith Dun (1948–9), Ne Win (1949–72), San Yu (1972–4), Tin Oo (1974–6), Kyaw Htin (1976–85), Saw Maung (1985–92), Than Shwe (1992–): Maung Aung Myoe (1998: 49).

99 This distinction follows that of Callahan (1998b: 16).

100 For a discussion of civil society, ethnic minority, human rights and international perspectives, see the essays by Steinberg, Smith, Lidell and Purcell (1999).

101 *The New Light of Myanmar*, 27 February 1998.

102 Houtman (1999: 167–71).

# 12

# Serbia and the Politics of the Yugoslav Armies

## Communism, Federalism and Democracy

JAMES GOW

Until late 2000, any discussion of democratic control of the military in the Federal Republic of Yugoslavia (Savezna Republika Jugoslavija) was an absurd topic. Only in a surreal sense could there be discussion of the issue. Without democracy, there could be no sense of democratic control – and in Serbia, the larger of the Federal Republic of Yugoslavia's constituent parts, there was no democracy. Despite a veneer of democratic features, the practices of communist rule remained, spiced with nationalist ideology and Mafia customs. In the other part of the federation, Montenegro, there was also no question of democratic control, but the situation was different. The development of democracy and pro-Western policies there gave rise to civil–military tension. On one side, there was the government. On the other, there was an army that still had the shadow of communism, nationalism and deeply anti-Western sentiment over its essence. Despite this, it is an irony of civil–military relations in the Federal Republic of Yugoslavia that the military, or rather elements within it, provided one of the main hopes upon which a transition to democracy in Serbia, and so in the Federal Republic as a whole, could be achieved – and, through intervention by the chief of the general staff, did so, at a key political moment on 5 October 2000. Thus, the military–political union from whence had sprung two Yugoslav armies and two challenged Yugoslavias under the influence of communist rulers (first Tito, then Milošević) finally brought the prospect of democracy to Serbia.[1]

In addition to the relative complexity of a civil–military relationship characterized by differing attitudes to and qualities of democracy in the constituent parts of the federation, there are additional layers that complicate the picture. First, each of the constituent states in the federation has its own Internal Force Service (*Ministerstvo Unutrašnjih Poslove*), each of which embraces police and paramilitary units. Second, the Serbian Security Service has been responsible for the organization and control of quasi-autonomous paramilitary forces and special military units. Third, on the territory of the Federal republic of Yugoslavia there has been an insurgent force, the Kosova Liberation Army (*Ushtria Clirimtare E Kosoves*) in the Serbian province of Kosovo, fighting for independence of its mainly ethnic

**297**

Albanian population. Fourth, this conflict has also led to the deployment of an international force in the province with NATO troops at its core. Fifth, the Army of Yugoslavia (Vojska Jugoslavije) and the Security Service paramilitary units have been engaged in war on the territory of two neighbouring former Yugoslavian states, Croatia and Bosnia–Herzegovina. Finally, a decade of war has defined civil–military relations in the Federal Republic of Yugoslavia.

After a decade of statehood defining war, the basic civil–military question in the Federal Republic of Yugoslavia, as in the other war-framed states that emerged from the dissolution of communist Yugoslavia, concerns legitimization and the need to arrive at a position where there is a correlation of statehood and regular armed forces.

## Democratic Control of the Military

The notion that the military can or should be controlled democratically is predicated on an understanding of democracy. The notion is linked to, but separate from, that of civilian control. While civilian authority could stop the military using its coercive capacity against the regime under communism, this did not constitute democratic control, even though it was clearly civilian. Civilian control under democracy concerns the principles and mechanisms by which political authority over the armed forces is maintained. These are the same principles and mechanisms by which all areas of political life and decision making are scrutinized.

Democracy is more than competitive multi-party, or multi-candidate, elections. While these may be the starting point, the essence of democracy lies elsewhere. In terms of value, the key to democracy is the admission of fallibility by the majority. This requires the recognition that it may well constitute a minority at another point as the possibility of change is accepted, and, because of this, there is a need for the majority to be restrained and responsible in its dealings. In terms of mechanisms, aside from permitting change through open elections, the representatives of the majority in government not only accept the need for self-limitation, but recognize the need for mechanisms of limitation on the exercise of power to prevent abuse. It is the mixture of self-limiting values and these mechanisms that defines democracy.

There are three levels at which democratic control operates: rules, management and policy communities. The first of these includes both formal rules, such as laws, and procedures. The second embraces accountability, structures and personnel. The final level is the one that most clearly defines a democracy and includes the institutions and arenas that are essential to public discussion of policy and to public scrutiny. This level most defines democracy because it provides the avenues of openness and the instruments of information and limitation on the exercise of power. All political systems have rules and forms of management, but only democracy depends on autonomous sources of knowledge, analysis and argument for both creative and critical input to policy making.

These three levels can be used to assess and to compare democratic control of civil–military relations and defence. However, two other elements are required for investigation of civil–military relations in formerly communist countries. The first of these is assessment of the restructuring process in a given country, as used in conjunction with the three elements described in my earlier work.[2] While this four-fold framework of analysis offers a clear basis for comparison (and was used in this way), it has been subject to appropriate criticism for omitting a crucial condition for civil–military relations in any of the post-communist countries: the degree of 'stateness'.[3] While the four elements identified enable investigation and, where appropriate, comparison, the framework is limited by the absence of a crucial variable that can assert difference as opposed to mere comparison – 'stateness' provides this. It is clear that one of the biggest factors in defining the degree to which a stable, democratic civil–military relationship has been achieved is the quality of statehood. Some former communist states began as states, such as Poland; others, such as Ukraine have sought to establish new statehood; some new states have been weak, such as Bosnia–Herzegovina; others have proved stronger, such as Estonia.

Nowhere is the importance of 'stateness' more important in civil–military relations than in the former Yugoslavian lands, especially in the Federal Republic of Yugoslavia and in Bosnia–Herzegovina, where issues of civil–military relations and democracy are clouded by two factors. The first of these is the absence of a clear correlation between states and armed forces. The second is the reason for that lack of correlation: a decade of war in pursuit of mutually exclusive state projects. The purpose of the war has been to define states and their borders. In pursuit of that goal, as will be seen below, links between the military and the state have not been straightforward in the case of the Federal Republic of Yugoslavia – its own statehood has been challenged, while the armed forces controlled by Belgrade, the capital, have included Serbian forces in neighbouring countries.

In a sense, the linked questions of state and military legitimization that confronted Yugoslavia before the end of communism and its collapse remain in new guises.[4] In both the Federal Republic of Yugoslavia and Bosnia–Herzegovina the legitimacy of the state is challenged because the key issue of political community is not agreed. In both cases, only when military legitimacy within the state is established will there be a real chance of consolidation and peace – or, indeed, the conditions for democratic control of the military. There is a need to correlate armed forces and states. Noting Edmonds' truism that 'every state has one',[5] there is a fairly clear principle: one country, one armed force. It is implicit that this armed force corresponds to a more or less agreed sense of political community – its main purpose, after all, is the effective defence of that political community from outside attack. Only when there is legitimate statehood can there be any chance of democratic civil–military relations. As Finer showed in one of the earliest and still one of the best studies of civil–military relations, the relative strength or weakness of regime legitimacy will determine whether or not the conditions for undue military involvement in politics exist.[6]

The Federal Republic of Yugoslavia does not represent an agreed political community. There is no more than a skin of democracy in its major component state, Serbia, and there is no settled correlation between armed forces and statehood. Although there are some democratic appearances in Serbia, such as the holding of elections and some elements of free information distribution, there is no reality to this democracy. Serbian leader and Federal Republic of Yugoslavia President Slobodan Milošević has ruled for a decade through a combination of security service operations and organized crime activity; domination, and ultimately control, of information flows to the majority of the Serbian population; and, crucially, the destruction and denial of alternatives.[7] Thus, Milošević's Serbia is antithetical to democracy. Where the latter is predicated on the existence of autonomous and alternative actors, in the former, there are none, in any conventional sense. Given these points, the study of civil–military relations in this case can only be understood by analysis of how the armed forces came to be in this indeterminate situation and through consideration of politics in Serbia and the Federal Fepublic of Yugoslavia . The point of departure for this is the legacy of civil–military relations from Tito's Yugoslav federation,[8] the warped root of the current Yugoslav army and its corruption by Slobodan Milošević.

## The Role and Character of the JNA in the Socialist Federal Republic of Yugoslavia

There can be few armies as truly political as the regular army (the Jugoslovenska Narodna Armija – JNA) was in Tito's Yugoslavia. Uniquely, the army, which was enmeshed in the political birth of the communist and federal Yugoslav state, was given formal roles in the political arena under the 1974 Socialist Federal Republic of Yugoslavia constitution and complementary arrangements in the League of Communists of Yugoslavia. This formal political mandate was an important factor in shaping the attitude and approach of the JNA command as, ten years after Tito's death, the communist federation he had created and managed hurtled towards dissolution and war.

The armed forces of the Socialist Federal Republic of Yugoslavia comprised two elements The first tier, the JNA, was a regular armed force, including ground, air and naval services. The second tier, a territorial defence force, was an irregular force derived from the tradition of the Partisans in guerrilla warfare. The Federal Secretariat for People's Defence was responsible for the JNA. Republican Secretariats for People's Defence were responsible for the various territorial defence forces. Both tiers were intended to be components of the doctrine of General People's Defence, adopted in 1969. The command structures of the JNA and the territorial defence forces were decentralized, because the maintenance of a command and control network across all Socialist Federal Republic of Yugoslavia territory would have been too difficult in the event of an invasion.

The origins of the JNA lie in the Second World War Partisan movement that brought Tito's regime to power. Originally a guerrilla force, as the war progressed, the Partisan army took the shape of a regular armed force and, in 1945, became the army of the new Yugoslavia. It was known first as the Yugoslav Army but renamed the Yugoslav People's Army after the 1948 Soviet–Yugoslav split. Supplemented by the territorial defence forces, the army was preoccupied with external threat. Initially, Yugoslavia perceived the threat as originating in the West and turned to the USSR for assistance.

In the 1950s, the Yugoslav military was primarily concerned with developing the military capability of the country and had no political role. Because of its emphasis on hierarchy, discipline and responsiveness to command, the JNA was regarded as being relatively successful at overcoming ethnic and political differences. It therefore saw itself as a champion of 'Yugoslavism'. However, a major political role emerged in the late 1960s. Through 1971 constitutional amendments and the new 1974 constitution, the JNA gained a leading role within the governing party, the League of Communists of Yugoslavia, receiving equal status with the two autonomous provinces in the new 166–member central committee. As Yugoslavia seemed to be falling apart in 1971, the JNA leadership became essential in maintaining the stability, cohesion and authority of civilian political institutions.

The JNA's political role increased in part because it was a pan-Yugoslav institution. Its loyalty was not to any one republic, but to the Yugoslav Federation. Its own legitimacy and survival depended on Yugoslavia's continuing to exist. As a result, the JNA leadership was cautious about intervening in politics, physically or otherwise, beyond its allotted constitutional role.

The constitution was central to the military's role in the political system. In 1971, General Ivan Miškovic said that 'only in cases where the constitutional order was threatened would the army become an instrument for solving internal difficulties'. As long as some central civil authority remained, the army would be the coercively instrumental partner in an alliance with that authority and would not itself usurp the political process.

This formalized, legitimate political role for the JNA was based on the notion that it would ensure a 'pan-Yugoslav' voice in politics, inheriting Tito's mantle when he died. Tito emphasized this:

> Brotherhood and Unity are inseparably linked with our army.... I believe that our army is still playing such a role today.... [O]ur army must not merely watch vigilantly over our borders, but also be present inside the country.... [T]here are those who write that one day Yugoslavia will disintegrate. Nothing like that will happen because our army ensures that we will continue to move in the direction we have chosen for the socialist construction of our country.[9]

This role was given substance by the appointment of generals to key government party leadership posts in the 1970s and 1980s.

In 1988, as nationalist sentiments grew stronger throughout Yugoslavia, civil–military relations deteriorated in Slovenia. In May, the JNA arrested and tried three journalists and a soldier on suspicion of betraying a military secret. The trial incited the Slovenes because it was conducted in camera and in the Serbo-Croat language, rather than in Slovene. Even though the 1974 constitution assured the equality of all Yugoslav languages in the JNA (article 243), the reality was that increasingly Serbo-Croat had become the *de facto* command language, used in almost all circumstances. The use of Serbo-Croat at the trial reinforced the notion among many Slovenes that an ever more vigorous Serb nationalism was emerging. It also catalysed Slovene national sentiment, decisively forcing pressure towards federal dissolution in 1991.

The JNA was increasingly enmeshed by tensions and in March 1991 the JNA supreme command schemed with Serbian political leaders in Belgrade to get the federal presidency to declare a state of emergency and allow the army to impose martial law. At two specially convened meetings, held not in the normal presidency building but in the cold basement of an army building, the eight members of the presidency were cajoled by General Kadijević and other military leaders.[10] They were also pushed to declare a state of emergency by the chair of the meeting, Borisav Jović. The latter was formally president of the Yugoslav presidency at that time and was also one of the closest confidants of Slobodan Milošević, the Serbian president. After two tense meetings, in which the Croatian representative pointed out that this was effectively a move towards war and General Kadijević replied that if the presidency would not act, the JNA would be forced to take matters into its own hands, there was a split decision. The representative from Bosnia, Bogić

Bogićević, although a Serb, surprised Jović and his allies by voting against the proposal.[11] This meant that a state of emergency was not declared.

Milošević and Jović had a fallback plan. This was to create the conditions in which the federal presidency would not function, so that the federal secretary for defence, General Kadijević, would become *de facto* commander-in-chief of the armed forces. He would then be able to effect a state of emergency and martial law himself. The president of the presidency, Serbian representative Jović, resigned in order to set the stage for General Kadijević's ascendance. However, this did not happen. Part of the explanation lies with activity in the presidency without Jović. The vice-president of the presidency, Croatian representative Stipe Mesić, surprised the JNA by preparing to take over the presidency in Jović's absence. This left the presidency functioning. The other factor was General Kadijević himself. He did not pursue the plan, because he could not bring himself to proceed with this momentous step if it meant acting in an unconstitutional manner.[12] Once it was clear that the JNA was not going to act as arranged with the Serbian political leadership, Jović quickly returned to his post after the Serbian parliament, controlled by Milošević, had rejected his resignation.

A final possibility for JNA intervention in the fading political life of the Yugoslav federation occurred in May 1991, but the JNA's proposals were again rejected, as the storm clouds literally and figuratively gathered over the lands of the South Slavs. In these situations, the JNA chief of staff, General Blagoje Adšić, appears to have argued for acting without an order from the presidency, but Kadijević opposed this. However, despite Kadijević's sense of constitutional propriety, as well as his aversion to Serbian President Milošević, he and his army had become ever more aligned with Belgrade's political leaders. This occurred perhaps predominantly by force of circumstance and the institutional prejudice and culture that remembered Croatian nationalist independence leading to the mass murder of Serbs. This political drift was to be confirmed by the approach and effects of war. These would see the demographic character of the army change, the JNA formally cease to exist and Milošević effecting increasing Serbian control over the army – in part through preference for other armed forces, as will be seen below.

## Serbianization: Milošević and the military

When Belgrade retired 42 generals after a meeting of the supreme defence council on 25–26 August 1993, President Slobodan Milošević's effective control of the Yugoslav military was confirmed and all but the last concrete traces of the JNA removed. Its principal successor, Belgrade's new military, the Army of Yugoslavia, continued a process of Serbianization already begun in the JNA during Yugoslavia's descent into war and dissolution. That process meant both transformation from a multi-ethnic armed force to an almost purely Serbian organization and the accrual of command and control of the military by the Serbian president. Yet not until the Kosovo campaign of 1999 would he have generals in charge upon whom he could absolutely rely. And even then, the prospect of adverse civil–military relations remained, as will be seen below.

Three confluent forces led to the Serbianization of the JNA and the creation of its *de facto* Serbian successors. These were the creation of paramilitary and successor forces as competitors (dealt with in a separate section below), the organic impact of federal break-up and ethnic homogenization and, lastly, a proactive political campaign by pro-Milošević forces outside, then inside, the army. The last of these was the *vojna linija* – the 'military line'.[13] This referred to a thread of Serbian officers in the JNA who had been colonized by approaches from the Serbian Security Service to serve the political interests of Serbia under the leadership of Slobodan Milošević. This small band of soldiers were identified as being frustrated at limited promotion opportunities, disaffected by the Yugoslavism of the army's higher command and, linking these two aspects, the apparent fact that good Serb officers were denied promotion because of the 'Yugoslav' philosophy of ensuring proportionate ethnic and republican representation in JNA's higher command positions. One of the most important of these mostly middle-ranking officers was (then) Colonel Ratko Mladić, deputy commander of the Knin Corps, based in the capital of the heavily Serb-inhabited Krajina region of Croatia. The colonel would be commander of that corps during the vital months in which war began and later would be commander of Serbian forces in Bosnia–Herzegovina. Another key figure was General Božidar Stevanović, who, like Mladić, would quickly be promoted as the conflict developed and the successful Serbianization of the JNA was transformed into the creation of new armed forces to serve the interests of Slobodan Milošević's Serbia.

Action within the JNA to turn it into a Serbian force was complemented by the impact of dissolution and war on the composition of the federal army and its eventual death. In the course of the armed conflict surrounding the dissolution of the Socialist Federal Republic of Yugoslavia, the character of the JNA changed substantially in ethnic and ethno-political terms. Prior to 1990–1, the JNA was a mixed force of regular soldiers, almost entirely officers and non-commissioned officers, and a conscript cadre. At the highest levels in the JNA, an 'ethnic key' principle operated to ensure proportional representation of all the major communities in the Socialist Federal Republic of Yugoslavia, although the most senior posts were almost invariably held by Serbs. The middle and junior ranks of the JNA were overwhelmingly dominated by Serbs.

Through defections to Slovenia, Croatia and then other republics, resignations from disillusioned officers who could not defect, and an apparent programme of retiring non-Serbs, the army progressively became Serbian-dominated. In May 1992, the JNA, by then over 90 per cent Serbian in composition, was formally disestablished and divided into two (although some parts of it, especially command and control, had already been inherited by the armed forces of the Krajina Serbs in Croatia, thus maintaining Belgrade control). This followed international recognition of the independence of Bosnia at the beginning of April and the proclamation of a new Yugoslav federation of Serbia and Montenegro at the end of that month. This proclamation and the division of the armed forces were a response to the imposition of comprehensive, mandatory UN sanctions on Serbia and Montenegro, aimed at getting the JNA to withdraw from Bosnia. Belgrade tried to sidestep the issue by dissolving the JNA and dividing its assets between the self-styled Serbian Republic of Bosnia and Herzegovina (*Srpska Republika Bosne i Hercegovine*)[14] and the new Federal Republic of Yugoslavia (*Savezna Republika Jugoslavija*), comprising Serbia and Montenegro. This was a move carefully conceived and planned several months beforehand. Following an assessment that Belgrade's campaign against Bosnia would meet with a hostile international response and accusations of aggression, Milošević and Jović prepared to deal with this possibility by deception.

As a result of the May division, the Army of the Serbian Republic (Vojska Republika Srpska, VRS) and the Army of Yugoslavia each gained around 80,000 personnel.[15] For the most part, the units involved kept the equipment at their disposal in both cases, although the VRS did not inherit some of the old JNA's most modern capabilities – most notably, aircraft.[16] Whilst formally divided, the chain of command within the old federal army did not change. The VRS continued to be under Belgrade's command,[17] albeit with broad operational authority given to the commander in Bosnia, General Ratko Mladić, who could be relied on to prosecute the campaign largely without reference to Belgrade, thereby enhancing the superficial fiction.

Mladić and the military in Bosnia served Belgrade's purposes and clearly acted in line with Serbian nationalist political objectives. However, problems of reliability remained regarding the Army of Yugoslavia. Great changes occurred in that army after the division of the JNA. These were an effective continuation of the pro-Milošević Serbianizing tendency within the army and were engineered by General Stevanović, who became air force chief in January 1992.

Stevanović organized an air force intelligence operation which was responsible for engineering greater Serbian political control of the armed forces. In May, following the removal of 20 generals in February, a further 38 generals were purged as 'traitors' and 'unreliable' elements. Stevanović and his team were responsible for preparing the list of those to be purged and, in some cases, arranging smear campaigns. The impact of this campaign on the 150-strong cadre of generals in the army has already been noted. This process sought to eradicate any residual 'Yugoslav' character in the armed forces.

Whilst Stevanović was constructing an army free from Yugoslav impurities and which would be wholly subordinate to Milošević from within, Milošević himself was strengthening the army's subordination to him from without. Command and control of the Army of Yugoslavia was established on a different basis from that of the JNA in the old state. Significantly, a body called the supreme defence council, rather than the federal presidency, became the ultimate authority over the armed forces. This council comprised the presidents of the federation, Serbia and Montenegro. The federal president acted formally as its spokesman, but orders were determined by the council.

This indicated that, whatever the policies and positions of federal politicians in Belgrade, command of the military had been transferred significantly into the hands of the republics. In particular, Serbian President Milošević now had some degree of official, direct and formal control over the Army of Yugoslavia. This was something that he did not have over the JNA. Indeed, he only needed the backing of one of the other members of the presidential troika for the Army of Yugoslavia to be following his orders, officially. Given that the appointment of the federal president was made by the federal parliament which was, in turn, controlled by Milošević's Serbian Socialist Party, the federal president was de facto a Milošević appointment. This was confirmed when, facing the prospect that constitutionally he could not stand again as president of Serbia, he had himself chosen as president of the Federal Republic of Yugoslavia by the parliament. His long-time political ally, Milan Milutinović, was appointed in his place as president of Serbia. More than ever before, therefore, Milošević was the key figure in Yugoslav military–political affairs.

# General Perišić and the Persistence of Ambiguities within the Army

Although so many generals had been removed, relatively few new appointments were made. When Ratko Mladić was promoted to the rank of general in October 1991, along with four others, he was among the last to achieve this status in the JNA. During the first half of 1992, the 42 generals removed from their positions by Stevanović's Serbianization campaign gave way to only one new appointment. This was the naming of Colonel-General Momčilo Perišić, formerly commander of the third army, as chief of staff to replace Colonel-General Žitova Panić. The promotion of Perišić was important in the context of civil–military trends in Belgrade following the declarations of independence by Slovenia and Croatia and the onset of war in June 1991. By far the most surprising element of the purge of generals was the retiring of General Stevanović and the appointment of General Perišić as chief of staff. As the man who had been whisked from the brink of retirement by Milošević in 1991 and who had been the scourge of anything pro-Yugoslav in the military, Stevanović seemed to be set to complete his renaissance by becoming chief of staff. Indeed, Belgrade circles were reported to have been buzzing with news of Stevanović's appointment as chief of staff the day before it was announced that Perišić was to have the job.

In this context, Perišić, at 49 and with a proven record in the field, represented a new generation of militarily competent officers to shape a professional army. General Perišić was born on 22 May 1944 in Koštuniši kod Gornjeg Milanovca. His secondary school education was in Čačak, after which he went to the military academy for ground forces, where he trained as an artillery officer. He was later to graduate in psychology from the higher military–political school of the then JNA. During active service, he held fifteen posts prior to being promoted to the top position in the Army of Yugoslavia. During the break-up of Yugoslavia, Perišić saw action at Zadar in Croatia, where he began the war with the rank of colonel as commandant of the artillery school there. He was uncompromising in his bombardment of the town, whilst under a Croatian blockade – although he later explained this action by saying that he was 'defending a still existing country against rebels'.[18] After successfully breaking the blockade, he was transferred from Zadar to Bileća in eastern Herzegovina, where he became corps commander. From there he was active in the Dubrovnik campaign. Later, in Bosnia, he was to be involved in engagements at Foča, as well as at Mostar, where he gained the nickname 'The Knight of Mostar' following his part in the destruction of the centuries-old town.[19] Both temperamental and intelligent, he was a man of verve whose mind was not closed. He was reported to have shown some remorse at the destruction of Mostar, but nonetheless retained a strong reputation as a tough soldier who inspired those who served with him. Before being nominated chief of staff, he was commander of the third army, with its headquarters at Niš.

It was the issue of Kosovo that, combined with the even more distressing case of Montenegro, led to the ousting of General Perišić at the end of 1998. On 24 November 1998, he was sacked as chief of staff. This was part of a purge that had begun the previous month. In that period Milošević, a leader who always dealt with problems cautiously and separately, had purged about 15 members of the Serbian Security Service who seem to have been regarded as potentially disloyal. Most significantly, he sacked two of the key figures from the military–political campaigns of the 1990s: General Perišić and the head of the security service, Jovica Stanišić.

General Perišić's sacking capped an uneasy relationship with President Milošević over the years, with the latter ever distrustful and unloving of the former and most of his colleagues. Reports in Belgrade had long suggested that Perišić was opposed to the campaign in Kosovo, just as he had been publicly reluctant in late 1996 to allow the army to be used against opposition demonstrators. This was confirmed by his being bypassed in the Kosovo campaign during 1998. The commander of the third military district at Niš, General Dušan Samardšić, was given formal command over the Army of Yugoslavia operation, while effective command lay with the 52nd Corps in Priština, in association with Internal Force Service commanders who took orders directly from the political leadership in Belgrade. Perišić may have feared a further diminution of the Army of Yugoslavia's position *vis-à-vis* the Internal Force Service, which was more actively involved in Kosovo. However, this same motivation caused some others in the army to draw the opposite conclusion to that of Perišić. He judged the Kosovo campaign to be against the army's better interest, whereas some of his colleagues concluded that the army had to be more involved so as not to fall further behind the Internal Force Service in institutional standing. The latter were, therefore, keen to commit the Army of Yugoslavia to the fray, while General Perišić attempted to limit its involvement. This was further evidence confirming Milošević's distrust of Perišić and the generals.

An even more decisive reason for distrust and for the general's sacking concerned Montenegro. Plausible rumours regarding Perišić's links with the Montenegrin leadership linked his removal to the sacking three weeks previously of security service chief Jovica Stanišić. Although no one but Milošević's wife knew more about the workings of power in the regime, or its involvement in war, there had been persistent rumours over several months of strong differences of opinion between Stanišić and Serbia's MacBeth and his Lady. These involved the security service chief's refusing to become involved in plans to remove the Montenegrin leadership. This tied in with Perišić's contact with Djukanović and signals that he would be reluctant to use the Army of Yugoslavia against Montenegro. Although it appears unlikely that the two would have been conspiring against Milošević together, either of them might have been exploring such possibilities.

Perišić charged that his removal had been 'inappropriate and illegal' and that his alleged new post as adviser to Bulatović was fictitious. At the same time, he confirmed the political thrust of the sackings by adding that the country's leaders were seeking to exclude those who thought for themselves and were of 'high integrity'. Both sackings confirmed that the Miloševićes felt deeply threatened as they sought to eliminate any potentially unreliable elements in their closed circle. However, they could feel more comfortable with Perišić's successor, General Dragoljub Ojdanić. A supporter of the pro-communist JUL party run by the president's wife, Mira Marković, and said to be close to her, his appointment put Milošević in a stronger position regarding the army than ever before. He finally had a chief of staff in Belgrade who was his and could be relied on to do what he wanted – even if it meant leading the country and its armed forces like lemmings into an unwinnable conflict with NATO over Kosovo. In the meantime, Milošević's campaign to acquire the means to prosecute war had seen the appearance, in name at least, of other armed forces.

# Serbian Ghosts of the JNA: the Army of Yugoslavia and the Krajina and Bosnian Serb forces

Implementing the decision to divide the JNA greatly reduced Belgrade's open participation in the war in Bosnia. This was part of an attempt to persuade the outside world that the new Federal Republic of Yugoslavia was not involved in, or responsible for, events there. The reality was, in fact, very different. In May 1992, the federal Yugoslav army divided itself into the Serbian Army in Bosnia (later the VRS) and the Army of Yugoslavia. While the VRS remained to carry the Serbian war against Bosnia–Herzegovina, the Army of Yugoslavia became the armed force of the Federal Republic of Yugoslavia , which consisted of Serbia and Montenegro. In fact, these two were part of a troika. An element of division had already occurred at the beginning of 1992 when the Armed Forces of the Republic of Serbian Krajina (Orušanih Snage Republika Srpska Krajina) were the manifestation of Serbian military might in Croatia after the 2 January 1992 ceasefire there.

The most important element of this troika remained the one formally attached to Belgrade's political leadership – the Army of Yugoslavia. The Army of Yugoslavia comprised all three services – land, air and sea. The ground forces were organized into three armies, with headquarters at Belgrade, Podgorica and Niš. Within each of these armies, there was a corps structure. For a time, command positions in the Army of Yugoslavia were unclear until on 7 September the supreme defence council nominated the following to become commanding officers of the three armies, the air force and the navy: Colonel-General Jevrem Djokić, first army; Major-General Boidar Babić, second army; Major-General Dušan Samarić, third army; Major-General Miloje Pavlović, air force and air defence; Contra-Admiral Dojčilo Isaković, navy. As noted above, however, none of these was to last as long as a year in his post.[20] While change continued in Belgrade, the spectre of the JNA loomed in Croatia and Bosnia.

This ostensible division and the apparent distance from Belgrade were belied by events. The Army of Yugoslavia offered great assistance to the military forces that remained in Bosnia and continued support to those in Croatia. The Krajina Serbs in Croatia had inherited a military capability and command and control structures from the JNA, as did the Bosnian Serb military after its division. This was unlike the JNA's conduct when it withdrew from its installations in the remainder of Croatia and in Slovenia, Macedonia and other parts of the former Yugoslavia. In the latter cases, it removed all of its equipment and destroyed everything, down to the light fixtures and electric outlets. However, the JNA left its installations intact in Bosnia and gave significant military equipment, including tanks and ammunition, to the VRS.

The Armed Forces of the Republic of Serbian Krajina took over from forces led by Milan Martić, the Serb who had been dismissed as police chief in Knin, the central town in Krajina, in July 1990. Although Martić remained a prominent figure, this was in the political sphere, as leader of Serbian Krajina. The armed forces themselves retained vital links with Belgrade, including membership of what was, effectively, a common officer corps. Although officially the officers were part of the Armed Forces of the Republic of Serbian Krajina, as with their Bosnian Serb brothers, they remained on the Belgrade military payroll – numerous then-current Belgrade pay and passbooks were found after Croatian operations in western Slavonia in 1995 – and in some cases were rotated with positions in the Army of Yugoslavia. The most notable example of this involved General Mile Mrkšić. General Mrkšić had been involved in the JNA first military district siege of Vukovar in Croatia before holding positions in the Army of Yugoslavia, including deputy chief of staff immediately before he was transferred to take command of the Armed Forces of the Republic of Serbian Krajina in May 1995. Although many perceived this as a move to strengthen the Armed Forces of the Republic of Serbian Krajina, which had just suffered defeats in western Slavonia, in reality the appointment of General Mrkšić was to manage military withdrawal from Croatia.

Another example from the VRS illustrates continued involvement in Bosnia after the 19 May division. This was Colonel-General Djordje Djukić, chief of logistics in General Mladić's army. In 1996, after the Bosnian peace agreement at the end of 1995, General Djukić was arrested by Bosnian forces.[21] The general was found to be carrying an Army of Yugoslavia passbook.[22] Although he was formally chief of logistics in the VRS, a putatively separate force, he was, in practice, co-ordinator of Army of Yugoslavia supplies into Bosnia through the VRS staff headquarters at Han Pijesak.

## Parallel Armies and Milošević's Final Bid for Control

While the JNA's officers might all have been forced into apparently different armies for the sake of Milošević's attempt at international deception, they retained common cause and common *esprit de corps*. As was seen in the discussion of General Perišić above, this did not mean that the army was wholly reliable from Milošević's point of view. Not until the Kosovo campaign of 1999 would the top levels of the regular armed forces be truly loyal to him. Even then this appeared to be loyalty from a small group at the top, led by Ojdanić, promoted to their positions by him. Underlying military disaffection among more junior officers that could turn into the use of armed force remained a potent risk for Milošević, even once he had full control of the supreme command. Because the army was a potential problem from the outset *vis-à-vis* reliability, it was always necessary for Milošević to bolster his efforts to marshal the regular military. He did so through the creation and strengthening of alternative sources of armed force. These were both complements to the regular armies and competition.

There were three reasons for President Milošević to nurture militarized alternatives to the JNA and its successors. The first of these was practical. The organization of 'volunteer' paramilitary units served the purposes of strategic deception and ambiguity. This meant that supposedly independent forces could be blamed for atrocities, the appearance of chaos could be maintained in the field and the army's professional reputation could be bolstered as a contrast. In operational terms, the paramilitary forces provided a cadre of infantry 'shock troops' that could carry out tasks the regular army could not be counted on to perform. These included close combat and street-to-street fighting. Crucially, their role also included commission of the catalogue of acts that added up to ethnic cleansing: murder, mutilation, torture, rape and terrorization.

The other purposes for the use of alternatives were more political. One of these involved paramilitary groups. Irregular armed forces could be used to set the pace. This meant carrying out action that required support from the JNA or its successors, thus putting pressure on the regular army to follow the Serbian line. In a similar sense, paramilitary groups organized by the Milošević security service apparatus were also competitors to those Serbian formations that might have been created independently. Thus, Milošević's paramilitaries could not only be used to drag the regular army into the Serbian corner, but also to burn off any competition for the Serbian mantle. In either case, the Serbian leader's control was consolidated.

The final purpose in building alternative sources of armed force was to secure loyalty. In this context, the development of the Internal Force Sevice in Serbia was crucial. Better trained, equipped, fed and paid than Belgrade's regular army, this force and its special units became Milošević's praetorian guard. The Internal Force Service was a vital competitor to the Army of Yugoslavia in terms of old-style communist bureaucratic politics. One of its roles was to keep the Army of Yugoslavia in its place. Another, more chilling role, was to be the avant-garde of ethnic cleansing when the Kosovo campaign came. Unlike its paramilitary counterparts, however, the Internal Force Service was a highly organized, large force, capable of action on a far greater scale than the various paramilitary forces that had peppered the war in Croatia and in Bosnia. First and foremost, the Internal Force Service remained Milošević's key instrument of power and terror. Although no formal Serbian army was to emerge from the ashes of the JNA, one effectively appeared with the Internal Force Service. This was the core of the campaign to have armed forces wholly subordinated and loyal to Milošević.

While the Internal Force Service as a whole could not outnumber or outgun the regular army, it was always in a position to use its cohesion and troop quality as a force multiplier in any conflict with the army. The latter would inevitably be less well prepared and was likely to be divided. This and the favourable allocation of resources and options to the Internal Force Service in comparison with the Army of Yugoslavia during the 1990s ensured that the army would be an institutional loser and kept at bay. However, with the Kosovo campaign in 1999, Milošević, by this time President of the Federal Republic of Yugoslavia, finally gained formal control as commander-in-chief of all the armed forces. On 24 March 1999 the force which Milošević had developed as his own in Serbia, the Internal Force Service, was placed under the authority of the Army of Yugoslavia, the regular force of which he had always been distrustful. By now, the man who had always hated the generals was in a position to love them. He had a chief of staff, in General Ojdanić, who was his to control, as well as others in the most senior positions whom he could afford to trust – including one of his wife's relatives, General Nebojša Pavković, as commander of the third army fighting in Kosovo. He had ensured that both the Internal Force Service and the Army of Yugoslavia would do his bidding in battle. However, even with his own men in command of the Army of Yugoslavia for the first time, the Internal Force Service continued to provide Milošević with the only force that would be wholly and truly his. This, however, was still not guaranteed to be enough if circumstances turned against him – along with the people and the bulk of the army. Most significantly, as a result of these developments, Milošević, for the first time, put himself in a position of indisputable formal and legal responsibility for the commission of crimes against humanity.

## Milošević's Downfall and the Military

It was therefore ironic that, when the forces of popular opinion finally turned against the president, it would be Pavković who maintained the tradition of military involvement in politics by obliging the defeated Milošević to leave office. Milošević had quite unnecessarily called early elections for the Federal Republic of Yugoslavia presidency, having first forced constitutional changes to give the office he held a popular rather than parliamentary mandate. This act of hubris was the Serbian leader's fateful error. The usually fractious Serbian opposition saw the chance to end the Milošević era and disciplined itself to unite behind the campaign of Vojislav Koštunica. When it emerged the latter had clearly won in the first round of the elections, in true style Milošević sought to deny the victory by a blend of fraud, denying his opponents outright victory in the first round, and provocation that would create conditions for a state of emergency as massive protests came to the streets of Serbia, including the capital, Belgrade. On 5 October 2000 the protesters in Belgrade withstood initial assaults by the Internal Force Service to break in to the Federal Republic of Yugoslavia parliament, where boxes of fraudulent ballot papers in Milošević's name could be found.

With a revolution on the streets, Milošević's position had become untenable, short of a massive use of force against the population. While this was well within his plans, it became clear that the police would not act against the people at the parliament and that tank units of the Army of Yugoslavia, which had already left their barracks outside Belgrade, were turning back. Whatever the positions of the higher command of the Internal Force Service and the Army of Yugoslavia, it was clear that the main body of both forces was not prepared to act against the people – indeed, it emerged that well over 70 per cent of the Army of Yugoslavia had voted for Koštunica, while the same was true of more than half the Internal Force Service – despite their traditional (paid) role as Milošević's praetorian guard. In these circumstances, while Milošević played for time and sought any way to stay in power, his loyal General Pavković arrived with a squad of troops and told the president at gunpoint that he should concede defeat and leave office – otherwise he would be dealt with, one way or another, by the army.

With this profound political act, the general helped to turn the tide of trouble that had swamped Serbia and its neighbours for over ten years. However, he also set the scene for a continuing political role for the army in Serbia – and certainly for the prominence of the Army of Yugoslavia as a factor in politics. Pavković's action gained him the initial loyalty of the new Federal Republic of Yugoslavia president, who, in one the few areas where he had some formal (as opposed to *de facto*) responsibility, resisted strong pressures from the rest of the coalition that had supported him, and which was forming a new government, to sack the general because of his record over Kosovo and, most of all, because of his known proximity to Milošević. While it seemed unlikely that a war crimes suspect who had been central in plans to take military action against Montengro had Milošević won the election (as well as at critical moments in the past) could retain his position indefinitely, in the delicate political situation that surrounded the transition, there could be no doubting the political need to restrain the army while the new democratic forces sought to bring Serbia under control and to normalize the Federal Republic of Yugoslavia – even to the point of naming it anew and reconstituting its components on a different footing.

## Conclusion

Legitimacy was the defining question for Serbia and other former Yugoslav states. This was the case at the end of the Socialist Federal Republic of Yugoslavia, beyond it, through dissolution and war, and ultimately with the end of the Federal Republic of Yugoslavia and the transition to democracy that began in Serbia. Legitimacy and the link to an agreed political community was the vital issue at all stages for the armed forces. The army gave birth to Tito's Yugoslavia, and played a unique and important formal role in its lifetime. It was decisive in making the difference between separation and separation accompanied by war. Finally, after a decade of bloodshed, it was the Belgrade army that ensured the ousting of Slobodan Milošević and his replacement by Vojislav Koštunica, in the name of the people who had elected him and the path of democracy that he was set to follow.

There were and remained two keys to the processes of military legitimization. One was the establishment of a sound civil–military relationship. The other was consolidation of statehood. Throughout its history, the various attempts to form something with the name Yugoslavia, as well the politics of inter-communal relation and violence across many of the territories involved, had failed to achieve agreed political communities that could form stable states. Arguments were always over what the political community should be, not how it should be run. In this context, the position of the armed forces was inevitably strained. The army needed a country, in different ways took roles in trying to create one, but, ultimately, was left in a continuously anomalous position.

With the ending of the Federal Republic of Yugoslavia, the Belgrade military had begun to adjust to a new environment, but it would be one in which its political profile would remain salient for some time to come. This was because of the need to achieve a correlation between armed forces and statehood – and the fact that this would mean major adjustment for the armed forces. Just as the role of the Partisan army had held the key to the formation of communist and federal Yugoslavia, and just as the political role of the JNA had offered the chance of readjustment and peace as Tito's Yugoslavia came to an end, so, with the transition from the Federal Republic of Yugoslavia to whatever the final successor arrangements would be, the Belgrade army held the political key to the difference between one outcome and another.

Fortunately, it seemed that the impact of ten years of war had not only drastically changed the ethnic composition and shape of the army commanded from Belgrade, but had also made it more sensitive to peaceful adjustment, rather than defending lost causes. Successful adjustment to whatever the new arrangements for statehood and political rule would be was destined to be a test of the army. There would have to be readjustment to relationships between Serbia, Montenegro and Kosovo that could not possibly involve continuation of the Army of Yugoslavia as it had been. And there would have to be an opening to co-operation and to eventual partnership with the countries of the West that had been at war with Serbia only a few years before. The armed forces, whatever their new name and form, held the key to a peaceful and stable future, for Serbia and for the region that had been Yugoslavia.

## Notes and References

1 The present chapter is based on Gow (forthcoming: Chapter 3).
2 Gow and Birch (1997).
3 Gogolewska (1999).
4 In Gow (1992) I argued that civil–military relations were a function of regime legitimacy and military legitimacy. The only possibility of restoring regime legitimacy in the deeply fractured federal polity was through relegitimization of the military on a new basis, harmonious with the political changes that had occurred.
5 Edmonds (1985: 1).
6 Finer (1978).
7 For an excellent study of this phenomenon across all spheres of society, see Gordy (1999).
8 Josip Broz, 'Tito', was leader of the Communist Party of Yugoslavia and Marshall of the National Liberation Army – the Partisans – who emerged as victors from the many-sided composite liberation war, civil war and revolution that occurred on the territory of Yugoslavia between 1941 and 1945.
9 Quoted in Johnson (1982: 189).
10 The Slovene representative to this collective body, Janez Drnovšek, did not attend the first of the meetings.
11 Whereas the Serbian camp – Serbia, its two autonomous provinces of Vojvodina and Kosovo, and Montenegro – supported the action, the four other republican representatives, from Slovenia, Croatia, Macedonia and Bosnia, rejected it.
12 While Kadijević seems to have had little sense that plotting with one part of the presidency against others, among other things, might have been an unconstitutional action, it seems clear that he was not prepared to intervene and declare martial law without some kind of an order from the presidency formally to authorize this. This assessment is confirmed by his predecessor as defence secretary and adviser, Admiral Branko Mamula, in *Death of Yugoslavia*, Part 2, Brian Lapping Associates for the BBC, 1995.
13 Judah (1999).
14 This entity was later to be renamed Republika Srpska.
15 Vego (1992: 445).
16 The VRS inherited, in fact, 43 aircraft, of which the most important were Yugoslav-produced Galeb G-4 ground attack aircraft.
17 See Vego (1992).
18 Quoted in *RFERL Newsline*, 13 August 1999.
19 It should be pointed out that the most significant part of the destruction of this beautiful medieval town was the responsibility of Croatian forces which, in a venal act of vandalism, deliberately destroyed the 700-year-old bridge that had survived all other wars through its history.
20 *Vojska*, 16 September 1992.
21 This operation was tantamount to entrapment, or a kidnapping, provoking strong protests and tension and obliging the Bosnian authorities to give an undertaking not to repeat this type of action.
22 See Vulliamy (1996).

# 13

## The Military in Politics: Old Wine in New Bottles?

### An Attempt at Stocktaking

EMANUEL DE KADT

## Military Interests and Civilian Domains

At the beginning of the twenty-first century the extent of political activity of the military in different parts of the world varies from virtually nil to near-absolute rule – though the latter situation has become exceptional after a decade during which military rule was challenged almost everywhere in the name of 'democratization'. As a result, even where the military have played a significant role on the national political stage until recently, the area on which they can now 'acceptably' make pronouncements, or be heard, has shrunk. Over the past 30 years the international context has also changed a great deal: whereas then military intervention was condoned and at times encouraged by the United States, in spite of its formal commitment to democracy, today such intervention is no longer regarded as acceptable.[1]

In various countries of Africa, Asia and Latin America the end of civil wars, and to a lesser extent certain changes at the 'surface' of the political system, notably 'democratization', have led to a restructuring of the armed forces, sometimes amalgamating former opponents in new national armies, sometimes changing command structures that had been determined by internal wars. These processes always directly touch the army's interest, giving the military a strong incentive to seek to influence them. This is so even in advanced countries with armed forces that have been politically 'abstinent' for as long as anyone can remember: there, too, they are heard in certain areas pertaining to their interests. Following Welch,[2] Griffiths has written: 'Despite the ideal of a politically neutral institution that simply serves the government of the day ... no military can be completely apolitical.'[3]

Nevertheless, there are now fewer areas which are accepted as falling within the military's legitimate interests. What remains within this minimal area are matters of pay, conditions of service, status and privileges. When these are experienced as 'out of joint' with those of comparable professions, military resentment may build up. In Chile this happened at various points in the twentieth century, culminating at the end of the 1960s in an expression of frustration by one garrison (a 'tantrum' as Agüero put it), which led to some of the demands of the military being granted. In Serbia, too, there are said to be significant sections of the professional officer corps who are dissatisfied with their pay and the conditions under which they work, particularly in the middle ranks.

As for military privileges, these are usually left-overs from earlier situations of power, when those privileges were first defined and exacted. While they rarely impinge significantly on the wider economy, they do often result in the military being considerably better off than civilians in comparable jobs – a kind of 'privileged caste'. Special housing is perhaps the most frequent advantage, but there may also be military clubs for the families of officers, or special shops where scarce goods may be bought, or where prices are subsidized. Occasionally, these subsidies can be so high that the resulting income in kind is of greater importance to military families than the breadwinner's regular salary, making their removal very problematic. In Sierra Leone, for example, in the mid-1990s the open market price for rice was 23 times the price paid by the military for their subsidized rice supplies, and the removal of the subsidy led to growing indiscipline in the army.[4]

However, privileges that set the military apart from civilians in legal status have a much greater impact than pecuniary advantages. Thus, for crimes committed while on active duty, members of the armed forces may be subject to a system of justice different from that which applies to civilians – even for breaches of the civilian code of law, such as torture, murder or abduction. This can be particularly significant for officers, for whom judgement by their peers may constitute a considerable advantage, especially in situations where the military retain significant residual power. A recent example was the uncertainty over whether Pinochet, after he returned to Chile from his enforced stay in the United Kingdom, could be summoned before a civil court in Chile. More generally, the military may grant themselves legal immunity from prosecution for crimes committed during the period of their rule by means of an amnesty – which is precisely what Pinochet enacted five years after the 1973 military coup.[5] Something similar happened in Peru in 1995, after the Fujimori self-coup and the drive to eliminate the threat from the Shining Path guerrillas, when an amnesty law granting immunity from prosecutions for human rights violations in war situations was passed.[6]

Yet, as we discuss in greater detail below, what the military define as their 'minimal interests' often go well beyond the privileges mentioned above. They may regard certain decisions that are formally reserved for government and parliament as falling quite legitimately within their purview – above all those related to issues of security, often broadly interpreted. It is only a small step for the armed forces to see themselves as the guardians of the nation, which is when they do become political armies. Koonings and Kruijt have defined political armies as armed forces that consider active participation in domestic politics as a normal, important and legitimate institutional role.[7] Political armies act either in a backroom capacity, visible only to those in government whom they try to influence, or they step into the limelight to take over power and exercise it directly.

## Types of Military Regime and Their Main Characteristics

It may be useful, here, to give a typology of military regimes that is simple yet able to capture the most important differences, such as the one elaborated by Hale.[8] He distinguishes three types. From the least intrusive to the most these are: moderator or veto regimes, guardian regimes and ruler regimes.

Moderator or veto regimes exercise veto power without formally taking over power. These regimes are usually supportive of the status quo; they may have carried out a 'displacement coup' to replace a civilian government that is undesirable in their eyes by one that is more acceptable. Guardian regimes take over direct government power, but declare that they intend to exercise it only for a limited time span (perhaps two to four years). These regimes tend to be authoritarian and limit civil rights, but the mutual expectation of a limited period constrains their degree of control over social and economic structures. Ruler regimes stay in power for longer, and they try to exercise much wider political control (their leaders often see themselves as radical modernizers).

Perhaps the most abiding characteristic of military regimes, and the most abiding self-justification for their intervention, is that they regard themselves as final arbiters of the political process, final judges as to whether a particular turn of events is acceptable from their standpoint as the guardians of national integrity. The threat of secession – an issue that (in East Timor) led to some of the worst excesses of the military in the history of Indonesia, and one that continues to rumble in the background there – is the ultimate menace to national integrity. It has also played a central role over a long period of time in the Ethiopia–Eritrea saga.[9] Not all the cases discussed fall unambiguously into one of these categories, but (while under military rule) Algeria and Indonesia could be classed as veto regimes, Turkey and Peru as guardian regimes, and the other Latin American cases and Nigeria as ruler regimes. In all regimes it is important for the military to show cohesion and a minimal unity of purpose and agreement. The army almost always sets the tone; in the case of an actual intervention, its capacity to occupy strategic locations makes it into the key actor which the other services tend to follow. The senior army commander often chairs the committee of chiefs of staff; through that kind of body the other services may be pressured into the needed 'consensus'. Sometimes, however, differences of view emerge and rifts may open up around the appropriate course of action, especially in situations of ruler or guardian regimes.

An interesting case was that of Chile. Less than a year after the 1973 coup, General Pinochet had himself designated president of the junta. He modelled this position on the well-known role of president, with a swearing-in ceremony, a ceremonial sash and so on. Six months later he had his title changed to president of the republic by decree law.[10] This brought about a

> clear separation … between the military as institution and the military as government, one that was made possible by the strong traditions of discipline and hierarchy in Chile's armed forces. Yet, this disjuncture did not create fundamental conflicts between the two roles, because Pinochet was successful in consolidating power, both as the final authority in the armed forces and as president of the republic.[11]

In general, Pinochet always took care of the legal niceties. During the 17 years of his military rule, the junta over which he presided remained the country's legislative power. This role it had taken over from the dissolved Congress – and it was a separate role, therefore, from that of commanding the armed forces, as well as from that of fulfilling the executive functions of government. However, inter-service disagreements did emerge into the open a few years after the coup, and these were dealt with quite ruthlessly by Pinochet, so that in due course the decision-making process of the junta became reasonably smooth, and consensus was arrived at without undue problems.[12] Gow tracks quite a similar course for Serbia under Milošević.

Any ruler regime has to face the problem of how to garner popular support and limit opposition, and it may attempt to create a base for itself by founding a mass party meant to promote its ideas and principles – as happened, for example, in Brazil.[13] In Chile, in contrast, that route of populist mobilization was not followed. As Valenzuela argues, Pinochet and the military went for the notion that 'structural transformation in the economy and in state–civil society relations would, over time, create a new citizen.... Pinochet's refusal to support a mobilization strategy helped him to maintain military obedience and neutrality....'[14] Even so, when the transition loomed Pinochet did encourage the foundation of a political party (the Independent Democratic Union) which presented itself unabashedly as heir to his ideas, but this never became a mass movement and Valenzuela argues that his refusal to seek support from organized popular groups helped lead to his electoral defeat in 1988.

Koonings and Kruijt point to one important characteristic of direct military rule (guardian or ruler regimes): where this exists, the military principle of hierarchy tends to determine the position of different persons in the government, limiting the possibilities of appointment of the most appropriate person to the most appropriate post. This will be felt particularly when changes are made; 'the internal succession of retiring general–ministers will follow a strictly hierarchical procedure'. Perhaps that is also one reason why even in fully fledged military regimes certain posts are entrusted to loyal civilian technocrats.

Military regimes are also likely to have certain repercussions on the armed forces themselves. Placing military men in government posts requires that someone else take up their erstwhile military duties; Kruijt and Tello mention that in the latter part of military rule in Peru 40–50 per cent of military officers served as political or administrative executives. Moreover, as a result of excessive rotation and rapid promotions there may not be sufficient time for them to familiarize themselves with command and staff posts; this can in turn lead to organizational problems lower down, issues signalled by Fayemi for Nigeria and by Schulte Nordholt for Indonesia. Finally, the chance of 'jobs' easily brings about political careerism, and this in turn can result in jealousy, rivalry and disunity among the officers.[15]

## Historical Reasons for the Political Role of the Military

In this section we review some of the historical reasons that have placed the military on the political stage in different countries. Such political activity tended to be ultimately justified by reference to the military as 'guardians of the nation'. While this epithet may have been self-awarded, it has often given armed forces arguments with which to justify or legitimize their intervention in the political process.

### Independence struggle

Where the precursors of today's armed forces played a decisive part in the struggle for independence and the subsequent founding of the independent state, the outcome has been a strong identification of the military with the nation.[16] Koonings and Kruijt refer to this as the 'birthright principle'. This principle operates clearly in Algeria.[17] There, in the formal sense, the president, elected for five years, runs the state according to the constitution. Yet Addi argues that he is in fact appointed by the military from among a number of candidates taking part in rigged elections. He speaks of the unwritten law of the Algerian political system, a law which states that the army is the only source of power and ultimately of absolute sovereignty, even though the army as such does not intervene in the political field. It makes itself felt through a political police, Military Security, whose mission it is to ensure that all political parties accept that unwritten law. This military–political police fulfils many of the functions undertaken by intelligence services elsewhere.

A variant of this case was found in the Horn of Africa. There, the armed struggle against the military machine of Ethiopia's ferociously repressive Derg, which attempted to impose national unity by force, eventually led to an agreed secession of Eritrea and brought governments to power backed by 'people's' armies with real popular legitimacy. These governments sought to reconstitute the state on a more democratic basis (at first along Marxist principles, later approximating liberal democracy and a market economy) and to rebuild a national army for each country, too. The inherent contradictions between the 'democratic' legacy of guerrilla bands and the hierarchical command structure required of a modern army did cause problems, at first. But in Ethiopia, where the concept of (ethnic) decentralization became constitutionally central, the ethnically mixed national army acquired a significant integrating role.[18] Koonings and Kruijt note that the armed forces in such situations can easily come to see themselves as guarding over the nation's 'core principles and basic values', or their 'permanent national objectives'. Of course, this does not mean that the military's definition of particular goals, values or objectives as 'core' will necessarily command a consensus in the society.

We should not forget, however, that there may well be different interpretations of the role of the armed forces during the independence struggle. As Schulte Nordholt notes for the case of Indonesia, some of these were clearly self-serving, notably the highly exaggerated role supposedly played by the battalion under Suharto's command. More generally, the Indonesian army's 'self-imputed heroic part in casting off the colonial yoke' underplays the role played by other sectors of society, notably politicians and diplomats. This may well be relevant, too, for some of the other cases considered.

*National integration*

A second argument historically used by the military to justify their involvement in politics (and an argument frequently accepted by civilians) is that only they could provide the impetus for national integration, needed as part of the process of modernization of state and society. The first notable case of this kind in the twentieth century was that of Turkey. Ever since the days of Atatürk, the Turkish military have considered themselves the guardians of the secular and democratic principles upon which the republic was founded, and they have intervened when they perceived threats to the maintenance of these principles.[19]

Under Atatürk the central aim of the army was to make Turkey into a secular republic, in contrast to the situation in the Ottoman Empire, where state and religion – Islam – had been closely intertwined. The rise of political Islam in Turkey over the past decade or so has brought this issue once again to the centre of the political stage. Thus President Kenan Evren, who saw himself as the guardian of secular Kemalist nationalism and who was widely regarded as the link between the military and civilians in the years following the military coup of 1980, leant on prime ministers in the later 1980s to hold them back from going too far in accepting the influence of the radical Islamic parties on government policy.[20] The issue sprang back into the limelight in 1996.[21] A coalition government, which had been formed under the Islamist prime minister Erbakan, took a number of measures that were anathema to the secularist military – such as rapprochement with Libya and the possible support this gave to armed internal groups; the stimulation of Islamic religious orders and associations and the expansion of the Islamic education system; instructions to Turkish diplomats to fulfil Islamic obligations; and even the use of dress that was 'illegal' under the so-called dress code. Things came to a head in mid-1997, when the Erbakan government resigned after intense pressure from the military and from secularist politicians and civil society organizations, who accused it of 'using democracy to destroy democracy'.

The Turkish army obviously saw itself as an honourable defender of democracy, which was perceived as threatened by the theocratic principles of Islamism. Yet, such intervention in the political process, even if it is indirect and against forces that might curtail the democratic rights of others, does raise all kinds of awkward questions and moral dilemmas, even when – in conspicuous contrast to the somewhat comparable case of Algeria – no military coup occurred and no blood was shed.

This issue of how Islamist forces might use democracy also arose in other countries where the majority of the population are Muslims, such as Indonesia. There, the old forces wishing to Islamize the political system have gained in strength over the last ten years, and they have nestled themselves within the army as well.[22] These forces challenge the (still) accepted state ideology of *pancasila*, which has kept an exclusive or fundamentalist interpretation of the role of Islam at bay for half a century. Virtually since independence the Indonesian army has regarded itself as playing a legitimate role in the process of national integration, a role given further substance in 1958, when the army formulated the so-called principle of dual function. This principle proclaims that, based on its role in the struggle for independence and its merits in having kept separatism at bay in the 1950s, the army can legitimately perform duties in the fields of government and administration, even including the economy, in addition to its conventional defensive functions.

In former Yugoslavia, too, such an integrating role was played by the armed forces – from the time of Tito onwards. However, when after his death the centrifugal forces in the country became so great that the previously accepted overarching political community fell part, it was equally no longer possible to have one army. In fact, the 'attachment' of parts of the former Yugoslav army to different communities sealed the disintegration of the country.[23]

Such processes of national integration and modernization can, of course, cause considerable disruption. In many countries entrenched elites did hold back necessary political and socio-economic reforms. That was the case in Chile, where the military intervened in 1924 to oust a conservative president unwilling to pass social legislation, to incorporate labour organizations into the political system and to make other much needed reforms.[24] Over forty years later a similar course of events occurred in Peru, when General Velasco staged a coup and conceived of a structural reform programme for the country that would integrate the poor majority, neglected by successive governments, into mainstream development. The military stayed in power for some 12 years and imposed their revolution from above, particularly through a much-expanded public sector. Kruijt and Tello paint a very positive picture of their achievements, notwithstanding their top-down, hierarchical methods (the major new 'mobilization' organization is said to have been full of 'control freaks'): security and justice, water and sewerage, education and literacy, health workers in remote places, labour-friendliness, and the promotion of indigenous language and culture. That kind of transition from an agrarian to an industrializing society brings about socio-economic and structural changes which also impinge on existing mechanisms of conflict management and resolution, including the role played by traditional legal systems.[25] Schulte Nordholt discusses this issue specifically for Indonesia, where the resulting institutional gaps were filled by the army and the bureaucracy.

*National security doctrine: counter-insurgency*
As Koonings and Kruijt point out, in Latin America there is a century-old tradition of 'geopolitical' thinking in the higher military academies, long supported by military missions from Europe. In the late 1930s and early 1940s this provided fertile ground for the reception of ideas on an 'Inter-American' defence concept, ideas which later developed into 'national security doctrines' during the period of the Cold War.

This doctrine was originally elaborated in the military academies and think tanks of the United States, where officers from developing countries – and particularly from Latin America – came to study, though further elaboration took place in the Latin American countries themselves. For example, in Guatemala the counter-insurgency doctrine directly informed the nature and conditions of the politico-military project of the Guatemalan army.[26] In general, as McSherry notes for Argentina, these counter-insurgency doctrines made the army consider 'liberal democratic freedoms of the press, of speech and of assembly … and so on as dangerous to national security and favourable to "subversion"'.[27] The 17-year dictatorship of Pinochet in Chile was based on similar principles, in that case topped up by the attitudes of one who deeply believed in his mission to conduct a holy war against communism.[28]

However, as Koonings and Kruijt remind us, such doctrines were also supported by and served the interests of beleaguered elites or even middle classes, afraid of changes in the class structure in which they had hitherto occupied a favoured position. That led in the 1970s and 1980s in Latin America to the civil-military alliances which promoted what Guillermo O'Donnell has called authoritarian developmentalism and the civilian–military 'coup coalitions'[29] that have striven to provide legitimacy for military interventions and the direct rule of the armed forces (see below).

# More Recent Sources of the Political Role of Armies

*Security doctrines and intelligence services*
The Cold War which threw up the national security doctrines is over, but significant remnants from that period remain, in the rationales for action as well as

in the structures of security and intelligence services, especially again in Latin America. This originates from the central role played by counter-intelligence for so many years, resulting in turn in the 'intelligence community' having developed a great deal of power within the armed forces.[30] Such prominence of intelligence interests does not easily disappear when times change.

Schirmer, writing about Guatemala, asks whether officers trained in counter-insurgency are able and/or willing to accommodate to the new forms of politics that arise out of the peace accords. Can they be relaxed about the everyday open conflicts of a democratic political structure and accept dissent as a part of demo-cracy rather than as an automatic threat to the system? She answers the question in the negative: officers appear to have a conception of human rights, of 'threats to stability' and of the rule of law which can easily lead to certain groups wishing to participate in the political process being labelled as 'illegal'. They also appear to have much more difficulty in adapting to a democratic form of politics than those with a more traditional training, and they have a tendency to integrate the political into the military domain. Yet officers with that kind of background remain in prominent positions in a number of other Latin American countries. In Peru under Fujimori there is said to be a 'network of petty betrayers, cash-paid village informants, office agents, and informers-by-blackmail'; after the basic threat from the guerrilla groups was eliminated this network turned its attention to the political opposition, the media, NGOs and the trade unions.[31] Schirmer points to quite similar developments in post-civil war Guatemala. In Indonesia the policy of dual function affected certain organizational aspects within the army itself, as it emphasized the development and importance of KOPASSUS and the intelligence agencies, and also brought the army into contact with a number of right-wing militia groups.[32]

The line of thinking developed in this volume is consistent with that of Griffiths in his analysis of southern Africa. He notes that under the apartheid regime the armed forces developed considerable expertise in internal security areas. To some extent this puts the post-reform government at their mercy, partly because such expertise is also needed in the new circumstances, and partly because it creates temptations for the armed forces to use that expertise, in the post-reform period, for their own benefit.[33]

*Problems of governance*

Today (apart from the occasional simple greedy impulse) military intervention is often brought about by the perception that civilian government is simply not functioning 'as it should' – that it is inefficient, ineffective and perhaps above all corrupt, and that such malfunctioning threatens the very institutions of the state itself. That is not a new perception. Finer wrote many years ago that the military are more likely to intervene in politics in times of a serious domestic crisis, such as violent internal conflicts, or in situations in which a power vacuum exists, so that the military remain as the only viable governing institution.[34] The military justify such interference by reference to what Koonings and Kruijt call 'the competence principle': compared to bumbling and incompetent civilians, the well-organized, united and 'modern' military are much better able to promote the national interest and run the affairs of state. There are two examples from the year 2000. Although the attempt to interfere with the structure and functioning of the army itself was the ostensible reason given by General Musharraf for the coup in Pakistan, that attempt was probably the last straw for a military command which had long perceived the government as incompetent and corrupt, and unable to govern 'honestly'.[35] In Ecuador, too, what effectively amounted to an army coup to remove the president, and secure his substitution by the vice-president, was justified by 'governance' concerns.[36] Such problems around governance have probably now become the central issues that impel military men to interfere with government.

More than just perceiving civilians as incompetent, the military may consider politics to be the root cause of evil in the state. They may, even in the year 2000, still see democracy as a threat to civil peace, as is notably the case in Algeria.[37] There, the Islamists have gathered considerable support, largely because of the continued exclusion of the poor by a system which is deeply corrupt and oligarchic, with the army being in cahoots with those who benefit economically from the situation. Even so, the military still aim for a body politic without conflict, and hence without parties. The Islamists (like the Leninists before them) would institute changes that then would become irrevocable, and they would impose their world view and lifestyle on people who might not agree. Thereby they would deny democracy itself. Yet for their opponents it is difficult to proclaim their democratic credentials and then exclude a large part of the population from the political process – even when they are essentially anti-democratic. Here is a dilemma that democrats have agonized over for much of this century. The military may also aim to replace politicians with professionals in government – believing that it is possible to depoliticize politics by way of militarization.[38] They often devise institutional mechanisms to safeguard such arrangements even after they will have relinquished power officially, in order to be able to neutralize the 'machinations' of the politicians well into the future. They will make use of supposedly neutral technocrats and are likely to build up coalitions with civilians, usually from the right, who favour such arrangements, possibly through creating or encouraging 'suitable' political parties. This sequence of events was prototypically followed in Chile between 1973 and 1989.

Problems of governance – not exclusively of government as such, but also of the context in which government has to operate – have a variety of causes. In his examination of the role of the military in Uganda, Brett discusses certain systemic factors that have led to democratic setbacks in Africa. He lists these as (1) regional, ethnic or religious conflicts; (2) poorly educated and corrupt military leaders; (3) the unwillingness of political elites to accept defeat and; (4) the organizational weakness of civil society.[39] There is a feedback system here, in which factors such as these affect the behaviour of the military, yet the latter in turn influence the prospects for the potential effectiveness of civilian government.

In very poor countries the effective functioning of civilian government is often seriously hindered by a general lack of resources. Donors have stepped in to try and help strengthen the institutions of government and administration; that is also regarded as a preventive measure against the kind of collapse that could lead to a military takeover. Nevertheless, there are usually other factors that play an even more important role. In many African countries central among these is the perception of government and politics as a domain of power rather than an arena of responsibility, a chance to appropriate resources more than an opportunity to provide service. Hence, such outside attempts at improving governance may only have very limited effects.[40]

*Resort to force and violence*

Another major problem of governance is caused by widespread resort to force and violence. Violence perpetrated by forces not under the direct control of the state is not a new phenomenon, but it has been particularly prominent in the last decade or so. It may occur either in confrontations between different groups vying for predominance, in situations that effectively constitute civil wars (Angola, Liberia, Sierra Leone, Sudan), or in less institutionalized or even random forms. Echoing what has been said by many predecessors, Brett reminds us that 'where violence is possible and profitable, history suggests that it will be used without mercy in pursuit of private or group advantage'.[41]

Some well-established states have lived with such violence for decades – a situation found particularly in Latin America. Colombia is the classic case. Politically inspired violence almost destroyed the country in the years around 1950; it was overcome by an unprecedented political pact of 'alternation' between the two major political parties. More recently, violence has flared up again as the enormous illegal earnings from drugs production and trafficking have given drugs barons immense power. This power has been exercised against established structures and institutions through violence perpetrated in alliance with left-overs from the guerrilla groups started in the heyday of the ideological politics of the 1960s. The level of this violence has seriously weakened the state itself.[42] Peru is another case in point: after the military handed back power to the civilians in 1980 the country was convulsed by the revolutionary and often cruel violence of the Shining Path guerrillas, 'a barren, totalitarian regime of terror and fear ... with fundamentalist traits and devotion'.[43] This led eventually to a self-coup by Alberto Fujimori, the third civilian president elected after the military bowed out. Fujimori dissolved parliament and became sole ruler, supported by the armed forces' commanders. In the intensifying battle against the guerrillas, the military commanders of the country's emergency zones were granted extraordinary political and judicial powers: they had direct command over the civilian administration, and military justice was applied to matters related to the insurgency. Shortly afterwards the army managed to capture the top leadership of Shining Path, a development that helped consolidate Fujimori's civilian dictatorship, which continued to lean heavily on support from the armed forces.

Resort to force and violence tends to be more acute in situations where the state has not been fully consolidated, where it is still in formation – as is the case in much of Africa, even today. There, the role of force is more salient 'because contending parties have not fully internalized the constraints which must be accepted if there is to be government by consent'.[44] Civilians do not as a matter of course settle their (political) differences without resorting to armed force. A tradition of its use may well exist, a legacy from colonial times which may also have become embedded in traditional society and culture. Wilson, writing of Mozambique, speaks of a deep-seated

> legacy of warlordism, slavery, forced labour and casually violent administration that have dominated the last five hundred years of history .... Organized violence appears to be considered by rural people of northern Mozambique a normal if somewhat undesirable tool of economic and political activity; and participating in it at some stage in life is seen as likely for men.[45]

He also notes that violence against women (especially rape) is very widespread; 'women (and sexual intercourse with them) are seen as the objects and objectives of violence and war'.[46] And such ritualized violence works: it cows the population, helps maintain control, prevents any organized resistance.

Wilson's further discussion of the link between 'magic' and violence, deeply embedded in the culture of Mozambican society, is compelling. Of course, it would be wrong to generalize from that single case: such cultural characteristics differ greatly between different African societies. Even so, the lessons from his analysis are likely to have wider relevance, notably for the conflicts in Sierra Leone and Angola. He concludes that the war in Mozambique was fought 'entirely' within a cultic framework. The cult of violence was a major tool of Renamo in its struggle for control, but the local chiefs and militias and the Frelimo military have 'competed for this same authority' and made good use of it.[47] This is a reflection of the weak penetration of the state in Mozambique, but it testifies above all to the strength of traditional beliefs. Wilson raises a significant question as a result, and the implicit answer to it is not particularly comforting:

> given the extent of military violence and civil war in Africa and other parts of the world, in situations where state power has virtually collapsed and international forces lack the understanding, capacity and will to intervene effectively, it is important to ask whether forces mobilizing popular culture and traditions really can pacify institutionalized warfare and defuse the cycle of violence.[48]

Violence was also the subject of Campbell's social–psychological study of African families in South Africa. She argued that violence is 'an option coherently related to social group memberships and power relations ... a comprehensible response by a particular group of people to a particular set of circumstances'.[49] In South Africa those circumstances were the 'erosion of patriarchy' in African families, with young men asserting their masculinity in an aggressive and arrogant way, also in the public (and political) sphere. For men, who were oppressed in society in terms of race and class, 'their socially sanctioned power over women and young men in the family was often the only arena in which they were able to exercise any dominance'.[50] This expressed itself in 'controlling their women' and dominating their girlfriends. Forced sex was seen as proof of such domination among young men; 'men first learn to view violence as a socially sanctioned means of resolving conflict in the context of violence by fathers against mothers and children, and the violence of older brothers against their sisters in their socially approved role of policing or "guarding" them'.[51]

So violence and masculinity are seen as closely intertwined in what at the time of Campbell's study was still a macho culture of resistance to the apartheid regime, itself in its worst days a very violent affair. Now that apartheid has gone, and blacks increasingly occupy positions of power and responsibility throughout society, South Africa continues to be a very violent place, with a high degree of criminal behaviour. As yet there are no signs that this is bringing the armed forces closer to active intervention in the state. But unless there is a reduction in the level of violence, the institutional foundations of the South African state may well be sorely tested.

## Civilian–Military Interplay

*Can civilians control the military?*

Brett reminds us that violence subjected to the rule of law is essential for the survival of democracy. In terms of institutionalized violence it requires separating the military and political commands and clearly subjecting the former to the latter.[52]

Beyond the politically institutionalized acceptance of such subordination, well established in North America and Europe (East and West), proper civilian control of the military requires expertise on the part of civilians and an ability to talk to the military professionals on their own terms. This revolves above all around budgets: how the demands of the military affect the proportion of government expenditure required for military rather than, say, social needs. Such expertise is usually thin on the ground, often available only through persons in politics who themselves have come from a military background. In established democracies this does not necessarily matter, but elsewhere the results can be more serious politically. Even in apartheid South Africa, 'members of parliament never developed an expertise in military matters and were content, for the most part, to accept the armed forces' assertions and explanations'.[53] As a result, civilian control was never fully established. Concerns about such lack of expertise are also expressed by Castro for Brazil and by Fayemi with regard to Nigeria. Fayemi points out that over time military control of the government can lead to a decrease in the 'culture of dialogue', with force increasingly seen as a sound option for action. That, in turn, raises the profile of the military, even under a civilian government, and contributes to a willingness to let them 'get on with it', and hence to a further loosening of control.

In countries where armies have played a political role in the past, civilian control may be hedged in by implicit threats of a coup. The more believable such a threat, the more will the military have freedom to do as they wish. Sabre-rattling can happen not only in reality, but also in the minds of the civilian politicians. The resulting compromises may be seen as 'necessary' in order to avoid direct intervention. Where the successor regime to one in which the military were dominant is itself strongly influenced by military (or ex-military) men – and Fayemi argues this is the case for present-day Nigeria – the situation easily becomes one of 'democracy without democrats'.

The Pinochet extradition case, so much in the news during 1999 and the early months of 2000, had significant reverberations for the relations of the military with the civilian authorities. When the top brass of all services gave him a hero's reception upon his return to Santiago, this indirectly called into question the authority of the government over the armed forces. In the eyes of many it foreshadowed further trouble in civil–military relations, something against which the then President Ricardo Lagos rather gingerly put the armed forces on guard. However, because of ex-President Frei's own ambivalent attitude, his publicly expressed satisfaction at preventing Pinochet's extradition from Britain to Spain, and the evidence of his deal making with the armed forces around the Pinochet case, the room for manoeuvre of the incoming president *vis-à-vis* the army may well have been unnecessarily restricted.

*Civilian support for military intervention*

As we have already noted, the military often justify their intervention by the apparent existence of governance 'chaos' in the country, and there may be broad civilian support for such intervention. In the last six months of the Allende government in Chile in 1973 conditions for much of the population were indeed chaotic. This resulted not merely from the organized opposition of the right and of the United States, and from their wrecking tactics, but to an even greater extent from the profound divisions within the government itself. Different partners in the coalition promoted policies that were incompatible and regarded the different ministries as their private fiefdoms, significant above all as providers of employment to their own militants and as power bases for their parties. Just before the military coup of September 1973 the Congress, in which the government's supporters were in the minority, declared the government illegitimate, and the coup was quite widely welcomed as a relief from increasing disorder, on the mistaken assumption that power would be returned to civilians within a matter of months.

There are other cases of widespread civilian support for military intervention when government fails to function properly, or when some widely agreed constitutional principle – such as secularism in Turkey – is seen to be endangered. Yet such support melts away if the military stay in power for longer than is deemed necessary: this happened in Chile to the early support from the centrist Christian Democrats around six months after the 1973 coup, and loss of support also affected the Turkish military well before the end (1993) of their last period of intervention.[54] In such cases it is interesting to consider which civilian groups are the main instigators and carriers of opposition to military rule. In more advanced political systems, as in much of Latin America, political parties on the left are the natural opponents of military rule, but in addition an important role may be played by other actors such as the judiciary, parts of the media, and even just the general population, as McSherry documents in the case of Argentina.[55]

Occasionally, civilian leaders of government try to use the military for their own ends. This tactic can work – it did, apparently, in the case of President Menem in Argentina. He is said to have drawn on military 'guardian capabilities', for example the fact that they continued to hover as a threat in the background, to secure his own neo-liberal project against much internal opposition.[56] But it is a dangerous game to play. In Uganda, as Mudoola argues, 'in their factional bid for power, groups ... work[ed] out their own private agenda for politicizing the military on their own terms', with tragic consequences.[57] Obote cowed his opponents and relied on the troops, nursing the army as his 'critical power constituency'. In turn, within the military, this 'generated a sense of politico-functional indispensability and relegated the crucial importance of civilian political institutions as legitimizing instruments to the background'.[58] It was the souring of relations between Obote and Amin which paved the way for Amin's coup. The army was thrust into a position of 'active power' as the civilian political institutions were undermined and rendered incapable of conflict resolution by Obote, a power-hungry politician. When civilian politicians try to use the military for their own ends, the latter may easily get the wrong idea.

*Economic interests of the military*
In many countries the military run considerable defence-related enterprises; in some cases enterprises *tout court*. This gives them access to resources independent from those voted by parliament or allocated by government, and leverage over their supposed civilian masters by decreasing their degree of dependence. An unusual mechanism that increases their room for manoeuvre is found in Chile,

where the armed forces, under a law instituted in the Pinochet years, have been receiving 10 per cent of the income of the State Copper Corporation every year, but without being directly involved in its management.

Military involvement in the economy can result in greatly increased opportunities for personal enrichment, and the availability of significant resources, such as oil in Nigeria, may 'sharpen the predatory instincts' of the military and their allies in the civil service or the business sector. Fayemi also notes that such alliances can outlast the particular period of military intervention: (ex-)officers who played significant roles during military rule are likely to find their way into business or politics subsequently, as a result of help received from those earlier contacts.

Indonesia, as Schulte Nordholt amply demonstrates, is an extreme case of such an entanglement of the military in the economy. The doctrine of the dual function[59] gave the justification for that involvement, which under the Suharto regime took on monumental proportions: between 30 and 50 per cent of all top functions at the national level (ministers to heads of department in ministries) and between 50 and 70 per cent of provincial governors and district officers had a military background. Schulte Nordholt argues that in the earlier part of Suharto's New Order this deployment of senior military personnel introduced much-needed discipline into the civil service, which in turn contributed to considerable economic growth (some 7 per cent annually on average over thirty years) and to greater efficiency in the attainment of objectives set in the development of physical as well as social infrastructure (health, education and credit programmes). Kruijt and Tello mention similar developments in Velasco's Peru, where the military were said to be 'pouncing on "lazy" civil servants', publicly admonishing them for anti-patriotic behaviour. In both countries the population benefited from this development, and considerable attention was paid to poor rural areas, even though in Indonesia this was conditional on electoral support to the government party, obtained through clientelistic practices that often verged on blackmail, as well as through intimidation. There, this economic involvement also pitted the army – as entrepreneur and employer – from the early days against the labour movement, and this may well have contributed to the bloody repression of the second half of the 1960s, when between half a million and one million people were killed for their supposed communist sympathies.

Schulte Nordholt emphasizes that, despite the supposed economic benefits, this intransparent and unaccountable system led over time to increasing 'KKN practices' – corruption, collusion and nepotism. The involvement in business of ex-generals and their relatives, aided by mostly Chinese business partners, grew by leaps and bounds. They also made extensive use of so-called non-profit foundations, through which vast sums could be channelled that were not subject to business accounting methods or the payment of tax. The largest beneficiaries were Suharto, who behaved increasingly like an oriental sultan, and his immediate family: exclusively by means of such foundations, Suharto's family is said to have controlled some 15 billion US dollars.

## The Military in the Democratic Era

*Transitions, hand-overs and left-overs*
It is difficult for the military to ignore the new international climate of the late 1990s. Apart from the manifest demise of communism (which, alive, had made

anti-communism into a credible doctrine), 'globalization' has weakened various key notions that underpinned the military's political claims, notably because the idea of nationalist development has been pushed into the background. Democracy is now at least formally regarded as a condition by all major countries in the North for friendly inter-state relations (and more expressly for development cooperation), and 'hard-boiled military regimes' are, albeit selectively, likely to be given the cold-shoulder treatment in the international arena. While in many countries of the South the military do continue to regard democracy as a kind of Pandora's box, full of danger for the country – hence their attempts to hedge it in by institutional means[60] – democracy has also to an extent become one of the canons of modernity.[61] This pressure for democratization is reinforced when the inherent weaknesses of military rule become visible as that rule is prolonged. Continued human rights violations will undermine civilian support; the institutional unity of the armed forces will be eroded; corruption among the military masters or their civilian servants may increase alarmingly – not to speak of the inappropriateness of the military's education and training for dealing with the affairs of government.

Even so, a transition to democracy will be hindered by various factors. In some countries, notably in Africa, military rule may have been deeply corrupt and practices such as favouritism and bribery may have become so strongly embedded that they have come to be regarded as 'normal' by the population and are continued even after the departure of the soldiers from government.[62] Also, and again especially in countries of Africa, there are many countries where there is little pre-dictatorship experience with democracy. Elsewhere, where military rule was particularly harsh, there will be a legacy of fear which may make it difficult to believe the soldiers will not be back, sometime.[63] Almost everywhere the transition is likely to be hedged in by terms set by the military, which may well make it more difficult. As Griffiths[64] argued for the case of post-apartheid South Africa, minimizing the legacy of support for the previous regime, and thereby facilitating the transition, requires that the armed forces be restructured, that they lose their old face. Only then can they regain legitimacy. The more the army's old face is preserved in transitional arrangements, the more has the institutional interest of the armed forces been predominant in the transitional compromise, and the more power the armed forces clearly retain. This is especially relevant if surviving elements include many of those who have been responsible for, or engaged in the dictatorship's excesses.

Beyond guarantees for the military themselves, agreed institutional arrangements will limit the room for manoeuvre in the political arena and will specifically exclude certain aspects of civilian–military relations from being formally subordinated to the civilian political authorities. The Chilean experience, again, is typical: senators appointed for life by the military; restrictions on the role of the president in the appointment (or firing) of the heads of the armed forces; high court judges who can be expected to hand down rulings that are to the liking of the generals; a council of state in which the military have a prominent role. In Indonesia, too, the left-overs of military rule linger; there, says Schulte Nordholt, the basic question is whether, and if so when, the army will give up its dual function and indeed will allow itself, both formally and *de facto*, to be placed under the primacy of a civil and democratic authority.

Yet the military may also, voluntarily, refrain from continuing to involve themselves directly in politics. As we have seen, this has happened in the case of

Turkey, where the armed forces regularly removed themselves from the scene once their 'democratizing' – or secularizing – objectives were fulfilled. Brazil is another case where, at least since handing over power in 1985, the generals have steered well clear of further political involvements, even on occasions when sceptics might have expected them to make their presence felt. Such occasions were the impeachment of President Collor in 1992, the decision in the late 1990s to create a civilian-dominated ministry of defence, with the commanders of the armed forces losing their long-standing ministerial status, as well as two instances of the (re-)opening of issues surrounding human rights abuses or the denial of justice.[65] Even if they had been tempted to manifest themselves, the fact that there was no clear civilian support for such a materialization would have held them back: neither in Brazil, nor elsewhere in Latin America, have the military intervened without support from some significant section of the civilian population. Such a brake does not necessarily operate on the military in other countries, particularly not where the involvement of the population with the state is (still) rudimentary, as it is in many African countries.

*How to deal with the repressive past*
An important left-over from the period of military rule is the memory of years of repressive rule and the issue of human rights violations. I have already referred to the self-accorded amnesties with which military or quasi-military governments tried to bury the violent past in Chile and Peru. I have also mentioned developments in the recent Pinochet 'extradition' case that seem to have strengthened the legal claims of international human rights covenants over other bodies of law – including those that underpin national sovereignty.[66]

Castro shows that in Brazil this issue of the repressive past remains one of the most sensitive zones of contemporary Brazilian historical memory. Over against the lofty image of founders of the nation, or even of defenders of its integrity and security, stands the picture of the military engaging in extensive torture practices to gather information or to cow the population into submission, or even 'disappearing' people. How to deal with this past? Should it be written off, forgotten – if not forgiven – for the sake of reconciliation and an orientation to the future, or should those who were most to blame be made to face up to this flaunting of some of the most basic rules of civilized society? In most cases there has at least been some process of recording the names of those who were killed as an act of remembrance and as an inherent pledge that it will 'never happen again'. Such memorializing of the victims, but without naming those who sent them to their fate, may be as much as the military are prepared to accept: it shows their residual power after the transition, often laid down in some kind of 'pact' that shaped its course.

An interesting comparison in this respect can be drawn between two neighbouring countries, Argentina and Chile. Not only did Argentina revert to civilian rule well before Chile, but a number of its senior commanders were tried for human rights abuses, something studiously avoided in Chile. 'For the military and their *golpista* ... allies, the trials made clear that human rights crimes and repression had consequences and costs. The political culture seems to have been permanently changed in Argentina as a result of the trials.'[67] The trials strengthened the foundations for democratic development, even though only the top brass were prosecuted and many of the worst actual perpetrators went scot-free.[68]

In contrast, the military in Chile would not accept any more than the Truth and Reconciliation Commission, which listed the known victims of military terror. Chile's generals were manifestly able to impose more conditions than their counterparts across the border – mainly because their defeat in the Falklands (Malvinas) War in 1982 seriously weakened the latter. After Chile's 1990 transition there was much talk of looking to the future, and the past was largely banned from the public arena. As a result, beyond those who had directly suffered from the military's outrages, large sections of the population – probably close to half – continued to believe that the tales of torture and death were, if not fabrications, at least exaggerations; without trials of the perpetrators, there was nothing to set the record straight. It was only with the arrest of Pinochet in the United Kingdom, and the extensive reporting in the conservative press of the accusations, that the issue came into the public eye; there are indications that it may have led to a new awareness among his past supporters.

In this volume, too, some attention is paid to the issue of living (or coming to terms) with the military past. Castro shows how in Brazil, since returning power to the civilians (now well over ten years ago) the military have become socially more isolated, have lost prestige and have yet to achieve a clearly defined role. But they have made efforts to ensure that the symbolic role of founders of the nation is preserved for the armed forces. Schulte Nordholt shows how in Indonesia the reformist Wahid administration, which came to power late in 1999, is trying to deal with the issue of past horrors. It is hindered by an unreformed judiciary and the fact that, according to some, the armed forces would lose their entire top echelon if all those apparently guilty were to be prosecuted. A Truth and Reconciliation approach, with those responsible named but not prosecuted, is thought to be the best that can be done to achieve national reconciliation.

Yet even the rather minimalist character of such an approach may not elicit much collaboration from the armed forces, even when 'reformed'. Schirmer tells us how in Guatemala the army tried systematically to destroy all evidence of the 'dirty war'. With the exception of three officers who provided information voluntarily, as individuals, the military as an institution refused to collaborate with what in Guatemala was called the Historical Clarification Commission, and most officers reacted with 'anger and disdain' to its report. And though there now is said to be internal dissension within the high ranks of the army about its future role, which holds out some hope for an unconditional subordination to civilian authority in due course, Schirmer emphasizes that the outcome is by no means a foregone conclusion. The predominant line continues to be a defiant and defensive one, with the powers of the intelligence services continuing largely unchecked and their approach largely unreformed.

*Prospects*
In looking to the future, some rather tentative and broad distinctions should be made between the different continents. Latin America and Africa are the most distinct; Asia seems to occupy an intermediate position.

In most of Latin America the armed forces have, to all appearances, been pushed into the background – even if their subordination to civilian authority remains half-hearted. There are two notable exceptions. Colombia, where guerrillas and drugs barons have forged an unholy alliance, seems to be sliding ever closer to anarchy, in spite of millions of dollars of military aid for the 'war on drugs' from the United States. In Chile the jury is still out on the extent to which the military and their right-wing allies are prepared eventually to countenance changes that would result in a clear-cut submission of the military to civilian authority – at least in formal terms (under the constitution inherited from Pinochet the president does not even have the authority to change the command structure of the armed forces). Yet while in Latin America the signs do look positive, on balance, there is no guarantee – there or anywhere – that the democratic transitions are truly irreversible, and that they will inevitably lead to democratic consolidation, especially where there have been pacted transitions.[69] A particularly poignant case is that of Peru, where the military withdrew from the political scene at the beginning of the 1980s, only to find themselves in the 1990s the instruments (some might say the victims) of an increasingly arbitrary and dictatorial, yet originally elected, president. He ruthlessly eliminated anyone from senior army positions not considered loyal to him personally. That military–civilian president's numerous boxes of dirty tricks are extensively described in this volume by Kruijt and Tello.

In a significant number of countries in Africa, the problems of governance and of violent intra-state conflicts are pushing some of the already weak states close to collapse. Armed force, there, is no longer the monopoly of the state. Armed actors proliferate; the continent is awash with small weapons, easily and openly acquired. Militias and rebel armies fight to influence the course of events in the political sphere, and the army itself may use rogue paramilitary groups to exercise political leverage. What limited transparency there was with regard to military issues disappears. (Serbia, incidentally, has shared these characteristics with the African cases.) If anything, in Africa 'political armies' are on the increase. Add to that the new social and economic challenges – regionalism and ethno-religious conflicts, social exclusion and environmental degradation – which are giving rise to new patterns of social instability that may run counter to the military notion of national order, and the outlook is far from reassuring.

## Notes and References

1 Yet the ambiguous reaction to the recent coup in Pakistan raises doubts about the depth of US opposition to military rule elsewhere in the world.
2 Welch (1976).
3 Griffiths (1996: 480).
4 Zack-Williams (1997: 378).
5 Though I shall be citing the views of other authors with respect to Chile, particularly Agüero (see his study of Chile, Chapter 5, pp. 111–34 in this volume), I am relying to a considerable extent on my own experience in that country. Brief accounts can be found in de Kadt (1994, 1996).
6 See Kruijt and Tello on Peru, Chapter 2, pp. 35–63 in this volume.
7 When we speak of a political army as an actor on the political scene it is implied that those who determine its actions are the men occupying the higher ranks at the top of the military hierarchy, the military high command, who can expect the obedience of those lower down.
8 See Hale (1994: 309 ff.).
9 See Luckham on Eritrea and Ethiopia, Chapter 10, pp. 238–69 in this volume.
10 Valenzuela (1995).
11 Valenzuela (1995: 23).
12 In the first period after the coup Pinochet came to be increasingly opposed by the air force, through its member of the junta, General Leigh. Eventually, the rift came out into the open, Leigh making a number of 'democratizing' proposals in May 1978 (ten years before the

transition to democracy eventually got under way), which included a formal limit of five years on the military government. This led Pinochet to have him 'fired' by the other junta members and locked out of his office, two months later. The tension between army and air force was great. Eleven generals resigned in solidarity with Leigh, but the air force was made to back down in due course, after Pinochet (in his role of 'president') had retired a further eight generals. See Valenzuela (1995).

13 See Koonings and Kruijt, Chapter 1, pp. 9–34; and Castro on Brazil, Chapter 4, pp. 90–110 in this volume.

14 Valenzuela (1995: 16).

15 See Fayemi on Nigeria, Chapter 9, pp. 204–37 in this volume.

16 This particular reason does not apply to Latin America, whose states attained independence in the early nineteenth century with 'popular' uprisings against colonial rule, nor is it applicable to those African and Asian states which were granted independence by the United Kingdom and France, mainly in the 1960s, without an armed struggle.

17 See Addi on Algeria, Chapter 8, pp. 179–203 in this volume.

18 See Luckham on Ethiopia and Eritrea, Chapter 10, pp. 238–69 in this volume.

19 On the whole the Turkish military have not retained direct power for very long and have moved out of politics within a relatively short period of time. See Güney on Turkey, Chapter 7, pp. 162–78 in this volume.

20 Hale (1994: 296).

21 See Güney on Turkey, Chapter 7, pp. 162–78 in this volume.

22 See Schulte Nordholt on Indonesia, Chapter 6, pp. 135–61 in this volume.

23 See Gow on Serbia, Chapter 12, pp. 297–312 in this volume.

24 See Agüero on Chile, Chapter 5, pp. 111–34 in this volume.

25 De Kadt (1999).

26 See Schirmer on Guatemala, Chapter 3, pp. 64–89 in this volume.

27 McSherry (1997: 271).

28 Valenzuela (1995).

29 See Koonings and Kruijt, Chapter 1, pp. 9–34 in this volume.

30 See Kruijt and Tello on Peru, Chapter 2, pp. 35–63 in this volume.

31 *Ibid.*

32 See Schulte Nordholt on Indonesia, Chapter 6, pp. 135–61 in this volume.

33 Griffiths (1996: 481).

34 See Fayemi on Nigeria, Chapter 9, pp. 204–37 in this volume; Finer (1988); Koonings and Kruijt, Chapter 1, pp. 9–34 in this volume.

35 See Koonings and Kruijt, *ibid.*

36 *Ibid.*

37 See Addi on Algeria, Chapter 8, pp. 179–203 in this volume.

38 See Koonings and Kruijt, Chapter 1, pp. 9–34 in this volume.

39 Brett (1995: 133).

40 De Kadt (in press).

41 Brett (1995: 131).

42 See, for example, Martz (1994); Pearce (1990), and Watson (2000).

43 See Kruijt and Tello on Peru, Chapter 2, pp. 35–63 in this volume.

44 Brett (1995: 130).

45 Wilson (1992: 534 ff.).

46 Wilson (1992).

47 Wilson (1992: 581–2).

48 Wilson (1992).

49 Campbell (1992: 616).

50 Campbell (1992: 618).

51 Campbell (1992: 626).

52 Brett (1995: 131).

53 Griffiths (1996: 482).

54 Hale (1994).
55 McSherry (1997).
56 McSherry (1997: 271).
57 Mudoola (1994: 195).
58 Mudoola (1994: 203).
59 See the section on national integration, pp. 317–19 above.
60 See the section on problems of governance, pp. 320–1 above.
61 See Koonings and Kruijt, Chapter 1, pp. 9–34 in this volume.
62 See Fayemi on Nigeria, Chapter 9, pp. 204–37 in this volume.
63 See Koonings and Kruijt, Chapter 1, pp. 9–34 in this volume.
64 Griffiths (1996).
65 See Castro on Brazil, Chapter 4, pp. 90–110 in this volume.
66 See the section on civilian–military interplay, pp. 324–6 above.
67 McSherry (1997: 8).
68 *Ibid.*
69 See Fayemi on Nigeria, Chapter 9, pp. 204–37 in this volume.

# Epilogue

## Political armies
## between continuity and demise

### KEES KOONINGS and DIRK KRUIJT

Political armies show a series of shared characteristics despite the many differences and variations over time and from one country to another. In the first chapter we suggested that both common elements and differences revolve around:

1   the (self-ascribed) role of the military in the long-term project of nation building;
2   the elaboration of specific and often explicit ideologies and doctrines that bring politics and governance into the core business of the military;
3   the architecture of military rule, centring upon a partial or full militarization of the state and the political arena; and
4   the ambivalent relationship between the military and democracy, especially in the post-Cold War context.

To what extent do the country studies presented in this volume lend substance to these similarities and differences among political armies? In this epilogue we will examine these four issues against the backdrop of the country cases analysed in the book. The first section looks at the configuration of political armies and military rule in its relation to nation building, politico–military ideologies and doctrines, and the militarization of the state and politics. The two remaining sections discuss in more detail the ambiguities that arise from the post-Cold War reconsideration of the relationship between political armies and democracy.

## The Configuration of Political Armies

*Political armies and nation building*
The notion that political armies are at the core of nation building (through birth-right and competence) can be found in all cases studied in this book. In a number of countries there has been a 'real' historical relationship between the coming into existence of the nation as an independent and sovereign state (such as after an anti-colonial independence struggle, separatist war, or revolutionary transformation) and the political aspirations of the military institution.

Political armies founded upon wars waged for national independence can be found in Algeria, Eritrea, and Indonesia, and to a certain extent also in the former Socialist Federal Republic of Yugoslavia (in the sense that Tito's initially Partisan army successfully ended Nazi-German occupation). In these countries, the key role of the military in building national sovereignty has led, up to the present, to an active and sometimes consistent role in domestic politics and governance. It has contributed in large measure to bestowing upon the military what Addi has called the effective source of legitimate power,[1] and to a strong identification of the military with the very existence of the nation-state.

Political armies founded upon revolutionary transformations have come to the fore in Burma, Ethiopia (twice: in 1974 and 1991), Peru, Turkey, and – again to a certain extent – Serbia. These revolutionary episodes have, however, been quite different one from the other. In Turkey, the revolution consisted of defining a modern, territorial, secular and culturally homogeneous nation-state out of the remnants of the Ottoman Empire, and of safeguarding this new state, between 1918 and 1923, against the allied occupation forces and during the war with Greece.[2] In Ethiopia, a first moment of the constitution of a Marxist-Leninist political army 'from below' followed the overthrow of the empire in 1974. The Derg regime quickly turned into a harsh and doctrinaire dictatorship, against which a regionally founded military opposition movement arose, with final success in 1991. This 'second' revolution marked the beginning of a period in which this country's 'new model army' regime had to deal with complex issues of democracy, ethnic pluralism, adjustment of the economy, governance and border conflict.[3] In Peru, the armed forces set about to make their 'own' social revolution, against elite privileges, poverty and foreign dependence. In this country more than anywhere else, revolutionary change was a predominantly military initiative that, in addition, was brought about by the top brass of an existing and well-consolidated apparatus.[4] Only in Serbia has the transformative role of the military been less clear, indeed highly ambiguous. The initial act of the dissolution of Yugoslavia as a socialist and federal state ruled by a single party and supported by a politically activated people's army was marked by the failure of this army to prevent the disintegration of the country and to resist Serbian nationalism. During the 1990s, this army was cajoled into supporting this nationalism both domestically and in some of the breakaway republics, with devastating consequences. Only after Milošević's downfall have we witnessed the possibility of the Serbian (or new Yugoslav) military being an active force in consolidating the country's political system on a new footing.

Political armies born out of a revolution see the continuity and legitimacy of their political role as being strongly dependent upon the overall trajectory of the revolution itself. If a revolutionary model erodes or breaks down, to be eventually toppled by civic or armed opposition, the ability of the revolutionary military to continue to play a (legitimate) political role will be seriously undermined or even ended completely. Either a successor civilian regime (more or less democratic) will take over, as in Peru and recently in Serbia, in which case the military as an institution may well remain relatively unaffected (and may even be strengthened as part of a 'reconversion' programme) but its role as a political actor will have become untenable.[5] Or a revolution is brought down by armed opposition, in which case this rebel force may turn into a new political army sustaining (or even forming) the successor regime, as was the case in Ethiopia.

This leaves us with a number of cases in which the military have appropriated a founding role with respect to the nation-state without such a clear historical connection between original nation building and state formation and the operations of the current military institution. From the countries studied in this book, Brazil, Chile, Guatemala, and Nigeria fall into this category. The first three Latin American countries gained their national independence early in the nineteenth century, with some armed struggle involved (minimal in the Brazilian case), but with a clear temporal and institutional separation between the independence campaigns and the formation of genuinely national military institutions that took place only towards the final decades of the nineteenth century or even later. In Nigeria, the process of decolonization was civil and institutional, and the military only lost their image as a colonial hand-me-down after bringing the civil war to a successful conclusion in 1970. What constitutes these political armies in terms of their identification with national destiny is basically the 'competence principle', or stated differently, the idea that the military are crucial for the maintenance of the existing national order, and particularly national unity and the integrity of the state.

The Latin American examples bring to the fore the identification of these political armies with the integrity and security of the state. State formation and nation building in Latin America go back to the nineteenth century, but in the first instance these processes were driven by civil, economic and political elites, or oligarchies. Many of the manifestations of political militarism from the early twentieth century onwards were directed against these oligarchies because they were seen as selfish, anti-modern, and anti-national. From the 1920s to the 1950s, most Latin American political armies sought connections with so-called populist forces that were economically nationalist, socially reformist and politically oriented towards state centralization and the controlled incorporation of the popular masses. Only after the Second World War did the Latin American political armies take on a more clearly defined conservative stance, in which the defence of the 'national order' was seen as guaranteeing state security against internal threats, and promoting national development along capitalistic lines. The eruption of political conflicts, in various ways related to the problems of reformist nationalism and populism, was now seen as the manifestation of internal threats to the state and the economic and social order this represented. So the connection between political militarism and the long-term fate of the nation was the protection of the state, and societal interests linked to that state, against real or perceived political opponents.[6]

Elsewhere, political armies appear to play a much more foundational role in state building although the military had no direct hand in bringing about national independence. In Nigeria from the mid-1960s onwards there was much more at stake, in the eyes of the military, than just the security of the state. The very survival of the country as a single nation seemed in jeopardy owing to political confrontations and imminent ethnic and regional fragmentation. In fact, this *raison d'être* of political armies is more deeply linked to the problems of state formation and nation building on the basis of socially and culturally highly diverse imperial or colonial constructs. In these situations the state itself has to be carved out almost from scratch. Ethiopia offers another example, where the monarchy ultimately failed to deliver upon the challenge of national unity, modernization and social reform leading to the socialist-military revolution of 1974.

In a certain sense, all political armies act as caretakers of national destiny, either through state protection or formation, the guaranteeing of core national values and objectives (such as secularism within the state and public life in Turkey), or even national unity as such. In some cases, political armies therefore consider themselves as the ultimate source of political legitimacy: quite clearly so in Algeria and Burma, in a more veiled way in Turkey and Guatemala. In most other cases analysed here, political armies respond to a more specifically defined need for their intervention and rule, while at the same time implicitly or explicitly acknowledging the 'people' or the 'nation' as the source of sovereignty.

*Ideologies and doctrines*
This brings us to the second issue: that of the ideology and doctrines of political armies. As we suggested in Chapter 1, such ideologies and doctrines serve to translate the foundational orientation of political armies into more specific guidelines for political intervention or direct rule. In Latin America, the doctrines of political armies stayed closest to notions derived from military life as a profession. New professionalism, as pointed out by Stepan, offered a doctrine for political intervention that was directly derived from conventional military strategizing.[7] The doctrine of 'national security' that underpinned the conservative military regimes of Brazil, Chile and Guatemala had at its core a notion of 'enemies' and 'threats' posed by radical ('communist') opposition against the prevailing order embodied in the state.[8] Since these threats were not only military, but also political, social and moral, a military counter-strategy that only addressed the issue of armed insurgency 'from within' would be insufficient. Potential armed opponents, the economic and social conditions that produced them, and the political space they might find as a result of 'civil inadequacy' could only be dealt with through the militarization of politics and of the state itself. Therefore, the comprehensive security doctrines of Latin America's conservative political armies included not only counter-insurgency,[9] but also political control, the neutralization (through state terror) of non-armed opponents, and economic and social development.[10] Nevertheless, for the *Latino* political armies this was clearly defined as a war to be won, even if in actuality very few armed confrontations took place, as in the case of Brazil.[11]

In other parts of the globe, ideologies and specific doctrines of political armies offer a more diverse panorama. Of the country cases discussed in this book, Indonesia's military developed the most explicit politico–military doctrine, one that bore resemblances to Latin American security doctrines (partly because of the similar insertion of the Suharto regime in a Cold War anti-Communist logic).[12] The dual function doctrine specified the key role of the Indonesian military, not only in defence matters but also in public administration and even in the economy, right down into every crack and hole of society. On the other end of the spectrum we find Turkey, where a 'guardian' political army adheres to Atatürkism, that is to say, the secular, democratic and unitary nature of Turkey.[13] This doctrine has spurred the military into directly taking over state power on three brief occasions, but the Turkish military use this doctrine principally to supervise civilian politics and to pressure these into conformity with the founding principles, for instance against the rise of political Islam during the 1990s. The military act as ultimate arbiters with respect to these core national values.

In between these two poles the case studies in this book show a variety of doctrinaire positions adopted by political armies. We may suggest another remarkable binary opposition: between military adherence to originally non-military ideologies and doctrines, particularly socialism, on the one hand, and the simple assertion of the birthright or duty to exercise power, on the other hand. Remarkably, some political armies discussed here have often oscillated between these two situations (or more precisely, combined the two in practice). The military of Algeria, Ethiopia and Burma at certain stages adhered to one or another form of homespun socialism. In Algeria and Ethiopia, this was originally linked to a broader political movement mobilizing against French colonial rule and the Haile Selassie imperial state, respectively, but this soon evolved into naked rule (directly by the military Derg in Ethiopia, indirectly through unconditional guardianship in Algeria). In Burma, the military's 'garrison socialism' also served to adorn its adopted position as the essence of state power: a government of 'first resort'.[14] Finally, in Yugoslavia, the military were drawn into supporting non-military party and regime ideologies, first that of socialism and pluri-national federalism and subsequently that of Serbian ethno-nationalism. It appears that, anyway, in the course of time exalted ideologies espoused by political armies tend to collapse or to be traded in for more realistic approaches to the use of military power in the political arena.

*The militarization of the state and politics*
The third issue that we pick up briefly here is that of the organization and orientation of military political involvement. Much of the ground has already been covered by De Kadt in the previous chapter, on the basis of Hale's typology of veto, guardian and ruler political armies.[15] Luckham provides another typology of military politics: corporate, instrumental, quasi-partisan, fragmented, or even non-state military involvement in politics.[16] These or other typologies are based on both the 'form' and the 'content' military involvement in politics (or the political absorption of the military) can adopt. Most political armies discussed in this book combine several of these characteristics or pass through them in sequences or cycles. In addition, distinctions can be drawn with respect to the developmental orientation of military regimes (neo-liberal in Chile, state capitalist in Brazil, Indonesia and Nigeria, nationalist-reformist in Algeria and Peru, or socialist in Ethiopia, Burma and Yugoslavia), or to the role of personalism in the consolidation of military rule: weak in Algeria (after Boumédiènne), Brazil, Guatemala, Turkey, stronger in Chile (Pinochet), Nigeria (Babangida and Abacha), Ethiopia (Mengistu), Burma (Ne Win), and Indonesia (Suharto). Here we just want to draw attention to two institutional dimensions of the organization of the military: the shaping of a militarized state political arena, and the problem of broader political (civil) support for political armies.

The shaping of a militarized state breaks down into several aspects. We can look at the way the strategic orientation of military involvement in politics takes shape, institutionally and politically. And then there is the issue of the organization of politico-military surveillance and control, which in turn leads to the examination of the potential tensions between the military-as-regime and the military-as-institution. The institutionalization of the strategic orientation of political armies particularly regards the ruler-type regimes. Usually, some combination of an intra-institutional *politburo* or political council and a (military-dominated) platform for civil–military political supervision and policy guidance is set up within or above the normal institutional framework of the state. Political councils can be seen as the strategic nucleus of military quasi-parties that directly prepare or direct politics and policies. We just list some examples: the high-level officers political committee (COAP) in Peru that advised President Velasco and the junta between 1968 and 1975; the successive bodies underpinning military rule in Burma (from the BSPP, a real military party, to the SLORC and SPDC councils in the late 1980s and the 1990s); in Nigeria the Supreme Military Council (SMC) oversaw the military commander/president, at least prior to the Babangida regime of the 1980s; a fourth typical example is provided by the Derg, the revolutionary committee of the Ethiopian regime between 1974 and 1991. In many cases, these policy bodies maintained links to high-level military training institutions with which basic doctrinal and policy orientations were shared and from which expertise could be recruited.

The creation of top-level entities to provide strategic guidance to politics and policy issues that involved the top military brass and the leading civilian representatives of military-dominated regimes was a common feature of all the political armies discussed here. The function of such entities in general was to assert military domination of policy formation while at the same time incorporating civil views and interests deemed legitimate. As a result, elementary consensus and legitimacy on broad policy issues could be engineered. The typical format for such an entity was the 'national security council' that supervised the domestic and foreign policy agendas. The usefulness of such councils lies among other things in their flexibility and durability: security councils serve both ruler and guardian regimes, as has been demonstrated in countries like Brazil, Chile, Guatemala and Turkey where national security councils continued to convey the military voice in policy matters after the formal transition or return to civil democracy. The attributes of national security councils were as a rule firmly institutionalized, which gave military tutelage a distinct flavour of legitimacy. The case of Algeria is an interesting exception, because there the usurpation of political power by the military has been by and large informal, implicit, or unspoken. The practice of controlling access to the office of the presidency rather than the institutionalization of military control was at the heart of military politics in this country.

Military surveillance and control – at least in ruler-type or corporate regimes – is closely linked to the fundamental problem of the separation between the military-as-regime and the military-as-institution. One could add a third and a fourth configuration to the latter: the military-as-repressive-apparatus and the military-as-economic-stakeholder. Without dwelling on details (many of which are analysed in the country chapters) the basic tensions here lie in the inherent threat posed to the military-as-institution by the military taking on any of the other three roles. Being immersed in the daily administrative details of government or business may be seen as a distraction from military professionalism. In countries such as Guatemala, Indonesia, Burma or Nigeria, the militarization of the routine administration of the country and significant parts of the economy seriously influenced the organization and outlook of the conventional armed forces. When political armies are drawn into the political arena (Brazil, Nigeria, Indonesia, and spectacularly Ethiopia under the Derg, among others) they may become receptive to political vices such as personalism, factionalism, infighting and reprisal, or corruption. Finally, the repression that almost certainly accompanies military rule is prone to affect the institution at large, with respect not only to its operational capabilities but also and especially to its moral standing and self-image. Therefore, without exception, the security apparatus has been taking on a pivotal role within military-dominated regimes. The open or hidden rise of intelligence and security agencies reflected the repressive practices of political armies, as well as the increasing need for internal and external surveillance and control through systematic information gathering, the organization of permanent supervision through informants or political commissars, and widespread practices of repression, intimidation and political blackmail.

We will only dwell briefly on the issue of broader political, hence civil support for political armies. As a general rule, political armies need civilian allies or backers for reasons of legitimacy, expertise, or policy implementation. The most immediate form this can take is the association of apolitical technocrats with the policy agenda of military regimes. This has been typical of Latin America, but also of countries like Nigeria, Thailand, South Korea and Indonesia.[17] In such cases, the ascendancy of technocrats is often associated with a more general affinity between the political army and economic and societal elite groups that share a common aim of economic development. More systematic political formulas for engineering support for military politics include the formation of political parties led by or supportive of the military, or alliances between a political army and social or popular movements, preferably under controlled conditions.

The formation of supportive parties has proved quite difficult for political armies, probably for the basic reason that the militarization of politics aims at the kind of 'anti-politics' that is supposed to do away with the 'vices' of political parties.[18] In countries where relatively sustainable political parties served as a back-up to military rule, these parties were set up and run by strong civilian actors within the reduced spaces of political society: ARENA in Brazil, the FLN in Algeria and Golkar in Indonesia are the clearest examples. Examples are also provided by Burma and Ethiopia, where the military regimes set up control parties in the 1970s and 1980s, respectively. In many other cases, efforts to set up military parties either failed or produced ephemeral results (as in Nigeria, where personalism, factionalism and prebendalism affected parties and the military alike), or were not even attempted at all.

The relationship between political armies and popular movements provides a number of fascinating situations. Political armies here tend to face the dilemma between, on the one hand, the political gain that can be derived from linking up to (or better: controlling) broad popular movements, and on the other hand the political risks that political armies fear from uncontrolled, radicalized or revolutionary movements. Two contrasting examples, Peru and Ethiopia, serve to illustrate this. During the reformist military regime of General Velasco in Peru (1968–75), the military came to realize the necessity of enlisting popular support for its reform agenda. Therefore, the regime allowed for the functioning of existing peasant and worker organizations and the setting-up of new mass movements. However, a bureaucratic structure was created to supervise and control the popular organizations. This bureaucracy, SINAMOS, was key to the formation, recognition and functioning of mass organizations, and was born out of explicit fear within the military hierarchy that linking up to a mass political party would be dangerous and undesirable.[19] In Ethiopia after 1974 a somewhat inverse process took place, as Luckham shows in Chapter 10 of this volume. Subaltern officers within the army rode the crest of a broader popular revolution against the imperial state. Soon, however, the military took control of the revolution, first by institutionalizing hierarchical relations with the popular movements through the Provisional Office for Mass Organizational Affairs (POMOA), but then by unleashing indiscriminate violence against civilian sectors during the 'Red Terror' of the late 1970s.

Political armies and mass organizations make for unlikely or at least uneasy bedfellows. This has been the experience of the successors to the Derg regime in Eritrea and Ethiopia. Both the EPLF and the TPFL/EPRDF faced the challenge of readdressing their legacy of army parties enjoying widespread popular support –successful during the war with the Derg regime – into something approaching the separation of a professionalized military institution, a state apparatus, and political and civil society under the professed *desideratum* of building democratic governance.[20]

## Political Armies after the End of the Cold War

The final key issue, the relationship between political armies and democracy, deserves separate attention. As we suggested in Chapter 1, political armies have been facing the democratization agenda despite the fundamental ambiguity that characterizes a military view of civil democratic politics. This has been especially pressing after the end of the Cold War as various combinations of internal and external pressure have been eating into efforts to prolong or reinstall direct military rule or military-controlled authoritarian regimes.

The key issues at stake appear to be: the institutionalization of democracy; the reassertion of civil supremacy in civil–military relations; dealing with legacies of violent repression and gross human rights violations; the abolishing of old and new forms of coercive capacity by the military, paramilitary and intelligence agencies; the formulation of new non-politicized military missions and corresponding self-images; and, last but not least, challenges in dealing in a non-coercive way with state rebuilding, territorial unity, societal diversity (especially ethnic), and globalized development. This and the following sections look into these problems. This section tries to do so by briefly picking up on the three post-Cold War scenarios suggested in Chapter 1 with respect to the fate of political armies. Obviously, these scenarios should be seen as ideal types, elements of which are visible in various combinations in all cases reviewed here. In addition, scenarios are not to be confused with firm trajectories or certain outcomes. Setbacks, reversals or turn-arounds are never far away in politics, and particularly when political armies are concerned. One could indeed imagine the three scenarios as connected poles of a triangular continuum; specific country cases being placed dynamically along the three sides of the triangle. The countries analysed in this book may be placed – with the necessary caution symbolized by the question marks in the headings of the following sections – close to one of the three scenarios.

*Withering away?*
This scenario presupposes the reconstitution of democratic rule and especially the reaffirmation of civilian dominance within civil–military relations. Necessary conditions for this scenario to materialize appear to be that there is an available resource pool of civil democratic institutions, party politics and civil society that can be drawn upon from a pre-military past. In addition, the transition to

democracy must be institutional and peaceful, supported by broad segments of the population. Finally, the transition has to be accepted by a military that maintains its institutional cohesion and is therefore able and willing to negotiate a pacted exit from the centre stage of politics.[21] Subsequent democratic consolidation has to progress under conditions of relative institutional stability, enjoying ongoing popular approval and contributing to a thorough reformulation of civil–military relations and military roles in a non-political direction.

Of the cases analysed here, Brazil seems to have come closest to this pole of the ideal-type triangle. Since 1985, or even earlier, the institutional dimension of democratic consolidation in Brazil has been remarkably successful and durable. Civil society has been greatly strengthened, opening up spaces for wider political participation. Electoral politics has contributed to the progressive removal of the military from politics. As Castro shows in Chapter 4 of this volume, the defeat of the military in the battle for 'memory' has also made a return to active political intervention by the Brazilian military increasingly difficult. This is not to say that democracy in Brazil is flawless. However, key problems related to the political institutions and above all to the problem of underclass exclusion, widespread poverty and endemic everyday (criminal, social, and police) violence unleashed against the excluded, do not appear to make political militarism imminent in this country.[22]

Chile and Turkey have shown comparable progress in the consolidation of institutional democracy, but both countries display some elements that remove them, perhaps, somewhat further from the 'withering away' ideal type. In the first place we can observe, in both countries, the maintenance of high levels of support for the army or the legacy of military politics within public opinion. As is argued by Güney in Chapter 7 of this volume, the Turkish army figures among the most trusted institutions in the country, while a public opinion majority subscribes to the military dogma of secular politics. In Chile, close to half of the electorate upholds support for a right-wing or conservative political platform that is the direct successor to the legacy of the Pinochet regime. This has been reflected in the preservation of a strong and confident position by the military-as-institution in relation to politics. In addition, both countries display actual or potential complications with respect to democratic consolidation that keep the military on edge: fundamentalist political Islam and Kurdish nationalism in Turkey, the legacy of human rights violations and the related issue of the charges brought to bear against Pinochet.

Finally, Nigeria also appears ready to experience a 'withering away'. After decades of erratic political militarism, the military seemed totally discredited in the face of widespread clamour for a return to democracy, voiced by a diverse and active civil society. During the past few years, progress has been made in the field of institutional changes. However, the traditional flaws of the political process have not yet been removed, while fault lines along regional, ethnic or religious lines are manifold. When one adds the proliferation of violence and the fundamental problem of the rule of law in the country to this, the prospect for ending political militarism seems by no means certain.

*Institutionalized modification?*

This scenario implies the preservation of political militarism as an institutional phenomenon, either as an impediment to full-fledged civil democracy or as a powerful force behind a thin veil of formal democratic rule. In this scenario political armies hold on to their trusted notions of political control, or redesign them to adapt to changing circumstances (like the discourse of democracy, the end of communism, etcetera). The clearest case discussed here has been Burma. Almost two decades of socialist military rule was followed, almost smoothly, by a new phase of military supremacy as a response to the outbursts of pro-democratic opposition in the late 1980s and during the 1990s. As Smith shows in Chapter 11 of this volume, the Burmese military have deliberately modified their political strategy by dumping the socialist doctrine and instead declaring themselves committed to nation building, modernization and development. In the process, democracy is accepted in theory (as long as it remains 'disciplined'), while appeasement of the ethnic uprisings in the borderlands has been more actively sought. At the same time, the democratic opposition appears to be too weak and disarticulated to make, up till now, serious inroads against military supremacy.

Similarly, in Guatemala, the military, a dominant force throughout the twentieth century and all-powerful between 1960 and 1985, espoused a new doctrine of 'national stability' that was meant to underscore continuing military control of national political life. Facing the challenge of accepting democracy and reaching a 'strategic peace' with the guerrillas, the preservation of the institutional foundations of the Guatemalan political army was set out in a 'plan' or a 'project' leading, as shown by Schirmer in Chapter 3 of this volume, to a practice of 'co-governance' for guided or armoured democracy, with the military as senior partners to the weak and divided civilian politicians. Although the peace agreement of 1996 and subsequent developments (especially the strengthening of an indigenous grassroots civil society)[23] seem to have weakened this project considerably, Guatemala is still a long way from putting a decisive end to political militarism.

Indonesia also shows many signs of the institutionalized modification scenario. Despite the popular dissatisfaction with the military, and the legacy of Suharto's New Order more generally, the military remain powerful players, especially in the face of the growing problems experienced by the Wahid government and the ongoing threats of regional separatism and destabilization. In the process, as Schulte Nordholt shows in Chapter 6 of this volume, the Indonesian military actively seek to redefine the doctrinaire foundations of their 'new' national role, conceived as 'back to the basics': military guardianship over basic national interests.

Algeria's institutional modification scenario is much harder to pin down, because it is not expressed in a formally acknowledged political role of the military. As Addi has argued in Chapter 8 of this volume, the military's claim to ultimate political sovereignty is almost unspoken but put into daily practice. Not unlike the Turkish case, the Algerian military claim to have protected the country against the demise of democracy that would certainly have followed the materialization of the Islamist victory in the 1991 elections. But since then the military have been quite active in pursuing a violent course against the Islamists, while controlling the government and society at large through the security apparatus. So political militarism is upheld to protect the state, which in practice means the undisputed hegemony of the military over state power.

Finally, Ethiopia and Eritrea provide examples of a quite thorough and unique form of institutional modification. In both countries, comparable and related army parties brought down a violent military regime in 1991. Since then, both armies have sought a partial rupture with their own backgrounds as leftist, revolutionary independence movements in order to adopt the paradigm of the non-political professional military under democratic surveillance. This has proved a difficult agenda in view of the initial strength and legitimacy of both movements and the fear that the fledgling process of national reconstruction could easily be jeopardized if the new armies let go too hastily of their political role.

The general conditions that make the institutional modification scenario likely are, in the first place, a weak or non-existent legacy of civil and democratic institutions and practices: this will weaken pro-democracy movements and actual civil governments. Second, if the military, while not necessarily enjoying prestige or support, have remained basically cohesive, they will be able to wield considerable power within the political arena and in controlling the state apparatus. Finally, if a perceived threat remains with respect to national unity or state security, this will nourish military fears of the adverse consequences associated with giving up their political role, and make institutional modification more likely.

*Perversion and corruption?*
When political armies are unable to put their political aspirations on a firm institutional footing, and at the same time the conditions for strengthening democratic governance seem to be bleak, a scenario of perversion and corruption of military politics becomes likely. Weak or contested civil rule often means a failure to settle basic bones of contention according to peaceful, consociational and institutional principles, with ongoing instability and violence as the most problematic result. Political armies and their non-military allies who, in such circumstances, have lost the capacity to revamp institutional militarism, are prone to seek recourse to more shadowy means to exert power. In many cases this means the use of informal types of coercion and violence that start to erode the nation-building role of the military, eat into their institutional integrity, and finally bring down their monopoly over the effective means of coercion. In such a situation, the result can be a *de facto* authoritarian regime in connivance with the formal military apparatus, but increasingly resting upon parallel power mechanisms provided by the intelligence services, paramilitary, private or criminal armed entities. In the most cynical form of this scenario, such regimes and their military pledge their adherence to democracy and the rule of law while at the same time making a mockery of these very principles. Since the perpetrators of the violations of these principles are formally outside the ambit of the state, perverted regimes and political armies may easily disclaim responsibility while in fact they seek to continue their control over power and resources through 'dark forces' and murky means.

Precisely because of the hidden quality of this scenario, it is hard to put any example squarely at this end of the triangle. At the same time, many of the cases discussed here provide elements that would fit into the scenario. At first sight, Peru and Serbia during the 1990s seem to fit the bill. In both countries, an eventually authoritarian non-military regime built up a power structure that, rather than responding to military interests, pressed the military into a broader system of arbitrary rule in which power mechanisms had to be shared with the secret service, parallel military and paramilitary entities, and various kinds of organized crime.[24] Both regimes coupled hardly hidden authoritarianism with arbitrariness and the routine use of political violence. Ironically, in both Peru and Serbia the emergence of this scenario brought the demise of political armies that, up to that time, had prided themselves on their key role in supporting national integration and social reform. It took years of protest by the civil opposition in both countries to bring down these regimes and to help redirect the military (in a still uncertain way) away from perversion and towards support for democracy.

Similar problems of perversion and corruption have come to the fore in many other cases such as Indonesia, Algeria, Nigeria and, emblematically, Colombia (not discussed here because of the absence of a clear political army, although with no lack of political violence). In Indonesia, many observers have pointed at the involvement of the military in organizing or allowing paramilitary and gang-like armed upheavals in East and West Timor and the Moluccan Islands. In Algeria, there may be no certainty with respect to the precise background of armed mass assassination gangs and their relationship to the Islamist militants or Military Security. In Nigeria, the proliferation of violence as part of the fragmented militarization of social and political relations is seriously questioning the feasibility of democratic restoration, as is argued by Fayemi in Chapter 9 of this volume. These examples are by no means complete but serve to show that the ultimate result of military politics and the use of coercion in politics may well be not nation building and the strengthening of the state, but the opposite.

## Political Armies in the Age of Democracy: elements of a reform agenda

Against such adversities, what prospects can we see, in a more normative sense, for curbing the role of political armies while strengthening civil supremacy and democratic governance? The armed forces are the strong arm of the state. Like all the other integral parts of the public sector – the ministries and the decentralized bureaucracies, the police, the tax and revenue institutions, etcetera – the armed forces ideally should be subject to control by parliament and government, the standard rule of a well-functioning democracy. The abolition of political army status and the self-attributed nation-building task of the armed forces is the basic problem of good civil–military relations under the democratic rule of law. That implies an undisputed equilibrium between the recognized and accepted security mission of the military institutions and the recognized and accepted power and control mechanisms of civilian society and elected rulers. This good balance between civilians and the military requires an *a priori* decision to strengthen and consolidate the vital functions of the public institutions that regulate the stability of civil – and not only electoral – democracy. Without a stable democracy and without a secure, efficient and coherent civilian public sector, a civilian legal and court system, a civilian police and public order system, the problem of military interference in politics, the threat of *pronunciamentos*, coups and self-coups will remain.

On the other side, a long-term consequence of political armies is a large group of officers who, during the better part of their military careers, were engaged in political activities – acting as minister, vice-minister, director-general, director or adviser in the public sector, or as manager in one of the public enterprises – during the long years of (civil–military or military) government in the past. Most of these military politicians and public administrators acquired managerial efficiency in civilian matters. Military interference in national politics does not depend on the magnitude of the armed forces, the volume of the military budget or the sophistication of the army's equipment. It depends mostly on the tradition of political soldiers, on the unfamiliarity of elected politicians with security issues and military matters, and on the remnants of 'societies of fear' created by the combined proclivity to state terror of most military regimes, and the enlarged role of the (military) intelligence and security apparatus that has tended to prosper and expand under military rule.[25] Ultimately, only the reinforcement of the competence of the public sector and the maturity and stability of the institutions of civil society will terminate the zero-sum situation in which the military necessarily play a prominent role in the political arena. As the contributors to a recent publication on the liquidation of the legacy of tutelage left by Latin American dictatorships conclude,[26] the 'transition from dictatorship to the normalcy of democratic rule' will take a period of 15 to 20 years. It involves the consolidation of a new generation of military thinkers and an officer corps familiar with the functioning of democracy. It calls for a new generation of politicians who can handle the paradoxical requirements of political stability and the necessity of compromise: a centre–left or centre–right coalition that incorporates the political middle instead of ultra–rightist or ultra–leftist political factions in control. And it involves a new generation of public servants and a mature electorate that has lost its fear of military leadership and will not remain silent under subtle threats.

A successful exit strategy from the dominance of political armies requires, in the first place, the re-design of an army, a navy and an air force in relation to the significance of their basic military tasks: professional defence of the national territory and professional defence against specified external threats and internal disasters. As Fayemi argues in Chapter 9 of this book,[27] that requires a parliamentary impetus towards the definition of new military and security missions, the development of civilian expertise for legislative supervision, the acceptance of professional autonomy of the military leadership under democratic control, and – in most countries with strong ethnic differences – an appropriate solution to the challenge of ethnonationalism in recruitment. Similar conclusions can be drawn from an ongoing research-cum-policy project in Guatemala, where – four years after the peace agreements that concluded 36 years of civil war – politicians and researchers, jointly with military representatives and government advisers, are redrafting the national security agenda.[28]

It also requires redefinition of the legal or semi-legal incentives for political presence within the nation-state, revising the existing too-vague constitutional provisions that allocate to the armed forces the task of 'protecting the national interest'. It requires, in the third place, an intelligent dismantling of the legal and semi-legal 'immunity and impunity climate' favouring the military and establishing their virtually separate status and exclusion from society: from armed forces' supermarkets to armed forces' banks. It requires, of course, a well-defined separation between military defence tasks and the tasks of the police in maintaining civil order. It requires the redefinition of army, navy and air force intelligence to confine these activities to core military affairs. An all-embracing and omnipotent state security apparatus, run by the military without explicit civilian control mechanisms, is a core element in the blueprint of a police state. It requires a certain modesty in the definition of the tasks and virtues of civil–military training institutions such as Brazili's National Intelligence Service, Peru's Centre of Advanced Military Services and Guatemala's Centre of National Stability Studies:[29] in the long run, civil society is better off with a competent public sector, whose able bureaucrats and capable technocrats are trained in civilian institutions, than with civil servants and leaders of organized civil society who are encouraged to think in terms of military solutions.

Perhaps a keen eye is also required in the definition of new missions. Involvement of the military in police tasks, use of the special forces in anti-riot operations and other duties against the civilian population will re-emphasize the role of the armed forces as repressive forces. Involvement in anti-narcotics operations implies the risk of institutional corruption. The use of the military as a police force or as anti-narcotics brigades undermines both the armed forces and civilian institutions like the urban and rural police and other, more specialized agencies with their own qualities, their own professionalism and their own *esprit de corps*. The protection of the environment does not justify the budget, the equipment and the specialized training spent on equipping the military institutions for this role. Besides, it disqualifies other civilian organizations such as the rangers, the foresters, even the boy scouts. A strong emphasis on civic–military action and other local development activities, again, does not justify the existence of the armed forces and weakens the functioning of the public sector and civilian authorities in the provinces. Only peacekeeping operations seem to be both prestigious and adequate as a new task for military professionals. Moreover, they give the armed forces a well-deserved standing and the multilateral postings abroad reduce overall dependence on unilateral foreign influences.

The basic problem, however, remains the strengthening of the civilian institutions of the state and society: a good and competent government, a respectable parliament, an efficient legal system with basic justice, and a competent public sector. That requires training institutions for civilian higher echelons. That requires a well-organized and well-paid urban and rural police with its own ambience of operations. It requires some new, competent professional agencies, operating against the narco-economy and narco-violence, against organized crime and criminal associations. It requires the presence of the public sector, with civilian authority and with a reasonable budget, in the remote regions and the under-developed areas. And it presupposes a long-term strategy against mass poverty, against second-class citizenship based on ethnic criteria and marginalizing characteristics, and against social exclusion. When the minimum conditions for social welfare are fulfilled, the stability of the democratic institutions and the foundations of civil society will be such that military hegemony in the national politics of societies like those studied in this book will cease to be an urgent and unavoidable topic.

## Notes and References

1 See Addi on Algeria, Chapter 8, pp. 178–203 in this volume.
2 See Güney on Turkey, Chapter 7, pp. 162–78 in this volume; also Özbudun (1995).
3 See Luckham on Ethiopia and Eritrea, Chapter 10, pp. 238–69 in this volume.
4 See Kruijt and Tello on Peru, Chapter 2, pp. 35–63 in this volume. See also Kruijt (1994) for a full treatment of the revolutionary period of the Peruvian military, 1968–75.
5 This might be a likely outcome, or at least one hoped for by many, in Burma as well.
6 See Perelli (1990) for a discussion of the notion of 'threat'.
7 See Stepan (1971, 1976).
8 See Zagorski (1992).
9 In fact, in countries such as Argentina, Brazil and Chile this was only a minor aspect of 'national security'. Military counter-insurgency was more prominent in countries where

open armed conflict developed: Guatemala, El Salvador, Colombia, among others. Counter-insurgency notions were mainly developed through the connections with the US military assistance and training programmes. See Barber and Neale Ronning (1966).

10 See also Silva (2000b: 12).
11 See Castro on Brazil, Chapter 4, pp. 99–110 in this volume.
12 See Schulte Nordholt on Indonesia, Chapter 6, pp. 135–61 in this volume.
13 See Güney on Turkey, Chapter 7, pp. 162–78 in this volume.
14 See Smith on Burma, Chapter 11, pp. 270–96 in this volume.
15 See De Kadt, Chapter 13, pp. 313–32 in this volume; also Hale (1994).
16 See Luckham on Ethiopia and Eritrea, Chapter 10, pp. 238–69 in this volume.
17 See O'Donnell (1973); Chai-Anan (1995); Silva (2000a); Steinberg (1995).
18 See Loveman and Davies (1978) for the notion of 'anti-politics' in the Latin American context.
19 See Kruijt (1994: 116–21).
20 See Luckham on Ethiopia and Eritrea, Chapter 10, pp. 238–69 in this volume.
21 See O'Donnell and Schmitter (1986).
22 See Koonings (1999); Kingstone and Power (2000).
23 See Krznaric (1999) and Koonings (2001) for overviews.
24 See Kruijt and Tello on Peru, Chapter 2, pp. 35–63, and Gow on Serbia, Chapter 12, pp. 297–312, both in this volume.
25 See our previous analysis in Koonings and Kruijt (1999).
26 We quote from the manuscript of the volume edited by Arévalo de León (in press).
27 See Fayemi on Nigeria, Chapter 9, pp. 204–37 in this volume.
28 See Arévalo de León et al. (2000). This document is the official first draft of a new security statement that defines revised missions for the armed forces, the police and the intelligence community.
29 See Chapter 1 of this book, p. 22.

# Bibliography

## A

Abbink, J. (1995) 'Breaking and making the state: the dynamics of ethnic democracy in Ethiopia', *Journal of Contemporary African Studies*, 13, 2, pp. 149–63.

Abbink, J (1998) 'Briefing: the Eritrean–Ethiopian border dispute', *Africa Affairs*, 97, pp. 551–65.

Addi, Lahouari (1990) *L'Impasse du populisme*, Alger: ENA.

Addi, Lahouari (1993) 'La notion d'autorité politiqueet d'idéologie étatique', *Cahiers Internationaux de Sociologie*, June 1993, pp. 145–60.

Addi, Lahouari (1994) *L'Algérie et la Democratie*, Paris: La Découverte.

Addi, Lahouari (1996) 'Algeria's tragic contradictions', *Journal of Democracy*, 7, 3, pp. 94–107.

Addi, Lahouari (1997) 'Algeria's army, Algeria's agony', *Foreign Affairs*, August 1997, pp. 44–54.

Addi, Lahouari (1998) 'L'armée algérienne à la conquête du pouvoir', *Le Monde Diplomatique*, February 1998.

Addi, Lahouari (1999a) 'L'armée algérienne se divise', *Le Monde Diplomatique*, March 1999.

Addi, Lahouari (1999b) *Les mutations de la société algérienne. Famille et lien social dans l'Algérie contemporaine*, Paris: La Découverte.

Adekanye, J. 'Bayo (1981) *Nigeria in Search of Stable Civil–Military Relations*, Boulder, Colorado: Westview Press.

Adekanye, J. 'Bayo (1993) *Military Occupation and Social Stratification*, Ibadan: University of Ibadan.

Adekanye, J. 'Bayo (1997) 'Ethiopian case: disarming ethnic guerrillas, power-sharing and transition to democracy'. Unpublished manuscript, PRIO, Oslo.

Adekanye, J 'Bayo (1997) 'The military'. In Larry Diamond *et al.*, *Transition Without End: Nigerian Politics and Civil Society under Babangida*, Colorado: Lynne Rienner.

Adhana Haile Adhana (1994) 'Mutation of statehood and contemporary politics'. In

Zegeye and Pausewang (eds), *Ethiopia in Change*, London: British Academic Press, pp. 12–29.

Ageron, Charles-Robert (1967) *Les Algériens Musulmans et la France*, Paris: PUF (2 vols).

Agüero, Felipe (1993) 'Chile: South America's success story?', *Current History*, 92, 572, March 1993, pp. 130–5.

Agüero, Felipe (1995) *Soldiers, Civilians, and Democracy: Post-Franco Spain in Comparative Perspective*, Baltimore and London: Johns Hopkins University Press.

Agüero, Felipe (1997) 'Toward civilian supremacy in South America'. In Larry Diamond, Marc. F. Plattner, Yun-han Chu, and Hung-mao Tien (eds), *Consolidating the Third Wave Democracies*, Baltimore: Johns Hopkins University Press, 1997.

Agüero, Felipe (1998a) *Brechas en la Democratización: Las visiones de la elite política sobre las fuerzas armadas*, Chile: Flacso (Nueva Serie Flacso).

Agüero, Felipe (1998b) 'Chile's lingering authoritarian legacy', *Current History*, 97, 616, February 1998, pp. 66–70.

Agüero, Felipe (1998c) 'Conflicting assessments of democratization: exploring the fault lines'. In Felipe Agüero and Jeffrey Stark (eds), *Fault Lines of Democracy in Post-Transition Latin America*, Coral Gables: North–South Center Press, pp. 1–20.

Agüero, Felipe *et al.* (1998) 'Votantes, partidos e información política: la frágil intermediación política en el Chile posautoritario', *Revista de Ciencia Política* (Santiago) XIX, 2.

Agüero, Felipe and Jaime Gazmuri (1988) *Chile en el Umbral de los Noventa, Quince Años que condicionan el Futuro*, Santiago: Editorial Planeta.

Agüero, Felipe and Jeffrey Stark (eds) (1998) *Fault Lines of Democracy in Post-Transition Latin America*, Coral Gables: North–South Center Press.

Aguilera Peralta (1988) 'The hidden war. Guatemala's counter-insurgency campaign'. In Nora Hamilton *et al.* (eds), *Crisis in Central America*, Boulder: Westview Press, pp. 153–72.

Agyeman-Duah, B (1998) 'Liberia: the search for stable civil–military relations', paper presented at the Workshop on State Rebuilding after State Collapse in Liberia, Centre for Democracy and Development, London, 19 June 1998.

Ahmad, Z. H. and H. Crouch (1985) *Military–Civilian Relations in South-East Asia*, New York: Oxford University Press.

Alemseged Tesfai (1999) 'Issues of governance in the Eritrean context'. In Martin Doornbos and Alemseged Tesfai, *Post-Conflict Eritrea*, Asmara: Red Sea Press, pp. 239–323.

Amnesty International (1992) *Myanmar: 'No Law at All': Human Rights Violations under Military Rule*, London: Amnesty International.

'An approach to the pacification strategy', *Comando en Acción*, 8, 28, pp. 44–51 (1999).

*Annuaire de l'Afrique du Nord*, Paris: CNRS (1966).

'A paso lento', *Informe Anual sobre la Región Andina*, Lima: Comisión Andina de Juristas (1999).

Arévalo de Leon, Bernardo (1998) *Sobre arenas movizadas. Sociedad, estado y ejército en Guatemala, 1997*, Guatemala: Flacso.

Arévalo de Leon, Bernardo *et al.* (2000) *Función Military Control Democratico. Conferencia Internacional Ciudad de Guatamala Junio 2000*. Guatemala: Amanuense.

Arriagada, Genaro (1985a) 'The legal and institutional framework of the armed forces in Chile'. In J. Samuel Valenzuela and Arturo Valenzuela (eds), *Military Rule in Chile: Dictatorship and Oppositions*, Baltimore: Johns Hopkins University Press.

Arriagada, Genaro (1985b) *La Política Militar de Pinochet,* Santiago: Editorial Anconcagua.

Arriagada, Genaro (1986) *El Pensamiento Político de los Militares*, Santiago: Editorial Aconcagua.

*Asiaweek* (1989) 27 January.

Asprey, Robert (1993) *The German High Command at War. Hindenburg and Ludendorff and the First World War*, London: Little, Brown and Company.

Aung San (1972, 1983) 'Blue Print for Burma'. In J. Silverstein (ed.), *The Political Legacy of Aung San*, Ithaca NY: Southeast Asia Program, Cornell University, pp. 18–42.

Aung San Suu Kyi (1995) *Freedom from Fear*, Harmondsworth: Penguin Books.

Aung San Suu Kyi (1997) *The Voice of Hope: Conversations with Alan Clements with contributions by U Kyi Maung and U Tin U*, Harmondsworth: Penguin Books.

# B

Babangida, Ibrahim (1990) 'The military and the nation: perspectives in development', address to the Command and Staff College, Jaji, Kaduna, 29 June.

Bahru Zewde (1991) *A History of Modern Ethiopia*, London: James Currey.

Bahru Zewde (1998) 'The military and militarism in Africa: the case of Ethiopia'. In Eboe Hutchful and Abdoulaye Bathily (eds), *The Military and Militarism in Africa*, Dakar: CODESRIA, pp. 257–89.

Barahona de Brito, Alexandra (1997) *Human Rights and Democratisation in Latin America: Uruguay and Chile*, Oxford: Oxford University Press.

Barber, William F. and C. Neale Ronning (1966) *Internal Security and Military Power. Counterinsurgency and Civic Action in Latin America*. Ohio: Ohio State University.

Barros, Robert (forthcoming in Spring 2001) 'Personalization and institutional constraints: Pinochet, the military junta, and the 1980 constitution', *Latin American Politics and Society*, forthcoming 43, 1.

Baynham, Simon (1988) *The Military and Politics in Nkrumah's Ghana*, Boulder: Westview Press.

Becka, Jan (1983) *The National Liberation Movement in Burma during the Japanese Occupation Period (1941–45)*, Prague: Dissertationes Orientales 42.

Béjar, Héctor (1973) *Las Guerrillas de 1965: Balance y Perspectiva*, Lima: PEISA.

Bereket Habte Selassie (1998) 'Creating a constitution for Eritrea', *Journal of Democracy*, 9, 2: pp. 164–74.

Berhane Woldemichael and Ruth Iyob (1999) 'Reconstruction and development in Eritrea: an overview'. In Martin Doornbos and Alemseged Tesfa (eds), *Post-Conflict Eritrea*, Asmara: Red Sea Press, for UNRISD, pp. 27–54.

Bevor, Anthony (1998) *Stalingrad*, London: Penguin Books.

Bhakti, I. N. *et al.* (1999) *Tentara Mendamba Mitra* (Military in Search of Partnership): *Hasil Penelitian LIPI tentang Pasang Surut Keterlibatan Militer dalam Kehidupan Kepartaian di Indonesia*, Jakarta: PPW–LIPI.

Bicheno, H. E. (1972) 'Antiparliamentary themes in Chilean history', *Government and Opposition*, 7, 3, pp. 351–88.

Billah, M. M. (1995) *Peran Ornop dalam Proses Demokratisasi Yang Berkedualatan Rakyat* (The Role of NGOs in the Democratization Process Which Is Based on People's

Sovereignty), Jakarta: LP3ES, Agenda LSM Menyongsong Tahun 2000.

Birand, Mehmet Ali (1991) *Shirts in Steel: an Anatomy of the Turkish Armed Forces*, London: I. B. Tauris.

Black, George with Milton Jamail and Norma Stolz Chinchilla (1984) *Garrison Guatemala*, New York: Monthly Review Press.

Boadi, Gyimah E. (1998) 'The rebirth of African liberalism', *Journal of Democracy*, 9, 2, pp. 18–31.

*Boletín, Agregado Militar de la Embajada de Guatemala* (1999) 19 July.

Bourchier, D. and J. Legge (1994) *Democracy in Indonesia: 1950s and 1990s*, Clayton: Centre of Southeast Asian Studies.

Bowen, Sally (2000) *El expediente Fujimori. El Perú y su presidente, 1990–2000*, Lima: Peru Monitor SA.

Bratton, Michael and Nicholas van de Walle (1997) *Democratic Experiments in Africa: Regime Transitions in Comparative Perspective*, Boulder, Colorado: Lynne Rienner.

Bray, John (1995) 'Burma: the politics of constructive engagement', Discussion Paper 58, Royal Institute of International Affairs, London.

Brett, E. A. (1995) 'Neutralising the use of force in Uganda: the rôle of the military in politics', *Journal of Modern African Studies*, 33, 1, pp.129–52.

Brietzke, Paul H. (1995) 'Ethiopia's "leap in the dark": federalism and self-determination in the new constitution', *Journal of African Law*, 39, 1, pp. 19–38.

Brown, David (1994) *The State and Ethnic Politics in Southeast Asia*, London: Routledge.

Bulut, Faik (1997) *Resmi Belgeler Işiğinda Ordu ve Din*, Ankara: Doruk Yayıncılık.

Burton, Michael, Richard Gunther and John Higley (1992) 'Introduction: elite transformations and democratic regimes'. In John Higley and Richard Gunther (eds), *Elites and Democratic Consolidation in Latin America and Southern Europe*, Cambridge: Cambridge University Press: 1992, pp. 323–48.

Bustamante, Fernando (1998) 'Democracy, civilizational change, and the Latin American military'. In Felipe Agüero and Jeffrey Stark (eds), *Fault Lines of Democracy in Post-Transition Latin America*, Coral Gables: North–South Center Press, pp. 345–70.

Byrne, Hugh (1999) 'The Guatemalan peace process after the referendum', memorandum, Washington Office on Latin America, 28 June 1999.

# C

Cahyono, H. (1998) *Pangkopkamtib Jenderal Soemitro Dan Peristiwa 15 Januari '74* (Commander-in-Chief General Soemitro and the 15 January 1974 Affair), Jakarta: Pustaka Sinar Harapan.

Callahan, Mary (1996) 'The origins of military rule in Burma', PhD thesis, Cornell University, Ithaca.

Callahan, Mary (1998a) 'On time warps and warped time: lessons from Burma's "Democratic Era"'. In Robert Rotberg (ed.), *Burma: Prospects for a Democratic Future*, Washington DC: Brookings Institute Press, pp. 49–67.

Callahan, Mary (1998b) 'Democracy in Burma: the lessons of history'. In National Bureau of Asian Research, *Analysis*, 1998, 9, 3, pp. 8–27.

Cameron, Maxwell A. (1994) *Democracy and Authoritarianism in Peru: Political Coalitions and Social Change*, Basingstoke: MacMillan.

Cameron, Maxwell A. and Philip Mauceri (eds), (1997) *The Peruvian Labyrinth: Polity,*

*Society, Economy*, University Park Pennsylvania: Pennsylvania State University Press.

Campbell, Catherine (1992) 'Learning to kill? Masculinity, the family and violence in Natal', *Journal of Southern African Studies*, 18, 3, pp. 614–28.

Cardona Recinos, Rokael (1999) 'Prologue'. In Hector Rosada Granados, *Soldados en el poder. Proyecto militar en Guatemala (1944–1990)*, San José: FUNDAPEM, pp. ii–xx.

Carey, P. (1996) *East Timor: Third World Colonialism and the Struggle for National Identity*, London: Current Affairs Research Services(Conflict Studies 293–294).

Carey, Peter (1997) *From Burma to Myanmar: Military Rule and the Struggle for Democracy*, London: Research Institute for the Study of Conflict and Terrorism.

Carriere, Rolf (1997) 'Responding to Myanmar's silent emergency: the urgent case for international humanitarian relief and assistance'. In Peter Carey (ed.), *Burma: the Challenges of Change in a Divided Society*, Basingstoke: Macmillans, pp. 209–34.

Carvalho, Ferdinando de (1981) *Lembraivos de 35!* Rio de Janeiro: Biblioteca do Exército.

Castedo, Leopoldo and Francisco Encina (1985) *Historia de Chile*, Santiago: Editorial Zig-Zag (15th edition).

Castro, Celso and Maria Celina D'Araujo (eds) (1997) *Ernesto Geisel*, Rio de Janeiro: Ed. FGV.

Castro, Celso, Maria Celina D'Araujo and Gláucio Ary Dillon Soares (eds) (1994a) *Visões do Golpe. A Memória Militar sobre 1964*, Rio de Janeiro: Relum-Dumará.

Castro, Celso, Maria Celina D'Araujo & Gláucio Ary Dillon Soares (eds) (1994b) *Os Anos de Chumbo. A Memória Militar sobre a Repressão*, Rio de Janeiro: Relume-Dumará.

Centeno, Miguel Angel (1998) 'Blood and debt: war and taxation in nineteenth-century Latin America', *American Journal of Sociology*, 102, 6, pp. 1565–1605.

Central Committee for Drug Abuse Control (1999) *The War on Drugs, Myanmar's Efforts for the Eradication of Narcotic Drugs*, Rangoon: Central Committee for Drug Abuse Control.

Chai-Anan Samudavanija (1995) 'Thailand: a stable semi-democracy'. In Larry Diamond, Juan J. Linz and Seymour Martin Lipset (eds), *Politics in Developing Countries. Comparing Experiences with Democracy*. Boulder: Lynne Rienner, pp. 323–67.

Chateau, Jorge (1977) *Antecedentes Teóricos para el estudio de la Geopolítica y Doctrinas Castrenses: Notas para una Investigación*, Santiago: FLACSO, Documento de Trabajo.

*Chavín de Huantar. Modelo de Estrategia Frente al Tercer Milenio*, Lima: Diario El Sol (1997).

Cilliers, Jakkie (1999) 'Private Security in War-Torn African States'. In Jakkie Cilliers and Peggy Mason (eds), *Peace, Profit or Plunder? The Privatisation of Security in War-Torn African Societies*, Halfway House: Institute for Security Studies, pp. 1–9.

Cizre-Sakallıoğlu, Ümit (1997) 'The anatomy of the Turkish military's political autonomy', *Comparative Politics*, January, pp. 151–200.

Clapham, Christopher (1988) *Transformation and Continuity in Revolutionary Ethiopia*, Cambridge: Cambridge University Press.

Clapham, Christopher (1994) 'Ethnicity and the national question in Ethiopia'. In Peter Woodward and Murray Forsyth, *Conflict and Peace in the Horn of Africa: Federalism and Its Alternatives*, Aldershot: Dartmouth, pp. 27–40.

Clapham, Christopher (1996) *Africa and the International System: the Politics of State Survival*, Cambridge: Cambridge University Press.

Clapham, Christopher (ed.) (1998) *African Guerrillas*, Oxford: James Currey.

Cleary, Sean (1999) 'Angola – a case study of private military involvement'. In Jakkie Cilliers and Peggy Mason (eds), *Peace, Profit or Plunder? The Privatisation of Security in War-Torn African Societies*, Halfway House: Institute for Security Studies, pp. 141–74.

Cliffe, Lionel (1994) 'Eritrea: prospects for self-determination'. In Peter Woodward and Murray Forsyth, *Conflict and Peace in the Horn of Africa. Federalism and Its Alternatives*, Aldershot: Dartmouth, pp. 52–69.

Cliffe, Lionel (1999) 'Regional dimensions of conflict in the Horn of Africa', *Third World Quarterly* 20, 2, pp. 89–111.

Cohen, John M. (1997) 'Decentralization and "ethnic federalism" in post-civil war Ethiopia'. In K. Kumar (ed.), *Rebuilding Societies after Civil War: Critical Roles for International Assistance*, Boulder: Lynne Rienner, pp. 135–53.

Coletta, N. J. *et al.* (1996) 'Case studies in war-to-peace transition', World Bank Discussion Paper No. 331, Africa Technical Department Series, section 1, Ethiopia: From Emergency to Development, World Bank, Washington.

Collier, David (ed.) (1979) *The New Authoritarianism in Latin America*, Princeton: Princeton University Press.

Collier, Simon (1993) 'From independence to the War of the Pacific'. In Leslie Bethell (ed.), *Chile Since Independence*, Cambridge: Cambridge University Press, pp. 1–32.

Comblin, Joseph (1979) *La Doctrina de la Seguridad Nacional*. Santiago: Vicaría de la Solidaridad.

Commission on Human Rights (1998) *Situation of Human Rights in Myanmar: Report of Special Rapporteur, Mr Rajsoomer Lallah*, Geneva: Commission on Human Rights, 15 January.

Constable, Pamela and Arturo Valenzuela (1991) *A Nation of Enemies: Chile under Pinochet*, New York: Norton.

*Constitución Política de la República de Chile* (1998) Santiago: Ediciones Publiley (1998 edition).

Cotler, Julio (1978) *Clases, Estado y Nación en el Perú*, Lima: IEP (Perú Problema No. 17).

Cotler, Julio (1995) 'Crisis política, *outsiders* y democraduras: El Fujimorismo'. In Carina Pirelli, Sonia Picado and Daniel Zovalto (eds), *Partidos y clase política en América Latina en los 90s*, San José: IIDH, pp. 117–41.

Crabtree, John and Jim Thomas (eds) (2000) *El Perú de Fujimori, 1990–1998*, Lima: Universidad del Pacífico/IEP (Perú Problema, No. 25).

Cribb, R. (1991) *The Indonesian Killings 1965–1966: Studies from Java and Bali*, Monash University: Centre of Southeast Asian Studies.

Crough, H. (1988) *The Army and Politics in Indonesia*, Ithaca: Cornell University Press.

Crowder, Michael (1970) *West Africa under Colonial Rule*, London: Hutchinson.

Cruz Salazar, Lieutenant-Colonel José Luis (1980) 'El Ejército como una fuerza política', *Estudios Políticos*, pp. 74–98.

# D

Dahl, Robert (1971) *Polyarchy: Participation and Opposition*, New Haven and London: Yale University Press.

*Daily Kompas* (2000) 1 March.

Davis, Anthony and Bruce Hawke (1998) 'Burma: the country that won't kick the habit', *Jane's Intelligence Review*, March, pp. 26–34.

Davis, Nathaniel (1985) *The Last Two Years of Salvador Allende*, Ithaca: Cornell University Press.

Decalo, Samuel (1976) *Coups and Army Rule in Africa: Studies in Military Style*, New Haven: Yale University Press.

'The *de facto* powers behind Fujimori's regime' (1996) In *Privilege and Power in Fujimori's Peru*. Special Issue of the *NACLA Report on the Americas,* 30, 1, July–August.

Degregori, Carlos Iván (1990) *Ayacucho 1969–1979. El surgimiento de Sendero Luminoso*, Lima: IEP.

Degregori, Carlos Iván (1994) 'Perú: redefinición del papel militar en un contexto de violencia subversiva y colapso del régimen democratico'. In Gabriel Aguilera Peralta (ed.), *Conversión Militar en América Latina*, Guatemala: Flacso, pp. 107–26.

Degregori, Carlos Iván (ed.) (1996) *Las Rondas Campesinas y la Derrota de Sendero Luminoso*, Lima: IEP/UNSCH.

'Democracia en la encrucijada' (2000) In *Informe Anual sobre la Región Andina*, Lima: Comisión Andina de Juristas.

Dessalegn Rahmato (1994) 'The Unquiet Countryside: the Collapse of "Socialism" and Rural Agitation, 1990 and 1991'. In Zegeye and Pausewang (eds), *Ethiopia in Change*, London: British Academic Press, pp. 242–79.

De Waal, Alex (1991) *Evil Days: Thirty Years of War and Famine in Ethiopia*, New York: Human Rights Watch.

De Waal, Alex (1997) *Famine Crimes: Politics and the Disaster Relief Industry in Africa*, Oxford: James Currey.

Diamond, Larry, Juan J. Linz and Seymour Martin Lipset (eds) (1995) *Politics in Developing Countries. Comparing Experiences with Democracy*, Boulder: Lynne Rienner.

Diamond, L. and M. Plattner (eds) (1997) *Civil–Military Relations and Democracy*, Baltimore: Johns Hopkins University Press.

*DIDE Comunicado de Prensa* (1997) Nos 58–97.

Dijk, C. van (1981) *Rebellion under the Banner of Islam*, The Hague: Martinus Nijhof.

Domínguez, Jorge I. and Abraham F. Lowenthal (eds) (1996) *Constructing Democratic Governance – Themes and Issues*, Baltimore and London: Johns Hopkins University Press.

Doornbos, Martin and Alemseged Tesfai (eds) (1999) *Post-Conflict Eritrea: Prospects for Reconstruction and Development*, Asmara: Red Sea Press, for UNRISD.

Dudley, Seers (1971) *Development in a Divided World*, Harmondsworth, Middlesex: Penguin Books.

# E

Eca, J. and J. C. Vatin (1976) *L'Algerie, institutions et régime*, Paris: FNSP.

Edmonds, Martin (1985) 'Introduction'. In Martin Edmonds (ed.), *Central Organisations of Defence*, London: Pinter, p. 1.

Ejército de Guatemala (1996a) *Analisis Estrategico Nacional, 1996*, Guatemala: National Defence Staff, January 1996.

Ejército de Guatemala (1996b) *Plan de Campana Integracion '96*, 060800MAR96.

Ejercito de Guatemala (1996c) *Proceso de Paz en Guatemala. Fortalecimiento del Poder Civil y Funcion del Ejercito en una Sociedad Democratica*, Guatemala: Departmento de Informacion y Divulgacion del Ejercito, September 1996.

Ejército de Guatemala (1997) *Plan de Operaciones Transicion Hacia la Paz '97*, Guatemala: National Defence Staff, February 1997.

Elaigwu, J. Isawa (1986) *Gowon: the Biography of a Soldier-Statesman*, Ibadan: West Books Publishers.

*El Comercio* (1994, 2000) 10 May 1994; 29 February 2000.

*El Periódico* (1997) 24 October.

Encina, Francisco Antonio (1984) *Historia de Chile*, Santiago: Editorial Ercilla.

Erlich, Haggai (1983) 'The Ethiopian army and the 1974 revolution', *Armed Forces and Society*, 9, 3, pp. 455–81.

*Expreso* (1994) 16 January; 2 February; 16 February.

## F

*Far Eastern Economic Review Yearbook* (1966, 1968) 16 September 1993.

Fay, Sidney Bradshaw (1937) *The Rise of Brandenburg-Prussia to 1786*, New York: Henry Holt and Company.

Fayemi, J 'Kayode (1994) 'Threats, military expenditure and national security: analysis of trends in Nigeria's defence planning, 1970–1990', unpublished PhD dissertation, University of London.

Fayemi, J 'Kayode (1996) *Nigeria: Crisis of Nationhood*, London: Parliamentary Human Rights Group.

Fayemi, J 'Kayode (1998) 'The future of demilitarisation and civil military relations in West Africa: challenges and prospects for democratic consolidation', *African Journal of Political Science*, 3, 1.

Fayemi, J 'Kayode (1999) 'Military hegemony and transition politics in Nigeria', *Issue: Journal of Opinion*, 41, 1 (African Studies Association Journal, Rutgers University).

Fayemi, J 'Kayode and Musah, Abdel-Fatau (2000) *Mercenaries: an African Security Dilemma*, London: Pluto Press.

Feaver, Peter (1996) 'The civil–military problematique: Huntington, Janowitz, and the question of civilian control', *Armed Forces and Society*, 23, 2.

Feith, H. (1962) *The Decline of Constitutional Democracy in Indonesia*, Ithaca: Cornell University Press.

Fernandes, Florestan (1981) *A Revolução Burguesa no Brasil*, Rio de Janeiro: Zahar.

Figueroa, Adolfo, Teófilo Altamirano and Denis Sulmont (1996) *Social Exclusion and Inequality in Peru*, Geneva: International Institute for Labour Studies.

Figueroa, Adolfo (2000) 'Distribución de ingresos en el Perú'. In John Crabtree and Jim Thomas (eds), *El Perú de Fujimori, 1990–1998*, Lima: Universidad del Pacífico/IEP (Perú Problema No. 25), pp. 219–54.

Finer, S. E. (1962, 1978) *The Man on Horseback. The Role of the Military in Politics*, London: Pall Mall Press/Harmondsworth: Penguin.

Finer, S. E. (1988) *The Man on Horseback. The Role of the Military in Politics*, Pinter: London (second enlarged edition).

Fitch, J. Samuel (1986) 'Armies and politics in Latin America, 1975–1985'. In

Abraham Lowenthal and J. Samuel Fitch (eds), *Armies and Politics in Latin America*, New York: Holmes and Meier.

Fitch, J. Samuel (1998) *The Armed Forces and Democracy in Latin America*, Baltimore: Johns Hopkins University Press.

Forrester, G. and R. J. May (1999) *The Fall of Soeharto*, Singapore: Select Books.

*Forward* (1968) 15 October.

Fuentes, Claudio (1997) 'Militares en Chile: ni completa autonomía ni total subordinación'. In FLACSO, *Chile 96: Análisis y Opiniones*, Santiago: Nueva Serie FLACSO.

Fuentes, Claudio (2000) 'After Pinochet: civilian policies toward the military in 1990s Chilean democracy', *Journal of Interamerican Studies and World Affairs* 42, 3, Fall, pp. 111–42.

Fuller, John F. C. (1933) *Grant and Lee. A Study in Personality and Generalship*, London: Eyre and Spottiswoode.

Fuller, John F. C. (1943) *Armoured Warfare. An Annotated Edition of Fifteen Lectures on Operations between Mechanized Forces*, London: Eyre and Spottiswoode.

Fuller, John F. C. (1954) *The Second World War, 1939–45. A Strategical and Tactical History*, New York: Duell, Sloan and Pearce.

Fuller, John F. C. (1961) *The Conduct of War, 1789–1961. A Study of the Impact of the French, Industrial, and Russian Revolutions on War and Its Conduct*, New York: Minerva Press.

Furnivall, J. S. (1956) *Colonial Policy and Practice*, New York: New York University Press.

## G

Gamarra, Ronal (1996a) 'Acerca de la nueva legislación antiterrorista', *Ideéle*, 86, July, pp. 1–4.

Gamarra, Ronal (1996b) 'Tribunales militares. Y después?' *Ideéle*, 86, July, pp. 5–9.

Gamarra, Ronal (1997) 'Jueces sin rostro. Inquisisión y justicia ciega en el Perú de los años noventa', *Ideéle*, 102, November, pp. 52–4.

Gambari, Ibrahim (1989) *Theory and Reality in Nigeria's Foreign Policy Making,* New Jersey/ London: Humanities Press.

Garba, Joseph and Jean Herskovits (1997) 'Militaries, democracies and security in Southern Africa'. In *Report of the Southern Africa Security Project*, New York: IPA.

García, P. Gonzalo and Juan Esteban Montes I (1994) *Subordinación Democrática de los Militares: Exitos y Fracasos en Chile,* Santiago: Centro de Estudios del Desarrollo.

Garretón, Manuel Antonio (1982) 'Modelo y proyecto político del régimen militar Chileno', *Revista Mexicana de Sociología*, 44, 2.

Garretón, Manuel Antonio (1986) 'Political processes in an authoritarian regime: the dynamics of institutionalization and opposition in Chile 1973–1980'. In J. Samuel Valenzuela and Arturo Valenzuela (eds), *Military Rule in Chile*, Baltimore: Johns Hopkins University Press.

Garretón, Manuel Antonio (1987) *Reconstruir la Política: Transición y Consolidación Democrática en Chile*, Santiago: Editorial Andante.

Garretón, Manuel Antonio (1999) 'Chile 1997–1998: the revenge of incomplete democratization', *International Affairs*, 75, 2, pp. 259–67.

Garrido, Luis Javier (1982) *El Partido de la Revolución Institucionalizada. La Formación del Nuevo Estado en México, 1928–1945*, Mexico: Siglo XXI.

Gebru Tareke (1996) *Ethiopia: Power and Protest: Peasant Revolts in the Twentieth Century*, Asmara: Red Sea Press.

Geisse, Guillermo (1989) *Economía y Política de la Concentración Urbana en Chile*, Mexico: Pispal–El Colegio de México.

Geisse, Francisco, and José Antonio Ramírez Arrayas (1989) *La Reforma Constitucional*, Santiago: CESOC–Ediciones Chile-América.

Ghazi, Hidouci (1996) *La libération inachevée*, Paris: La Découverte.

Gilkes, Patrick and Martin Plaut (1999) 'War in the Horn. The Conflict between Eritrea and Ethiopia', discussion paper, Royal Institute for International Affairs, London.

Gogolewska, Agnieszka (1999) 'Comparing post-communist civil–military relations: Poland, the Czech Republic, Lithuania and Ukraine', unpublished PhD draft, Kings College, London.

González, Simeón Emilio (1990) *Sociología del 'Torrijismo'. Mito y Realidad de un Proceso*, Panamá: Universidad de Panamá/ECU.

Goodman, Louis W., Johanna S. R. Mendelson and Juan Rial (eds) (1990) *The Military and Democracy. The Future of Civil–Military Relations in Latin America*, Lexington, Mass.: Lexington Books.

Gordy, Eric D. (1999) *The Culture of Power in Serbia: Nationalism and the Destruction of Alternatives*, University Park, PA: Pennsylvania State University Press.

Government of the Union of Burma (1960) *Is Trust Vindicated?* Rangoon: Ministry of Information.

Gow, James (1992) *Legitimacy and the Military: the Yugoslav Crisis*, London: Pinter.

Gow, James (forthcoming) *The Serbian War Project and Its Advesaries: a Strategy of War Crimes*.

Gow, James and Carole Birch (1997) *Security and Democracy: Civil–Military Relations in Central and Eastern Europe*, London: Brassey's for the Centre for Defence Studies (London Defence Studies No. 40).

Gramajo Morales, Héctor Alejandro (1989) *Tesis de Estabilidad Nacional*, Guatemala: Editorial del Ejercito.

Gramajo Morales, Héctor Alejandro (1991a, b) 'Political transition in Guatemala (1980– 1990): a perspective from inside Guatemala's armed forces'. Two separately edited versions in Jorge Domíngues and Marc Lindenburg (eds), *Democratic Transitions in Central America and Panama*, Gainesville, Florida: University Press of Florida.

Griffiths, Robert J. (1996) 'Democratisation and civil–military relations in Namibia, South Africa and Mozambique', *Third World Quarterly*, 17, 3, pp 473–85.

Grompone, Romeo (1999) *Las Nuevas Reglas del Juego. Transformaciones Sociales, Culturales y Políticas en Lima*, Lima: IEP (Urbanización, Migraciones y Cambios en la Sociedad Peruana No. 13).

*Guardian, The* (1988) 26 July.

Güney, Aylin (forthcoming) 'Turkey beyond the Customs Union?' In Fulvio Attina and Stelios Stavridis (eds), *The Barcelona Process and Euro-Mediterranean Issues from Stuttgart to Marseille*, Ilford and Portland: Frank Cass Publishing Company.

Güney-Avci, Aylin (1996) 'Politique interieure et politique exterieure dans la Turquis d'ajourdhui', *Le Trimestre du Monde*, 4, 36, pp. 70–89.

Güney, Aylin and Metin Heper (1996) 'The military and democracy in the Third Turkish Republic', *Armed Forces and Society*, 22, Summer, pp. 619–42.

Güney, Aylin and Metin Heper (2000) 'The military, political Islam and democracy in Turkey', *Armed Forces and Society*, 26, Summer, pp. 635–57.

Guyot, Dorothy (1967) 'The Burma Independence Army: a political movement in military garb'. In Josef Silverstein (ed.), *Southeast Asia in World War II*, New Haven: Yale University Southeast Asia Program.

# H

Hale, William (1994) *Turkish Politics and the Military*, London and New York: Routledge.

Halliday, Fred and Maxine Moyneux (1981) *The Ethiopian Revolution*, London: Verso.

Handy, Jim (1984) *Gift of the Devil. A History of Guatemala*, Boston: South End Press.

Harbeson, John W. (1998) 'A bureaucratic-authoritarian regime, *Journal of Democracy*, 9, 4: pp. 62–9.

Harbi, Mohamed (1974) *Aux origines du FLN*, Paris: Ch. Bourgois.

Harbi, Mohamed (1982) *Le FLN, mirage et réalités*, Algeria: Ed. Jeune Afrique.

Harbi, Mohamed (1994) *L'Algérie et son destin. Croyants ou citoyens*, Algeria: Médias Associés.

Harris, George (1988) 'The role of the military in Turkey: guardians or decision-makers?' In Metin Heper and Ahmet Evin (eds), *State, Democracy and the Military in Turkey in the 1980s*, Berlin and New York: Walter de Gruyter.

Henze, Paul B. (1990) 'Three decades of arms for the Horn of Africa: a statistical analysis', *Conflict*, 10: 135–72.

Henze, Paul B. (1998) 'Is Ethiopia democratic? A political success story', *Journal of Democracy*, 9, 4, pp. 40–54.

Heper, Metin and Ahmet Evin (1998) (eds) *State, Democracy and the Military. Turkey in the 1980s*, Berlin and New York: Walter de Gruyter and Co.

Heper, Metin and Aylin Güney (1996) 'The military and democracy in the Third Turkish Republic', *Armed Forces and Society*, 22, 4, pp. 619–42.

Heper, Metin and Aylin Güney (2000) 'Military and the consolidation of democracy. The recent Turkish experience', *Armed Forces and Society*, 26, 4, pp. 635–57.

Heper, Metin and Frank Tachau (1983) 'The state, politics and the military in Turkey', *Comparative Politics*, 16, 3, pp. 17–33.

Hla Min, Colonel (1999) *Political Situation of Myanmar and its Role in the Region*, Rangoon: Ministry of Defence, Office of Strategic Studies.

Horne, Alistair (1977) *A Savage War of Peace. Algeria, 1954–1962*, London: MacMillan Ltd.

Houtman, Gustaaf (1999) *Mental Culture in Burmese Crisis Politics*, Tokyo: Tokyo University of Foreign Studies, Institute for the Study of Languages and Cultures of Asia and Africa.

Human Rights Watch/Africa (1997) 'Ethiopia: the curtailment of rights', *Human Rights Watch/Africa Report*, 9, 8, pp. 3–54.

Huneeus, Carlos (1998) 'Tecnócratas y políticos en un régimen autoritario: los "ODEPLAN Boys" y los "gremialistas" en el Chile de Pinochet', *Revista de Ciencia Política* (Santiago de Chile) 19, 2.

Huneeus, Carlos and Jorge Olave (1987) 'La partecipazione dei militari nei nuovi autoritarismi: il Cile in una prospettiva comparata', *Rivista Italiana di Scienza Politica*, 17, 1, April, pp. 57–104.

Hunter, Wendy (1997) *Eroding Military Influence in Brazil – Politicians against Soldiers*,

Chapel Hill: University of North Carolina.

Huntington, Samuel P. (1957) *The Soldier and the State. The Theory and Politics of Civil–Military Relations*, Cambridge, Mass.: Belknap Press of Harvard University Press.

Huntington, Samuel P. (1968) *Political Order in Changing Societies*, New Haven: Yale University Press.

*Hürriyet* (1997) 12 January; 20 January; 3 March; 4 November; 25 December.

Hurtado, Carlos (1966) *Concentración de Población y Desarrollo Económico*, Santiago: Instituto de Economía de la Universidad de Chile.

Hutchful, Eboe (1986) 'New elements in militarism: Ethiopia, Ghana and Burkina Faso', *International Journal*, 41, 4, pp. 802–30.

Hutchful, Eboe and Abdoulaye Bathily (eds) (1998) *The Military and Militarism in Africa*, Dakar: CODESRIA.

Hutchful, Eboe and Abdoulaye Bathily (1998) 'Military policy and reform in Ghana', *Journal of Modern African Studies*, 35, 2, pp. 251–78.

## I

Iba, Saban (1998) *Milli Güvenlik Devleti. Dünyada be Türkiye'de Belgeleriyle Milli Güvenlik Ideolojisi ve Kurumlasma*. Istanbul: Çiviyazıları.

Iguiñiz, Javier (2000) 'La estrategia económica del gobierno de Fujimori: una visión global'. In John Crabtree and Jim Thomas (eds), *El Perú de Fujimori, 1990–1998*, Lima: Universidad del Pacífico/IEP (Perú Problema No. 25), pp. 15–43.

IISS (several years) *Military Balance*, London: Brassey Publishers for IISS.

'The Indonesian military in the mid–1990s: political manoeuvring or structural change?' (1996) In *Indonesia*, autumn.

'In His Own Words: Colonel Chit Myaing' (1997) *Burma Debate*, IV, 3, July/August, pp.10–24.

'In Huancayo. Testimony of pacification' (1999) *Commando en Acción*, 8, 27, pp. 58–69.

Iswandi (1998) *Bisnis Militer Orde Baru* (Military Business During New Order): *Keterlibatan Abri Dalam Bidang Ekonomi Dan Pengaruhnya Terhadap Pembentukan Rezim Otoriter*, Bandung: ROSDA.

Iyob, Ruth (1997) 'The Eritrean experiment: a cautious pragmatism?', *Journal of Modern African Studies*, 35, 4, pp. 647–73.

## J

Janowitz, Morris (1964) *The Military in the Political Development of New Nations*, Chicago: University of Chicago Press.

Janowitz, Morris (1977) *Military Institutions and Coercion in the Developing Nations*, Chicago: University of Chicago Press.

Jenkins, D. (1984) *Suharto and His Generals: Indonesian Military Politics 1975–1983*, Ithaca: Cornell University Press.

Johnson, John J. (1962) 'Introduction'. In John J. Johnson (ed.), *The Role of the Military in Underdeveloped Countries*, Princeton: Princeton University Press, pp. 3–6.

Johnson, John J. (ed.) (1962) *The Role of the Military in Underdeveloped Countries*, Princeton: Princeton University Press.

Johnson, A. Ross (1982) 'The role of the military in Yugoslavia'. In R. Kolkowicz and A. Korbonski (eds), *Soldiers, Peasants and Bureaucrats: Civil-Military Relations in*

*Communist and Modernising Systems*. London: Allen and Unwin, pp. 181–97.

Joireman, Sandra F. (1996) 'The minefield of land reform: comments on the Eritrean land proclamation', *African Affairs*, 95, pp. 269–85.

Joireman, Sandra F. (1997) 'Opposition politics and ethnicity in Ethiopia: we will all go down together', *Journal of Modern African Studies*, 35, 3, pp. 387–407.

Joseph, Richard (1991) *Democracy and Prebendal Politics in Nigeria: the Rise and Fall of the Second Republic*, Ibadan: Spectrum.

Joseph, Richard (ed.) (1998) *State, Conflict and Democracy in Africa*, Boulder, Colorado: Lynne Rienner.

Joxe, Alain (1970) *Las Fuerzas Armadas en el Sistema Político de Chile*, Santiago: Editorial Universitaria.

Judah, Tim (1999) *The Serbs*, New Haven and London: Yale University Press.

## K

Kadt, Emanuel de (1993) 'Poverty–focused policies: the experience of Chile', IDS Discussion Paper No. 319, January, Institute of Development Studies, Brighton, Sussex.

Kadt, Emanuel de (1996) 'On promoting better policy management', *Asien Afrika Lateinamerika*, 24, pp. 605–18.

Kadt, Emanuel de (1999) 'Back to society and culture. On aid donors' overblown concern with "governance" and democratization', inaugural lecture, Utrecht University, Utrecht.

Kadt, Emanuel de (in press) 'Goed bestuur in Afrika. De realiteit in het licht van traditie en geschiedenis'. In Wetenschappelijke Raad voor het Regeringsbeleid (WRR), *Goed Bestuur en Ontwikkelingsbeleid, Rapporten aan de Regering*, The Hague: Staatsuitgeverij.

Kaldor, Mary and Robin Luckham (2001) 'Global transformations and new conflicts', *IDS Bulletin* (forthcoming).

Kamanu, O. S. (1977) 'Nigeria: reflections on defence posture for the 1980s', *Geneve Afrique*, 4,1, p. 35.

Kammen, D. (1999) 'Akhir "Kedirgadayaan" ABRI?' (The End of the Indonesian Military's 'Invulnerability'?), paper XII.II.1., Twelfth INFID conference, Kuta, Bali, Indonesia, September.

Kapuscinski, Ryszard (1983) *The Emperor*, London: Quartet Books.

Kean, Leslie and Denis Bernstein (1998) 'The Burma–Singapore axis: globalizing the heroin trade', US Department of State International Narcotics Control Strategy Report, *CovertAction Quarterly*, Spring.

Kennedy, Gavin (1974) *The Military in the Third World*, London: Duckworth.

Khin Nyunt, Brigadier-General (1989) *The Conspiracy of Treasonous Minions with the Myanmar Naign-Ngan and Traitorous Cohorts Abroad*, Rangoon: Guardian Press.

Kingstone, Peter R. and Timothy J. Power (eds) (2000*) Democratic Brazil: Actors, Institutions, and Processes*, Pittsburgh: Pittsburgh University Press.

Kinross, Patrick (1993, 1999) *Atatürk. The Rebirth of a Nation*, Frome and London: Butler and Tanner Ltd.

Klarén, Peter Findell (1973) *Modernization, Dislocation and Aprismo. Origins of the APRA Party, 1870–1932*, Austin: University of Texas Press.

Klarén, Peter Findell (2000) *Peru. Society and Nationhood in the Andes*, New York/ Oxford: Oxford University Press.

Knight, Alan (1999) 'Political violence in post-revolutionary Mexico'. In Kees Koonings and Dirk Kruijt (eds), *Societies of Fear. The Legacy of Civil War, Violence and Terror in Latin America*, London: Zed Books, pp. 105–24.

Koonings, Kees (1991) 'La sociología de la intervención militar en la política Latinoaméricana'. In Dirk Kruijt and Edelberto Torres-Rivas (eds), *América Latina: Militares y Sociedad*, San José: Flacso, 1, pp. 19–61.

Koonings, Kees (1996) 'Onder het zwaard van Damocles. Militairen en politiek sinds 1930'. In Kees Koonings and Dirk Kruijt (eds), *Democratie en Dictatuur in Latijns-Amerika*, Amsterdam: Thela Publishers, pp. 59–77.

Koonings, Kees (1999) 'Shadows of violence and political transition in Brazil: from military rule to democratic governance'. In Kees Koonings and Dirk Kruijt (eds), *Societies of Fear. The Legacy of Civil War, Violence and Terror in Latin America*, London: Zed Books, pp. 197–234.

Koonings, Kees (2001) 'Civil society, transitions, and post-war reconstruction in Latin America: a comparison of El Salvador, Guatemala, and Peru'. Paper for the international conference on 'The Role of Civil Society in Conflict Resolution', February, National University of Ireland, Maynooth.

Koonings, Kees and Dirk Kruijt (eds) (1996) *Democratie en Dictatuur in Latijns-Amerika*, Amsterdam: Thela Publishers.

Koonings, Kees and Dirk Kruijt (eds) (1999) *Societies of Fear. The Legacy of Civil War, Violence and Terror in Latin America*, London: Zed Books.

Kruijt, Dirk (1991) 'Perú: relaciones entre civiles y militares, 1950–1990'. In Dirk Kruijt and Edelberto Torres-Rivas (eds), *América Latina: Militares y Sociedad*, San José: Flacso, 2, pp. 29–142.

Kruijt, Dirk (1994) *Revolution by Decree. Peru 1968–1975*, Amsterdam: Thela Thesis Publishers.

Kruijt, Dirk (1996a) 'Peru: the state under siege'. In Richard L. Millett and Michael Gold-Biss (eds), *Beyond Praetorianism. The Latin American Military in Transition*, Miami: North– South Center Press, pp. 261–89.

Kruijt, Dirk (1996b) 'Politicians in uniform: dilemmas about the Latin American military', *European Review of Latin American and Caribbean Studies*, 61, pp. 7–19.

Kruijt, Dirk (1998) 'Alte Sünder im neuen Gewand? Militär und Gesellschaft in Lateinamerika', *Lateinamerika. Analysen und Berichte*, 22 (special issue, *Die Macht und die Herlichkeit*), pp. 125–48.

Kruijt, Dirk (2000) *Baile de Disfraces. Ensayos sobre Viejos y Nuevos Actores en la Sociedad Militar y la Sociedad Civil de América Latina*, San José: Flacso.

*Kyemon* (1996) 4 July.

*Kyodo* (2000) 9 December.

Kznaric, Roman (1999) 'Civil and uncivil actors in the Guatemalan peace process', *Bulletin of Latin American Research* 18, 1, pp. 1–16.

## L

Lefort, Rene (1983) *Ethiopia: an Heretical Revolution?* London: Zed Books.

Lintner, Bertil (1990) *Outrage: Burma's Struggle for Democracy*, Bangkok: White Lotus.

*Living Colour Magazine* (in Burmese) (1999) February.

Lock, Peter (1999) 'Africa: military downsizing and the growth in the security industry'. In Jakkie Cilliers and Peggy Mason (eds), *Peace, Profit or Plunder? The Privatisation of Security in War-Torn African Societies*, Halfway House: Institute for Security Studies, pp. 11–36.

López-Alves, Fernando (2000) *State Formation and Democracy in Latin America, 1810–1900*, Durham: Duke University Press.

López Urrutia, Carlos (1969) *Historia de la Marina de Chile*, Santiago: Editorial Andres Bello.

Loveard, K. (1999) *Suharto: Indonesia's Last Sultan*, Singapore: Horizon Books.

Loveman, Brian (1988) *Chile: the Legacy of Hispanic Capitalism*, New York: Oxford University Press.

Loveman, Brian (1994) 'Protected democracies and military guardianship: political transitions in Latin America, 1978–1993', *Journal of Interamerican Studies and World Affairs*, 36, 2, pp. 105–90.

Loveman, Brian (1995) *The Constitution of Tyranny: Regimes of Exception in Spanish America*, Pittsburgh: Pittsburgh University Press.

Loveman, Brian (1999) *For la Patria: Politics and the Armed Forces in Latin America*, Wilmington, Delaware: Scholarly Resources Inc.

Loveman, Brian and Thomas M. Davies (eds) (1978) *The Politics of Anti-Politics. The Military in Latin America*, Lincoln: University of Nebraska Press.

Lowry, R. (1996) *The Armed Forces of Indonesia*, Sydney: Allen and Unwin.

Luckham, Robin (1966) 'Democracy and the military: an epitaph for Frankenstein's monster?', *Democratization*, 3, 2, Summer, pp. 1–16.

Luckham, Robin (1971a) 'A comparative typology of civil–military relations', *Government and Opposition*, 6, 1, pp. 15–35.

Luckham, Robin (1971b) *The Nigerian Military. A Sociological Analysis of Authority and Revolt 1960–67*, Cambridge: Cambridge University Press.

Luckham, Robin and Dawit Bekele (1984) 'Foreign powers and militarism in the Horn of Africa', *Review of African Political Economy*, 30 and 31, pp. 9–20 and pp. 7–28.

Luckham (1994) 'The military, militarization and democratization in Africa: a survey of the literature and issues', *African Studies Review*, 37, 2, pp. 13–75.

Luckham, Robin (1996) 'Faustian bargains: democratic control over military and security establishments'. In Robin Luckham and Gordon White (eds), *Democratization in the South: the Jagged Wave*, Manchester: Manchester University Press, pp. 119–77.

Luckham, Robin, Anne Marie Goetz and Mary Kaldor (2000) 'Democratic institutions and politics in contexts of inequality, poverty and conflict', IDS Working Paper 104, Sussex: Institute of Development Studies.

## M

MacDonald, Brian (1997), *Military Spending in Developing Countries: How Much Is Too Much?* Ottawa: Carleton University Press.

MacFarling, I. (1994) 'The evolution of the Indonesian armed forces: a case study in the fusion of civil and military roles', PhD thesis, University of New South Wales.

Makki, Fouad (1996) 'Nationalism, state formation and the public sphere: Eritrea 1991–96', *Review of African Political Economy*, 70, pp. 475–97.

Mangunwijaya, Y. B. (1994) *The Indonesian Raya Dream and Its Impact on the Concept of Democracy in Indonesia: 1950s and 1990s*, Clayton: Centre of Southeast Asian Studies.

Markakis, John (1974) *Ethiopia: Anatomy of a Traditional Polity*, Oxford: Clarendon Press.

Markakis, John (1987) *National and Class Conflict in the Horn of Africa*, Cambridge: Cambridge University Press.

Martínez, Javier and Alvaro Díaz (1996) *Chile: the Great Transformation*, Geneva: United Nations Research Institute for Social Development and Brookings Institute.

Martins Filho, João Roberto and Daniel Zirker (1998) 'The Brazilian armed forces after the Cold War: overcoming the identity crisis', paper presented at the Latin American Studies Association Congress, Chicago.

Martz, John D. (1994) 'Colombia: democracy, development and drugs', *Current History*, 93, 581, pp. 134–9.

Masterson, Daniel M. (1991) *Militarism and Politics in Latin America. Peru from Sánchez Cerro to Sendero Luminoso*, New York: Greenwood Press.

Matos Mar, José (1984) *Desborde Popular y Crisis del Estado. El Nuevo Rostro del Perú en la Década del 1980*, Lima: IEP (Perú Problema No. 21).

Mauceri, Philip (1996) *State under Siege: Development and Policy Making in Peru*, Boulder: Westview Press.

Maung Aung Myoe (1998) 'Building the Tatmadaw: the organisational development of the armed forces in Myanmar, 1948–98', Working Paper No. 327, Strategic and Defence Studies Centre, Australian National University, Canberra.

Maung Maung (1999) *The 1988 Uprising in Burma*, New Haven: Yale University South East Asian Studies.

McCoy, Alfred (1972) *The Politics of Heroin in SE Asia*, New York: Harper Torchbooks.

McSherry, J. Patrice (1997) *Incomplete Transition: Military Power and Democracy in Argentina*, Houndmills and London: Macmillan.

Mello, Evaldo Cabral de (1997) *Rubro Veio. O Imaginário da Restauração Pernambucana*, Rio de Janeiro: Topbooks (second edition).

*Milliyet* (1996, 1997, 1999, 2000) 5 October, 19 November 1996; 1 March, 2 May, 22 May, 11 June, 13 August 1997; 18 December 1999; 2 February, 6 April, 14 April, 18 June, 25 July, 23 September, 15 November 2000.

MINUGUA (1996) *Cuarto Informe del Director de la Mision de las Naciones Unidas de Verificacion de los Derechos Humanos del Cumplimiento de los Compromisos del Acuerdo Global sobre Derechos Humanos en Guatemala*, Guatemala: United Nations Mission for Guatemala, March.

MINUGUA (1998a) *Informe del Secretario General de las Naciones Unidas sobre la Verificacion de los Acuerdos de Paz en Guatemala (1 de enero–31 de julio 1998)*, Guatemala: United Nations Mission for Guatemala.

MINUGUA (1998b) *The Situation in Central America: Procedures for the Establishment of a Firm and Lasting Peace and Progress in Fashioning a Region of Peace, Freedom, Democracy and Development*. Report of the Secretary-General to the General Assembly, 52nd Session, Agenda Item 45, Guatemala: A/52/757, 4 February.

MINUGUA (1998c) *Suplemento al Octavo Informe del Director de la Mision de las Naciones Unidas en Guatemala*, Guatemala: United Nations Mission for Guatemala, June.

MINUGUA (1998d) *Acta Final. Relativa al Cumplimiento del Compromiso 63b del Acuerdo sobre Fortalecimiento del Poder Civil y Funcion del Ejercito en una Sociedad Democratica, en Relacion con la Reduccion de los Efectivos del Ejercito de Guatemala*, Guatemala: United Nations Mission for Guatemala, 23 September.

MINUGUA (1998e) *Plan de Verificacion del Ejercito,* Guatemala: United Nations Mission for Guatemala.

Molina Mejia, Raul (1998) 'Demilitarizing Guatemalan state and society, CEDMUC and FDNG', paper for the 21st Latin American Studies Association Conference, 24–27 Chicago, September.

Mudoola, Dan (1994) 'The role of the army in society: lessons from Uganda'. In Asmelash Beyene and Gelase Mutuhaba, *The Quest for Constitutionalism in Africa. Selected Essays on Constititionalism, the Nationality Problem, Military Rule,* Frankfurt am Main: Peter Lang, pp. 190–217.

Muñoz, Oscar (1977) 'Estado e industrialización en el ciclo de expansión del salitre', *CIEPLAN,* 6, January.

**N**

National Democratic Institute (1997) *Report of the Civil–Military Relations Assessment Mission: West and Central Africa,* Washington, DC: NDI.

*New Light of Myanmar, The* (1998, 2000) 27 February 1998; 23 December 2000.

*New Nigerian* (1966) 18 January.

*News Magazine, The* (1994, 1999) 24 Januar, May 1994; 4 October 1999.

*Noticiário do Exército* (1999) No. 9,626, 27 November.

Notosusanto, N. (1985) *Pejuang dan Prajurit* (Freedomfighter and Soldier), Jakarta: Sinar Harapan.

Nun, José (1967) 'The middle-class military coup'. In Claudio Véliz (ed.), *The Politics of Conformity in Latin America,* Oxford: Oxford University Press, pp. 66–118.

Nun, José (1986) 'The middle-class military coup revisited'. In Abraham Lowenthal and J. Samuel Fitch (eds), *Armies and Politics in Latin America,* New York: Holmes and Meier, pp. 71–124.

Nunn, Frederick (1970) 'Emil Körner and the Prussianization of the Chilean army: origins, process and consequences, 1885–1920', *Hispanic American Historical Review,* May.

Nunn, Frederick (1976) *The Military in Chilean History: Essays on Civil–Military Relations, 1810–1973,* Albuquerque: University of New Mexico Press.

Nunn, Frederick (1978) 'An overview of the European military missions in Latin America'. In Brian Loveman and Thomas M. Davies (eds), *The Politics of Anti-Politics,* Lincoln: University of Nebraska Press, pp. 38–45.

**O**

Oakley R., M. Dziedic and W. Goldberg (1998) *Policing the New World Disorder: Peace Operations and Public Security,* Washington, DC: National Defence University Press.

Obando, Enrique (1993) 'Subversion and anti-subversion in Peru, 1980–1992. A view from Lima', *Low Intensity Conflict and Law Enforcement,* 2, 2, pp. 318–30.

Obando, Enrique (1996) 'Fujimori and the armed forces', *Privilege and Power in Fujimori's Peru. Special Issue of the NACLA Report on the Americas,* 30,1, July–August, pp. 26–30.

Obando, Enrique (2000) 'Fujimori y las fuerzas armadas'. In John Crabtree and Jim Thomas (eds) *El Perú de Fujimori, 1990–1998,* Lima: Universidad del Pacífico/IEP (Perú Problema No. 25), pp. 353–78.

Obasanjo, Olusegun (1990) *Not My Will: An Autobiography of a Former Head of State,* Ibadan: University Press Limited.

O'Brien, Philip and Paul Cammack (eds) (1985) *Generals in Retreat. The Crisis of Military Rule in Latin America*, Manchester: University of Manchester Press.

O'Donnell, Guillermo (1973) *Modernization and Bureaucratic-Authoritarianism: Studies in South American Politics*, Berkeley: Center for International Studies, University of California.

O'Donnell, Guillermo and Philippe C. Schmitter (1986) *Transitions from Authoritarian Rule: Tentative Conclusions about Uncertain Democracies*, Baltimore: Johns Hopkins University Press.

Oliveira, Eliézer Rizzo de and Samuel Alves Soares (forthcoming in 2001) 'Forças armadas, direção política e formato institucional'. In: Maria Celina D'Araujo and Celso Castro (eds), *Democracia e Forças Armadas no Cone Sul*, Rio de Janeiro: Editorial FGV.

Olonisakin, Funmi (forthcoming) 'Bridging the conceptual gap in peace-keeping: peace creation in Liberia', Occasional Paper 2, Centre for Democracy and Development, London.

Orrego, Claudio *et al.* (1979) *Siete Ensáyos sobre Arturo Alessandri Palma*, Santiago: Instituto Chileno de Estudios Humanísticos.

O'Shaughnessy, Hugh (2000) *Pinochet, the Politics of Torture*, New York: New York University Press.

Ottaway, Marina (1995) 'The Ethiopian transition: democratization or new authoritarianism?', *Northeast African Studies*, 2, 3, pp. 67–84.

Özbudun, Ergun (1995) 'Turkey: crisis, interruptions, and reequilibrations'. In Larry Diamond, Juan. J. Linz and Seymour Martin Lipset (eds), *Politics in Developing Countries. Comparing Experiences with Democracy*. Boulder: Lynne Rienner, pp. 219–61.

**P**

Palmer, David Scott (1992a) 'The Shining Path in Peru: insurgency and the drug problem'. In Edwin G. Corr and Stephen Sloan (eds), *Low Intensity Conflicts. Old Threats in a New World*, Boulder: Westview Press, pp. 151–70.

Palmer, David Scott (1992b) 'Peru, the drug business and Shining Path: between Scylla and Charybdis?', *Journal of Interamerican Studies and World Affairs*, 32, 3, pp. 65–88.

Pankhurst, Richard (1990) *A Social History of Ethiopia*, Addis Ababa: Institute of Ethiopian Studies.

Pansters, Wil (1999) 'The transition under fire: rethinking contemporary Mexican politics'. In Kees Koonings and Dirk Kruijt (eds), *Societies of Fear. The Legacy of Civil War, Violence and Terror in Latin America*, London: Zed Books, pp. 325–63.

Pateman, Roy (1991) 'Soviet arms transfers to Ethiopia', *Transafrica Forum*, 8, 1, pp. 43–57.

Pearce, Jenny (1990) *Colombia. Inside the Labyrinth*, New York: LAB.

Pécaut, Daniel (1999) 'From the banality of violence to real terror. The case of Colombia'. In Kees Koonings and Dirk Kruijt (eds), *Societies of Fear. The Legacy of Civil War, Violence and Terror in Latin America*, London: Zed Books, pp. 141–67.

Perelli, Carina (1990) 'The military's perception of threat in the Southern Cone of South America'. In Louis W. Goodman, Johanna S. R. Rial, and Juan Rial (eds), *The Military and Democracy: the Future of Civil–Military Relations in Latin America*, New York: Free Press, pp. 93–105.

Perlmutter, Amos (1977) *The Military and Politics in Modern Times*, New Haven: Yale University Press.

Pettifer, James (1997, 1998) *The Turkish Labyrinth. Atatürk and the New Islam*, Harmondsworth, Penguin Books.

Peukert, Dieter (1992) *The Weimar Republic*, Harmondsworth: Penguin Books.

Philip, George (1985) *The Military in South American Politics*, London: Croom Helm.

'La Plate-forme de Rome', *Le Monde Diplomatique*, February 1995.

Pliny the Middle Aged (1978, 1979) 'The PMAC, origins and structure'. Part 1 in *Ethiopianist Notes*, 2, 3 and Part 2 in *Northeast African Studies*, 1, 1.

Pool, David (1998) 'The Eritrean People's Liberation Front'. In Christopher Clapham (ed.), *African Guerrillas*, Oxford: James Currey, pp. 35–52.

Prats, Carlos (1985) *Memorias: Testimonio de un Soldado*, Santiago: Pehuén Editores.

Prendergast, John and Mark Duffield (1999) 'Liberation politics in Ethiopia and Eritrea'. In Taiser Ali and Robert O. Matthews (eds), *Civil Wars in Africa: Roots and Resolution*, Montreal: McGill and Queens University Press, Chapter 2.

*Prensa Libre* (1999) 12 June, 30 June, 19 July, 16 October.

*Privilege and Power in Fujimori's Peru* (1996) Special issue of the *NACLA Report on the Americas*, 30, 1, July–August.

Pye, Lucian W. (1962) 'Armies in the process of political modernization'. In John J. Johnson (ed.), *The Role of the Military in Underdeveloped Countries*, Princeton: Princeton University Press, pp. 69–89.

*Radikal* (2000) 12 April.

# R

Ramage, D. E. (1995) *Politics in Indonesia: Democratics, Islam and the Ideology of Tolerance*, London: Routledge.

Ramírez Necochea, Hernán (1985) *Fuerzas Armadas y Política en Chile, 1810–1970*, La Habana: Casa de las Américas.

'Rangoon Home Service, 8 September' (1991). In British Broadcasting Corporation, *Survey of World Broadcasts*, 11 September 1991.

Remmer, Karen (1989) *Military Rule in Latin America*, Boston: Unwin Hyman.

Reporters San Frontières (1996) *Le drame Algerien*, Paris: La Découverte.

*Report of the Chilean National Commission on Truth and Reconciliation* (1993) Translated by Phillip E. Berryman, introduction by José Zalaquett, Notre Dame: Notre Dame University Press .

*Revista do Clube Militar* (1999) July.

*Reuters* (2000) 12 December.

*RFERL Newsline* (1999) 13 August.

Rial, Juan (1990) 'The armed forces and the question of democracy in Latin America'. In Louis W. Goodman, Johanna S. R. Mendelson and Juan Rial (eds), *The Military and Democracy. The Future of Civil–Military Relations in Latin America*, Lexington and Toronto: Lexington Books, pp. 3–21.

Robison R. (1986) *Indonesia: the Rise of Capital*, Canberra: Asian Studies Association of Australia.

Rochabrun, Guillermo (1996) 'Deciphering the enigmas of Alberto Fujimori', *Privilege and Power in Fujimori's Peru*, special issue of the *NACLA Report on the Americas*, 30, 1, July–August, pp. 16–24.

Rojas, Francisco and Claudio Fuentes (1998) 'Civil–military relations in Chile's geopolitical transition'. In David Mares (ed.), *Civil–Military Relations: Building Democracy and Regional Security in Latin America, Southern Asia, and Central Europe*, Boulder: Westview Press.

Rojas Aravena, Francisco, Bernardo Arevalo and Carlos Sojo (1998) *La Nueva Agenda de Seguridad en Centroamerica*, Guatemala: Flacso.

Roniger, Luis and Mario Sznajder (1999) *The Legacy of Human Rights Violations in the Southern Cone: Argentina, Chile, and Uruguay*, Oxford: Oxford University Press.

Rosada-Granados, Hector (1999) *Soldados en el Poder. Proyecto Militar en Guatemala, 1944–1990*, Amsterdam: Thela Thesis Publishers (Latin America Series No. 15).

Rosenthal, Stephen (1992) 'The missing piece: the role of the United States in supporting civilian control over the militaries in El Salvador and Guatemala', Bachelor of Arts Honours thesis, Department of Government, Harvard.

Rospigliosi, Fernando (1995) 'El enfrentamiento entre los poderes ejecutivo y legislativo y la formación del parlamentalismo en América Latina'. In Carina Pirelli, Sonia Picado and Daniel Zovalto (eds), *Partidos y Clase Política en América Latina en los 90*, San José: IIDH, pp. 311–34.

Rospigliosi, Fernando (1997) 'Al desnudo: El SIN y la cúpula militar', *Ideéle*, 97, May, p. 58.

Rouquié, Alain (ed.) (1981) *La politique du Mars: les processus politiques dans les partis militaires*, Paris: Sycomore.

Rouquié, Alain (1987, 1989) *The Military and the State in Latin America*, Berkeley: University of California Press.

Rustow, Dankwart A. (1957) 'The army and the founding of the Turkish Republic', *World Politics*, 11, 4, pp. 513–52.

## S

*Sabah* (1996, 1997) 25 December 1996; 22 May, 12 June 1997.

Said, Salim (1998) 'Suharto's armed forces: building a power base in New Order Indonesia, 1966–1998', *Asian Survey*, 38, 6, pp. 535–52.

Samego, I. (1998) *Bila Abri Menghendaki: Desakan-Kuat Reformasi Atas Konsep Dwifungsi Abri* (When the Armed Forces Want: Strong Pressure to Reform the Concept of Dual Function of the Armed Forces), Bandung: Mizan.

Samego, I. *et al.* (1998) *Bila Abri Berbisnis* (When the Armed Forces Go Business): *Buku Pertama Yang Menyingkap Kata Dan Kasus Penyimpangan Dalam Praktik Bisnis Kalangan Militer*, Bandung: MIZAN.

Schirmer, Jennifer (1991) 'Interview with General Gramajo', *Harvard International Review*, 8, 3, Spring, pp. 10–13.

Schirmer, Jennifer (1998) *The Guatemalan Military Project. A Violence Called Democracy*, Philadelphia: University of Pennsylvania Press

Schulte Nordholt, N. G. (1996, 2000) 'Corruption and legimacy in Indonesia'. In N. G. Schulte Nordholt and Heleen E. Bakker, *Corruption and Legimacy*, Amsterdam: SISWO/ Instituut voor Maatschappijwetenschappen, pp. 65–94.

Schulte Nordholt, N. G. (1999) 'More than just watchdogs: reflections on the role Indonesian NGOs could play to enhance their civil society', paper XII.I.2, Twelfth INFID Conference, Kuta, Bali, Indonesia, September.

Schulte Nordholt, N. G. (2000a) 'De Molukken als oefenterrein van een Jakartaans machtsspel' (The Moluccas as playing field of a Jakartan power play), *Allerwegen*, March, pp. 24–36.

Schulte Nordholt, N.G. (forthcoming) 'Violence and the anarchy of the modern Indonesian state'. In F. Hüsken and H. de Jong (eds), *Violence in Indonesia*.

Schwarz, A. (1999) *A Nation in Waiting: Indonesia's Search for Stability*, Sydney: Allen and Unwin.

Schwarz, A. and J. Paris (1999) *The Politics of Post-Suharto Indonesia*, New York: Brookings Institute Press.

Sein Win (1959) *The Split Story*, Rangoon: The Guardian Ltd.

Selth, Andrew (1996) *Transforming the Tatmadaw: the Burmese Armed Forces since 1988*, Canberra: Strategic and Defence Studies Centre, Australian National University.

Selth, Andrew (1997) 'Burma's defence expenditure and arms industries', Working Paper No. 309, Strategic and Defence Studies Centre, Australian National University, Canberra.

Selth, Andrew (2000) 'The future of the Burmese armed forces'. In Morten Pedersen, Emily Rudland and R. J. May (eds), *Burma: Myanmar: Strong Regime Weak State*, London: C. Hurst and Co., pp. 54–92.

*Seven Days Update* (1998) 23 December.

Shaw, Stanford J. and Ezel Kural Shaw (2000) *History of the Ottoman Empire and Modern Turkey. Reform, Revolution and Republic. The Rise of Modern Turkey 1808 – 1975*, Cambridge: Cambridge University Pess.

Shearer, David (1997) *Private Armies and Military Intervention*, Oxford: Oxford University Press for IISS (Adelphi Paper).

Shils, Edward (1962) 'The military in the political development of the new states'. In John J. Johnson (ed.), *The Role of the Military in Underdeveloped Countries*, Princeton: Princeton University Press, pp. 7–67.

Shirer, William S. (1983) *The Rise and Fall of the Third Reich. A History of Nazi Germany*, New York: Ballantine Books.

*Siglo Veintiuno* (1999) 16 March, 8 May, 21 May.

Silva, Patricio (1999) 'Collective memories, fears, and consensus: the political psychology of the Chilean democratic transition'. In Kees Koonings and Dirk Kruijt (eds), *Societies of Fear: the Legacy of Civil War, Violence and Terror in Latin America*, London: Zed Books, pp. 171–96.

Silva, Patricio (2000a) *State Capacity, Technocratic Insulation, and Government–Business Relations in South Korea and Chile*. Santiago: FLACSO.

Silva, Patricio (2000b) 'The soldier and the state in South America: introduction'. In Patricio Silva (ed.), *The Soldier and the State in South America. Essays in Civil–Military Relations*, Hampshire: Palgrave, pp. 1–12.

Silverstein, Josef (1977) *Burma: Military Rule and the Politics of Stagnation*, Ithaca: Cornell University Press.

Silverstein, Josef (1980) *Burmese Politics: the Dilemma of National Unity*, New Brunswick: Rutgers University Press.

Simanjuntak, M. (1989) *Unsur Hegelian dalam Pandangan Negara Intergralistik* (Hegelian Element in the Integralistic State View), University of Indonesia thesis, Jakarta.

Singh, B. (1994) *Abri and the Security of Southeast Asia: the Role and Thinking of General L. Benny Moerdani*, Singapore: Singapore Institute of International Affairs.

Smith, Martin (1994) *Ethnic Groups in Burma: Development, Democracy and Human Rights*, London: Anti-Slavery International.

Smith, Martin (1996) *Freedom of Expression and the Right to Health in Burma*, London: Article 19.

Smith, Martin (1999) *Burma: Insurgency and the Politics of Ethnicity*, London: Zed Books.

Smith Dun, General (1980) *Memoirs of the Four Foot Colonel*, Cornell Data Paper No. 113, South East Asia Program, Ithaca.

Soares, Gláucio Ary Dillon and D'Araujo, Maria Celina (eds) (1994) *21 Anos de Regime Militar: Balanços e Perspectivas*, Rio de Janeiro: Editorial FGV.

Soares, Gláucio Ary Dillon, Maria Celina D'Araujo and Celso Castro (eds) (1995) *A Volta aos Quartéis. A Memória Militar sobre a Abertura*, Rio de Janeiro: Relume-Dumará.

Stanley, William and David Holiday (1999) 'From fragmentation to a national project? peace implementation in Guatemala' (draft, 28 February).

Stavenhagen, Rodolfo (1990) *The Ethnic Question: Conflicts, Development and Human Rights*, Tokyo: United Nations University Press.

Stein, Steve (1980) *Populism in Peru: the Emergence of the Masses and the Politics of Social Control*, Madison: University of Wisconsin Press.

Steinberg, David I. (1995) 'The Republic of Korea: pluralizing politics', in Larry Diamond, Juan. J. Linz and Seymour Martin Lipset (eds), *Politics in Developing Countries. Comparing Experiences with Democracy*. Boulder: Lynne Rienner, pp. 369–415.

Steinberg, David I. (1997) 'The Union Solidarity and Development Association: mobilization and orthodoxy in Myanmar', *Burma Debate*, IV, 1, January/February, pp. 4–11.

Steinberg, David (2000) 'The state, power and civil society in Burma–Myanmar'. In Morten Pedersen, Emily Rudl and R. J. May (eds), *Burma: Myanmar: Strong Regime, Weak State*, London: C. Hurst and Co.

Steinberg, David I., Martin Smith, Zunetta Lidell and Marc Purcell (1999). Contribution to Burma Center Nederlands (ed.), *Strengthening Civil Society in Burma: Possibilities and Dilemmas for International NGOs*, Chieng Mai: Silkworm Books.

Stepan, Alfred (1971) *The Military in Politics. Changing Patterns in Brazil*, Princeton: Princeton University Press.

Stepan, Alfred (1976) 'The new professionalism of internal warfare and military role expansion'. In Abraham F. Lowenthal (ed.), *Armies and Politics in Latin America*, New York and London: Holmes and Meier, pp. 244–60.

Stepan Alfred (1978) *The State and Society. Peru in Comparative Perspective*, Princeton: Princeton University Press.

Stepan, Alfred (1988) *Rethinking Military Politics: Brazil and the Southern Cone*, Princeton: Princeton University Press.

Stern, Steve, J. (ed.) (1973) *Resistencia, Rebelión y Conciencia Campesina en los Andes. Siglos XVIII al XX*, Lima: IEP.

Sudoplatov, Pavel and Anatoli Sudoplatov with L. Jerrold and Leona P. Schechter (1994) *The Memoirs of an Unwanted Witness – a Soviet Spymaster*, London: Little, Brown and Company.

Sulmont, Denis (1981) *El Movimiento Obrero Peruano (1890–1980)*, Lima: TAREA.

Sundhausen, U. (1982) *The Road to Power: Indonesian Military Politics 1945–1967*, Kuala Lumpur: Oxford University Press.

## T

Tapia, Carlos (1995) *La Autodefensa Armada del Campesinado*, Lima: CEDEP.

Tapia, Carlos (1997) *Las Fuerzas Armadas y Sendero Luminoso. Dos Estrategias y su Final*, Lima: IEP.

Taylor, Robert (1987) *The State in Burma*, London: C. Hurst and Co.

Taylor, Robert (1998) 'Myanmar: army politics and the prospects for democratisation', *Asian Affairs*, XXIX, Part 1, February, pp. 3–12.

Teferra Haile-Selassie (1997) *The Ethiopian Revolution 1974–1991*, London: Kegan Paul.

Tello, Maria del Pilar (1983) *Golpe o Revolución? Hablan los Generales del 68*, Lima: SAGSA, 2 vols.

Tello, Maria del Pilar (1989) *Sobre el Volcán. Dialogo Frente a la Subversión*, Lima: SAGSA.

Tello, Maria del Pilar (1994) *El Pacto. Perú: De la Crisis al Acuerdo Nacional*, Lima: SAGSA.

*Tempo Magazine* (1997) 28 August.

*Tentara Mendaba Mitra* (The Military in Search of Partnership) (1999) Jakarta: LIPI.

Thein Han, Lieutenant-Colonel (1998) 'Human resource development and nation building in Myanmar: unity in diversity'. In Ministry of Defence, *Human Resource Development and Nation Building in Myanmar*, Rangoon: Ministry of Defence, pp. 215–26.

Thein Pe Myint (1956) 'The world peace camp and Burma'. In *Political Experience in the Revolutionary Period*, Rangoon: Shwe Pyi Tan.

Thein Swe, Colonel (1998) 'Human resource development in nation building: the role of the armed forces'. In Ministry of Defence, *Human Resource Development and Nation Building in Myanmar*, Rangoon: Ministry of Defence.

Tilly, Charles (1985) 'War and the power of war makers: Western Europe and elsewhere, 1600–1980'. In P. Wallerstein *et al.* (eds), *Global Militarization*, Boulder: Westview.

*Time Magazine* (1999) 14 February.

*Times, The* (1958, 1962) 1 November 1958; 3 March 1962.

Tin Maung Maung Than (1989) 'Burma's national security and defence posture', *Contemporary Southeast Asia*, 11, 1, June, pp. 40–55.

Tironi, Eugenio (1988) *Los Silencios de la Revolución*, Santiago: Puerta Abierta, 1988.

Tironi, Eugenio and Felipe Agüero (1999) 'Chili: quel avenir pour le nouveau paysage politique?', *Problemes D'Amérique Latine* (Paris) 35, October–December.

*TNI Abad XXI: Redefinisi Reposisi, Dan Reaktualisasi Peran TNI Dalam Kehidupan Bangsa* (Redefinition, Repositioning, and Reactualization of the Armed Forces in the Life of the Nation) (1999) Jakarta: Jasa Buma.

Toland, John (1970) *The Rising Sun. The Decline and Fall of the Japanese Empire*, New York: Random House/Bantam Books.

Tollefson, Scott D. (1995) 'Civil–military relations in Brazil: the myth of tutelary democracy', paper presented at the Latin American Studies Association Congress, Washington.

Torres-Rivas, Edelberto (1989) *Repression and Resistance*, Boulder: Westview Press.

Torres-Rivas, Edelberto and Gabriel Aguilera (1998) *Del Autoritarismo a la Paz*, Guatemala: Flacso.

Torumtay, Necip (1993) *Orgeneral Torumtay'in Anilari*, Istanbul: Milliyet Yayinlari.

Touraine, Alain (1974) *Production de la Societe*, Algeria: Seuil.

Tronvoll, Kjetil (1999) 'Borders of violence – boundaries of identity: demarcating the Eritrean nation-state', *Ethnic and Racial Studies*, 22, 6, pp. 1037–60.

Trudeau, Robert (1989) 'The Guatemalan election of 1985: prospects for democracy'. In John A. Booth (ed.), *Elections and Democracy in Central America*, Chapel Hill: University of North Carolina Press, pp. 93–125.

'The truth behind General Abacha's anti-corruption crusade' (1996) *Nigeria Now* , 5, 5, June, pp. 20–4.

Tsadkan Gebre Tensae (1994) 'A vision of a new army for Ethiopia'. In *Proceedings of the Symposium on the Ethiopian Constitution*, Addis Ababa: Inter-Africa Group, pp. 187–92.

Tsegaye Tegenu (1996) *The Evolution of Ethiopian Absolutism: the Genesis and the Making of the Fiscal Military State*, Uppsala: Uppsala University.

Tucker, Steven P. (1998) *Ethiopia in Transition, 1991–1998,* Writenet.

## U

U Ba Than (1962) *The Roots of the Revolution*, Rangoon: Government Printing Press.

Unidad Revolucionaria Nacional Guatemalteca (1998) *III Informe sobre el Cumplimiento de los Acuerdos de Paz. Abril–diciembre 1997*, Guatemala: URNG.

United Nations General Assembly (1997) *Fifth Report of the Director of the UN Mission for the Verification of Human Rights and of Compliance with the Commitments of the Comprehensive Agreement on Human Rights in Guatemala*, Geneva: A52/330, 10 September.

United Nations General Assembly (nd) *Acuerdo sobre Cronograma para la Implementacion, Cumplimiento y Verificacion de los Acuerdos de Paz* (draft).

UN Working Group (1998) *Human Development in Myanmar*, Rangoon: UNDP.

## V

Valenzuela, Arturo (1978) *The Breakdown of Democratic Regimes: Chile*, Baltimore and London: Johns Hopkins University Press.

Valenzuela, Arturo (1991, 1995) 'The military in power: the consolidation of one-man rule'. In Paul W. Drake and Iván Jaksi´c (eds), *The Struggle for Democracy in Chile, 1982–1990*, Lincoln: University of Nebraska Press, pp. 298–318.

Valenzuela, Arturo (1994) 'Party politics and the crisis of presidentialism in Chile: a proposal for a parliamentary form of government'. In Juan Linz and Arturo Valenzuela (eds), *The Failure of Presidential Democracy, Volume 2 – The Case of Latin America*, Baltimore and London: Johns Hopkins University Press.

Valenzuela, Arturo (1999) 'Chile: origins and consolidation of a Latin American democracy'. In Larry Diamond, Jonathan Hartlyn, Juan J. Linz and Seymour Martin Lipset (eds), *Democracy in Developing Countries: Latin America*, Boulder, Colorado: Lynn Rienner Publishers (second edition), pp. 159–206.

Varas, Augusto and Felipe Agüero (1984) *El Proyecto Político Militar*, Santiago: Flacso.

Varas, Augusto (1987) *Los Militares en el Poder: Régimen y Gobierno Militar en Chile 1973–1986*, Santiago: Pehuén-Flacso.

Varas, Augusto (1991, 1995) 'The crisis of legitimacy of military rule in the 1980s'. In Paul W. Drake and Iván Jaksić (eds), *The Struggle for Democracy in Chile, 1982–1990*, Lincoln: University of Nebraska Press, pp. 237–56.

Varas, Augusto and Claudio Fuentes (1994) *Defensa Nacional, Chile 1990–1994:*

*Modernización y Desarrollo*, Santiago: Flacso.

Varas, Augusto, Felipe Agüero and Fernando Bustamante (1980) *Chile, Democracia, Fuerzas Armadas*, Santiago: Flacso.

Villalobos, Sergio, Osvaldo Silva, Fernando Silva and Patricio Estelle (1974) *Historia de Chile*, Santiago: Editorial Universitaria.

Vatikiotis, M. (1993) *Indonesian Politics under Suharto: Order, Development and Pressure for Change*, London: Routledge.

Vargas Llosa, Mario (1993) *El Pez en el Agua. Memorias*, Barcelona: Seix Barral.

Vego, Milan (1992) 'Federal army deployments in Bosnia-Hercegovina', *Jane's Intelligence Review*, October 1992, p. 445.

Vidal, Ana Maria (1993) *Los Decretos de la Guerra*, Lima: IDS.

Villagran Kramer, Francisco (1993) *Bibliografía Política. Los Pactos Políticos de 1944 a 1970*, Guatemala/San José: Flacso.

Villanueva, Victor (1962) *El Militarismo en el Perú*, Lima: Empresa Gráfica T. Scheuk.

Villanueva, Victor (1972) *El CAEM y la Revolución de la Fuerza Armada*, Lima: IEP/ Campodónico.

Villanueva, Victor (1973) *La Sublevación Aprista del 48. Tragedia de un Pueblo y un Partido*, Lima: Editorial Milla Batres.

Villanueva, Victor (1975) *El APRA en la Buzca del Poder*, Lima: Horizonte.

Villanueva, Victor (1977a) *El APRA y el Ejército, 1940–1950*, Lima: Horizonte.

Villanueva, Victor (1977b) *Así Cayó Leguía*, Lima: Editorial Retama.

*Vojska* (1992) 16 September.

Vulliamy, Ed (1996) 'Serbian lies world chose to believe', *The Guardian*, 29 February 1996.

# W

Wahid, Abdurrahman (1999) *Berpolitik Atau Kembali Ke Barak: Militer Dalam Wacana Masyarakat Madani* (Playing Politics or Back to the Barracks: Military in the Perspective of the Madani Society), Yogyakarta: Biograf Publishing.

Wandelt, I. (1989) *Der weg zum Pancasila-Menschen: Die Pancasila-Lehre unter dem P4–Beschluss des Jahres 1978: Entwicklung und Struktur der indonesischen Staatslehre*, Frankfurt am Main: Lang.

Watson, Cynthia A. (2000) 'Civil–military relations in Colombia: a workable relationship or a case for fundamental reform?' *Third World Quaterly*, 21, 3, pp. 529–49.

Weber, M. (1947)*Wirtschaft und Gesellschaft*, Tübingen: Mohr.

*Week Magazine, The* (1999) 4 October; 6 December.

Welch, Claude (1976) *Civilian Control of the Military,* Albany New York: SUNY Press.

Wiant, Jon (1986) 'The vanguard army: the Tatmadaw and politics in revolutionary Burma'. In Edward A. Olsen and Stephen Jurika (eds), *The Armed Forces in Contemporary Asian Societies*, Boulder and London: Westview Press, pp. 235–57.

Williams, Rocky (1998) 'Towards the creation of an African civil–military relations tradition', *African Journal of Political Science*, 3, 1.

Wilson, K. B. (1992) 'Cults of violence and counter-violence in Mozambique', *Journal of South African Studies*, 18, 3, pp. 527–82.

Winters, J. A. (1999) 'Criminal Department', additional paper at Twelfth INFID Conference, Kuta, Bali Indonesia, September.

Wirahadikusumah, A. (1999) *Indonesia Baru dan Tantangan TNI* (New Indonesia and the Challenges of the Armed Forces), Jakarta: Pustaka Sinar Harapan.

Wise, Carol (1997) 'State policy and social conflict in Peru'. In Maxwell A. Cameron and Philip Mauceri (eds), *The Peruvian Labyrinth: Polity, Society, Economy*, University Park: Pennsylvania State University Press, pp. 70–103.

*Working People's Daily, The* (1990, 1992) 10 January, 9 October, 11 October.

World Bank (1994) *World Debt Tables: Country Tables*, Washington, DC: World Bank, data on Nigeria.

## Y

*Yeni Yüzyil* (1997, 2000) 2 February, 18 June, 21 June 1997; 19 February 2000.

Young, John (1996a) 'The Tigray and Eritrean people's liberation fronts: a history of tensions and pragmatism', *Journal of Modern African Studies*, 34, 1, pp. 105–20.

Young, John (1996b) 'Ethnicity and power in Ethiopia', *Review of African Political Economy*, 70, pp. 531–42.

Young, John (1998) 'The Tigray People's Liberation Front'. In Christopher Clapham (ed.), *African Guerrillas*, Oxford: James Currey, pp. 36–52.

## Z

Zack-Williams, A. B. (1997) 'Kamajors, "sobel" and the militariat: civil society and the return of the military in Sierra Leone politics', *Review of African Political Economy*, 73, pp. 373–98.

Zagorski, Paul W. (1992) *Democracy vs National Security. Civil–Military Relations in Latin America*, Boulder: Lynne Rienner.

Zaverucha, Jorge (1994) *Rumor de Sabres: Tutela Militar ou Controle Civil?* São Paulo: Ática.

Zaverucha, Jorge (1998) 'Sarney, Collor, Itamar, FHC e as prerogativas militares', paper presented at Latin American Studies Association Congress, Chicago.

# Index

# Zed Books Titles on Conflict and Conflict Resolution

*The hope that conflicts within societies might decrease markedly with the demise of the Cold War has been cruelly disappointed. Zed Books has published a number of titles which deal specifically with the diverse forms of modern conflict, their complex causes, and some of the ways in which we may realistically look forward to prevention, mediation and resolution.*

Adedeji, A. (ed.), *Comprehending and Mastering African Conflicts: The Search for Sustainable Peace and Good Governance*

Allen, T. and Seaton, J. (eds), *The Media of Conflict: War Reporting and Representations of Ethnic Violence*

Bishara, M., *Palestine/Israel: Peace or Apartheid*

Cockburn, C., *The Space Between Us: Negotiating Gender and National Identities in Conflict*

Cristalis, I., *Bitter Dawn: East Timor – A People's Story*

Duffield, M., *Global Governance and the New Wars: The Merging of Development and Security*

Evans, G., Goodman, J., and Lansbury, N. (eds), *Moving Mountains: Communities Confront Mining and Globalization*

Fink, C., *Living Silence: Burma under Military Rule*

Fisher, S. et al, *Working with Conflict: Skills and Strategies for Action*

Gopal, S., *Anatomy of a Confrontation: Ayodhya and the Rise of Communal Politics in India*

Guyatt, N., *The Absence of Peace: Understanding the Israeli-Palestinian Conflict*

Jacobs, S., Jacobson, R. and Marchbank, J. (eds), *States of Conflict: Gender, Violence and Resistance*

Kapadia, K. (ed.), *The Violence of Development: The Political Economy of Gender*

Koonings, K. and Kruijt, D. (eds), *Societies of Fear: The Legacy of Civil War, Violence and Terror in Latin America*

Koonings, K. and Kruijt, D. (eds), *Political Armies: The Military and Nation Building in the Age of Democracy*

Lewer, N. and Schofield, S., *Non-Lethal Weapons – Military Strategies and Technologies for 21st Century Conflict*

Lumpe, L. (ed.), *Running Guns: The Black Market in Small Arms*

Macrae, J., *Aiding Recovery? The Crisis of Aid in Chronic Political Emergencies*

Mare, G., *Ethnicity and Politics in South Africa*

Melvern, L., *A People Betrayed: The Role of the West in Rwanda's Genocide*

Moser, C. and Clark, F. (eds), *Victims, Perpetrators or Actors? Gender, Armed Conflict and Political Violence*

Nzongola-Ntalaja, G., *The Congo from Leopold to Kabila: A People's History*

Ohlsson, L., *Hydro Politics: Conflicts over Water as a Development Constraint*

Pirotte, C., Husson, B. and Grunewald, F. (eds), *Responding to Emergencies and Fostering Development – The Dilemmas of Humanitarian Aid*

Shiva, V., *The Violence of the Green Revolution*

Suliman, M. (ed.), *Ecology, Politics and Violent Conflict*

Turshen, M. and Twagiramariya, C. (eds), *What Women Do in War Time: Gender and Conflict in Africa*

Turshen, M., Meintjes, S., and Pillay, A. (eds), *The Aftermath: Women in Post-conflict Transformation*

Vickers, J., *Women and War*

For full details of this list and Zed's other subject and general catalogues, please write to: The Marketing Department, Zed Books, 7 Cynthia Street, London N1 9JF, UK or email Sales@zedbooks.demon.co.uk

Visit our website at: www.zedbooks.demon.co.uk